HANDBOOK OF
WORK–FAMILY INTEGRATION

HANDBOOK OF WORK-FAMILY INTEGRATION

Research, Theory, and Best Practices

Edited by

Karen Korabik, Donna S. Lero and Denise L. Whitehead
University of Guelph, Guelph, Ontario, Canada

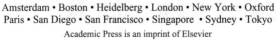

Amsterdam • Boston • Heidelberg • London • New York • Oxford
Paris • San Diego • San Francisco • Singapore • Sydney • Tokyo

Academic Press is an imprint of Elsevier

ELSEVIER

ACADEMIC
PRESS

Academic Press is an imprint of Elsevier
84 Theobald's Road, London WC1X 8RR, UK
Radarweg 29, PO Box 211, 1000 AE Amsterdam, The Netherlands
30 Corporate Drive, Suite 400, Burlington, MA 01803, USA
525 B Street, Suite 1900, San Diego, CA 92101-4495, USA

H

First edition 2008

British Library Cataloguing in Publication Data
A catalogue record for this book is available from the British Library

Library of Congress Cataloging-in-Publication Data
A catalog record for this book is available from the Library of Congress

ISBN: 978-0-12-372574-5

For information on all Academic Press publications
visit our web site at books.elsevier.com

Typeset by Charon Tec Ltd (A Macmillan Company), Chennai, India
www.charontec.com

Printed and bound in the United States of America
08 09 10 11   10 9 8 7 6 5 4 3 2 1

To my wonderful daughter, Michelle, who every day teaches me the true meaning of work-family enrichment; and to my parents who provided me with a strong foundation and a commitment to social justice.

Karen Korabik

To my mother and grandparents, my brother, and my husband, Vincent, who have always supported and encouraged me, and to my dear colleagues and friends who help me integrate work and life.

Donna S. Lero

To an extraordinary group of special people: my husband Mark Hunter and our daughters Laura and Sarah, who are the center of my universe and make every day worthwhile; my parents, Dr. Paul and Doreen Whitehead, who have always given me boundless encouragement, love and support; and my parents-in-law Doug and Carol Hunter, who have always expressed their pleasure and pride in my accomplishments, big or small.

Denise L. Whitehead

CONTENTS

Preface   xi
Acknowledgments   xiii
About the contributors   xv

SECTION I

THEORIES AND MEASUREMENT ISSUES

CHAPTER 1
Work-Family Integration: Introduction
and Overview   3

Denise L. Whitehead, Karen Korabik and Donna S. Lero

CHAPTER 2
Historical Trends in Work-Family:
The Evolution of Earning and Caring   13

Denise L. Whitehead

CHAPTER 3
A Conceptual Model of the Work-Family
Interface   37

Patricia Voydanoff

CHAPTER 4
Reflections and Future Directions on
Measurement in Work-Family Research   57

Dawn S. Carlson and Joseph G. Grzywacz

CHAPTER 5
On Multiple Roles: Past, Present, and Future
Rosalind Chait Barnett

75

CHAPTER 6
Toxic Job Ecologies, Time Convoys, and Work-Family Conflict: Can Families (Re)Gain Control and Life Course "Fit"?
Phyllis Moen and Noelle Chesley

95

SECTION II
ANTECEDENTS, OUTCOMES & MODERATORS

CHAPTER 7
Too Much To Do, and Not Enough Time: An Examination of Role Overload
Linda Duxbury, Sean Lyons and Christopher Higgins

125

CHAPTER 8
Positive Spillover Between Personal and Professional Life: Definitions, Antecedents, Consequences, and Strategies
Steven Poelmans, Olena Stepanova and Aline Masuda

141

CHAPTER 9
Work-Related Outcomes of the Work-Family Interface: Why Organizations Should Care
Jay M. Dorio, Rebecca H. Bryant and Tammy D. Allen

157

CHAPTER 10

**The Emotional Dimensions of Family Time
and Their Implications for
Work–Family Balance**   177

Shira Offer and Barbara Schneider

CHAPTER 11

**Health and Well-being Outcomes of the
Work–Family Interface**   191

Jane Mullen, Elizabeth Kelley and E. Kevin Kelloway

CHAPTER 12

**Integrating Gender-Related Issues into
Research on Work and Family**   215

Karen Korabik, Allyson McElwain and Dara B. Chappell

CHAPTER 13

**Viewing 21st Century Motherhood Through
a Work–Family Lens**   233

Sarah Damaske and Kathleen Gerson

CHAPTER 14

Work–Life Issues for Fathers   249

Kerry Daly, Lynda Ashbourne and Linda Hawkins

SECTION III

**CONTEXT, PROCESSES, PRACTICES &
POLICIES**

CHAPTER 15

**Coping with Work–Family Conflict:
Integrating Individual and Organizational
Perspectives**   267

Anat Drach-Zahavy and Anit Somech

CHAPTER 16

Social Support and Work–Family Conflict   287

Roya Ayman and Amy Antani

CHAPTER 17

Face-Time Matters: A Cross-Level Model of How Work-Life Flexibility Influences Work Performance of Individuals and Groups   305

Ellen Ernst Kossek and Linn Van Dyne

CHAPTER 18

Work–Family Culture: Current Research and Future Directions   331

Jeanine K. Andreassi and Cynthia A. Thompson

CHAPTER 19

Cross-Cultural Approaches to Work–Family Conflict   353

Zeynep Aycan

CHAPTER 20

Assumptions, Research Gaps and Emerging Issues: Implications for Research, Policy and Practice   371

Donna S. Lero and Suzan Lewis

Appendix: Work-Family Websites, Resources, and Organizations   399
Author Index   403
Subject Index   421

PREFACE

This handbook is a compendium of up-to-date theories, research, and best practices on topics pertaining to the work-family interface. In today's industrialized societies, the majority of parents are engaged in full-time work while raising their children and, increasingly, while caring for aging parents. Fulfilling these roles while also managing household upkeep and work responsibilities has become a challenge for many individuals. Workplace demands have contributed to the precarious balance of work and family. More hours, shift work, downsizing, travel, commuting, and increased job expectations have added to the sense of not having enough time to be a good worker and a good parent, child, and citizen. Yet, work is important. People define their identity and self-worth through the opportunities that work provides for personal growth, interaction with co-workers, and the income and benefits on which families rely. Understanding the ways stress, job burn-out, self-esteem, gender, work demands, overload, spillover, and parenting come together and affect individuals, families, and experiences at work are important. So, too, is new research on how work and family experiences can facilitate or enrich role quality in both domains, and how work redesign and work culture can facilitate a positive integration of work and family roles.

Currently, there is a burgeoning interdisciplinary research literature on work and family issues that encompasses psychology, family studies, business, sociology, health, and economics. Many papers on the topic are being published and presented at conferences each year. In addition, specialized conferences on the topic are being held at locations around the world. New developments in theory and methodology are also evident. Due to the sheer amount of new information that is being produced and its scattered nature, it is difficult even for experts in the field to keep up with everything they need to know. This handbook is intended as a resource that will fill this gap by synthesizing theory, research, policy, and workplace practice/organizational policy issues in one place for a wide readership.

The authors of each chapter in this handbook are well-known academic experts in various areas pertaining to work-family issues. Each has written on a topic that encapsulates the state-of-the-art knowledge in their area. Where appropriate, in their chapters they discuss the theoretical, conceptual, and methodological considerations that are relevant to their topic; provide a critique of existing work in the area; identify opportunities for future theory and research; and note implications for policy and practice at the individual, organizational or societal level.

This handbook should serve as an essential reference for researchers in the area of work-family, as a guide to human resource professionals and policy makers, and as a teaching and learning resource for students in undergraduate and graduate courses. The chapter authors represent many disciplines (e.g., psychology, sociology, family studies, health and education, business and management) as well as countries and continents (e.g., USA, Canada, Turkey, Israel, United Kingdom). Thus, the handbook should appeal to an interdisciplinary and international audience.

ACKNOWLEDGMENTS

It requires a somewhat Herculean effort to bring together this many expert authors from around the world and mesh them between two covers. One of the unfortunate ironies is that the specialists in the domain of work and family research often acutely experience the very issues of role overload, stress, and negative spillover about which they study and write. To bring a book of this magnitude to fruition has required a team of authors committed to the effort of seeing this book come to life. Our heart felt thanks to our authors who consistently met our requests for drafts, revisions, and final chapters, and the multitude of other requests we sent their way. Their belief in, and dedication to this project is a testament to their passion, interest, and commitment to furthering our understanding of work and family.

Our time as editors of this volume has been preceded by many more years of working together on various projects under the auspices of the Centre for Families, Work and Well-being at the University of Guelph, Ontario, Canada. We are extremely grateful to the network of support and encouragement that resides within this centre. We owe particular thanks to the Centre's Executive Director, Linda Hawkins, who always finds little ways to support each of us in our times of need.

We also wish to acknowledge the support that comes from our academic departments within the university, including the Psychology Department, the Department of Family Relations and Applied Nutrition, and the overarching College of Social and Applied Human Sciences.

The Centre for Families, Work and Well being gratefully acknowledges the generous endowment provided through the Stephen A. Jarislowsky Foundation. The Jarislowsky Chair in Families and Work, currently held by Dr. Donna Lero, is the first academic chair in Canada addressing the healthy integration of work and family responsibilities as a critical economic and social policy issue. As an outspoken proponent of business ethics and accountability of corporate governance, Stephen Jarislowsky is a unique visionary in understanding the critical intersections between work and family and the bottom line.

ABOUT THE CONTRIBUTORS

THE EDITORS

Karen Korabik is a Professor of Industrial/Organizational and Applied Social Psychology at the University of Guelph, Ontario, Canada. She is the Research Director for Women and Work at the Centre for Families, Work, and Well-Being and a Research Associate at the University's Centre for Leadership Studies. Dr. Korabik regularly serves as a consultant to the Guelph Centre for Occupational Research. She is a Fellow of the American Psychological Association and has served in several administrative roles in the Canadian Psychological Association. Since receiving her Ph.D. from St. Louis University in 1976, Dr. Korabik has carried out research in a wide variety of public and private sector organizational settings both in Canada and internationally. She has published more than 50 book chapters and scientific articles on topics such as work/family balance; leadership and conflict management; stress, coping, and social support; job change; gender issues; acculturation; and program evaluation.

Donna S. Lero holds the Jarislowsky Chair in Families and Work and is an Associate Professor in the Department of Family Relations and Applied Nutrition at the University of Guelph, Ontario, Canada. She is co-founder of the Centre for Families, Work and Well-Being, where she directs a program of research on Public Policies, Workplace Practices and Community Supports. Dr. Lero has served on many government task forces and recently chaired the Ontario government's Expert Panel on Quality and Human Resources in Early Learning and Child Care Services. Donna received her Ph.D. from Purdue University and has served on the Advisory Board of Purdue's Center for Families. Dr. Lero has published more than 50 book chapters, articles, and government reports on topics such as parental leave policies, child care policies and services, work-family conflict, supports for parents of children with disabilities, and policies affecting father involvement. Her current research includes an international study of work-family conflict, research on student parents in colleges and universities, institutional support for work-family balance and greater equity among women in science and engineering programs, and policies and programs to support employees caring for seniors and/or ill family members.

Denise L. Whitehead is a trained lawyer (LL.B., Osgoode Hall Law School) and a member of the bar of Ontario. She is a Ph.D. candidate in the

Department of Family Relations and Applied Nutrition at the University of Guelph, Ontario, Canada. Her research is focused on social policy as it relates to gender, work and family, father involvement, and the care and support of children following divorce. Past work has examined policy options for self-employed women and their economic security, the sociolegal implications for dependent self-employment, and an inventory of policies as they relate to father involvement. Her dissertation research is exploring the fragility of shared custodial relationships and the factors that contribute to its changes.

THE AUTHORS

Tammy D. Allen is Professsor of Psychology at the University of South Florida. She received her doctorate in industrial and organizational psychology from the University of Tennessee. Her research interests include work and family relationships, mentoring, career development, occupational health psychology, and organizational citizenship behavior.

Jeanine K. Andreassi, Ph.D. is an Assistant Professor of Management at the John F. Welch School of Business at Sacred Heart University. Her research interests are in the work-family area. She has published in the areas of work-life culture, personality, and coping. She is an active contributor to the Sloan Work and Family Research Network, and has presented at the Society for Industrial and Organizational Psychology and the Academy of Management. She has also published in the Journal of Managerial Psychology.

Amy K. Antani received her M.S. and Ph.D. from the Illinois Institute of Technology. Her areas of research interest and focus are work-family conflict and social support. Dr. Antani is currently the director of organizational development for Advocate Health Care in Chicago.

Lynda M. Ashbourne recently completed her Ph.D. in the Department of Family Relations and Applied Nutrition at the University of Guelph, Ontario, Canada. Dr. Ashbourne has more than 15 years experience as a registered couple and family therapist, and has worked with both fathers and mothers who are negotiating the work/family interface. Her research interests include social policy influences on father involvement and parent–adolescent relationships.

Zeynep Aycan is a Professor of Industrial and Organizational Psychology at Koç University, Turkey. Trained as a cross-cultural psychologist, Dr. Aycan's research focuses on the impact of culture on various aspects of organizational processes, including leadership, human resource management, women's career development, and work-life balance. She has published in journals, including *Annual Review of Psychology, International Journal of Human Resource Management, Journal of Cross-Cultural Psychology, Applied Psychology: An International Review.* She is the Editor of *The International Journal of Cross-Cultural Management* (with Terence

Jackson), and the President of the International Society for the Study of Work and Organizational Values.

Roya Ayman, Ph.D. is a Professor at the Illinois Institute of Technology, Institute of Psychology, where she is the director of the Industrial and Organizational Psychology program. She was a co-editor of a book on leadership theory and research and has published extensively on issues related to leadership, culture, and gender. She has also consulted on topics of diversity in the workplace with major corporations.

Rosalind Chait Barnett is a senior scientist at Brandeis University's Womens Studies Research Center, and executive director of the Community, Families & Work Program. She received her Ph.D. from Harvard. She has published over 100 articles, 37 chapters, and 7 books. Her most recent book is *Same Difference: How Gender Myths are Hurting Our Relationships, Our Children and Our Jobs* (Basic, 2004). Her primary interests are work-family issues, alternative work arrangements, and gender and education.

Rebecca H. Bryant is currently pursuing her doctoral degree in industrial and organizational psychology at the University of South Florida. Additionally, she works as a Research Associate for Personnel Decisions Research Institutes. Her research interests include work and family relationships, organizational citizenship behavior, and team-related phenomena.

Dawn S. Carlson is an Associate Professor of Management at Baylor University. Her Ph.D. is in Organizational Behavior and Human Resource Management from Florida State University. Dr. Carlson's general research interests are in the areas of the work-family interface, ethics, and impression management. She has published in journals such as *Journal of Management, Journal of Organizational Behavior,* and *Human Relations.*

Dara Chappell completed her undergraduate degree in psychology at the University of Guelph and her Master's degree in industrial relations and human resources at the University of Toronto. Her research areas include work-family conflict, employee adaptive skills, and career development for women.

Noelle Chesley is an Assistant Professor in the Department of Sociology at the University of Wisconsin—Milwaukee. Her research interests include gender and the life course, the work/family interface, health and well-being, and aging. Current projects address the social implications of technology use for workers and their families, assessing whether and how gender and employment patterns interact to influence the propensity to provide care for a parent or in-law, and the health consequences associated with combining work and informal care to parents.

Kerry Daly is a Professor in the Department of Family Relations and Applied Nutrition and is one of the founding directors of the Centre for Families, Work and Well-Being at the University of Guelph in Ontario, Canada. He received his Ph.D. in Sociology from McMaster University, Hamilton, Ontario.

He is co-chair of the Father Involvement Research Alliance, a Canadian national organization of researchers, practitioners and policy-makers. His current research interests focus on the changing practices of fatherhood, the way that families negotiate and navigate time pressures in their lives, and the challenges families face in trying to harmonize their work and family life.

Sarah Damaske is a doctoral candidate in sociology at New York University, where her primary research interests focus on gender, the family, and social inequality. She is currently conducting research for her dissertation, "Moving on Up? Work and Family in Women's Mobility Paths." Her research is supported by a Woodrow Wilson Women's Studies fellowship and a doctoral dissertation improvement grant from the National Science Foundation.

Jay M. Dorio is a doctoral student in industrial and organizational psychology at the University of South Florida. He received his Master's degree in I/O psychology from the University of South Florida, and his Master's degree in marriage and family counseling from the University of Massachusetts, Boston. Jay's research interests include work and family relationships, mechanisms of social support, and gender role issues.

Anat Drach–Zahavy is a staff member at the faculty of Health and Welfare Sciences at the University of Haifa, Israel. She received her Ph.D. degree in the Department of Industrial Engineering and Management at the Technion, the Israel Institute for Technology, with an emphasis on behavioral sciences and management (1997). Her research focuses on stress and support within the organization from a multilevel perspective.

Linda Duxbury is a Professor at the Sprott School of Business at Carleton University in Canada. She has published widely in both the academic and practitioner literatures in the areas of work-life conflict, supportive management, tele-work, managing the new workforce, and the use and impact of office technology. Her most recent books (with Christopher Higgins) include *Voices of Canadians: A View from the Trenches*, and *Work-life Conflict in the New Millennium: A Status Report*.

Kathleen Gerson is Professor of Sociology at New York University and President Elect of the Eastern Sociological Society. She is the author or co-author of numerous books and articles focusing on the connections among gender, work, and family change in post-industrial societies, including *Hard Choices: How Women Decide About Work, Career, and Motherhood (1985)*; *No Man's Land: Men's Changing Commitments to Family and Work* (1993); and *The Time Divide: Family, Work, and Gender Inequality* (with Jerry A. Jacobs, 2004). She is nearing completion of a new book, *Children of the Gender Revolution: Family, Work, and Social Change in the Lives of a New Generation*, which examines young women's and men's strategic responses to growing up in an era of changing families and blurring gender boundaries.

Joseph G. Grzywacz, Ph.D., is Associate Professor, Department of Family and Community Medicine, Wake Forest University School of Medicine,

North Carolina. He is an interdisciplinary social scientist who has studied work, family, and health for 10 years. His research is consistently recognized as among the "best of the best" research in work and family, and it has been published in journals such as the *Journal of Marriage and Family*, *Social Science and Medicine*, *Journal of Occupational Health Psychology*, and the *American Journal of Health Promotion*. His research is supported by public and private sponsors including the National Institute of Health and the Alfred P. Sloan Foundation.

Linda Hawkins is the Executive Director of the Centre for Families, Work & Well-Being at the University of Guelph, Ontario, Canada, where she works to develop and facilitate complex interdisciplinary research programs around gender, work, and care. Her current research interests are in everyday fathers and work-family, women in the academy, and community–university partnerships for change.

Chris Higgins is a Professor at The Richard Ivey School of Business, The University of Western Ontario, London, Canada. Higgins' research focuses on the impact of technology on individuals, including such areas as champions of technological innovation, alternative work arrangements, and, most recently, work and family issues and their impact on individuals and organizations. Higgins has published articles in several top journals including *The Journal of Applied Psychology*, *Communications of the ACM*, *Administrative Sciences Quarterly*, *Sloan Management Review*, *Information Systems Research*, and *Management Information Systems Quarterly*.

Elizabeth Kelley is a Professor in the School of Business Administration at Dalhousie University, Halifax, Nova Scotia. Her research interests center on leadership, particularly the antecedents and outcomes of transformational leadership styles in various environments, as well as the impact of organizational and societal context on management theory and practice.

E. Kevin Kelloway is Professor of Management and Psychology at Saint Mary's University, Halifax, NS, and a Senior Research Fellow at the CN Centre for Occupational Health and Safety. His research interests include occupational health psychology, leadership, and unionization.

Ellen Ernst Kossek (Ph.D., Yale University) is a Professor of Human Resources and Organizational Behavior at Michigan State University's School of Labor & Industrial Relations. She is a Fellow of the American Psychological Association and the Society of Industrial Organizational Psychology. She served on the Board of Governors of the National Academy of Management and as Chair of the Gender and Diversity in Organizations Division. She is Associate Director of the Center that is part of the National Work, Family and Health Network and has received several major grants from the Alfred P. Sloan Foundation to study organizational, managerial, and career processes related to work and family relationships and new ways of working.

Suzan Lewis is Professor of Organisational Psychology at Middlesex University Business School, London. Her research interests include "work-personal life" and gender issues, workplace practice, culture and change in diverse national contexts, the relationships between national and organizational policies and practices and the impacts on work-life integration across the life course. She is a founding editor of the international journal *Community, Work and Family*. Her publications include: *The Work Family Challenge: Rethinking Employment* (Sage, 1996); *Work-Life Integration: Case Studies of Organisational Change* (Wiley, 2005), and, with Rhona Rapoport and Richenda Gambles, *The Myth of Work-Life Balance: The Issue of Our Time for Men, Women and Societies* (Wiley, 2006).

Sean Lyons, Ph.D., is an Assistant Professor of Organizational Behaviour in the College of Management and Economics at the University of Guelph. Dr. Lyons's research concerns work-life balance and the impact of inter-generational differences on workplace dynamics and managing people.

Aline D. Masuda received a Master's degree at Missouri State University and a Ph.D. from the University at Albany, State University of New York, in Industrial Organizational Psychology. She has previously had consultant experience in the areas of organizational surveys working at a global consultant firm in Chicago, and in the areas of workforce and marketing intelligence at IBM. She has been conducting research on work-family conflict, motivation, and leadership with a cross-cultural perspective. Currently, she is working as a post-doctoral researcher at IESE Business School, University of Navarra.

Allyson McElwain is a Ph.D. candidate in Industrial/Organizational Psychology at the University of Guelph. Her research areas include work-family conflict, attitudes toward employment equity, the history of diversity in I/O psychology, and community and societal influences on violence in the workplace.

Phyllis Moen holds the McKnight Presidential Chair in Sociology at the University of Minnesota. She also directs the Flexible Work and Well-Being Center, part of a larger NIH-funded research network initiative. An underlying theme in her work concerns the dynamic intersections between individual life paths and societal institutions. Dr. Moen has published many articles and books on social transformations in the family, workplace, gender roles, and longevity, her most recent being *It's About Time: Couples and Careers* and *The Career Mystique: Cracks in the American Dream*, co-authored with Patricia Roehling.

Jane Mullen has a Ph.D. in Business Administration (Management) from the Sobey School of Business, Saint Mary's University. She is an Assistant Professor in the Department of Commerce at Mount Allison University. Her research interests focus on occupational health and safety, leadership, workplace violence and work-related stress, and she currently holds a grant from the Social Sciences and Humanities Research Council of Canada (SSHRC) to study safety socialization of young workers.

Shira Offer is Assistant Professor in the Department of Sociology and Anthropology at Bar Ilan University, Israel. She received her Ph.D. in Sociology from the University of Chicago, where she worked as a research associate at the Alfred P. Sloan Center on Working Families. Her research focuses on family and community processes in the urban context, with an emphasis on social support networks. She has recently published articles about social support in poor and middle-class communities in the US and about processes of segregation and social marginalization among Ethiopian immigrants in Israel.

Steven A.Y. Poelmans has a Master's degree in Organizational Psychology and Marketing Management and a Ph.D. in Management/Organizational Behavior (IESE Business School/University of Navarra). He is Associate Professor at the IESE Business School and teaches organizational behavior, managerial communication, and self-management. He is Academic Director of the International Center of Work and Family. His research focuses on work-family conflict, managerial stress, family-friendly policies, and cultural intelligence. He is author of three books and a dozen articles in peer-reviewed academic journals, such as *Human Resource Management Review, Personnel Psychology*, and *Academy of Management Journal*. He did training, consulting and executive coaching for companies like Henkel, Randstad, Sun Microsystems, Roche Diagnostics, and Nike.

Barbara Schneider is currently the John A. Hannah Chair in the College of Education and Professor in the Department of Sociology at Michigan State University. She was the co-director of the Alfred P. Sloan Center on Parents, Children, and Work at the University of Chicago. Interested in the lives of families and adolescent transitions into adulthood, Schneider has written widely on these topics. Her most recent publications include: *The Ambitious Generation: America's Teenagers, Motivated but Directionless*, co-authored with David Stevenson (Yale University Press) and *Being Together, Working Apart: Dual-Career Families and the Work-Life Balance* (Cambridge University Press).

Anit Somech is the head of the Educational Leadership & Policy Department at the University of Haifa, Israel. She received her Ph.D. degree in the Department of Industrial Engineering and Management at the Technion, the Israel Institute for Technology, with an emphasis on behavioral sciences and management (1994). Her research is in the areas of management (participative management), burn-out, and work motivation from a cross-cultural perspective.

Olena Stepanova holds a Master's degree in the Psychology of Intercultural Actions (University of Nancy 2, France). She graduated in psychology after studying in the Ukraine and the US. She has worked in a personnel consulting company and collaborated with various academic and social institutions. Currently she is working as Research Assistant in the International Center of Work and Family (ICWF) at IESE Business School, University of Navarra. Her research focuses on cultural change, family-friendly policies, work-family and cross-cultural issues, coaching and mentoring.

Cynthia Thompson is a Professor of Management in the Zicklin School of Business at Baruch College New York, where she teaches courses in organizational behavior, human resource management, and work-life balance. Her research focuses on the integration of work and life, and in particular the extent to which supportive work-family cultures affect employee attitudes and organizational effectiveness. Her research has been published in both scholarly and practitioner journals, including *Journal of Applied Psychology, Journal of Vocational Behavior*, and *Journal of Occupational Health Psychology*. Two of her articles were nominated for the Rosabeth Moss Kanter Award for Excellence in Work-Family Research.

Linn Van Dyne, Professor (Ph.D. University of Minnesota), has research programs on proactive employee behaviors, cultural intelligence, roles, and effects of flexibility on performance. She has published in the *Academy of Management Journal, Academy of Management Review, Journal of Applied Psychology, Organizational Behavior and Human Decision Processes, Research in Personnel and Human Resources Management*, and *Research in Organizational Behavior*. She is a fellow in the Society of Organizational Behavior, and a member of the Academy of Management, the Society for Industrial and Organizational Psychology, the American Psychological Association, and the American Psychological Society.

Patricia Voydanoff, Ph.D., is Senior Research Associate at the Fitz Center for Leadership in Community, University of Dayton. Her research has focused on issues of work and family and the consequences of economic distress, adolescent childbearing, and remarriage and stepfamilies on families and children. Her most recent book, *Work, Family, and Community: Exploring Interconnections*, was published by Lawrence Erlbaum Associates (2007). She is a Fellow of the National Council on Family Relations and a former editor of *The Journal of Family Issues*.

SECTION I

Theories and Measurement Issues

CHAPTER 1

Work–Family Integration: Introduction and Overview

Denise L. Whitehead, Karen Korabik and Donna S. Lero
Centre for Families, Work and Well-being, University of Guelph, Guelph, ON, Canada

In the last twenty years research, policy discussions and public discourse about the challenges and the importance of integrating work and family life have expanded and attained a degree of visibility that is hard to ignore. Researchers have gone beyond earlier studies that focused mostly on the "struggle to juggle," believed to be the particular purview of women or dual-earner couples with children, to develop a complex, multidimensional understanding of the factors that influence the experiences at the work-family interface for all.

The work-family or work-life interface itself reflects the variety of experiences, constraints, supports, and opportunities that individuals and groups experience in the unique cultures that make up their workplace—and their specific role in it. To understand and support a healthy integration of work and life within the wide range of public, private, and non-profit organizations now requires a complex understanding of individual, group, and organizational forces. Furthermore, there has been a growing appreciation of both the negative and positive aspects of this interface. On the negative side of the work-family and productivity ledger are items such as work-family conflict, role strain, job stress and poor performance; on the positive side is the recognition of work-family enrichment, enhancement, and effective performance in work and family roles.

Policy makers and business leaders require information and tools to support work-life integration amidst the many changes in business, the economy, and in workers' lives. Our goal in developing this handbook is to provide readers with an overview of key understandings from internationally recognized experts who have synthesized the many different facets of work and life. We believe their contributions provide important and distinctive views on the challenges faced by individuals, families, and organizations. They have also raised important questions as we move forward in the quest to utilize research and theory to effect best practices in the work-family field.

Handbook of Work-Family Integration: Research, Theory, and Best Practices

WHAT YOU WILL FIND IN THIS BOOK

All authors were asked to discuss the theoretical, conceptual, and methodological considerations that were appropriate to their topic; to provide a critique of existing work in the area; to delineate implications for future theory and research; and to reflect on the implications for policy and practice at the individual, organizational, or societal level. In addition, authors were invited, where appropriate, to provide examples of exemplary policies, progressive companies, and innovative/exemplary practices.

Specifically, this book embraces the interdisciplinary research literature on work and family issues that encompasses psychology, family studies, business, sociology, health, and economics. Moreover, it takes a multilevel approach by addressing issues from individual, family, organizational, and sociocultural perspectives. We recognize that work-family issues are a global concern. To address this, we have invited authors from several different countries (the US, Canada, the United Kingdom, Spain, Israel, and Turkey) representing three continents to contribute chapters to this book. In addition to a chapter specifically on the topic of cross-cultural research on the work-family interface, all of the chapter authors were asked to make reference to research that was done outside of the North American context where relevant. Therefore, this book draws upon international comparisons as a way to relate theory, research, policy, and workplace practice/organizational policy issues in one place. It is hoped that this book will serve as a useful reference for academics and researchers in the area, as a guide to practitioners and policy makers, and as a resource for teaching in both undergraduate and graduate courses.

OVERVIEW OF THE CHAPTERS

The organization of this book is broadly conceptualized around three key themes: (1) Theories and measurement issues, (2) Antecedents, outcomes and moderators, and (3) Context, processes, practices, and policies.

THEORIES AND MEASUREMENT ISSUES

The focus of the first part of this book is on theories and measurement. The five chapters in this section lay the foundation for the book. The first three set the historical context, articulate an overarching theory of work-family integration, and discuss issues pertaining to measurement and methodology. The remaining two chapters concentrate on providing conceptual formulations of a more specific nature (i.e., on multiple roles and the life-course perspective).

In Chapter 2, Denise Whitehead uses broad brush strokes to outline the key historical trends that have brought discussions about work and family to the foreground. Utilizing various sources of statistical data, her chapter chronicles the often perceived competing spheres of earning and caring. Various demographic and social trends are described to illustrate their impact: the influence of women entering the labor force, the aging workforce, the changing nature of work, and trends in business and government policies. Recognizing the entrenchment of women in the labor force and the growing quest for work-life balance amongst a diversity of workers (men and women, mothers and fathers, younger and older) this chapter sets the stage for the in-depth discussions that follow throughout this handbook.

Patricia Voydanoff draws upon an ecological systems approach to articulate a conceptual model of the work-family interface in the third chapter. Voydanoff discusses the nature of within-domain and cross-domain (i.e., boundary spanning) demands and resources and demonstrates how they are directly related to role performance and well-being. Her model lays out the relationships between demands and resources and work-family linkages (e.g., work-family conflict, facilitation, and fit). She postulates that individuals engage in preventative, therapeutic or buffering boundary-spanning strategies to reduce the degree of misfit between the work and family aspects of their lives. Voydanoff also suggests that there is a difference in the manner in which within-domain demands, within-domain resources, and boundary-spanning demands and resources relate to work-family conflict versus work-family facilitation. She believes that within-domain demands are positively associated with work-family conflict, whereas within-domain resources are positively related to work-family facilitation.

In Chapter 4, Dawn Carlson and Joseph Grzywacz provide an overview of the measurement of constructs relating to the negative, positive, and integrative perspectives on the work-family interface. They clarify the conceptual distinctions among several constructs in the work-family literature, examine the variety of measures being used for these constructs, and discuss the measurement issues associated with the manner in which various constructs are conceptualized. They also critique existing measures, make recommendations for future research and scale development, and discuss implications for practice. They suggest that research examining the interrelationship of work-family balance with work-family conflict and work-family enrichment will be useful in testing and refining existing models of the work-family interface.

The focus of the fifth chapter by Rosalind Barnett, is the impact of holding multiple roles. Barnett chronicles how far we have come from the notion that the number of roles an individual can attend to is limited to women as keepers of hearth and home and to men as family breadwinners. She shows how current research has refuted these assumptions. As Barnett discusses, contrary to earlier theories, research has consistently shown that men and women who hold the multiple roles of spouse, parent, and employee report better mental and physical well-being. Barnett and Hyde's expansionist theory extends the research beyond the notion of scarcity to consider the positive effects that multiple roles play. As she reports, it is role quality rather than quantity that is the key factor in determining positive health and well-being outcomes with adults as well as their children reaping the benefits.

In Chapter 6 Phyllis Moen and Noelle Chesley present a life-course perspective on work and family. This involves understanding individuals' life histories and how the timing of life events affects the decisions that individuals make about the structure of their work and family lives. Moen and Chesley discuss a number of life-course constructs (e.g., time cages, time convoys, linked lives). As well, they explain how the timing, duration, and sequencing of life events in the work and family domains over time can result in temporal fit or misfit between the domains that will affect well-being.

ANTECEDENTS, OUTCOMES AND MODERATORS

To adequately understand the work-family interface, it is necessary to understand why problems with integrating the work and family domains of life arise and what consequences result from a lack of work-family integration. As well, insight into the role of moderating variables is important. The second section of this volume is devoted to examining these matters. Among the eight chapters in this section are two that review the empirical research regarding the antecedents and outcomes of role overload and of positive spillover, respectively. Three other chapters look at the outcomes associated with the work-family interface in the work domain, the family domain, and the health and well-being domain. Men and women do not experience the work-family interface similarly, nor do parents and people who do not have children. Moreover, not all men and women are alike nor are all mothers and fathers. The final three chapters in this section address these issues by focusing on gender, motherhood, and fatherhood as moderating variables.

In Chapter 7, Linda Duxbury, Christopher Higgins and Sean Lyons document the existence of high levels of role overload in today's workforce and delineate the consequences that this has for the quality of workers' lives. They provide a theoretical framework for understanding role overload and discuss the issues involved in defining the role overload construct. They then review the literature on the antecedents and consequences of role overload. Finally, they present findings from the 2001 Canadian National Work-Life Study that are pertinent to role overload and offer suggestions for research and practice.

Steven Poelmans, Olena Stepanova and Aline Masuda examine the issue of positive spillover between the work and family domains of life in Chapter 8. They begin by making a distinction between the positive and negative aspects of the work-family interface and discuss how positive and negative spillover are related to one another. Then they differentiate between the various constructs that have been used in the work-family literature to characterize the positive side of the work-family interface (e.g., positive spillover, work-family facilitation, work-family enhancement, work-family engagement, and work-family enrichment). Next they review the literature on the antecedents and outcomes of positive spillover between work and family. Finally, they examine some individual and organizational strategies that may be useful for creating positive spillover between the life domains.

In Chapter 9, Jay Dorio, Rebecca Bryant and Tammy Allen review the North American and international literature regarding the work-related outcomes associated with the work-family interface. They begin by examining outcomes pertaining to work-family conflict. They review the research that has been done on job attitudes (i.e., job satisfaction and organizational commitment), career outcomes (i.e., career satisfaction and career success), performance-related outcomes (i.e., work performance, productivity and organizational citizenship behaviour), and withdrawal intentions and behaviours (i.e., turnover and absenteeism). Then they turn their attention to outcomes associated with the "positive side" (i.e., work-family enhancement) of the work-family interface, once again reviewing the literature pertaining to the same four general categories of outcomes. Following this they present a synopsis of the results of cross-cultural and multinational studies. Finally, a summary and critique of the literature, as well as directions for future research and implications for practice are provided.

Chapter 10 by Shira Offer and Barbara Schneider affirms how family time and togetherness has many positive outcomes for parents and their children. Finding the time to forge family activities, however, has become more difficult as parents have become busier, particularly in dual-earner and single-parent households. The changing nature of work (e.g., more full-time dual earners, longer hours, nonstandard work hours) and increased pressure to engage in quality time with children has increased the pressures on families. Utilizing findings from their research from the *Family 500 Study*, Offer and Schneider examine some of the emotional dimensions associated with family time such as experiences at work, quality of marriage, parent–child relationships, the division of household labor, and psychological well-being. They conclude by noting that emotionally positive family time was associated with the parents' perceptions of their ability to balance their work and family lives.

Jane Mullen, Elizabeth Kelley and E. Kevin Kelloway explore the important nexus between health and well-being outcomes and the work-family interface in Chapter 11. As the authors delineate, the connections between work stress and poor physical well-being outcomes such as cardiovascular problems, sleep disturbances, suppressed immune functioning, and hypertension, to name a few, is irrefutable. Yet, a focus on only negative effects ignores the existence of positive benefits as well. To that end the authors provide a comprehensive overview of the dominant theoretical perspectives with attendance to both negative and positive spillover. This chapter then explores the outcomes of the work-family interface in a variety of domains, including the individual (e.g., psychological well-being, physical well-being, health-related behaviours, and family/dyadic effects), family characteristics (e.g., single, presence of children), and organizational characteristics (e.g., hours of work, type of job, supervisory support). Finally, the authors discuss the importance of considering moderators of the work-family interface to address the complexities of including gender, personality or age in explaining outcomes.

In Chapter 12 Karen Korabik, Allyson McElwain and Dara Chappel review the research that has been carried out on gender and the work-family inter-face and offer suggestions for integrating gender-related issues into work-family research. They begin by defining the construct of gender and identifying problems with the manner in which gender has been studied in the work-family literature. These include research that is atheoretical in nature, that uses sex as a proxy for different aspects of gender, and that examines only mean differences rather than relationships among variables. They, then review and critique studies on the dif-ferences between men and women on work-family conflict. Following this, they examine the relationship between work-family conflict and other aspects of gen-der (i.e., gender-role ideology/attitudes, gender-role orientation, and gender-role values). Finally, they suggest a number of ways that research in this area could be improved.

In Chapter 13 Sarah Damaske and Kathleen Gerson start their chapter on motherhood by articulating an established fact, "mothers are far more likely than not to be paid workers." The fact that most mothers work and remain committed to the workplace throughout their lives is still not without its tensions. The gen-dered and cultural role of mothers and what it means to engage in "mothering" and caring are still often seen to be in direct conflict with earning. That women are penalized on the work and earning front for engaging in care work, and that they are criticized for their care work when devoting too much time to work is one of the ongoing juxtapositions faced by many mothers. As Damaske and Gerson observe, the resulting "politics of motherhood" persists and poses ongoing challenges as women continue to navigate the dilemmas associated with providing care and maintaining a workplace presence.

Chapter 14 is concerned with the issue of fatherhood. In this chapter Kerry Daly, Lynda Ashbourne and Linda Hawkins discuss how the debate and concerns about work-life balance are rooted and perpetuated in discourse on the uptake of paid employment by women and the resulting concerns with their ability to manage work and home. The privilege accorded to mothers and their experiences has relegated fathers to the periphery of these discussions and, often, business and government policies. The positive role that father involvement plays in the lives of their children is well established and documented. Reconciling the provider role with father involvement is one of the ongoing contradictions faced by men. The reality is that there is considerable diversity of experiences for both men and women in managing the work-life interface. For men, however, changes in workplace cultures and policies, societal expectations, and government policies require a shift from viewing work-life as a private issue to a public one.

CONTEXT, PROCESSES, PRACTICES AND POLICIES

The chapters that make up the last section of this handbook examine issues related to process, context and workplace policies and practices. Here you will find chapters on coping and social support as processes that can be used to deal with the work-family interface. Chapters pertaining to context in the form of both workplace culture and national culture are also included in this section. There is also a chapter that discusses the dynamics of face time and how it influences co-worker relationships at work and the uptake of family-friendly policies.

In Chapter 15 Anat Drach-Zahavy and Anit Somech discuss three perspectives for coping with work-family conflict: the individual perspective, the organization-calculative perspective, and the organization-humanistic perspective. They then review the literature on coping with work-family conflict. First, they discuss a number of typologies pertaining to the strategies that individuals use to cope with work-family conflict. Next, they discuss how workplace family-friendly policies relate to coping with work-family conflict. Following this, they propose three models that depict different ways of integrating the individual and organizational perspectives: the compensatory model, the complementary model, and the spiral model.

Roya Ayman and Amy Antani review the existing knowledge on social support and its relation to work-family conflict in Chapter 16. They discuss the various definitions of social support and approaches to its operationalization and measurement. They present a typology that includes: (1) the types of support that exist (instrumental vs. emotional), (2) whether support is received or perceived, (3) the various work (supervisors, co-workers) and nonwork (friends and family) sources that can provide support, and (4) the domains in which support occurs (for work vs. family issues). They introduce a measure that they have developed that captures these dimensions by including items relating to instrumental and emotional support from work and nonwork sources for work and family issues. Furthermore, they delineate several potential models of the relationship between social support, work-family conflict and organizational outcomes and review the empirical evidence relating to each one.

In Chapter 17 Ellen Ernst Kossek and Linn Van Dyne present a cross-level model of the impact of the reduced face time that results when workers make use of family-friendly policies. They first review the literature on three types of workplace flexibility (time, timing, and place). They discuss motivational and coordination effects as they pertain to both individual workers and to work groups. Situating their argument in the context of social comparison processes and equity theory, they consider cross-level effects by explicating how family-friendly policy use by a worker could lead to resentment by co-workers and decrements in group performance. They propose that because more intense policy use (e.g., using more policies over a longer time period) results in greater face time reductions, it will be associated with more detrimental consequences and greater co-worker resentment compared to less intense policy use. Moreover, they propose that policies related to place flexibility (the location of work) will have more significant effects on co-worker resentment than policies related to either time (reduced hours) or timing (flextime) flexibility.

In Chapter 18 Jeanine Andreassi and Cynthia Thompson address the impact of work-family culture. Despite the increase in work-related supports such as telecommuting or access to childcare, there often persists an underlying corporate culture that emphasizes "face time" and a penalty for those who take a leave of absence or parental leave. As Andreassi and Thompson discuss, the critical notion of perceived organizational support, some of which is reflected in formal organizational policies, is a critical factor in whether such policies are deemed to be supportive and whether they will be utilized. Workplace culture is a complex weaving of organizational time demands, perceived career consequences, and managerial support. Each is critical in assessing the actual climate or culture of the organization and whether there are positive or negative benefits for the health and well-being of employees. This chapter also addresses the important consideration of a national context for understanding work-family culture and offers insights for future research.

Zeynep Aycan provides a review of the cross-cultural literature on the work-family interface in Chapter 19. She discusses the role of culture in understanding the work-family interface and why the study of culture is important. She presents a conceptual model in which culture can be seen both as having a main effect and as being a moderator of work-family conflict. One implication of this model is that culture influences the strength of the relationship among work-family conflict, its antecedents and consequences. Aycan reviews the literature regarding how work-family conflict is conceptualized in different cultures and its prevalence across cultures. She also examines the impact of culture on demands and support mechanisms in the work and family domains. Furthermore, she looks at how culture moderates the relationship between work-family conflict, its antecedents and consequences. She concludes that cultural context influences the ways in which family and work demands are perceived and appraised in different societies. For example, cross-cultural differences in appraisal and coping relate to differences in the prevalence of work-family conflict as well as its impact on outcomes (e.g., well-being, job and marital satisfaction, turnover intentions). Finally, Aycan points out the need to consider the *emic* or indigenous manifestations of work-family dynamics.

The purpose of the concluding chapter by Donna Lero and Suzan Lewis is to tie together the themes that emerged in the book. They do so by surfacing the multiple assumptions that are made about work and the ideal worker, families and the roles of mothers and fathers, and organizations and their policies. They point out some of the gaps that exist between research and policy planning. They identify emerging issues (e.g., the ageing workforce, challenges of combining work and eldercare) and the need to address under-researched issues, including immigration, low wage workers, and occupation-specific issues, as in paid care work.

At the end of this handbook is an appendix listing websites, major research centers, organizations, and other subject matter of interest to work-family scholars and practitioners. This compilation is the effort of all of the authors of this volume who contributed their suggestions and favorites. With the volume of new information being constantly generated the Internet has become a valuable resource and highly accessible means by which to distribute information and research results. It is hoped that you will find something of interest and will utilize this appendix to obtain additional information, contacts, and to track emerging issues and policy changes.

CHAPTER 2

Historical Trends in Work–Family: The Evolution of Earning and Caring

Denise L. Whitehead

Centre for Families, Work and Well-being University of Guelph, Guelph, ON, Canada

Appreciating how work and family have risen to the forefront of organizational and individual's agendas and policy is to understand the development of the perfect storm. There is no one single policy, societal or business trend that has driven this evolution and the accompanying discussions and research. Rather, like a perfect storm, it is the commingling of these spheres, each with their own unique aspects, as they feed into, and back onto the other, that has taken the discussions about integrating work and family from its earliest inklings during World War II to the current modern age. Increased female labor force participation and increased stress and pressures, both at home and at work, have given rise to concerns about how to combine both roles of earner and caregiver (Beaujot, 2000). This chapter chronicles some of the key trends that have played a large role in this field including: the impact of dual-earner families in the paid labor force, the changing nature of work, and the influence and response of business and government policies.

WOMEN IN THE PAID LABOR FORCE

While it is certainly true that women entering the workforce in ever-increasing numbers since World War II is not the sole societal shift that has brought work and family issues to the fore, it is nonetheless acknowledged as a major contributor (Menaghan & Parcel, 1990). It is the combination of more intensive work for women and men, increasing family diversity, the importance of women and work in the economy and the necessity of two incomes, while also addressing the need to care for both the young and old, that sets the context for current work-life research and discourse.

In the US, in 2004, more than 59% of women were in the paid labor force, an increase of 16% over the last 24 years (Bureau of Labor Statistics, 2005c). In contrast, men's labor force participation has decreased from 90% in 1970 to just

Handbook of Work-Family Integration: Research, Theory, and Best Practices

above 80% in 2005 (Lang & Risman, 2007). A similar trend is evident in Canada, which has some of the highest rates of female labor force participation in the world, with 81% of women engaged in paid work, only 10 percentage points lower than for men (Marshall, 2006). The societal transition from families headed by men as primary breadwinners to a majority of families consisting of dual-earner couples is a dramatic change (59.5% in 1997, up from 35.9% in 1970) and highlights why balancing work and family has become such a concern (Jacobs & Gerson, 2001).

The proportion of men and women in the labor force is now nearly equal in both Canada and the US (Bond, Thompson, Galinsky & Prottas, 2002) and reflects the social movement towards greater individual autonomy and gender equality (McLanahan, 2004). While a recent slight dip in women's labor force participation has raised the question as to whether there is a reversal towards traditional family roles, Lang and Risman (2007) argue that a shift towards gender convergence and egalitarian attitudes is occurring with increasing similarity between men and women and their desires for work and life. The labor force participation of mothers with children under age 18 reflects how entrenched employment has become; from 47% in 1975 to 73% in 2000 (Bureau of Labor Statistics, 2005c). While women continue to increase their work participation in managerial and professional occupations, administrative work and part-time employment is a significant part of women's labor force participation. In the US, 25.7% of women usually work part-time as compared to 10.8% of men (Bureau of Labor Statistics, 2005c).

INCREASING WORK HOURS: PAID AND UNPAID

Not only are the number of dual-earner couples increasing, but the number of hours that these couples are spending at work has also increased. Bond et al. (2002) report that combined work hours for dual-earner couples with children in the US have increased 10 hours a week, from 81 hours per week in 1977 to 91 hours per week. While women engage in paid work, on average six hours less per week than men (35.9 hours compared to 41.6 hours), nearly 60% of women who worked in 2003 worked full-time and year round, compared to only 41% in 1970 (Bureau of Labor Statistics, 2005c). Jacobs and Gerson's (2001) research has emphasized that little has changed by way of individuals' allocation of time to paid work, but rather what has changed is the combined amount of time allocated to work by dual-earner couples (and similarly single parents), particularly among couples with high educational attainment, who often experience the greatest conflict in demands between work and home.

While much early research on maternal employment focused on possible negative effects on children's well-being, this concern has abated somewhat as increased attention has focused on explorations of the impact of stress and time strains faced by dual-earner couples (Nomaguchi, Milkie & Bianchi, 2005;

Perry-Jenkins, Repetti & Crouter, 2000). Arlie Hochschild's (1989) description of women working a "second shift" in addition to their work-related duties has helped define the challenges and burdens associated with women entering the workforce while still attending to and retaining responsibility for the domestic tasks of housekeeping and child rearing.

The trend towards increased time spent in the paid labor force is accompanied by two other distinct trends: less time on unpaid tasks, such as cooking and household upkeep, and increased time spent caring for children. Overall, the increase in paid working hours among women has been accompanied by a decrease in the amount of time spent by women on household tasks and an increase in the unpaid work of men (Ciscel, Sharp & Heath, 2000). As Coltrane (2000) notes, women's decrease in housework has been steeper than men's increase in contributions to engaging in housework. Overall, the actual time spent in unpaid work is decreasing, as families increasingly outsource domestic chores by hiring other individuals to clean their house or rely on convenience meals and take-outs (Bianchi, Milkie, Sayer & Robinson, 2000; Marshall, 2006), though women still continue to spend more hours in unpaid work than men (Coltrane, 2000).

In contrast to housework, time spent in childcare and child-related activities is increasing. When combined, the time that parents with children spend on caring for and doing things with their children on workdays has increased (Bond et al., 2002). Bianchi, Robinson & Milkie (2006) report that in 2000 fathers in the US devoted 6.5 hours per week to caring for their children, an increase of 153% from 1965, and married mothers spent an average of 12.9 hours per week, an increase of 21%. And single mothers, whom one would anticipate are the most time-pressed, have increased their time spent in childcare by 57% to 11.8 hours a week.

Time, however, is only part of the equation. It is the cultural shift in expectations that parents engage in more intensive and professionalized parenting of fewer children that partly accounts for the increased time expenditures associated with childrearing (Bianchi et al., 2006). As a consequence of more time being devoted to paid work and the care and education of children, both mothers and fathers report far less time for themselves and their own hobbies: in 2002 fathers reported 1.3 hours spent on time to themselves per workday, down from 2.1 hours 25 years ago, and mothers reported 0.9 hours versus 1.6 hours in 1977 (Bond et al., 2002). Not all children, however, are sharing in increased parenting time. Sara McLanahan (2004) has noted a divergence in the access to time and resources; children of mothers with the highest educational attainment and income and increased father involvement, have experienced the greatest gains, often as a result of delayed childbearing and maternal employment, as compared to children who have experienced losses, often as the result of divorce and nonmarital childbearing. Nonmarital childbearing accounts for 32% of all births to women aged 15 to 44 in the US, with most of these births occurring to teenage women and women in their early twenties (Lawler Dye, 2005).

There are many normative social expectations associated with the care of children, although there are changes underway. There is considerable evidence to suggest that many women still feel obligated to pursue the quest to maintain the dual roles of both *ideal worker* and *ideal parent* (Stone & Lovejoy, 2004; Williams, 2000) (see also Chapter 13 by Damaske & Gerson in this volume). While fathers of the pre-World War II birth cohort were largely exempted from the *ideal parent* presumption in deference to their primary role as family breadwinner, there is a growing wave of changing norms regarding paternal involvement (Carr, 2002; Gavanas, 2002). As a consequence, fathers, too, are facing greater work-life stress in response to time shortages and the increasing demands associated with involved and responsible fatherhood (Silverstein, 2002; Winslow, 2005) (see also Chapter 14 by Daly, Ashbourne & Hawkins in this volume). That a father's responsibilities are still largely defined by their ability to provide cash rather than care continues to be reinforced by laws, policies and social norms (Hobson & Morgan, 2002).

FAMILY DIVERSITY

When it comes to family structure, diversity is the new norm—couples with children, some married, some cohabitating, couples without children, same-sex couples, single parents, and blended families created through re-marriage and re-partnering have relegated the concept of the "nuclear" family to the distant past. While households composed of married couples (52%) still predominate (an 11% increase from 1990 to 2000), the increase in people living alone (26%) (a 23% increase from 1990 to 2000) is noteworthy (Simmons & O'Neill, 2001). Increasing numbers of single parents due to high rates of marital dissolution and even higher rates of partnership dissolution amongst cohabitors (Heuveline & Timberlake, 2004) further add to the stress of managing earning and caring. In this wake are the increasing numbers of women and children who rely on a woman's income for their primary source of financial support; US family households maintained by women with no husband present (12.9 million) are three times greater than single-father households (Simmons & O'Neill, 2001).

In part, women's rising stature in the workplace has facilitated the independence of women and their financial capacity to leave marital and other relationships that are no longer satisfactory (Beaujot, 2000). The rising rates of sole support parents (from 13% in 1970 to 32% in 2003) has necessitated a strong attachment to the labor force, while also putting further pressure on and increasing the stress level for the individual who plays the roles of both worker and primary parent with less income to purchase childcare and home-related supports (Fields, 2004; Jacobs & Gerson, 2001). Therefore, the allocation of time and energy to paid and unpaid work is not so straightforward. The dichotomy of earning and caring is central to this discussion, as is the gendered nature of such care. Canadian demographer Rod

Beaujot (2000) has noted the central fact that "men...are more likely to be living in relationships, while women are more likely to be living with children" (p. 83).

THE IMPORTANCE OF WOMEN AND WORK IN THE ECONOMY

Discussions about women's presence in the workforce is not just about the fact that more women are working, but that society and business need women to work. Increasing numbers of women are attaining a post-secondary education. The US Bureau of Labor Statistics (2005c) reports that young women are more likely to enroll in college than young men (72% versus 61%). Many professional schools, such as law and medicine, frequently graduate classes of at least equal numbers of men and women. Undergraduate programs, with exceptions such as engineering, are increasingly finding that women are outnumbering men. Long gone are the days when a woman, upon her marriage, was expected to vacate her employment (Boris & Lewis, 2006). Such a marriage bar would be impractical in society today. With increased education and employment opportunities, in 2004 women were filling half of all management, professional and related occupations in the US (Bureau of Labor Statistics, 2005c). It is noteworthy that in 2000 labor force participation was much higher for women with the most education, as compared to women with the least education (65% versus 30%) (McLanahan, 2004), suggesting wider income inequality and potential life-long poverty for less educated women (and men) and their families.

In the wake of these educational and work realities are two other factors: delayed childbearing and falling fertility (Martin, 2000). In the US, fertility rates peaked during the baby boom at 3.5 births per woman, declined to all-time lows of 1.8 births per woman in the mid-1970s and have risen to what is considered replacement levels of 2.1 births per woman (Lawler Dye, 2005). In Canada and many European countries, however, fertility rates are considerably lower than in the US, a fact that concerns policy-makers who project a shrinking workforce. Indeed, the labor and expertise that women have to contribute to most industrialized societies has become a necessity. It is anticipated that the up and coming wave of retiring baby boomers will continue to exacerbate the need for pools of labor from women and, increasingly, from immigrants (US Department of Labor, 1999).

THE TWO-INCOME NECESSITY

The preceding discussion on the *need* for women to work dovetails with the increasing necessity of two incomes in most families as the value of a single earner as the source of family income recedes (Ciscel et al., 2000). Moreover, in some instances, the striving for increased material consumption continues to drive what that standard of living should look like (e.g., a large house, two cars, vacations), having an impact on the time needed for work and the time needed to acquire and maintain the goods (Daly, 2003). While this may create additional time burdens for middle-class families, the reality for many other families is that the stagnation in real income growth experienced in the 1990s has increasingly meant that two-wage earners are a necessity, not a luxury, as wages have been eroded (Ciscel et al., 2000; Sauvé, 2007). While low-income women have long fulfilled their community-defined gendered obligation of working to improve the standard of living of their families (Abramovitz, 2001), women's wages are no longer perceived as simply "gravy" for household extras, and instead have become a part of the economic force to help families maintain their standard of living in an economy driven by purchasing power (Sauvé, 2007).

These realities are further complicated by the increasing presence of households led by a single parent where opportunities for sharing the childcare burdens and obtaining flexibility to meet work demands are further challenged (Jacobs & Gerson, 2001; Menaghan & Parcel, 1990). In 2003, the earnings of wives accounted for 35% of their families' incomes (up from 26% in 1973) and in 2003, 25% of women out-earned their working husbands (up from 18% in 1987) (US Bureau of Labor Statistics, 2005c). Nevertheless, on average, women's annual earnings are still significantly lower than men's earnings ($36,716 versus $52,908) (Bond et al., 2002). Women college graduates, while earning 76% more than women with only a high school diploma, only earned 75% of what their male counterparts earned in 2004 (Bureau of Labor Statistics, 2005c). Concerns surrounding glass ceilings and lack of pay parity for women persist in both Canada and the US (Stone & Lovejoy, 2004).

THE PROVISION OF CARE

While the discourse on work and family balance at times extends to all workers and their quest for balancing work, family and leisure, it is often around issues of providing care that the discussion is most focused. Childcare was the first area to be identified. During World War II it was acknowledged that recruiting women to contribute their labor to the war effort was dependent on providing care for their children. This association, however, was not maintained once men returned home and women were expected to vacate their jobs and return to the homefront (Boris & Lewis, 2006). Childcare continues to remain a low priority for many industrialized countries. Conflicting normative expectations around the rearing of children has complicated such initiatives with the suggestion that parental care is optimal, but in conflict with the demands of work, thus inhibiting progress in creating more unified and state-sponsored programs for childcare delivery (Crittenden, 2001; Harrington, 1999; Lewis & Haas, 2005).

The advent of aging baby boomers and increasing life spans is now direct-ing attention to care needs at the other end of the life cycle, as a growing propor-tion of employees seek ways to care for aging parents and relatives (Garey, Hansen, Hertz & Macdonald, 2002). It is predicted that by the year 2030 Americans over the age of 65 will comprise 20% of the population, with those 80 and older con-stituting the fastest growing segment (Rubin, 2001, as cited in Garey et al., 2002). The *2005 National Study of Employers* noted that 35% of employees had elder care responsibilities within the past year (Bond, Galinsky, Kim & Brownfield, 2005). The combination of later-age childbearing and increasing life expectancy will result in more individuals caught in the throes and challenges of child and elder care; the *sandwich generation*. Increasingly, employers are recognizing this trend and providing information with respect to elder care resources to their employees (up 11% from 23% in 1998 to 34% in 2005) (Bond, Galinsky, Kim & Brownfield, 2005).

These social realities, in turn, have spurred employers to take into further consideration the nonworking, parental and personal aspects of their employees' lives. Governments are being called upon to institute social policies that address the realities of individuals engaged in work and caregiving across the life-course. In the young years, paid maternity and parental leaves have become common, as many industrialized nations (e.g., Sweden, Canada, France) legislated time off work and income replacements to allow new parents the opportunity to bond and care for their children while also maintaining some level of income and work-place security. Such initiatives are far more tenuous in the US where extremely modest efforts have been expended to introduce very limited family leave with no income replacement (see Block, Malin, Kossek & Holt, 2006). Overall, a debate exists as to where and how to expend efforts to facilitate both work and family; an onus on the state to provide universally accessible benefits to all or encouragement for employers to individually sponsor and support their employees (see Chapter 20 by Lero & Lewis in this volume). The ongoing challenge over the next decades will be to deal with the growing need for more care for children, and for ill or disabled family members amidst a declining supply (Hochschild, 1998).

THE CHANGING NATURE OF WORK

Discussions regarding work and family are not simply about whether people are or are not working, but rather what type of work they are doing. The social, technological and economic forces that have led to the transition from agricultural to manufacturing to service-oriented jobs are significant and have had an impact on the type of work most people perform, the nature of the employee–employer relationship, and the restructuring of work itself.

Part of the changing landscape around the fluidity between work and family can be found in the shift from rural agricultural occupations to urban, industrialized centers. Working on the family farm and in local endeavors often enabled parents, and particularly mothers, to contribute to the financial well-being of the household while integrating childrearing responsibilities (Boris & Lewis, 2006). The migration from rural communities to urban factories brought with it an increased need and mandate for the separateness of work and home life from each other. Organizational work introduced more rigid expectations regarding time expectations and an increasing focus on expecting and measuring efficiency. With the promise of better wages, workers were drawn to urban centers where work in the manufacturing sector was predominant.

Opportunities for employment in manufacturing and other goods-producing industries have traditionally been associated with "good jobs" in North America (Lowe & Schellenberg, 2001). Often unionized, these jobs have been seen to have the advantages of both good wages and benefits. Nevertheless, manufacturing jobs are on the decline worldwide. In the US, manufacturing accounts for only half of the share in non-farm employment that it did in 1970 (US Department of Labor (DOL), 1999). The DOL projected a total loss of 18.1 million jobs in the 10-year period between 1996 and 2006. In the US only construction is expected to increase due to the demand for new housing, while Canada is also seeing growth in industries related to natural resources (Statistics Canada, 2006a).

Technological advances and innovations that have saved time and money by replacing human workers, coupled with the relocation of many manufacturing jobs to foreign countries with cheaper labor costs, have been identified as the drivers behind this momentum. The resulting trade deficit—the ongoing demand for manufactured goods necessitating a reliance on imports in the presence of decreased domestic production—is estimated to account for 58% of the decline in manufacturing employment of more than 3 million jobs between 1998 and 2003 and a 34% decline from 2000 to 2003 (Bivens, 2004). The decline in the goods-producing sector of the economy has been characterized as the deindustrialization of America (US Department of Labor, 1999). Further, the loss of some jobs due to efforts to invoke cost-saving measures have resulted in the increase in the contracting-out of service jobs, such as janitorial services and accounting, often resulting in the trading-off of secure, good paying jobs with benefits, for insecure work with lower pay and no benefits (Canadian Centre for Policy Alternatives, 2007).

Service-oriented businesses and jobs now account for the greatest increase in employment. In the US, service sector work accounted for approximately 76% of employment in 2004 (Bureau of Labor Statistics, 2005a). This is expected to increase as the number of related jobs, such as businesses that service the work of larger businesses, are contracted out (projected to rise to 78.5% in 2014) (Bureau of Labor Statistics, 2005a). The transformation from a manufacturing to a service-based economy has created large numbers of jobs that require increased skills, a good portion of which have often been the types of jobs for which women are traditionally hired (Menaghan & Parcel, 1990). Jobs in computer services and health care are among some job categories where ongoing growth is projected (US Department of Labor, 1999). Furthermore, the nature of blue-collar work is changing, as well-paid industrial jobs are deemed expendable in favor of cheaper labor in developing countries, the increase in poorly paid service jobs, the weakening of labor unions and the influx of migrant workers. The increase in service-oriented jobs also increases the prevalence of those working nonstandard work hours such as in call-centers, health aides and those individuals servicing the expansion of e-commerce over the Internet, which in part, is being utilized by individuals who work nonstandard hours. Even managers and professionals are not immune to the precariousness of the workplace. The economic recessions of the 1980s and early 1990s, as well as increasing global competition, have brought about downsizing, outsourcing and mergers, such that even professionals and managers find themselves "working scared" (Hochschild, 1998).

DIVERSITY IN THE WORKPLACE

The workplace is now the visible melting pot as cultural, linguistic and multinational groups commingle. In part, this is attributable to the fact that the US expects a 50% increase in population by 2050. This will be due primarily to immigration, which is estimated will account for two-thirds of the growth, in an attempt to off-set decreasing fertility (US Department of Labor, 1999). Discrimination in the workplace as a result of gender and race has declined, though immigrants and racial minorities continue to experience exceptional challenges and, increasingly, older workers are facing lack of work opportunities due to ageism. Employment opportunities by class, age, and race are not uniformly available to all individuals and this can have profound implications for work-life integration (see Marks, 2006, for an expansive discussion on diversity in the workplace).

This diversity is also attributable to the increase in multinational corporations with a worldwide presence and to technological advances and travel which have made globalization an everyday aspect of doing business. In multinational corporations, and when obtaining specialized technical support, conducting business increasingly calls on workers to connect with fellow employees who are thousands of miles away. In turn, corporate organizations need to re-orient policies that increasingly need to respect different religious, ethnic and cultural norms.

There is also considerable diversity in the structure of the working day. Working in nonstandard or shift work is a reality for many families (Presser, 2003). Two-fifths of all employed Americans work at mostly nonstandard times, outside of the traditional 9 to 5 brackets. For some this is their preferred work arrangement, while others equate this with the nature of the job. For some families, this facilitates parents providing care to children. In the future, diversity across so many domains will require that the workplace generates diversity in family and work policies. As Levin-Epstein (2006) has noted, family-supportive policies should contemplate not only aspects related to flexibility, but also focus on the conditions of work that are related to individual and family functioning.

THE EMPLOYEE–EMPLOYER RELATIONSHIP AND UNIONIZATION

The expectation that the employee–employer relationship would last for the duration of one's adult work life has been slowly eroded. At one time there were few expectations that an employee could have of an employer except a regular paycheck, and, if all went well, a gold watch at retirement and a pension. The unwritten contract that this was a job for life defined the relationship with an expectation of loyalty on both sides. Erosion of this psychological contract has brought decreased organizational commitment and job satisfaction (Sparrow, 2000). Over time, the increased demands by employers on employees have also contributed to the changed nature of the relationship. The reality for many workers is that they are working longer and harder. Galinsky et al. (2005) report that one in three US workers report being overworked, which was associated with greater incidences of high stress levels, clinical depression, and poorer health. (See also Chapter 7 by Duxbury, Higgins & Lyons in this volume.)

The increasing demands of work are being generated in other ways. Technology, with its original promise of labor saving, has, in fact, allowed workers to feel that they are "on call" 24/7 (Presser, 2003). Cellular phones, e-mail and Blackberries have facilitated a work culture where the lines between home and work have become blurred (Bond et al., 2002). On the other hand, the advent of computers, both at work and at home, coupled with the rising availability of Internet access, has transformed the nature of work and the way in which it is performed for some workers. In 2004, 15% of men and women reported working at home at least once per week as part of their job (Bureau of Labor Statistics, 2005d), with working at home being more common for parents than for non-parents (Bureau of Labor Statistics, 2005c). The opportunity for working at home, however, is concentrated in occupations that lend themselves more readily to such arrangements, particularly managers and professionals (which constitute 50% of such workers) and those in sales (20%) (Bureau of Labor Statistics, 2005c; Major & Germano, 2006). Though such work arrangements can negatively impact work and home life due to the blurring of boundaries, in many instances the work genres of telework and telecommuting do provide some workers with flexibility and thus enhance work-life integration (Sparrow, 2000).

One of the resulting aspects of the advent of sweeping job loss and downsizing is that many employees are seen to have the onus for their own career progression, rather than the employer, with the responsibility to pursue professional development and to continually increase work-related skills and capacities (Cavanaugh & Noe, 1999, as cited in Major & Germano, 2006). In addition, workers also face constant interruptions and distractions in a work environment that expects ongoing multi-tasking in the context of increased pressure related to job performance. The numbers of US employees who work while on holiday and who fail to use some or all of their vacation days (one-third of those with access to paid vacations) is indicative of the increasing pressures faced by employees, particularly those in managerial, professional or high-earning occupations (Galinsky et al., 2005). In addition, the reality of living in a global economy creates demands on some workers to commit to continental hours that are not family-friendly, such as the growing number of overseas call centers that service trans-Atlantic markets which require that employees be available when the customers call.

Unions are also undergoing significant changes. During the periods of advancing industrialization unions brought better wages and working conditions and, in time, also addressed issues pertaining to safety and time off. In the last 20 years unions find that the benefits that they have lobbied for are no longer needed as manufacturing jobs disappear as a result of corporate relocation to countries with lower wages and as domestically produced products are no longer deemed as desirable. Overall, union representation has fallen for both men and women: 15% of men were unionized in 2004 as compared with 28% in 1983, and 13% of women in 2004 were union members compared to 18% in 1983 (Bureau of Labor Statistics, 2005c).

Canada has also been experiencing declining rates of unionization though the statistics reflect a different pattern. First, the US unionization rate in 2006 stands at approximately 12% (down from 20.1% in 1983) compared to 30% in Canada (down from 38% in the late 1980s) (Block et al., 2006; US Department of Labor, 2007). Block et al. posit that the US has typically had lower unionization rates because of a social-economic policy that places a greater emphasis on market-driven demands and an emphasis on individualism. The other stark difference is that in Canada slightly more women are unionized than men (30.1% as compared to 29.4%, respectively, in 2006) reflecting their presence in public sectors of health and teaching (Statistics Canada, 2006b). Yet the story is more subtle. In the US, rates of unionization have tripled among those employed in the public sector, increasing from 10% to 37% between 1950 and 1998. In contrast, private sector unionization has declined from 35% to 10% during the same period, primarily due to offshore manufacturing and increased resistance to union efforts to organize by the private sector (US Department of Labor, 1999). Similar to the US, rates of unionization amongst Canadian workers in the public sector, not only experienced a slight increase compared to a decline in the private sector, but the rate of unionization in the public sector greatly exceeds the rate in the private sector (71.4% versus 17%, respectively, in 2006) (Statistics Canada, 2006b).

The ongoing juxtaposition for workers is that some individuals have too much work and some individuals have too little work, often at low hourly wage rates and on a precarious basis (Jacobs & Gerson, 2001). Both the US and Canada have seen a decrease in the number of employees with access to paid sick days, vacation or personal leave days—only 25% of working parents with a child under three, and four in ten workers who are low-income have access to paid leave (Levin-Epstein, 2006). In the US, the proportion of employees with access to sick days dropped from 69% to 56% between 1988 and 1997; those with paid holidays dropped from 96% to 89%, and paid vacation from 98% to 95% for employees in medium and large firms (Levin-Epstein, 2006). Low-income workers are the most vulnerable group amongst all categories of workers, having less access to paid sick days, and other employer-provided benefits, including health care coverage.

THE RESTRUCTURING OF WORK

The preceding discussion reflects the changing nature of the employer–employee relationship (Bond et al., 2002). For 1 in 5 workers, however, the reality is that they work for themselves rather than for someone else (Bond et al., 2002). This trend is part of the growing discourse on the changing nature of employment in most industrialized countries from traditional, full-time secure employment to work patterns that are characterized by a lack of security and considerable precariousness (Cranford, Vosko & Zuke, 2003; Eardley & Corden, 1996; Gabel & Mansfield, 2003; Sarfati & Bonoli, 2002). The 1990s brought to the fore the impact that a recession can have on the workforce as jobs disappeared and downsizing and restructuring became the operative words. The corporate quest for savings and shareholder profits has brought about other changes that have impacted workers. Outsourcing and "just in time" delivery have both reduced good paying jobs within organizations and increased pressure on businesses, and hence workers, who must stage the delivery of products and services to coincide with the business model where inventory will not take up needed space and costs are minimized.

Job losses and the combination of outsourcing and technological advancements have led to the growth in the number of individuals who are now working as contingent workers, defined as persons who do not expect their jobs to last or who report their jobs as temporary. These workers account for 5.7 million US workers, or 4% of total employment (US Bureau of Labor Statistics, 2005b). Furthermore, the growth in independent contractors has been significant. In 2005 the US Bureau of Labor Statistics estimated that 10.3 million individuals, or roughly 7.4% of the labor force, worked as independent contractors (2005b).

While self-employment has often been viewed as a capital-based business with employees, the reality is that most newly generated self-employed individuals are nonemployers—a business owner with no employees. This segment of the self-employed (which includes a wide range of individuals—from highly specialized consultants to those providing individual services such as home childcare) accounted for 19.5 million workers in the US in 2004 (US Census Bureau, 2006). The growth of knowledge and service based industries has seen the largest growth and individuals starting businesses are increasingly loners with no or one or two employees providing services and information. Push and pull theories predominate (Delage, 2002)—some workers have been pushed into these jobs when previous employers downsized (Dennis, 1996; Kalleberg, Reskin & Hudson, 2000), while others, particularly mothers, have utilized self-employment as a work strategy to balance the demands of work and family (Heilman & Chen, 2003). In 2004, 5.6% of employed women were self-employed compared with 8% of men (Bureau of Labor Statistics, 2005c), and women now comprise 38% of self-employed persons compared to 27% in 1976.

POLICY TRENDS

In the context of understanding the larger historical picture of work and family, it is necessary to consider the role and impact that changes in welfare reform, employment insurance, health care, retirement funding and work–family policies across countries have had. This chapter will highlight some of the overarching key trends that have come into play regarding the conceptualizations of work–family polices. The reader is referred to Chapter 20 by Lero & Lewis in this volume for further discussion.

Part of the key to understanding policy trends is to understand the central and often pivotal role that government plays both in terms of its direct involvement (e.g. through public policies such as maternity leave) and indirectly by influencing employees and employers' rules, norms, practices and beliefs that underlie work-life practices and cultures (Lewis & Haas, 2005). One of the central themes in work-family policies is that much of it is predicated on the basis of labor force attachment that is still often rooted in gendered norms, assumptions about paid employment, and ideals about work and family.

FAMILY-RELATED LEAVE AND BENEFITS

At a global level there is a growing recognition of the importance of work and family issues among industrialized nations. The United Nations Declaration of the Rights of the Child emphasizes the importance of sharing work and family responsibilities and society's responsibility for providing adequate childcare. Article 18-3 stipulates that "state parties shall take all appropriate measures to ensure that children of working parents have the right to benefit from childcare services and facilities" (Wolcott & Glezer, 1995, p. 145, as cited in Lewis & Haas, 2005, p. 366). Coupled with this is the acknowledgement that children need engaged parents while also encouraging ongoing attachment to the labor force. Concerns about declining fertility and delayed childbearing in most industrialized countries have brought to the fore the need to consider issues related to work and family. Current directives to European Union member states encourage a minimum allowance of three months of unpaid leave by mothers and fathers and equal sharing of childcare responsibilities. This indicates a shift not only toward state-sponsored leave, but also a fundamental shift in the social constructions of the roles of both mothers and fathers. As Lewis and Haas (2005) have noted, how society deals with the issues of how paid leave and family caregiving will be combined is a central question in understanding the gender contract.

The US continues to be notable as one of the few industrialized countries to not have any kind of paid leave following a child's birth or adoption. The introduction of the *Family Medical Leave Act of 1993* (FMLA) ushered in 12 weeks of unpaid leave after the birth or adoption of a child, for an employee's serious health condition, or to care for a spouse, parent or minor or disabled child who has a serious health condition. Job and health insurance protection are covered during the leave of absence. As Block et al. (2006) summarize, the use of the FMLA leave provisions has been primarily by employees to deal with their own health conditions (52.4%), followed by employees who need to attend to a newborn or adopted child (18.5%).

Childcare services, in both Canada and the US, continue to be haphazardly provided. The lack of childcare options that consider both quality and affordability is a concern that has plagued most working families since before the postwar years, but has intensified as women's labor force participation has accelerated, especially among mothers with young children (Boris & Lewis, 2006). Despite the fact that families with dual-earners is now firmly entrenched, neither country offers any kind of national daycare system, thus forcing most parents to rely on their own financial and personal resources in finding and maintaining care and making decisions about the type of care to use—whether regulated or unregulated, private or public.

While subsidies may be available for unemployed and low-income families, to facilitate labor force participation, middle and upper income parents primarily reap assistance through tax deductions and credits (Kelly, 2006). In 2006 the Canadian federal government introduced the $100 per month Universal Child Care Benefit, suggesting that this offered childcare "assistance" to those seeking childcare and "choice" for those choosing to stay home. The reality is that such funding does little to increase spaces or assure affordability and access. Furthermore, childcare workers, who are almost all women, find that this work often offers poor pay; a similar trend for those who provide caring services to the elderly. While Canada's parental leave policies are far more progressive than the US, its childcare policies (with the important exception of Quebec) share many common traits with its close US neighbor. Ultimately, a focus on individual responsibility for matters pertaining to family and family-related issues continues to dominate (Bogenschneider, 2006). In contrast, member states of the European Union have developed more accessible and affordable childcare services to facilitate increased female labor force participation, though with mixed results in terms of achievement to date (Block et al., 2006).

Ultimately, the flexibility that workers experience in the day-to-day aspects of their working life is often in the form of workplace policies. As Stone and Lovejoy conclude, access to workplace flexibility is critically important for the retention of all workers, but especially true for women (2004). The US Bureau of Labor Statistics reported that in 2004, 27 million full-time wage and salary workers (27.5%) had flexible work schedules that allowed them to vary the start and end time of their workday (2005a). Men had somewhat more flexible schedules than women (28.1 and 26.7%, respectively) with white workers more likely to have access to flexible work than black or Hispanic workers (28.7%, 19.7% and 18.4% respectively). Similar to access to telework and telecommuting options (as discussed above), individuals in management, professional, and related occupations as well as salespersons and office workers, are more likely to have flexible work options (36.8% and 29.5%). Interestingly, although 1 in 4 workers has access to a flexible work schedule, only 1 in 10 workers are enrolled in a formal employer-sponsored flextime program. Stone and Lovejoy argue that there is a great need "to create meaningful part-time opportunities in the professions that do not penalize workers who take advantage of them; and second, to fully institutionalize these arrangements to shield them from arbitrary and individualized implementation" and, most crucially, that they be gender neutral (2004, pp. 81–2).

WELFARE REFORM

Welfare policies, particularly with respect to the level of support provided and the degree of income testing, have played a central role in the support of single mothers and their children. Between 1955 and 1975 cash benefits available to single mothers in the US increased along with the introduction of services such as Medicaid, food stamps, housing and childcare subsidies (McLanahan, 2004). As McLanahan chronicles, as cash benefits were reduced in the mid-1970s, in-kind transfers increased, but on an income-tested basis. As a result, when low-income women worked or had income through a partner's work, much of the benefits disappeared.

Since the 1990s both the US (Abramovitz, 2001) and Canada (Schafer, Emes & Clemens, 2001) have experienced welfare activism in their efforts to reduce the number of individuals receiving state-sponsored benefits. The US has been more aggressive than Canada in its efforts. The federal US passage of the 1996 *Personal Responsibility and Work Opportunity Reconciliation Act* (PRWORA) has been central to the efforts to implement extensive government reforms, privatize service delivery, and increase the use of private and faith-based organizations in efforts to reduce welfare dependency (Schafer et al., 2001). Both countries have increasingly mandated that recipients of welfare submit to some kind of employment uptake. Furthermore, time limits on the receipt of welfare in the US (five years federally and even less in some states), have driven caseloads down. In the US welfare caseloads experienced significant drops, falling by 46% nationwide from 5.5% in 1994 to 2.1% of the population in 2000 (US Department of Labor, 1999). Canada experienced significant declines as well, from 10.7% of the population in 1994 to 6.8% in 2000. While these welfare reforms are often touted as successful, the requirements, particularly with respect to mandated employment, often ignore other realities. Women, often with young children, find themselves relegated to the lowest paying jobs, with little support for affordable, quality childcare, training and educational opportunities, health care and transportation. Permanent work is often at minimum wage rates that do not allow for a family's living wage. The fact that women, and predominantly women of color, fill this niche ignores the ongoing burden of pregnancy, childrearing and caretaking associated with gender, and ignores the particularly heavy burden of work–family obligations that some citizens bear. As Jacobs and Gerson have noted, the ambivalence associated with the presence of mothers in the workforce is apparent in that "welfare mothers are criticized for not working enough, [while] middle-class women are castigated for spending too much time in paid-employment" (2001, p. 60).

[Un]Employment Insurance

Insurance for some part of one's income earnings in the event of job loss was one of the first work–family policies to come into reality. In response to high rates of unemployment during the Great Depression, employment insurance, both in the US and Canada, was initially conceived as a preservation of the man's wage and ability to provide for the family, with early employment insurance specifically excluding women, even if they worked (Boris & Lewis, 2006; Porter, 2003). Modern-day employment insurance is still predicated on organizational workforce attachment, often with the provision of minimum work requirements in order to qualify. In Canada, EI is administered through the federal employment insurance system based on mandatory contributions from employers and employees. This pooled fund provides partial income replacement for those experiencing unemployment as well as new parents, both mothers and fathers, who can qualify for a combined total of up to 50 weeks of income replacement following the birth of their child.

Other forms of "employment insurance" provide income support for illness, absence following a workplace injury and for disability claims. Qualifying for employment insurance has become more difficult over time. Precarious and seasonal workers often fail to qualify due to lack of sufficient employment hours or earnings. Additionally, the increased movement to self-employment has generated a category of workers who do not qualify for job-related insurance benefits.

THE AGING LABOR FORCE

As discussed previously, an aging population and an aging workforce are creating care issues for those employees seeking to balance work and caring for children and/or aging parents, spouses and relatives. While the advent of issues surrounding their care has already been discussed, two other critical issues are looming on the horizon: the shortage of replacement workers and the adequacy of retirement funds. The anticipated shortage of workers as the baby boomers continue to age and fertility rates are insufficient to ensure that there will be enough workers to fill positions looms large over the next two decades of the 21st century (Piktialis & Morgan, 2003). For example, 11% fewer Americans were born between 1966 and 1985, and it is anticipated that the number of young workers available to take the place of retiring older workers will continue to fall below replacement levels. On the one hand, a trend towards earlier retirement seems to have stopped, yet the accelerated increase in the numbers of older individuals is starting to create, and will likely continue to create, increasing gaps in work sectors.

ADEQUACY OF RETIREMENT FUNDS

Work in the retirement years will likely fall into three categories: those who retire early or at least with sufficient income to fully retire; those who continue to work to off-set or compensate for the lack of retirement savings; and those who choose to work, most likely because they have marketable skills and thus are able to negotiate favorable terms and conditions for their work. While the latter group will have a great deal of input and control into what their work situation looks like, it is the group that *must* work in their older years who will face unique challenges, due to declining health and the challenges of providing care for spouses, siblings and parents. Approximately half of the private sector workforce is not covered by an employer-sponsored retirement plan (US Department of Labor, 1999). Fewer than 40% of working women in the private sector are entitled to a company-based pension as compared to 46% of men and only 32% of female retirees in the US are receiving a pension (US Department of Labor, 1999). Women have an elevated risk for poverty in their old age. Compromised earnings due to caregiving in earlier periods result in lower lifetime earnings and a lack of access to pensions despite a greater need due to longer life expectancies (Spratlin & Holden, 2000).

Furthermore, concerns about the instability of public funds, particularly given the predicted lack of sufficient labor to meet current job demands, downturns in the economy, and precariousness of corporate retirement plans are creating concerns around gaps for providing for retirees. For many private sector employers, significant legacy costs associated with retiree health and pension benefits are a significant burden and some retired employees face the loss of their earned benefits with the demise of some businesses (Bivens, 2004). For other workers, the rise in precarious and self-employment has left a growing number of individuals without adequate plans or funds to see them through their retirement years.

For those who do have access to employer-sponsored plans, changes in how those plans are funded and allocated have also been significant. "Defined benefit" plans (in which an employee was guaranteed a specific dollar amount upon retirement) have increasingly been replaced with "defined contribution" plans. Defined contribution plans allocate more of the responsibility to the employee to plan for their own retirement and to bear the burden of both rising and falling financial market performance as the employee's own contributions and the employer contributions are vested within individual retirement accounts. Of the approximately 50% of US private sector workers who have coverage through a retirement plan, those covered by a defined contribution plan more than doubled from 33% in 1975 to 80% by end of the century (US Department of Labor, 1999). Men are more likely than women (45% versus 35%) to have a defined-benefits pension plan or guaranteed-benefits pension plan through work, thus facilitating their economic transition to retirement (Bond, Galinsky, Pitt-Catsouphes & Smyer, 2005). While defined-contribution plans offer less security in terms of the lack of guaranteed payout, the defined-contribution plan is seen as allowing greater flexibility for the employee who changes jobs.

ACCESS TO GOVERNMENT REGULATED AND FUNDED SOCIAL SECURITY

US social security benefits are based on the average of the highest 35 years of the worker's covered earnings. In the event of no earnings during any of those years a zero is assigned in the averaging. In contrast, Canada's "childrearing dropout" provision of the Canada Pension Plan (CPP) allows workers to remove those years for which they had no income due to childcare responsibilities for children under the age of seven. While no money is added in for those years, removing those years with zero income before averaging lifetime earnings does have the effect of increasing the overall payout of the retirement pension.

HEALTH CARE

The preceding discussion on the increasing numbers of the elderly and increased longevity highlights the issue of the need for and access to health care. The discussion, however, is not limited to only this segment of the population, but necessarily applies to all citizens. The issue of health care provides a study in contrasts between Canada and the US. Canada has had state-sponsored health care available to all citizens since 1966 with the introduction of the *Medical Care Act* (Health Canada, 2005). The core principles of universality, comprehensiveness, public administration and portability have been affirmed with the passing of the *Canada Health Act* in 1984, which included the prohibition of user fees, and most recently in 2004 with distinct federal cash funding through the Canada Health Transfer. In contrast, the US does not have a government-sponsored plan (with the exception of Medicare for seniors 65 and older and Medicaid for the very poor), thus making employer-sponsored health insurance one of the most important benefits received by US workers and their families. Large employers (those with 100 or more employees) offer 98% of full-time employees health coverage and 94% offer family coverage (Bond, Galinsky, Kim & Brownfield, 2005). Overall, 15.3% of the US population was without any health insurance in 2005 (US Census Bureau, 2007).

IMPLICATIONS FOR FUTURE RESEARCH AND PRACTICE

The entrenchment of dual-earners in most industrialized countries has had profound implications for families who must deal with the realities of earning and caring, and for the workplaces which must increasingly acknowledge and address the issues faced by a diverse workforce. Women's entrance into the labor force can no longer be conceived as a mere trend or blip—their presence in the labor force is crucial with respect to gender equality and for the skills they bring and the income they provide to their families and to the economy. The need for ongoing attachment to the labor force will continue to be a pressing concern for employers as the workforce continues to age at a rapid rate. Offering workplace flexibility to attract and retain workers at different places along the life-course will be key. Younger workers will want to balance work with caring for children and in time, the means to care for an ageing or ill spouse or parents. Older workers will want flexibility to smooth the transition from work to full retirement, particularly critical as they too search for ways to care for aging spouses and relatives.

REFERENCES

Abramovitz, M. (2001). Learning from the history of poor and working-class women's activism. *Annals of the American Academy, 577*, 118–129.

Beaujot, R. (2000). *Earning and Caring in Canadian Families*. New York: Broadview Press.

Bianchi, S. M., Milkie, M. A., Sayer, L. C. & Robinson, J. P. (2000). Is anyone doing the housework? Trends in the gender division of household labor. *Social Forces, 79*, 191–228.

Bianchi, S. Robinson, J. P. & Milkie, M. A. (2006). *Changing Rhythms of American Family Life*. New York: Russell Sage Foundation.

Bivens, J. (2004). Shifting blame for manufacturing job loss: Effect of rising trade deficit shouldn't be ignored. Briefing Paper #149. Washington, DD: Economic Policy Institute. Available at www.epi. org/content.cfm/briefingpapers_bp149

Block, R. N., Malin, M. H., Kossek, E. E. & Holt, A. (2006). The legal and administrative context of work and family leave and related policies in the USA, Canada and the European Union. In F. Jones, R. J. Burke & M. Westman (eds), *Work-life Balance: A Psychological Perspective* (pp. 39–68). New York: Psychology Press.

Bogenschneider, K. (2006). *Family Policy Matters: How Policymaking Affects Families and What Professionals Can Do* (2nd edn). Mahwah, N. J.: Lawrence Erlbaum.

Bond, J. T., Galinsky, E., Kim. S. S. & Brownfield, E. (2005). *2005 National Study of Employers*. New York: Families and Work Institute.

Bond, J. T., Galinsky, E. M., Pitt-Catsouphes, M. & Smyer, M. A. (2005). *The Diverse Employment Experiences of Older Men and Women in the Workforce*. New York: Families and Work Institute.

Bond, J. T., Thompson, C., Galinsky, E. & Prottas, D. (2002). *Highlights of the National Study of the Changing Workforce*. New York: Families and Work Institute.

Boris, E. & Lewis, C. H. (2006) Caregiving and wage-earning: A historical perspective on work and family. In M. Pitt-Catsoupes, E. E. Kossek & S. Sweet (eds), *The Work and Family Handbook: Multidisciplinary Perspectives and Approaches* (pp. 73–97). Mahwah, NJ: Lawrence Erlbaum.

Bureau of Labor Statistics. (2005a). BLS releases 2004–2014 employment projections (USDL 05-2276). Washington, DC: US Government Printing Office. Retrieved May 30, 2007 from http://www.bls. gov/news.release/ecopro.nr0.htm

Bureau of Labor Statistics. (2005b). Contingent and alternative employment arrangements, February 2005 (USDL 05-1433). Washington, DC: US Government Printing Office. Retrieved April 20, 2007 from www.bls.gov/news.release/conemp.nr0.htm

Bureau of Labor Statistics. (2005c). Women in the labor force: A databook (USDL 05-849). Washington, DC. Available at http://www.bls.gov/cps/wlf-databook-2005.pdf

Bureau of Labor Statistics. (2005d). Work at home summary (2004) (USDL 05-1768). Washington, DC: Us Government Printing Office. Retrieved November 12, 2006 from www.bls.gov/news.release/ homey.nr0.htm

Canadian Centre for Policy Alternatives. (2007). Lots of insecure jobs created in 2006, but more good jobs lost. *The CCPA Monitor, 13*(9), 5–9. Available at http://www.policyalternatives.ca

Carr, D. (2002). The psychological consequences of work-family trade-offs for three cohorts of men and women. *Social Psychology Quarterly, 65*, 103–124.

Ciscel, D. H., Sharp, D. C. & Heath, J. A. (2000). Family work trends and practices: 1971 to 1991. *Journal of Family and Economic Issues, 21*, 23–36.

Coltrane, S. (2000). Research on household labor: Modeling and measuring the social embeddedness of routine family work. *Journal of Marriage and the Family, 62*, 1208–1233.

Cranford, C. J., Vosko, L. F. & Zukewich, N. (2003). Precarious employment in the Canadian labour market: A statistical portrait. *Just Labour, 3*, 6–21.

Crittenden, A. (2001). *The Price of Motherhood: Why the Most Important Job in the World is Still the Least Valued*. New York: Henry Holt and Company.

Daly, K. J. (2003). Family theory versus the theory families live by. *Journal of Marriage and Family, 65*, 771–785.

Delage, B. (2002). Results from the survey of self-employment in Canada. Ottawa, ON, Canada: Applied Research Branch, Human Resources Development Canada.

Dennis, W. J. (1996). Self-employment: When nothing else is available? *Journal of Labor Research, 17*, 645–661.

Eardley, T. & Corden, A. (1996). *Low Income Self-employment: Work, Benefits and Living Standards*. Brookfield USA: Avebury.

Fields, J. (2004). *America's Families and Living Arrangements: 2003*. Current Population Reports, P20-553. Washington, DC: US Census Bureau.

Gabel, J. T. A. & Mansfield, N. R. (2003). The information revolution and its impact on the employment relationship: An analysis of the cyberspace workplace. *American Business Law Journal, 40*, 301–353.

Galinsky, E., Bond, J. T., Kim, S. S., Backon, L., Brownfield, E. & Sakai, K. (2005). *Overwork in America: When the Way We Work Becomes Too Much* (Executive Summary). New York: Families and Work Institute.

Garey, A. I., Hansen, K. V., Hertz, R. & Macdonald, C. (2002). Care and kinship: An introduction. *Journal of Family Issues, 23*, 703–715.

Gavanas, A. (2002). The fatherhood responsibility movement: The centrality of marriage, work and male sexuality in reconstructions of masculinity and fatherhood. In B. Hobson (ed.), *Making Men Into Fathers: Men, Masculinities and the Social Politics of Fatherhood* (pp. 213–242). New York: Cambridge University Press.

Harrington, M. (1999). *Care and Equality: Inventing a New Family Politics*. New York: Knopf.

Health Canada (2005). Canada's health care system. Ottawa, ON: Health Canada. Retrieved May 14, 2007 from http://www.hc-sc.gc.ca/hcs-sss/pubs/system-regime/2005-hcs-sss/back-context_e.html#1

Heilman, M. E. & Chen, J. J. (2003). Entrepreneurship as a solution: The allure of self-employment for women and minorities. *Human Resource Management Review, 13*, 347–364.

Heuveline, P. & Timberlake, J. M. (2004). The role of cohabitation in family formation: The Unite States in comparative perspective. *Journal of Marriage and Family, 66*, 1214–30.

Hobson, B. & Morgan, D. (2002). Introduction. In B. Hobson (ed.), *Making Men into Fathers: Men, Masculinities and the Social Politics of Fatherhood* (pp. 1–21). New York: Cambridge University Press.

Hochschild, A. (1989). *The Second Shift: Working Parents and the Revolution at Home*. New York: Viking.

Hochschild, A. R. (1998). Ideals of care: Traditional, postmodern, cold-modern, and warm-model. In K. Hansen & A. Garey (eds), *Families in the US: Kinship and Domestic Politics* (pp. 527–538). Philadelphia: Temple University Press.

Jacobs, J. A. & Gerson, K. (2001). Overworked individuals or overworked families? Explaining trends in work, leisure, and family time. *Work and Occupations, 28*, 40–64.

Kalleberg, A. L., Reskin, B. F. & Hudson, K. (2000). Bad jobs in America: Standard and nonstandard employment relations and job quality in the United States. *American Sociological Review, 65*, 256–278.

Kelly, E. L. (2006). Work-family policies: The United States in international perspective. In M. Pitt-Catsoupes, E. E. Kossek & S. Sweet (eds), *The Work and Family Handbook: Multi-disciplinary Perspectives and Approaches* (pp. 99–123). Mahwah, NJ: Lawrence Erlbaum.

Lang, M. M. & Risman, B. J. (2007, May). The continuing convergence of men's and women's roles. A discussion paper for the 10th Anniversary Conference of the Council on Contemporary Families, University of Chicago. Retrieved May 22, 2007 from http://www.contemporaryfamilies.org

Lawler Dye, J. (2005). *Fertility of American women: June 2004 (population characteristics)*. Washington, DC: US Census Bureau.

Levin-Epstein, J. (July, 2006). *Getting punched: The job and family clock (It's time for flexibility work for workers of all wages)*. Washington, DC: Center for Law and Social Policy. Available at www.clasp.org.

Lewis, S. & Haas, L. (2005). Work-life integration and social policy: A social justice theory and gender equity approach to work and family. In E. E. Kossek & S. J. Lambert (eds), *Work and life Integration: Organizational, Cultural, and Individual Perspectives* (pp. 349–374). Mahwah, NJ: Lawrence Erlbaum.

Lowe, G. S. & Schellenberg, G. (2001). *What's a Good Job? The Importance of Employment Relationships.* Ottawa, ON, Canada: Canadian Policy Research Networks.

Major, D. A. & Germano, L. M. (2006). The changing nature of work and its impact on the work-home interface. In. F. Jones, R. J. Burke & M. Westman (eds), *Work-life Balance: A Psychological Perspective* (pp. 13–38). New York: Psychology Press.

Marks, S. R. (2006). Understanding diversity of families in the 21st century. In M. Pitt-Catsoupes, E. E. Kossek & S. Sweet (eds), *The Work and Family Handbook: Multi-disciplinary Perspectives and Approaches* (pp. 41–65). Mahwah, NJ: Lawrence Erlbaum.

Marshall, K. (2006, July). Converging gender roles. Perspectives on labour and income, 7. Ottawa, ON: Statistics Canada.

Martin, S. P. (2000). Diverging fertility among US women who delay childbearing past age 30. *Demography, 37,* 523–533.

McLanahan, S. (2004). Diverging destinies: How children are faring under the second demographic transition. *Demography, 41,* 607–627.

Menaghan, E. G. & Parcel, T. L. (1990). Parental employment and family life: Research in the 1980s. *Journal of Marriage and the Family, 52,* 1079–1098.

Nomaguchi, K. M., Milkie, M. A. & Bianchi, S. (2005). Time strains and psychological well-being: Do dual-earner mothers and fathers differ? *Journal of Family Issues, 26,* 756–792.

Perry-Jenkins, M., Repetti, R. L. & Crouter, A. C. (2000). Work and family in the 1990s. *Journal of Marriage and the Family, 62,* 981–998.

Piktialis, D. & Morgan, H. (2003, January/February). The aging of the US workforce and its implications for employers. *Compensation and Benefits Review, 35,* 57–63.

Porter, A. (2003). *Gendered States: Women, Unemployment Insurance, and the Political Economy of the Welfare State in Canada, 1945–1997.* Toronto, ON: University of Toronto Press.

Presser, H. B. (2003). *Working in a 24/7 Economy: Challenges for American Families.* New York: Russell Sage Foundation.

Sarfati, H. & Bonoli, G. (eds) (2002). *Labour Market and Social Protection Reforms in International Perspective.* Burlington, VT: Ashgate Publishing Company.

Sauvé, R. (February, 2007). The current state of Canadian family finances: 2006 report. Ottawa, ON, Canada: The Vanier Institute of the Family. Available at www.vifamily.ca

Schafer, C., Emes, J. & Clemens, J. (2001). Surveying US and Canadian welfare reform. The Fraser Institute: British Columbia, Canada. Retrieved May 14, 2007 from http://www.fraserinstitute.ca/admin/books/files/SurveyingWelfare.pdf

Silverstein, L. B. (2002). Fathers and families. In J. P. McHale & W. S. Grolnick (eds), *Retrospect and Prospect in the Psychological Study of Families* (pp. 35–64). Mahwah NJ: Lawrence Erlbaum.

Simmons, T. & O'Neill, G. (2001, September). Household and families: 2000 (Census 2000 Brief). Washington, DC: US Census Bureau.

Sparrow, P. (2000). The new employment contract: Psychological implications of future work. In R. Burke & C. L. Cooper (eds), *The Organization in Crisis* (pp. 167–187). Oxford: Blackwell.

Spratlin, J. & Holden, K. C. (2000). Women and economic security in retirement: Implications for social security reform. *Journal of Family and Economic Issues, 21*(1), 37–63.

Statistics Canada (2006a). Study: Labour market shifts in manufacturing, construction and natural resources. *The Daily, Friday January 27, 2006.* Ottawa, ON: Statistics Canada. Retrieved May 7, 2007 from www.statcan.ca/Daily/English/060127/d060127c.htm

Statistics Canada. (2006b). Unionization. Ottawa, ON: *Perspectives on Labour and Income.*

Stone, P. & Lovejoy, M. (2004). Fast-track women and the "choice to stay home". *Annals of the American Academy of Political and Social Science, 596,* 62–83.

US Census Bureau. (2006). Non-employer statistics: 2004 (NS04-00A-1). Washington, DC: Government Printing Office. Available at www.census.gov/prod/2006pubs/ns0400a01.pdf. Retrieved April 30, 2007

US Census Bureau. (2007). Census Bureau revises 2004 and 2005 health insurance coverage estimates. Washington, DC: US Census Bureau. Retrieved May 14, 2007, from http://www.census.gov/Press-Release/www/releases/archives/health_care_insurance/009789.html

US Department of Labor. (1999). Futurework: Trends and challenges for work in the 21st century. Washington, DC: Author.

US Department of Labor. (2007). Union members summary. Washington, DC: US Bureau of Labor Statistics.

Williams, J. (2000). *Unbending Gender.* New York: Oxford University Press.

Winslow, S. (2005). Work-family conflict, gender, and parenthood, 1977–1997. *Journal of Family Issues,* *26*(6), 727–755.

CHAPTER 3

A Conceptual Model of the Work-Family Interface

Patricia Voydanoff
Fitz Center for Leadership in Community, University of Dayton, Dayton, OH

INTRODUCTION

Empirical research on the work-family interface has exploded in recent decades. These studies represent disciplines such as sociology, psychology, organizational behavior, family science, human development, social work, gerontology, family therapy, law, and occupational health. The diversity of approaches associated with this multiplicity of disciplines has advantages and disadvantages. Its breadth is useful in documenting the complexity involved in understanding the work-family interface. However, it creates a lack of theoretical focus, which makes it difficult to develop comprehensive yet manageable theoretical frameworks and models for research. Eventually, this multi-disciplinary complexity needs to be embraced to create more meaningful models and theories.

This chapter draws upon several theoretical approaches to formulate and articulate a conceptual model of the work-family interface. These frameworks are useful for understanding various aspects of the interface. They include ecological systems theory; individual and occupational stress theories; resilience theory; and work-family border theory. The next section presents the general conceptual model, which is derived from ecological systems theory. The following sections elaborate upon specific linkages presented in the model and discuss their theoretical grounding in theories of stress, resilience, and borders. The chapter closes with a brief discussion of implications of the model for future research and policy.

THE GENERAL CONCEPTUAL MODEL

This chapter uses an ecological systems approach as a general framework for the development of a conceptual model of the work-family interface. This approach suggests that aspects of each domain occur at multiple ecological levels. The ecological model of human development articulated by Bronfenbrenner (1989) focuses on four ecological levels, each nested within the next according to their immediacy

Handbook of Work-Family Integration: Research, Theory, and Best Practices

to the developing person. The most immediate level, the microsystem, consists of a pattern of activities, roles, and interpersonal relations experienced by a person in a network of face-to-face relationships, which occur in settings such as the workplace, the family, and the community. The mesosystem is the interlinked system of microsystems in which a person participates—for example, linkages between family and school. The external environments in which a person does not participate but which exert indirect influence on the person are referred to as exosystems. An example is the work setting of a family member. Finally, the macrosystem is the overarching pattern of the culture or subculture in which the micro-, meso-, and exosystems are nested. The macrosystem consists of the institutional patterns and broad belief systems that provide the context for human development.

Mesosystems consist of interrelationships among the microsystems in which an individual participates. Four mesosystems can be formed through the connections among the work, family, and community microsystems. Three of these consist of relationships between two microsystems, that is, the work-family, work-community, and family-community mesosystems. The work-family-community mesosystem is created when an individual participates in all three microsystems. Direct relationships occur in which characteristics of one or more microsystems are related to characteristics of another microsystem. However, relationships among microsystems also may operate through linking mechanisms and processes. This chapter proposes and elaborates a conceptual framework and model for examining these relationships and processes. The most general form of the model is presented in Figure 3.1. Although the model focuses on linkages between the work and family domains, the community domain also is incorporated in terms of the influence of community demands and resources on the work-family interface and effects of the work-family interface on community outcomes.

The top part of the model indicates that economic, workplace, family, community, and social contexts are expected to influence the relationships and processes that comprise the work-family-community mesosystem. According to ecological systems theory, microsystems, mesosystems, and exosystems are influenced by the larger macrosystem in which they are embedded. The macrosystem forms a "societal blueprint" for a given culture or subculture that consists of opportunity structures, resources and hazards, life-course options, patterns of social interaction, shared belief systems, and life styles (Bronfenbrenner, 1989). Thus, the demands, resources, and strategies associated with the work-family-community mesosystem operate within these larger structural and cultural contexts. These contexts include the structure of the economy and the workplace, family demographics and ideology, community structure and participation, and social categories such as social class, race and ethnicity, and gender.

The remainder of the model proposes several ways in which characteristics associated with the work, family, and community microsystems are related to work, family, and community role performance and quality and individual well-being.

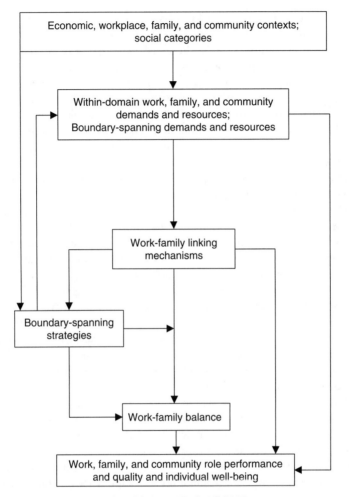

Figure 3.1   The general conceptual model. *Source*: Voydanoff (2007)

The wide range of work, family, and community characteristics that have shown relationships to role performance and quality and to individual well-being can be subsumed under two categories: demands and resources. Demands are structural or psychological claims associated with role requirements, expectations, and norms to which individuals must respond or adapt by exerting physical or mental effort. Resources are structural or psychological assets that may be used to facilitate performance, reduce demands, or generate additional resources.

Work, family, and community demands and resources are derived from a range of work, family, and community characteristics. For example, the structure of work, family, and community life encompasses the organization and timing of work life, the size and composition of family structures, and the social networks making up community life. The social organization of work incorporates the demands and content of jobs, family social organization consists of the division of labor among family members, and community social organization reflects formal and informal organizations. Norms and expectations associated with work include job descriptions, employment policies, and work culture. Families operate within the context of role expectations and gender ideology. Community norms are associated with the reciprocity and trust incorporated in social capital. In addition, the work, family, and community domains include various types of support from supervisors and coworkers at work, family members at home, and friends and neighbors in the community.

The model in Figure 3.1 distinguishes between two types of demands and resources: within-domain and boundary-spanning. Within-domain demands and resources are associated with characteristics such as the structure and content of activities in one domain (e.g. job pressure and autonomy, time spent caring for family members, or friend and neighbor support), whereas boundary-spanning demands and resources are inherently part of two domains (e.g. bringing work home and a supportive work-family culture). Although boundary-spanning demands and resources originate in one domain, they serve as demands and resources in other domains. For example, when individuals work at home or perform family activities at work, they are operating in both domains at the same time. When employers acknowledge and address employee family needs through a supportive work-family culture and policies, the two domains are partially integrated.

The model proposes that within-domain and boundary-spanning demands and resources are directly related to work, family, and community role performance and quality and to individual well-being. Role performance encompasses behaviors performed at work and in the home, whereas role quality refers to positive and negative affect, such as positive and negative moods and emotions derived from work, family, and community activities. Work outcomes include job performance and productivity, attendance-related issues, and job satisfaction and stress. Family outcomes encompass family role performance, family role quality, and child development outcomes. Community outcomes consist of participation in formal and informal community activities as well as community satisfaction. Individual outcomes incorporate several aspects of psychological and physical well-being, for example depression, psychological distress, and physical health and illness. These outcomes have implications for the system-level functioning of workplaces, families, and communities.

The proposition of direct relationships between demands and resources and outcomes is the basis for much of the extant research on relationships among work, family, and community life. The model also serves as a framework for proposing a chain of relationships and processes through which these direct effects may operate. Demands and resources lead to linking mechanisms (e.g. work-family conflict, facilitation, and fit). Linking mechanisms lead to boundary-spanning strategies, which are actions taken by individuals and families to reduce misfit between work, family, and community demands and resources. These strategies are proposed to have both mediating and moderating effects on relationships between work-family linking mechanisms and work-family balance. In addition, feedback effects are proposed from boundary-spanning strategies to work, family, and community demands and resources. Linking mechanisms also are expected to be related directly to work-family balance, which in turn is associated with work, family, and community role performance and quality and individual well-being. The following sections explore the model in greater detail and provide theoretical and conceptual underpinnings to its various propositions. See Voydanoff (2007) for a more detailed explication of the model, its theoretical grounding, and extent of empirical support.

DIRECT RELATIONSHIPS BETWEEN DEMANDS AND RESOURCES AND OUTCOMES

The general model presented in Figure 3.1 posits direct relationships between within-domain and boundary-spanning work, family, and community demands and resources and work, family, and community role performance, role quality, and individual well-being. However, the rationale for these relationships differs for within-domain demands, within-domain resources, boundary-spanning demands, and boundary-spanning resources.

WITHIN-DOMAIN DEMANDS

Within-domain demands, which are characteristics associated with the structure and content of a domain, are of two types: time-based and strain-based. Time-based demands reflect the idea that time is a fixed resource, that is, time spent in activities in one domain is not available for activities in another domain. Time-based demands are related to outcomes through a process of resource drain in which the time or involvement required for participation in one domain limits the time or involvement available for participation in another domain (Tenbrunsel, Brett, Maoz, Stroh & Reilly, 1995). Resource drain from one domain limits role performance and quality in other domains and reduces individual well-being. Time-based demands include the amount of time in paid work (the number and scheduling of work hours), in family work (time caring for children and elderly parents and time in household work), and in community activities (time volunteering and informal helping).

Strain-based demands influence work, family, and community role performance, role quality and individual well-being through a process of negative psychological spillover in which the strain associated with participating in one domain is carried over to another domain such that it creates strain in the second domain. This strain hinders role performance and quality, thereby reducing individual well-being. Psychological spillover operates through transmission processes in which conditions in one domain are associated with psychological responses, which are then transferred into attitudes and behavior in another domain. Negative transmission processes include negative emotional arousal, interpersonal withdrawal, energy depletion, and stress (Piotrkowski, 1979; Rothbard, 2001). Strain-based demands include characteristics associated with the social organization of work (job demands and job insecurity), family social organization (marital conflict, children's problems, caregiver strain, and unfairness in household work), and community social disorganization (neighborhood problems and demands from friends).

Strain-based demands may be more strongly related to role performance and quality and individual well-being than time-based demands are. The relative weakness of the effects of time-based demands on outcomes may derive from the ability of individuals to maintain a balance between the demands and resources associated with spending time in a given activity. Strain-based demands operate through processes of negative psychological spillover, which may be more difficult to prevent. In addition, some time-based demands may produce strain-based demands, for example the time spent caring for children and elderly parents may create strain-based demands such as role overload (Voydanoff, 2007).

WITHIN-DOMAIN RESOURCES

Within-domain work, family, and community resources engender processes that improve role performance and quality and individual well-being when they are applied across domains. They include enabling resources and psychological rewards. Enabling resources from one domain may generate resources in another domain that provide the means for enhancing participation in the second domain. Enabling resources generally are associated with the structure or content of domain activities, for example skills and abilities developed through domain activity, behaviors associated with role activities, and the availability of social support from others involved in the domain. Enabling resources in one domain increase the competence and capacities of individuals to perform in other domains. For example, interpersonal communication skills developed at work, at home, or in the community may facilitate constructive communication with members of other domains. In addition, positive participation in domain activities may be associated with energy creation that enhances participation in other domains (Marks, 1977). This improved performance is accompanied by role quality and individual well-being. Enabling resources include job autonomy, skill utilization, and workplace support in the work domain; family adaptation and cohesion and spouse and kin support in the family domain; and formal community support, neighborhood cohesion, and friend support in the community domain.

In early work on psychological rewards, Sieber (1974) proposed that rewards from one domain may facilitate participation in another domain. These rewards included privileges, status security and enhancement, and personality enrichment. Rewards also include psychological resources that are associated with feeling esteemed and valued and intrinsic rewards such as meaningful activities. These rewards may be accompanied by psychological benefits, such as motivation, a sense of accomplishment, self-esteem, and ego gratification. They may affect other domains through processes of positive psychological spillover. Positive transmission processes include positive emotional arousal, interpersonal availability, energy creation, and gratification (Piotrkowski, 1979; Rothbard, 2001). Psychological rewards include meaning, pride, and respect associated with performing work, family, and community activities.

BOUNDARY-SPANNING DEMANDS

Boundary-spanning demands and resources are expected to influence outcomes through different processes than do within-domain demands and resources. Work-family border theory (Clark, 2000) provides a useful framework for understanding the processes through which boundary-spanning demands and resources influence outcomes. It views relationships between domains as a continuum ranging from segmentation to integration. At the segmentation end of the continuum, the work and family domains are mutually exclusive with distinctive mentalities and no physical or temporal overlap. At the integration end of the continuum, work and family are indistinguishable in terms of the people, tasks, and thoughts involved (Clark, 2000; Nippert-Eng, 1996). Work-family border theory further posits that the extent of segmentation or integration is associated with the degree of permeability and flexibility of the boundaries between domains. Permeability refers to the degree to which elements from one domain enter into another domain, for example an individual making family-related appointments while at work. Flexibility is the extent to which temporal and spatial boundaries allow roles to be enacted in various settings and at various times, for example flexible work schedules in which an individual can vary starting and ending work times to meet family needs. Segmentation is characterized by low permeability and inflexible boundaries, whereas integration is associated with high permeability and flexible boundaries (Clark, 2000).

Boundary-spanning work, family, and community demands and resources derive from the boundary permeability and flexibility associated with varying degrees of segmentation or integration. Boundary-spanning demands encompass boundary permeability across domains, whereas boundary-spanning resources incorporate boundary flexibility. Low boundary permeability is accompanied by more difficult transitions across domains, which may result in decreased role performance and quality and individual well-being. Demands associated with difficult role transitions include overnight travel for work, commuting time, and the hours and schedules of community services and schools. High permeability also is associated with role blurring or blending, in which distinctions between roles become unclear. Demands associated with role blurring include the performance of work responsibilities at home or family duties at work, permeable work-family boundaries, and work- or family-based community involvement.

BOUNDARY-SPANNING RESOURCES

Boundary-spanning resources address how work, family, and community domains connect with each other in terms of boundary flexibility. Boundary flexibility refers to the degree to which temporal and spatial boundaries permit role activities to be performed in various settings and at various times, that is, flexibility regarding when and where activities are performed. Work-based boundary-spanning resources include the availability of workplace policies and programs that enhance the flexibility of the temporal boundary between work and family. These policies and programs may improve flexibility in two ways: via work supports and/or family supports. Work supports (e.g. flexible work schedules and dependent care benefits) help employees accommodate their family responsibilities without reducing work hours or the amount of work that is performed. Family supports (e.g. parental leave, the ability to take time off from work for family responsibilities, and part-time work) enhance flexibility by reducing an individual's time at work. In addition, normative support can increase boundary flexibility by providing organizational support for workers to use these policies and programs to coordinate work and family obligations and activities.

Family-based and community-based boundary-spanning resources also include work supports, family supports, and normative support. Spouses and kin can increase the ability of individuals to meet the temporal demands of their work roles by performing additional dependent care and household work activities, which frees up time for work activities. Community programs (e.g., childcare and after-school programs) provide a similar type of support by caring for family members when individuals are at work. In addition, one spouse may be the major provider so that the other spouse can devote more time to family activities. Family and community members and friends also may provide normative support to individuals who are attempting to combine work and family activities by acknowledging the value of such attempts and giving instrumental and emotional social support. Boundary-spanning resources may enhance cross-domain role performance and quality and individual well-being through increased flexibility of the temporal boundary between work and home, legitimacy for the use of work-family policies, spouse and kin assistance, community-based programs, and normative work-family support from family, community, and friends.

CROSS-DOMAIN BUFFERING EFFECTS OF RESOURCES ON DEMANDS

Theories of occupational stress and family resilience propose that resources may buffer the effects of demands on outcomes. These within-domain approaches provide a framework for examining similar relationships that may occur across domains. Occupational stress theory includes two approaches that are relevant to understanding the combined effects of demands and resources on outcomes within the work domain. The most prominent is the job demand-control model in which job resources are expected to buffer the effects of job demands on job strain and individual well-being. This model is based on the assumption that the level of psychological demands combines with the level of decision latitude to influence psychological strain or physical illness and psychological growth. Job demands focus on time demands, monitoring demands, and problem-solving demands, whereas decision latitude includes decision or task authority and skill discretion. Recently, social support has been added to the model as a resource that operates similarly to control in relation to job demands and health outcomes (de Lange et al., 2003; van der Doef & Maes, 1999). The second approach focuses on rewards rather than enabling resources as a potential buffer. The effort-reward approach proposes that an imbalance between work effort and rewards (i.e. situations of high effort and low reward) leads to adverse physical and psychological health consequences. (See Mullen, Kelley & Kelloway, this volume.) High effort results from the demands of the job or the motivations of workers in demanding situations such as need for control. Rewards include money, esteem, and status control (Siegrist, 1998).

The family resilience literature views resilience as a process in which risks and protective factors interact in relation to a family's ability to fulfill important family functions such as family solidarity, economic support, nurturance and socialization, and protection. Risks that endanger these family outcomes include nonnormative family demands and the family's shared meanings of these demands. Family protective factors, such as family cohesiveness, flexibility, and communication patterns, may buffer the relationships between risks and outcomes. Individual and community level resources also may serve as protective factors (Patterson, 2002).

These approaches suggest that, in addition to additive effects of work, family, and community demands and resources on outcomes, resources from one domain may buffer the negative effects of demands from another domain on outcomes. The implications for work-family policy differ for additive and buffering effects. When demands and resources have additive effects on role performance and quality and individual well-being, resources reduce negative outcomes but do not address the negative effects of demands on outcomes. Thus, the negative consequences associated with demands remain unchanged, whereas resources have independent compensating effects on outcomes. However, if resources buffer the effects of demands on outcomes, the negative effects of demands are reduced or eliminated. Thus, demands no longer contribute to outcomes and increasing resources is sufficient to protect against the negative effects of demands. When additive effects occur, policies that only increase resources are insufficient to reduce the negative effects of demands on well-being. Thus, it is important to investigate such relationships further.

WORK-FAMILY FIT AS A LINKING MECHANISM

In addition to proposing direct effects of demands and resources on outcomes, the conceptual model in Figure 3.1 indicates that demands and resources influence outcomes indirectly through a series of mediating and moderating processes. The first of these is work-family linking mechanisms, which include work-family fit, work-family conflict, and work-family facilitation. Linking mechanisms are cognitive appraisals of the effects of the work (family) domain on the family (work) domain. According to Lazarus and Folkman (1984), cognitive appraisal is the process of deciding whether an experience is positive, stressful, or irrelevant with regard to well-being. A stressful appraisal occurs when individuals perceive that the demands of the environment exceed their resources, thereby endangering their well-being. Thus, linking mechanisms derive from assessing the relative demands and resources associated with work, family, and community roles.

Work-family fit is conceptualized from the perspective of the person-environment fit approach to occupational stress. The basic tenet of person-environment fit theory is that stress arises from the lack of fit or congruence between the person and the environment rather than from either one separately (Edwards & Rothbard, 2005). Fit is of two types: demands–abilities and needs–supplies. Demands include quantitative and qualitative job requirements, role expectations, and group and organizational norms, whereas abilities include aptitudes, skills, training, time, and energy that may be used to meet demands. Fit occurs when the individual has the abilities needed to meet the demands of the environment. Strain is expected to increase as demands exceed abilities. Needs encompass biological and psychological requirements, values, and motives; whereas supplies consist of intrinsic and extrinsic resources and rewards that may fulfill the person's needs, such as food, shelter, money, social involvement, and the opportunity to achieve. Fit exists when the environment provides the resources required to satisfy the person's needs, whereas stress occurs when needs exceed supplies. Misfit, which occurs when demands and needs exceed abilities and supplies, results in strains and illness as well as coping behavior and cognitive defense to improve fit, whereas fit can create positive mental and physical health outcomes.

Others have extended the principles of the person-environment fit approach from the fit of demands and resources within the work domain to the consideration of fit across the work and family domains. Pittman (1994) and Barnett, Gareis, and Brennan (1999) focused on family demands-work resources fit. Pittman's conceptualization of fit suggested that family members weigh the demands on them with the benefits that the job and work organization provide. Barnett et al. considered fit in terms of the ability of employees to develop and optimize strategies to meet family needs in the workplace. Expanding on this approach, DeBord, Canu, and Kerpelman (2000) and Teng (1999) proposed a two-dimensional model of work-family fit. The first dimension conceives of fit as the match of work demands with family abilities or expectations regarding meeting work demands, whereas the second dimension is the match of work supplies or rewards with family needs or goals. Work demands and family needs consist of time-based and strain-based work and family demands. Family abilities or expectations and work supplies or rewards focus on organizational and social rewards at work and family coping abilities.

Building on this previous work, this chapter defines work-family fit as a form of inter-role congruence in which the resources associated with one role are sufficient to meet the demands of another role such that participation in the second role can be effective. Work-family fit has two dimensions: work demands-family resources fit in which family-related resources are adequate to meet the demands of the work role and family demands-work resources fit in which work-related resources are sufficient to satisfy family demands. The two dimensions range from fit in which resources are adequate to meet demands to misfit in which there is a discrepancy between demands and resources. For example, a fit scale could range from −4 (*resources are less than needed to meet demands*) through 0 (*resources meet demands*) to +4 (*resources are greater than needed to meet demands*). The perception of work-family fit may reflect various combinations of demands and resources, for example the extent to which a given resource in one domain buffers a specific demand in another domain. Drawing on the demands and resources approach articulated earlier, the first stage of the model presented in Figure 3.2 proposes that work demands and family resources are related to work demands-family resources fit, whereas family demands and work resources are associated with family demands-work resources fit. Because boundary-spanning demands and resources increase demands or resources in both domains, they are related to both types of fit.

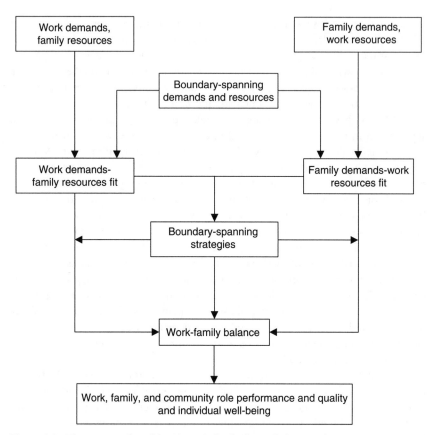

Figure 3.2 The conceptual model with work-family fit as a linking mechanism. *Source:* Voydanoff (2005)

WORK-FAMILY BALANCE, BOUNDARY-SPANNING STRATEGIES, AND OUTCOMES

The second stage of the model in Figure 3.2 proposes that the two dimensions of fit result in an overall assessment of work-family balance, either directly or through the use of boundary-spanning strategies. Work-family balance is the global assessment that work and family resources are sufficient to meet work and family demands such that participation is effective in both domains. It combines the appraisals that resources are adequate to meet demands with the effects of boundary-spanning strategies to yield an overall appraisal of the extent of harmony, equilibrium, and integration of work and family life. It ranges from high levels of balance to high levels of imbalance.

Boundary-spanning strategies are actions taken on the part of individuals and families to reduce or eliminate a lack of congruence between work and family demands and resources. Some strategies change work, family, and community roles so that time-based and strain-based demands are reduced, for example cutting work hours, reducing work responsibilities, limiting dependent care and household work, and performing less volunteer work and informal helping. When time and strain demands are reduced in one domain, enabling resources and psychological rewards in another domain are better able to meet these lowered demands. Other strategies increase resources, for example taking a more enriching job, gaining job flexibility by becoming self-employed, hiring dependent care and household services, and using community services. These strategies provide additional resources for individual and family efforts to meet demands in another domain.

Depending on the timing, these strategies may prevent work-family misfit in the first place, for example using flextime may reduce the need to cut work hours. Thus, a given strategy can have a positive relationship to work-family fit (a preventive effect), or can be positively related to work-family balance (a therapeutic effect), or can have a buffering effect on relationships between work-family fit and work-family balance (Bowen, 1998). All three types of relationship may exist simultaneously.

Preventive strategies are encompassed by the resources discussed earlier as predictors of work, family, and community role performance and quality and individual well-being, for example supportive supervisors, co-workers, and family members and the availability of quality childcare. Therapeutic strategies may mediate negative effects such that misfit leads to the use of strategies, which in turn improves balance. Strategies also may moderate the effects of fit on balance by buffering the negative effects of misfit on balance. In this situation, the negative relationship between misfit and balance decreases when boundary-spanning strategies are used. For example, the negative relationship between work-family misfit and balance may be weaker for those who cut work hours, increase work-family support, or use community services such as after-school programs.

When work-family fit occurs, boundary-spanning strategies may be unnecessary. However, some individuals who experience work-family fit may increase resources as an additional source of role quality and well-being, for example taking a more enriching job, hiring household services, or using community services. These strategies may have direct effects on balance or they may amplify positive relationships between work-family fit and balance.

The general model presented in Figure 3.1 also proposes that boundary-spanning strategies have feedback effects on within-domain and boundary-spanning demands and resources. The successful use of these strategies may change within-domain and boundary-spanning demands and resources such that they can prevent work-family misfit.

The final stage of the conceptual model proposes that work-family balance is positively associated with work, family, and community role performance and quality and individual well-being. A global assessment of balance between the work and family domains is posited to improve performance and quality in both domains as well as to have positive effects on community role performance, role quality, and individual well-being. It also is possible that role performance is a precursor of role quality. Greenhaus and Powell (2006) propose that performing well in a role is likely to be reflected in increased positive affect.

WORK-FAMILY CONFLICT AND FACILITATION AS LINKING MECHANISMS

Two other important linking mechanisms include work-family conflict and work-family facilitation. Similar to work-family fit, work-family conflict and facilitation are cognitive appraisals of the effects of the work (family) domain on the family (work) domain. Work-family conflict is a form of inter-role conflict in which the demands of work and family roles are incompatible in some respect so that participation in one role is more difficult because of participation in the other role (Greenhaus & Beutell, 1985). This conflict can take two forms: work-to-family conflict in which the demands of work make it difficult to perform family responsibilities and family-to-work conflict in which family demands limit the performance of work duties. Although these two forms of work-family conflict are moderately correlated, work demands generally are associated with work-to-family conflict, whereas family demands are the proximal sources of family-to-work conflict (Byron, 2005).

Work-family facilitation is a form of synergy in which resources associated with one role enhance or make easier participation in the other role. It can operate from work to family or from family to work. Work resources are expected to influence work-to-family facilitation, whereas family resources affect family-to-work facilitation. Work-family conflict and facilitation are only slightly correlated with each other and the four components of conflict and facilitation form separate factors in a factor analysis (Grzywacz & Marks, 2000). Thus, work-family conflict and work-family facilitation can be viewed as independent constructs rather than opposite ends of a single continuum.

Figure 3.3 suggests that within-domain demands, within-domain resources, and boundary-spanning demands and resources operate differently in relation to work-family conflict and facilitation. Within-domain demands are expected to be positively associated with work-family conflict, whereas within-domain resources are expected to be positively related to work-family facilitation. This differential salience approach proposes that within-domain demands are relatively salient for work-family conflict because they are associated with processes that limit the ability of

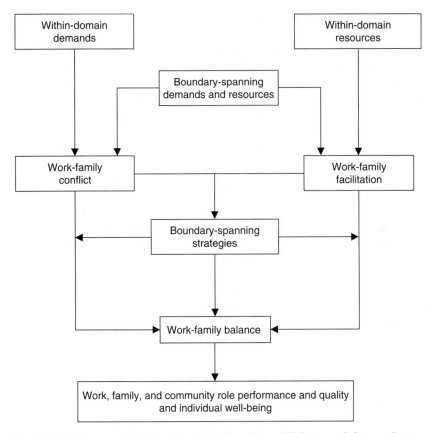

Figure 3.3 The conceptual model with work-family conflict and facilitation as linking mechanisms

individuals to meet obligations in another domain. Within–domain resources are relatively salient for work-family facilitation because they engender processes that improve one's ability to participate in other domains (Voydanoff, 2004).

In contrast to the prediction of differential salience of within–domain demands and resources for work-family conflict and facilitation, boundary-spanning demands and resources are expected to have comparable salience for work-family conflict and facilitation. Boundary-spanning demands and resources also are expected to be related to both directions of conflict and facilitation, for example work-based demands are expected to be associated with both work-to-family and family-to-work conflict and facilitation. Because boundary-spanning demands and resources focus on aspects of role domains that directly address how they connect with each other, the processes relating them to conflict and facilitation are expected to operate similarly in both directions and for both demands and resources.

These proposed relationships are the first step through which work-family conflict and facilitation serve as linking mechanisms between demands and resources and work, family, and community role performance and quality and individual well-being. Similar to Figure 3.2, the rest of the model presented in Figure 3.3 suggests that work-family conflict and facilitation influence outcomes via their relationships with boundary-spanning strategies and work-family balance.

Work-family conflict, facilitation, fit, and balance are cognitive appraisals that reflect work and family demands and resources in different ways. Work and family demands generally are related to work-to-family and family-to-work conflict respectively, whereas work and family resources are associated with work-to-family and family-to-work facilitation respectively. In contrast, work-family fit and balance are derived from the extent to which resources associated with one role are sufficient to meet the demands of another role. Conflict and facilitation are useful for understanding the differential or independent effects of demands and resources, whereas fit and balance address the intersection or joint effects of demands and resources. Thus, the two types of linking mechanisms are useful for addressing different questions. For example, if one were concerned about the effects of time caring for young children on job performance, family-to-work conflict would be a useful appraisal to examine. If one were interested in whether job autonomy would be helpful in meeting the demands associated with caring for young children, it would be more important to assess family demands-work resources fit.

IMPLICATIONS FOR FUTURE RESEARCH AND POLICY

Using a general conceptual model as a framework, this chapter has integrated theoretical and conceptual literature that underpins our understanding of the work-family interface. Despite relatively extensive analysis of parts of the conceptual model, additional conceptual and empirical work is needed to further develop the model and its implications for policies and programs. An agenda for future research includes investigating more of the relationships proposed in the model, incorporating more demands and resources in the analysis, including more aspects of the community domain, improving measures of the variables being examined, exploring the model as a temporal process using longitudinal research, and specifying the individual, contextual, and family circumstances under which the relationships in the model occur (Voydanoff, 2007).

The relationships proposed in the conceptual model provide implicit implications for policy and practice. Insufficient testing of the model, however, precludes the development of explicit policy and practice recommendations based solely on the model. Nevertheless, it is possible to formulate a broad strategy regarding policies and programs that would encourage the integration of the work, family, and community domains so that they operate together to assist working families coordinate and fulfill their work, family, and community obligations in a way that enhances role performance and quality and individual well-being.

For example, the model reveals the importance of examining not only the demands that may reduce role performance, role quality, and individual well-being, but also the resources that may enhance them. Thus, policies and programs should include the enhancement of work, family, community, and boundary-spanning resources as well as the reduction of work, family, community, and boundary-spanning demands. Both can occur either by developing policies and programs that reduce demands and increase resources independently (e.g. by reducing work hours or increasing job autonomy) or by designing policies that address demands and resources jointly (e.g. by creating a supportive work-family culture that focuses on flexibility in meeting family demands such as caregiving for children or parents).

A strategy based on the development of the resources and the reduction of the demands associated with work, family, and community role performance and quality and individual well-being represents a preventive rather than a therapeutic approach. For this preventive approach to be effective, work, family, and community demands must be limited and resources must be adequate and accessible to working families. When these conditions do not exist, boundary-spanning strategies are needed that reduce work-family conflict and misfit after they occur. However, these are viewed as secondary in importance to the preventive approach.

A special emphasis on boundary-spanning demands and resources is warranted because they represent a critical point of intervention for policies and programs designed to enhance role performance and quality and well-being in the context of the work-family-community mesosystem. By addressing the intersection of two domains simultaneously, reducing boundary-spanning demands or increasing boundary-spanning resources are more likely to influence outcomes than altering within-domain demands or resources.

We also need to understand the work context in which boundary-spanning community demands and resources operate. For example, how do boundary-spanning community resources (e.g. after-school and elder-care programs) combine with within-domain work demands (e.g. long work hours) and boundary-spanning work resources (e.g. time off work for family needs or flexible work schedules) to reduce work-family conflict and enhance family well-being?

Work-based policies and programs are a critical part of a strategy designed to enhance family well-being. These policies include increasing the flexibility of work, for example by developing more flexible employment schedules, providing dependent-care assistance, and creating opportunities for family leave and time off from work to address family needs. Others have reported that these work-family policies are necessary but not sufficient to reduce work-family conflict and increase work-family facilitation. It also is essential to reduce the level of within-domain work demands. For example, Rapoport and her colleagues (2002) have documented the importance for work-family integration of job design efforts that increase worker autonomy and decrease work stress. Additional research will provide conceptual and empirical grounding for the development of workplace, community, and government policies and programs that enhance rather than hinder the well-being of working families.

REFERENCES

Barnett, R. C., Gareis, K. C. & Brennan, R. T. (1999). Fit as a mediator of the relationship between work hours and burnout. *Journal of Occupational Health Psychology, 4*, 307–317.

Bowen, G. L. (1998). Effects of leader support in the work unit on the relationship between work spillover and family adaptation. *Journal of Family and Economic Issues, 19*, 25–52.

Bronfenbrenner, U. (1989). Ecological systems theory. *Annals of Child Development, 6*, 187–249.

Byron, K. (2005). A meta-analytic review of work-family conflict and its antecedents. *Journal of Vocational Behavior, 67*, 169–198.

Clark, S. C. (2000). Work/family border theory. *Human Relations, 53*, 747–770.

DeBord, K., Canu, R. G. & Kerpelman, J. (2000). Understanding work-family fit for single parents moving from welfare to work. *Social Work, 45*, 313–324.

de Lange, A. H., Taris, T. W., Kompier, M. A. J. & Houtman, I. L. D. (2003). "The *very* best of the millennium": Longitudinal research and the demand-control-(support) model. *Journal of Occupational Health Psychology, 8*, 283–305.

Edwards, J. R. & Rothbard, N. P. (2005). Work and family stress and well-being. In E. E. Kossek & S. J. Lambert (eds), *Work and Life Integration* (pp. 211–242). Mahwah, NJ: Lawrence Erlbaum.

Greenhaus J. H. & Beutell, N. J. (1985). Sources of conflict between work and family roles. *Academy of Management Journal, 10*, 76–88.

Greenhaus, J. H. & Powell, G. N. (2006). When work and family are allies. *Academy of Management Review. 31*, 72–92.

Grzywacz, J. G. & Marks, N. F. (2000). Reconceptualizing the work-family interface. *Journal of Occupational Health Psychology, 5*, 111–126.

Lazarus, R. S. & Folkman, S. (1984). *Stress, Appraisal, and Coping*. New York: Springer.

Marks, S. R. (1977). Multiples roles and role strain. *American Sociological Review, 42*, 921–936.

Nippert-Eng, C. E. (1996). *Home and Work*. Chicago: University of Chicago Press.

Patterson, J. M. (2002). Integrating family resilience and family stress theory. *Journal of Marriage and Family, 64*, 349–360.

Piotrkowski, C. (1979). *Work and the Family System*. New York: Free Press.

Pittman, J. F. (1994). Work/family fit as a mediator of work factors on marital tension. *Human Relations, 47*, 183–209.

Rapoport, R., Bailyn, L., Fletcher, J. K. & Pruitt, B. H. (2002). *Beyond Work-Family Balance*. San Francisco: Jossey-Bass.

Rothbard, N. P. (2001). Enriching or depleting? The dynamics of engagement in work and family roles. *Administrative Science Quarterly, 46*, 655–684.

Sieber, S. D. (1974). Toward a theory of role accumulation. *American Sociological Review, 39*, 567–578.

Siegrist, J. (1998). Adverse health effects of effort-reward imbalance at work. In C. L. Cooper (ed.), *Theories of Organizational Stress* (pp. 190–204). New York: Oxford University Press.

Tenbrunsel, A. E., Brett, J. M., Maoz, E., Stroh, L. K. & Reilly, A. H. (1995) Dynamic and static work-family relationships. *Organizational Behavior and Human Decision Processes, 63*, 223–246.

Teng, W. (1999). Assessing the work-family interface. Dissertation, Auburn University.

van der Doef, M. & Maes, S. (1999). The job demand-control (-support) model and psychological well-being: A review of 20 years of empirical research. *Work & Stress, 13*, 87–114.

Voydanoff, P. (2004). The effects of work demands and resources on work-to-family conflict and facilitation. *Journal of Marriage and Family, 66*, 398–412.

Voydanoff, P. (2005). Toward a conceptualization of work-family fit and balance: A demands and resources approach. *Journal of Marriage and Family, 67*, 822–836.

Voydanoff, P. (2007). *Work, Family, and Community: Exploring Interconnections*. Mahwah, NJ: Lawrence Erlbaum.

CHAPTER 4

Reflections and Future Directions on Measurement in Work–Family Research

Dawn S. Carlson* and **Joseph G. Grzywacz†**

*Baylor University, Department of Management, Hankamer School of Business, Waco, TX

†Wake Forest University School of Medicine, Department of Family and Community Medicine, Winston-Salem

Concepts in the work-family literature reflect three primary points of view: negative, positive, and integrative. The conceptual evolution of the work-family literature has varied greatly across these three perspectives and there is substantial variation in the sophistication of measurement of core concepts from each perspective. More specifically, the core concept from the negative perspective—work-family conflict—has received substantial measurement research. By contrast, considerably less attention has been given to emerging concepts from the positive perspective like positive spillover, enrichment, or facilitation. Virtually no attention has been given to the measurement of concepts like "balance" reflecting the integrative perspective. In some cases measurement has developed before conceptualization. In still others concepts are heavily influenced by popular culture and there is a lag between popularity and scholarly theorizing. All this suggests the need to be very careful in understanding and measuring work-family concepts.

The purpose of this chapter is to clarify the different conceptualizations and overview measurement of constructs reflecting the negative, positive, and integrative perspectives of the work-family interface. First we will provide an overview of the conceptual distinctions among several constructs in the work-family literature. Next we examine the variety of measures being used for several of these constructs, measurement issues associated with the conceptualizations, and implications for practice. Finally, we make recommendation for areas of future research and development. Given that several reviews have already been done on work-family conflict (Bellavia & Frone, 2005; MacDermid, 2005; Tetrick & Buffardi, 2006) we focus our attention on measures intended to capture concepts reflecting the positive and integrative perspectives of the work-family interface. Our goal is to reduce conceptual confusion and guide researchers in the choice of constructs most relevant to their research and applied interests.

THE NEGATIVE PERSPECTIVE ON WORK-FAMILY INTERFACE

The dominant view of the work-family interface is negative. Deeply entrenched beliefs that individuals have a finite amount of time and energy, and that work and family compete for these finite resources have contributed to a nearly exclusive focus on work-family conflict. Work-family conflict, according to the most commonly used definition, is "a form of inter-role conflict in which the role pressures from the work and family domains are mutually incompatible in some respect" (Greenhaus & Beutell, 1985). In the wake of rapid growth in women's labor force participation and presumed deleterious effects of women's, particularly mothers', employment, researchers quickly capitalized on the offered definition of work-family conflict. Over the past 20 years, several measures of work-family conflict have been used to study the phenomenon.

MAJOR MEASURES OF WORK-FAMILY CONFLICT

Given the developed nature of the construct as well as its primacy in the work-family literature, there have been several recent reviews of measures of work-family conflict. Rather than provide yet another review of work-family conflict we will summarize the key findings of three recent reviews (Bellavia & Frone, 2005; MacDermid, 2005; Tetrick & Buffardi, 2006). We then highlight additional measurement issues related to work-family conflict that have not been addressed in previous reviews.

Comments from Recent Critiques

Both Bellavia and Frone (2005) and MacDermid (2005) provide a broad summary of the construct and deal with conceptual issues underlying the measurement of work-family conflict. Tetrick and Buffardi (2006) give a detailed examination of measures of conflict broken down by use, directionality in terms of work-to-family or family-to-work conflict, type of conflict (i.e., time-, strain-, and behavior-based), and reliability and correlation of directions of conflict. Tetrick summarizes seven major measures of work-family conflict and the other two reviews refer to most of these measures (Bohen & Viveros Long, 1981; Carlson, Kacmar & Williams, 2000; Frone, Russell & Cooper, 1992; Gutek, Searle & Klepa, 1991; Kopelman, Greenhaus & Connolly, 1983; Netemeyer, Boles & McMurrian, 1996; Stephens & Sommer, 1996). For the most part the scales are paper and pencil questionnaires that ask respondents to indicate the degree one domain interferes with the other. There is solid evidence indicating that work-to-family and family-to-work conflict are distinct and that researchers should include measures of both directions in their study designs (Byron, 2005; Frone et al., 1997; Mesmer-Magnus & Viswesvaran, 2005). The internal consistency of existing measures is generally acceptable suggesting that most instruments are reliable. However, more evidence of validity has been provided for some scales than others (i.e., Carlson, et al., 2000; Netemeyer et al., 1996). The reviews agree that measures of work-family conflict have become more sophisticated and that most contemporary measures have desirable features, but the reviewers also agree that more refinements are needed.

Measurement Issues

There are several measurement issues that are considered for the existing measurement scales. Bellavia and Frone (2005) are critical of the response options used in existing measures of work-family conflict because vague frequency anchors (e.g., never to always) and affective response formats (agree/disagree) do not allow researchers to determine how frequently work-family conflict occurs. Bellavia and Frone (2005) also argue that the lack of parallel construction of work-to-family and family-to-work conflict scales undermine a researcher's ability to directly compare the frequency and significance of each direction of conflict. Tetrick and Buffardi (2006) point out that many of the measures fail to distinguish between family and non-work, thus failing to provide a pure assessment of work-family conflict. Whereas Tetrick and Buffardi (2006) find the multidimensional nature of the Netemeyer et al. (1996) and the Carlson et al. (2000) measures comprehensive and appealing, Bellavia and Frone (2005) believe that scales assessing different types of conflict risk conceptually confounding conflict and its antecedents. On the other hand, MacDermid (2005) questions if measures of work-family conflict are meaningfully distinct from outcomes of interest like strain. Finally, MacDermid (2005) questions whether respondents have the cognitive capacity to complete typical work-family conflict items because of the inherent complexity of the phenomenon.

CONCEPTUAL CLARIFICATION BETWEEN CONFLICT AND INTERFERENCE

The distinction between work-family conflict and work-family interference has not been discussed in previous reviews of the literature. Greenhaus and Beutell (1985), in their original formulation of the concept, explicitly stated that work-family conflict is non-directional in nature and that it only takes on direction when the individual makes a decision to resolve the incompatibility, at which point either work or family is interfered with. From this perspective it is clear that work-family conflict and work-family interference are distinct phenomena separated by time and individual behavior. However, work–family conflict and work–family interference are used interchangeably in the literature.

The distinction between work–family conflict and work–family interference has important implications for measurement and work–family research. All of the existing instruments purporting to measure work–family conflict actually measure work–family interference. Distinguishing these concepts is more than semantic because instruments assessing work–family interference confound episodes or experiences where work and family exerted mutually incompatible pressures (i.e., work–family conflict) and differences in how individuals respond to the incompatible pressures. Obviously, confounded measures undermine the ability to interpret observed associations. For example, does an observed association between high job demands and high work–family conflict (operationalized with scales purporting to measure work–family conflict but, in fact, measuring work–family interference) reflect the possibility that job demands increase the risk of experiencing mutually incompatible work and family-related pressures, or does it reflect the tendency for job demands to elicit a behavioral response from individuals to resolve incompatible pressures by favoring work? Although subtle, these two interpretations have different implications for theory development and they also have different implications for intervention.

Measurement development focused on work–family conflict, as it was originally conceptualized, is needed. Items would need to tap how frequently an individual experiences mutually incompatible work- and family-related pressures. Such an item might be something like, "How often do your work and family-related responsibilities require you to be in two different places at the same time?" Or, an individual might describe their level of agreement with an item like, "There is little difference in the way I need to behave at work and at home." A measure comprised of items like these capturing the construct as originally conceptualized would be invaluable for understanding how frequently work–family conflict occurs and for clearly delineating its antecedents. Further, being able to measure both work–family conflict and work–family interference would build greater understanding of the personal and contextual factors shaping how individuals resolve episodes of work–family conflict and how work–family conflict transitions into work interference with family or family interference with work.

THE POSITIVE PERSPECTIVE ON WORK-FAMILY INTERFACE

The positive side of the work–family interface or the idea that work and family may actually be mutually beneficial has begun to receive attention as the field attempts to respond to the call to provide a more complete picture of the work–family interface (Frone, 2003; Parasuraman & Greenhaus, 2002).

Unfortunately, research taking a positive view of the work-family interface has developed without clear direction and there is a great need for more clearly distinguished concepts and measures. The concepts of positive spillover, enrichment, and facilitation have been used simultaneously (Greenhaus & Powell, 2006). However, we believe they are conceptually distinct and this distinction is critical to theory development as well as measurement (to get a detailed review of the conceptual differences, see Hanson, Hammer & Colton, 2006; Grzywacz, Carlson, Kacmar & Wayne, 2007). In this section we briefly examine positive spillover, enrichment, and facilitation with the goal of articulating conceptual distinctions among the concepts and subsequent implications for measurement.

CONCEPTUALIZATION OF POSITIVE CONSTRUCTS

Positive spillover was originally defined broadly as how an individual's activities in one role "supports, facilitates, or enhances" the other (Crouter, 1984). This broad definition was later refined as when "experiences, thoughts, and feelings of one role spillover to positively influence the experiences, thoughts, and feelings in another role" (Stephens & Sommer, 1997). More recently, drawing on Edwards and Rothbard's (2000) framework, Hanson, Hammer and Colton defined positive spillover as "the transfer of positively valenced affect, skills, behaviors, and values from the originating domain to the receiving domain, thus having beneficial effects on the receiving domain" (2006, p. 251).

Enrichment is a positively-oriented concept that has changed slightly over time. Initially, enrichment was used simultaneously with positive spillover and even measured with the same items (Cohen & Kirchmeyer, 1995; Kirchmeyer, 1992a; Kirchmeyer, 1992b). Building from role expansion theory (Sieber, 1974), early views of enrichment focused on role occupancy in one life domain, such as family, and the benefits that role occupancy confers to the individual in another life domain, such as work. Recently, Greenhaus and Powell (2006) defined and conceptualized work-family enrichment as "the extent to which experiences in one role improved performance or the quality of life in the other role". Thus, whereas the original conceptualization implied that an individual's activity in one role could benefit activities in another, the current conceptualization makes this benefit explicit.

Facilitation was originally introduced to the literature to represent the synergies or complementarities that occur between an individual's work and family life (Frone, 2003; Grzywacz, 2002; Wayne, Musisca & Fleeson, 2004). As it was originally defined and used there was great overlap with the concepts of enrichment and positive spillover. However, recently Grzywacz, Carlson, Kacmar and Wayne (2007) offered a new definition of work-family facilitation that allowed for clear distinction from both work-family enrichment and positive spillover. They define facilitation as the extent to which an individual's engagement in one social system (e.g., work or family) contributes to growth in another social system (e.g., family or work). Grzywacz and colleagues further argued that facilitation differs from enrichment and positive spillover in that it focuses on the implications for either the work or family system of its individual members' activities in another life domain.

Differentiation

Although we are unable to cover all of the conceptual differences among positive spillover, enrichment, and facilitation, even this brief overview illustrates key distinctions among these constructs. First, positive spillover focuses primarily on the transfer of positively valenced individual attributes (e.g., mood, behaviors) between work and family (Hanson et al., 2006). By contrast, although enrichment and facilitation recognize these individual attributes they also highlight the possibility that work and family can affect each other through other means. Next, whereas positive spillover gives only general attention to the consequences of individual-level transfers that occur between work and family, enrichment focuses squarely on how these transfers shape performance and quality of life in one domain or the other (Greenhaus & Powell, 2006). Further, facilitation focuses on the system-level implications of these transfers (Grzywacz et al., 2007). Finally, whereas facilitation emphasizes the system-level consequences of a member's involvement in another life domain, positive spillover and enrichment are both focused on individual-level consequences.

Major Measures of Positive Work–Family Concepts

Although some progress has been made recently, measures of positive phenomenon of the work–family interface reflect the conceptual ambiguity among concepts discussed above. The two most commonly used scales to measure the positive side of the work–family interface are the MIDUS scale and the Kirchmeyer scale (Grzywacz, 2000; Kirchmeyer, 1992). The Kirchmeyer items have been reported to measure "positive spillover" (Kirchmeyer, 1995) as well as "enrichment" (Witt & Carlson, in press); likewise, the MIDUS items have been reported to measure positive spillover (Grzywacz & Marks, 2000) and facilitation (Ayree et al., 2005; Grzywacz & Bass, 2003). The interchangeable use of concepts across common items clearly illustrates the conceptual confusion in the literature.

Positive Spillover

Neither the MIDUS scale nor the Kirchmeyer scale incorporate enhanced functioning in the receiving domain, suggesting that they are actually measures of positive spillover as defined above. The Kirchmeyer (1992) scale includes items assessing four types of rewards of role accumulation (i.e., role privileges, status security, resources for status enhancement, and ego gratification), but was developed to capture the rewards of family role occupancy on work. The MIDUS scale includes items tapping both directions (work to family and family to work), but there are few parallels among the work-to-family and family-to-work items. Moreover, it fails to consider the multidimensional nature of the construct. Neither scale was validated on development. Recently Hanson et al. (2006) developed and validated a multidimensional scale of perceived work-family positive spillover. The scale consists of 22 items, includes multiple forms of positive spillover (affective, behavior, value), and has both a work-to-family and a family-to-work dimension.

While this scale has many clear advantages over previous scales, one weakness is that it combines items assessing positive spillover with items assessing enrichment. For example, "Being happy at home improves my spirits at work" clearly captures the transfer of positive affect from home to work; however, we don't know if it improved functioning in the receiving domain (work, in this case). Items such as this are combined with items that measure enrichment. For example, the item "[V]alues that I learn through my family experiences assist me in fulfilling my work responsibilities," clearly reflects the enrichment concept because it captures the application of values acquired at home to tasks in the workplace and the implications of that application for performance. This limitation notwithstanding, Hanson and colleagues' measure is superior to those commonly used because of its theoretical basis, its multidimensional nature, and its rigorous testing and evaluation.

Enrichment

In order for an item to capture Greenhaus and Powell's (2006) conceptualization of work-family enrichment, it has to have three elements: the individual's activity in one domain, the type of benefit derived from that activity, and an appraisal of improved performance or quality of life for the individual in the other role. Most of the previously developed scales such as MIDUS (Grzywacz & Marks, 2000) and Kirchmeyer (1992) do not capture all three elements consistently across their items. Carlson and colleagues (2006) developed an instrument to measure work-family enrichment as it was conceptualized by Greenhaus and Powell (2006). The instrument is comprised of 18 items reflecting different mechanisms by which enrichment occurs (development, affect, gain, efficiency) and it captures both work-to-family and family-to-work enrichment.

The largest concern we have with this scale is that respondents may not consider all the ideas in the items when formulating their response. An example item is "My involvement in my work puts me in a good mood and this helps me to be a better family member." This requires the respondent to not only assess if their involvement in work put them in a good mood, but also if this good mood actually makes them a better family member. This double-barreled form of the item was intentionally designed to reflect the construct as it has been conceptualized. Based on data collected in the formative stages of instrument development and presented in the article, Carlson and colleagues suggest that respondents do consider all of the elements in items. However, recognizing that items assessing work-family phenomena tend to be cognitively challenging (MacDermid, 2005), future research should continue to evaluate the Carlson and colleagues enrichment scale. In the meantime, however, Carlson and colleagues' instrument is the strongest in the literature because of its theoretical foundation and its reported solid evidence of validity and reliability.

Facilitation

While Grzywacz and Bass (2003), Wayne et al. (2004), and Hill (2005) have all claimed to measure the concept of facilitation, the items used more closely reflect enrichment or positive spillover than facilitation as distinguished above as a system-level construct. In fact, to our knowledge there are not any existing measures that capture the multilevel phenomenon inherent in facilitation.

It is necessary to develop multidimensional scales that capture key aspects of the receiving system such as family functioning or work group performance. Items might be written similarly to the enrichment items following the general formula of: "My engagement in my family/work provides me with [*insert spillover-like effects* such as 'new skills' or 'a positive attitude'] which improves functioning in my workplace/family." A similar structure such as "My engagement in work *provides my family members* with unique opportunities, and this improves overall functioning in my family" could be used to assess work-to-family facilitation that occurs outside of individual spillover effects. Of course, these types of items are problematic because they are "triple-barreled" in that respondents may agree with one or two, but not all three elements of the item. Moreover, they require respondents to make multiple attributions (see Bellavia & Frone, 2005). These concerns notwithstanding, we contend future research must grapple with and overcome the difficult measurement issues so that researchers and practitioners can assess absolute levels of facilitation to evaluate programs and interventions, and to relate them to individual, work, and family correlates.

THE INTEGRATIVE PERSPECTIVE OF THE WORK-FAMILY INTERFACE

The least developed area of measurement consists of concepts reflective of the integrative perspective of work and family. Here we are referring to concepts such as work-family balance or work-family fit. We focus on work-family balance here because it is the dominant concept reflecting the integrative perspective. The lack of development in this area is interesting because most research is predicated on the goal of promoting integrative concepts like work-family balance, yet few studies measure these concepts directly. The lack of measurement is driven by poor conceptual development. For example, while the concept is widely used, very few authors explicitly define work-family balance (Greenhaus & Allen, 2006; Grzywacz & Carlson, 2007). When definitions are offered, there is very little consistency among definitions. Some conceptualize it to be like a scale reflecting perfect equality across work and family life. Still others conceptualize it as the absence of conflict and the presence of enrichment. To the extent that conceptual foundation is critical for measurement, we are first going to examine the prevailing conceptualizations of balance and then consider implications for measurement.

CONCEPTUALIZATION OF BALANCE

Equality

One stream of theorizing is that work-family balance is the consequence of equality in work and family. Role-balance theory suggests that people seek full and meaningful experiences in their work and family lives (Marks, Huston, Johnson & MacDermid, 2001; Marks & MacDermid, 1996). Further, this conceptualization of balance suggests that in order to achieve balance one must distribute their personal resources across all life roles in an "evenhanded" fashion (Kirchmeyer, 2000; Marks & MacDermid, 1996). This definition is characterized by equal engagement, attention, investment of time, psychological involvement or identification across all role obligations (Ayree & Luk, 1996; Greenhaus, Collins & Shaw, 2003).

Fit

Another conceptualization of balance is as fit. This perspective suggests that balance is not merely the investments an individual makes across their roles, but rather the critical feature is the individual's satisfaction with the roles. Further, some theorists propose that balance in not necessarily equal investment, but investment consistent with underlying values (Bielby & Bielby, 1989; Kofodimos, 1993; Lambert, 1990; Milkie & Peltola, 1999). Greenhaus and Allen (2006), for example, define balance as the extent to which an individual's effectiveness and satisfaction in work and family roles are compatible with the individual's life-role priorities at a given point in time. Similarly, Sheldon and Niemiec (2006) recently argued that balance is not shaped by the amount of time or energy spent on different aspects of life; rather it is the extent to which an individual's need for autonomy, competence, and connection with others is met. Thus, the fit perspective of work-family balance emphasizes an individual's affective appraisal of role-related performance across different domains of life and activities across diverse areas of life relative to some personalized ideal.

Role Performance

Whereas the previous conceptualizations of work-family balance are largely psychological in nature, Grzywacz and Carlson (2007) argued that greater attention needs to be placed on the social basis of work-family balance. They point out that an individual's perception of work-family balance may occur at the expense of another (e.g., a working wife who picks up the slack at home as her husband climbs the corporate ladder), which raises significant questions about whether work and family are indeed "balanced". They further argued that purely psychological views of work-family balance are problematic because they have little observable meaning outside of the individual, and they confound an individual's activities within a role with his/her appraisals of those activities in terms of satisfaction. To avoid these and other challenges of purely psychologically-oriented views of balance, Grzywacz and Carlson (2007) defined work-family balance as accomplishment of role-related expectations that are negotiated and shared between an individual and his/her role-related partners in the work and family domains. By focusing on an individual's role-related performance, work-family balance takes on meaning outside of the individual, and it allows researchers to uncouple individuals' behavior from their own appraisals of that behavior.

MEASUREMENT OF WORK-FAMILY BALANCE

Measurement of work-family balance is nascent and underdeveloped. Measurement approaches for work-family balance, with few exceptions, (Greenhaus et al., 2003; Marks & MacDermid, 1996), have been developed without solid theoretical or conceptual underpinning. In general, there are three strategies people have used to measure balance: (1) singe-item global measure, (2) multi-item scale, and (3) algorithmic approaches. Each of these will be reviewed.

Single-item

One approach used by researchers to capture work-family balance is that of a single-item global indicator. For example, Ezra and Deckman (1996) used the item "I am satisfied with the balance I have achieved between my work and family life." Milkie and Peltola (1999) used "How successful do your feel in balancing your paid work and family life?" Although global indicators such as these are valuable for describing work-family balance in a sample or population, they are less ideal for rigorously studying this complex phenomenon. It is not at all clear, for example, whether individuals use the same reference for "balance" when they respond to these types of questions. Furthermore, single-item scales are limited in that they cannot adequately and accurately capture the broader concept being measured (Nunnally, 1978).

Multiple-item

A second approach to measuring balance is to use a scale consisting of multiple items. However, unlike conflict and enrichment, which have several well-developed scales, there are no scales of balance that have been developed around a commonly agreed upon definition that have undergone extensive development and validity testing. We found two multi-item measures of work-family balance in the literature. Marks and MacDermid (1996) developed an eight-item scale based on their definition of role balance. The Marks and MacDermid scale has marginally acceptable internal consistency ($\alpha = .68$). They also present results that are consistent with theory, such as greater role balance was associated with greater well-being and role ease. The primary problem with these items is that they were not developed to measure work-family balance per se; rather, they were designed to measure the extent to which an individual engages comparably across all role-related responsibilities. Hill, Hawkins, Ferris & Weitzman (2001) used five items to assess work-family balance. Although the items had good internal consistency ($\alpha = .83$), they combined items tapping appraisals of work-family balance (e.g., "all in all, how successful do you feel in balancing your work and personal/family life?") with items assessing work-family conflict (e.g., "How often do you feel drained when you go home from work because of work pressures and problems?"). The lack of a clear focus on a specific underlying construct undermines enthusiasm for this measure. Thus, there is clearly a need for a well-defined multiple-item measure of balance.

Algorithm

The third major approach researchers have taken to study balance is through algorithmic methods. Frone (2003) suggests that balance is a combination of decreased conflict and increased facilitation. However, it is not clear how the two are to be combined to determine actual level of balance. For example, Ayree et al. (2005) used 16 items from Grzywacz and Marks (2000) that capture both directions of conflict and facilitation and combined them to create what they called balance. However, it is not clear how they combined them or what that score would mean. Another approach was taken by Greenhaus et al. (2003) who measured work-family balance by directly measures of the components of balance: time, involvement, and satisfaction. They used measures and created different score coefficients. However, these measures suffer from the fact that they are getting at the potential causes of balance, but not at the construct of balance itself. Grzywacz and Bass (2003) attempted to examine different combinations of conflict and facilitation and their impact on outcomes. They suggest that a combination of reduced conflict and enhanced facilitation is the best, but it is still not clear that balance is being measured. Likewise, Grzywacz and Carlson (2007) recently demonstrated how the use of the four components of balance (work-to-family conflict, family-to-work conflict, work-to-family enrichment, family-to-work enrichment) explained greater variance that a single-item general measure of balance. However, they point out that while the components approach has superior predictive power, it remains unknown whether or not the components really capture the higher order "balance" construct.

IMPLICATIONS FOR FUTURE RESEARCH AND PRACTICE

So, where do we go from here? Given our understanding of the current state of the work-family literature it is our belief that there is substantial need for further measurement development and research. While opportunities for development are wide we choose to focus on three major areas that we think have the highest potential to advance the field: conceptual clarification, measurement of balance, and systems-level conceptualizing and measurement. Finally, we will discuss implications for practice.

CONCEPTUAL CLARIFICATION

One area that researchers have not given sufficient attention to is the conceptual distinction among different work-family concepts. The concepts of work-family interference and work-family conflict are confounded. In fact, we suggest that work-family conflict as originally conceptualized has never been measured and the existing work-family conflict scales are actually measuring work-family interference. Thus, measurement research is needed to develop measures of work-family conflict as originally conceptualized. Furthermore, research is needed for examining the inter-relationships between work-family conflict (as it needs to be measured) and work-family interference (as it is currently measured with work-family conflict scales) to better understand when conflict translates into interference. Further, understanding of the situational and personal factors influencing whether or not conflict translates into work interference with family or family interference with work would provide great insight into the interaction of work and family.

On the positive side, progress clarifying concepts recently has been made. However, much more work is needed to clearly differentiate positive spillover, enrichment, and facilitation. It is imperative that measures reflect the important, albeit subtle, distinctions among these concepts, and that researchers avoid the tendency to use these concepts interchangeably. It is important, for example, that measures of positive spillover include only items reflecting the transfer of skills, behaviors, and moods between work and family. Spillover scales should avoid "enrichment-like" items that tap the effect of spillover in a receiving domain. This would enable research that is designed to determine if spillover and enrichment are, in fact, distinct phenomena. Further, as facilitation begins to diverge from enrichment and capture the systems-level aspect of the positive side of work and family, it is in need of theoretically developed and validated measures.

MEASUREMENT OF BALANCE

A second major of area of research that would be invaluable to the work-family literature is measurement work focused on work-family balance. Balance, despite its widespread popularity as a construct, is in desperate need of attention. Only recently have we begun to try and define and clarify what work-family balance means, and there is no real consensus on the best way to define the concept. Further, there are a variety of measures and measurement approaches to balance that are being used; however, it is not clear what these approaches are actually measuring. Research is needed that critically evaluates existing approaches to measuring work-family balance, and researchers need to develop and validate a theoretically-based measure of work-family balance. Furthermore, recognizing that different conceptualizations of balance will require different measures, and research will need to evaluate which conceptualization is most plausible and useful. Finally, research examining the interrelationship of work-family balance with conflict and enrichment will be useful in testing and refining existing models of the work-family interface (e.g., Voydanoff, 2005).

SYSTEMS-LEVEL CONCEPTUALIZING AND MEASUREMENT

A third area that is in need of attention in the work-family arena is the development of more systems-level thinking and measurement of systems-level constructs. To date almost all of the work-family research has considered individual-level analysis and has not provided a more systems-level perspective. Systems-level thinking is critical to adequately represent the complexity of both the work and family domain and the inter-relationship between the domains. It is only in expanding to systems-level thinking that we can better understand the inter-relatedness between members of a system, such as co-workers or husband and wife, and systems-level outcomes, such as organizational performance or quality of marriage.

Very little systems-level theorizing has been done and virtually no measurement development. The positive side of the work–family interface has begun to see some initial theoretical development through the concept of facilitation (Grzywacz et al., 2007). Facilitation is defined as the next step beyond enrichment which incorporates the transfer of resources to the systems level. The negative side and balance have not yet been framed from a systems-level perspective, thus limiting the ability of researchers to make connections and thus conclusions regarding any systems-level outcomes. Further, the measurement to capture these systems-level phenomena is needed for all three areas. We see the development of systems-level thinking in the work–family area as one of the most challenging yet promising arenas for future development.

IMPLICATIONS FOR PRACTICE

The information provided in this chapter is focused on measurement and as such provides only minimal insights for the practitioner. The different conceptualizations of the work–family interface are important as practitioners monitor different perspectives in their organizations. If they want to know if their work–family policies are working, it will be important to know how to accurately examine work–family conflict and work–family enrichment, as well as the aspect of balance. The roles that a program plays in impacting these and the fact that a single intervention might impact these aspects of the work–family interface uniquely, makes the measurement and understanding of them more critical.

CONCLUSION

The goal of this review was to clarify key concepts reflecting different perspectives of the work–family interface and to evaluate measures of these concepts. As work–family research has evolved, so too has the sophistication and focus of measurement. On the negative side of the work–family interface, the measurement of work–family conflict is highly developed. However, we raise the concern that existing "work–family conflict" scales actually measure work–family interference rather than conflict as it was originally conceptualized, and we contend that conflict per se needs more explicit measurement. The positive side of the work–family interface is receiving increased attention and several measures are emerging; unfortunately, these measures generally do not give adequate attention to important distinctions among different concepts. Measurement research and evaluation clearly differentiating positive spillover and enrichment is needed. Finally, work–family balance is the least developed area in terms of measurement. This is in part due to lack of conceptual clarity, but substantial measurement research and development is needed to provide a more comprehensive understanding of work-family balance.

REFERENCES

Ayree, S. & Luk,V. (1996). Balancing two major parts of adult life experience:Work and family identity among dual-earner couples. *Human Relations, 49,* 465–487.

Ayree, S., Srinivas, E. S. & Tan, H. H. (2005). Rhythms of life: Antecedents and outcomes of work-family balance in employed parents. *Journal of Applied Psychology, 90,* 132–136.

Bellavia, G. & Frone, M. R. (2005).Work-family conflict. In J. Barling, E. K. Kelloway, and M.R. Frone (eds), *Handbook of Work Stress.*Thousand Oaks, CA: Sage.

Bielby,W. T. & Bielby, D. D. (1989). Family ties: Balancing commitments to work and family in dual-earner households. *American Sociological Review, 54,* 776–789.

Bohen, H. H. & Viveros-Long, A. (1981). *Balancing Jobs and Family Life: Do Flexible Schedules Really Help?* Philadelphia:Temple University Press.

Byron, K. (2005). A meta-analytic review of work-family conflict and its antecedents. *Journal of Vocational Behavior, 67,* 169–198.

Carlson, D. S., Kacmar, K. M.,Wayne, J. H. & Grzywacz, J. G. (2006). Measuring the positive side of the work-family interface: Development and validation of a work-family enrichment scale. *Journal of Vocational Behavior, 68,* 131–164.

Carlson, D. S., Kacmar, K. M. & Williams, L. J. (2000). Construction and validation of a multidimensional measure of work-family conflict. *Journal of Vocational Behavior, 56,* 249–276.

Cohen, A. & Kirchmeyer, C. 1995. A multidimensional approach to the relation between organizational commitment and nonwork participation. *Journal of Vocational Behavior, 46,* 189–202.

Crouter, A. C. (1984). Spillover from family to work: The neglected side of the work-family interface. *Human Relations, 37,* 425–442.

Ezra, M. & Deckman, M. (1996). Balancing work and family responsibilities: Flextime and child care in the federal government. *Public Administration Review, 56,* 174–179.

Frone, M. R., Russell, M. & Cooper, M. L. (1992). Antecedents and outcomes of work-family conflict: Testing a model of the work-family interface. *Journal of Applied Psychology, 77,* 65–78.

Frone, M. R., Russell, M. & Cooper, M. L. (1997). Relation of work-family conflict to health outcomes:A four-year longitudinal study of employed parents. *Journal of Occupational and Organizational Psychology, 70,* 325–335.

Frone, M. R. (2003). Work-family balance. In J. C. Quick & L. E. Tetrick (eds), *Handbook of Occupational Health Psychology* (pp. 143–162). Washington, DC: American Psychological Association.

Greenhaus, J. H. & Allen, T. D. (2006).Work-family balance: Exploration of a concept. Paper presentation, *Families and Work Conference.* (March). Provo, UT.

Greenhaus, J. H. & Beutell, N. J. (1985). Sources of conflict between work and family roles. *Academy of Management Review, 10,* 76–88.

Greenhaus, J. H., Collins, K. M. & Shaw, J. D. (2003). The relation between work-family balance and quality of life. *Journal of Vocational Behavior, 63,* 510–531.

Greenhaus, J. H. & Powell, G. N. (2006). When work and family are allies: A theory of work-family enrichment. *Academy of Management Review, 31,* 72–92.

Grzywacz, J. G. & Bass, B. L. (2003).Work, family, and mental health:Testing different models of work-family fit. *Journal of Marriage and Family, 65,* 248–261.

Grzywacz, J.G. (2002). Toward a theory of work-family facilitation. Paper presentation, *34th Annual Theory Construction and Research Methodology Workshop* (November). Houston,TX.

Grzywacz, J. G. & Carlson, D. S. (2007). Conceptualizing work-family balance: Implications for practice and future research. *Advances in Developing Human Resources, 9*(4), 455–471.

Grzywacz, J. G., Carlson, D. S., Kacmar, K. M. & Wayne, J. H. (2007). Work-family facilitation: A multilevel perspective on the synergies between work and family. *Journal of Occupational and Organizational Psychology, 80*(4), 559–574.

Grzywacz, J. G. & Marks, N. F. (2000). Reconceptualizing the work-family interface: An ecological perspective on the correlates of positive and negative spillover between work and family. *Journal of Occupational Health Psychology, 5*, 111–126.

Gutek, B., Searle, S. & Klepa, L. (1991). Rational versus gender-role explanations for work family conflict. *Journal of Applied Psychology, 76*, 560–568.

Hanson, G. C., Hammer, L. B. & Colton, C. L. (2006). Development and validation of a multidimensional scale of perceived work-family positive spillover. *Journal of Occupational Health Psychology, 11*, 249–265.

Hill, E. J. (2005). Work-family facilitation and conflict, working fathers and mothers, work-family stressors and support. *Journal of Family Issues, 26*, 793–819.

Hill, E. J., Hawkins, A. J., Ferris, M. & Weitzman, M. (2001). Finding and extra day a week: The positive influence of perceived job flexibility on work and family life balance. *Family Relations, 50*, 49–58.

Kirchmeyer, C. (1992a). Nonwork participation and work attitudes: A test of scarcity vs. expansion models of personal resources. *Human Relations, 45*, 775–795.

Kirchmeyer, C. (1992b). Perceptions of nonwork-to-work spillover: Challenging the common view of conflict-ridden domain relationships. *Basic and Applied Social Psychology, 13*, 231–249.

Kirchmeyer, C. (1995). Managing the work-nonwork boundary: An assessment of organizational responses. *Human Relations, 48*, 515–536.

Kirchmeyer, C. (2000). Work-life initiatives: Greed or benevolence regarding workers' time? In C. L. Cooper & D. M. Rousseau (eds), *Trends in Organizational Behavior* (Vol. 7, pp. 79–93). West Sussex, UK: Wiley.

Kofodimos, J. R. (1993). *Balancing Act*. San Francisco: Jossey-Bass.

Kopelman, R. E., Greenhaus, J. H. & Connolly, T. F. (1983). A model of work, family, and interrole conflict: A construct validation study. *Organizational Behavior and Human Performance, 32*, 198–215.

Lambert, S. J. (1990). Processes linking work and family: A critical review and research agenda. *Human Relations, 43*, 239–257.

MacDermid, S. M. (2005). (Re)Considering conflict between work and family. In E. E. Kossek, & S. Lambert (eds), *Work and Family Integration in Organizations: New Directions for Theory and Practice* (pp. 19–40). Mahwah, NJ: Lawrence Earlbaum Associates.

Marks, S. R., Huston, T. L., Johnson, E. M. & MacDermid, S. M. (2001). Role balance among white married couples. *Journal of Marriage and Family, 63*, 1083–1098.

Marks, S. R. & MacDermid, S. M. (1996). Multiple roles and the self: A theory of role balance. *Journal of Marriage and the Family, 58*, 417–432.

Mesmer-Magnus, J. R. & Viswesvaran, C. (2005). Convergence between measures of work-to-family and family-to-work conflict: A meta-analytic examination. *Journal of Vocational Behavior, 67*, 215–232.

Milkie, M. A. & Peltola, P. (1999). Playing all the roles: Gender and the work-family balancing act. *Journal of Marriage and the Family, 61*, 476–490.

Netemeyer, R. G., Boles, J. S. & McMurrian, R. (1996). Development and validation of work-family conflict scales and family-work conflict scales. *Journal of Applied Psychology, 81*, 433–410.

Nunnally, J. (1978). *Psychometric Theory*. New York: McGraw-Hill.

Parasuraman, S. & Greenhaus, J. H. (2002). Toward reducing some critical gaps in work-family research. *Human Resource Management Review, 12*, 299–312.

Sheldon, K. M. & Niemiec, C. P. (2006). It's not just the amount that counts: balanced need satisfaction also affects well-being. *Journal of Personality and Social Psychology, 91*, 331–341.

Sieber, S. D. (1974). Toward a theory of role accumulation. *American Sociological Review, 39*, 567–578.

Stephens, M., Franks, M. & Atienza, A. (1997). Where two roles intersect: Spillover between parent care and employment. *Psychology and Aging, 12,* 376–386.

Stephens, G. K. & Sommer, S. M. (1996). The measurement of work to family conflict. *Educational and Psychological Measurement, 56,* 475–486.

Tetrick, L. E. & Buffardi, L. C. (2006). Measurement issues in research on the work-home interface. In F. Jones, R. J. Burke & M. Westman (eds), *Work-life Balance: A Psychological Perspective* (pp. 90–114). Hove, East Sussex: Psychology Press.

Voydanoff, P. (2005). Toward a conceptualization of perceived work-family fit and balance: A demands and resources approach. *Journal of Marriage and Family, 67,* 822–836.

Wayne, J. H., Musisca, N. & Fleeson, W. (2004). Considering the role of personality in the work-family experience: Relationships of the big five to work-family conflict and facilitation. *Journal of Vocational Behavior, 64,* 108–130.

Witt, A. & Carlson, D. S. (in press). The work-family interface and job performance: Moderating effects of conscientiousness and perceived organizational support. *Journal of Occupational Health Psychology.*

CHAPTER 5

On Multiple Roles: Past, Present, and Future

Rosalind Chait Barnett
Brandeis University Women's Studies Research Center Mailstop, Waltham, MA

There has been a remarkable change in both theory and research on multiple roles over the past 50 years. So much has changed that the assumptions underlying the seminal early works of the major theoreticians seem almost quaint today. In the 1950s, and for about 20 years thereafter, the accepted wisdom was that men and women had innate or deeply socialized differences that ideally suited them for the very different social roles they occupied. Men took charge; women took care. Heavy social sanctions operated to keep "men and women in their place." Women who had careers were seen as unfeminine, selfish, and unmarriageable "old maids." Men who were active parents and shared the housework with their wives were considered henpecked, mama's boys. Moreover, it was thought that if women assumed non-nurturant roles it was unnatural and by necessity would have negative effects on them and their families.

In this chapter, I first discuss current demographic trends, and then look at the early research on multiple roles—examining the then dominant underlying theoretical perspectives and the findings that grew out of that viewpoint. I then turn to the present, once again laying out newer theories and associated empirical results. Most of the chapter is devoted to this section primarily because the research results, while compelling, still have not had the effect of changing earlier and still popular ideas about the effects of multiple roles, especially for women with children. Finally, I comment on the implications of projected demographic and attitudinal changes for multiple roles in the future.

DEMOGRAPHIC TRENDS

In spite of strong social pressures, increasing numbers of women entered the U. labor force in the 1950s and thereafter. Many got their start during World War II, when vacancies opened because so many men were sent overseas. The need for women to "man" the assembly lines created new opportunities that were previously closed off to women. Rosie the Riveter was born. With the end of the

Handbook of Work-Family Integration: Research, Theory, and Best Practices

war, women were shooed out of the workplace and into the home. Why? Because their jobs were needed for the returning troops. But many women who had a taste of life beyond the front door did not want to return to full-time domesticity. Following the end of the war, there was a relatively steep but short-lived decline in women's labor force participation. But by 1970, women began what has been called the quiet revolution. Since then there has been a steady increase in women's labor force participation. In 2005, women constituted 46% of the labor force, and that percentage is projected to increase (U. Department of Labor, 2005). And, this increase was not just among single, divorced, or widowed women. The steepest increase was among married women and most notably among married women with young children. Moreover, women's labor force participation increasingly resembles the male pattern: more and more women are working full-time, full-year, whereas not long ago the typical female labor-force participation pattern was part-time, part-year (Barnett, 2005).

With the rise in women's labor force participation, there has been a related rise in the prevalence of dual-earner families. As of 2002, 78% of employees were in dual-earner families, compared to 66% in 1977 (Bond, Thompson, Galinsky & Prottas, 2003). Thus, the dual-earner family was on its way to becoming what it is today—the modal American family. Not only are more women in the labor force than before, but individual women are working more weeks per year than in the past (Jacobs & Gerson, 2004). As a result, their contribution to the household income has increased over time. In three-quarters of dual-earner couples, both partners work full-time, and as of 2007, wives in 33% of dual-earner families earned more than their husbands (Bureau of Labor Statistics, Table 25, 2005). These demographic trends have made full-time employed dual-earner families a major force in the US population.

More and more women are combining full-time employment with marriage and children. And, on average, women take short maternity leaves. Today, the majority of mothers in the US who return to work after having a child do so before their child's first birthday. In the National Institute of Child Health and Human Development (NICHD) Study of Early Child Care, the overwhelming majority of mothers who were employed in their infants' first year returned to work and placed their children in some kind of routine non-maternal care arrangement before the child was six months of age (Hofferth, 1996; NICHD Early Child Care Research Network, 1997a, 1997b). As of 2002, 54% of women with infants under one year of age were in the labor force (Downs, 2002; Bureau of Labor Statistics, personal communication, May 14, 2007); comparable rates in 1970 and 1984 were 24% and 53%, respectively (Hofferth, 1996; Hoffman, 1989). As of 1997, the majority of children in the US had mothers and fathers who were employed full-time (Bond, Galinsky, & Swanberg, 1998). In 2006, 52% of dual-earner couples had a child under 18 in the home (Bureau of Labor Statistics, 2007).

THE PAST: A FOCUS ON NEGATIVE EFFECTS OF MULTIPLE ROLES

These demographic changes represent striking shifts in the relationships between gender, work, and family. Yet most theories and popular beliefs about multiple roles date from the 1950s, a time of remarkable sex segregation, gender asymmetry, and stability in work and family patterns. Women's labor-force participation peaked during World War II at 36.3% in 1944 but then immediately fell back to 30.8% in 1946 (US Bureau of the Census, 1975), as women were fired from their factory jobs to make way for returning veterans. Perhaps more important than the reality was the ideology of the time, with a strong resurgence of the doctrine of separate spheres, which originated among the English upper-middle classes in the 19th century, and held that woman's proper place was in the home and that man's was in the world of commerce (Reskin & Padavic, 1994). Mothers of the 1950s and their atypically large families were isolated from the world of work in which their husbands spent long hours. Fathers, who were fully employed at a family wage, i.e., "the amount that a single wage earner requires to financially support a family" (Albelda, Drago & Shulman, 1997, p. 157) rarely engaged in a meaningful way with their children (Christiansen & Palkovitz, 2001; Griswold, 1993). At that time, marriage and motherhood were the only acceptable and socially sanctioned roles for adult women, who would otherwise be stigmatized as spinsters or old maids, shunned socially, and deprived economically because women at that time were barred from occupations that might provide a reasonable livelihood. The marriage-and-motherhood imperative was reinforced by severe social and religious sanctions against divorce. Indeed, social mores at the time provided little latitude in gender roles. These trends were characteristic mainly of the middle class; working-class and poor women had to work throughout these decades, whatever the ideology.

It is important to note that the early research on multiple roles focused almost exclusively on women, especially on women who occupied the roles of wife, mother, and employee. As discussed below, research on men and multiple roles became increasingly more prevalent only in the last 20 years, in part, accompanying the striking growth among dual-earner families.

TRADITIONAL THEORIES OF GENDER, WORK, AND FAMILY

The eminent family sociologist Talcott Parsons (1949) observed the uniformity of gender differentiated marital/family roles and the high marital stability of his time and concluded that family functioning is optimized when the husband specializes in market work and the wife in domestic work. Each partner then trades the fruits of her or his different skills, ensuring the stability of the marriage.

In other words, gender-role specialization and complementarity (or asymmetric mutual dependence) were considered key to marital stability and presumably to marital quality. From this, it follows that gender symmetry (both parents working) should increase the risk of marital dissatisfaction and disruption.

Parsons and his colleagues (e.g., Parsons & Bales, 1955) believed that the functional asymmetry in marital roles they observed was inevitable and attributable to the biological fact that women bear and nurse children, which establishes a presumptive primacy of the relationship between mother and child. The related presumption then is that men, who cannot perform these biological functions, should specialize in the instrumental realm of work. Parsons believed, therefore, that he had articulated a universal theory of family functioning. In his words,

> the broad structural outlines of the American nuclear family, as we have delineated it, are not fortuitous in the sense of being bound to a particular highly specific social situation, but are of generic significance with respect to the structure and functions of the family in all societies.

(Parsons & Bales, 1955, p. 355)

These views, albeit modified somewhat, continued to be dominant within sociology until the mid-1980s and continue today to dominate in family studies (Thompson & Walker, 1989), corporate policy, and public policy.

The Cost of Multiple Roles

It was widely held that multiple roles would have negative effects on women because human energy was conceived of as a limited quantity. According to this scarcity hypothesis, the more energy expended on one social role, the less energy is available for other social roles. Thus, if a married woman with children, who already occupied two demanding social roles, added the employee role, also a demanding role, she would have less energy available for each of her multiple roles. Based on predictions from both the Parsonian functionalist perspective and the scarcity hypothesis, women who occupied multiple roles (i.e., wife, mother, and paid employee), were expected to have troubled marriages, children who felt abandoned and rejected, and poor personal health. For example, it was assumed that such women would report high levels of depression, anxiety, and work-family conflict. Predictions from sociology were also gloomy. Jessie Bernard (1982), among others, claimed that as women became more educated and as their earning potential increased, they would be less likely to find eligible marital partners. The so-called "marriage gradient," according to which women married up and men married down, would leave highly competent women with no one above them as possible mates.

THE PRESENT: A FOCUS ON POSITIVE EFFECTS OF MULTIPLE ROLES

Several important research studies challenged the predictive power of the scarcity hypothesis. Specifically, these studies indicated that men and women who occupy "non-traditional" roles actually report positive rather than negative effects, that women and men benefit from multiple roles (Barnett 2005; Gore & Mangione, 1983), and that the quality of one's role experiences was a more significant predictor of health and well-being outcomes than the number of roles occupied *per se*. In light of these empirical findings, a new theoretical model, referred to as an Expansionist theory (Barnett & Hyde, 2001) was developed. What were some of the key research findings that led to this new theoretical development?

RESEARCH FINDINGS

A key question was whether women who occupied solely "natural" domestic roles experienced higher psychological well-being than their counterparts who combined those roles with that of paid employee. An early answer came from a systematic study of middle-class women 35–55 years of age who varied in employment, marital, and parental status. Importantly, the parameter that accounted for most of the variance in psychological well-being was employment status (Barnett & Baruch, 1985). That is, employed women, whether they were married or parents, reported greater well-being than the nonemployed women. Moreover, married women who had children and who held high-prestige jobs reported the greatest well-being of all. Again, these findings would not have been predicted by previous theories. These findings presented a serious challenge to traditional theories. The results of other studies continued to undermine the earlier and dominant functionalist perspective.

In 1992, Peggy Thoits found more similarity between the sexes in the importance men and women attached to their various social roles than would have been predicted by earlier theories. Specifically, men and women ranked the roles of partner and parent similarly in prominence and higher than the role of employee (which was also ranked similarly by women and men). In addition, little support has been found for the prediction that women and men who engage in "unnatural" roles, for example the employee role for women and the parental role for men, will experience distress. Indeed, study after study has demonstrated that women and men who engage in multiple roles report lower levels of stress-related mental and physical health problems and higher levels of subjective well-being than do their counterparts who engage in fewer roles (Barnett & Marshall, 1993; Crosby & Jaskar, 1993; Simons, 1992; Thoits, 1992; Wethington & Kessler, 1989).

Furthermore, in current research, the low distress of women in multiple roles has been attributed primarily to the effects of the employee role.

With respect to men's well-being, several studies have highlighted the centrality of the paternal role. For example, Simons (1992) reported that fathers were as reactive to strains in their relationships with their children as mothers were. Dual-earner fathers who dropped their children off at day-care centers experienced at least as much separation anxiety as did their wives (Deater-Deckard, Scarr, McCartney & Eisenberg, 1994). Furthermore, several studies of men having sole custody of their children reported that they were as nurturant and caring as were mothers. As noted above, these men resembled mothers more than other (less involved) fathers with respect to their caring behaviors (Coltrane, 1996; Greif, 1992; Risman, 1986).

Based on the cumulating research evidence from contemporary samples, a new consensus has been developing. Specifically, the weight of empirical data indicates that women and men are not naturally suited for either domestic or non-domestic social roles and that multiple roles are beneficial for both women and men. This consensus is reflected in a new theory about multiple roles—*An Expansionist Theory of Women, Men, Work, and Family* (Barnett & Hyde, 2001).

BENEFITS OF MULTIPLE ROLES

Based on the empirical literature, the first of the four principles of the Expansionist theory is that multiple roles, rather than being harmful, are, in general, beneficial for women and men as reflected in mental health, physical health, and relationship health. (For a complete discussion of this theory, including a discussion of the other three principles, namely that: several processes contribute to the relationship between multiple roles and beneficial outcomes; there are upper limits to the benefits of multiple roles; and psychological gender differences are generally small, see Barnett & Hyde, 2001). Here are several of the key findings on which the principle that multiple roles are beneficial for women and for men rests.

Mental Health

In an early review of both British and American research through 1980, Warr and Parry (1982) found no differences overall between employed women and homemakers on measures of psychological distress and well-being. However, the authors cautioned that a variety of other variables needed to be taken into account, including role quality (as discussed in the third principle below).

Reviewing the next decade of research, Repetti, Matthews and Waldron (1989) concluded that employment was associated with improved health for single and married women who held a positive attitude toward employment. They noted that the effects were less consistent for mental health than for physical health. Several studies have found employed women to be less depressed than nonemployed women (see, e.g., Aneshensel, 1986; Kandel, Davies & Raveis, 1985), whereas there were no significant differences between the groups in other studies (e.g., Baruch & Barnett, 1986; Repetti & Crosby, 1984). In no studies were employed women more depressed than nonemployed women. In another review, Crosby (1991) concluded that women who juggle multiple roles are less depressed than other women.

In a longitudinal study, Wethington and Kessler (1989) examined changes in labor force participation over time in the US in relation to psychological distress in a sample of White women. They found that women who increased their workforce participation from homemaker (not employed or employed less than 10 hours per week) to part-time worker (10–34 hours per week) or to full-time worker (employed 35 or more hours per week) showed lower levels of depression over the three-year period of the study. Over the same period of time, employed women who decreased their hours of paid employment from full-time to low part-time (i.e., between 10–19 hours per week) or who became homemakers reported an increase in symptoms of depression. These findings were net of the effect of initial level of depression, family income, years of education, age of respondent, and number and ages of children in the household.

Importantly, most of the studies cited above looked at employed women as an aggregate, not differentiating them according to parental status; however Repetti et al. (1989) concluded, after reviewing studies that examined interactions between work status and parental status, that the mental health effects of employment are consistent across different parental statuses. Kessler and McRae (1982) found that, although the presence of preschool children in the home was associated with psychological distress among women, employed women showed less distress than nonemployed women and the effect remained even when the number of children was controlled. Russo and Zierk (1992), using a large national sample, found that after childbearing was controlled, women's well-being was positively related to employment, although it was negatively related to the total number of children.

Studies have also indicated that men's mental health benefits from their occupancy of multiple roles. Several early studies (Farrell & Rosenberg, 1981; Lein et al., 1974) concluded that men "seek their primary emotional, personal, and spiritual gratification in their family setting" (Lein et al., 1974, p. 118). Using a nationally representative probability sample, Veroff, Douvan, and Kulka (1981) reported similar findings. Male respondents who held all three roles of spouse, parent, and paid worker rated family roles as more critical to their well-being than occupational roles. In another study, men's psychological well-being benefitted equally from their experiences in their employee, spouse, and father roles (Barnett & Gareis, in press; Barnett, Marshall & Pleck, 1992; Ozer, Barnett, Brennan & Sperling, 1998).

Physical Health

Men who were engaged in the roles of employee, spouse, and father reported fewer physiological symptoms of distress than men who occupied fewer roles (typically, men who were not fathers; Gore & Mangione, 1983). These results are in sharp contrast to conclusions drawn about social roles and men's physical health from earlier studies influenced by functionalist views. The influential Western Collaborative Group Study (Rosenman et al., 1975), the first major prospective study that identified psychosocial stressors as independent risk factors in cardiovascular disease, did not even ask the 3,000 male participants whether they were married or had children! So convinced were the investigators that men's primary role was that of worker that they inferred that whatever psychosocial stressors or benefits were operative would be at the workplace.

For women, the data provide no evidence of a negative effect of multiple roles on physical health, and some studies have found a positive relationship (Repetti et al., 1989). For example, using longitudinal data from a sample of middle-aged women, Waldron and Jacobs (1989) found that labor-force participation had beneficial effects on health for unmarried women and for African-American married women and no significant effect on health for White married women.

Relationship Health

Here, too, when relationship health is the outcome, again the evidence indicates that multiple roles—and, in particular, employment for women and family involvement for men—are beneficial. Whereas functionalist theories (and past folk wisdom) predicted that women's educational attainment and employment would threaten marital stability as well as a woman's chances of being married, the reverse now seems to be true. According to Oppenheimer (1997), women who complete higher levels of education have a greater likelihood of marriage than those who do not. As noted earlier, in spite of some support for the functionalist position, historical evidence indicates that income equality within couples is not synonymous with complications for marriage and, in fact, may be associated with benefits (Oppenheimer). In one study of couples' relative earnings, to be discussed in greater detail below, Ono (1998) found that marital dissolution was highest in couples in which the wife had no earnings. This analysis controlled for husband's race and income, each partner's age, age of the husband at marriage, education, length of marriage, home ownership, presence of children, age of the youngest child, percentage of weeks worked in the previous year, and husband's and wife's percentage of years worked since school completion.

Men, too, benefit from multiple roles. Data on fathers support the view that men's family roles are central to their mental and physical well-being and, in fact, may be more critical to their psychological state than are their employee roles

(Pleck, 1985). Wilkie, Ferree and Ratcliff (1998), for example, found that more equitable sharing of breadwinning offered benefits to marital satisfaction for both husbands and wives; the benefits were somewhat greater for husbands. In practice, most research relating multiple roles to health outcomes is tantamount to the study of nontraditional roles and their health effects. For women, the research focus is on the influence of the paid-employee role among married women with children; for men, the focus is on the roles of partner and parent among employed men. (See Daly, Ashbourne & Hawkins in this volume for a review of the literature on fathers and work-life balance.)

DUAL-EARNER COUPLES

In contrast to early research that was limited to studying the relationship between multiple roles and outcomes in individual women and men, several methodological advances in the past 20 years have made it possible to study the effects of multiple roles and a host of outcomes within couples. With data from 300 primarily White and middle-class, full-time-employed, dual-earner couples who were interviewed three times over a two-year period, Ozer and her colleagues asked whether fathers' involvement in childcare relative to their wives was associated with either partner's marital-role quality or psychological distress (Ozer et al., 1998). Hypotheses derived from earlier theories would have led to the prediction that men should engage in such tasks only under duress (e.g., wife is ill) or that higher involvement per se should have negative effects because it was unnatural and therefore stressful. Contrary to those predictions, the husbands who did more childcare relative to their wives reported lower psychological distress. Interestingly, husbands' relative participation was unrelated to their reports of their own marital quality; however, compared with wives whose husbands participated less, wives whose husbands were highly participatory reported higher marital quality. Milkie and Peltola (1999) have argued that women and men can derive a subjective sense of success from balancing work and family demands. Analyzing data from married, employed Americans in the 1996 General Social Survey, they developed a measure of sense of success in balancing work and family and found that women and men reported similarly high levels of success.

Overall, when women and men combine both work and family, as occurs in dual-earner couples, their daily life experiences become more similar, facilitating spousal communication and marital quality (Cowan et al., 1985; Schwartz, 1994). Other benefits to men and women in dual-earner couples include added income, social support, opportunities to experience success, expanded frame of reference, and increased self-complexity. Of course, these processes or factors need not be mutually exclusive.

DUAL-EARNER FAMILIES

In a recent study (Barnett & Gareis, 2007), the unit of analysis was broadened to include the mother, father, and all children 8–14 years of age. The mothers were all registered nurses employed full-time on either the evening or the day shift. The fathers were all employed at least half-time and the large majority worked days. The study was designed to see whether the socio-emotional well-being of children varied depending on parental work schedules. One of the main findings was that fathers whose wives worked the evening shift (i.e., 3 p.m. to 11 p.m.) compared to the day shift (i.e., 7 a.m. to 3 p.m.), spent significantly more time alone with their children, felt more competent as a parent, rated their parenting skills higher, and knew more about their children's everyday activities. Their children reported fewer risky behaviors and said that they spontaneously disclosed more about their lives to their fathers. Significantly, the more time children spent with their father, the fewer risky behaviors they report and the fewer internalizing and externalizing behaviors they exhibit, according to the mothers. Importantly, neither the time the mothers spend interacting with their children, nor their children's rating of their mothers' parenting skills, nor the children's tendency to spontaneously disclose to their mothers was affected by the mothers' shift schedule.

These findings support a growing consensus that children do not suffer if their parents are both employed outside the home (Galinsky, 2003; NICHD Early Child Care Research Network, 1998). If mothers are warm and responsive, children do well whether their mothers are at home with them or in the paid labor force. At least in some families, as just described, fathers increase their time with their children when mothers are not available. However, the benefits to children might be compromised if the child care is poor and extensive (Waldfogel, 2006).

CONDITIONING FACTORS

There are, however, conditions under which the effects of multiple roles may be attenuated. For example, overload and distress may occur beyond certain limits. This may occur when the number of roles becomes too great (e.g., a woman adds care of an elderly and ailing parent to her roles of wife, mother, and president of a small business) or when the demands of one role are excessive (e.g., the young lawyer who is a husband and father and must work 80 hours per week at his job). Voydanoff and Donnelly (1999) tested for the latter effect by estimating the curvilinear relationships between time spent in roles and psychological distress, the hypothesis being that increased time in a role decreases psychological distress up to a certain point and, beyond that point, increases distress. These researchers did indeed find the expected curvilinear relationship between hours of paid work and psychological distress. They found a similar curvilinear relationship between time spent with spouse and psychological distress. Both findings support the hypothesis that there are upper limits to the benefits of multiple roles and, in particular, that there are upper limits to the benefits of hours spent in particular roles.

With regard to the effect of the sheer number of roles, in a study attempting to discern the upper limits of these benefits, Thoits (1986) noted that most studies relating multiple-role occupancy to well-being indicators have focused on the three major social roles of parent, partner, and employee. To rectify this situation, she expanded the number of roles to include friend, neighbor, relative, student, church member, and organizational member. Her results indicated that five roles seem optimal for psychological well-being. However, in her large representative sample of adults in Chicago, Illinois, and New Haven, Connecticut, the average respondent possessed fewer than six role identities. Thus, for all intents and purposes, she was unable to test whether there might be a curvilinear relationship between number of roles and mental health.

Finally, role quality is more important than number of roles or time spent in a role. For example, mental health benefits do not accrue from the work role when the job is not satisfying or when the person is the victim of discrimination or harassment. Similarly, people may work long hours but benefit psychologically if the work is satisfying. In a review of the multiple roles literature of the 1990s, Perry-Jenkins, Repetti and Crouter (2000) reported that researchers were now attending more to role quality than to role occupancy. Greenberger and O'Neil (1993), in a study of men and women in dual-earner marriages who were parenting a preschool child, found that satisfactory experiences in parental, marital, and work roles were particularly potent predictors of psychological distress (depression and anxiety) for women, but less so for men. High levels of role satisfaction were associated with low levels of depression and anxiety. Results of an analysis regressing men's stress-related physical health problems on their subjective experiences in their work role as well as their family roles (i.e., spouse and parent) support this view (Barnett et al., 1992).

Role quality is also key in family roles. Among full-time-employed men in dual-earner couples, those who experienced more concerns in their parenting role also reported higher levels of stress-related physical symptoms (e.g., insomnia, lower back pain, fatigue; Barnett & Marshall, 1993). In the Wisconsin Maternity Leave and Health Project, a longitudinal study of couples following the birth of a child, Hyde, Klein, Essex and Clark (1995) found that women's depressive symptoms at 4 months postpartum (with prebirth symptoms controlled) were not significantly predicted by hours worked per week but were significantly predicted by rewards in the work role; higher levels of work rewards were associated with lower levels of depressive symptoms. When anxiety was the outcome variable, number of hours worked per week was a significant predictor (more hours were associated with more anxiety), but with that controlled, work-role quality was significantly associated with anxiety above and beyond work hours (which remained significant). Analyses with the same sample at 12 months after the birth indicated that hours worked per week was not significantly associated with depression or anxiety; however, a sense of overload in the work role was positively associated with depressive symptoms, and a sense of compatibility with one's spouse was associated with fewer depressive symptoms (Klein et al., 1998).

WORK-FAMILY CONFLICT

Finally, there is a widespread belief, based largely on the scarcity hypothesis, that there is an inherent and inevitable conflict between involvement in work and family roles, such that conflict and tension are inevitable, especially for women. Yet the empirical literature does not support this prediction. In study after study, men report as high or higher work-family conflict as women (e.g., Bond et al., 1998). At first, this finding seems counterintuitive. However, when we focus on the benefits of multiple roles, we learn that performance in each role is facilitated so that strong commitment to work does not preclude strong commitment to family and vice versa. In sharp contrast to predictions from the functionalist perspective and the scarcity hypothesis, research shows a modest positive correlation between work commitment and family commitment (Marks & MacDermid, 1996). For example, a study of male and female senior managers, in which commitment was operationalized as hours spent in paid work and family work, found a modest positive correlation between these two indicators of role commitment (Gutek, Searle & Klepa, 1991). In the Wisconsin Maternity Leave and Health Project, work commitment and spouse commitment were significantly positively correlated for wives, but were not significantly related for husbands (Hyde, DeLamater & Durik, 2001). These findings contradict the functionalist assumption that work commitment and family commitment are negatively correlated.

THE FUTURE

Several demographic and attitudinal trends suggest that the dual-earner family will continue to be the dominant American family form. The trends that lead to this conclusion include:

- a rising age at first marriage for both women and men over the course of the past five decades
- declining fertility rates and lengthening of the life span for men and women
- the increasing prevalence of egalitarian gender-role attitudes

- increasing numbers of women students at all levels of post-secondary education; and
- a growing reliance on wives' earnings to enable couples to maintain a middle-class standard of living.

RISING AGE AT FIRST MARRIAGE

Since the 1950s, there has been a steady increase in age at first marriage for both women and men. As of 2005, the median age at first marriage was 25.8 years for women and 27.1 years for men; in 1950, the comparable ages were 20.5 years for women and 23.7 years for men (US Census Bureau, 2005 Current Population Survey's (CPS) Annual Social and Economic Supplement). In part, this trend reflects women's increasing educational attainment. As of 2000, women in the US earned 56% of bachelor's degrees, 55% of master's degrees, and 41% of doctorates. These figures reflect a sharp and steady increase from 1950, when the comparable percentages were 25%, 26%, and 10% (Caplow, Hicks & Wattenberg, 2001). The increasing median age at first marriage may also reflect changes in earning patterns for men. Men tend to postpone marriage until they can adequately provide for a family, therefore when men's wages stagnate or decline, their age at first marriage tends to increase (Oppenheimer, 1997).

DECLINING FERTILITY AND LENGTHENING LIFE SPAN

The trend toward increasing age at first marriage also reflects women's increasing commitment to the labor force and expanding control over fertility. As of 2000, US fertility was hovering around 1.9 children per couple, a level below that required for the natural replacement of the population (Bachu, 2001). It is important to note that fertility rates are higher in the US than in most other industrialized countries, due largely to differences in immigration policies. Another indicator of women's commitment to the workforce is the percentage of women who are employed and who have dependent children. In 1990, 58.9% of married women with children under age six were in the labor force, as compared to 59.3% in 2004 (Bureau of Labor Statistics, 2005). Of married women with older children (6 to 17 years of age), 73.6% were in the labor force in 1990 and 72.8% were in the labor force in 2006 (US Department of Labor, 2006). It is instructive to see the low fertility figures in the context of the lengthening life span for women and men. As of 2004, women in the US had a life expectancy at birth of 80.4 years compared to a life expectancy at birth of 75.2 years for men (Office of Analysis & Epidemiology, NCHS, 2006). Thus, today fewer children are being born and reared in a narrower band of years within a longer life span. As a result of these trends, it is less likely that today's women will center their long lives solely around rearing one or two children. As the maternal role has been compressed, the employee role has been expanding.

INCREASING PREVALENCE OF EGALITARIAN GENDER-ROLE IDEOLOGY

There is convincing evidence that women's and men's gender-role ideology is increasingly supportive of women's new social roles. A Gallup poll in 1936 asked a national sample the following question, "Should a married woman earn money if she has a husband capable of supporting her?" Eighty-two percent of men and women said NO. A similar question ("Do you approve or disapprove of a married woman earning money in business or industry if she has a husband capable of supporting her?") has been asked regularly since 1972 as part of the General Social Survey (Caplow et al., 2001). By 1996, there had been a complete reversal in responses: 83% of respondents—men and women—approved. When responses to similar questions are broken down by gender, there is a consistent pattern. Men are typically less liberal in their attitudes toward multiple roles for women; however, over time and for males from high-school age on, there has been a steady and impressive increase in the percentages who endorse multiple roles for women (James, Barnett & Brennan, 1998; Moen, 1999; Radcliffe Public Policy Center, 2000; Twenge, 1997). Lastly, the most recent National Study of the Changing Workforce (Bond et al., 2003) revealed a 32% decline in traditional gender role attitudes among men over the course of the previous 25 years: 42% of men surveyed in 2002 felt that women's "appropriate" role was to tend the home and children while men earned money for the household, down from 74% of male respondents in 1977 (Bond et al.). Taken together, these studies suggest widespread and growing acceptance of egalitarian social roles for women and men.

A similar trend appears in data on men's and women's actual behavior. Between 1977 and 2002 in two nationally representative samples, full-time employed men significantly increased the time that they spent on household and child-care tasks, whereas women's time on these chores remained the same or decreased (Bond et al., 2003). If the present trend continues there is every reason to believe that within a relatively short period of time, employed men and women will be spending roughly equal amounts of time in these two forms of domestic labor.

WOMEN ARE NOW A MAJORITY OF STUDENTS AT ALL LEVELS OF POST-SECONDARY EDUCATION

After many years of increasing enrollments, women are now the majority of US college students and of those receiving bachelor's degrees. One reason for this trend, according to Goldin, Katz, and Kuziemko (2006), is young women's increased expectations for future long-term labor force participation. Yet major media stories have painted a picture of women college graduates from leading universities as leaving the workforce in favor of a life of domesticity (Belkin, 2003; Story, 2005; Wallis, 2004). These largely anecdote-based stories notwithstanding, evidence from several recent studies strongly challenge that conclusion. According to Claudia Goldin, women who graduated 25 years ago from the nation's top colleges did not "opt out" in large numbers, and today's graduates aren't likely to do so either (2006). Moreover, in 2004, the impact of having children in the home on women's labor force participation ("the child penalty") fell compared to prior years (Boushey, 2005). In fact, college-educated women have a labor force participation rate of 80% compared to roughly 75% for all women between the ages of 25 and 64 (Bradbury & Katz, 2005). These studies point to continued growth in dual-earner couples and in multiple roles for women and men.

WIVES' EARNINGS ARE NEEDED FOR MOST COUPLES TO MAINTAIN A MIDDLE-CLASS STANDARD OF LIVING

Finally, changes in workforce participation among married men and women have affected median family income for more than a generation. The gap between the median household incomes for families with and without a mother in the workforce increased steadily between 1967 and 2001. In 1967, the gap was about $10,000; in 2001, it was approximately $30,000 (US Census Bureau, Table F-7, 2002). Moreover, a significant proportion of married women are now earning as much as or more than their husbands. As of 1998, 40% of white college-educated women earned more than their husbands (Freeman, 1998). The prevalence of this pattern was underscored in the summer of 2003 in a cover story in *Newsweek* magazine (Tyre & McGinn, 2003).

Clearly, evidence from several quarters suggests that women and men will continue to occupy multiple roles.

In summary, a number of processes or factors may contribute to the beneficial effects of multiple roles, including buffering, added income, social support, increased opportunities to build self-efficacy, expanded frame of reference, increased self-complexity, similarity of experiences, and gender-role ideology.

IMPLICATIONS FOR FUTURE RESEARCH AND PRACTICE

Research on multiple roles has progressed from challenging assumptions based on stereotypical gender roles and beliefs about role scarcity to identifying the benefits that accrue for men, women, and families in occupying multiple roles.

Researchers have confirmed that role quality and conditioning factors are essential influences in understanding how multiple roles influence various health and well-being outcomes. Today's current research on positive spillover, work–family facilitation, and work–family enrichment (Carlson, Kacmar, Wayne & Grzywacz, 2006; Edwards & Rothbard, 2000; Greenhaus & Powell, 2006; Poelmans, Stepanova & Masuda, 2008) builds on the legacy of research on multiple roles. Future research can expand our understanding of how personal, familial, and organizational factors influence the ways multiple roles are experienced at the work–family interface and in other domains. This new understanding has practical applications for individuals, workplaces, and public policies, since optimizing the benefits of multiple roles is valuable for all.

REFERENCES

Albelda, R., Drago, R. & Shulman, S. (1997). *Unlevel Playing Fields: Understanding Wage Inequality and Discrimination*. New York: McGraw-Hill.

Aneshensel, C. S. (1986). Marital and employment role-strain, social support, and depression among adult women. In S. E. Hobfoll (ed.), *Stress, Social Support, and Women* (pp. 99–114). New York: Hemisphere.

Bachu, A. & O'Connell, M. (2001). Fertility of American women: June 2000 (Current Population Reports No. P20-543). Washington, DC: US Census Bureau.

Barnett, R. C. (2005). Dual-earner couples: Good/bad for her and/or him? In D. F. Halpern & S. E. Murphy (eds), *From Work-Family Balance to Work-Family Interaction: Changing the Metaphor* (pp. 151–171). Mahwah, NJ: Lawrence Erlbaum.

Barnett, R. C. & Baruch, G. K. (1985). Women's involvement in multiple roles and psychological distress. *Journal of Personality and Social Psychology, 49*(1), 135–145.

Barnett, R. C. & Gareis, K. C. (2007). Shift work, parenting behaviors, and children's socioemotional well-being: A within-family study. *Journal of Family Issues, 28*(6), 727–748.

Barnett, R. C. & Hyde, J. S. (2001). Women, men, work, and family: An expansionist theory. *American Psychologist, 56*, 781–796.

Barnett, R. C. & Marshall, N. L. (1993). Men, family-role quality, job-role quality, and physical health. *Health Psychology, 12*, 48–55.

Barnett, R. C., Marshall, N. L. & Pleck, J. H. (1992). Men's multiple roles and their relationship to men's psychological distress. *Journal of Marriage and the Family, 54*, 358–367.

Baruch, G. K. & Barnett, R. C. (1986). Role quality, multiple role involvement, and psychological well-being in midlife women. *Journal of Personality and Social Psychology, 51*, 578–585.

Belkin, L. (2003, October 26th). Q: Why don't more women get to the top? A: They don't want to. Abandoning the climb and heading home. *New York Times Magazine*, 42–59.

Bernard, J. S. (1982). *The Future of Marriage*. New Haven: Yale University Press.

Bond, J. T., Galinsky, E. & Swanberg, J. E. (1998). *The 1997 National Study of the Changing Workforce*. New York: Families and Work Institute.

Bond, J. T., Thompson, C., Galinsky, E. & Prottas, D. (2003). *Highlights of the 2002 National Study of the Changing Workforce* (No. 3). New York: Families and Work Institute.

Boushey, H. (2006). *Are Mothers Really Leaving the Workplace?* Council on Contemporary Families and the Center for Economic and Policy Research.

Bradbury, K. & Katz, J. (2005). Women's rise: A work in progress. *Regional Review, Q1*.

Caplow, T., Hicks, L. & Wattenberg, B. J. (2001). *The First Measured Century. An Illustrated Guide to Trends in America, 1900–2000*. Washington DC: AEI Press.

Carlson, D. S., Kacmar, K. M., Wayne, J. H. & Grzywacz, J. G. (2006). Measuring the positive side of the work-family interface: Development and validation of a work-family enrichment scale. *Journal of Vocational Behaviour, 68*, 131–164.

Christiansen, S. L. & Palkovitz, R. (2001). Why the "good provider" role still matters. *Journal of Family Issues, 22*, 84–106.

Coltrane, S. (1996). *Family Man: Fatherhood, Housework, and Gender Equity*. New York: Oxford University Press.

Cowan, C. P., Cowan, P. A., Heming, G., Garrett, E., Coysh, W. S., Curtis-Boles, H. & Boles, A. J. (1985). Transition to parenthood: His, hers and theirs. *Journal of Family Issues, 6*, 451–481.

Crosby, F. (1991). *Juggling: The Unexpected Advantages of Balancing Career and Home for Women and their Families*. New York: Free Press.

Crosby, F. J. & Jaskar, K. L. (1993). Women and men at home and at work: Realities and illusions. In S. Oskamp & M. Costanzo (eds), *Gender Issues in Contemporary Society* (pp. 143–171). Newbury Park: Sage .

Deater-Deckard, K., Scarr, S., McCartney, K. & Eisenberg, M. (1994). Paternal separation anxiety: Relationships with parenting stress, child-rearing attitudes, and maternal anxieties. *Psychological Science, 5*, 341–346.

Downs, B. (2002). *Fertility of American Women, June 2002* (Current Population Survey No. P20-548). Washington, DC: US Census Bureau.

Edwards, J. R. & Rothbard, N. P. (2000). Mechanisms linking work and family: Clarifying the relationship between work and family constructs. *Academy of Management Review, 25*, 178–199.

Farrell, M. P. & Rosenberg, S. D. (1981). *Men at Midlife*. Dover, MA: Auburn.

Freeman, R. B. (1998, January–February). Unequal incomes: The worrisome distribution of the fruits of American economic growth. *Harvard Magazine, 100*, 62–64.

Galinsky, E. (2003, February 22). Children's perspectives of employed mothers and fathers: Closing the gap between public debates and research findings. Paper presented at the 13th Annual Kravis-de Roulet Conference: Leadership in Work/Family Balance, Claremont McKenna College.

Goldin, C. (2006, March 15). Working it out. *New York Times*, p. A27.

Goldin, C., Katz, L. F. & Kuziemko, I. (2006). *TheHhomecoming of American College Women: The Reversal of the College Gender Gap* (Working Paper No. 12139). Cambridge, MA: National Bureau of Economic Research.

Gore, S. & Mangione, T. W. (1983). Social roles, sex roles, and psychological distress: Additive and interactive models of sex differences. *Journal of Health and Social Behavior, 24*, 300–312.

Greenberger, E. & O'Neil, R. (1993). Spouse, parent, worker: Role commitments and role-related experiences in the construction of adults' well-being. *Developmental Psychology, 29*, 181–197.

Greenhaus, J. H. & Powell, G. N. (2006). When work and family are allies: A theory of work-family enrichment. *Academy of Management Review, 31*,(1), 72–92.

Greif, G. L. (1992). Lone fathers in the United States: An overview and practice implications. *British Journal of Social Work, 22*, 565–574.

Griswold, R. L. (1993). *Fatherhood in America*. New York: Basic Books.

Gutek, B. A., Searle, S. & Klepa, L. (1991). Rational versus gender role explanations for work-family conflict. *Journal of Applied Psychology, 76*, 560–568.

Hofferth, S. L. (1996). Effects of public and private policies on working after childbirth. *Work and Occupations, 23*, 378–404.

Hoffman, L. W. (1989). Effects of maternal employment in the two-parent family. *American Psychologist, 44*, 283–292.

Hyde, J. S., DeLamater, J. D. & Durik, A. M. (2001). Sexuality and the dual-earner couple, part II: Beyond the baby years. *Journal of Sex Research, 38*, 10–23.

Hyde, J. S., Klein, M. H., Essex, M. J. & Clark, R. (1995). Maternity leave and women's mental health. *Psychology of Women Quarterly, 19*, 257–285.

Jacobs, J. A. & Gerson, K. (2004). *The Time Divide: Work, Family and Gender Inequality*. Cambridge, MA: Harvard University Press.

James, J. B., Barnett, R. C. & Brennan, R. T. (1998). The psychological effects of work experiences and disagreements about gender-role beliefs in dual earner couples: A longitudinal study. *Women's Health: Research on Gender, Behavior, and Policy, 4*, 341–368.

Kandel, D. B., Davies, M. & Raveis, V. H. (1985). The stressfulness of daily social roles for women: Marital, occupational, and household roles. *Journal of Health and Social Behavior, 26*, 64–78.

Kessler, R. C. & McRae, J. A. (1982). The effect of wives' employment on the mental health of married men and women. *American Sociological Review, 47*, 216–227.

Klein, M. H., Hyde, J. S., Essex, M. J. & Clark, R. (1998). Maternity leave, role quality, work involvement, and mental health one year after delivery. *Psychology of Women Quarterly, 22*, 239–266.

Lein, L., Durham, M., Pratt, M., Schudson, M., Thomas, R. & Weiss, H. (1974). *Final Report: Work and Family Life*. Cambridge: Center for the Study of Public Policy.

Marks, S. R. & MacDermid, S. M. (1996). Multiple roles and the self: A theory of role balance. *Journal of Marriage and the Family, 58*, 417–432.

Milkie, M. A. & Peltola, P. (1999). Playing all the roles: Gender and the work-family balancing act. *Journal of Marriage and the Family, 61*, 476–490.

Moen, P. (1999). *The Cornell Couples and Careers Study*. Ithaca, New York: Cornell Employment and Family Careers Institute, Cornell University.

NICHD Early Child Care Research Network. (1997a). Child care in the first year of life. *Merrill-Palmer Quarterly, 43*, 340–360.

NICHD Early Child Care Research Network. (1997b). Mother–child interaction and cognitive outcomes associated with early child care: Results of the NICHD study. Paper presented at the Biennial Meeting of the Society For Research in Child Development, Washington, DC.

NICHD Early Child Care Research Network. (1998). Relations between family predictors and child outcomes: Are they weaker for children in child care? *Developmental Psychology, 34*(5), 1119–1128.

Office of Analysis and Epidemiology, NCHS (2006). *Health, United States*. Retrieved May 14, 2007. from http://www.cdc.gov/nchs/data/hus/hus06.pdf#027.

Ono, H. (1998). Husbands' and wives' resources and marital dissolution. *Journal of Marriage and the Family, 60*, 674–689.

Oppenheimer, V. K. (1997). Women's employment and the gain to marriage: The specialization and trading model. *Annual Review of Sociology, 23*, 431–453.

Ozer, E. M., Barnett, R. C., Brennan, R. T. & Sperling, J. (1998). Does child care involvement increase or decrease distress among dual-earner couples? *Women's Health: Research on Gender, Behavior, and Policy, 4*, 285–311.

Parsons, T. (1949). The social structure of the family. In R. Anshen (ed.), *The Family: Its Function and Destiny* (pp. 173–201). New York: Harper.

Parsons, T. & Bales, R. F. (1955). *Family, Socialization and Interaction Process*. Glencoe, Il: Free Press.

Perry-Jenkins, M., Repetti, R. L. & Crouter, A. C. (2000). Work and family in the 1990s. *Journal of Marriage and the Family, 62*, 981–998.

Pleck, J. H. (1985). *Working wives, working husbands*. Beverly Hills: Sage.

Poelmans, S., Stepanova, O. & Masuda, A. (2008), in this volume Radcliffe Public Policy Center. (2000). *Life's Work: Generational Attitudes Toward Work and Life Integration*. Cambridge, MA: Harvard University, Radcliffe Institute for Advanced Study.

Repetti, R. L. & Crosby, F. (1984). Gender and depression: Exploring the adult-role explanation. *Journal of Social and Clinical Psychology, 2*, 57–70.

Repetti, R. L., Matthews, K. A. & Waldron, I. (1989). Employment and women's health: Effects of paid employment on women's mental and physical health. *American Psychologist, 44*, 1394–1401.

Reskin, B. F. & Padavic, I. (1994). *Women and Men at Work*. Thousand Oaks: Pine Forge Press.

Risman, B. A. (1986). Can men "mother"? Life as a single father. *Family Relations, 35*, 95–102.

Rosenman, R. H., Brand, R. J., Jenkins, C. D., Friedman, M., Straus, R. & Wurm, M. (1975). Coronary heart disease in the Western Collaborative Group Study: Final follow-up experience of 81/2 years. *Journal of the American Medical Association, 233,* 872–877.

Russo, N. F. & Zierk, K. L. (1992). Abortion, childbearing, and women's well-being. *Professional Psychology: Research and Practice, 23,* 269–280.

Schwartz, P. (1994). *Peer Marriages: How Love Between Equals Really Works.* New York: Free Press.

Simons, R. (1992). Parental role strains, salience of parental identity and gender differences in psychological distress. *Journal of Health and Social Behavior, 33,* 25–35.

Story, L. (2005, September 20). Many women at elite colleges set career path to motherhood. *New York Times,* pp. A1, A18.

Thoits, P. A. (1986). Multiple identities: Examining gender and marital status differences in distress. *American Sociological Review, 51,* 259–272.

Thoits, P. A. (1992). Identity structures and psychological well-being: Gender and marital status comparisons. *Social Psychology Quarterly, 55,* 236–256.

Thompson, L. & Walker, A. J. (1989). Gender in families: Women and men in marriage, work, and parenthood. *Journal of Marriage and the Family, 51,* 845–871.

Twenge, J. M. (1997). Attitudes toward women, 1970–1995: A meta-analysis. *Psychology of Women Quarterly, 21,* 35–51.

Tyre, P. & McGinn, D. (2003, May 12). She works, he doesn't. *Newsweek,* p. 44.

US Census Bureau. (1975). *Historical Statistics of the United States, Colonial Times to 1970s.* Washington, DC: Bureau of the Census.

US Census Bureau. (2002). *Historical Income Tables-Families. Table F-7. Type of Family (all races) by Median and Mean Income: 1947 to 2001.* Washington, DC: Retrieved from http://www.census.gov/hhes/income/histinc/f07.html on October 22, 2003.

US Census Bureau. (2005). Current Population Survey's (CPS) Annual Social and Economic Supplement (ASEC): Washington, DC: US Census Bureau.

US Department of Labor. (2005). *Women in the Labor Force in 2005.* Retrieved May 14, 2007. from http://www.dol.gov/wb/factsheets/Qf-laborforce-05.htm.

US Bureau of Labor Statistics. (2005). Women in the labor force: A databook (Report 985). Retrieved September 26, 2005, from http://www.bls.gov/cps/wlf-databook-2005.pdf

US Bureau of Labor Statistics. (2007). *Employment Characteristics of Families Summary.* Retrieved May 14, 2007. from http://www.bls.gov/news.release/famee.nr0.htm.

Veroff, J., Douvan, E. & Kulka, R. A. (1981). *The Inner American.* New York: Basis Books.

Voydanoff, P. & Donnelly, B. W. (1999). Multiple roles and psychological distress: The intersection of the paid worker, spouse, and parent roles with the role of the adult child. *Journal of Marriage and the Family, 61,* 725–738.

Waldfogel, J. (2006). *What Children Need.* Cambridge MA: Harvard University Press.

Waldron, I. & Jacobs, J. A. (1989). Effects of multiple roles on women's health: Evidence from a national longitudinal study. *Women and Health, 15,* 3–19.

Wallis, C. (2004). The case for staying home. *Time Magazine, 163,* 50–59.

Warr, P. & Parry, G. (1982). Paid employment and women's psychological well-being. *Psychological Bulletin, 91,* 498–516.

Wethington, E. & Kessler, R. C. (1989). Employment, parental responsibility, and psychological distress: A longitudinal study of married women. *Journal of Family Issues, 10,* 527–546.

Wilkie, J. R., Ferree, M. & Ratcliff, K. S. (1998). Gender and fairness: Marital satisfaction in two-earner couples. *Journal of Marriage and the Family, 60,* 577–594.

CHAPTER 6

Toxic Job Ecologies, Time Convoys, and Work-Family Conflict: Can Families (Re)Gain Control and Life-Course "Fit"?

Phyllis Moen* and **Noelle Chesley†**
*Department of Sociology, University of Minnesota
†Department of Sociology, University of Wisconsin-Milwaukee

Paid work is the lynchpin connecting individuals to institutions, families to economies, identities to roles, and gender (as well as other structural locations) to inequality. We argue that scholars from a range of disciplines have based their theoretical arguments and empirical investigations of work, mobility, and inequality on conventional taken-for-granted framings, what we term the *career mystique* (Moen & Roehling, 2005), the widely accepted belief that continuous, hard work from the time one leaves school to the time one retires or dies (whichever comes first) is both the way things *are* and the way things *should be*. North Americans commonly view this lock-step as the only path to success—occupational mobility, economic and job security, and personal fulfillment. Moreover, this mystique has been legitimized in a regime of age-graded temporal polices and practices (time cages and convoys) around education, employment, and retirement in America and Europe, producing an "expected" clockwork of paid work days, work weeks, work years, work lives, and the lock-step life course (Kohli & Meyer, 1986; Moen, 2003a; Moen & Roehling, 2005; Settersten, 2003).

A parallel but independent line of theory development and research has examined *families* as institutional arrangements that are also temporally organized, another legitimated regime of time cages and convoys in the form of within-household distributions and divisions of resources and labor, along with bundles of intergenerational, interpersonal and intimate relationships (Bianchi, Robinson & Milkie, 2006; Daly, 2003). The temporal clockworks of family life were recognized early by family scholars, such as Reuben Hill, who developed a life-cycle theory of family development based on the ages of children and the employment of the (primary) breadwinner. This clockwork pattern was, like the clockwork of paid work, depicted as the way families *are* and the way they *should be*. It was criticized because it ignored the variety of family forms and family timetables observed in empirical

Handbook of Work-Family Integration: Research, Theory, and Best Practices

research (Elder & O'Rand, 1995; O'Rand & Krecker, 1990). Still, scholars accept Hill's thesis that the bearing of and caring for children is tied to biological and developmental clocks, making their timing, sequencing, and duration throughout the life course less "optional" than other institutional arrangements.

But it is the *interface* between family and work that has increasingly dominated the (often interdisciplinary) focus of family scholars (Bellavia & Frone, 2005; Chesley, 2005; Chesley & Moen, 2006; Crouter, 1984; Gareis, Chait Barnett & Rennan, 2003; Greenhaus & Beutell, 1985; Lewis & Cooper, 1999; Swisher, Sweet & Moen, 2004; Zedeck, 1992). Looking at the nexus between these two institutions—work and family—underscores the temporal aspects of both occupational careers and family careers, and especially the temporal "fit" and "misfit" between them. We propose that an ecology of the gendered life-course perspective (Moen & Chermack, 2005; Moen, Elder & Lüscher, 1995; Moen, Kelly & Chermack, 2008; Moen, Kelly & Magennis, 2008; Moen & Spencer, 2006) provides a fruitful framing for understanding the multilayered social and temporal ecologies and dynamisms operating as women and men, as individuals, and as family members, seek to create or sustain work-family "fit," or, more broadly, life-course "fit" at different ages and life stages (see also Swisher et al., 2004).

Women and men as members of couples, as parents, as adult children of aging parents, and as workers make *strategic selections* (a concept we describe in detail later) about whether or how to combine work and family roles and relationships. But their choices are constrained by existing institutional and social ecologies, what we describe in this chapter as the customs, rules and regulations functioning as *time cages* at any one point and *time convoys* over the life course. We argue that some types of cages and convoys around paid work constitute potentially *toxic job ecologies*, harmful to the health and life quality of both employees and their families (see also Moen, Kelly & Chermack, 2008).

In this chapter we sketch the intellectual history and development of the life-course perspective, delineate mechanisms that produce work-family conflicts, and describe possible consequences of this conflict for employees and families. The concepts we introduce can help to: (1) identify potentially "toxic" psychosocial work environments, (2) highlight the absence of institutionalized arrangements (time cages and convoys) designed to minimize work-life conflicts, and (3) document the strategic role and relationship selections workers and families make as they seek to gain or retain a sense of control over their lives and to promote both personal and family well-being.

There are six concepts that we see as crucial to understanding the work-family interface as an ecologically embedded and gendered process. We draw on these concepts—*time convoys, structural lag, life-course fit, cycles of control, adaptive strategies, and converging divergences*—to develop a dynamic ecology of the gendered life-course framework that links work-family conflict, "fit," and control to individual and family health and well-being.

THE LIFE COURSE: A SOCIAL INSTITUTION AND A SENSITIZING DEVICE

The term *life course* refers to (1) an institution in the form of an *age-graded lock-step regime* of shared cultural understandings and taken-for-granted rules, roles, relationships, resources, and risks available or seen as appropriate at different ages and life stages (Chudacoff, 1989; Heinz, 1992; Krüger, 2001, 2003; Mayer & Schopflin, 1989). It also denotes (2) *identifiable patterns* of successive role entries, durations, overlaps, and exits of people located in different parts of the social structure and in different cohorts (Abbott, 1995; Elder, 1995; Nydegeer; 1986; Wheaton, 1990). A life-course approach can (3) link micro- and macro-processes by connecting people's individual and family experiences to continuities, changes, and lags in institutionalized regimes of work, family, education, and civic life. This linkage is dynamic, in that individual behaviors shape larger social institutions and social institutions shape individual choices and behavior (by producing or reinforcing particular opportunity structures). For scholars and practitioners, the life course can also be broadly viewed as: (4) an intellectual framework emphasizing the importance of examining historical context as well as the timing, duration, and sequencing of events, in other words, attending to patterns of continuity or change over time.

The life course as an analytical approach developed in response to an effort to understand the implications of social change on individual lives—examining historical events such as immigration (Thomas & Znaniecki, 1918–20) and the Great Depression (Elder, 1974). The emergence of the life-course paradigm in the 1970s fostered an emphasis on the dynamic, interlocking nature of work and family paths, placing them in the context of history, relationships, and strategic action (Elder 1974, 1978; Hareven, 1978). Life-course scholars began to investigate multiple temporal layers: the historical, organizational and cultural dynamics in which life paths unfold, the uneven rates of social and institutional change, the complex interplay between biology, biography, identity, and history.

This chapter incorporates all these meanings of the life course, but is grounded in the first definition: the life course as an *institution*. The life course as a bundle of legitimated rules and regulations is a product of primarily 20th century policies and practices emerging in conjunction with industrialization, urbanization, bureaucratization, and technological innovation. Ultimately, these processes have created a life-course temporal regime organized around *paid work*, fully anchored within the tripartite, age-graded institutions of education, employment, and retirement (see Kohli, 1986; Kohli & Meyer, 1986; Riley, 1987; Settersten & Mayer, 1997). Meyer and Rowan (1977, p. 341) define institutionalization as occurring when "social processes, obligations, or actualities come to take on a rule-like status in social thought and action." Mayer (1986, p. 167) describes the orderly flow of persons through segmented institutions.

In Europe, career and life-course regimes emerged as a function of the *state*: educational, welfare, and labor policies developed that fostered entry and exit portals into and out of various roles for individuals of particular ages and in particular circumstances. European social policies addressing sources of social risks (of poor health, lay offs, unemployment, childcare, aging) have long been in place, providing security and support at different ages and stages, thereby further structuring the life course (e.g., Leisering, 2003).

In the United States and Canada, the career and life-course regime emerged more as a consequence of the *economy* and the *labor market* than from state (public policy) initiatives. Myriad corporate policies developed around hiring, firing, promotions, geographical mobility, occupational mobility, career paths, retirement, security, compensation, benefits. These business policies, in combination with related government regulations, have created and perpetuated a *career mystique*, the belief (most widely endorsed in the US) that a lifetime of full-time commitment and hard work (in other words, following the normative path of mostly white-collar or unionized blue-collar male workers in the 1950s) is the path to individual and family fulfillment (Moen & Roehling, 2005).

Both Europe and North America have deeply rooted organizational and cultural practices that reify this "normal" lock-step life course of first full-time, uninterrupted education, then full-time, uninterrupted employment, then full-time, uninterrupted retirement. For Americans, this lock-step path became value-laden, intertwined with the American Dream. But this *career* mystique, the belief that continuous hard work, enterprise and talent is the (only) path to fulfillment and success, developed in tandem with the *feminine* mystique in the post-war boom economy of the 1950s. Workers (especially white-collar and unionized blue-white men) could devote time, energy, and effort to their jobs precisely because they had *someone else*—a homemaker—to do the unpaid care work of family life: taking care of children, aging parents, and the myriad details of daily living.

With the women's movement of the 1970s, women came to reject the feminine mystique, only to embrace the career mystique as the path to equality. Early feminists did not recognize that the foundation of the social organization of paid work rests on the social organization of family carework as women's unpaid work. This created a mismatch between the cultural endorsement of gender equality and the rigidity of occupational policies and practices presuming total devotion to one's job. The result has been increasing gender *equality* in educational attainment and labor market regulations, coupled with persistent (though lessening) gender *inequality* in occupational status and income, concomitant with persistent gender differences in the time devoted to both unpaid care work and paid work. Policies functioning as if workers have no family responsibilities, together with the declining numbers of families with homemakers, have created a "crisis" in caregiving, increasing work-family pressures and conflicts. Consider US welfare reform, the Personal Responsibility and Work Opportunity Reconciliation Act of 1996.

It argues, at its core, that all women should work for pay in the same way that men do: full-time and continuously, regardless of their family care obligations. But the absence of community-based, reliable and affordable childcare makes this welfare "solution" impossible for some.

Against and parallel with this historical backdrop have emerged important advances in the life course as a frame for research and policy (Elder, 1985; Moen et al., 1995; Mortimer & Shanahan, 2003). This is evident in studies locating individuals and families within the ecologies of *linked lives* (Elder, 1974; 1985). We build on this life-course concept of linked lives to capture continuity and change in both relationships and institutional arrangements. To do so we invoke the notion of "time convoys," a dynamic ecological approach that is particularly useful in capturing the work-family-gender interface as it unfolds over time.

TIME CONVOYS: THE SOCIAL AND INSTITUTIONAL CONTEXTS OF LIVES

We coin the concept *time convoys* (see also Moen, Kelly & Chermack, 2008; Moen et al., 2007) to capture the taken-for-granted organizational and cultural rules, routines, and regulations about time *durations* (such as the 40-hour [or more] work week), *rhythms* (such as the work day, the work week, and the school-work-retirement path), *timing* (such as norms about the age children "should" leave their parents' home), and *biographical pacing* (such as individuals' and families' unique timing and ordering of transitions and turning points, for example those related to schooling, marriage, parenting, and job shifts and exits). Time *cages* constitute these rules and routines at any one point in time; but the payoff comes in thinking about them as *convoys*, propping up and/or problematizing roles and relationships over time.

SOCIAL CONVOYS

There are two types of time convoys. First are *social convoys*: one's friends, classmates, and neighbors constitute a collection of people moving more or less in tandem through adulthood (Kahn & Antonucci, 1980). Sometimes birth cohorts of people (all born in the same historical time period) constitute a distinctive social convoy, with all having similar experiences at similar ages. This was especially true for the pre-boomer generation, proceeding into marriage, parenthood, employment, and retirement at roughly the same ages. But people born at different time periods are also part of a person's social convoy: the friends, parents, children, schoolmates and workmates of different ages and life stages that are sources of support and/or stress along the way.

The life-course concept of *linked lives* (Elder, 1995, 2003) highlights the notion of social convoys, the ways individuals' choices are always embedded in and shaped by the beliefs, expectations, and actions of the people in their lives. Adulthood often requires synchronizing or otherwise accommodating these relationships over time, including managing sometimes conflicting goals, expectations, and obligations—as adult children of aging parents, as siblings, as husbands and wives, and as parents themselves. Couples frequently must coordinate two careers and, increasingly, "blended" families. Single parents must coordinate with their former spouses and current partners. Mothers and fathers must coordinate with their children's school and recreational timetables. Caregivers to aging or infirm relatives must coordinate with other relatives, and with obligations to their own children.

INSTITUTIONAL CONVOYS

Second, there are *institutional convoys*: legitimated, routinized and expected rules, rhythms, and timetables that "kick in" at different ages and stages. For example, adults may well not think about the timetables of childcare and elementary education until they become parents. It is then they become acutely aware that childcare arrangements and schooling are available only for children of certain ages, only for certain days of the week, only for certain times of the day and the year. Similarly, as adults move into the role of caregivers for their ailing parents they find they must take on the institutionalized clockworks and regimes of health care services, Medicare, long-term care insurance, and other bureaucratic regimes. And the architecture of time embodied in the cages and convoys of labor market policies and practices and business rules and regulations are so commonly accepted as to be virtually invisible.

BIOGRAPHICAL PACING

People leave old roles and enter new ones—such as that of spouse, parent, retiree—at particular points in their lives. Han and Moen (1999a, 1999b) term this *biographical pacing*, defined as the age at which individuals undergo key status passages—whether and when one marries, has children, takes a job, goes back to school, changes employers, opts out of the workforce, retires, goes back to work, remarries, or moves (see also Sweet & Moen, 2006).

This highlights the *social clock* aspects of transitions. Institutional convoys foster the taken-for-granted but socially constructed culture of timing, with individuals defining the passages in their lives (and the lives of others) as being either "on" or "off" time—for example, marrying or retiring earlier or later than the conventional norm (Hagestad & Neugarten, 1985; Mortimer, Oesterle & Krüger,

2005; Mortimer, Vuolo, Staff, Wakefield & Xie, 2006; Neugarten & Hagestad, 1976; Settersten & Hagestad, 1996a, 1996b). Biographical pacing shapes not only individual life pathways but the subjective side of adulthood as well, coloring expectations, self-concepts, goals, identities, and affinities (Downey, Chatman, London, Cross, Hughes, Moje, Way & Eccles, 2005; Moen, Sweet & Swisher, 2005). Thus, the predictability, timing, and clustering of work and family role transitions shape their meaning, along with their implications for identity and adult development. This is, in part, because time convoys—the institutionalized nature of the life course—provide individuals at different life stages with "available lists of reasons, motives, and aspirations" that shape individual and family decisions (Meyer, 1986), such as expectations regarding parenthood, employment, and retirement (see also Gerson, 1985; Han & Moen, 1999a, 1999b; Moen et al., 2005; Brines, 1994; Altucher & Williams, 2003; Pixley & Moen, 2003; Wethington, Pixley & Kavey, 2003).

TIME CONVOYS AND THE LIFE COURSE

Biographical pacing in employment, family, and their interface is patterned by social class, race and ethnicity, and other social markers, as well as by health and ability. There are distinctive expectations for women and men at different ages and life stages. Biographical pacing is further shaped by the interplay between individual experiences and large-scale technological, economic, and policy transformations.

A life-course theoretical lens (e.g., Elder, 1985, 1998a, 1998b; Moen & Wethington, 1992) also points to the importance of *prior* as well as coterminous events for understanding the gendered nature of adulthood. While considerable advance has been made in capturing the patterned constellations of paths shaping adolescent development (Booth, Crouter & Shanahan, 1999; Mortimer, Staff & Lee, 2005; Shanahan, 2000), we know relatively little about the dynamic interplay between work, family, gender, and human development in middle and later adulthood. This points to the need to capture, through life histories or longitudinal data, the patterned dynamics of work and family lives, including work-family conflicts, as they are constructed and reconstructed over time.

An important theoretical and practical implication of the life-course approach is the insight that occupying particular roles at any one point in time may matter less, in terms of adult development (in the form of health, identity, and psychological well-being), than the number, predictability, durations, and timing of role entries and exits in relation to gender and age. In particular, we see the combination of global and technological trends producing a speedup in work activities, more hours on the job, and additional workloads. These chronic time pressures, together with little work-time control and heightened job insecurities, constitute *toxic social ecologies* (see also Garbarino, 1995) for workers and their families.

STRUCTURAL LAG AND MISMATCH

Matilda White Riley (see Riley, Kahn & Foner, 1994) built on the early body of life-course research to theorize the twin and often uneven processes of social change—changing lives and changing institutions. Riley introduced the concept of *structural lag*, the fundamental mismatch between the age-graded social and organizational policies and practices systematizing careers and the life course as an institution, on the one hand, and the shifting demographic, technological, economic and social exigencies in which real lives play out, on the other. For example, retirement as an institution is unraveling, replaced with the ambiguities and uncertainties confronting many contemporary workers approaching "retirement" age.

What Riley showed was the datedness of conventional age scripts and structures. The lock-step career and retirement mystiques belie the increasing vitality, health, and longevity of today's and tomorrow's older population, as well as the economic insecurity of the rising numbers of workers in their 50s and 60s encouraged or forced to retire. The retirement mystique also lags behind technological transformations of paid work that have eliminated age-related physical strength and endurance requirements of most jobs.

This "lag" is also reflected in the fundamental mismatches between the clockworks of paid work and family, along with the mismatches between time investments in paid work and job protections. There is evidence of a mismatch between work-hour preferences and available work schedules; research shows growing numbers of workers are suffering from a time squeeze that is connected to the rise of the dual-earner household and that spills over into their family lives (Clarkberg & Moen, 2001; Gornick & Meyers, 2003; Jacobs & Gerson, 2004). Conventional time clocks shaping work and careers are clearly at odds with the needs of today's families. Structural lag in the social organization of work time and in the ineffectiveness of existing safety nets means that *time* and *security* have joined *income* as scarce resources in most American households.

Permeating the *age*-stratification system is a *gender*-stratification system, as well as other systems of stratification that privilege some people over others due to their social statuses or credentialing. Thus occupational and family careers are both gender-graded and age-graded. These stratifying systems have profound effects on the patterning of men's and women's work and family lives. Life-course scholars have identified very different work and family trajectories for men and women that are linked to income and health disparities throughout the life course (Han & Moen, 1999a, 1999b; Pavalko & Woodbury, 2000; Reichart, Chesley & Moen, 2007).

It is these *macro*-level age- and gender-segmentations that serve to construct individuals' *micro*-level expectations and options throughout the life course (Henretta, 1992; Meyer, 1986; Riley et al., 1994; Uhlenberg, 1978). Recall that most age-graded policies and practices developed in terms of the lock-step career path. Sociologists, economists, and other scholars usually characterize as "typical" the orderly progression from full-time career preparation (education) to full-time occupational engagement (employment) to full-time leisure (retirement). This normative life-course path was the characteristic experience of only a subgroup of the workforce in the post–World War II economy, typically middle-class, white-collar and unionized blue-collar men with full-time homemakers to facilitate their whole-hearted investment in their jobs. In contrast, women's life paths tend to be neither orderly nor neatly segmented. Rather, women have always been more apt to move in and out of education, employment, and community roles, often in conjunction with changing family care obligations and/or accommodating their husbands' job-related moves (Moen, 2003a, 2003b; Moen & Roehling, 2005).

Today's workforce is almost equally composed of men and women, with few having the luxury of a full-time homemaker. It is also an aging workforce, as members of the vast baby-boom cohort move toward retirement and confront health limitations (their own and their partners) as well as aging parents requiring their care. For the first time in history, couples are experiencing two retirements, "his" and "hers." And yet current retirement policies developed based on a single (male) breadwinner per household. The concept of structural lag is useful in capturing these mismatches between the changing labor force (without the backup of full-time homemakers) and a labor market and retirement regime based on the (male) career mystique of continuous full-time employment. The lag produced by policies and practices geared to a male breadwinner workforce now constrains the universe of options available for men and women to shape their occupational career paths and life courses at every life stage (e.g., Kohli, 1986; Marshall, Heinz, Krüger & Verma, 2001; Moen 2003a, 2003b)

The structural lag concept is also useful in thinking about and framing another form of work, rarely acknowledged as such. The social organization of *unpaid work*, especially the unpaid family care of dependents (children, ailing relatives, disabled children, and other people with health conditions), is conspicuously absent from the policy agenda. Differences in the pattern and intensity of men's and women's caregiving careers is a key factor producing and reproducing the gendered life course, along with attendant disparities in economic and social resources. A large body of research shows that women are more likely than men to provide informal adult care, that women caregivers provide higher levels of assistance than male caregivers, that married women often provide assistance to their husband's relatives as well as their own kin, and that women caregivers experience more distress as a result of caregiving responsibilities than their male counterparts (see review in Cancian & Oliker, 2000).

Structural lag is also evident in the fact that family clockworks are in disarray. Young adults sometimes move back home when they can't support themselves and, as Mortimer, Staff and Lee (2005) point out, what it means to be an adult is no longer self-evident to young people in the midst of that transition. People are postponing marriage, never marrying, or leaving marriage, while parenthood now occurs on a variety of timetables. Women are having their first child at 15 and 40, or not having children at all. Men in their 80s are fathering kids, often with second or third (younger) wives. Demographic changes are also reconfiguring the adult years, as baby boomers move toward and through the traditional retirement years. Increasing longevity means that adult children are now more apt to share more years with their aging parents, meaning that daughters (and perhaps, increasingly, sons), are likely to care for infirm relatives.

Life-course and feminist research points out how the growing care needs of families do not match (lagging) institutional arrangements (see review in Reichart et al., 2007). Ample evidence exists showing how (paid) employment and (unpaid) caregiving produce and reproduce the gendered age-stratification system, as well as a crisis of care. Employed parents of young children feel the time squeeze of one-size-fits-all employment arrangements equating work hours with commitment. Older workers can also confront the same time squeeze as they seek to help ailing or infirm parents, adult children, and other kin (Gerstel & Gallagher, 1994). The lag between existing institutional arrangements and a workforce that is, wants to be, or will care for the people in their lives plays out in ways that are often detrimental to employers as well as to employees and their families.

Classic studies in the sociology of work, occupations and stratification were based on men's lives, as were the social policies that developed around the concept of continuous full-time employment. (Re)framing research questions about mobility, careers, and retirement using the concept of structural lag locates them in the moving stream of uneven cultural and structural change. Inequalities in opportunities for social participation, in streams of resources, and in exposure and vulnerability to stress characterize contemporary paid work and unpaid family and community care work. This plays out in the diverging life courses of men and women, even though they may begin life with similar backgrounds and abilities (Han & Moen, 1999b; Moen & Roehling, 2005; Reichart et al., 2007). The key life-course concept of structural lag underscores the political, institutional and organizational forces producing inequality by constraining the paid and unpaid work, retirement, and family care options of people located in different positions within society.

WORK-FAMILY CONFLICT AND LIFE-COURSE "FIT"

Stress at its most basic can be defined as the gap between resources and needs [or demands, such as between A and B on Figure 6.1, leading to role strains C (see also Goode, 1960)]. The absence of life-course "fit" between personal/family time needs and existing (and emerging) institutional convoys of time regulated by the market and by public policy is creating a tension between jobs and family life

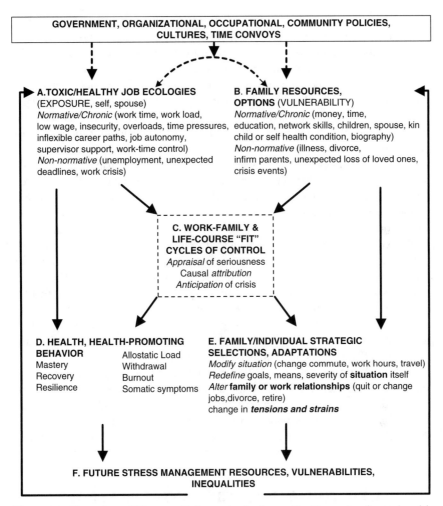

Figure 6.1   The ecology of life-course "fit," strategic selections and health: a cycles of control model

conducive to neither life quality nor health, much less optimal functioning on the job. This tension is often experienced as *work-family conflict*, an important correlate of stress (Bellavia & Frone, 2005).

It has always been true that some families—those with adults with little education, few job skills, and minimal social or economic resources, such as single parents, immigrant and minority families—are more vulnerable to toxic job events and chronic job stress. Evidence suggests that the number of vulnerable families is growing (Bellavia & Frone, 2005). While poor families have always been at risk, today many middle-class professionals raising children are also under chronic stress

(Moen & Huang, 2007). Currently, even families with educated and skilled adults in "good" jobs are stretched thin in time, economic, and emotional resources.

An understanding of the contemporary work-family interface as it unfolds over the life course requires information on characteristics of the person (including education, race and ethnicity, age, gender, and prior experiences), features of the environment (including the broader social and structural milieu of both family and work), and documentation of the process that shapes both and binds the two over time (Bronfenbrenner, 1995; 2005). What an ecology of the life-course perspective provides is insight into the embeddedness of workers in the ecologies of their families and their jobs, as well as the linking of changes in individual lives and changes in their environments over time (see Voydanoff in this volume). For example, Chesley (2005) finds that cell phone use over a two-year time period (environment) is linked to increased *work*-family conflict for both working women and men. For women, cell phone use also produces an increase in *family*-work conflict. The consequences? Increased distress and decreased family satisfaction, given that cell phones facilitate access to individuals in ways that intensify the demands of both work and family life, depending on one's gender. The case of cell phones as both a convenience and an intrusion makes the larger point that life changes can be both beneficial and detrimental to individual and family development. Moreover, at different ages and stages, including different family stages, there may well be more or less life-course "fit" between individual and family goals and needs and different work and family demands and resources.

Cumulative gendered experiences throughout the life course mean that men and women typically confront work-family conflict or achieve life-course "fit" through different experiences, expectations, and options, often leading to a perpetuation of gender differences, with women still accommodating their career paths to their husbands' careers as well as to the needs of their children and/or ailing relatives, and men accommodating their family participation to the primacy of their jobs.

ADAPTIVE STRATEGIES AND STRATEGIC SELECTIONS

Women's and men's paid and unpaid work and family career courses are products of individual action (agency), as well as structural opportunities and constraints. An important concept linking structure, agency, and social change is the notion of family *strategies of adaptation* (see E on Figure 6.1). The concept of adaptive strategies points to individuals and families as active decision-makers, the architects of their own biographies even as they are enabled or constrained by existing (and often lagging) institutional arrangements. In particular, workers seek "fit" between their occupational and family environments through strategies of adaptation: changing the circumstances of their work or family lives, shifting their goals and expectations, or redefining or accepting existing strains or conflicts (Conger & Elder, 1994; Elder, 1974, 1978; Hareven, 1982; Moen & Wethington, 1992).

In times of social stability, adaptive strategies draw on taken-for-granted scripts: cultural blueprints about gender- and age-appropriate roles and relationships that require little conscious decision-making about work, retirement, marriage, family. In times of social change, these taken-for-granted scripts no longer "fit," forcing women and men, as purposive actors, to make strategic choices about whether or when to marry, become a parent, take a job, change jobs, move across the country. We term these processes of *strategic selection*, in that people make adaptations to meet their goals or needs on a moving platform of multilayered change (in families, in the labor market, in a global economy, in technology, in gender expectations) and outmoded cultural scripts. Such strategies may be conscious choices, but they invariably reflect a lifetime of *socialization* into gender, age, family, and occupational norms and expectations (e.g. Moen & Wethington, 1992; Pavalko & Woodbury, 2000; Reichart et al., 2007).

There are as well (often unrecognized) *allocation* mechanisms (recruitment, hiring, retention, discrimination) that channel men and women of different ages and stages into distinctive work and family arrangements. These processes—socialization, allocation, and strategic selection—produce patterned roles and routines over the life course, in employment histories and family processes. They are also relational processes, as couples, adult children, and aging parents make strategic selections about who will work for pay and how many hours, for example, or who will care for infants or aging family members (Dentinger & Clarkberg, 2002; Drobnič & Blossfeld, 2004; Elder, 1996; Hynes & Clarkberg, 2005; Pavalko & Elder, 1993).

Life-course research underscores the embeddedness of these strategic choices in historically situated institutional and relational contexts. In their classic paper, Pavalko and Elder (1993) show how women's involvement in and support of their husbands' careers in the early part of the 20th century varied both within and between husbands' occupations. They found that many women performed activities that directly or indirectly supported their husband's paid work in keeping with cultural expectations that were prevalent at that particular time in American history. The value of this study is Pavalko and Elder's emphasis on how historical time (early 20th century) and place (United States) shape individual responses to the perpetual challenge of which family members should participate in the paid and unpaid work that undergirds family life.

Research on contemporary couples shows that women's involvement in family roles continues to shape their work behavior much more than does men's family involvement (Raley, Mattingly & Bianchi, 2006, Reichart et al., 2007). Thus women's career trajectories tend to be more variable than men's career patterns (Han & Moen, 1999a, 1999b). Further, men and women in dual-earner couples who exhibit unstable career trajectories (i.e., many job changes) also tend to report that family needs prompt job changes (Williams & Segal, 2003). For example, the transition to parenthood is a critical event that tends to recalibrate the nature and direction of both work and family careers for both men and women (Reichart et al., 2007). Caring for sick and infirm relatives also shapes occupational paths (Ettner, 1995). Older women who care for their ailing husbands are more likely to exit the workforce as a response to these care responsibilities, whereas men caring for ailing wives are unlikely to leave their jobs (Dentinger & Clarkberg, 2002).

The life-course concept of adaptive strategies—the ways individuals and families strategically select certain jobs, family arrangements, working hours, child and eldercare arrangements—places choices within the constraint of time cages and convoys shaping expectations and options. It also incorporates the notion of timing; *when* a particular transition (e.g., parenthood, retirement, caregiving) occurs has major implications for the subsequent life course (Elder, 1998a; 1998b; Elder, George & Shanahan, 1996). Institutional as well as social convoys are key; both relationships and *norms about* relationships shape the strategic choices around work and family of those embedded in them: singles, parents of young children, adult children with aging parents, couples, and even co-workers.

CYCLES OF CONTROL

The notions of *control cycles* (Elder, 1974, 1985; Moen & Yu, 2000) and *capital* (human, cultural, social, economic) are important factors in understanding the distribution of health and well-being by gender and age. Gaps between resources and needs (or expectations) occur both on home and job fronts, with individuals and families at more (or less) risk at various life stages (see Figure 6.2). "Needs" or "demands" at home include both time requirements (for caregiving of older relatives and children), as well as income requirements (for housing, health care, food and other costs of living, and a sense of security). "Needs" or "demands" at work include the requirements of long hours, shift work, frequent travel, demanding workloads, and arduous (physical or mental) job conditions. Resources can include human/cultural capital (education, autonomy and perceived control, information, workplace flexibility, initiative), social capital (family, friends, community ties, co-worker relationships, supportive supervisors), and economic capital (income, pensions, job security). Individuals feel that they are in charge of their lives, that they have a sense of mastery or *perceived control*, when they see their resources as adequate to meet prepackaged job demands, expected family demands and their own personal needs at particular ages and life stages.

Both paid work (as a result of downsizing and restructuring) and parenting (as a result of a cultural push toward intensive mothering—see Hays, 1996) are increasingly "greedy" institutions. Tensions play out (in long-term as well as day-to-day strategic adaptations) as women seek to meet—and integrate—their work

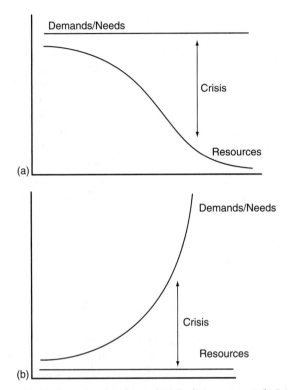

Figure 6.2   Strategic selections and cycles of control: (a) Declining resources; (b) Spiralling claims

and family obligations, and men seek to provide economically for their families while also being available to their children.

We have previously mentioned the rising demands, longer hours, and faster pace at work which produce potentially toxic ecologies, especially in the face of little work-time control and declining job security. But the linkages between work and health as they develop across time are both complex and interdependent (Chesley & Moen, 2006; Moen & Yu, 1999; Pavalko & Smith, 1999; Pavalko & Woodbury, 2000; Pavalko & Henderson, 2006). For example, the disparities between men and women in mental health problems narrow with age, suggesting that a *cycles of control* model fits better than a *cumulation of (dis)advantage* one (see National Survey on Drug Use and Health, 2002) Another example is men's retirement transition. Looking at panel data collected on men around retirement age (55–64), Mutchler and colleagues (1997) show that (poor) health affects the likelihood of men leaving the workforce, especially if their spouses are employed. Poor health also dampens the likelihood they will re-enter the workforce.

Studies that link employees' demands and control at work to health and gender conclude that women tend to experience more job stress and report worse health, even at the same occupational levels (Bosma, Stansfeld & Marmot, 1998; Muhonen & Torkelson, 2004). One possible explanation for this is the amount of social support that men and women use to moderate occupational stress. Generally, negative interpersonal relationships in the workplace are associated with more mental and physical complaints of illness (Repetti, 1998). From their 2003 study of 204 Australian men and women managerial-level employees, Bellman and colleagues (2003) conclude that perceived social support predicts less occupational stress in the workplace for both men and women. But men typically perceive more of "need for recognition" stress than women, while women generally report being in poorer health (Bellman, Forster, Still & Cooper, 2003). Taken-for-granted schema and scripts (such as expectations about work or family) combined with experience (such as stress and social support) affect women's and men's quest for biographical coherence and a sense of *control* as they seek to integrate and synchronize the public and private aspects of their lives.

CONVERGING DIVERGENCES

We draw on the concept of *converging divergences* to denote trends in within-group as well as across-group differences in family, work, and health, and how trends are in flux (Dannefer, 2003; Henretta, 1992; Moen & Spencer, 2006; O'Rand & Henretta, 1999; Shanahan, 2000). The term *convergence* invokes processes of increasing similarity (in, for example, labor force participation or health across gender) over various time dimensions. *Divergence* points to widening variations across or within subgroups. Thus we see widening gender income disparities with age as a consequence of processes of cumulative advantages for men (in earnings, status, pensions) and cumulative disadvantages for women (linked, for example, to caregiving responsibilities, see Moen & Roehling, 2005; O'Rand, 1996; O'Rand & Henretta, 1999). We combine both concepts to capture the growing heterogeneity (by age and by gender, but also by other locational markers) in work-related roles, resources, and social relations.

We see paid work as a fundamental organizing force in contemporary family life, shaping disparities (within and across age, gender, class, households, and other divides) in life chances and choices: men's and women's values and control over their lives, resources (e.g. health insurance, income, retirement, status, pensions), risks (layoffs, stress, burnout, injuries), relationships and integration, and behaviors (e.g. getting sufficient sleep or scaling back on work to provide care for children and other family members). Women and men's lives are converging in that increasingly *neither* can count on secure life-time employment. For both, security and skills obtained in early adulthood quickly grow out of date. Growing numbers of men and women are also moving in and out of roles—in families, in the workplace, and in educational institutions—at unprecedented rates. In part this reflects the dislocations of a global economy; today even middle-class white-collar and unionized blue-collar workers find that neither job nor economic security comes with seniority, as corporations merge, downsize, and become bankrupt—in good times as well as bad.

Family dislocations also exist, and are characterized by increased risk of divorce, increased rates of remarriage, and the growing geographic mobility of family members. What life-course scholars increasingly find in both men's and women's biographies are more *discontinuities* than continuities—in families, in paid work, across the generations, and in personal experience and development (Elder & O'Rand, 1995; Moen & Han, 2001a, 2001b; Pavalko & Smith, 1999; Rindfus, Swicegood & Rosenfeld, 1987; Settersten & Mayer, 1997).

Varying involvement in work and family roles over the life course is a key factor shaping divergences in later-life resources, health, and prospects for the future (Moen, Robison & Dempster-McClain, 1995; Pavalko & Artis, 1997; Pavalko & Smith, 1999, Pearlin & Aneshensel, 1994; Pearlin, Schieman, Fazio & Meersman, 2006). We propose that there is converging divergence with age as well as across social class, race and ethnicity, and other locational markers. Many people, regardless of age or class, find themselves at risk of layoffs and economically hard times, whether they are young or located in what was previously "secure" middle age. The scholarship of Greg Duncan and colleagues (1988) provides evidence from the US Panel Study of Income Dynamics of this process, showing that few families remain on welfare or below poverty for any extended period of time, but many experience poverty over the course of their lives. Longitudinal research on caring for parents and other infirm relatives identifies a similar pattern. While many potential "carers" may not care for a relative for an extended period of time, the "risk" of taking on carework has increased, and it is expected that more people will experience multiple caregiving episodes over the course of their lives (Evandrou & Glaser, 2004).

Drobnic and Blossfeld (2004) use longitudinal data from twelve countries to assess how the employment strategies of husbands and wives evolve across stages of family development, given shifts in household composition, family needs and resources, and country-specific opportunities and constraints. The results from this work indicate that, first, the majority of people in couples are now similar in terms of their occupational resources when they pair off and that this is the case across countries. Second, over the course of marriage the paths of men and women diverge in ways that correlate with government structures and policies. Thus, in conservative welfare state environments (the Netherlands, Germany, Belgium) or in Mediterranean welfare state regimes (Italy, Spain), there tends to be a traditional division of labor and a growing within-couple gap between male and female careers that results in greater economic dependency of a wife on her husband over time. This is in contrast to former socialist states (Hungary, Urban China,

East Germany—see Reichart et al., 2007) or Social Democratic states (Denmark, Sweden) in which married women are much less likely to exit the labor force.

CONCLUSIONS

Scholars are beginning to move beyond snapshot assessments of work and family life, focusing on how both work and family careers develop, intersect, and change over time, and the implications of these changes for individuals, families, and society at large. A life-course perspective has promoted understanding of family caregiving arrangements (Altucher & Williams, 2003; Chelsey & Moen, 2006; Drobnic, Blossfeld & Rohwer, 1999; Marks, 1998), spousal interactions and relationships (Chesley & Moen, unpublished; Moen 2001; Singley & Hynes, 2005; Spitze, Logan, Joseph & Lee, 1994; Williams & Umberson, 2004), and the linkages of work and family roles to health and life quality (Dentinger & Clarkberg, 2002; Moen & Huang, 2007; Swisher et al., 2004; Wethington, Moen, Glasgow & Pillemer, 2000).

Building on and extending this body of work (see Figure 6.1), we encourage a focus on both the micro- (changing biographical) and the macro- (changing social-organizational) ecology of the gendered life course as it plays out in distinctive ways for women and men within the work-family nexus. The goal is to understand the dynamic processes individuals and families use to seek to gain or regain control over their lives, identifying the series of strategic selections about work and family that influence individual lives, often reproducing gender differences, but also creating gender similarities. These selections are located within, respond to, and change social institutions (though sometimes glacially).

We argue that time cages and convoys—the taken-for-granted, age-graded and gender-graded constellations and institutionalized clockworks of roles, risks, and relationships embodied in the career and retirement mystiques—are examples of *structural lag* given the deinstitutionalization of traditional arrangements at work and at home in the face of a moving platform of demographic, labor market, technological, and economic changes. Despite their unraveling, cultural, institutional and policy blueprints nevertheless continue to frame real and perceived options at every life stage. As such, they are part of a process which creates and reinforces potentially toxic job ecologies as well as potentially toxic work-family pressures and conflicts for women, men, and children—as individuals and as family units.

(Re)Gaining Control and Life-course "Fit"?

Rapid social and technological changes are proliferating the kinds of psychosocial environments that evidence suggests are toxic to workers' health and well-being: those with high job demands and little job autonomy, job security, or work-time control (de Jonge, Bosma, Peter & Siegrist, 2000; Karasak, 1979; Karasek, Brisson, Kawakami, Houtman, Bongers & Amick, 1998; Karasek & Theorell, 1990). These toxic job ecologies also generate work-family conflict, with the subsequent strain spilling over into family life, including the lives of family members.

Women and men as partners, parents, and adult children of aging parents are not passive victims of either toxic job arrangements or social change. Many can and do seek to gain or regain a sense of control and life-course "fit" through reflexive processes of *strategic selection*. Unfortunately, the options from which they can choose most often relate to the *family* side of the work-family equation. In other words, couples cannot "select" to have each partner work part-time, since there are few "good" part-time jobs offering sufficient income and benefits much less any long-term tie to the workforce. But employees can strategically select to delay marriage or parenting, have fewer (or no) children, or otherwise reconfigure family life through divorce or geographic separation. On the job side, strategies may include a reduction or increase in work hours, leaving a demanding or inflexible job for a less-demanding or more flexible one, accepting an employer buy-out or retiring early, or else opting out of the workforce altogether. These pragmatic strategies of adaptation by individuals and couples tend to reproduce existing age and gender scripts around paid work and unpaid care work. For example, with new parenthood women may scale back on their hours or career goals (Becker & Moen, 1999) while their husbands may well increase their work commitments.

Can workers and family members regain control and life-course "fit"? In some cases, the answer is yes. But most are simply seeking to weather the perfect storm they find themselves in, the fundamental mismatch of high demands at work and at home, high goals for job and family, and little control over where and when they work, low job security, and few supports at work or in their communities. The issue for policy and research is whether and how potentially toxic job ecologies (especially related to work hours, work demands, inflexibility, insecurity, and little work-time control), can be changed in ways that reduce, if not eliminate, work-family conflicts and chronic strains.

IMPLICATIONS FOR FUTURE RESEARCH AND PRACTICE

There remain considerable unmined payoffs of the conceptual framework we have described, particularly as they link with other theoretical approaches. How do organizations and states acknowledge and respond to outdated policies and practices fostering toxic working conditions? What is the process of institutional change in response to recognized and deleterious work-family conflict?

How are resulting innovations legitimized and disseminated to other organizations and groups (Kelly, 2005; Kelly, Dahlin, Spencer & Moen, 2007; Kelly & Moen, 2007)? The challenge is to capture the embeddedness of lives within time convoys of rules and relationships that are themselves undergoing change. Documenting the institutional arrangements that serve to generate or amplify work-family conflicts can enable researchers and policymakers to identify strategies and solutions that could minimize such conflicts in working families, along with clarifying the health, development, productivity and turnover costs of current arrangements.

The concepts of adaptive strategies and *strategic role selections* can similarly be located in institutional as well as relational time. What are the life-course, well-being, and career implications, expected and unexpected, of the strategic adaptations of workers, family members and retirees in the face of both institutional changes and institutions failing to change? This points to the opportunity for scholars to engage in dynamic, multilevel analysis of family and occupational career paths, as well as social innovations. Consider the age wave of boomers on the precipice of retirement. How and when will they retire from their career jobs? How and when will they seek to create new arrangements that better "fit" with their self-concepts, needs, and aspirations?

Institutional change occurs side by side with individual biographical change. Life-course scholars in the US have directed attention to the interplay between historical events and individual lives, but have given less attention to the institutional forces that open up or close down options at various ages and stages. Life-course colleagues in Europe do attend to the role of the state and the market in constructing life courses (e.g. Mayer & Schoepflin, 1989; Weymann, 2003), but have theorized much less about processes of institutional change in response to alternative "strategic selections" of significant numbers of men and women (such as having fewer children; Balter, 2006), or as a consequence of globalization, new technologies, and/or shifts in workforce composition or motivation.

Capturing *converging divergences* in life chances and life quality also requires multilevel comparative analysis, incorporating within- as well as across-group theorizing and investigation. The goal would be not only to specify age, gender, or societal differences, for example, but to understand the ecological conditions (organizational, cultural, temporal) which produce desired or undesired outcomes (see also Reichart et al., 2007). Structural locations should not be "controlled for", but rather examined and understood as processes of strategic selection and institutional allocation. These selection and allocation dynamics produce long-term as well as short-term differences in roles, resources, and relationships, contributing to both divergences and convergences across social groupings.

Methodological innovations, such as the collection of panel and life history data as well as new analytical techniques, went hand in hand with the establishment of the life course as a field of inquiry in the second half of the 20th century

(Giele & Elder, 1998; Hardy, 1997; Pavalko, 1997). Today, new methods are emerging for studying lives in multiple contexts and for identifying moving constellations of both contexts and pathways (e.g. Abbott, 1995; Macmillan & Eliason, 2003). These methods open up possibilities for understanding the social organization of work as it exists and as it changes in different industries, occupations, economies, and cultures, along with the implications for individual lives and family life quality.

Can businesses and governments foster truly "family-friendly" ecologies that enhance individual and family health and well-being? We know that promoting people's sense of control has enormous payoffs in their effectiveness, at work, at home, and in their communities, as well as in their health and life quality (e.g. Bandura, 1982; Keyes, 1998; Muhonen & Torkelson, 2004; Ryff & Keyes, 1995; Thoits, 1999; Umberson, Williams & Sharp, 2000). The challenge is to identify specific job ecologies, as well as specific policies and practices that foster mastery. For example, job security is a key ingredient of individual and family mastery, health and well-being (Moen & Huang, 2007; Sweet, Moen & Meiksins, 2007). But job security is seldom on work-family research and policy agendas. Instead, the focus is often on smaller changes, such as childcare referrals or flextime arrangements that aren't, in fact, that flexible.

FROM WORK-FAMILY CONFLICT TO HEALTH AND LIFE QUALITY

The future for research, policy, and practice involves asking new questions, questions that move beyond work-family conflict at any one point in time, or of only one family member and not others, questions that consider job ecologies that both promote and detract from individual and family health. How and why do businesses and states retain the time cages and convoys designed for factory production and jobs in the middle of the 20th century? Rigid work days, work weeks, work lives, with little work-time control or career flexibility, may be conventional and taken for granted, but are not immutable. What are pockets of imaginative innovation in broadening the options around the temporal organization of paid work? Are there organizations, occupations, or particular industries that are leading change? Can scholars document the costs of retaining outdated regulations in a society where simply being present at a workplace no longer means being productive, and where being at home no longer means not being distracted by one's job? The challenge for policy is to widen employees' pool of options around exit portals from and entry portals into jobs at different ages and life stages, to widen the pool of community supports for working families, and to widen the range of work-hour options and employees' control over them. The challenge for research is to chronicle the costs and benefits of such innovations, as well as the costs of doing nothing.

ACKNOWLEDGEMENT

This research was conducted as part of the Alfred P. Sloan Foundation's work-family initiative, led by Kathleen Christensen, providing support for Noelle Chesley's postdoctoral fellowship at the University of Minnesota. Additional support was provided by the Work, Family, and Health Network, which is funded by a cooperative agreement through the National Institutes of Health and the Centers for Disease Control and Prevention: National Institute of Child Health and Human Development (Grant # U01HD051217, U01HD051218, U01HD051256, U01HD051276), National Institute on Aging (Grant # U01AG027669), Office of Behavioral and Science Sciences Research, and National Institute of Occupational Safety and Health (Grant # U01OH008788). The contents of this publication are solely the responsibility of the authors and do not necessarily represent the official views of these institutes and offices. We are grateful to Jane Peterson for all the bibliographic and editing assistance she provided.

REFERENCES

Abbott, A. (1995). Sequence analysis: New methods for old ideas. *Annual Review of Sociology, 21*, 93–113.

Altucher, K. A. & Williams, L. B. (2003). Family clocks: Timing parenthood. In P. Moen (ed.), *It's About Time: Couples and Careers* (pp. 49–59). Ithaca: Cornell University Press.

Balter, M. (2006). The baby deficit. *Science, 312*, 1894–1897.

Bandura, A. (1982). Self-efficacy mechanism in human agency. *American Psychologist, 37*, 122–147.

Becker, P. E. & Moen, P. (1999). Scaling back: Dual-career couples' work-family strategies. *Journal of Marriage and the Family, 61*, 995–1007.

Bellavia, G. M. & Frone, M. R. (2005). Work-family conflict. In J. Barling, E.K. Kelloway & M.R. Frone (eds), *Handbook of Work Stress* (pp. 113–147). Thousand Oaks, CA: Sage.

Bellman, S., Forster, N., Still, S. & Cooper, G. L. (2003). Gender differences in the use of social support as a moderator of occupational stress. *Stress and Health, 19*, 45–58.

Bianchi, S. M., Robinson, J. P. & Milkie, M. A. (2006). *Changing Rhythms of American Family Life*. New York: Russell Sage Foundation.

Booth, A., Crouter, A. C. & Shanahan, M. J. (eds) (1999). *Transitions to Adulthood in a Changing Economy*. Westport, CT: Praeger.

Bosma, H., Stansfeld, S. A. & Marmot, M. G. (1998). Job control, personal characteristics, and heart disease. *Journal of Occupational Health Psychology, 3*, 402–409.

Brines, J. (1994). Economic dependency, gender, and the division of labor at home. *American Journal of Sociology, 100*(3), 652–689.

Bronfenbrenner, U. (1995). The bioecological model from a life course perspective: Reflections of a participant observer. In P. Moen, Glen H. Elder Jr. & K. Lüscher (eds), *Examining Lives in Context: Perspectives on the Ecology of Human Development* (pp. 599–618). Washington DC: American Psychological Association.

Bronfenbrenner, U. (2005). *Making Human Beings Human: Bioecological Perspectives on Human Development*. Thousand Oaks: Sage.

Cancian, F. M. & Oliker, S. J. (2000). *Caring and Gender*. Walnut Creek: Altamira Press.

Chesley, N. (2005). Blurring boundaries? Linking technology use, spillover, individual distress, and family satisfaction. *Journal of Marriage and Family, 67*, 1237–1248.

Chesley, N. & Moen, P. (2006). When workers care: Dual-earner couples' adult caregiving, benefit use, and psychological well-being. *American Behavioral Scientist, 49*(9), 1–22.

Chesley, N. & Moen, P. (2007). The Stress Transfer Process in Dual-Earner Couples: Stress Contagion or Something Else? Unpublished manuscript.

Chudacoff, H. P. (1989). *How Old Are You? Age Consciousness in American Culture*. Princeton, NJ: Princeton University Press.

Clarkberg, M. & Moen, P. (2001). Understanding the time-squeeze: Married couples preferred and actual work-hour strategies. *American Behavioral Scientist, 44*, 1115–1136.

Conger, R. D. & Elder, G. H., Jr. (1994). *Families in Troubled Times: Adapting to Change in Rural America*. Hawthorne, NY: Aldine.

Crouter, A. C. (1984). Spillover from family to work: the neglected side of the work-family interface. *Human Relations, 37*(6), 425–442.

Daly, K. (2003). Family theory versus the theories families live by. *Journal of Marriage and Family, 65*, 771–784.

Dannefer, Dale (2003). Toward a global geography of the life course: Challenges of late modernity to the life course perspective. In J.T. Mortimer & M. Shanahan (eds), *Handbook of the Life Course*. New York: Kluwer.

de Jonge, J., Bosma, H., Peter, R. & Siegrist, J. (2000). Job strain, effort-reward imbalance and employee well-being: A large-scale cross-sectional study. *Social Science & Medicine, 50*, 1317–1327.

Dentinger, E. & Clarkberg, M. (2002). Informal caregiving and retirement timing among men and women. *Journal of Family Issues, 23*, 857–878.

Downey, G., Chatman, C., London, B., Cross, W., Hughes, D., Moje, E., Way, N. & Eccles, J. (2005). Navigating self and context in a diverse nation: How social identities matter. In G. Downey, J. Eccles & C. Chatman (eds), *Navigating the Future: Social Identity, Coping, and Life Tasks*. New York: RSF Press.

Drobnič, S. & Blossfeld, H -P. (2004). Career patterns over the life course: Gender, class, and linked lives. In A. L. Kalleberg, S. L. Morgan, J. Myles & R. A. Rosenfeld (eds), *Inequality: Structures, Dynamics and Mechanisms. Essays in Honor of Aage B. Sørensen, Research in Social Stratification and Mobility, Volume 21* (pp. 139–164). Amsterdam: Elsevier.

Drobnič, S, Blossfeld, H-P. & Rohwer, G. (1999). Dynamics of women's employment patterns over the family life course: A comparison of the United States and Germany. *Journal of Marriage and the Family, 61*, 133–146.

Duncan, G., Hill, M. & Hoffman, S. (1988). Welfare dependence within and across generations. *Science, 239*, 467–471.

Elder, G.H., Jr. (1974). *Children of the Great Depression*. Chicago: University of Chicago Press.

Elder, G.H. Jr. (1978). Approaches to social change and the family. *American Journal of Sociology, 84*, S1–S38.

Elder, G. (1985). *Life Course Dynamics: Trajectories and Transitions, 1968–1980*. Ithaca, NY: Cornell University Press.

Elder, G. H., Jr. (1995). The life course paradigm: Social change and individual development. In P. Moen, G. H. Elder, Jr. & K. Lüscher (eds), *Examining Lives in Context: Perspectives on the Ecology of Human Development* (pp. 101–140). Washington, DC: American Psychological Association.

Elder, G. H., Jr. (1996). Human lives in changing societies: Life course and developmental insights. In R. B. Cairns, G. H. Elder, Jr. & E. J. Costello (eds), *Developmental Science*: (pp. 31–62). New York: Cambridge University Press.

Elder, G. H., Jr. (1998a). The life course and human development. In R. M. Lerner (ed.), *Handbook of Child Psychology* (Vol. 1. *Theoretical Models of Human Development*) (pp. 939–991). New York: Wiley.

Elder, G. H., Jr. (1998b). The life course as developmental theory. *Child Development, 69*(1), 1–12.

Elder, G. H., Jr. (2003). The life course in time and place. In W. R. Heinz & V. W. Marshall (eds), *Sequences, Institutions and Interrelations Over the Life Course*, New York: Aldine de Gruyter.

Elder, G. H., Jr., George, L. K. & Shanahan, M. J. (1996). Psychosocial stress over the life course. In H. B. Kaplan (ed.), *Psychosocial Stress: Perspectives on Structure, Theory, Life Course, and Methods* (pp. 247–292). Orlando, FL: Academic Press.

Elder, G. H., Jr. & O'Rand, A.M. (1995). Adult lives in a changing society. In K. Cook, G. Fine & J. House (eds), *Sociological Perspectives on Social Psychology* (pp. 452–475). Needham Heights, MA: Allyn and Bacon.

Ettner, S. L. (1995). The opportunity costs of elder care. *The Journal of Human Resources, 31*(1), 189–205.

Evandrou, M. & Glaser, K. (2004). Family, work, and quality of life: Changing economic and social roles through the life course. *Aging & Society, 24*, 771–791.

Garbarino, J. (1995). *Raising Children in a Socially Toxic Environment.* San Francisco: Jossey-Bass Publishers.

Gareis, K. C., Chait Barnett, R. & Rennan, R. T. (2003). Individual and crossover effects of work schedule fit: A within couple analysis. *Journal of Marriage and Family, 65*, 1041–1054.

Gerson, K. (1985). *Hard Choices: How Women Decide about Work, Career, and Motherhood.* Berkley: University of California Press.

Gerstel, N. & Gallagher, S. (1994). Caring for kith and kin: Gender, employment, and the privatization of care. *Social Problems, 41*, 519–539.

Giele, J. A. & Elder, G. H., Jr. (eds) (1998). *Methods of Life Course Research: Qualitative and Quantitative Approaches.* Thousand Oaks: Sage.

Goode, W. I. (1960). A theory of role strain. *American Sociological Review, 25*, 483–496.

Gornick, J. C. & Meyers, M. K. (2003). *Families That Work: Policies for Reconciling Parenthood and Employment.* New York: Russell Sage Foundation.

Greenhaus, J. H. & Beutell, N. J. (1985). Sources of conflict between work and family roles. *Academy of Management Review, 10*(1), 76–88.

Hagestad, G. O. & Neugarten, B. L. (1985). Aging and the life course. In E. Shanas & R. Binstock (eds), *Handbook of Aging and the Social Sciences* 2nd edn (pp. 36–61). New York: Van Nostrand Reinhold.

Han, S.-K. & Moen, P. (1999a). Clocking out: Temporal patterning of retirement. *American Journal of Sociology, 105*, 191–236.

Han, S.-K. & Moen, P. (1999b). Work and family over time: A life course approach. *Annals of the American Academy of Political and Social Sciences, 562*, 98–110.

Hardy, Melissa. (ed.) (1997). *Studying Aging and Social Change: Conceptual and Methodological Issues.* Thousand Oaks, CA: Sage.

Hareven, T. K. (1978). *Transitions: The Family and the Life Course in Historical Perspective.* New York: Academic Press.

Hareven, T. K. (1982). The life course and aging in historical perspective. In T. K. Hareven & K. J. Adams (eds), *Aging and Life Course Transitions: An Interdisciplinary Perspective* (pp. 1–26). New York: Guilford

Hays, S. (1996). *The Cultural Contradictions of Motherhood.* New Haven, CT: Yale University Press.

Heinz W. R. (1992). *Institutions and Gatekeeping in the Life Course.* Weinheim: Deutscher Studien Verlag.

Henretta, J.C. (1992). Uniformity and diversity: Life course institutionalization and late-life work exit. *Sociological Quarterly, 33*, 265–279.

Hynes, K. & Clarkberg, M. (2005). Women's employment patterns during early parenthood: A group-based trajectory analysis. *Journal of Marriage and Family, 67*, 222–239.

Jacobs, J. & Gerson, K. (2004). *The Time Divide: Work, Family, and Gender Inequality.* Cambridge: Harvard University Press.

Kahn, R. L. & Antonucci, T. C. (1980). Convoys over the life course: Attachment, roles, and social support. In P. B. Baltes & O. Brim (eds), *Life-Span Development and Behavior* (Vol. 3, pp. 254–283). New York: Academic Press

Karasek, R.A., Jr. (1979). Job demands, job decision latitude, and mental strain: Implications for job redesign. *Administrative Science Quarterly, 24*, 285–308.

Karasek, R. & Theorell, T. (1990). *Healthy Work: Stress, Productivity, and the Reconstruction of Working Life.* New York: Basic Books.

Karasek, R., Brisson, C., Kawakami, N., Houtman, I., Bongers, P. & Amick, B. (1998). The job content questionnaire (JCQ): An instrument for internationally comparative assessments of psychosocial job characteristics. *Journal of Occupational Health Psychology, 3*, 322–355.

Kelly, E. (2005). Work-family policies: The United States in international perspective. In M. Pitt-Catsouphes, E. Kossek & S. Sweet (eds), *Work-Family Handbook: Multi-disciplinary Perspectives and Approaches* (pp. 99–123). New York: Lawrence Erlbaum.

Kelly, E., Dahlin, E., Spencer, D. & Moen, P. (2007). Making sense of a mess: Phased retirement policies and practices in the United States. *Journal of Workplace & Behavioral Health*, forthcoming.

Kelly, E. & Moen, P. (2007). Rethinking the clockwork of work: Why schedule control may pay off at home and at work. *Advances in Developing Human Resources, 9*(4), 487–506.

Keyes, C. L. M. (1998). Social well-being. *Social Psychology Quarterly, 61,* 121–140.

Kohli, M. (1986). The world we forgot: A historical review of the life course. In V. W. Marshall (ed.), *Later Life: The Social Psychology of Aging* (pp. 271–303). Beverly Hills, CA: Sage.

Kohli, M. & Meyer, J. W. (1986). Social structure and social construction of life stages. *Human Development, 29*: 145–180.

Krüger, H. (2001). Social change in two generation: Employment patterns and their costs for family life. In V. W. Marshall, W. R. Heinz, H. Krüger & A. Verma (eds), *Restructuring Work and the Life Course* (pp. 401–423). Toronto: University of Toronto Press.

Krüger, H. (2003). The life course regime: Ambiguities between interrelatedness and individualization. In W. R. Heinz & V. W. Marshall (eds), *Social Dynamics of the Life Course* (pp. 33–56). New York: Aldine de Gruyter Press.

Leisering, L. (2003). Government and the life course. In J. T. Mortimer & M. J. Shanahan (eds), *Handbook of the Life Course* (pp. 205–225). New York: Kluwer Academic/Plenum?.

Lewis, S. & Cooper, C. L. (1999). The work-family research agenda in changing contexts. *Journal of Occupational Health Psychology, 4*(4), 382–393.

Macmillan, R. & Elliason, S. (2003). Characterizing the life course as role configurations and pathways: A latent structure approach. In J. T. Mortimer & M. J. Shanahan (eds), *Handbook of the Life Course* (pp. 529–554). New York: Kluwer Academic/Plenum.

Marks, N. F. (1998). Does it hurt to care? Caregiving, work-family conflict, and midlife well-being. *Journal of Marriage and the Family, 60,* 951–966.

Marshall, V. H., Heinz, W. R., Krüger, H. & Verma, A. (eds). (2001). *Restructuring Work and the Life Course.* Toronto: University of Toronto Press.

Mayer, K. U. (1986). Structural constraints on the life course. *Human Development, 29,* 163–170.

Mayer, K. U. & Schoepflin, U. (1989). The state and the life course. *Annual Review of Sociology, 15,* 187–209.

Meyer, J. W. (1986). The institutionalization of the life course and its effects on the self. In A. B. Sorensen, F. E. Weindert & L. R. Sherrod (eds), *Human Development and the Life Course: Multidisciplinary Perspectives* (pp 119–216). Hillsdale, NJ: Lawrence Erlbaum.

Meyer, J. & Rowan, B. (1977). Institutionalized organizations: Formal structure as myth and ceremony. *American Journal of Sociology, 83*: 333–363.

Moen, P. (2001). The gendered life course. In R. H. Binstock & L. K. George (eds), *Handbook of aging and the Social Sciences* (5th edn, pp. 179–196). San Diego, CA: Academic Press.

Moen, P. (ed.). (2003a). *It's About Time: Couples and Careers.* Ithaca, NY: Cornell University Press.

Moen, P. (2003b). Midcourse: Navigating retirement and a new life stage. In J. Mortimer and M. J. Shanahan (eds), *Handbook of the Life Course* (pp. 267–291). New York: Kluwer Academic/Plenum.

Moen, P. & Chermack, K. (2005). Gender disparities in health: strategic selection, careers, and cycles of control. *Journal of Gerontology,* Series B, Vol. 60B (Special Issue II), 99–108.

Moen, P., Elder, G. H., Jr. & Lüscher, K. (eds) (1995). *Examining Lives in Context: Perspectives on the Ecology of Human Development.* Washington, DC: American Psychological Association.

Moen, P. & Han, S. -K. (2001a). Gendered careers: A life course perspective. In R. Hertz & N. Marshall (eds), *Working Families: The Transformation of the American Home* (pp. 42–57). Berkeley: University of California Press.

Moen, P. & Han, S. -K. (2001b). Reframing careers: Work, family, and gender. In V. Marshall, W. Heinz, H. Krüger & A.Verma (eds), *Restructuring Work and the Life Course* (pp. 424–445).Toronto: University of Toronto Press.

Moen, P. & Huang, Q. (2007). Dual-earner ecologies, gender, and life-course "fit": Middle-class couples stretched thin. (unpublished manuscript).

Moen, P., Kelly, E. & Chermack, K. (fourthcoming 2008). "Learning from a natural experiment: Studying a corporate work-time policy initative."Work-life policies that make a real difference for individuals, families, and organizations.Washington, DC: Urban Institute Press.

Moen, P., Kelly, E. & Magennis, R. (forthcoming 2008). Gender strategies: Social and institutional clocks, convoys, and cycles of control. In C. M. Smith & Reio, T. G. Jr. (eds), *Handbook of Research on Adult Development and Learning.?*

Moen, P., Robison, J. & Dempster-McClain, D. (1995). Caregiving and women's well-being: A life course approach. *Journal of Health and Social Behavior, 36*(3), 259–273.

Moen, P. & Roehling, P. (2005). *The Career Mystique: Cracks in the American Dream.* Boulder, CO: Rowman & Littlefield.

Moen, P. & Spencer, D. (2006). Converging divergences in age, gender, health, and well-being: Strategic selection in the third age. In R. Binstock & L. George (eds), *Handbook of Aging and the Social Sciences* (6th edn, pp. 171–187). Burlington, MA: Elsevier Academic Press.

Moen, P., Sweet, S. & Swisher, R. (2005). Embedded career clocks:The case of retirement planning. In R. Macmillan (ed.) *Advances in Life Course Research: The Structure of the Life Course: Individualized? Standardized? Differentiated?* (pp. 237–265).New York: Elsevier.

Moen, P. & Wethington, E. (1992).The concept of family adaptive strategies. *Annual Review of Sociology, 18*, 233–251.

Moen, P. and Yu,Y. (2000). Effective work/life strategies:Working couples, work conditions, gender and life quality. *Social Problems, 47*, 291–326.

Moen, P. & Yu, Y. (1999). Having it all: Overall work/life success in two-earner families. In T. Parcel and R. Hodson (eds), *Work and Family: Research in the Sociology of Work*, (Vol. 7, pp. 109–139). Greenwich, CT: JAI Press.

Mortimer, J. T., Oesterle, S. & Krüger, H. (2005). Age norms, institutional structures, and the timing of markers of transition to adulthood. In R. Macmillan (ed.), *The Structure of the Life Course: Standardized? Individualized? Differentiated? Advances in Life Course Research* (Vol. 9, pp. 175–203). Greenwich, CI: JAI, Elsevier Science Ltd.

Mortimer, J.T. & Shanahan, M.J. (eds) (2003). *Handbook of the Life Course.* New York: Kluwer Academic/Plenum

Mortimer, J.T., Staff, J. & Lee, J.C. (2005). Agency and structure in educational attainment and the transition to adulthood. In R. Levy, P. Ghisletta, J-M. Le Goff, D. Spini & E. Widmer (eds), *Towards an Interdisciplinary Perspective on the Life Course. Advances in Life Course Research* (Vol. 11, pp. 131–153). New York: Elsevier.

Mortimer, J. T., Vuolo, M., Staff, J., Wakefield, S. & Xie, W. (2006). Tracing the timing of "career" aquisition in a contemporary youth cohort. Presentation at American Sociological Association Annual Meeting.August 13th, 2006.

Muhonen, T. & Torkelson, E. (2004).Work locus of control and its relationship to health and job satisfaction from a gender perspective. *Stress and Health, 20*, 21–28.

Mutchler, J. E., Burr, J. A., Pienta, .M. & Massagli, M. P. (1997). Pathways to labor force exit:Work transitions and work instability. *Journal of Gerontology: Social Sciences, 52B*(1), S4–S12.

National Survey on Drug Use and Health. National Findings. (2002). Department of Health and Human Services Substance Abuse and Mental Health Services Administration Office of Applied Studies. Retrieved from http://www.oas.samhsa.gov/nhsda/2k2nsduh/Results/2k2Results. htm#chap9.

Neugarten, B. L. & Hagestad, G. O. (1976). Age and the life course. In R. H. Binstock & E. Shanas (eds), *Handbook of Aging and the Social Sciences* (pp. 35–55). New York:Van Nostrand Reinhold.

Nydegger, C. N. (1986). Age and life course transitions. In C. Fry & J. Keith (eds), *New Methods for Old Age Research: Strategies for Studying Diversity* (pp. 131–161). South Hadley, MA: Bergin & Garvey.

O'Rand, A. M. (1996). The precious and the precocious: Understanding cumulative disadvantage and cumulative advantage over the life course. *Gerontologist, 36*, 230–238.

O'Rand, A. M. & Henretta, J. C. (1999). *Age and Inequality: Diverse Pathways Through Later Life*. Boulder, CO: Westview Press.

O'Rand, A. M & Krecker, M. L. (1990). Concepts of the life cycle: Their history, meanings and uses in the social sciences. *Annual Review of Sociology, 16*, 241–262.

Pavalko, E. K. (1997). Beyond trajectories: Multiple concepts for analyzing long-term process. In M. A. Hardy (ed.), *Studying Aging and Social Change: Conceptual and Methodological Issues* (pp. 129–147). Thousand Oaks, CA: Sage.

Pavalko, E. K. & Artis, J. E. (1997). Women's caregiving and paid work: Causal relationships in late mid-life. *Journal of Gerontology: Social Sciences, 52B*, S1–S10.

Pavalko, E. K. & Elder, G. H. Jr. (1993). Women behind the men: Variations in wives' support of husbands' careers. *Gender & Society, 7*, 548–567.

Pavalko, E. K. & Henderson, K. A. (2006). Combining care work and paid work: Do workplace policies make a difference? *Research of Aging, 28*(3), 359–374.

Pavalko, E. K. & Smith, B. (1999). The rhythm of work: Health effects of women's work dynamics. *Social Forces, 77*(3), 1141–1162.

Pavalko, E. K. & Woodbury, S. (2000). Social roles as process: Caregiving careers and women's health. *Journal of Health and Social Behavior, 41*, 91–105.

Pearlin, L.I. & Aneshensel, C.S. (1994). Caregiving: The unexpected career. *Social Justice Research, 7*, 373–390.

Pearlin, L. I., Schieman, S., Fazio, E. M. & Meersman, S. C. (2005). Stress, health, and the life course: Some conceptual perspectives. *Journal of Health and Social Behavior, 46*(2), 205–219.

Pixley, J. & Moen, P. (2003). Prioritizing careers. In P. Moen (ed.), *It's About Time: Couples and Careers* (pp. 183–200). Ithaca, NY: Cornell University Press.

Raley, S. B., Mattingly, M. J. & Bianchi, S. M. (2006). How dual are dual-income couples? Documenting change from 1970 to 2001. *Journal of Marriage and Family, 68*, 11–28.

Reichart, E, Chesley, N. & Moen, P. (Forthcoming 2007). Beyond the career mystique? Policies structuring gendered paths in the United States and Germany. *Journal of Family Research, 3*.

Repetti, R. L. (1998). Multiple roles. In E. A. Blechman & K. D. Brownell (eds), *Behavioral Medicine and Women: A Comprehensive Handbook* (pp. 162–168). New York: Guilford Press

Ryff, C.D. & Keyes, C.L.M. (1995). The structure of psychological well-being revisited. *Journal of Personality and Social Psychology, 69*, 719–727.

Riley, M. W. (1987). On the significance of age in sociology. *American Sociological Review, 52*: 1–14.

Riley, M. W., Kahn, R. L. & Foner, A. (1994). *Age and Structural Lag: Society's Failure to Provide Meaningful Opportunities in Work, Family, and Leisure*. New York: Wiley.

Rindfus, R. R., Swicegood, C. G. & Rosenfeld, R. A. (1987). Disorder in the life course: How common is and does it matter? *American Sociological Review, 52*, 785–801.

Settersten, R. A. (2003). Age structuring and the rhythm of the life course. In J. T. Mortimer & M. J. Shanahan (eds), *Handbook of the Life Course* (pp. 81–98). New York: Kluwer Academic/Plenum.

Settersten, R. A., Jr. & Hagestad, G.O. (1996a). What's the latest? Cultural age deadlines for family transitions. *Gerontologist, 36*(2),178–188.

Settersten, R. A., Jr. & Hagestad, G.O. (1996b). What's the latest? II. Cultural age deadlines for educational and work transitions. *Gerontologist, 36*, 602–613.

Settersten, R. A., Jr. & Mayer, K. U. (1997). The measurement of age, age structuring, and the life course. *Annual Review of Sociology, 23*, 233–261.

Shanahan, M. (2000). Pathways to adulthood in changing societies: Variability and mechanisms in life course perspective. *Annual Review of Sociology, 26*, 667–692.

Singley, S. G. & Hynes, K. (2005). Gender, workplace policies, and the couple context. *Gender & Society, 19*, 376–397.

Spitze, G., Logan, J. R., Joseph, G. & Lee, E. (1994). Middle generation roles and the well-being of men and women. *Journal of Gerontology, 49*(3), S107–S116.

Sweet, S. & Moen, P. (2006). Advancing a career focus on work and family: Insights from the life course perspective. In M. Pitt-Catsouphes, E. Kossek & S. Sweet (eds), *The Work and Family Handbook: Multi-disciplinary Perspectives and Methods* (pp. 189–208). Mahwah NJ: Lawrence Erlbaum.

Sweet, S., Moen, P. & Meiksins, P. (2007) "Dual earners in double jeopardy: Preparing for job loss in the new risk economy. In Beth A. Rubin (ed.), *Research in the Sociology of Work*, Vol. 17: Work Place Temporalities (pp. 445–469). New York: Elsevier.

Swisher, R., Sweet, S. & Moen, P. (2004). The family-friendly community and its life course fit for dual-earner couples. *Journal of Marriage and Family, 66*, 281–292.

Thoits, P. (1999). Self, identify, stress, and mental health. In C. S. Aneshensel & J. C. Phelan (eds), *Handbook of the Sociology of Mental Health* (pp. 345–368). New York: Kluwer.

Thomas, W. I. & Znaniecki, F. (1918–20). *The Polish Peasant in Europe and America*. Chicago: University of Chicago Press.

Uhlenberg, P. (1978). Changing configurations of the life course. In T. Hareven (ed.), *Transitions: The Family and the Life Course in Historical Perspective* (pp. 65–97). New York: Academic Press.

Umberson, D., Williams, K. & Sharp, S. (2000). Medical sociology and health psychology. In C. E. Bird, P. Conrad & A. M. Fremont (eds), *Handbook of Medical Sociology* (pp. 353–364). Upper Saddle River: Prentice Hall.

Wethington, E., Moen, P., Glasgow, N. & Pillemer, K. (2000). Multiple roles, social integration, and health. In K. Pillemer, P. Moen, E, Wethington & N. Glasgow (eds), *Social Integration in the Second Half of Life* (pp. 48–71). Baltimore: Johns Hopkins University Press.

Wethington, E., Pixley, J. & Kavey, A. (2003). Turning points in work careers. In P. Moen (ed.), *It's About Time: Couples and Careers* (pp. 168–182). Ithaca, NY: Cornell University Press.

Weymann, A. (2003). Future of the life course. In: J. T. Mortimer & M. J. Shanahan (eds), *Handbook of the Life Course* (pp. 703–714). New York: Kluwer Academic/Plenum.

Wheaton, B. (1990). Life transitions, role histories, and mental health source. *American Sociological Review, 55*, 209–223.

Williams, K. & Umberson, D. (2004). Marital status, marital transitions, and health: A gendered life course perspective. *Journal of Health and Social Behavior, 45*(1), 81–98.

Williams, J. C. & Segal, N. (2003). Beyond the maternal wall: Relief for family caregivers who are discriminated against on the job. *Harvard Women's Law Journal, 26*, 77–162.

Zedeck, S. (1992). *Work, Families, and Organizations*. San Francisco, CA: Jossey-Bass Publishers.

SECTION II

Antecedents, Outcomes & Moderators

CHAPTER 7

Too Much to do, and Not Enough Time: An Examination of Role Overload

Linda Duxbury[*], **Sean Lyons**[†] **and Christopher Higgins**[‡]

[*]Sprott School of Business, Carleton University, Ottawa, Canada
[†]Gerald Schwartz School of Business and Information Systems
St. Francis Xavier University, Canada
[‡]Richard Ivey School of Business, University of Western Ontario,
London, Ontario, Canada

INTRODUCTION

"I have almost no personal time at all. I'm chronically tired and feel I can never catch up on all the things I need to get done at home and at the office. I spend most of my coffee breaks and lunches running errands for the family."

"The trade off with job vs family is not only one of time, it is also one of energy. Much of my time not on the job is spent recharging my batteries for time on the job. I do not have a lot of energy when I get home at night to do a lot of 'fun' things with my spouse and children."

"Life is a constant run from task to task. It seems that 24 hours is not enough."

"Time is so tight. It seems wherever I am I should really be somewhere else, because everything is such a rush."

These quotes were provided by individuals who responded to our 2001 National Work-Life Study (Duxbury, Higgins & Coghill, 2003) and speak directly to the issue of role overload which can be defined simply as having too much to do and not enough time in which to do it. Role overload means feeling rushed and time crunched, feeling physically and emotionally exhausted and drained, and not having enough time for oneself.

High levels of role overload have become systemic within the population of employees working for Canada's largest employers. In our 2001 survey of over 30,000 Canadians, we found that the majority of survey respondents (58%) reported high levels of role overload. Another 30% reported moderate levels, while only 12% reported low levels. The percentage of the workforce with high role overload has increased by 11 percentage points over the past decade (based on data from our 1991 research).

Analysis of the 2001 survey suggests that much of this increase in role over-load can be linked to increased time in work, new information and communication technology (e.g., laptops, e-mail, cell phones, Blackberrys), organizational norms that reward long hours at the office rather than performance and "organizational anorexia," a situation in which downsizing leaves too few remaining employees to do the work. At the same time, the proportions of working mothers, dual-career families and employed individuals with eldercare responsibilities have increased dra-matically. The culmination of these influences has resulted in a struggle by employ-ees to accommodate the various demands placed on them by their work and family lives. At the same time, work-family research has striven for a better understanding of the ways in which work and family intersect. However, although a burgeon-ing work-family literature has evolved since the mid-1970s, the critical concept of role overload has garnered relatively scant research attention. The paucity of role overload literature is notable, as recent research indicates that role overload is both prevalent and consequential for individuals, organizations, and society at large.

The evidence suggests that over the last several decades employed men and women have increased the amount of time that they spend in paid employment. As Jacobs and Gerson noted, since "time at work sets an upper boundary on the time left to spend in other pursuits, working time constitutes a starting point for under-standing the shifting balance between work and family" (2001, p. 41). It also provides a useful point to start talking about the idea of role overload, as work demands are the single most important predictor of role overload (Duxbury & Higgins, 2005).

An important and unresolved question in the work-family research literature is whether or not the sheer amount of time that people spend working matters for the quality of their lives (Crouter, Bumpus, Head & McHale, 2001). This issue has gained importance in the past decade in the face of mounting evidence that work-loads (and likely role overload) have increased globally. For example, data from the US National Study of the Changing Workforce can be used to illustrate the magni-tude of this phenomenon. In 2002, Bond and his colleagues observed that over the past 25 years, "the combined weekly work hours of dual-earner couples with chil-dren under 18 at home has increased by an average 10 hours per week, from 81 to 91 hours" and that "the combined weekly work hours (paid and unpaid) at all jobs of all couples has increased significantly over the past 25 years, from 70 hours to 82 hours" (p. 15). Galinsky et al. (2005) report that in 2004, 26% of employees within the US frequently felt overworked and overwhelmed by how much work they had to do. Similar findings come from a US Department of Labor report (2000), which notes that the number of workers in the US workforce that are working 49 hours or more per week increased by 1.8 million between 1994 and 1999 and that almost 11 million American workers now work at least 49 hours per week.

The Organization for Economic Co-operation and Development (OECD) makes a similar point through the use of a comprehensive measure of working time called "hours worked per capita," which is calculated by totalling the hours worked for pay by employees in the economy and dividing this by the population size. They note that this measure "reflects the combined impact of employment rates, the age structure of the population and the average hours actually worked by people with jobs" (p. 5) and, as such, allows for valid comparisons across different countries. Their calculations indicate that between 1970 and 2002, per capita hours rose by 20% in the US and by more than 15% in Canada and New Zealand (OECD, 2004). They concluded their report by observing that the long-term decline in average annual working hours has stopped and many countries are observing the reverse (i.e., time in work has increased). They also reported that many employees in the US, Canada and many OECD countries are "time squeezed" and that the number of organizations with a "long-hours culture" has increased (OECD, 2004).

A number of researchers (e.g., Bond, Galinsky & Swanberg, 1997; Hochschild, 1989; Schor, 1991) contend that workers are spending more hours in paid employment than their parents or grandparents. Data from the US (Arora, 2004; Bond, Thompson, Galinsky & Prottas, 2002; Kodz et al., 2003), Australia (Gray, Qu, Stanton & Weston, 2004), Europe (Arora, 2004; OECD, 2004), Japan, (Kodz et al., 2003) and Canada (Arora, 2004; Statistics Canada, 2000) indicate that this phenomenon can be observed around the world. Data also suggest that employees who are spending more than 45 hours per week in paid employment feel that they are working too much and would like to reduce their working hours (Duxbury & Higgins, 2001; Gray et al., 2004; Kodz et al., 2003).

Jacobs and Gerson (2001) suggest that the perception that people are working more hours is part of a larger social shift from the male breadwinner family to the dual-earner and single-parent household. In other words, it may be that it is a decline in support at home as much as an increase in the working time of individuals that underlies the growing sense that families are squeezed for time and individuals are overloaded

This chapter is divided into six sections. The theoretical framework from which role overload arises is presented first. This is followed by a discussion of the definitional issues associated with the role overload construct. The antecedents and consequences of role overload are presented and discussed in sections three and four respectively. Key findings with respect to role overload coming from the 2001 Canadian National Work-Life Study are outlined in the fifth section of the chapter. The final section offers conclusions and implications for research and practice.

THE THEORETICAL UNDERPINNINGS OF ROLE OVERLOAD

The theoretical underpinnings of the role overload construct can best be understood by examining the sociological theory of social roles. The concept of social roles was first introduced by Linton (1936), who used the term "role" to refer to the pattern of behaviours expected and demanded of a person in a given social position by others within the social system. The notion of role conflict was explored most vividly in Khan, Wolfe, Quinn, Snoek and Rosenthal's (1964) theory of role dynamics. In this theory, roles are defined as the set of behaviours and activities that are expected of an individual in a certain position by those people who rely on and interact with the person in that position. Individuals who interact with a person in a given role are referred to as *role senders*. These role senders hold a set of beliefs and attitudes about what should and should not be done within the role in question, which form their *role expectations*. Because various members of the role set hold varying role expectations for a given role, there is potential for conflict in their role expectations. Role conflict is defined by Khan et al. (1964) as a situation in which differing role expectations result in incompatible role pressures, resulting in psychological conflict for an individual as the pressures and role forces compete and conflict. Kahn and his colleagues identified the following types of role conflict: (a) *Intra-sender conflict*—conflicting role expectations emanating from a single member of the role set; (b) *Inter-sender conflict*—pressures from one sender oppose those from another sender; (c) *Inter-role conflict*—role pressures associated with the organizational role are opposed to those from external roles; (d) *Person-role conflict*—conflict between external role pressures and internal forces such as the values and needs of the individual; and (e) *Role overload*—a type of inter-sender conflict in which various role senders hold legitimate expectations for the role holder that are mutually compatible in the abstract, but which are brought into conflict by the limits of time. In other words, according to Kahn et al. "overload involves a kind of person-role conflict and is perhaps best regarded as a complex, emergent type combining aspects of inter-sender and person-role conflicts" (1964, p. 20).

CURRENT CONCEPTUALIZATIONS OF ROLE OVERLOAD

The extant literature concerning role overload suffers from a number of critical deficiencies, including wide variations in the definitions of key constructs, insufficient consideration of overload of roles across, rather than within, work and family domains, and the lack of a comprehensive theoretical model. These issues are highlighted below.

DEFINITIONAL ISSUES

Unfortunately, there has been a wide variation in the way that role overload has been conceptualized and situated within the nomological network of the work-family interface. The term role overload has been used interchangeably with role strain (e.g., Goode, 1960; Guelzow, Bird & Koball, 1991; Komarovsky, 1976; Marks & MacDermid, 1996), role stress (e.g., Jackson & Schuler, 1985), time-based strain (e.g., Bacharach, Bamberger & Conley, 1991; Greenhaus & Beutell, 1985), role conflict (Coverman, 1989) and the psychological discomfort that is felt when one is not able to meet one's own expectations or one's perceptions of the expectations of others with respect to a single role (Sieber, 1974). This confusion has undoubtedly hampered the advancement of role overload as an important construct in the study of work and family.

Overload was originally conceptualized as a subcategory of the broader construct of role strain, which refers to any difficulty that one experiences in fulfilling role obligations (Bohen & Viveros-Long, 1981; Goode, 1960; Khan et al., 1964; Komarovsky, 1976; Marks & MacDermid, 1996). The other component of role strain, role conflict, has received significantly more attention in the work-family literature. Scholars have been particularly interested in the inter-role conflict between work and family roles. Greenhaus and Beutell argued that inter-role conflict is "experienced when pressures arising in one role are incompatible with pressures arising in another role … when participation in one role is made more difficult by virtue of participation in another role" (1985, p. 77). They defined two types of inter-role conflict: time-based conflict, in which time spent in one role detracts from the time available for other roles, and strain-based conflict, in which strains in one role spill over to affect the individual's performance of other roles. Gutek, Searle, and Klepa (1991) later suggested that work-family conflict can take two forms: work interference with family and family interference with work. Both of these ideas have shaped subsequent research on inter-role conflict.

The type of inter-role conflict described by Greenhaus and Beutell (1985) and Gutek et al. (1991) focuses on the impact of one set of roles on the performance of another, rather than on the pressures that an individual faces in meeting the demands of his or her total role set. Coverman observed that "role conflict and role overload tend to be used interchangeably in the literature, when, in fact, they are related but distinct concepts" (1989, p. 986). Coverman distinguishes between these two constructs as follows. Role conflict is a type of inter-role conflict that emerges when multiple roles create conflicting demands on an individual, such that they are unable to adequately fulfill one or both of the roles. Role overload, on the other hand, occurs when the conflicting demands of various roles are so great that they inhibit the individual's ability to fulfill the roles adequately. Thus, role overload is a type of role conflict that is specifically related to the total time and energy needed to fulfill role demands and may occur even when the role demands are *compatible*, simply because the individual does not have sufficient time and energy to fulfill them all. Thus, although the individual's various roles may not directly conflict with each other in terms of their independent demands, strain is experienced on the whole due to the perceived limits of one's time to dedicate to the entire role set (Khan et al., 1964; Kopelman, Greenhaus & Connolly, 1983).

As such: "a person may experience conflicting demands of multiple roles (role conflict) but, unless time pressure is an issue, he or she will not necessarily encounter role overload" (Coverman, 1989, p. 968).

WHAT IS ROLE OVERLOAD?

We define role overload as a time-based form of role conflict in which an individual perceives that the collective demands imposed by multiple roles (e.g., parent, spouse, employee) are so great that time and energy resources are insufficient to adequately fulfill the requirements of the various roles to the satisfaction of self or others. This definition incorporates a number of noteworthy conceptual points. First, role overload is a specific type of time-based role conflict in which the individual perceives the amount of time available to be insufficient to fulfill all of the demands imposed by the various roles he or she occupies. It can therefore be distinguished from other types of time-based conflict, which occur because of simultaneously occurring demands from two or more roles (e.g., having a work-related meeting and a child's doctor's appointment scheduled at the same time). Overload can also be distinguished from strain-based forms of role conflict, which occur when the strains of one role spill over into other roles (e.g., marital problems affecting one's concentration and performance on the job) (Greenhaus & Beutell, 1985).

DOMAIN-SPECIFIC OVERLOAD

Although role strain research in the 1980s (e.g., Barnett & Baruch, 1985; Kelly & Voydanoff, 1985; Voydanoff, 1980) included both role conflict and role overload, more recent work-family research (e.g., Frone, Russell & Cooper, 1992a; Frone, Yardley & Markel, 1997) has focused almost exclusively on role conflict in the form of work interference with family roles and family interference with work roles. The few studies published in the past 15 years that have incorporated the concept of overload have focused specifically on overload within the separate domains of work (e.g., Bacharach et al., 1991; Brett & Stroh, 2003; Elloy & Smith, 2003; Frone, Russell & Cooper, 1997) and family (e.g., Aryee, Luk, Leung & Lo, 1999; Frone, Russell & Cooper, 1997). These variations of the overload concept relate to the scope of demands one faces within a given role rather than the aggregation of demands experienced within one's entire set of roles. Such domain-specific forms of overload are theorized to be antecedent to various forms of work-family conflict (Aryee et al., 1999; Frone, Russell & Cooper, 1997). In their pioneering work on role theory, Khan et al. (1964) argued that overload within any single role is not a necessary precondition for overload in the total role set. Even when the demands of specific roles are not over-demanding when considered in isolation, the combination of multiple roles can lead to perceived overload in total. Therefore, although domain-specific overload has been shown to be important in its own right, we believe that there is value in considering overload in the total role set as a separate construct. Thus, we conceptualize role overload in terms of "total role overload," which refers to the culminating outcome of over-demand across one's total role set.

TOTAL ROLE OVERLOAD

While the concept of role overload has been theoretically and empirically linked to a wide range of antecedents and consequences, little attempt has been made to generate a comprehensive theoretical model of role overload itself. Instead, role overload has generally been incorporated into models of related concepts, such as role strain and work-family conflict (e.g., Bohen & Viveros-Long, 1981; Goode, 1960; Guelzow, Bird & Koball, 1991). For instance, Cooke and Rousseau (1984) proposed a model of role strain which hypothesizes that work and family role expectations lead to both inter-role conflict (i.e., work interference with family and family interference with work) and work overload, which in turn lead to job dissatisfaction, life dissatisfaction and physical symptoms of strain (i.e., stress). The model proposed by Guelzow et al. (1991) suggests that the perception of role strain (which includes overload) is influenced by a number of environmental antecedents: number of hours worked, flexibility of working hours, number of children and age of the youngest child. Role strain is then proposed to lead to professional, marital, and parental stress. Coverman (1989), however, argued that role overload and role conflict are distinct concepts that may have different impacts on stress. Several researchers (e.g., Bacharach et al., 1991; Frone, Yardley & Markel, 1997) have modeled role overload as an antecedent of work-life conflict.

What is needed is a comprehensive model of total role overload including its antecedents and consequences. In the sections that follow, we review the existing evidence concerning the antecedents and consequences of overload as a step in this direction.

THE ANTECEDENTS OF ROLE OVERLOAD

While a large body of literature exists to inform our understanding of the antecedents of work-life conflict, much of what exists in this area does not focus specifically on the role overload construct. Moreover, it is limited by methodological issues (excellent discussions of these issues can be found in the following comprehensive reviews: Barnett, 1998; Frone, 2002; Guerts & Demerouti, 2003; Hammer, Colton, Caubert & Brockwood, 2002). This section presents a summary of what we know about the risk factors for role overload. The discussion is divided into three parts. The relationship between work demands and role overload is considered first. This is followed by an examination of the link between family demands and overload. The final part of this section identifies other factors associated with increased levels of role overload.

Conceptually we can expect that increases in role overload will be concomitant with the number of obligations and responsibilities that an individual has at work (i.e., their employer, superior, colleagues, subordinates, etc.) and outside of work (i.e., their spouse, children, parents, friends, community, etc.). The idea that increased work-role and family-role demands are closely related to increased time pressures and an increased perception of role overload is consistent with a substantial body of research in the area (e.g., Barnett, Gareis & Brennan, 1999; Cooke & Rousseau, 1984; Coverman, 1989; Frone, Yardley & Markel, 1997).

While we have chosen to consider work and family demands separately in this discussion, such a distinction may not be one that is easy for employees to make. As Guerts and Demerouti (2003) point out, the question of what constitutes work as opposed to nonwork demands has become more complicated over the past decade due to a number of irreversible changes in the context of work. These include an increase in the number of people who work: overtime; at a location other than a central office building; and hours outside a traditional 9 to 5 schedule. Guerts and Demerouti (2003) also note a similar phenomenon with respect to nonwork demands. Personal activities are, for example, often brought into the workplace by different kinds of employee benefits (e.g., fitness or daycare centers at work, concierge services offered by employers), and working hours are spent on family or personal activities (i.e., personal phone calls and e-mail). Similarly, Lewis and Dyer (2002) note that office technology such as e-mails and laptop computers and the shift to a knowledge economy has, in many cases, meant that the boundaries between work and nonwork domains have become blurred.

THE RELATIONSHIP BETWEEN WORK DEMANDS AND ROLE OVERLOAD

Work demands have generally been defined as the set of prescribed tasks that an individual performs while occupying a position in an organization (Guerts & Demerouti, 2003). Work hours are one of the most widely studied structural aspects of employment in the work-life literature (Barnett et al., 1999). It is generally agreed that the number of hours worked contributes to the experience of job demands (i.e., pressures arising from excessive workloads and workplace time pressures), which has been identified as a major workplace stressor (Barnett, et al., 1999).

Research in the area suggests that when job demands require "too much" effort and time (i.e., deadlines are too tight, resources are insufficient to allow the employee to fulfill their responsibilities at work during regular hours) energy and time resources are depleted. Over time, high job demands have been found to build up and hamper one's ability to function outside of work, such as fulfilling one's obligations to spouse, children, elder parents, and community (Guerts & Demerouti, 2003).

The amount of time required by the job (i.e., working hours per week, working overtime) has been frequently studied as an antecedent of work–life conflict (Guerts & Demerouti, 2003). One of the most consistent findings in the empirical literature is the strong positive association between weekly hours devoted to work and the incidence of work interference with family, work–life conflict, role overload, and negative spillover from work to family. Examples include Frone et al. (1992b); Frone, Yardley and Markel (1997), Guerts and Demerouti (2003) and Guelzow et al. (1991). Voydanoff (1988) provides citations for a number of earlier studies that have been done using diverse samples, which have also found a direct relationship between the number of hours worked and greater work–life conflict.

Barnett (1998), on the other hand, contends that the effect of long work hours on role overload is not straight forward, as the relationship might be confounded by other variables, such as degree of flexibility in/control over work schedule or type of job being performed. She further argues that working long hours may be a risk factor only for specific groups under specific conditions.

THE RELATIONSHIP BETWEEN NONWORK DEMANDS AND ROLE OVERLOAD

There is much less of a consensus on what should be included within the umbrella of nonwork demands. Nonwork may refer to activities and responsibilities associated with the family domain as well as activities and obligations that go beyond one's own family situation (Guerts & Demerouti, 2003). Social roles typically included within this category include leisure (interpreted to mean "spare time"), obligations and responsibilities associated with family membership (e.g., household activities, caregiving,), as well as social obligations (e.g., volunteer activities, community activities) and education (Frone, 2002; Guerts & Demerouti, 2003).

Frone et al. (1992a) define family demands as time pressures associated with tasks like housekeeping and child and elder care. Family demands have been found to increase as a function of family characteristics like a greater number of dependents and a larger family size (Frone et al., 1992a; Greenhaus & Beutell, 1985), an increased amount of time spent in family roles, a larger number of children and children who are younger (Greenhaus & Beutell, 1985; Voydanoff, 1988), and greater responsibilities for childcare and eldercare (Duxbury & Higgins, 1998). Other family-related sources of time-based conflict identified by Greenhaus and Beutell (1985) include marriage, parenthood, having responsibility for childrearing, and number of hours worked outside of the home by the primary caregiver. Finally, Coverman

(1989) cites a number of studies that found that greater participation of husbands in domestic work alleviates some of the role overload of employed women.

Early work by Rapoport and Rapoport (1976) also gives us insights into the link between family demands and what they referred to as "overload dilemmas." They determined that overload was positively associated with a tendency to treat housework as "overtime" work rather than the responsibility of the woman. In addition, they found that overload was increased when having children and a family life (as opposed to just being married) was salient. This was both because of added time demands and the increased psychic strain from being committed to two very different roles. Other important factors in determining the level of role overload experienced were: the degree to which the couple aspired to a high standard of domestic living; the degree to which family tasks were re-apportioned satisfactorily; and the degree to which social-psychological overload compounded physical overload.

In their study of dual-career couples, Rapoport and Rapoport (1976) observed that while relaxation of standards at home was a useful way to cope with social-psychological overload, this strategy was never used in relation to the care of children, as there was too much guilt associated with lowering standards for parenting. This finding was confirmed more recently by Brett and Stroh who observed that employees with children do not let the amount of time they spend in paid work impact on the amount of time they spend with their children and that "regardless of whether parents worked 40 or 60 hours per week, managers with children devoted about the same amount of time to their children" (2003, p. 72).

Little empirical research exists on the connection between role overload and specific nonwork roles other than those associated with the family (Frone, 2002). A number of studies have, however, found that the number of weekly hours devoted to family activities and chores to be positively associated with family interference with work (Frone, Yardley & Markel, 1997; Grzywacs & Marks, 2000; Gutek et al., 1991). Frone and colleagues (Frone et al., 1992a; Frone, Yardley & Markel, 1997) determined that parental workload was positively associated with family to work interference. Hours devoted to family activities have also been found to be positively related to family interference with work (Frone, Yardley & Markle, 1997; Gutek et al., 1991). Studies remain to be done, however, establishing the link between family and nonwork demands to role overload.

There are also other antecedents of role overload. These include personality, gender (see Chapter 12), and various aspects related to holding multiple roles (see Chapter 5).

THE CONSEQUENCES OF ROLE OVERLOAD

The importance of role overload is evidenced by its numerous detrimental outcomes for individuals, organizations, and society at large. For instance, role overload has been linked to increased levels of anxiety, fatigue, burnout, depression and emotional and physiological stress, and to decreased satisfaction with family and work (Bacharach et al., 1991; Barnett & Baruch, 1985; Cooke & Rousseau, 1984; Coverman, 1989; Duxbury & Higgins, 2003a; Guelzow et al., 1991; Khan et al., 1964). Duxbury and Higgins (2003b) also found high role overload to be related to higher rates of absenteeism on the job, lower levels of organizational commitment, increased thoughts of quitting, poorer physical and mental health, greater use of Canada's health care system and greater health care costs.

A number of studies have examined the stress–related outcomes associated with inter-role conflict between family and work (Frone et al., 1992a; Frone et al., 1997; Greenhaus & Beutell, 1985). A smaller number of studies have examined the relationship between overload and stress and have generally linked overload to increased incidence of emotional and physical stress (e.g., Cooke & Rousseau, 1984; Guelzow et al., 1991; Paden & Buehler, 1995). Other studies have found associations between role overload and increased levels of stress-related outcomes such as anxiety (Barnett & Baruch, 1985; Guelzow et al., 1991; Khan et al., 1964), fatigue and burnout (Bacharach et al., 1991) and depression (Guelzow et al., 1991). Overload has also been linked to decreased well-being in the form of diminished job satisfaction (Bacharach et al., 1991; Khan et al., 1964), family satisfaction (Coverman, 1989), and reduced satisfaction with relationships at home (Gray et al., 2004). Most recently Galinsky and colleagues (2005) reported the following consequences of overload: higher levels of depressive symptoms; higher levels of stress; lower levels of satisfaction with one's social life and one's ability to pursue leisure pursuits, and an increased likelihood that an individual will report that they are in poorer physical health and that they are not successful in taking good care of themselves.

KEY FINDINGS FROM THE 2001 NATIONAL WORK-LIFE STUDY

The 2001 National Work-Life Study involved the collection of data from over 31,000 working Canadians on a wide variety of work–life integration issues, including role overload. We believe that this study represents the largest and most comprehensive investigation to date of the phenomenon of role overload and its causes and consequences.

The data from the study provide a number of critical insights. First, the key predictor of role overload for both men and women was the amount of time spent in unpaid overtime a month. There was only one other predictor of role overload that was important for both men and women—the total number of hours spent in work per week, which was the second most important predictor of overload for men and the fourth most important predictor for women. These findings suggest that overload is not just a function of the amount of time spent working at the office per week, but also of work demands and expectations that must be fulfilled outside of regular work hours. This seems to be particularly true for men where the number of hours spent in supplemental work at home was the fourth most important predictor of role overload.

For men, holding a supervisory position was the third most important predictor of high levels of role overload. This suggests that there is a strong association between being a manager and engaging in the types of behaviour (e.g., working long hours, the performance of unpaid overtime, performing supplemental work at home) that lead to role overload. It is hard to determine the direction of causality of these data. Do they indicate that the workloads and the work expectations associated with being a manager encourage men to engage in the types of behaviours that contribute to role overload? Alternatively, do they indicate that men who work long hours and unpaid overtime are more likely to be promoted into management positions within their organization? In either case, the data from this research suggest that men who work longer hours will pay the price in terms of increased levels of role overload.

For women, on the other hand, three out of five of the most important predictors of role overload (i.e., time spent commuting to work, week day and weekend nights away from home on business-related travel) pertained to job-related travel. The fact that none of these work demands were significant predictors of overload in men suggest that the etiology of role overload varies by gender. It would appear that for men, role overload appears to be a function of being a manager and engaging in work extension activities, while for women this form of work-life conflict is linked to being away from home on business-related travel.

What is it about business-related travel that contributes to role overload for women? Again, we can only speculate as to why this strong relationship exists. It may be that women who do a lot of business-related travel try to make arrangements at home before they leave so that their absence will cause fewer problems for their family. Alternatively, it may be that women who travel on business spend a lot of their time on the road engaged in work-related activities rather than relaxing. Finally, it may also be that the activities associated with travel itself are more problematic for women than men, perhaps because they have fewer people to help them cope with these extra demands (i.e., support staff at work, spouse at home).

The link between time spent commuting to work and role overload for women (but not for men) is also interesting. Again, it is difficult to know with certainty why this relationship exists. It may be that women, more than men, are expected to combine family chores with the commute to and from work, such as dropping off and picking up children. Alternatively, it may be that women make different use of public transit than men or that women have less access to flexible work arrangements than men and hence are more likely to have to commute during the rush hour. Future research should focus on determining the causal mechanisms behind this finding.

Finally, it is important to note that role overload is impacted more strongly by demands generated from the work domain rather than from the nonwork domain. Nonwork demands such as time in childcare, eldercare and home chores are not substantive predictors of role overload for either men or women.

Taken together these findings indicate that while the relationship between role overload and work demands has a slightly different etiology for men than women, if one knows how much time an employee spends per week in unpaid work and work, all factors considered, then they will be able to predict with a fair degree of confidence the amount of role overload they will experience.

A number of other important conclusions about the occurrence of role overload can be drawn from the 2001 data. First, it would appear that objective facts about the nature of an employee's family (such as whether it is dual-career or single-parent), community (such as its size and whether it is rural versus urban), or work situation (such as one's sector of employment) do not help us to predict the amount of role overload they will experience. Rather, it would appear that along with work demands, the organizational culture is the most powerful predictor of role overload. For both men and women, the single most important aspect of work culture in the prediction of role overload was the extent to which the employee believed that the organization promoted a culture that was supportive of work-life balance. The results indicate that supportive work cultures serve a protective function within the organization, as the more supportive the environment, the lower the levels of role overload reported. Two other types of work cultures proved to be predictive of increased levels of role overload: a culture of hours and a culture of "work or family" (i.e., one in which employees perceive that family responsibilities limit career advancement). With respect to the culture of hours, employees who perceive that it is not acceptable for them to say no to more work and that an inability to work long hours would limit their career advancement are more likely to report higher levels of role overload regardless of their gender. Working for an organization that promotes a culture of work or family is also linked to higher role overload—perhaps because employees in such circumstances try to do it all.

Finally, it is important to note that with relatively few exceptions, the key predictors of role overload are the same for men and women.

CONCLUSIONS AND IMPLICATIONS FOR FUTURE RESEARCH AND PRACTICE

Given the prevalence of role overload and the number of negative consequences it engenders, it is unfortunate that role overload has largely disappeared from the work-family literature. It would appear that academics, practitioners and policymakers alike would benefit from a deeper understanding of the total role overload construct. Role overload has importance as a separate concept from role conflict in general, because it has important consequential differences. While conflict may be disheartening and distracting when it involves the amelioration of competing role demands, getting to a state of subjective overload—feeling like there is too much to do and too little time—is an altogether different state of affairs. Using the definition of role overload proffered by Khan and his associates, we can say that it is a form of role conflict, but it is a unique form of conflict that merits its own attention because of its potential effects. Frone, Russell and Cooper (1997) make a strong argument that work overload and family overload have different antecedents and different outcomes. Notably, they have separate direct and indirect effects on work interference with family and family interference with work. However, their model does not account for the notion that overload may not occur within the work or family roles, but may be the cumulative effect of too many role expectations within the role set. This chapter has made the case that researchers need to make the distinction between work-role overload, family-role overload and role-set overload, which may be the result of too many roles, including nonwork and nonfamily roles, or excessive demands in any number of roles. In other words, researchers need to include the role overload construct in their study of work-life conflict because as Coverman notes, that while role overload and role conflict overlap, it is important to our understanding of work-life conflict to "maintain their conceptual and analytical distinctions" (1989, p. 968).

REFERENCES

Arora, R. (2004). Are Americans really abject workaholics? Gallup Poll Briefing, Oct. 5th, pp. 1–4.

Aryee, S., Luk, V., Leung, A. & Lo, S. (1999). Role stressors, interrole conflict and well-being: The moderating influence of spousal support and coping behaviors among employed parents in Hong Kong. *Journal of Vocational Behavior, 54,* 259–278.

Bacharach, S. B., Bamberger, P. & Conley, S. (1991). Work-home conflict among nurses and engineers: Mediating the impact of role stress on burnout and satisfaction at work. *Journal of Organizational Behavior, 12,* 39–53.

Barnett, R. C. (1998) Toward a review and reconceptualization of the work/family literature, *Genetic, Social and General Psychology Monographs, 124,* 125–182.

Barnett, R. C. & Baruch, G. K. (1985). Women's involvement in multiple roles and psychological distress. *Journal of Personality and Social Psychology, 49,* 134–145.

Barnett, R., Gareis, K. & Brennan, B. (1999). Fit as a mediator of the relationship between work hours and burnout. *Journal of Occupational Health Psychology, 4,* 307–317.

Bohen, H. H. & Viveros-Long, A. (1981). *Balancing Jobs and Family Life: Do Flexible Work Schedules Help?* Philadelphia: Temple University Press.

Bond, J., Galinsky & Swanberg, J. (1997). *The 1997 National Study of the Changing Workforce: Synthesis of Findings.* New York: Families and Work Institute.

Bond, J., Thompson, C., Galinsky, E. & Prottas, D. (2002). *Highlights of the National Study of the Changing Workforce, Number Three.* New York: Families and Work Institute.

Brett, J. & Stroh, L. (2003). Working 61 hours a week: Why do managers do it? *Journal of Applied Psychology, 88* (1), 67–78.

Cooke, R. A. & Rousseau, D. M. (1984). Stress and strain from family roles and work-role expectations. *Journal of Applied Psychology, 69,* 252–260.

Coverman, S. (1989). Role overload, role conflict, and stress: Addressing consequences of multiple role demands. *Social Forces, 67,* 965–982.

Crouter, A., Bumpus, M., Head, M. & McHale, S. (2001). Implications of overwork and overload for the quality of men's family relationships. *Journal of Marriage and the Family, 63,* 404–416.

Duxbury, L. & Higgins, C., (2005). *Who is at Risk? Predictors of Work-Life Conflict* (Report Four). Ottawa: Health Canada.

Duxbury, L. & Higgins, C. (2003a). *Where to Work in Canada? An Examination of Regional Differences in Work-life Practices.* Vancouver, B.C.: B.C. Council of the Families.

Duxbury, L. & Higgins, C. (2003b). *Work-life Conflict in Canada in the New Millennium: A Status Report* (Report Two). Ottawa: Health Canada.

Duxbury, L., Higgins, C. & Coghill, D. (2003). *Voices of Canadians: Seeking Work-life Balance.* Human Resources Canada, Cat. No. RH54-12/2003.

Duxbury, L. & Higgins, C. (2001). Work-life balance in the new millennium: Where are we? Where do we need to go? Canadian Policy Research Network (CPRN) Discussion Paper No. W/12, CPRN: Ottawa.

Duxbury, L., Higgins, C., Lee, C. & Mills, S. (1991). *Balancing Work and Family: A Study of the Canadian Federal Public Sector.* Ottawa: Department of Health and Welfare Canada (NHRDP).

Duxbury, L. & Higgins, C. (1998). *Work-life Balance in Saskatchewan: Realities and Challenges,* Regina: Government of Saskatchewan.

Duxbury, L., Higgins, C. & Coghill, D. (2003). *Voices of Canadians* (2003). Ottawa: Department of Labour, Human Resources Development Canada..

Elloy, D. F. & Smith, C. R. (2003). Patterns of stress, work-family conflict, role conflict, role ambiguity and overload among dual-career and single-career couples: An Australian study. *Cross Cultural Management, 10,* 55–66.

Frone, M., Russell, M. & Cooper, M. (1992a). Antecedents and outcomes of work-family conflict: Testing a model of the work-family interface. *Journal of Applied Psychology, 77,* 65–78.

Frone, M., Russell, M. & Cooper, M. (1992b). Prevalence of work-family conflict: Are work and family boundaries asymmetrically permeable? *Journal of Occupational Behaviour, 13,* 723–729.

Frone, M., Russell, M. & Cooper, M. (1997). Relation of work-life conflict to health outcomes: A four-year longitudinal study of employed parents, *Journal of Occupational and Organizational Psychology, 70,* 325–335.

Frone, M., Yardley, J. & Markel, K. (1997). Developing and testing an integrative model of the work-family interface. *Journal of Vocational Behaviour, 50,* 145–167.

Frone, M. (2002). Work-life balance. In J.Quick & L. Tetrick (eds). *Handbook of Occupational Health Psychology* (pp. 143–162). Washington, DC: American Psychological Association.

Galinsky, E., Bond, J., Kim, S., Backon, L., Brownfield, E. & Sakai, K. (2005). *Overwork in America: When the Way We Work Becomes Too Much.* New York: Families and Work Institute.

Goode, W. J. (1960). A theory of role strain. *American Sociological Review, 25,* 483–496.

Gray, M., Qu, L., Stanton, D. & Weston, R. (2004). Long work hours and the well-being of fathers and their families. *Australian Journal of Labour Economics, 7,* 255–273.

Greenhaus, J. H. & Beutell, N. J. (1985). Sources of conflict between work and family roles. *Academy of Management Review, 10,* 76–88.

Guelzow, M. G., Bird, G. W. & Koball, E. H. (1991). An explanatory path analysis of the stress process for dual-career men and women. *Journal of Marriage and the Family, 5,* 151–164.

Guerts, S. & Demerouti, E. (2003). Work/non-work interface: A review of theories and findings. In M. Schabracq, J. Winnubst & C. Copper (eds), *The Handbook of Work and Health Psychology*(pp. 279–312). Chichester, England: Wiley.

Gutek, B., Searle, S. & Klepa, L. (1991). Rational versus gender role explanations for work-family conflict. *Journal of Applied Psychology, 76*, 560–568.

Hammer, L., Colton, C., Caubert, S. & Brockwood, K. (2002). The unbalanced life: Work and family conflict. In J. Thomas & M. Hersen, *Handbook of Mental Health in the Workplace* (pp. 83–102). Thousand Oaks, CA: Sage.

Higgins, C. & Duxbury, L. (2002). *The 2001 National Work-life Conflict Study: Report One*. Ottawa: Health Canada.

Hochschild, A. (1989), *The Second Shift*. New York: Viking Penguin.

Jacobs, J. & Gerson, K. (2001). Overworked individuals or overworked families, *Work and Occupations, 28*, 40–63.

Jackson, S. & Schuler, R. (1985). A meta-analysis and conceptual critique of research on role ambiguity and role conflict in work settings. *Organizational Behavior and Human Decision Processes, 36*, 16–78.

Kelly, R. F. & Voydanoff, P. (1985). Work/family role strain among employed parents, *Family Relations, 34*, 367–374.

Khan, R, L., Wolfe, D. M., Quinn, R. P., Snoek, J. D. & Rosenthal, R. A. (1964). *Organizational Stress: Studies in Role Conflict and Ambiguity*. New York: Wiley.

Kodz, J., Davis, S., Lain, D., Sheppard, E., Rick, J., Strebler, M., Bates, P., Cummings, J., Meager, N., Anxo, D., Gineste, S. & Trinczek, R. (2003). *Working Long Hours in the U.K.: A Review of the Research Literature, Analysis of Survey Data and Cross-national Organization Case Studies*. Employment Relations Research Series No. 16. London: Department of Trade and Industry.

Komarovsky, M. (1976). *Dimensions of Masculinity: A Study of College Youth*. New York: W. W. Norton and Company.

Kopelman, R. E., Greenhaus, J. H. & Connolly, T. F. (1983). A model of work, family, and interrole conflict: A conflict validations study. *Organizational Behavior and Human Performance, 32*, 198–215.

Lewis, S. & Dyer, J. (2002). Toward a culture for work-life integration. In C. Cooper & R. Burke (eds). *The New World of Work*. (pp. 302–316). London, England: Blackwell

Linton, R. (1936). *The Study of Man*. New York: D. Appleton-Century.

Marks, S. R. & MacDermid, S. H. (1996). Multiple roles and the self: A theory of role balance. *Journal of Marriage and the Family, 58*, 417–432.

Organization for Economic Co-operation and Development (OECD) (2004). *Clocking In and Clocking Out: Recent Trends in Working Hours*. Policy brief., retrieved October 16, 2006, from: http://www.oecd.org/dataoecd/42/49/33821328.pdf

Paden, S. L. & Buehler, C. (1995). Coping with the dual-income lifestyle. *Journal of Marriage and the Family, 57*, 101–110.

Rapoport, R. & Rapoport, R. (1976). *Dual-career Families Re-examined*. New York: Harper Row.

Schor, J. B. (1991). *The Overworked American: The Unexpected Decline of Leisure*. New York: Basic Books.

Sieber, S. D. (1974). Toward a theory of role accumulation. *American Sociological Review, 39*, 567–578.

Statistics Canada (2000 Spring). Long working hours and health. In *Perspectives on Income and Labour*. Ottawa: Statistics Canada.

United States Department of Labor (2000). Are managers and professionals really working more? *Issues in Labour Statistics*. Washington DC: Bureau of Labour Statistics.

Voydanoff, P. (1980). Work roles as stressors in corporate families. *Family Relations, 4*, 489–494.

Voydanoff, P. (1988). Work-role characteristics, family structure demands, and work/family conflict. *Journal of Marriage and the Family, 50*, 749–761.

CHAPTER 8

Positive Spillover Between Personal and Professional Life: Definitions, Antecedents, Consequences, and Strategies

Steven Poelmans, Olena Stepanova and Aline Masuda
IESE Business School University of Navarra, Barcelona, Spain

INTRODUCTION

Over the last few decades Western societies have gone through a number of major transformations creating a pressing need to study the interface between work, family, and personal life. Among these trends we can count the increased participation of women in the labor market, longer life expectancy, and a growing number of divorces. Combined, these trends have boosted the prevalence of dual-earner, mono-parental and combined families that, in addition to their caring responsibilities for children, sometimes have to support elderly parents or children of their partner's previous marriage (Bond, Galinsky & Swangberg, 1998). These new families have one thing in common: the intensification and higher complexity of caring responsibilities, and as a consequence, more frequent and intense conflicts between the professional and personal spheres of life.

Work and family conflict will intensify especially now with the availability of technically sophisticated gadgets (i.e., blackberries, cell phones) that will improve employees' flexibility at work but at the same time increase work demands and expectations. In other words, employees will have the autonomy to choose *where* to work but not necessarily *when* to work. Instead, employees will be expected to be available all the time and, as they perform work functions at home, the boundaries between work and life will be less clear. Given these changes in life style, it is not surprising that studies on work and family interactions have focused mostly on the negative side of the work-family interface: work-family conflict (WFC) (Barnett, 1998; Greenhaus & Parasuraman, 1999; Lambert, 1990).

This negative perspective is based on the scarcity hypothesis, which states that individuals have a finite amount of time and energy. As such, their participation in various roles (e.g., professional, family and leisure activities) leads to role ambiguity, role overload, and role conflict that can eventually result in the deterioration of quality of life (Greenhaus & Parasuraman, 1999). In the vein of "positive psychology" that focuses on the positive side of well-studied psychological constructs, more and more researchers are shifting their attention to positive relationships between life domains. Based on the early work of Sieber (1974) and Marks (1977), who suggested an expansionistic view of work and family relationships, scholars in the work/family domain now argue that role accumulation is beneficial for individuals and society and that human energy is not finite but rather recreates itself within limits. Barnett and Hyde (2001) agree with the view that active engagement in one domain provides access to resources and experiences that contribute to individual fulfillment. Additionally, positive experiences obtained in one role can buffer the strain experienced in another one (Greenhaus & Powell, 2006). In this chapter, we will focus mainly on this emerging literature, as reviews of the conflict literature can be found elsewhere (Frone, 2003; Poelmans, O'Driscoll & Beham, 2005). First, we define and distinguish the concept of work-family enrichment from the concept of work-family conflict by explaining the different types of positive interactions between work and family domains. Second, we examine the causes and consequences of these interactions. Third, we propose strategies to actively seek and create positive spillover between life domains.

DEFINITIONS

The positive side of the work-family interface is labeled differently: positive spillover, enhancement, engagement, work-family enrichment and facilitation (Carlson, Kacmar, Wayne & Grzywacz, 2006; Crouter, 1984; Greenhaus & Powell, 2006; Kirchmeyer, 1992; Ruderman, Ohlott, Panzer & King, 2002). In their review of the literature, Carlson et al. pointed out that these concepts are distinct, varying in their focus on received benefits, experiences, and improvement of role performance. For example, *work-family facilitation* has been defined as a form of *synergy* where resources associated with one role (e.g., *affect, skills, self-esteem, monetary benefits*, etc.) make participation easier in the other role (Wayne, Musica & Fleeson, 2004). *Enhancement* refers to social and psychological *resources* acquired by the participation in multiple life roles (Ruderman, Ohlott, Panzer & King). *Work family enrichment*, defined by Greenhaus & Powell, emphasizes that "*experiences* in one role improve the quality of life in the other role" (2006, p. 73). Finally, *positive spillover* is a term used to describe experiences such as moods, skills, values, and behaviors transferred from one role to another (Carlson et al.).

See Figure 8.1 for an illustration of these terms. Despite the existence of different terms for these positive work-life interactions, to simplify communication we will use *positive spillover* generally to refer to these positive cross-domain influences.

Work-family enrichment and WFC should be considered independent constructs, as research has found almost no evidence of their correlation (Frone, 2003). As such, positive and negative spillover can be experienced concurrently

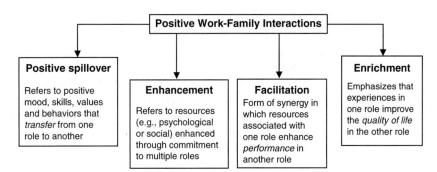

Figure 8.1   Positive interactions between work and life domain

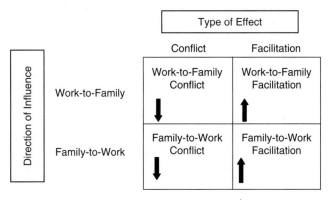

Figure 8.2   Dimension of work-family balance (From Frone, 2003)[1]

and are distinct (Frone; Grzywacz & Butler, 2005). Thus, one can experience negative spillover from family to work (e.g., stress from raising a child and handling multiple tasks during the day can have a negative affective impact at work) while, at the same time, skills learned from these family experiences can have a positive impact at work (i.e., positive spillover).

Although distinct, positive spillover and WFC have similarities in that both concepts are bidirectional, occurring from family-to-work and work-to-family domains (Crouter, 1984; Frone, Russell & Cooper, 1992 (a) & (b); Frone, Yardley & Markel, 1997). The four-fold taxonomy of work-family balance supported by Grzywacz & Marks (2000) distinguishes between the direction (work-to-family or family-to-work) and type of effect occurring (facilitation or conflict). As shown in Figure 8.2, a

[1]Reprinted from Frone, M. R. (2003). Work-family balance. In J. C. Quick & L. E. Tetrick (eds), *Handbook of Occupational Health Psychology* (pp. 143–162). Washington, DC: American Psychological Association. Copyright © 2006 by the American Psychological Association. Reprinted with permission of Michael R. Frone.

low degree of *interrole* conflict and a high level of *interrole* facilitation lead to work-family balance.

Research has identified several types of spillover: mood, values, skills, and behavior (Edwards & Rothbard, 2000). For example, mood spillover occurs when a positive mood experienced at work transfers to a positive mood at home. Value spillover takes place when a person who is expected to be punctual, also demands it from his/her children. In other words, the values lived out at work spill over to home. Skills and behavior spillover follow the same pattern as in mood and values and are described in more detail below.

The initial research on work-family enrichment described the benefits obtained from multiple roles as encompassing: role privileges, status security, status enhancement, and enrichment in personality (Sieber, 1974). Subsequently, Hanson, Colton and Hammer (2003) suggested a conceptualization that used two types of enrichment. *Instrumental enrichment* refers to skills and abilities acquired in one domain and applied in another, and it can be illustrated as follows: employees who acquired team-management and conflict-resolution skills at work can apply them in their family, resolving conflicts more effectively and managing better children (Crouter, 1984; Kirschmeyer, 1992). Other benefits such as perspective, flexibility, and psychological, physical, social–capital, and material resources also belong to this category (Greenhaus & Powell, 2006). *Affective enrichment* refers to positive emotions or affect transmitted from one role to another. This is similar to mood spillover explained above (Edwards & Rothbard, 2000).

In the work-family enrichment scale, developed and validated by Carlson et al. (2006), three dimensions of work-family and family-work enrichment are identified (see Figure 8.3). Work-to-family enrichment refers to (1) *work-family*

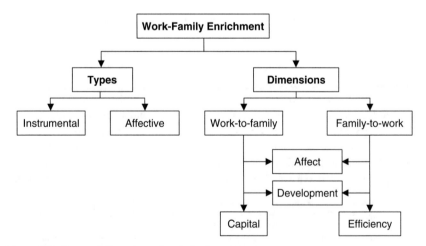

Figure 8.3 Types and dimensions of work-family enrichment

affect (moods and attitudes), for example work "puts me in a good mood and this helps me be a better family member"; (2) *work-family development* (skills, knowledge, behavior), for example work "helps me to gain knowledge and this helps me be a better family member"; and (3) *work-family capital* (work enhances psychological resources as sense of security, confidence, self-fulfillment), for example work "helps me feel personally fulfilled and this helps me be a better family member". Family-to-work enrichment has two similar dimensions (*family-work affect* and *family-work development*) but differs in the third one: *family-work efficiency*. The latter refers to the situation where family involvement encourages concentration on tasks, which helps one be a better worker; for example family obligations "requires me to avoid wasting time at work and this helps me be a better worker". Research shows that family-to-work enrichment is significantly higher than work-to-family enrichment (Greenhaus & Powell, 2006).

Another body of literature describing positive interactions between work and life domains focuses on the positive aspects of multiple role participation. For example, the multiple role participation theory (Froberg, Gjerdingen & Preston, 1986) contends that the outcome of participating in various roles depends on the type of roles a person is involved in, the degree of role quality experienced in each nonwork domain, and the relationships and outcomes that can support and enhance work differently from these other domains. Kirchmeyer (1992) conducted a study to uncover the relationship between participation in nonwork domains such as parenting, community involvement, and recreation and positive nonwork-work spillover. Participants believed that parenting creates a buffer against work problems, while community involvement generated new ideas and enhanced one's value at work, and recreation energized and provided a means to disconnect from problems. Participation in nonwork domains, moreover, helped develop delegation, teamwork, presentation, and self-management skills.

Finally, we should mention inter-individual transmissions of both stress and life satisfaction between spouses/partners, known as *crossover* (Demerouti, Bakker & Schaufeli, 2005; Westman, 2001). In these circumstances, transmission happens not from one domain to another for the same person as in spillover, but one person's experiences affect their spouse within the same or another domain. A study of 191 dual-earner couples with children in the Netherlands showed that life satisfaction of men predicted life satisfaction of their spouses (Demerouti et al., 2005). In other words, women viewed their own life satisfaction as closely connected to that of their partner's. In contrast, men viewed their life satisfaction as being independent of their partner's and based their feelings on work-related aspects. Similar results were obtained in a study of 49 dual-earner couples in the US, where wives were reported to be more reactive to their husband's experience compared to their husbands (Doumas, Margolin & John, 2003). These findings may be explained by the greater social involvement of women and their susceptibility to their significant others' contentment.

Greenhaus and Powell (2006) identified three ways positive outcomes can result from multiple role participation. First, it has *additive effects* on well-being, implying that role accumulation positively influences physical and psychological well-being. Satisfaction with family and with work additionally adds to one's feeling of happiness, life satisfaction, and quality of life. Second, participation in family and work roles can *buffer* the strain experienced in one of the roles; for example having a satisfying family or work life can decrease the impaired well-being in one of the domains. Third, participation in multiple roles can foster the *transfer of positive experiences* from one role to another. Besides, the creation of energy in one role can be transferred to the other, creating new experiences and outcomes (Marks, 1977). Individuals learn certain behaviors in one sphere and can apply them in another. For example, one manager reports, "I think being a mother and having patience and watching someone else grow has made me a better manager" (Greenhaus & Powell). The third mechanism appears to best describe work-family enrichment.

To conclude, scholars have used different terms to describe positive interactions between work and family domains. These concepts are similar to each other because they describe the optimistic side of participating in both domains. Researchers have shown that these factors are distinct from work-family conflict and, for this reason, have unique antecedents and outcomes. We will now review factors that determine positive spillover and describe the benefits of promoting positive interaction between multiple life roles.

ANTECEDENTS OF POSITIVE SPILLOVER

Scholars studying work and family argue that any psychological or environmental resource that can be acquired in one domain (i.e., at work), but that can be utilized in another domain (i.e., family), is likely to promote work and family enrichment (Carlson et al., 2006; Grzywacz & Butler, 2005). Examples of these factors are: job characteristics, personality, and organizational culture. Below we describe these factors and the consequences of positive spillover for both employees and organizations.

Characteristics inherent in a job can promote work-family facilitation (Edward & Rothbard, 2000; Grzywacz & Butler 2005; Thompson & Prottas, 2005; Williams et al., 2006). Specifically, perceived *job autonomy*, defined as discretion over how one's job is to be performed, is related to more positive spillover between work and life domains (Grzywacz & Marks, 2000; Williams, Franche, Ibrahim, Mustard & Layton, 2006). According to Thompson and Prottas, employees with more *decision latitude* experience more positive spillover between life domains as they also experience a greater sense of *control* over the important things in their lives. To illustrate how job autonomy can promote positive spillover we take as an example a full-time employed wife and mother of two children.

Although she could have acquired multitasking skills from her experiences juggling between work and family roles, she may not feel motivated to apply her skills at work if she does not believe she has the freedom to decide where, when, and how to work. Without this flexibility, she would experience high levels of stress and lower levels of satisfaction at work. These factors could hinder her ability to utilize, at full capacity, her broad range of work skills. For example, if she had the freedom to choose where to work, she could prepare a business report at home while supervising her son in completing his homework; however, if she is not allowed to work from home, her ability to multitask becomes limited.

Another important job-related factor that promotes work-family enrichment is *skill variety and complexity* (Grzywacz & Butler, 2005). Workers in complex jobs requiring high levels of social skills and authority are more likely to experience benefits from positive spillover between work and family compared with workers in jobs that do not require social interaction. Returning to the example above, the full-time employed mother of two who is also a project manager and who constantly deals with conflicts between team members at work can use her conflict resolution skills to solve conflicts between her two children. Hence, having a job that is highly complex and that requires high levels of skills can lead to a positive spillover from work to family.

Besides job-related factors, *personal characteristics* also contribute to a positive interaction between multiple life roles (Wayne et al., 2004). Researchers found that extroverted, female, and older employees are more likely to take advantage of the benefits of work-life facilitation (Grzywacz, Almeida & McDonald, 2002; Grzywacz & Marks, 2000). According to Wayne et al., an extroverted person is more likely to utilize resources that can be transferred from work to family or vice versa. Wayne et al. explained that because extroverts experience more positive affect, they are also likely to experience more positive mood compared to introverts. In fact, as previously stated, mood is a spillover factor between different life domains (Hellen & Watson, 2005). For example, Williams and Alliger (1994) found that employed parents who experienced unpleasant moods at work were likely to experience them at home and vice versa. Based on these studies, extroversion and positive affectivity are potential personal factors that promote work-family facilitation; happy and extroverted employees are more likely to utilize psychological or environmental resources to promote work-family enrichment. In fact, a "happy employee" who demonstrates open-mindness, imagination, curiosity, hardiness, positive affectivity, and a secure attachment pattern, viewed as personal resources, might take an active stand in life and choose creative strategies to utilize several resources and promote positive outcomes in both roles (Frone, 2003; Sumer & Knight, 2001). For example, employees who score high on traits such as openness to experience, agreeableness, and conscientiousness are more likely to experience work and family facilitation (Wayne et al.).

Finally, enrichment in a specific domain is also determined by individuals' *self concept* or *values*. For example, Carlson et al. (2006) suggest that employees are more likely to apply resources to their family role if family is more salient to their self-concept. That is, if one's self-concept is more closely connected to family as opposed to work, then positive spillover from family to work is likely to occur and vice versa (Carlson et al.).

Besides personal and job-related factors, environmental or contextual factors are also important determinants of work-family facilitation. Among environmental factors we can count a family-friendly organizational culture, characterized by *supervisor* and *co-worker support* (Mennino, Rubin & Brayfield, 2005; Thompson, & Prottas, 2005). Managers and co-workers who support a family-friendly workplace culture are likely to promote an environment where employees are more likely to take advantage of the benefits derived from work and family interactions (Grzywacz & Marks, 2000; Mennino et al. 2005; Thompson & Prottas, 2005). To illustrate, we can take the example of a single, female employee of a small consulting firm with formal policies allowing employees to work from home. Despite these policies, she felt uncomfortable working from home. Although company policies allowed telecommuting, her co-workers' behaviors created an environment that was not amenable to the implementation of such policy. For example, when she left home from work around 3 p.m. she was faced with sarcastic remarks from her colleagues such as, *"Are you going home already?"* and *"Oh, I wish I were you and I would be able to go home now."* Often, her colleagues would stop at her desk when they were leaving early to emphasize that they were leaving early, but were taking work home. This example shows that formal policies alone are not enough to create a family-friendly working environment. Instead, having an environment supportive of such policies is essential. Several studies have shown that the company culture and more specifically the attitude of the supervisors toward company policies play an important role in the successful implementation of work and family policies (see Andreassi & Thompson in this volume). This is because supervisors decide if and how formal procedures are implemented on a daily basis. Interestingly, Thompson, Beauvais and Lyness (1999) showed that top managers, managers in general, and peers have different attitudes and behaviour for or against employees with family care responsibilities which contribute to a family-supportive or family-hostile culture. Allen (2001) found that work/family policies would reduce work-family conflict and enhance commitment and job satisfaction *only if* employees perceive their organizations as "family-supportive". Additionally, in a study of managers, O'Driscoll, Poelmans, Spector, Cooper, Allen and Sanchez (2004) found that having established organizational policies is no guarantee of reduced levels of conflict or strain in the workforce. Perceptions of the organization as family-supportive and supervisor support for work-family balance are what really make the difference.

In sum, studies investigating the antecedents of positive spillover have demonstrated so far that both individual and environmental factors are important contributors to work-family facilitation. Specifically, friendly and supportive

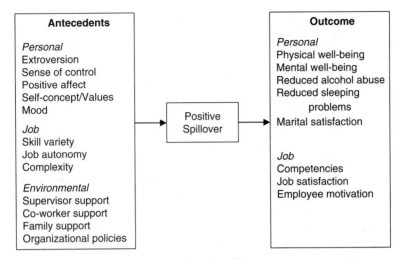

Figure 8.4 Antecedents and consequences of positive spillover

supervisors and co-workers promote an environment amenable to work and family facilitation. Also, several job and personal-related factors can promote positive spillover (Thompson & Prottas, 2005; Wayne et al., 2004). Figure 8.4 describes the antecedents of positive spillover.

CONSEQUENCES OF POSITIVE SPILLOVER

The study of antecedents of positive spillover is important because positive spillover has several benefits both for individuals and for organizations. For example, indicators of work-family facilitation have been associated with enhanced mental and physical well-being, and lower stress (Grzywacz, 2000; Grzywacz et al., 2002; Grzywacz & Bass, 2003; Ruderman et al., 2002). Interestingly, positive spillover has also been linked to a lower likelihood of developing problem drinking behaviors (Grzywacz & Marks, 2000), and also a higher likelihood of developing better sleep quality (Williams et al., 2006). Studies have also shown that employees who experienced work-family enrichment are likely to work above and beyond their required work (Rogers & May, 2003; Thompson & Werner, 1997). Specifically, Thompson and Werner found that employees who believed they could benefit from participating in multiple roles in their lives were also likely to take more initiative at work, help their co-workers, and perform above and beyond the call of duty. Interestingly, employees who perceived role facilitation were more likely to exhibit these behaviors because they were also more likely to commit to the organization. Moreover, women who participate in multiple roles are likely to benefit from multitasking and leadership practices that enhance their performance in management roles (Ruderman et al.). Finally, employees who experience positive spillover are also more likely to be satisfied at their work (Aryee, Srinivas & Hoontan, 2005; Rogers & May, 2003). Rogers and May observed couples for a period of 12 years and found that marital quality and job satisfaction were positively related. Interestingly, they found evidence for positive and negative spillover from marital quality to job satisfaction. Additionally, Aryee et al. found that parents who experienced work and family facilitation were more likely to be satisfied at work and to be more committed to their organization; hence, there is evidence that positive spillover influences job satisfaction.

Given all the benefits for organizations and individuals (listed in Figure 8.4), it is essential that practitioners become aware of the determinants and consequences of positive spillover so that they can better develop strategies to help create a family-friendly culture that promotes work–family enrichment. In the next section, we review useful strategies that companies can implement to promote a better relationship between work and life domains.

IMPLICATIONS FOR FUTURE RESEARCH AND PRACTICE

The research described above demonstrates the importance of exploring positive spillover between various life domains. Above we described the antecedents of positive spillover, as well as the beneficial effects for employees, such as enhanced well-being, increased competence, higher job satisfaction, and greater commitment. What is striking in this research, though, is that the process of facilitation is described with a certain detachment, making an abstraction of the actors behind those processes. The study of personality in relationship to facilitation suggests that certain people are more actively engaged in creating positive spillover, but very little is known about the strategies and processes through which actors actively create positive spillover (Wayne et al., 2004). Books such as *The 7 Habits of Highly Effective Families* (Covey & Covey, 2003) suggest that people can go beyond merely striving to reduce conflict, by looking for ways to find synergies between their personal and professional lives. A study of 221 Canadian managers suggests that the alteration of one's attitudes, rather than those of others, increases efficiency and thus helps coping with multiple roles (Kirchmeyer, 1993). Ideas described by these authors, with some exceptions, are seldom described in academic journals. Even studies that have examined coping with work-family conflict (for a review, see Thompson, Allen, Poelmans & Andreassi, 2007) are typically restricted to the broad categories of problem-focused or emotion-focused coping and rarely address the issue of actively and consciously seeking the transfer of moods, skills, or material benefits from one domain to the other.

Nippert-Eng (1996) distinguishes between the processes of segmentation and integration, suggesting that some individuals consciously strive for boundary separation to keep work and family roles apart, thus also avoiding positive spillover. Other individuals strive to integrate the two worlds. With integration, Nippert-Eng indirectly refers to synergies or transfers—for instance by using time or resources provided in one role (e.g., a company phone) to attend to demands associated with the other role (e.g., to call a school teacher for an appointment). Kossek, Noe and DeMarr (1999) refer to work-family role synthesis as the strategy an individual uses to manage the joint enactment of work and family roles and make a distinction between boundary management and role embracement of multiple roles. Whereas their concept of boundary management is based on Nippert-Eng's work, the concept of role embracement refers to the zeal or intensity with which one enacts roles. These authors do not explicitly comment on cross-fertilization between domains, but it is obvious that this zeal is a function of self-confidence and competence gained in the other domain.

In the decision-process theory of work and family, Poelmans (2005) integrates insights from equity theory and social exchange theory, arguing that work-family conflict is an intermediate state in an ongoing process of evaluating alternative ratios of inputs, costs, resources, and rewards associated with both work and family domains. This theory explains why multiple roles can be salutary instead of detrimental. Rewards from work (e.g., use of a company car) can be used as valuable inputs for the family (to transport children to school); rewards from family (e.g., support of a spouse) can offset the costs experienced from work (e.g., strain as a consequence of a conflict with a supervisor spills over to the family); or rewards obtained from work (e.g., competency gained during a time management training at work) increase the resources of the actor, which increases his/her ability to cope with family issues (to be better organized and as a consequence more available at home). Second, the decision-process theory of work-family conflict offers a language to understand positive spillover: work-family enhancement occurs when rewards gained in one domain (e.g., work) positively affect experiences or performance in the other domain (e.g., family). Negative spillover can be reduced by preventing unwanted consequences or costs in one domain that would affect the other domain. Decision-makers can scrutinize the implications of their choices and mentors can help them to do so. An example is a human resource manager who helps a high-potential employee to seriously consider the implications of accepting a promotion that involves frequent traveling on his capacity to attend to caring responsibilities. Company policies like flexible work arrangements or work-life programs can be directed at increasing rewards (by offering fringe benefits like medical insurance for family members), reducing costs (e.g., by offering a stress management program to help employees avoid the spillover of negative mood to the private sphere), or reducing demands or inputs (e.g., by offering childcare or on-site services, so that employees have to put in less time commuting between kindergarten, work, and home, or running errands).

Companies can indeed support their employees in their efforts to create synergies and take an active stand in the promotion of work-family enrichment in their employees' lives. For example, training programs focused on stress and coping strategies could be beneficial to employees and organizations. Kirchmeyer's (1993) study of the coping strategies used by men and women suggests that what is important is not how actively men and women are involved in nonwork activities, but how well they cope and manage both life domains. Certain coping strategies would not only reduce work conflict but also encourage the transfer of skills and knowledge acquired from one domain to another. As previously stated, women who participate in multiple roles acquire leadership skills that benefit their organization (Ruderman et al., 2002). Hence, it is in the interest of companies to provide supports and services to their employees. Other useful training programs in promoting positive spillover are those that teach employees conflict management or win-win negotiation skills.

Although the implementation of work-family policies and training programs is a crucial strategy to promote work-family facilitation, it is important to note that what really creates an impact, by enhancing commitment and job satisfaction, is the employees' perception of the organization as supportive of work-family balance (Allen, 2001; Mennino et al., 2005). As mentioned previously, informal organizational support has been found to promote positive spillover (Thompson & Prottas, 2005). Hence, environmental factors (e.g., managers' and co-workers' support) are necessary for a successful implementation of family-friendly policies. Research points out that supervisors play a key role in how employees experience the workplace and whether they believe that their organizations care for their well-being (Dormann & Zapf, 1999; Shanock & Eisenberger, 2006). For instance, in a private conversation a manager may find out that an associate is suffering severely from the consequences of a divorce and is trying his best to keep up with work, despite the constant hassles associated with a divorce. Instead of ignoring the needs of this employee or assuming that he will solve his own problems, the supervisor could refer her colleague to the company lawyer or to the employee assistance program of the firm so that an expert counsellor can attend him in resolving financial, legal, or social problems that arose during the divorce. As pointed out in the decision-process theory, this positive spillover of company resources will be considered as much more than a "perk" by the employee. It will create a bond of trust and support, which will most likely translate in an exchange relationship, and by a reciprocation by the employee in commitment and support to his company a year down the line, when the problems are smoothed out. In this effort, companies should look for a fit between employees' needs and the support they can offer. For instance, Ernst & Young encourages female employees taking a leave to participate in part-time projects to keep in touch with the firm (Ramachandran, 2005). Segmentors may not be very happy with this arrangement, whereas integrators could be enthusiastic. Instead of offering this as a general work-life policy, it is recommended that managers consider the needs and personal situation of each employee and evaluate the costs and benefits for the firm of various ways of providing support and flexibility (Poelmans & Beham, 2005). As much as each employee is unique in what circumstances create work-family conflict, each employee has a unique capacity for transferring specific moods, skills, or resources. As much as some policies can be very effective for reducing conflict without incurring too much expense for the company, some policies for creating enrichment can be easy to implement. For instance, instead of inviting spouses to company training, which could be too costly for the firm, the training department could include cases of work-family conflict in the content examples used when training business competencies like negotiation and conflict management. Finally, it is important to stress that for a successful implementation of family-friendly policies and training programs, it is necessary to obtain support from upper management and encourage an organizational culture that is amenable to the use and implementation of such policies (Mennino et al., 2005).

To conclude, whereas our understanding of the positive effects of work-family facilitation is growing, there is, as yet, little research that examines the conscious tactics and strategies individuals and companies use to create facilitation, and to improve the fit between company benefits and employee needs. Both academics and practitioners are invited to systematically explore these strategies in order to go beyond what seems to have been the sole focus until now: to avoid conflict. For example, practitioners and researchers alike could advocate for the importance of encouraging an organizational culture that supports formal work-family policies (Thompson, Beauvais & Lyness, 1999). Unfortunately, little is known about the specific strategies that can be used to promote such a positive work-family culture in organizations. This may require some creative thinking, taking into account suggestions from work-family facilitation and enrichment theory, and decision-making and coping; but more than anything, it will require actively looking for "out-of-the box" solutions that fit the needs of individual employees and the financial, material, and human resources available in each workplace.

REFERENCES

Allen (2001). Family-supportive work environments: The role of organizational perceptions. *Journal of Vocational Behavior, 58*, 414–435.

Andreassi, J.K & Thompson, C.A. (2008). Work-family culture: Current research and future directions This volume

Aryee, S. Srinivas, E.S. & Hoontan, H. (2005). Rhythms of life: Antecedents and outcomes of work-family balance in employed parents. *Journal of Applied Psychology, 90*, 132–146.

Barnett, R. C. (1998). Toward a review and reconceptualization of the work/family literature. *Genetic, Social, and General Psychology Monographs, 124*, 125–182.

Barnett, R. C. & Hyde, J. S. (2001). Women, men, work, and family. *American Psychologist, 56*, 781–796.

Bond, J. T., Galinsky, E. & Swangberg, J.E. (1998). *The 1997 National Study of the Changing Workforce.* New York: Families and Work Institute.

Carlson, D. S., Kacmar, K. M., Wayne, J.H. & Grzywacz, J. G. (2006). Measuring the positive side of the work-family interface: Development and validation of a work-family enrichment scale. *Journal of Vocational Behavior, 68*, 131–164.

Covey, S. R. & Covey, M. C. (2003). *The 7 Habits of Highly Effective Families.* New York: Golden Books Publishing Co.

Crouter, A. (1984). Spillover from family to work: The neglected side of the work-family interface. *Human Relations, 37*, 425–442.

Demerouti, E., Bakker, A. B. & Schaufeli, W. B. (2005). Spillover and crossover of exhaustion and life satisfaction among dual-earner parents. *Journal of Vocational Behavior, 67*, 266–289.

Doumas, D. M., Margolin, G. & John, R. S. (2003). The relationship between daily marital interaction, work, and health-promoting behaviors in dual-earner couples: An extension of the work-family spillover model. *Journal of Family Issues, 24*(1), 3–20.

Dormann, C. & Zapf, D. (1999). Social support, social stressors at work, and depressive symptoms: Testing for main and moderating effects with structural equations in a three-wave longitudinal study. *Journal of Applied Psychology, 84*, 874–884.

Edwards, J. R. & Rothbard, N. P. (2000). Mechanisms linking work and family: Clarifying the relationship between work and family constructs. *Academy of Management Review, 25*, 178–199.

Froberg, D., Gjerdingen, D. & Preston, M. (1986). Multiple role and women's mental health: What have we learned? *Women and Health Review, 11*, 79–96.

Frone, M. R. (2003). Work-family balance. In J. C. Quick & L. E. Tetrick (eds), *Handbook of Occupational Health Psychology* (pp. 143–162). Washington, DC: American Psychological Association.

Frone, M. R., Russell, M. & Cooper, M. L. (1992a). Antecedents and outcomes of work-family conflict: Testing a model of the work-family interface. *Journal of Applied Psychology, 77*, 65–78.

Frone, M. R., Russell, M., & Cooper, M. L. (1992b). Prevalence of work-family conflict: Are work and family boundaries asymmetrically permeable? *Journal of Organizational Behavior, 13*, 723–729.

Frone, M. R., Yardley, J. K. & Markel, K. S. (1997). Developing and testing an integrative model of the work-family interface. *Journal of Vocational Behavior, 50*, 145–167.

Greenhaus, J. H. & Parasuraman, S. (1999). Research on work, family, and gender: Current status and future directions. In G. N. Powell (ed.), *Handbook of Gender and Work* (pp. 391–412). Newbury Park, CA: Sage.

Greenhaus, J. H. & Powell, G. N. (2006). When work and family are allies: A theory of work-family enrichment. *Academy of Management Review, 31*(1), 72–92.

Grzywacz, J. G. (2000). Work-family spillover and health during midlife: Is managing conflict everything? *American Journal of Health Promotion, 14*, 236–243.

Grzywacz, J. G., Almeida, D. M. & McDonald, D. A. (2002). Work-family spillover and daily reports of work and family stress in the adult labor force. *Family Relations, 51*, 28–36.

Grzywacz, J. G. & Bass, B. L. (2003). Work, family, and mental health: Testing different models of work-family fit. *Journal of Marriage and Family, 65*, 248–261.

Grzywacz, J. G. & Butler, A.B. (2005). The impact of job characteristics on work-to-family facilitation: Testing a theory and distinguishing a construct. *Journal of Occupational Health Psychology, 10*, 97–109.

Grzywacz, J. G. & Marks, N. F. (2000). Reconceptualizing the work-family interface: An ecological perspective on the correlates of positive and negative spillover between work and family. *Journal of Occupational Health Psychology, 1*, 111–126.

Hanson, G. C., Colton, C. L. & Hammer, L. B. (2003). Development and validation of a multidimensional scale of work-family positive spillover. Paper presented at the 18th Annual Meeting of SIOP, Orlando.

Hellen, D. & Watson, D. (2005). The dynamic spillover of satisfaction between work and marriage: The role of time and mood. *Journal of Applied Psychology, 90*, 1273–1279.

Kirchmeyer, C. (1992). Perceptions of nonwork-to-work spillover: Challenging the common view of conflict-ridden domain relationships. *Basic and Applied Social Psychology, 13*, 231–249.

Kirchmeyer, C. (1993). Nonwork-to-work spillover: A more balanced view of the experiences and coping of professional women and men. *Sex Roles: A Journal of Research, 28*, 531–552.

Kossek, E. E., Noe, R. A. & DeMarr, B. J. (1999). Work-family role synthesis: Individual and organizational determinants. *The International Journal of Conflict Management, 10* (2, April), 102–129.

Lambert, S. J. (1990). Processes linking work and family: A critical review and research agenda. *Human Relations, 43*, 239–257.

Marks, S. R. (1977). Multiple roles and role strain: Some notes on human energy, time and commitment. *American Sociological Review, 42*, 921–936.

Mennino, S. F., Rubin, B. A. & Brayfield, A. (2005). Home-to-job and job-to-home spillover: The impact of company policies and workplace culture. *The Sociological Quarterly, 46*, 107–135.

Nippert-Eng, C. E. (1996). *Home and Work: Negotiating Boundaries Through Everyday Life*. Chicago: University of Chicago Press.

O'Driscoll, M., Poelmans, S., Spector, P. E., Cooper, C. L., Allen, T. D. & Sanchez, J. (2004). The buffering effect of family-responsive interventions, perceived organizational and supervisor support in the work-family conflict-strain relationship. *International Journal of Stress Management, 10*(4), 326–344.

Poelmans, S. A. Y. (2005). The decision process theory of work and family. In E. E. Kossek & S. J. Lambert (eds), *Work and Life Integration: Organizational, Cultural, and Individual Perspectives* (pp. 263–285). Mahwah, NJ: Lawrence Erlbaum.

Poelmans, S. & Beham, B. (2005). A conceptual model of antecedents and consequences of managerial work/life policy allowance decisions. Presented at the Founding Conference of the International Center of Work and Family. Barcelona, Spain.

Poelmans S., O'Driscoll, M. & Beham, B. (2005). A review of international research in the field of work and family. In: Steven A.Y. Poelmans (ed.), *Work and Family: An International Research Perspective* (pp. 3–46). Mahwah NJ: Lawrence Erlbaum.

Ramachandran, N. (2005). Career spotlight: Mommy track can derail career. *Newsweek*. http://www. usnews.com/usnews/biztech/articles/050718/18career.htm

Rogers, S. J. & May, D. C. (2003). Spillover between marital quality and job satisfaction: Long-term patterns and gender differences. *Journal of Marriage and Family, 65*, 482–495.

Ruderman, M. N., Ohlott, P. J., Panzer, K. & King, S. N. (2002). Benefits of multiple roles for managerial women. *Academy of Management Journal, 45*, 369–386.

Shanock, L. R. & Eisenberger, R. (2006). When supervisors feel supported: Relationships with subordinates' perceived supervisor support, perceived organizational support, and performance. *Journal of Applied Psychology, 91*, 689–695.

Sieber, S. D. (1974). Toward a theory of role accumulation. *American Sociological Review, 39*, 567–578.

Sumer, H. C. & Knight, P. A. (2001). How do people with different attachment styles balance work and family? A personality perspective on work-family linkage. *Journal of Applied Psychology, 86*, 653–663.

Thompson, C. A., Beauvais, L. L. & Lyness, K. S. (1999). When work-family benefits are not enough: The influence of work-family culture on benefit utilization, organizational attachment, and work-family conflict. *Journal of Vocational Behavior, 54*, 392–415.

Thompson, C. A. and Prottas, D. J. (2005). Relationships among organizational family support, job autonomy, perceived control, and employee well-being. *Journal of Occupational Health Psychology, 10*, 100–118.

Tompson, H. B. & Werner J. M. (1997). The impact of role conflict/facilitation on core and discretionary behaviors: Testing a mediated model. *Journal of Management, 23*, 583–601.

Wayne, J. H., Musisca, N. & Fleeson, W. (2004). Considering the role of personality in the work-family experience: Relationships of the big five to work-family conflict and facilitation. *Journal of Vocational Behavior, 64,* 108–130.

Westman, M. (2001). Stress and strain crossover. *Human Relations, 54,* 557–591.

Williams, K. J. & Alliger, G. M. (1994). Role stressors, mood spillover, and perceptions of work-family conflict in employed parents. *The Academy of Management Journal, 37,* 837–868.

Williams, A., Franche, R. L., Ibrahim, S., Mustard, C. A. & Layton, F. R. (2006). Examining the relationship between work-family spillover and sleep quality. *Journal of Occupational Health Psychology, 11,* 27–37.

CHAPTER 9

Work-Related Outcomes of the Work-Family Interface: Why Organizations Should Care

Jay M. Dorio, Rebecca H. Bryant and Tammy D. Allen
Department of Psychology, University of South Florida

INTRODUCTION

Despite prior claims that work and family are independent domains (Blood & Wolfe, 1960), few researchers or laypersons today would dispute their interdependence. Research has demonstrated that the work-family interface relates to a variety of variables, with implications for individuals, families, and organizations (e.g., Allen, Herst, Bruck & Sutton, 2000). This chapter focuses on work-related outcomes in particular, providing support for the notion that organizations cannot afford to ignore the interconnectedness between work and family.

The objective of this chapter is to review the existing literature regarding outcomes associated with the work-family interface. The chapter is organized as follows. First, work-related outcomes pertaining to the "negative side" (i.e., work-family conflict) are reviewed. We then review outcomes associated with the "positive side" (i.e., work-family enhancement) of the work-family interface. Next, a summary of multinational studies is presented. Finally, a summary and critique of the literature, as well as directions for future research, are provided. Throughout the chapter, work-related outcomes are grouped into four categories: job attitudes, career outcomes, performance-related outcomes, and withdrawal behaviors and intentions.

WORK-FAMILY CONFLICT AND WORK-RELATED OUTCOMES

Although researchers have suggested a variety of possible mechanisms linking work and family domains (see Edwards & Rothbard, 2000), a depletion argument underlies the majority of research. Drawing from a resource drain model (Edwards & Rothbard, 2000) and role theory (Kahn, Wolfe, Quinn, Snoek & Rosenthal, 1964), the depletion argument assumes that engaging in multiple roles leads to role conflict, given that individuals have a fixed amount of time and energy. Due to the emphasis on this viewpoint, research linking work-family conflict (WFC) to work-related outcomes dominates the literature. A summary of this body of research is discussed in this section.

JOB ATTITUDES

Job Satisfaction

The relationship between WFC and job satisfaction has received a wealth of empirical investigation, with the vast majority of research indicating that greater WFC relates to less job satisfaction. Meta-analytic reviews have reported weighted-mean correlations of $-.12$ to $-.24$ for WIF, $-.14$ for FIW, and $-.27$ for bi-directional WFC (Allen et al., 2000; Kossek & Ozeki, 1998; Mesmer-Magnus & Viswesvaran, 2005). It is important to note that the majority of studies employed global measures of job satisfaction, rather than facet-level or composite scales.

WIF has been negatively associated with global measures of job satisfaction in studies conducted in the US (e.g., Allen, 2001; Netemeyer, Maxham & Pullig, 2005; Thompson & Prottas, 2005), India (Aryee, Srinivas & Tan, 2005), Hong Kong (Ngo & Lui, 1999), Singapore (Aryee, 1992), and the Netherlands (Demerouti & Geurts, 2004). WIF has also been negatively associated with composite measures of job satisfaction in the US (e.g., Anderson, Coffey & Byerly, 2002). In one of the few studies that measured job satisfaction at the facet-level, Boles, Howard and Donofrio (2001) found that WIF related to satisfaction with work and promotion but not to satisfaction with co-workers, highlighting the multidimensionality of the job satisfaction construct. Moreover, Bruck, Allen and Spector (2002) found that WIF related to global, composite, and facet measures of job satisfaction, though relationships were significantly greater for composite versus global job satisfaction. Differential relationships have also been found across dimensions of WIF, with behavior-based WIF demonstrating the strongest relationship with job satisfaction (Bruck et al., 2002).

Other studies have examined FIW or bi-directional WFC and job satisfaction, uncovering similar results. Negative relationships have been reported between FIW and job satisfaction using samples from the US (e.g., Anderson et al., 2002; Netemeyer et al., 2005; Thompson & Prottas, 2005), Hong Kong (Aryee, Luk, Leung & Lo, 1999), and India (Aryee et al., 2005). At the facet level, FIW has been associated with satisfaction with pay, work, co-workers, and supervision (Boles et al., 2001). Type of FIW has also been investigated. Carlson, Kacmar and Williams (2000) found a relationship between global job satisfaction and strain-based FIW only. Bruck et al. (2002) found the strongest relationship between behavior-based FIW and job satisfaction. Using bi-directional measures of WFC, significant negative relationships have been found in studies conducted in Canada (Beatty, 1996), Hong Kong (Hang-yue, Foley & Loi, 2005), Israel (Drory & Shamir, 1988), and

Singapore (Chan, Lai, Ko & Boey, 2000). Although the majority of research has demonstrated a significant relationship between job satisfaction and WFC, several studies found no relationship (e.g., Lyness & Thompson, 1997).

An increasing number of studies have investigated moderating and mediating variables of the WFC–job satisfaction relationship. Based on samples from the US (Grandey, Cordeiro & Crouter, 2005) and Finland (Kinnunen, Geurts & Mauno, 2004), WIF predicted job satisfaction one year later for women but not men. In terms of type of satisfaction, Boles, Wood and Johnson (2003) found that WIF predicted satisfaction with work, co-workers, and policy for women, but satisfaction with pay, supervisor, promotion, and policy for men. Finally, research has found the WFC–job satisfaction relationship to be partially mediated by value attainment (Perrewe, Hochwarter & Kiewitz, 1999) and by job stress (Judge, Boudreau & Bretz, 1994).

Overall, research has supported a negative relationship between WFC and job satisfaction, using diverse samples and measures of WFC/job satisfaction. Although few researchers examined job satisfaction at the facet level, those that did uncovered differential relationships across dimensions. Thus, future research should continue to explore how relationships vary across facets of job satisfaction.

ORGANIZATIONAL COMMITMENT

Organizational commitment has also received much empirical attention, with research indicating that greater WFC relates to less organizational commitment. In terms of meta-analytic findings, Allen et al. (2000) reported a weighted-mean correlation of −.23 between commitment and WIF, and Kossek and Ozeki (1999) reported weighted-mean correlations of −.05 for WIF, −.17 for FIW, and −.27 for WFC.

Studies have found a negative association between WIF and organizational commitment in the US (e.g., Hogan, Lambert, Jenkins & Wambold, 2006; Netemeyer, Boles & McMurrian, 1996; Netemeyer et al., 2005) and India (Aryee et al., 2005), though others have reported no relationship (e.g., Geurts, Taris, Kompier, Dikkers, van Hooff & Kinnunen, 2005). Similarly, FIW has been negatively related to organizational commitment across diverse samples from the US (e.g., Carlson et al., 2000; Netemeyer et al., 1996; Netemeyer et al., 2005), India (Aryee et al., 2005), and the Netherlands (e.g., Geurts et al., 2005). On the other hand, null results have also been found between FIW and commitment (Hill, 2005; Hogan et al, 2006). Carlson et al. (2000) used a multidimensional measure of WFC, finding that only behavior-based FIW related to commitment. Finally, several studies found bi-directional measures of WFC related negatively to affective commitment (e.g., Allen, 2001; Blau, 1995) and to general organizational commitment (Good, Sisler & Gentry, 1988).

While research has supported a negative link between WFC and organizational commitment, most studies have focused on general or affective commitment, rather than continuance or normative. Meta-analytic support for divergent relationships across types of commitment was found by Meyer, Stanley, Herscovitch and Topolnytsky (2002), with weighted-mean correlations of −.20 for affective, −.04 for normative, and .24 for continuance, across various measures of WFC. Similarly, Lyness and Thompson (1997) found that WIF negatively related to affective commitment, positively related to continuance commitment, and was unrelated to normative commitment. Additionally, Casper, Martin, Buffardi and Erdwins (2002) reported a positive association between WIF and continuance commitment, but no relationship for affective commitment. Thus, most research supports a negative association between organizational commitment and WFC, though the relationship seems to vary by type of commitment.

CAREER OUTCOMES

Career Satisfaction

While much research has examined the relationship between WFC and job attitudes, relatively little has investigated career-related attitudes. Allen et al. (2000) reported a weighted-mean correlation of −.04 across two studies. Null results have also been reported in other studies (e.g., Beutell & Wittig-Berman, 1999; Lyness & Thompson, 1997). However, more recently, Martins, Eddleston, and Veiga (2002) found that WIF negatively related to women's career satisfaction, but for men it was related to the career satisfaction of older men only. Parasuraman and Simmers (2001) found WFC negatively related to career satisfaction among organizationally-employed, but not among self-employed individuals. These moderators may help explain the null findings in previous studies.

Studies examining the relationship between FIW and career satisfaction have produced more consistent results. Both Beutell and Wittig-Berman (1999) and Parasuraman, Purohit, Godshalk, and Beutell (1996) reported a negative relationship between the two variables. Focusing on career commitment, Carmeli (2003) found that Israeli chief financial officers high in emotional intelligence (EI) demonstrated a negative relationship between FIW and career commitment whereas a positive relationship existed for those low in EI. Overall, career satisfaction appears to have a stronger relationship with FIW than WIF. However, given the paucity of research, as well as the potential for moderators, more studies are needed.

CAREER SUCCESS

Even less research has examined career success as an outcome of WFC. Peluchette (1993) found that WIF and subjective career success were negatively related among full-time faculty members. More recently, Ngo and Lui (1999) found a negative association between WIF and subjective career achievement in a sample of Hong Kong managers. Gender differences have also been uncovered, though inconsistently. While Ngo and Lui (1999) found that the relationship between WIF and subjective career achievement was stronger for women, Aryee (1993) found that WIF (job-parent and job-spouse conflict) was positively related to perceived lack of career progress among husbands but not wives. Using an objective index of success, Aryee and Luk (1996) found a positive relationship between WIF and monthly salary among wives but not husbands, with a sample of dual-earner couples in Hong Kong.

In terms of FIW, Chi-Ching (1992) found that family-related barriers to work (e.g., a lack of spousal support regarding respondent's career) was not predictive of career mobility or salary among female business graduates in Singapore. Ngo and Lui (1999) found that the relationship between FIW and subjective career achievement was stronger for men than for women. Butler and Skattebo (2004) provided further support for the notion that FIW differentially impacts career success across gender in a laboratory study. Specifically, they found participants gave lower reward recommendations to a hypothetical male manager experiencing FIW (as compared to a male manager without FIW). Conversely, no differences were found for females. Finally, Carnicer, Sanchez, Perez and Jimenez (2004) found a bi-directional measure of WFC was negatively related to functional mobility but unrelated to upward mobility among employees in Spain. Thus, the literature on WFC and career success has produced mixed results, with findings varying by direction of conflict, gender, and the operationalization of career success.

PERFORMANCE-RELATED OUTCOMES

In-role Performance and Productivity

Results of studies examining WFC and in-role performance have been mixed. In terms of meta-analytic results, Allen et al. (2000) reported a weighted mean correlation of $-.12$ between WIF and performance, while Kossek and Ozeki (1999) reported weighted-mean correlations of $-.03$ for WIF, $-.45$ for FIW, and $-.19$ for bi-directional WFC, though the latter two were based on only one study each. Although the majority of studies have used self-ratings of performance, supervisor ratings have been used as well.

Significant negative relationships have been found between WIF and self-rated performance among employed adults (Frone, Yardley & Markel, 1997); between job-parent conflict and self-reported work quality among married professional women in Singapore (Aryee, 1992); and between WIF and supervisor ratings of performance among online electronics retailers (Kossek, Colquitt & Noe, 2001). Conversely, null findings have been reported between both job-spouse and job-homemaker conflict and self-reported work quality (Aryee, 1992); between

WIF and self-reported sales performance among accountants and female real estate agents (Greenhaus, Bedeian & Mossholder, 1987; Netemeyer et al., 1996, respectively); and between WIF and supervisor-ratings of performance in a sample of New Zealand salespeople (Bhuian, Menguc & Borsboom, 2005) and professionals in Fortune 500 firms (Kossek, Lautsch & Eaton, 2006). Kossek et al. (2001) found a significant, albeit small, positive correlation between WIF and performance among employees of a public Midwestern university.

Research examining FIW and performance has produced mixed results as well. Researchers have found negative relationships between FIW and self-rated performance (Kossek et al., 2001; Netemeyer et al., 1996), as well as supervisor ratings of performance (Netemeyer et al., 2005). Conversely, Carmeli (2003), using self-reported performance, and Kossek et al. (2006), utilizing supervisor ratings of performance, found no relationship. Furthermore, in the experiment described previously, Butler and Skattebo (2004) found that FIW negatively impacted performance ratings for males but not females.

Finally, a few studies have utilized bi-directional WFC measures, or examined potential mediators of the WFC-performance relationship. Kossek and Nichol (1992) found a negative relationship between WFC and supervisor-rated performance. Similarly, inter-role conflict was negatively related to work quality/effort among automotive retail employees, and the relationship was mediated by job satisfaction (Hom & Kinicki, 2001). Netemeyer et al. (2005) found support for a mediator as well, with job stress mediating the relationship between WIF and performance.

Although several studies have examined the impact of WFC on performance, more research is necessary given the inconsistent findings across directions of WFC and sources of performance ratings. It seems important to uncover contextual factors that impact these relationships. Additionally, it is critical to note that for some researchers, a performance decrement is inherent to the conceptualization of WFC. For example, Greenhaus, Allen and Spector (2006) define WFC as "the extent to which experiences in one role result in diminished performance in the other role" (p. 83), which corresponds to Edwards and Rothbard's (2000) proposition that role performance is a necessary component of interference. Other studies have not utilized this definition, instead considering WFC as occurring when the demands in one role make it *difficult* to meet the requirements of the other role. Thus, it is important to consider the definition of WFC when discussing its impact on performance, given these discrepancies.

Organizational Citizenship Behavior (OCB)

A few studies have examined the WFC–OCB relationship; generally finding that greater WFC relates to less OCB. Netemeyer et al. (2005) reported that both WIF and FIW negatively related to supervisor ratings of extra-role performance.

Similarly, Bragger, Rodriguez-Srednicki, Kutcher, Indovino and Rosner (2005) found that WFC negatively related to self-rated OCB among teachers. Tompson and Werner (1997) found a negative association between role conflict and OCB (self-report); however, their measure of role conflict placed conflict and facilitation on a continuum, thus blurring the results. In another study, Bolino and Turnley (2005) suggested that engaging in more OCB would increase WFC. The authors did find a positive relationship between spouse ratings of individual initiative (a dimension of OCB) and WFC. However, this study, as most research in this area, was cross-sectional, so causality could not be determined. Researchers have also examined potential mediators between WFC and OCB, including job stress, organizational commitment, and job satisfaction (Netemeyer et al., 2005; Tompson & Werner, 1997). Among the tested mediators, support was only found for organizational commitment, and this only held for the loyalty dimension of OCB (Tompson & Werner, 1997). Although the mechanisms underlying the relationship between WFC and OCB remain unclear, research generally converges to support a negative association between the variables. However, more research is needed to determine whether relationships differ depending on the direction of WFC and the type of OCB, and longitudinal research is necessary to offer insight into the direction of causality.

WITHDRAWAL BEHAVIORS AND INTENTIONS

Absenteeism

Although research has revealed a positive relationship between WFC and absenteeism, findings are by no means conclusive. In fact, even meta-analytic reviews have reported divergent results. Allen et al. (2000) found no relationship between WIF and absenteeism ($r = -.02$) using two studies. On the other hand, Kossek and Ozeki (1999) found one study which reported a positive relationship between absenteeism and WIF ($r = .18$) and reported a positive relationship between absenteeism and a bi-directional measure of WFC ($r = .17$) across four studies. Finally, Mesmer-Magnus and Viswesvaran (2005) reported a weighted-mean correlation of .18 between both FIW and WIF and a composite of organizational withdrawal, which included tardiness and turnover.

The research linking WFC and absenteeism appears to be strongest for studies using bi-directional WFC measures, while the relationships between WIF/FIW and absenteeism are more tenuous. For example, researchers have reported null results between WIF and both self-reported absenteeism (e.g., Gignac, Kelloway & Gottlieb, 1996; Kirchmeyer & Cohen, 1999) and company records of absenteeism (Boyar, Maertz & Pearson, 2005; Cohen & Kirchmeyer, 2005), across diverse samples in the US, Canada, and Israel. Additionally, Hackett, Bycio and Guion (1989) found that WIF was related to a desire to be absent but not to actual absences, and Hammer, Bauer and Grandey (2003) found that WIF related to self-reported absences among husbands but not wives. Thus, despite the generally null findings, there may be certain situations in which WIF and absenteeism are positively related.

Research examining FIW and absenteeism has found positive, null, and even negative relationships. Positive relationships have been reported, utilizing self-report measures of absenteeism, in the US (e.g., Anderson et al., 2002) and Canada (e.g., Gignac et al., 1996; Kirchmeyer & Cohen, 1999). On the other hand, Hammer et al. (2003) found that FIW was unrelated to self-reported absences for both husbands and wives, but wives' FIW was negatively related to husbands' absences.

Studies examining the relationships between bi-directional measures of WFC and absenteeism have tended to reveal positive findings. Kossek (1990), examining public utility workers, and Kossek, DeMarr, Bachman, Bachman and Kollar (1993), studying eldercare providers, found positive relationships between WFC and self-reported absenteeism. Additionally, Kossek and Nichol (1992) found a positive relationship between WFC and supervisor ratings of absenteeism, and Hom and Kinicki (2001) found that inter-role conflict impacted self-reported job avoidance (which included absenteeism) among employees at an automotive retail store. Conversely, no relationship was found between WFC and self-reported absenteeism by Thomas and Ganster (1995).

Despite the generally positive findings between bi-directional WFC and absenteeism, Kossek and Ozeki (1999) point out that results differ depending on the measure of absenteeism. Specifically, studies conducted by Kossek and colleagues asked about family-related absences in particular, and their findings tended to reveal stronger relationships. Thus, it is important to consider how absenteeism is measured when assessing its relationship with work-family variables. The relationship may also vary by gender. Using company records of absenteeism, Boyar et al. (2005) found that women with high WIF or FIW had absenteeism, whereas there was little relationship among men. Overall, the literature has produced mixed results regarding WFC and absenteeism, and more research is needed before conclusions can be drawn.

Partial Absenteeism

Partial absenteeism includes such behaviors as arriving to work late, leaving early, or experiencing family-related interruptions while at work. Although no reviews have focused on the impact of WFC on partial absenteeism, Mesmer-Magnus and Viswesvaran (2005) included tardiness in their analysis of organizational withdrawal behaviors (see "Absenteeism" for a summary). Studies have examined the impact of both WIF and FIW on indices of partial absenteeism, generally finding a positive relationship between these variables.

WIF has been positively associated with leaving work early (Boyar et al., 2005), though the same study found no relationship between WIF and tardiness. WIF has also been related to interruptions from work (husbands and wives) and lateness (wives only) in a sample of dual-earner couples (Hammer et al., 2003), and work-eldercare conflict has been related to partial absenteeism (Barling, MacEwan, Kelloway & Higginbottom, 1994). In a study spanning 20 days, work-parent conflict was positively correlated with partial absenteeism, though SEM results were not significant (Hepburn & Barling, 1996). Barrah, Schultz, Baltes and Stolz (2004) also reported null results regarding starting late/leaving early among eldercare providers.

Regarding FIW, Barrah et al. (2004) found a positive relationship between FIW and starting late/leaving early among men but not women, and Hepburn and Barling (1996) found FIW (parent-work conflict) positively related to partial absenteeism. Moreover, Hammer et al. (2003) found that FIW positively related to work interruptions but not lateness. Interestingly, the study also found crossover effects, with husband FIW predicting wife lateness, and wife FIW being related to husband interruptions.

Two moderators that have been examined include gender and kinship responsibilities. Boyar et al. (2005) found a significant interaction between WIF/FIW and gender in predicting leaving early; specifically, women with high WIF/FIW were more likely to leave work early than were all other groups. They also found that the relationship between WIF and leaving early was stronger when kinship responsibilities were high. Finally, the relationship between FIW and tardiness was moderated by kinship responsibilities as well, with the highest tardiness being exhibited for individuals with low FIW and low kinship responsibilities. The authors suggest that this group may have been less committed to their jobs. Future research should examine this possibility and continue to study the relationship between WFC and partial absenteeism.

Turnover

A great deal of research has examined the relationship between WFC, particularly WIF, and turnover intentions, consistently finding a positive relationship. Allen et al. 's (2000) review found that, among the work-related outcomes, turnover intentions had the highest relationship with WIF ($r = .29$). Similarly, Kossek and Ozeki (1999) reported that turnover intentions related to WIF ($r = .32$) and FIW ($r = .17$). Mesmer-Magnus and Viswesvaran (2005) included turnover intentions in their composite of organizational withdrawal as well, as summarized earlier. While these reviews emphasize the positive relationship between WFC and turnover intentions, studies examining actual turnover found weaker results, as described below.

Positive relationships between WIF and turnover intentions have been reported among diverse samples in the US (e.g., Batt & Valcour, 2003; Netemeyer et al., 1996), Canada (e.g., Kirchmeyer & Cohen, 1999), and in a multi-country study that examined married expatriates in 46 countries (Shaffer, Harrison, Gilley & Luk, 2001). Additionally, Kelloway, Gottlieb and Barham (1999) found that strain-based WIF correlated with turnover intentions, though time-based WIF did not. Two studies examined WIF and actual turnover. Specifically, Cohen and Kirchmeyer (2005) found that WIF was unrelated to turnover among Israeli nurses, and Greenhaus, Parasuraman and Collins (2001) found that WIF did not relate to withdrawal from public accounting 22 months later.

Fewer studies have investigated FIW and turnover intentions/decisions, but the results have shown positive relationships. FIW positively related to turnover intentions in the US (e.g., Kossek et al., 2006; Netemeyer et al., 1996), and across multiple countries (Shaffer et al., 2001). Null relationships have also been found (e.g., Greenhaus et al., 2001; Netemeyer et al., 1996). Kelloway et al. (1999) found that strain-based but not time-based FIW related to turnover intentions six months later.

Results of studies using bi-directional measures of WFC have mirrored the results for WIF, exhibiting a positive relationship that is stronger for intentions than actual turnover. Positive relationships have been found in the US (e.g., Good et al., 1988) and Hong Kong (e.g., Hang-yue et al., 2005). Moreover, Hom and Kinicki (2001) found that inter-role conflict led to withdrawal cognitions, which predicted actual turnover, and Greenhaus, Collins, Singh and Parasuraman (1997) found a positive relationship between WFC and actual turnover as well.

Mediators of the relationship between WFC and turnover intent have also been examined, with researchers finding support for job satisfaction (Hom & Kinicki, 2001), stress symptoms (Kirchmeyer & Cohen, 1999), emotional exhaustion, and burnout (Hang-yue et al., 2005). In terms of moderators, Shaffer et al. (2001) found that the relationships between WIF/FIW and withdrawal cognitions were exacerbated by high affective commitment, while Greenhaus et al. (2001) found the relationships to be weaker among those with low career involvement.

The relationship between WFC and turnover is robust, though it appears to be stronger for WIF and turnover intentions as compared to FIW and actual turnover. Additionally, different types of WFC (e.g., time-based, strain-based) exhibited dissimilar relationships with turnover intentions, highlighting the importance of investigating dimensions of WFC separately.

Summary

Overall, a wealth of research exists regarding the relationship between WFC and work-related outcomes. However, job attitudes tended to be over-represented in the literature, while research that links WFC to career attitudes/outcomes and OCB is sparse. Despite the vast amount of research on job attitudes, researchers have tended to focus on global job satisfaction and affective organizational commitment. Given the multidimensionality of these constructs, and the support for differential relationships across dimensions, future research should continue to examine how various components of job satisfaction and organizational commitment relate to

WFC. Similarly, more research is needed on how WFC differentially relates to facets of career satisfaction, in addition to other career-related outcomes.

With regard to behavioral outcomes, the literature generally supports a negative relationship between WFC and performance, and a positive relationship between WFC and withdrawal behaviors/intentions. However, relationships tended to be stronger for self-reported compared to other-reported outcomes, and for measures that specifically tapped into family as the cause for withdrawal (i.e., family-related versus general absences). These findings highlight the role that methodological factors play in relationships between WFC and outcomes. Still, it is important to note that significant relationships were found using non-self-report data, including supervisor ratings of performance/OCB, objective indices of productivity, and archival records of absenteeism/turnover, providing compelling support that WFC impacts the bottom-line.

Despite these findings, relationships were by no means conclusive. Across all work-related outcomes, some studies reported no relationship with WFC. Moreover, findings were more inconsistent for some outcomes than others. Research linking WFC to job satisfaction, affective organizational commitment, and turnover intentions appears to be particularly robust, while less consistent results were reported for career-related outcomes, performance, and absenteeism. Discrepancies across studies highlight the importance of searching for moderator variables, and several researchers have already begun this task. Some support has been found for the moderating role of gender, dispositional factors, family responsibilities, and other variables, though more research is needed. The field would also benefit from more research on mediators.

Another important observation is that relationships were generally found for both WIF and FIW. This contradicts the domain specificity hypothesis, which posits that situational variables associated with a given domain relate to conflict originating from that domain (Frone, Russell & Cooper, 1992). Thus, researchers are encouraged to study both WIF and FIW when assessing how WFC relates to outcomes, rather than focusing on one direction. While most studies examined WIF and FIW separately, surprisingly little research investigated time-, strain-, and behavior-based conflict. Among the few that did, relationships often differed across dimensions of WFC, underscoring the importance of examining each type. Finally, the field would also benefit from using more diverse methodological approaches, as the majority of studies were cross-sectional and self-report.

WORK-FAMILY BALANCE, FACILITATION, AND ENHANCEMENT AND WORK-RELATED OUTCOMES

Given that work-family research has been dominated by a conflict paradigm (Rothbard, 2001), far fewer studies have examined the facilitative aspects of the work-family interface. Those that did used various terms to describe similar, yet distinct, constructs, including work-family enrichment, positive spillover, and facilitation (see Chapters 3–5 for a thorough discussion). Despite differences, the argument underlying these constructs is that engaging in multiple roles can be beneficial, rather than draining (Rothbard, 2001). Empirical studies linking such constructs to work-related outcomes are reviewed in this section.

JOB ATTITUDES

Of the few studies that investigated facilitative effects of the work-family interface, most examined job attitudes. WF and FW facilitation were positively related to job satisfaction in the US (e.g., Carlson, Kacmar, Wayne & Grzywacz, 2006; Hanson, Hammer & Colton, 2006) and job satisfaction and affective commitment in India (Aryee et al., 2005) and the Netherlands (Geurts et al., 2005). However, in another study, WF facilitation but not FW facilitation related to job satisfaction (Wayne, Musisca & Fleeson, 2002). Moreover, Hill (2005) reported that WF facilitation was positively related to job satisfaction but unrelated to organizational commitment, while FW facilitation was *negatively* related to organizational commitment for males and unrelated to job satisfaction. Using data from the 2002 National Study of the Changing Workforce, Thompson and Prottas (2005) found that job satisfaction related to bi-directional positive spillover. Work-family balance has also been positively related to job satisfaction (Barnett, Del Campo, Del Campo & Steiner, 2003) and organizational commitment (Finegold, Mohrman & Spreitzer, 2002). Finally, Cohen (1997) found that nonwork-to-work positive spillover was unrelated to job satisfaction using a Canadian sample. Thus, despite many positive findings, inconsistent results have emerged.

CAREER OUTCOMES

Little research has investigated the relationship between the "positive side" of the work-family interface and career-related outcomes, and those that did often reported null results. For example, Aryee, Chay and Tan (1994) found that the integration of work and family was unrelated to career satisfaction among managers in Singapore. Though somewhat peripheral to work-family enrichment and related constructs, researchers have found that parental role quality was positively associated with career satisfaction, though marital role quality was not (Aryee et al., 1994). Moreover, spousal support has been linked to career satisfaction among dual-earner couples in Hong Kong (Aryee & Luk, 1996).

Performance-related Outcomes

Although researchers have offered various definitions for such constructs as work-family facilitation, enrichment, and positive spillover, some of the definitions specify a performance increase as inherent to the construct. For example, Greenhaus and Powell (2006) define enrichment as when experiences in one role improve the quality of life (i.e., affect or performance) in the other role. Similarly, Rothbard (2001) describes the enrichment process as occurring when engagement in Role A leads to positive emotion, which leads to engagement in Role B. Engagement is conceptualized as being fully absorbed in role performance. Thus, one would expect a positive association between family-to-work enrichment and work performance.

Despite these definitions, there is very little research linking work-family enrichment and related constructs to performance. Tompson and Werner (1997) found that role facilitation was unrelated to self-reported performance but positively related to OCB; however, as mentioned earlier, they placed role conflict and role facilitation on a continuum, so their measure is tapping both constructs. Moreover, Baruch-Feldman, Brondolo, Ben-Dayan and Schwartz (2002) found that family support was unrelated to productivity among traffic enforcement agents.

Withdrawal Behaviors and Intentions

A few studies have examined turnover intentions in relation to positive spillover, reporting mixed results. Thompson and Prottas (2005) found that bi-directional positive spillover negatively related to turnover intent. Conversely, Cohen (1997) reported no relationship between positive nonwork-to-work spillover and withdrawal cognitions among employees of a western Canadian school district. Social support from one's significant other was also unrelated to turnover intentions among public child welfare workers (Nissly, Barak & Levin, 2005). Bretz, Boudreau and Judge (1994) found that a desire for more work-family balance did not predict actual separation a year later.

Summary

In summary, there is a paucity of research examining how positive work-family variables impact work-related outcomes, with the majority of research to date investigating job attitudes. Additional research on the construct, measurement, and outcomes of work-family facilitation/enrichment is sorely needed, though recent strides have been made (e.g., Carlson et al., 2006; Greenhaus & Powell, 2006). Furthermore, as with WFC research, studies are needed that investigate potential moderators and mediators of these relationships. Given the theoretical and practical importance of this topic, future research examining potential links between the positive side of the work-family interface and work-related outcomes is clearly warranted.

INTERNATIONAL COMPARISONS

As evidenced by the review in the preceding sections, the majority of work-family research has utilized Western samples, predominantly from the US. However, individuals from Singapore, Israel, the Netherlands, and Hong Kong have also been investigated, among others. Studies conducted in other countries often replicate those in the US, testing whether the relationship between WFC and a work-related outcome extends to a non-US sample. More recently, researchers have begun to conduct cross-national comparative studies. Five such studies are summarized in this section.

Hill, Yang, Hawkins and Ferris (2004) tested the veracity of a work-family model across four cultural groups of IBM employees (Eastern, West-Developing, West-Affluent, and West-US), composed of 48 countries. They found that WIF and FIW related to job satisfaction via work-family fit. Moreover, the relationships were similar across cultural groups. Further support for the generalizability of work-family relationships with work outcomes across culture was found by Spector, Cooper, Poelmans, Allen, O'Driscoll, Sanchez, et al. (2004). Managers in 15 countries were categorized into three culturally distinct regions: Anglo, China, and Latin America. Across all regions, work-family pressure was associated with job satisfaction and turnover intentions.

Other studies have compared a US sample to a sample from one other country. Posthuma, Joplin and Maertz (2005) compared American and Mexican grocery employees; in both samples, WFC was not related to turnover intentions but was negatively related to job satisfaction. Conversely, Janssen, Peeters, Jong, Houkes and Tummers (2004) discovered that WFC was associated with job satisfaction among Dutch but not American nurses. Finally, Wang, Lawler, Walumbwa and Shi (2004) examined the impact of culture among American and Chinese employees in the banking sector. The moderating effect of country as well as individual-level allocentrism (an individual's tendency to put the collective unit first) and idiocentrism (an individual's tendency to put personal interests first) were examined. They found WIF related to job withdrawal intentions in the US sample, while FIW related to job withdrawal intentions in the Chinese sample. Moreover, the relationship between WIF and withdrawal intentions was stronger for individuals high on idiocentrism, while the relationship between FIW and withdrawal intentions was stronger for those high on allocentrism. This study highlights the importance of considering culture at both the individual- and country-level.

Overall, cross-cultural studies have uncovered more similarities than differences. Still, more research is necessary, particularly examining a wider range of outcomes and studying the impact of culture at multiple levels of analysis.

OVERVIEW OF EXISTING WORK, PRACTICAL CONSIDERATIONS, AND FUTURE DIRECTIONS

As the current review demonstrates, there has been an abundance of research examining the work-family interface and work-related outcomes. However, the emphasis has been on job attitudes and uni-dimensional measures of WFC, with less research on WF enrichment, cross-cultural comparisons, and multidimensional WFC measures. Moreover, while results are robust for certain outcomes (e.g., job satisfaction), relationships concerning other variables (e.g., performance) are less clear-cut. Divergent findings across studies highlight the need to identify contextual factors that impact the strength and direction of relationships.

With regard to methodology, the vast majority of studies relied on cross-sectional designs and self-report measures. Cross-sectional designs are problematic in their inability to determine the direction of causality. More studies utilizing longitudinal designs and experience sampling methodology are needed. With regard to the over-reliance on self-report measures, it is important to note that findings have generally been stronger between WFC and self-reported, rather than other-reported outcomes. This speaks to the possibility of common method bias, as well as potential discrepancies between participants' reports and intentions versus their actual behavior. Finally, researchers have criticized current measures of WFC (see MacDermid, 2005), and measures of positive work-family variables are just beginning to be developed (e.g., Carlson et al., 2006). Given that existing measures of the work-family interface may be subject to numerous cognitive errors (MacDermid, 2005), further development of psychometrically sound measurement tools is needed (see Chapter 4 of this volume for further discussion of this issue).

Another area that would benefit from additional research is the theory underlying the relationships reviewed in this chapter. Many studies did not provide well-developed theoretical arguments for *why* relationships exist. Although many researchers cited role theory, a resource drain model, or role accumulation, a description of how and why work-family variables should relate to *specific* outcomes was lacking. The field would benefit from more descriptive theories and a heightened emphasis on theory-driven approaches. Research examining potential mechanisms linking work-family variables and outcomes is also warranted, as is integration between the positive and negative sides of the work-family interface.

Despite limitations in the literature, it is clear that work-family variables relate to work-related outcomes, ranging from job and career attitudes to withdrawal behaviors. These findings have definitive implications for policy and practice at the individual, organizational, and societal level. Individuals need better tools to manage the work and family domain, and organizations need to be aware of the significant impact that family has on business-related outcomes. Researchers have already begun investigating the role that family-friendly initiatives have on mitigating the negative impact of WFC (see Chapters 18, 19 and 20 of this volume), but a broader consideration of interventions is necessary. For example, research should explore whether employees can be trained to better manage their work and family lives, and interventions designed to enhance facilitation and minimize conflict should be considered. Moreover, the field would benefit from a life-course perspective (see Chapter 6 by Moen & Chesley in this volume), examining how family-related variables impact one's job and career over time. Finally, in an age of growing globalization, more multicultural comparisons are necessary; such research has important theoretical and practical implications regarding the impact of work-family variables. While past research has clearly shown that organizations cannot afford to ignore the work-family interface, future research should continue to provide guidance regarding what companies can do about it.

REFERENCES

Allen, T. D. (2001). Family-supportive work environments: The role of organizational perceptions. *Journal of Vocational Behavior, 58*, 414–435.

Allen, T. D., Herst, D. E. L., Bruck, C. S. & Sutton, M. (2000). Consequences associated with work-to-family conflict: A review and agenda for future research. *Journal of Occupational Health Psychology, 5*, 278–308.

Anderson, S. E., Coffey, B. S. & Byerly, R. T. (2002). Formal organizational initiatives and informal workplace practices: Links to work-family conflict and job-related outcomes. *Journal of Management, 28*(6), 787–810.

Aryee, S. (1992). Antecedents and outcomes of work-family conflict among married professional women: Evidence from Singapore. *Human Relations, 45*, 813–837.

Aryee, S. (1993). Dual-earner couples in Singapore: An examination of work and non-work sources of their experienced burnout. *Human Relations, 46*, 1441–1468.

Aryee, S., Chay, Y. W. & Tan, H. H. (1994). An examination of the antecedents of subjective career success among a managerial sample in Singapore. *Human Relations, 47*, 487–509.

Aryee, S. & Luk, V. (1996). Work and non-work influences on the career satisfaction of dual-earner couples. *Journal of Vocational Behavior, 49*, 38–52.

Aryee, S., Luk, V., Leung, A. & Lo S. (1999). Role stressors, inter-role conflict, and well-being: The moderating influence of spousal support and coping behaviors among employed parents in Hong Kong. *Journal of Vocational Behavior, 54*, 259–278.

Aryee, S., Srinivas, E. S. & Tan, H. H. (2005). Rhythms of life: Antecedents and outcomes of work-family balance in employed parents. *Journal of Applied Psychology, 90*, 132–146.

Barling, J., MacEwan, K. E., Kelloway, K. & Higginbottom, S. F. (1994). Predictors and outcomes of eldercare-based inter-role conflict. *Psychology and Aging, 9*(3), 391–397.

Barnett, K. A., Del Campo, R. L., Del Campo, D. S. & Steiner, R. L. (2003). Work and family balance among dual-earner working-class Mexican Americans: Implications for therapists. *Contemporary Family Therapy: An International Journal, 25*, 353–366.

Barrah, J. L., Shultz, K. S., Baltes, B. & Stolz, H. E. (2004). Men's and women's eldercare-based work-family conflict: Antecedents and work-related outcomes. *Fathering, 2*, 305–330.

Baruch-Feldman, C., Brondolo, E., Ben-Dayan, D. & Schwartz, J. (2002). Sources of social support and burnout, job satisfaction, and productivity. *Journal of Occupational Health Psychology, 7*, 84–93.

Batt, R. & Valcour, P. M. (2003). Human resources practices as predictors of work-family outcomes and employee turnover. *Industrial Relations: A Journal of Economy & Society, 42,* 189–220.

Beatty, C. A. (1996). The stress of managerial and professional women: Is the price too high? *Journal of Organizational Behavior, 17,* 233–251.

Beutell, N. J. & Wittig-Berman, U. (1999). Predictors of work-family conflict and satisfaction with family, job, career, and life. *Psychological Reports, 85,* 893–903.

Bhuian, S. N., Menguc, B. & Borsboom, R. (2005). Stressors and job outcomes in sales: A triphasic model versus a linear-quadratic-interactive model. *Journal of Business Research, 58,* 141–150.

Blau, G. (1995). Influence of group lateness on individual lateness: A cross-level examination. *Academy of Management Journal, 38,* 1483–1496.

Blood, R. O. & Wolfe, D. M. (1960). *Husbands and Wives.* New York: Macmillan.

Boles, J. S., Howard, W. G. & Donofrio, H. H. (2001). An investigation into the interrelationships of work-family conflict, family-work conflict and work satisfaction. *Journal of Managerial Issues, 13,* 376–390.

Boles, J. S., Wood, J. A. & Johnson, J. (2003). Interrelationships of role conflict, role ambiguity, and work-family conflict with different facets of job satisfaction and the moderating effects of gender. *Journal of Personal Selling & Sales Management, 23,* 99–113.

Bolino, M. C. & Turnley, W. H. (2005). The personal costs of citizenship behavior: The relationship between individual initiative and role overload, job stress, and work-family conflict. *Journal of Applied Psychology, 90*(4), 740–748.

Boyar, S. L., Maertz, C. P. J. & Pearson, A. W. (2005). The effects of work-family conflict and family-work conflict on nonattendance behaviors. *Journal of Business Research, 58,* 919–925.

Bragger, J. D., Rodriguez-Srednicki, O., Kutcher, E. J., Indovino, L. & Rosner, E. (2005). Work-family conflict, work-family culture, and organizational citizenship behavior among teachers. *Journal of Business and Psychology, 20,* 303–324.

Bretz, Jr., R. D., Boudreau, J. W. & Judge, T. A. (1994). Job search behavior of employed managers. *Personnel Psychology, 47*(2), 275–301.

Bruck, C. S., Allen, T. D. & Spector, P. E. (2002). The relation between work-family conflict and job satisfaction: A finer-grained analysis. *Journal of Vocational Behavior, 60,* 336–353.

Butler, A. B. & Skattebo, A. (2004). What is acceptable for women may not be for men: The effect of family conflicts with work on job-performance ratings. *Journal of Occupational and Organizational Psychology, 77,* 553–564.

Carlson, D. S., Kacmar, K. M., Wayne, J. H. & Grzywacz, J. G. (2006). Measuring the positive side of the work-family interface: Development and validation of a work-family enrichment scale. *Journal of Vocational Behavior, 68*(1), 131–164.

Carlson, D. S., Kacmar, K. M. & Williams, L. J. (2000). Construction and initial validation of a multidimensional measure of work-family conflict. *Journal of Vocational Behavior, 56,* 249–276.

Carmeli, A. (2003). The relationship between emotional intelligence and work attitudes, behavior and outcomes: An examination among senior managers. *Journal of Managerial Psychology, 18,* 788–813.

Carnicer, M. P. d. L., Sánchez, A. M., Pérez, M. P. & Jiménez, M. J. V. (2004). Work-family conflict in a southern European country: The influence of job-related and non-related factors. *Journal of Managerial Psychology, 19,* 466–489.

Casper, W. J., Martin, J. A., Buffardi, L. C. & Erdwins, C. J. (2002). Work-family conflict, perceived organizational support, and organizational commitment among employed mothers. *Journal of Occupational Health Psychology, 7,* 99–108.

Chan, K. B., Lai, G., Ko, Y. C. & Boey, K. W. (2000). Work stress among six professional groups: The Singapore experience. *Social Science & Medicine, 50,* 1415–1432.

Chi-Ching, E. Y. (1992). Perceptions of external barriers and the career success of female managers in Singapore. *Journal of Social Psychology, 132,* 661–674.

Cohen, A. (1997). Nonwork influences on withdrawal cognitions: An empirical examination of an overlooked issue. *Human Relations, 50*(12), 1511–1536.

Cohen, A. & Kirchmeyer, C. (2005). A cross-cultural study of the work/non-work interface among Israeli nurses. *Applied Psychology: An International Review, 54,* 537–567.

Demerouti, E. & Geurts, S. (2004). Towards a typology of work-home interaction. *Community, Work & Family, 7,* 285–309.

Drory, A. & Shamir, B. (1988). Effects of organizational and life variables on job satisfaction and burnout. *Group & Organization Studies, 13,* 441–455.

Edwards, J. R. & Rothbard, N. P. (2000). Mechanisms linking work and family: Clarifying the relationship between work and family constructs. *The Academy of Management Review, 25*(1), 178–199.

Finegold, D., Mohrman, S. & Spreitzer, G. M. (2002). Age effects on the predictors of technical workers' commitment and willingness to turnover. *Journal of Organizational Behavior, 23,* 655–674.

Frone, M. R., Russell, M. & Cooper, M. L. (1992). Antecedents and outcomes of work-family conflict: Testing a model of the work-family interface. *Journal of Applied Psychology, 77*(1), 65–78.

Frone, M. R., Yardley, J. K. & Markel, K. S. (1997). Developing and testing an integrative model of the work-family interface. *Journal of Vocational Behavior, 50,* 145–167.

Geurts, S. A. E., Taris, T. W., Kompier, M. A. J., Dikkers, J. S. E., van Hooff, M. L. M. & Kinnunen, U. M. (2005). Work-home interaction from a work psychological perspective: Development and validation of a new questionnaire, the SWING. *Work and Stress, 19,* 319–339.

Gignac, M. A. M., Kelloway, E. K. & Gottlieb, B. H. (1996). The impact of caregiving on employment: A mediational model of work-family conflict. *Canadian Journal on Aging, 15,* 525–542.

Good, L. K., Sisler, G. F. & Gentry, J. W. (1988). Antecedents of turnover intentions among retail management personnel. *Journal of Retailing, 64,* 295–314.

Grandey, A. A., Cordeiro, B. L. & Crouter, A. C. (2005). A longitudinal and multi-source test of the work-family conflict and job satisfaction relationship. *Journal of Occupational and Organizational Psychology, 78,* 305–323.

Greenhaus, J. H., Allen, T. D. & Spector, P. E. (2006). Health consequences of work-family conflict: The dark side of the work-family interface. In P. L. Perrewe & D. C. Ganster (eds), *Research in Occupational Stress and Well being* (Vol. 5, pp. 61–99). Amsterdam: Elsevier.

Greenhaus, J. H., Bedeian, A. G. & Mossholder, K. W. (1987). Work experiences, job performance, and feelings of personal and family well-being. *Journal of Vocational Behavior, 31,* 200–215.

Greenhaus, J. H., Collins, K. M., Singh, R. & Parasuraman, S. (1997). Work and family influences on departure from public accounting. *Journal of Vocational Behavior, 50,* 249–270.

Greenhaus, J. H., Parasuraman, S. & Collins, K. M. (2001). Career involvement and family involvement as moderators of relationships between work-family conflict and withdrawal from a profession. *Journal of Occupational Health Psychology, 6,* 91–100.

Greenhaus, J. H. & Powell, G. N. (2006). When work and family are allies: A theory of work-family enrichment. *Academy of Management Review, 31*(1), 72–92.

Hackett, R. D., Bycio, P. & Guion, R. M. (1989). Absenteeism among hospital nurses: An idiographic-longitudinal analysis. *Academy of Management Journal, 3,* 424–453.

Hammer, L. B., Bauer, T. N. & Grandey, A. A. (2003). Work-family conflict and work-related withdrawal behaviors. *Journal of Business and Psychology, 17*(3), 419–436.

Hang-yue, N., Foley, S. & Loi, R. (2005). Work role stressors and turnover intentions: A study of professional clergy in Hong Kong. *International Journal of Human Resource Management, 16*(11), 2133–2146.

Hanson, G. C., Hammer, L. B. & Colton, C. L. (2006). Development and validation of a multidimensional scale of perceived work-family positive spillover. *Journal of Occupational Health Psychology, 11*(3), 249–265.

Hepburn, C. G. & Barling, J. (1996). Eldercare responsibilities, interrole conflict, and employee absence: A daily study. *Journal of Occupational Health Psychology, 1*(3), 311–318.

Hill, E. J. (2005). Work-family facilitation and conflict, working fathers and mothers, work-family stressors and support. *Journal of Family Issues, 26*(6), 793–819.

Hill, E. J., Yang, C., Hawkins, A. H. & Ferris, M. (2004). A cross-cultural test of the work-family interface in 48 countries. *Journal of Marriage and Family, 66,* 1300–1316.

Hogan, N. L., Lambert, E. G., Jenkins, M. & Wambold, S. (2006). The impact of occupational stressors on correctional staff organizational commitment. *Journal of Contemporary Criminal Justice, 22*(1), 44–62.

Hom, P. W. & Kinicki, A. J. (2001). Toward a greater understanding of how dissatisfaction drives employee turnover. *Academy of Management Journal, 44*(5), 975–987.

Janssen, P. P. M., Peeters, M. C. W., Jonge, J. Houkes, I. & Tummers, G. E. R. (2004). Specific relationships between job demands, job resources and psychological outcomes and the mediating role of negative work-home interference. *Journal of Vocational Behavior, 65,* 411–429.

Judge, T. A., Boudreau, J. W. & Bretz, Jr., R. D. (1994). Job and life attitudes of male executives. *Journal of Applied Psychology, 79*(5), 767–782.

Kahn, R. L., Wolfe, D. M., Quinn, R. P., Snoek, J. D. & Rosenthal, R. A. (1964). *Organizational Stress: Studies in Role Conflict and Ambiguity.* New York: Wiley.

Kelloway, E. K., Gottlieb, B. H. & Barham, L. (1999). The source, nature, and direction of work and family conflict: A longitudinal investigation. *Journal of Occupational Health Psychology, 4*(4), 337–346.

Kinnunen, U., Geurts, S. & Mauno, S. (2004). Work-to-family conflict and its relationship with satisfaction and well-being: A one-year longitudinal study on gender differences. *Work and Stress, 18*(1), 1–22.

Kirchmeyer, C. & Cohen, A. (1999). Different strategies for managing the work/non-work interface: A test for unique pathways to work outcomes. *Work and Stress, 13*(1), 59–73.

Kossek, E. E. (1990). Diversity in child care assistance needs: Employee problems, preferences, and work-related outcomes. *Personnel Psychology, 43,* 769–791.

Kossek, E. E., Colquitt, J. A. & Noe, R. A. (2001). Caregiving decisions, well-being, and performance: The effects of place and provider as a function of dependent type and work-family climates. *Academy of Management Journal, 44*(1), 29–44.

Kossek, E. E., Demarr, B., Bachman, K., Bachman, K. & Kollar, M. (1993). Assessing employees' emerging elder care needs and reactions to dependent care benefits. *Public Personnel Management, 22,* 617–638.

Kossek, E. E., Lautsch, B. A. & Eaton, S. C. (2006). Telecommuting, control, and boundary management: Correlates of policy use and practice, job control, and work-family effectiveness. *Journal of Vocational Behavior, 68,* 347–367.

Kossek, E. E. & Nichol, V. (1992). The effects of on-site child care on employee attitudes and performance. *Personnel Psychology, 45*(3), 485–509.

Kossek, E. E. & Ozeki, C. (1998). Work-family conflict, policies, and the job-life satisfaction relationship: A review and directions for organizational behavior-human resources research. *Journal of Applied Psychology, 83,* 139–149.

Kossek, E. E. & Ozeki, C. (1999). Bridging the work family policy and productivity gap: A literature review. *Community, Work & Family, 2,* 7–32.

Lyness, K. S. & Thompson, D. E. (1997). Above the glass ceiling? A comparison of matched samples of female and male executives. *Journal of Applied Psychology, 82*(3), 359–375.

MacDermid, S. M. (2005). (Re)Considering conflict between work and family. In E. E., Kossek & S. Lambert (eds), *Work and Life Integration: Organizational, Cultural, and Individual Perspectives* (pp. 19–40). Mahwah, NJ: Lawrence Erlbaum.

Martins, L. L., Eddleston, K. A. & Veiga, J. F. (2002). Moderators of the relationship between work-family conflict and career satisfaction. *Academy of Management Journal, 45,* 399–409.

Mesmer-Magnus, J. R. & Viswesvaran, C. (2005). Convergence between measures of work-to-family and family-to-work conflict: A meta-analytic examination. *Journal of Vocational Behavior, 67,* 215–232.

Meyer, J. P., Stanley, D. J., Herscovitch, L. & Topolnytsky, L. (2002). Affective, continuance, and normative commitment to the organization: A meta-analysis of antecedents, correlates, and consequences. *Journal of Vocational Behavior, 61*, 20–52.

Netemeyer, R. G., Boles, J. S. & McMurrian, R. (1996). Development and validation of work–family conflict and family–work conflict scales. *Journal of Applied Psychology, 81*(4), 400–410.

Netemeyer, R. G., Maxham, J. G. I. & Pullig, C. (2005). Conflicts in the work–family interface: Links to job stress, customer service employee performance, and customer purchase intent. *Journal of Marketing, 69*, 130–143.

Ngo, H. & Lui, S. (1999). Gender differences in outcomes of work–family conflict: The case of Hong Kong managers. *Sociological Focus, 32,* 3, 303–316.

Nissly, J. A., Barak, M. E. M. & Levin, A. (2005). Stress, social support, and worker's intentions to leave their jobs in public child welfare. *Administration in Social Work, 29*(1), 79–100.

Parasuraman, S., Purohit, Y. S., Godshalk, V. M. & Beutell, N. J. (1996). Work and family variables, entrepreneurial career success, and psychological well-being. *Journal of Vocational Behavior, 48,* 275–300.

Parasuraman, S. & Simmers, C. A. (2001). Type of employment, work–family conflict and well-being: A comparative study. *Journal of Organizational Behavior, 22*, 551–568.

Peluchette, J. V. E. (1993). Subjective career success: The influence of individual difference, family, and organizational variables. *Journal of Vocational Behavior, 43*, 198–208.

Perrewe, P. L., Hochwarter, W. A. & Kiewitz, C. (1999). Value attainment: An explanation of the negative effects of work–family conflict on job and life satisfaction. *Journal of Occupational Health Psychology, 4*, 318–326.

Posthuma, R. A., Joplin, J. R. W. & Maertz, Jr., C. P. (2005). Comparing the validity of turnover predictors in the United States and Mexico. *International Journal of Cross Cultural Management, 5*(2), 165–180.

Rothbard, N. P. (2001). Enriching or depleting? The dynamics of engagement in work and family roles. *Administrative Science Quarterly, 46*(4), 655–684.

Shaffer, M. A., Harrison, D. A., Gilley, K. M. & Luk, D. M. (2001). Struggling for balance amid turbulence on international assignments: Work–family conflict, support, and commitment. *Journal of Management, 27*, 99–121.

Spector, P. E., Cooper, C. L., Poelmans, S., Allen, T. D., O'Driscoll, M., Sanchez, J. I. et al. (2004). A cross-national comparative study of work–family stressors, working hours, and well-being: China and Latin America versus the Anglo world. *Personnel Psychology, 57*, 119–142.

Thomas, L. T. & Ganster, D. C. (1995). Impact of family-supportive work variables on work–family conflict and strain: A control perspective. *Journal of Applied Psychology, 80*, 6–15.

Thompson, C. A. & Prottas, D. J. (2005). Relationships among organizational family support, job autonomy, perceived control, and employee well-being. *Journal of Occupational Health Psychology, 10*(4), 100–118.

Tompson, H. B. & Werner, J. M. (1997). The impact of role conflict/facilitation on core and discretionary behaviors: Testing a mediational model. *Journal of Management, 23*(4), 583–601.

Wang, P., Lawler, J. J., Walumbwa, F. O. & Shi, K. (2004). Work–family conflict and job withdrawal intentions: The moderating effect of cultural differences. *International Journal of Stress Management, 11*(4), 392–412.

Wayne, J. H., Musisca, N. & Fleeson, W. (2002). Considering the role of personality in the work–family experience: Relationships of the big five to work–family conflict and facilitation. *Journal of Vocational Behavior, 64*, 108–130.

CHAPTER 10

The Emotional Dimensions of Family Time and Their Implications for Work-Family Balance

Shira Offer* and **Barbara Schneider†**
*Department of Sociology and Anthropology Bar Ilan University
Ramat Gan, Israel
†Department of Sociology and College of Education Michigan
State University, East Lansing

INTRODUCTION

Family dinners have attracted national attention. The advantages of shared meals have made headlines and the popular media, citing findings from recently conducted studies—most notably the National Center on Addiction and Substance Abuse's (CASA) latest report has highlighted their contribution for child development, individual health, and family functioning. For example, adolescents who reported at least five family dinners per week were substantially less likely to smoke cigarettes, use drugs and alcohol, and had higher grades at school compared to their counterparts who ate dinner with their family less frequently (2006). Gathering at the dinner table has been celebrated as a recipe for family connectedness, a powerful yet simple means to improve well-being and promote the next generation's success.

Family dinners, however, are not an easy thing to do considering the hectic schedules of both parents and children in contemporary western society. Parents' long work hours and children's participation in many after-school programs have made getting together a challenge that requires considerable effort and strategizing (Bianchi, Robinson & Milkie, 2006; Presser, 2003). For example, in CASA's study, 57% of parents reported that because of work-related reasons, such as conflicting schedules and working late, family dinners were not as frequent as they wished them to be (2006).

The challenge of family gathering around the dinner table, once a major pillar of family life, is just one illustration of the serious time squeeze that many families are currently experiencing. It is not surprising that in light of the growing complexity of work and family lives, integrating between the two has become difficult. Stress, feelings of overwork, role strain, and the wish to spend more time with family are at the heart of the work-family conflict.

Handbook of Work-Family Integration: Research, Theory, and Best Practices

In this chapter, we seek to shed light on the emotional dimensions of family time. Family time can be a form of interactive togetherness or a contested terrain where antagonistic relations develop (Shaw 1997). We argue that generally being together is a positive experience that can be an important source of support for working parents. By decomposing family time, we seek to reveal the emotional experiences associated with different family activities and their implications for parents' well-being, particularly as they relate to their perception of balancing work and family demands.

CONTEMPORARY FAMILIES AND THE GROWING COMPLEXITY OF WORK AND FAMILY LIVES

Changes in the nature of work, the organization of the workplace, and the move toward a 24/7 economy have created new challenges for workers and their families. Longer work hours, declining job security, nonstandard work schedules, lack of flexibility, and extended commutes have brought about new sources of stress and have made it more difficult for working parents to negotiate their multiple roles at home and work (Carnoy, 2000; Mishel, Bernstein & Schmitt, 2001; Presser, 2003).

The challenge of integrating work and family lives has become especially acute for dual-earner families, a growing proportion of all families in the population (Casper & Bianchi, 2002; Waite & Nielsen, 2001), who need to orchestrate between three jobs, two at work and one at home. For this reason, it is important that social scientists treat the family as a whole unit of investigation in their attempt to describe and explain the impacts of work on family well-being and functioning. Consistent with this approach, contemporary research indicates that dual-earner families have experienced an important increase in their joint-work effort; parents' combined number of work hours has steadily grown in the last three decades (Jacobs & Gerstel, 2004; Mishel et al., 2001).

The need to juggle work and family demands has also become a major challenge for single parents, another group that has increased in size in the last few decades. Single-parent families need to support their children with one income and cannot rely on a spouse or partner to help with childcare and household tasks. Following the 1996 Welfare Reform, many single parents, particularly low-income mothers, have been pressured to leave the welfare rolls and join the labor force. However, the move from welfare to work has not been a smooth one. Welfare leavers, as do other single parents, typically hold low-skilled low-paying jobs that do not provide much economic security and often require them to work under highly inconvenient circumstances (Casper & Bianchi, 2002; Loperst, 1999).

These trends have had important implications for individual well-being. A large number of workers feel overworked. For example, Jacobs and Gerstel (2004) report that the gap between actual and ideal weekly work hours is especially high among the married and parents of young children (the number of actual work hours is higher by more than 10 hours than the number of ideal work hours). They further note that many parents wished to work less or to have shorter work-weeks (see also Galinsky et al., 2001). Long work hours was also perceived as a problem among single parents, especially among those who worked multiple jobs, a common strategy to increase income, and experienced difficulties in coordinating childcare arrangements for their children (Chaudry, 2005).

TIME SQUEEZE AND WORK–FAMILY CONFLICT

Increased involvement in paid work has created new time squeezes at home and set constraints on what working families can do together. As Nock and Kingston point out "as the husband and wives in dual-earner families seek to fulfill all of their roles, they must wrestle with the combined time demands of work on the family as a unit" (1984, p. 334). Being a scarce commodity in contemporary society, time is a highly sensitive issue understood in terms of competition and substitution. Typically, more time spent at work, or on work–related activities, is interpreted as less time available for children and family.

Studies show that parents' time with children has not decreased dramatically in the last few decades, contrary to what one would have predicted considering parents' greater labor force participation (Bianchi, 2000; Bond, Galinsky & Swanberg, 1998; Sandberg & Hofferth, 2001). Rather, pressured by multiple demands at work and home, parents have developed strategies to maximize their time with children and with family (Bianchi et al., 2006). Spending "quality time" has been treated as a way for busy parents to be more involved with their children and family, which can compensate for increasing time spent at work (Snyder forthcoming; Voydanoff, 2002)

Yet, feeling rushed, a sense of life speed-up, and feelings of frustration that one does not have enough time are very common (Robinson & Godbey, 1999). Using time diary measures, Bianchi and her associates report that more than a third of parents reported always feeling rushed (2000). According to Daly this stems in part because "family time is a *prescriptive* term that upholds a set of traditional family values that may not be easily realized in the face of today's work and family challenges" (2001, p. 293). Daly's study describes the yearning for more family time and the feeling of guilt that accompanies it in working families (see also Chaudry, 2005; Voydanoff, 1988).

The experience of time deficit is especially acute among parents. Almost half of parents in a study using nationally representative samples felt that they do not spend enough time with their children (Milkie et al., 2004). This study further found that the likelihood of feeling time strain increased as parents' work hours increased. Similar patterns were observed for single and married parents. Scholars have pointed out that the experience of a time squeeze is also the result of rising standards of parenting, which have created, besides high work expectations, additional sources of stress for parents (Bianchi et al., 2006; Lareau, 2002).

Job-related time constraints can also impair a parent's ability to fulfill home obligations (Voydanoff, 1988), and the need to coordinate between two work schedules can contribute to the development of family conflicts about time allocation and time usage. Thus, the perception of a shortage of time constitutes a crucial dimension of the work-family conflict. This is especially the case for parents. Depending on the measure used to gauge work-family conflict, in some cases as many as 60 % of parents, either men or women, reported tension between their work and family lives (Jacobs & Gerstel, 2004). Numbers for men and women without children were substantially lower (see also Roehling, Zarvis & Swope, 2005).

THE EFFECT OF OCCUPATIONAL CONDITIONS

Research indicates that the experience of work-family conflict is affected by occupational conditions and the workplace culture. Some argue that occupational conditions can matter more than the actual number of work hours (Jacobs & Gerstel, 2004). Especially important are autonomy and control over scheduling and job content, which are not only associated with job satisfaction and well-being at work, but have also been found to ease work-family conflict. Moen and Yu (2000), for example, show that among both men and women job autonomy was associated with higher levels of work-family balance (see also Voydanoff, 1988).

Supportive supervisors, access to benefits, and the ability to use family-friendly options are also important in this matter and can help parents better deal with the competing demands of work and family (Blair-Loy & Wharton, 2002; Hill, 2005). The organizational culture often prevalent in the professions and the corporate world, which requires complete time and energy devotion to the job, can be a serious obstacle to family life. Indeed, for some people in top positions, particularly women, being successful means remaining childless (Blair-Loy, 2003; Goldin, 2004).

Nonstandard work hours, on the other hand, have been shown to be detrimental. Rotating and night shifts are associated with greater marital instability (Presser, 2000) and work-family conflict (Moen & Yu, 2000). Shift work is also a source of stress for single parents, not only due to high levels of physical stress but also because this type of jobs makes it more difficult for them to secure childcare, thus increasing stress and parental concern over their children's well-being (Chaudry, 2005).

The disadvantage of single parents also stems from the fact that they are substantially more likely to work nonstandard work hours compared to other parents. Because they are typically younger and less well-educated, single parents are more likely to be concentrated in low-status occupational sectors that have inconvenient and rigid schedules, provide little control over the work process, and offer few if any benefits (Casper & Bianchi, 2002; Loperst, 1999). As such, single parents are especially vulnerable to experience severe time squeezes.

FAMILY TIME AS A SOURCE OF SUPPORT

In their attempt to better understand the causes and consequences of parents' daily struggle to juggle family life with paid work and other obligations, social scientists have typically examined the effects of occupational conditions, social policies, and access to informal sources of support on the experience of work-family conflict. Much less attention, however, has been dedicated to the role that the family itself can play in helping parents balance their work and family responsibilities.

Scholars such as Hochschild (1997) argue that in contemporary society the traditional emotional and supportive functions of the family have been seriously eroded. Because of the growing complexity of everyday life, people, most notably professionals, would rather spend more time at work than at home. In this way, the workplace has become a major source of support and personal fulfillment. We argue, however, that the family is still an important integrative entity that can help shield parents and children from the stressors of everyday life. Specifically, spending time with family can provide working parents and their children with a much needed break in the form of "time-out-of-time" (Gillis, 1996).

It is important to note that we do not want to portray a romanticized picture of family life. Rather, by examining the emotional experiences associated with family time and by decomposing it into different types of activity, we emphasize that family time is a complex and multidimensional concept that needs to be studied critically. We believe that this approach will also help reveal the aspects of family time that are most likely to affect working parents' well-being.

THE 500 FAMILY STUDY

To examine the emotional dimensions associated with family time, we present below a series of analyses based on data from the 500 Family Study. The 500 Family Study, conducted by the Alfred P. Sloan Center on Parents, Children, and Work, was designed to collect comprehensive information about the experiences of middle-class dual-earner parents and their children at work and at home. It deals with a variety of issues, such as experiences at work, quality of marriage, parent-child relationship, household division of labor, and psychological well-being (for more information about the sample see Hoogstra, 2005).

Multiple methods were used to collect data about the complex dynamics of work and family life among dual-earner families. In this study we use data from two sources: surveys and time diaries. The survey administered to the parents provides detailed information about a variety of work-related issues, including occupational conditions and job duties. The experience sampling method (ESM), a form of time diary, provides comprehensive data about activities and emotional experiences in the course of a typical day. It uses preprogrammed wristwatches to randomly beep participants several times a day during their waking hours. When signaled, respondents are asked to fill out a questionnaire in which they describe their feelings and activities and provide information about their location and the people with whom they interact. The ESM provides an invaluable opportunity for studying real-time emotional experiences and activities as they occur in a natural setting. It is considered a valid and reliable instrument for examining time uses, subjective experiences, and emotional states (Csikszentmihalyi & Larson, 1987; Robinson, 1999). The analyses presented here are based on a subsample of families that includes 246 dual-earner couples with children who filled both the ESM and the survey questionnaires.

MEASURING FAMILY TIME, ITS EMOTIONAL DIMENSIONS, AND PARENTAL WELL-BEING

We began by examining the amount of time dual-earner couples spend with their family. One of the questions in the ESM asked respondents to indicate whom they were with when signaled. We used this item to calculate family time, a variable indicating the proportion of beeps (out of total number of beeps) respondents spent together with her/his spouse and at least one child.

We then decomposed family time into various types of family activities by categorizing responses to the ESM question of "What was the main thing you were doing?" (primary activity). The family activities we examined are: (1) direct interaction, which includes items such as talking to, playing with, holding and kissing spouse and/or child; (2) household-related tasks, which includes activities such as cleaning, repairing, and cooking; (3) religious activity, which refers to participation in various religious events; (4) leisure activity, which includes activities such as watching a movie, going to the theatre, watching TV, and playing a board or computer game; (5) social activity, which refers to talking to and playing with friends or relatives, partying, and celebrating; (6) assistance to child, which includes activities such as taking or picking up child, putting child to bed, and helping child with homework; and (7) family meals, which refers to eating meals together.

In the next stage, we looked at the emotional dimensions of family time. We constructed three ESM measures to describe the emotional states associated with different family activities and with family time in general: positive affect, negative affect, and feeling engaged. Each of these variables is a composite measure ranging from 0 to 3, which was computed as the average of several emotional items from the ESM. Positive affect is based on four items asking the extent to which respondent was feeling happy, cheerful, relaxed, and good about herself/himself when signaled. Negative affect is based on the items of feeling irritated, frustrated, and stressed. Feeling engaged is measured by how interesting the activity was, to what extent respondent enjoyed what she/he was doing, and how excited she/he was.

We also calculated the mean scores on positive affect, negative affect, and engagement for beeps with family only. These variables indicate how respondents feel when they are with family (as opposed to their general emotional assessment) and are used as predictors in a series of OLS regression models of parental well-being.

Work-family balance refers to parents' assessment of how well they handle family and work responsibilities and was used as a measure of parental well-being. It was computed as the mean of the following three survey items: "I feel confident about my ability to handle personal or family matters," "I feel confident about my ability to handle work-related matters," and "I feel I can't cope with everything I have to do" (reverse coded). Responses range from 0 to 4 with higher scores indicating a higher degree of balance of family and work lives.

In examining the association between the emotional states of family time and work-family balance, we included several survey-based measures as controls. The first set of variables controls for occupational conditions and includes whether respondent is working 46 or more hours a week; whether he/she works standard work hours; and how much work autonomy he/she has. Because how parents feel when they spend time with family (and how much time they spend with it) is likely to be affected by the quality of their relationship with their spouse and children, we also controlled for marital quality and parent-child relationship.

THE EMOTIONAL DIMENSIONS OF FAMILY TIME

DISTRIBUTION OF FAMILY TIME

How much time do dual-earner families spend together and what do they typically do? We found that overall the mean proportion of beeps spent with family was 11% (SD = .07 and .08 for mothers and fathers respectively), meaning that families spent almost 12 hours per week together (.11 × 7 days × 15 hours) engaging in different family activities.

Interesting variation was found when we decomposed family time into types of activities. Families spent almost half of their time together in direct interaction (31.8 and 30.3% of beeps out of all family beeps for mothers and fathers respectively) or eating meals together (15.6 and 17.8% for mothers and fathers respectively). Not surprisingly, a substantial amount of time was also spent on household-related tasks (15.1% for mothers and 12.7% for fathers). Leisure activities came fourth (7.4 and 9.1% for mothers and fathers respectively). Finally, less than 3% of all family beeps were spent on either assistance to children, religious, or social activities.

Note that there were minor differences between mothers' and fathers' responses because parents may not necessarily engage together in the same type of activity, although both of them are present. For example, mother may be cooking while father is helping child with homework in the kitchen. In this case, all family members are together in the same place although they engage in very different types of activities. It is therefore not surprising that mothers' share of family time spent on household-related tasks and assistance to children was slightly higher than that of fathers.

THE EMOTIONAL EXPERIENCE OF FAMILY TIME

How do parents feel when they spend time with family and do their emotional experiences vary by type of activity? In a series of ANOVA's we first examined how mothers and fathers feel in general when they are with family compared to other situations. The results revealed similar emotional patterns for fathers and mothers. Overall, being with family was a positive experience. Parents reported higher scores on positive affect, lower scores on negative affect, and higher scores on engagement for family versus non-family beeps. All these differences, although moderate in size, were significant. Furthermore, mothers and fathers expressed similar daily emotional experiences. Differences in mean scores on positive affect, negative affect, and engagement by gender were very small and non-significant.

Although spending time with family was in general a positive experience, an examination of the emotional states associated with different types of family activities portrayed a slightly more complex picture of family time. For mothers, the highest score on positive affect was reported for social activities (3.3), for fathers it was leisure activities (3.1). Direct interaction and eating meals together were also associated with especially high scores (above 3) on positive affect for mothers and fathers alike. But most importantly, in all activities *except* household-related tasks, a mother's mean score on positive affect was higher when she indicated being with family than in other situations. In other words, spending time with family while doing household-related tasks was perceived by mothers to be a significantly less positive experience.

This finding was further supported by the results for negative affect. Mothers' mean score on negative affect for family time spent on household-related tasks was substantially higher than in other situations (.6 compared to .37). Mean scores on negative affect associated with family time spent on direct interaction, eating meals, and especially leisure activities, on the other hand, were lower compared to other situations. A similar pattern was found for fathers. In all family activities, except household-related tasks, father's mean score on negative affect was lower than in other situations. The difference for family time spent on household-related tasks, however, was not significant for fathers.

Similarly, mean scores on engagements were higher for all family activities except household-related tasks. For both mothers and fathers, family time spent on household-related tasks was perceived as significantly less interesting, enjoyable, and exciting than other activities in general (a gap of .3 and .4 for mothers and fathers respectively). Mothers felt especially engaged while involved in religious and social activities with their family (mean scores of 3.5 and higher). Fathers felt most engaged while spending time with their families in social activities and having meals together (mean scores of 3.2 and higher).

FAMILY ACTIVITIES AS A SOURCE OF SUPPORT

To what extent does time spent with family constitute a source of support that can contribute to working parents' well-being? In the next analyses, we examined how parents' emotional experiences of family time are related to their assessment of work-family balance. We sought to understand how family time can fulfill important emotional needs required for dealing with the competing demands of work and family lives.

In a first series of regression analyses (results not shown here) we used proportion of time spent with family to predict work-family balance. Because no significant relationship was found between the two variables, we decided to focus on the emotional dimensions of family time. Table 10.1 presents the results of a series of OLS models regressing work-family balance on the emotional experiences associated with family time, controlling for occupational conditions and relational quality in the family. Scores on positive affect, negative affect, and engagement for beeps with family were entered respectively in Models 1–3.

The results indicate that for both mothers and fathers, positive family time (i.e., scores on positive affect when parents spend time with their family) is associated with a higher degree of work-family balance, whereas negative family time (i.e., scores on negative affect when parents spend time with their family) is associated with a lower degree of work-family balance. The effect of negative affect was especially pronounced for fathers ($\beta = -.219$, p $<$ .001). For mothers, although negative in sign, the coefficient of negative affect was not significant. Parents' assessment of work-family balance was not related to the extent to which they felt family time was interesting, enjoyable, and exciting.

Interestingly, work-family balance was not related to most occupational conditions. No significant association was found with either hours of work or work schedule. Work-family balance, however, was significantly related to work autonomy. Consistent with past research, for both mothers and fathers, greater

Table 10.1

Ordinary least squares regression results for work-family balance (standardized coefficients and standard errors in parentheses)

	Mothers			Fathers		
	Model 1	Model 2	Model 3	Model 1	Model 2	Model 3
Emotional experience of family time						
Positive affect	.179★★	–	–	.178★★	–	–
	(.067)			(.066)		
Negative affect	–	−.061	–	–	−.219★★★	–
		(.100)			(.09)	
Engagement	–	–	.025	–	–	.051
			(.065)			(.07)
Job characteristics						
>46 work hrs/week	−.021	−.033	−.025	.024	.008	.014
	(.088)	(.089)	(.090)	(.081)	(.081)	(.082)
Work autonomy	.242★★★	.249★★★	.242★★★	.252★★★	.266★★★	.264★★★
	(.044)	.045)	(.045)	(.052)	(.051)	(.052)
Standard work schedule	.003	.021	.023	−.013	.007	−.008
	(.079)	(.080)	(.08)	(.112)	(.111)	(.114)
Relational quality						
Marital quality	.286★★★	.308★★★	.316★★★	.133★	.117+	.141★
	(.003)	(.003)	(.003)	(.003)	(.003)	(.003)
Parent-child relationship	.144★	.174★★	.177★★	.216★★	.218★★★	.237★★★
	(.084)	(.084)	(.085)	(.069)	(.068)	(.069)
R-square	0.243	0.217	0.213	0.205	0.22	0.176
N	205	206	205	188	187	188

work autonomy was related to a higher degree of work-family balance. As expected, family relational quality, measured by marital quality and parent-child relationship, was positively and significantly associated with work-family balance. This finding in itself suggests that good family relations can emotionally help parents deal with work-family conflict.

IMPLICATIONS FOR FUTURE RESEARCH AND PRACTICE

The case provided here supports our argument that the nuclear family can be an important source of support for working parents. We found that controlling for relational quality in the family, the more emotionally positive family time was, the better parents' assessment of the ability to balance their work and family lives. Conversely, emotionally negative family time was associated with a lower degree of work-family balance. What could be the underlying mechanism by which the emotional dimension of family time affects parents' well-being? We suggest that when time spent with family is a positive experience it can help busy working parents take a break from the stressors of everyday life and regain much needed energy. In this way, family time can boost parents' self-esteem and contribute to their confidence in their ability to manage the complexities of contemporary work and family lives (Barnett & Rivers, 1996).

This study further sheds light on the types of activities that are most likely to be emotionally enhancing. We found that for both mothers and fathers, most family activities were positive and engaging in nature, especially leisure and social activities and eating meals together. Time spent on unstructured direct interaction, such as talking and playing with spouse and child, was also an important positive experience of family time. Family time spent on household-related tasks, however, was a much more negative and less engaging experience. Considering that, on average, the dual-earner families in this study spent about 15% of their time together doing household-related tasks, this effect cannot be overlooked.

Interestingly, the negative emotional dimension of family time spent on household-related tasks suggests that "quality time" cannot be simply defined as time being together. Using a subsample of families from the 500 Family Study, Snyder and Lewin (2006) report that once controls for occupational conditions and work hours were included in their model, parents who defined quality time as "all the time they spent with family" did not differ in their level of work-family conflict from parents who defined quality time in terms of joint planned and structured activities.

The idea that quality time does not constitute family time in general is further supported by our finding that the proportion of time spent with family was not significantly related to parents' assessment of work-family balance. Rather than quantity, this study indicates that the quality of family time, that is how parents feel when they spend time with their family, is what matters for parents' well-being. This finding highlights the complex and multidimensional nature of family time.

Finally, it is important to stress that because of the nature of the sample, the results reported here best apply to dual-earner middle-class families and cannot be generalized to the overall population of working families. Nevertheless, it has important implications for low-income families. One of the strategies middle and upper middle-class families adopt to deal with the shortage of time is to use their disposable income to purchase household services in the market (Hochschild, 2003; Stuenkel, 2005). Low-income families, on the other hand, have a much more limited ability to do so. As a result, they may need to spend more of their precious family time on household-related activities, which are associated with more negative emotional experiences. Viewed in this way, in low-income families the time squeeze may be more severe and its effects on family well-being more detrimental.

REFERENCES

Barnett, R. C. & Rivers, C. 1996. *She Works He Works: How Two-Income Families are Happy, Healthy, and Thriving*. Cambridge, MA: Harvard University Press.

Bianchi, S. M. (2000). Maternal employment and time with children: Dramatic change or surprising continuity? *Demography, 37*, 401–414.

Bianchi, S. M., Robinson, J. P. & Milkie, M. A. (2006). *The Changing Rhythm of American Family Life*. New York: Russell Sage Foundation.

Blair-Loy, M. (2003). *Competing Devotions: Career and Family Among Women Executives*. Cambridge, MA: Harvard University Press.

Blair-Loy, M. & Wharton, A. S. (2002). Employees' use of work-family policies and the workplace social context. *Social_ Forces, 80*, 813–845.

Bond, J. T., Galinsky, E. & Swanberg, J. E. (1998). *The 1997 National Study of the Changing Workforce*. New York: Families and Work Institute.

Carnoy, M. (2000). *Sustaining the New Economy: Work, Family, and Community in the Information Age*. New York: Russell Sage Foundation.

Casper, L. & Bianchi, S. M. (2002). *Continuity and Change in the American Family*. Thousand Oaks, CA: Sage.

Chaudry, A. (2005). *Putting Children First: How Low-Wage Working Mothers Manage Child Care*. New York: Russell Sage Foundation.

Csikszentmihalyi, M. & Larson, R. (1987). Validity and reliability of the experience sampling method. *Journal of Nervous and Mental Disease, 175*, 526–536.

Daly, K. J. (2001). Deconstructing family time: From ideology to lived experience. *Journal of Marriage and Family, 63*, 283–294.

Galinsky, E., Kim, S. S. & Bond, J. T. (2001). *Feeling Overworked: When Work Becomes too Much*. New York: Families and Work Institute.

Gillis, J. (1996). Making time for families: The intervention of family time(s) and the reinvention of family history. *Journal of Family History, 21*, 4–21.

Goldin, C. (2004). The long road to the fast track: Career and family. *Annals of the American Academy of Political and Social Sciences, 596*, 20–35.

Hill, E. J. (2005). Work-family facilitation and conflict, working fathers and mothers, work-family stressors and support. *Journal of Family Issues, 26*, 793–819.

Hochschild, A. R. (2003). *The Commercialization of Intimate Life*. Berkeley, CA: University of California Press.

Hochschild, A. R. (1997). *The Time Bind: When Work Becomes Home and Home Becomes Work*. New York: Metropolitan Books.

Hoogstra, L. (2005). Design and sample characteristics of the 500 Family Study. In B. Schneider & L. J. Waite (eds), *Being Together, Working Apart: Dual-Career Families and their Work-Life Balance* (pp. 23–48). Cambridge, UK: Cambridge University Press.

Jacobs, A. J. & Gerson, K. (2004). *The Time Divide: Work, Family, and Gender Inequality*. Cambridge, MA: Harvard University Press.

Lareau, A. (2002). Invisible inequalities: Class, race, and child rearing in black families and white families. *American Sociological Review, 67*, 747–776.

Loperst, P. (1999). *How Families that Left Welfare are Doing*: A National Picture (Assessing the New Federalism Policy Brief no. B-1). Washington, DC: Urban Institute.

Milkie, M. A., Mattingly, M. J., Nomaguchi, K. M., Bianchi, S. M. & Robinson, J. P. (2004). The time squeeze: Parental statuses and feelings about time with children. *Journal of Marriage and Family, 66*, 739–761.

Mishel, L. R., Bernstein, J. & Schmitt, J. (2001). *The State of Working America*. Ithaca, NY: Cornell University Press.

Moen, P. & Yu, Y. (2000). Effective work-life strategies: Working couples, work conditions, gender, and life quality. *Social Problems, 47*, 291–326.

National Center on Addiction and Substance Abuse. (2006). The importance of family dinners III. New York: Columbia University.

Nock, S. L. & Kingston, P. W. (1984). The family work day. *Journal of Marriage and Family, 47*, 333–343.

Presser, H. B. (2003). *Toward a 24-hour Economy*. New York: Russell Sage Foundation.

Robinson, J. P. (1999). The time-diary method. In W. Pentland, A. Harvey, M. Lawton & M. McColl (eds), *Time Use Research in the Social Sciences* (pp. 47–89). New York: Kluwer Academic/Plenum Publisher.

Robinson, J. P. & Godbey, G. (1999). *Time for Life: The Surprising Ways Americans Use Their Time* (2nd edn). University Park, PA: Pennsylvania State University Press.

Roehling, P. V., Jarvis, L. H. & Swope, H. E. (2005). Variations in negative work-family spillover among white, black, and Hispanic American men and women: Does ethnicity matter? *Journal of Family Issues, 26*, 840–865.

Sandberg, J. F. & Hofferth, S. L. (2001). Changes in children's time with parents : United States, 1981–1997. *Demography, 38*, 423–436.

Shaw, S. M. (1997). Controversies and contradictions in family leisure: An analysis of conflicting paradigms. *Journal of Leisure Research, 29*, 98–112.

Snyder, K. A vocabulary of motives: How parents understand quality time. *Journal of Marriage and Family*. Forthcoming.

Snyder, K. & Lewin, A. (2006). Balancing work and home: The relationship between quality time and work-family conflict. Paper presented at the annual meeting of the American Sociological Association. Montreal.

Stuenkel, C. P. (2005). A strategy for working families: The commodification of household services. In B. Schneider & L. J. Waite (eds), Being Together, Working Apart: Dual-Career Families and their Work-Life Balance (pp. 252–272). Cambridge, UK: Cambridge University Press.

Voydanoff, P. (1988). Work role characteristics, family structure demands, and work-family conflict. *Journal of Marriage and Family, 50*, 749–761.

Voydanoff, P. (2002). Linkages between the work-family interface and work, family, and individual outcomes: An integrative model. *Journal of Family Issues, 23*, 138–164.

Waite, L. J. & Nielsen, M. (2001). The rise of the dual-career family: 1963–1997. In R. Hertz & N. L. Marshall (eds), *Women and Work in the Twentieth Century* (pp. 23–41). Berkeley, CA: University of California Press.

CHAPTER 11

Health and Well-Being Outcomes of the Work-Family Interface

Jane Mullen*, **Elizabeth Kelley**[†] **and E. Kevin Kelloway**[‡]
*Mount Allison University, Sackville, NB
[†]Dalhousie University, Halifax, NS
[‡]Saint Mary's University, Halifax, NS

Sufficient data have now accumulated to allow the unequivocal assertion of the link between work stress and both physical and psychological health. With respect to the former, work stress has been associated with conditions ranging from minor psychosomatic complaints such as sleep disturbances and digestive problems (e.g., Schat, Kelloway & Desmarais, 2005), through increased risk of infectious disease (e.g., Cohen & Williamson, 1991; Schaubroeck, Jones & Xie, 2001) suppressed immune functioning (O'Leary, 1990) and musculoskeletal problems (e.g., Carayon, Smith & Haims, 1999; Lundberg et al., 1999). Evidence for the link between job stress and physical health is particularly strong for cardiovascular outcomes including elevated blood pressure (Barling & Kelloway, 1996), chronic hypertension (Schwartz, Pickering & Landsbergis, 1996), and coronary heart disease (CHD) (Karasek & Theorell, 1990; Krantz, Contrada, Hill & Friedler, 1988; Theorell and Karasek, 1996). Importantly, prospective evidence from the Whitehall studies suggested that individuals in "low control" occupations were 1.5 to 1.8 times as likely to experience new heart disease at 5-year follow-up (Bosma, Stansfeld & Marmot, 1998). In addition to these "disease" outcomes, there is also evidence that suggests that individuals may increase their smoking (e.g., Conway, Vickers, Ward & Rahe, 1981; Parrott, 1995) or consumption of alcohol and other drugs (Grunberg, Moore, Greenberg & Anderson-Conolly, 1999; Jones & Boye, 1992) under periods of increased stress. Paradoxically, individuals in high-stress jobs report engaging in less exercise than do individuals in low-stress jobs (e.g., Payne, Jones & Harris, 2002). With regard to psychological health, disturbances in affect and cognitive functioning are also consistently identified as outcomes of work stress (e.g., Kelloway & Day, 2005). For example, Wang and Patten (2001) found support for the association between work stressors and major depressive disorders in Canadian workers.

These observations provide a starting point for considering the effect of the work-family interface on individual health and well-being. To the extent that the work-family interface is a source of stress, the available data would suggest

Handbook of Work-Family Integration: Research, Theory, and Best Practices

that work-family interactions also have consequences for individual well-being. However, we suggest that the impact of the work-family interface on well-being is not entirely negative and that the available data suggest the existence of both positive and negative effects. The goal of this chapter is to review this evidence. In doing so, we depart from previous reviews (e.g., Allen, Herst, Bruck & Sutton, 2000; Bellavia & Frone, 2005; Frone, 2003; Geurts & Demerouti, 2003) by going beyond an exclusive focus on negative effects. From this basis, we examine current research practices as well as organizational, individual, and governmental policy and practices. Specifically, we provide an overview of the dominant theoretical perspectives that are used to guide research on the work-family interface. Subsequently, the nature of the work-family interface is reviewed, followed by a comprehensive review of the work-family literature. We conclude with a discussion of the future research needs and the implications for practice and policy.

THE WORK-FAMILY INTERFACE: LEVELS OF CONCEPTUALIZATION AND ANALYSIS

Most research on the work-family interface has focused on work-family conflict (Allen et al., 2000). This may reflect the fact that individuals are more likely to experience work interference in their family lives than family interference at work (Bellavia & Frone, 2005; Duxbury & Higgins, 2001; Eagle, Miles & Icenogle, 1997; Frone, 2003). While Duxbury and Higgins documented an increase in both work-to-family (WTF) and family-to-work (FTW) conflict in the decade between 1991 and 2000–2001, they also noted a change in the balance between them. Employees in 2001 were still far more likely to experience WTF interference than they are to experience FTW interference. Between 1991 and 2001, the rates of individuals reporting high WTF interference increased from 27% to 31% while the percentage of those reporting high FTW interference increased from 5% in 1991 to 10% in 2001 (Duxbury & Higgins).

Because most of the literature in this area has taken the conflict perspective, the dysfunctional consequences of the interference of one domain on the other (Hill, 2005; Parasuraman & Greenhaus, 2002) has been extensively explored. Both Frone's (2003) and Geurts and Demerouti's (2003) reviews suggest that a different perspective is beneficial: the interface between work and family may also have positive consequences, more recently referred to as "facilitation" (Frone, 2003; Grzywacz & Butler, 2005; Hill, 2005; Kirchmeyer, 1993), "enrichment" (Greenhaus & Powell, 2006; Rothbard, 2001) or positive spillover (Barnett, 1998; Crouter, 1994; Grzywacz & Marks, 2000; Kirchmeyer, 1992, 1993). These are salient distinctions in this discussion of outcomes because it has been suggested that the manifestations of the work-family interface, which encompasses both conflict and facilitation, have different antecedents, outcomes, and moderators (Aryee, Tan & Srinivas, 2005; Demerouti & Geurts, 2004; Frone, 2003; Grzywacz & Marks, 2000b).

THEORETICAL PERSPECTIVES

The predominant theoretical perspectives that have guided research in the work-family domain include role theory and ecological systems theory. Prior to reviewing the health-related outcomes in the work-family literature, it is important to briefly review each of these theories.

Role Theory

Most of the research on the work-family interface has been guided by role theory (e.g., Kahn, Wolfe, Quinn, Snoek & Rosenthal, 1964; Katz & Kahn, 1978). Within role theory, researchers have described the work-family relationship in terms of the number of roles occupied by an individual. Some researchers suggest that individuals have a limited amount of time and energy, thus engaging in multiple roles tends to be overly demanding. This perspective is known as the scarcity hypothesis (Goode, 1960), and assumes that conflict and strain are probable outcomes of performing multiple roles. The more roles an individual occupies, the greater the likelihood that an individual will experience stress. Kahn et al. defined this type of work-family relationship as role conflict, which is the "simultaneous occurrence of two (or more) sets of pressures such that compliance with one would make more difficult compliance with the other" (1964, p. 19). Based on Kahn et al.'s conceptualization of role conflict, Greenhaus and Beutell defined WTF conflict as "a form of interrole conflict in which the role pressures from the work and family domains are mutually incompatible" (1985, p. 77). It is now generally recognized that work-family conflict is bidirectional, such that work can interfere with family and family can interfere with work (Frone, 2003). Much of the work-family research continues to call attention to the negative outcomes associated with conflicting roles between work and the family.

Within the role accumulation perspective, several theorists proposed an expansion hypothesis (Marks, 1977; Sieber, 1974) in which the roles in one area (e.g., work) can benefit one's role in another area (e.g., family). Similar to the scarcity hypothesis, the expansion hypothesis also focuses on the number of roles that an individual occupies. Expansion theorists do not disagree that occupying multiple roles can lead to conflict and stress. However, occupying multiple roles may also lead to positive effects on psychological health and well-being (Barnett & Baruch, 1985) and tend to be overlooked in the literature.

Stemming from the work of early expansion theorists, several researchers have examined enrichment (Greenhaus & Powell, 2006; Rothbard, 2001), enhancement (Rudderman, Ohlott, Panzer & King, 2002), and positive spillover (Edwards & Rothbard, 2000; Grzywacz & Marks, 2000a; Hanson, Hammer & Colton, 2006). There is a growing body of empirical evidence supporting the notion that participation in multiple work and family roles can lead to positive effects on individuals' physical and psychological health (Barnett & Hyde, 2001; Barnett & Marshall, 1993; Grzywacz & Marks, 2000a, 2000b; Hammer, Cullen, Neal, Sinclair & Shafiro, 2005; Hanson et al., 2006; Poelmans, Stepanova & Masuda, this volume).

Ecological Systems Theory

To develop a broader conceptualization of the work-family interface, researchers have drawn on ecological theory. Bronfenbrenner (1979) suggests that individual development occurs throughout one's lifespan and is shaped by dynamic, reciprocal interactions between one's self and the experiences one has as a consequence of immediate and broader social contexts.

There are four hierarchical environmental systems that influence individual development including the microsystem, the mesosystem, the exosystem, and the macrosystem (for a review see Voydanoff, this volume). The microsystem is "the complex of relations between the developing person and environment in an immediate setting (e.g., home, workplace)" and "a setting is defined as a place with particular physical features in which the participants engage in particular roles (e.g., parent, employee) for particular periods of time" (Bronfenbrenner, 1977, p. 514). Secondly, the mesosystem is a "system of microsystems" (Bronfenbrenner, 1977, p. 514) and comprises the interactions among the major systems in the microsystem. Thirdly, the ecosystem is defined as "an extension of the mesosystem embracing other specific social structures, both formal and informal, that do not themselves contain the developing person but impinge upon or encompass the immediate settings in which that person is found" (Bronfenbrenner, 1977, p. 515). Within the context of the work-family interface, for example, the exosystem could include the interaction between an individual's experience at home and their partner's work life (Bellavia & Frone, 2003). Lastly, the macrosystem is the "overarching institutional patterns of the culture or subculture, such as the economic, social, educational, and political systems, of which micro, meso, and exo are the conceived manifestations" (Bronfenbrenner, 1977, p. 515).

These environmental systems interact to have an effect on individuals' work-family experiences and serves as a useful framework for understanding the work-family interface (Bronfenbrenner, 1986; Grzywacz & Marks, 2000b). Much of the research focuses on the mesosystem level of the ecological model as it focuses specifically on how roles, relationships, and experiences at work are related to roles, relationships, and experiences in one's family (Carlson & Perrewe, 1999; Frone, Russell & Cooper, 1993; Grzywacz & Marks, 2000b; O'Driscoll, Ilgen &

Hildreth, 1992; See also Voydanoff, this volume). Others have focused on the exo-system level by examining the effects of one family member's experiences on another family member (e.g., Kohn, 1969; Morgan, Alwin & Griffin, 1979). For example, Parasuraman, Greenhaus, Rabinowitz, Bedeian and Mossholder (1989) examined the effects of women's' employment status on their partners' well-being and job satisfaction, and Harrison and Ungerer (2002) examined the effects of mothers' work experiences on child-mother attachment security. Researchers have also examined the work-family interface at the macrosystem level (Barnett, 1996). For example, Aryee, Fields and Luk (1999) examined the cross-cultural generalizability of a work-family conflict model (see also Aycan, this volume).

Overall, there is a growing body of empirical evidence supporting each level of the ecological model (Bellavia & Frone, 2003). The theory is useful for under-standing the work-family interface as it encompasses a broader range of factors that influence both the positive and negative work-family experiences of indi-viduals. Furthermore, ecological theory is a valuable conceptual model that can be used to examine how environmental systems interact and influence individual health and well-being (e.g., Grzywacz & Marks, 2000b; Stokols, 1996).

THE NATURE OF THE WORK-FAMILY INTERFACE

WORK-FAMILY CONFLICT MODELS

One of the earlier comprehensive frameworks of WTF conflict was pro-posed by Frone, Russell and Cooper (1992). The framework extends previous theories of WTF conflict (e.g., Greenhaus & Beutell, 1985; Kopelman, Greenhaus & Connelly, 1983) by specifically testing and providing empirical support for the reciprocal relationship between WTF and FTW conflict. In this theoretical frame-work, WTF conflict mediates the relationship between stressors and job character-istics and family distress. FTW conflict, in turn, mediates the relationship between family demands and job distress. Furthermore, both WTF conflict and FTW con-flict are positively and directly related to overall psychological distress.

Research supports Frone et al.'s (1992) bidirectional theoretical framework suggesting that WTF and FTW conflict are two distinct forms of conflict that each have unique, although not mutually exclusive outcomes (Frone, 2000; Grzywacz & Marks, 2000; Hammer et al., 2005) such as increased psychological distress (Frone, Russell & Cooper, 1997; Frone, Yardley & Markel, 1997; MacEwen & Barling, 1994; Wayne, Musisca & Fleeson, 2004) and alcohol abuse (Frone et al., 2003). However, the results reported in the literature are not consistent and researchers suggest that gender and personality may moderate the link between WTF con-flict and FTW conflict and psychological distress. For example, Rantanen and col-leagues found that WTF conflict, resulting from number of hours spent working, occupational status, and work demands, was shown to be associated with increased psychological distress. The link between WTF conflict and psychological distress in women was moderated by neuroticism. FTW conflict, resulting from parental demands associated with children under school age, also predicted psychological distress. The relationship was moderated by gender such that young children had a positive impact on men's well-being and a negative effect on women's well-being (Rantanen, Pulkkinen & Kinnunen, 2005).

In a longitudinal study of employed parents, WTF conflict was associated with increased levels of alcohol consumption, and FTW conflict was associated with increased levels of depression and poor physical health (Frone, Russell & Cooper, 1997). Hammer, Neal, Newsom, Brockwood and Colton (2005) found similar results in their longitudinal study of the effects of the work-family interface on depression among dual-earner couples, demonstrating a significant effect of FTW conflict on depression, yet a non-significant relationship between WTF conflict and depression. Gender differences were also found such that the effects of FTW conflict on depression were significant for men but not for women. Thus, only men reported increased levels of depression when FTW conflict increased.

WORK-FAMILY POSITIVE SPILLOVER

In response to the over-emphasis on role conflict in the work-family literature, researchers have proposed various constructs to explain the positive and reciprocal effects of combining work and family roles. Greenhaus and Powell (2006) proposed a model of work-family enrichment that describes the positive outcomes associated with combining work and family roles. Work-family enrichment is defined as "the extent to which experiences in one role improve the quality of life in the other role" (Greenhaus & Powell, p. 73). The relationship between work and family is reciprocal, such that WTF enrichment occurs when an individual's experience at work improves the quality of their family life, and vice versa.

The enrichment model suggests that resources generated in Role A (work or family) can have a direct impact on one's quality of life in Role B (work or family), as measured by performance and positive affect. For example, skills or psychological resources (e.g., self-efficacy) generated in one area of our life (work or family) can directly impact our performance in another area. Moderators of the direct path between resources generated in Role A and quality of life in Role B include salience, perceived relevance of a resource, and consistency with norms of Role B. In addition, the model incorporates an affective path (Hanson et al., 2006) in which the relationship between resources generated by Role A have an effect on positive affect, which in turn affects an individual's performance in Role B. The relationship between affect in one role and performance in another is moderated by the salience of role B. Researchers have yet to empirically test and validate the enrichment model proposed by Greenhaus and Powell (2006); however, it provides a very useful framework for extending research on the interface between work and family.

Theoretical frameworks and a measure of work-family positive spillover have been proposed by other researchers (Edwards & Rothbard, 2000; Hanson et al., 2006). Hanson et al. defined work-family positive spillover as "the transfer of positively valenced affect, skills, behaviours, and values from the originating domain to the receiving domain, thus having beneficial effects on the receiving domain" (p. 251), and suggested that positive spillover can be divided into six sub-dimensions including (a) WTF affective positive spillover, (b) WTF behaviour-based instrumental positive spillover, (c) WTF value-based instrumental positive spillover, (d) FTW affective positive spillover, (e) FTW behaviour-based instrumental positive spillover, and (f) FTW value-based instrumental positive spillover. Empirical support was provided for the multidimensional scale in addition to the reciprocal nature of the types of spillover, such that positive spillover occurs in both directions (WTF, FTW). Furthermore, there is a growing body of evidence that suggests that positive spillover is related to improved attitudes and well-being (Grzywacz, 2000; Hammer et al., 2005; Poelmans et al., this volume). For example, family role commitment is associated with decreased psychological strain, through FTW positive spillover (Graves, Ohlott & Ruderman, 2007). Family role commitment has also been shown to enhance leadership skills and well-being at work (Rudderman et al., 2002). With respect to WTF positive spillover, research suggests that characteristics of the job such as variety and authority positively impact employee attitudes, self-esteem, and motivation, which in turn enhances functioning in the family domain (e.g., Friedman & Greenhaus, 2000; Grzywacz & Butler, 2005).

FAMILY CARE

Demographic changes such as the increased participation rates of women in the labour force and an aging population have resulted in various types of family care roles that employees occupy. In a recent survey of over 31,000 employed Canadians, 70% of the sample were parents, 60% reported eldercare responsibilities, and 13% reported having both child and eldercare responsibilities (Duxbury & Higgins, 2003) referred to as the sandwiched generation (e.g., Ingersoll, Dayton, Neal & Hammer, 2001). In addition, approximately 13% of the respondents indicated that they provided care for a disabled family member.

There is a growing body of research that examines the caregiving roles that individuals occupy (e.g., Barling, MacEwen, Kelloway & Higginbottom, 1994; Bainbridge, Cregan & Kulik, 2006; Stephens & Townsend, 1997). Research on the effects of combining work and caregiving roles has predominantly been examined from the role conflict perspective (e.g., Goff, Mount & Jamison, 1990; Hammer et al., 2005) and has largely focused on parent-employee conflict. For example, research suggests that childcare responsibilities create time-based conflict such that participation in the family role makes it difficult to perform work roles (e.g., Baltes & Heydens-Gahir, 2003; Frone et al., 1992).

The roles of providing eldercare or care for a person with a disability or chronic illness has also received increasing attention (e.g., Barling, et al., 1994; Hepburn & Barling, 1996; Marks, 1998; Sahibzada, Hammer, Neal & Kuang, 2005). There is a considerable body of research suggesting that dependent care responsibilities are associated with poor health and increased work-family conflict (e.g., Frone, et al., 1992; Greenhaus & Beutell, 1985; Hammer, Allen & Grigsby, 1997). Researchers have identified various stressors related to the care provider role such as the type of disability/illness, and the amount of care required or time required to provide care, as well as the effects of these stressors on psychological strain (e.g., Cannuscio, Jones, Kawachi, Colditz, Berkman & Rimm, 2002). The role conflict perspective (e.g., Kahn et al., 1964) suggests that commitment to the caregiving role may reduce the resources and energy that could be devoted to work roles.

A small number of studies have examined the effects of family care from the enrichment perspective (Bainbridge et al., 2006; Scharlach, 1994) and are raising questions about the adequacy of the role conflict perspective (e.g., scarcity hypothesis) to explain the experiences of individuals who occupy work and caregiving roles. In fact, based on the results of a recent study, Bainbridge et al. caution against the exclusive use of the role scarcity framework and suggest that researchers should examine the effects of role enrichment by measuring the benefits associated with the caregiving role. Consistent with the view of enrichment/expansionist theorists (Marks, 1977; Sieber, 1974), research suggests that the benefits of occupying multiple roles (e.g., work and family roles) outweigh the detrimental factors (Rothbard, 2001).

OUTCOMES OF THE WORK-FAMILY INTERFACE

INDIVIDUAL EFFECTS

Psychological Well-Being

A significant body of research across several disciplines has examined the various psychological outcomes of the work-family interface (Allen et al., 2000; Frone, 1992, 2003; Frone et al., 1997; Grzywacz & Bass, 2003; Kossek & Ozeki, 1998). Although it is unequivocal that conflict between the two domains has negative consequences, there have been contradictory findings about the specific associations. In his 2003 review, Frone notes that many studies have assessed only WTF conflict, or have used global measures that confound what has been more recently assessed as separate constructs (Allen et al., 2000; Demerouti & Geurts, 2004; Geurts & Demerouti, 2003; Hill, 2005; Voydanoff, 2002). Most studies have been cross-sectional and achieve results that differ from findings of longitudinal studies. For example, Allen et al. observed that all cross-sectional studies have found significant correlations between work-family interference and depression, while Frone's (1997) longitudinal study found no such association. Bellavia and Frone (2004) noted that generally there are a multitude of negative effects of both WTF and FTW conflict on the individual including, for example, stress (Kelloway, Gottlieb & Barham, 1999), general psychological strain (Grzywacz & Marks, 2000a), alcoholism (Frone, Russell & Cooper, 1993), somatic/physical symptoms (Burke & Greenglass, 1999), burnout and depression (Allen et al., 2000; Frone, 1992), medication use (Burke & Greenglass, 1999), and decreased life satisfaction (Allen et al., 2000; Brotheridge & Lee, 2005; Demerouti & Geurts, 2004; Hill, 2005; Kossek & Ozeki, 1998).

Many studies have reported correlations between WTF conflict and life satisfaction; two meta-analyses reported similar weighted mean correlations with bidirectional work-family conflict: .28 (Kossek & Ozeki, 1998) and .31 (Allen et al., 2000). Hill (2005) found that FTW conflict was positively related to individual stress, but not to life satisfaction.

Some findings suggest that the bidirectional effects are not of equal magnitude; Brotheridge and Lee (2005), for example, found that general well-being is primarily predicted by work-related conditions, such as WTF conflict. Kelloway et al. (1999), in a longitudinal study, highlighted the need to consider both the source and the nature of work and family conflict and noted the ambiguous nature of WTF conflict effects. These findings suggest that only strain-based FTW conflict is a precursor to perceived stress; in fact, it appears that perceptions of WTF conflict may result from, rather than predict, stress reactions. Demerouti and Geurts (2004) found that when employees perceive their work-home interaction as primarily negative, they experience psychological health symptoms at a higher level than employees who perceived a positive influence from their jobs.

The relationship between positive aspects of the work-family interface and individual outcomes has not been empirically investigated to any great extent (Demerouti & Geurts, 2004). Greenhaus and Powell (2006) support their theoretical model of the work-family enrichment process with an integrated review of a disparate body of work. In their analysis of 19 studies that measured work-family enrichment, they found that the average enrichment score was at least as high as the average conflict score, and generally was substantially higher. Although there is little data on specific psychological outcomes of work-family enrichment or positive spillover, this finding suggests that employees perceive that their work and family roles do enrich one another. Demerouti's and Geurts' (2004) findings support this argument. Their analysis identified five clusters. Approximately one-third of respondents experienced work and family as two separate spheres (i.e., with no interaction between work and family). A very small number (approximately 5%)

experienced primarily negative interactions between work and family. The majority of participants experienced some kind of positive interaction, including approximately 40% who perceived a primarily positive interaction, with the remaining participants experiencing both negative and positive interactions.

Interestingly, those who experienced separation did not enjoy better outcomes than participants in the other clusters; they had the second lowest scores on the negative health indicators and only average scores on positive health indicators. This suggests that interaction between work and family, if positive, offers the best quality of life (Demerouti & Geurts, 2004). Grzywacz's and Bass's (2003) research supports this suggestion. They contend that work-family fit is more than the absence of conflict; their results suggest that FTW facilitation is a family protective factor that buffers the negative effects of work-family conflict on mental health and that adult mental health is optimized when FTW facilitation is high and FTW and WTF conflict are low.

Physical Well-being

A large amount of research has shown a correlation between work-family conflict and reduced physical well-being. Outcomes such as obesity (Grzywacz, 2000), hypertension (Frone et al., 1997), psychosomatic symptoms (Burke & Greenglass, 1999), and substance use (e.g., Frone et al., 1994, 1997) have all been associated with the work-family conflict. This is both a significant personal and societal issue. For example, Duxbury and Higgins (2001) calculated the societal cost of increased visits to physicians associated with declines in physical health at almost half a billion Canadian dollars.

Two recent reviews of the relevant literature support the connection between negative experience of the work-family interface, in either direction, and decreased physical health (Allen et al., 2000; Bellavia & Frone, 2004). Bellavia and Frone noted that the direction of the conflict has been linked to specific health problems, with FTW conflict predicting the onset of hypertension in a longitudinal study (Frone et al., 1997), and WTF conflict predicting obesity (Grzywacz, 2000). In their meta-analysis, Allen et al. obtained a weighted mean correlation of .29 between work-family conflict and increased physical symptoms or somatic complaints.

There has been little empirical investigation of the potential for positive physical effects emerging from the work-family interface; however, there are grounds for positing such a relationship. In a recent investigation, for example, Williams, Franche, Ibrahim, Mustard and Layton (2006) reported that hospital workers who reported positive FTW spillover also experienced better sleep quality. Barnett and Hyde (2001) reviewed the literature relating to multiple roles and summarized their findings by stating that research consistently demonstrates that women and men who engage in multiple roles report lower levels of stress-related mental and physical health problems and higher levels of subjective well-being than do those who engage in fewer roles. More recent research has attributed these positive effects primarily to the employee role. Grzywacz and Marks (2000b) observed that research in related bodies of literature consistently finds that employed married mothers enjoy better physical and psychological health than unemployed married mothers, suggesting that work and family life can benefit each other. In their own investigation, they found that all forms of work-family spillover (negative FTW, negative WTF, positive FTW, and positive WTF) were uniquely associated with both physical and mental health after controlling for the other forms of spillover.

Health-Related Behaviors

The psychological and physical effects of a negative work-family interface may contribute to unhealthy behaviors as well. Bellavia and Frone (2004) have noted research that documents various health-related behaviors that have a deleterious effect, such as substance use, overeating, and eating poorly or skipping meals completely. Ng and Jeffery (2003) demonstrated that high stress for both men and women was associated with a higher fat diet, less frequent exercise, and increased cigarette smoking. The use of medications (Burke & Greenglass, 1999), cigarettes (e.g., Frone et al., 1994), and alcohol (Frone et al., 1997; Grzywacz & Bass, 2003) have also been associated with work-family conflict.

FAMILY/DYADIC EFFECTS

It is a given that most employees live in some kind of a family structure and that what happens to one family member affects others. Barnett (1998) found that negative job experiences for one partner created psychological distress for the other, an example of emotional contagion as a crossover effect. Some research has demonstrated that negative family/dyadic effects occur in one direction, with WTF conflict associated with family-related distress and dissatisfaction, poor family performance, and family-related withdrawal. In contrast, FTW conflict is hypothesized to mainly relate to organizational outcomes (Frone, 1992). Subsequent studies (Aryee et al., 2005) suggest that both forms of work-family conflict predict lower family satisfaction, directly or indirectly (Bellavia & Frone, 2004). Perry-Jenkins, Repetti and Crouter (2000) in their review of the impact of occupational stress on families, note that there is a substantial body of research that suggests that chronic job stressors affect families when they induce feelings of role overload or role conflict between the two spheres. In Allen et al.'s (2000) meta-analysis, the link between work-family conflict and family-related stress was clear; the weighted mean correlation was .31. Generally, researchers have found that increased levels of WTF conflict are inversely related to marital functioning or adjustment (Barling, 1986). WTF conflict has also been inversely related to family satisfaction in most studies (Allen et al.; Frone, 2003). From the perspective of WTF facilitation, Greenhaus and Powell (2006) noted that research suggests that positive aspects of the work environment, such as supportiveness and flexibility, have been associated with positive outcomes in the family domain such as family satisfaction (Frone et al., 1997; Voydanoff, 2001). It has also been suggested that work satisfaction is related to family satisfaction, and to positive parenting and child outcomes (Barling, 1986; Rothbard, 2001).

Paths to Well-being

Bellavia and Frone (2005) suggest that the effect of work-family conflict on physical health may occur through multiple, and perhaps complementary, pathways. As a preliminary specification, consideration of the data reviewed above suggests several of these pathways. First, work-family conflict is associated with numerous health behaviors including substance use, smoking, and overeating (Greeno & Wing, 1994). Thus, one effect of increased work-family conflict would be to decrease engagement in health promoting behaviors (e.g., nutrition and exercise) while at the same time increasing adverse health behaviors such as smoking or drinking alcohol.

As noted above, work-family conflict also has an impact on psychological well-being including stress, anxiety, and depression. The links between these outcomes and physical health are also well documented (e.g., Hurrell & Kelloway, in press) and work-family conflict may impact physical health indirectly by adversely affecting psychological well-being. Using longitudinal data, Kelloway and Barling (1994) directly tested and supported this suggestion finding that job stress led to depression which, in turn, impaired family relationships. We further note the potential for these effects to spiral, that is, for negative family or dyadic effects to exacerbate the stress experienced by individuals, perhaps leading to more adverse health behaviors.

Family Characteristics

The role of family configuration and context has been extensively explored, although findings about several variables are inconclusive. Family characteristics such as marital status, the presence of children, the number and age of children, amount of marital support, family roles, and the availability and suitability of childcare have all been investigated and generally found to have some effect on work-family relationships. For example, there is evidence that spousal support (or related constructs such as spousal criticism) moderate the effect of work-family conflict (Grzywacz & Marks, 2000; Suchet & Barling, 1986). There are mixed findings about the presence and age of children. For example, Voydanoff (1988) found that age of children significantly affects the work-family interface, with conflict being highest among those with younger children. Duxbury and Higgins (2001) found no relation between life-cycle stage and WTF conflict, while FTW conflict was strongly associated with life-cycle parameters. Hughes and Galinsky (1994) found that the presence of children younger than 13 in the family moderated the relationships between job characteristics and family functioning. In their recent review, Eby, Casper, Lockwood, Bordeaux and Brinley (2005) reviewed the research on potential moderators and concluded that family structure is an important construct in work-family research and that simultaneous consideration of several family characteristics may be required to fully understand the work-family interface.

ORGANIZATIONAL CHARACTERISTICS

A number of work-related variables have been shown to moderate the relationships involved in the work-family interface. Hours spent working has been shown to be related to levels of WTF and FTW conflict (Bellavia and Frone, 2004). Grzywacz and Marks found that working more than 45 hours/week was associated with more negative WTF spillover for both men and women. The findings relating to hours of work have been mixed however (Hill, 2005), and appear to be linked to type of job (professional/nonprofessional) (Duxbury & Higgins, 2001) and gender (Hill, 2005). Another moderator that has been extensively researched is supervisory support. Levels of supervisory support have been found to moderate the relationship between work role conflict and WTF conflict (Bellavia & Frone, 2004; Eby et al., 2005). Hill found that manager support of the employee on the job had a stronger impact on work-family conflict and facilitation than did manager support of the parent in his/her parental responsibilities. More broadly, support from one's supervisor, organizational culture, or a mentor has been found to positively influence the work-family interface (Brotheridge and Lee, 2005; Duxbury and Higgins, 2001; Eby et al.) through various mechanisms, such as reducing job strain (Demerouti & Geurts, 2004) and increasing perceived control (Clark, 2002; Grzywacz & Marks, 2000).

MODERATORS OF THE WORK-FAMILY INTERFACE

Allen (2000) observed that the range of differential findings in this literature suggests the existence of undetected moderator variables. We would expand this suggestion to include the potential for a variety of indirect effects including both moderated and mediated relationships. Viewed from an ecological systems theory or fit theory perspectives, in which the work-family interface is a joint function of process, person, context, and time characteristics (Eby et al., 2005; Grzywacz & Marks, 2000; Perry-Jenkins et al., 2000), the list of potential moderators is long indeed.

Gender is perhaps the most researched individual characteristic (Korabik, McElwain & Chappell, this volume). Bellavia and Frone (2004) report that, as with research into gender differences in the prevalence of work-family conflict, there is little evidence that gender plays a moderating role in the relationship between either direction of work-family conflict and its antecedents and outcomes (Demerouti & Geurts, 2004; Frone, et al., 1997; Geurts & Demerouti, 2003; Kinnunen & Mauno, 1998; Kirchmeyer, 1992). Some studies have found differences along gender lines, both in the prevalence of work-family conflict and in the pathways by which work factors influence WTF conflict. For example, Duxbury and Higgins (2001) found that mothers reported higher levels of role overload than fathers, and that motherhood was associated with higher levels of stress and depression than was fatherhood. Hill (2005) found that gender moderated the strength of five different relationships, such as between job hours and WTF conflict, and concludes that gender should always be included as a variable in this type of research. The limited research into work-family facilitation suggests that gender may moderate the amount and direction of positive spillover, with women reporting slightly more positive spillover from work to family than men (Grzywacz & Marks, 2000). Age moderated this relationship as well, with younger women reporting higher levels of positive and negative spillover. Given the mixed findings that emerge from these studies, it appears that more research is required into the role gender may play in the experience of the work-family interface.

The role of personality factors in the experience of work-family interface has been minimally investigated. Extraversion has been positively related to both directions of work-family conflict (Grzywacz & Marks, 2000). Wayne and colleagues (2004), however, found that extraversion was related to greater facilitation but not conflict, whereas neuroticism was related to greater conflict, but was only weakly related to facilitation. Conscientiousness was related to lower levels of conflict, which was generally negatively related to work-family outcomes, whereas facilitation was positively related to the same outcomes. Other studies suggest that lower levels of work-family conflict are perceived for those who are high self-monitors, exhibit Type A tendencies, and have less negative affect (Eby et al., 2005). Finally, attachment style has been linked to work-family spillover; specifically those with preoccupied attachment styles report more negative spillover between work and home while those with secure attachment styles report more positive spillover in both directions (Sumer & Knight, 2001).

MEDIATIONAL PROCESSES

In an extensive recent review of the work-family literature, Eby et al. (2005) report on the various configurations in which general or unidirectional work-family conflict has been examined as a mediator variable. For example, general work-family conflict has been found to mediate relationships between job expectations and quality of work and family life (Higgins, Duxbury & Irving, 1992), supervisory support and improved health (Thomas & Ganster, 1995), and work and family overload with work and personal outcomes (Greenhaus, Collins, Singh & Parasuraman, 1997).

More generally, we suggest that the work-family interface has to be understood within a broader context of the effects of work on the individual. The literature on work stress is far too large to be reviewed herein, but we note that a variety of factors that have been identified as predictors of individual well-being also plausibly have an impact on the work-family interface. The model of job stressors proposed by the National Institute for Occupational Safety and Health (NIOSH) (Sauter, Murphy & Hurrell, 1990) identifies the principal stressors as comprising: (a) work load and work pace, (b) role stressors (conflict, ambiguity), (c) career concerns, (d) work scheduling, (e) interpersonal relations, and (f) job content and control. These stressors have an impact on both work-family conflict (Bellavia & Frone, 2005) and individual well-being (Kelloway & Day, 2006). The extent to which the effects of work stressors on well-being conflict are fully mediated or partially mediated by the work-family interface remains an empirical question.

IMPLICATIONS FOR FUTURE RESEARCH AND PRACTICE

FUTURE RESEARCH

Several key research needs have been identified in the work-family literature. Although theorists support the reciprocal nature of the work-family relationship, Bellavia and Frone (2003) call for researchers to measure both work to family and family to work dimensions, as such studies have been lacking. Furthermore, the need for a common conceptual definition and valid measure of work-family conflict has also been expressed in recent reviews of the literature (see Bellavia & Frone for a detailed discussion of conceptual and measurement issues).

Given the emphasis on the negative effects associated with work-family conflict, researchers have identified the need for a more balanced approach which recognizes the positive effects associated with combining work and family roles (Bellavia & Frone, 2003; Greenhaus & Powell, 2006; Grzywacz, 2002; Rothbard, 2001). Frone (2003) and others have suggested that an individual's experience in one role can facilitate one's experience in another role. A variety of constructs have been proposed to describe the positive effects of combining the work and family domains, including positive spillover (Edwards & Rothbard, 2000; Hanson et al., 2006) and work-family facilitation (Wayne et al., 2004). Greenhaus and Powell provided a definition and a comprehensive theoretical framework of work-family enrichment to guide future research. Given the proposed constructs that explain the benefits associated with combining work and family roles, there is a need for clear construct definition, the development of a comprehensive theoretical model, and the development of valid measures. In addition, research on work-family enrichment must also address similar measurement challenges that have been identified in the work-family conflict research (see Bellavia & Frone, 2003; Greenhaus & Powell, 2006).

Greenhaus and Powell (2006) also recommended further investigation of the relationship between work-family depletion, work-family enrichment, and their correlates. Previous research suggests that enrichment and depletion have different correlates (Grzywacz & Marks, 2000) and work-family facilitation can buffer the negative effects of work-family conflict on well-being. Thus, additional research is necessary to empirically examine the relationships between work-family conflict and work-family enrichment to gain a more complete understanding of the work-family interface and its effects on health and well-being.

Frone (2003) suggests that research should move beyond work-family balance to explore balance between work and other non-work roles (e.g., caregiver, student, spouse) and to assess the characteristics of each role separately. There are a limited number of studies that have examined the role of caregiving from an enrichment perspective (Bainbridge, 2006). Future researchers should examine different types of caregiving roles that individuals occupy (childcare, eldercare, care for a disabled person, etc.) to better understand both the positive and negative outcomes of combining work and family-care roles. Eldercare, for example, has not been examined to the same extent that work-childcare balance has (Lee, Walker & Shoup, 2001). Furthermore, the effects of multiple caregiving roles (e.g., sandwiched generation) occupied by individuals and the personal characteristics of the care provider also warrant further investigation (Bainbridge et al., 2006).

Finally, on a more methodological note, we would be remiss not to comment on the overwhelming predominance of cross-sectional survey research designs in the literature. While we do not suggest that such designs are without value, we do note the need for research to move toward the use of alternative research designs such as longitudinal, experimental, and quasi-experimental research. Further we note the advisability of explicitly examining non-self report indicators of well-being. These suggestions are not unique to our review but, to date, researchers have largely ignored these methodological challenges and we suggest that it is now time to move in that direction.

IMPLICATIONS FOR PRACTICE AND POLICY

Organizational Practice

With Duxbury and Higgins' (2001) findings that work-family conflict is on the rise and daily news reports about the difficulty of attracting and retaining staff in almost all industries, there is a very strong imperative for organizations to implement policies that effectively reduce negative spillover and increase positive spillover between work and family life (Barnett & Hyde, 2001). Grzywacz and Marks (2000) make an interesting argument for organizations determining the goals of their policies. Given the orthogonal nature of the four variations of spillover (Demerouti & Geurts, 2004; Grzywacz & Marks, 2000; Hill, 2005), one set of interventions may not be effective. Based on their research, Grzywacz and Marks argue that if the goal is to reduce negative WTF spillover, then programs, policies, and job redesign efforts that aim to reduce work pressure, build supportive cultures, and promote close family relationships are indicated. If, however, the goal is to enhance the positive potential of the work-family interface, organizations need to focus on increasing decision latitude and control (Clark, 2002). Hill notes that because spending more time with one's children enhances FTW outcomes, organizations should consider implementing flexible programs that enable parents to do so. Bellavia and Frone (2004) argue that companies have provided these kinds of family-supportive interventions to reduce FTW conflict, mitigating the adverse impact of family responsibilities on the organization, and recommend that organizations should find ways to help employees manage the invasion of work into family.

Given the substantial research that demonstrates the importance of various forms of supervisory support (Eby et al., 2005; Hill, 2005), Duxbury and Higgins (2001) recommend that organizations invest in sound management development to ultimately enhance work-family facilitation and reduce conflict. Other programs that enhance employees' perception of the supportiveness of the organizational culture, such as orientation and opportunities for collective socialization, are beneficial (Eby et al., 2005; Hill, 2005). Recent research on workplace culture (Andreassi & Thompson in this volume; Duxbury & Higgins, 2005) highlights the impediments to using family-friendly workplace arrangements and identifies the importance of workplace culture per se as a factor influencing role overload and work-family conflict. The culture in place in many organizations discourages the use of alternative work arrangements and caregiving leave, especially for professionals, suggesting that implementing such programs is not enough—building a truly supportive corporate culture is essential to minimize work-family conflict and enhance facilitation. Kirchmeyer (1992) suggests that organizations' human resource policies should reflect the findings of the preponderance of research that shows no gender difference in the prevalence of work-family interference (Bellavia & Frone, 2004), which was previously used as an excuse to deny women responsibility and advancement. Batt & Valcour (2003) argue that the most effective organizational responses to work-family conflict are drawn from the concept of high involvement work systems, in which work-family policies are combined with other human resource practices, including work design and commitment-enhancing incentives.

Individual Behavior

The research on the implications for individuals in managing the work-family interface is sketchy and mixed. Kirchmeyer (1992) found that strategies that were effective in coping with the demands of multiple life domains involved altering one's own attitudes rather than trying to alter those of others, and increasing one's efficiency rather than decreasing one's activity level or trying to rely on others. A study of police officers' ability to cope with work and non-work strain found that an emotion-focused strategy (putting the situation in perspective) was more effective than praying, meditating, or developing a plan of action and following it (Beehr, Johnson, Nieva & Hurrell, 1995). Duxbury and Higgins (2001) suggest that employees take full advantage of any support policies that exist in their organizations, raise work-life balance issues in the community and the organization, and educate themselves on how to effectively deal with stress.

Social Policy

Duxbury and Higgins (2001) recommend that unions have an important role to play in establishing family-friendly workplaces. They suggest that unions can play a strong advocacy and educational role in organizations. For governments, they recommend changes to legislation to ensure common labor standards relating to family-friendly issues, such as time off in lieu of overtime pay. Outside of legislation, there are other ways in which governments can further the work-family agenda, for example by being a model employer, developing national child and eldercare programs, revising the taxation system to facilitate child and eldercare options, and finally funding research in this area. On a more macro level, several authors have called for governments in North America to investigate and adopt the supportive policy structures of European countries (Frazee, 1998; Gornick & Meyers, 2004; Lero & Lewis this volume; White, 1999).

CONCLUSION

The suggestion that both the nature and the quality of the work-family interface have implications for individual health and well-being is, by no means, novel. Indeed, research dealing with the nature and consequences of work-family relationships goes back over 75 years (Barling, 1990). While most of this research has focused on the potential for conflict or negative interactions, more recent theorists have also suggested a facilitation role whereby performance in one role enhances performance in another. With regard to health-related outcomes, it is plausible to suggest that engaging in one role may provide some "respite" from the other, and that support gleaned at either home or work may mitigate the stresses associated with role performance.

Researchers are now beginning to consider these issues in more detail. Although it is not novel to assert the existence of an effect of the work-family interface on individual well-being, we suggest that the pervasiveness of the effect has been largely overlooked in the existing literature. There is no doubt that both work and family roles are critical for individual well-being (Kelloway & Day, 2005). The work-family interface represents the intersection of those capabilities and, and, as such has a demonstrable impact on individual well-being. For this reason, work-family relationships were identified as one of the leading causes of stress (Sauter, Murphy & Hurrell, 1990) and the quality of those relationships may emerge as an issue of public health for the 21st century.

REFERENCES

Allen, T. D., Herst, D. E. L., Bruck, C. S. & Sutton, M. (2000). Consequences associated with work-to-family conflict: A review and agenda for future research. *Journal of Occupational Health Psychology, 5*(2), 278–308.

Andreassi & Thompson, this volume.

Aryee, S., Fields, D. & Luk, V. (1999). A cross-cultural test of a model of the work-family interface. *Journal of Management, 25*(4), 491–511.

Aryee, S., Tan, H. H. & Srinivas, E. S. (2005). Rhythms of life: Antecedents and outcomes of work-family balance in employed parents. *The Journal of Applied Psychology, 90*(1), 132.

Aycan, Z., this volume.

Bainbridge, T. J., Cregan, C. & Kulik, C. T. (2006). The effect of multiple roles on caregiver stress outcomes, *Journal of Applied Psychology, 91*(2), 490–497.

Baltes, B. B. & Heydens-Gahir, H. A. (2003). Reduction of work-family conflict through the use of selection, optimization, and compensation. *Journal of Applied Psychology, 8,* 1005–1018.

Barling, J. (1986). Interrole conflict and marital functioning amongst employed fathers. *Journal of Occupational Behavior, 7,* 1–8.

Barling, J. (1990). *Employment Stress and Family Functioning.* Chichester: Wiley.

Barling, J. & Kelloway, E. K. (1996). Job insecurity and health: The moderating role of workplace control. *Stress Medicine, 12,* 253–260.

Barling, J., MacEwen, K. E., Kelloway, E. K. & Higginbottom, S. F. (1994). Predictors and outcomes of eldercare-based interrole conflict. *Psychology and Aging, 9,* 391–397.

Barnett, R. C. (1996). *Toward a Review of the Work-family Literature: Work in Progress.* Boston: Wellesley College Center for Research on Women.

Barnett, R. C. (1998). Toward a review and reconceptualization of the work/family literature. *Genetic, Social & General Psychology Monographs, 124*(2), 125–182.

Barnett, R. & Baruch, G. K. (1985). Women's involvement in multiple roles and psychological distress. *Journal of Personality and Social Psychology, 49*(1), 135–145.

Barnett, R. C. & Hyde, J. S. (2001). Women, men, work and family. *American Psychologist, 56,* 781–796.

Barnett, R. C. & Marshall, N. L. (1993). Men, family-role quality, job-role quality, and physical health. *Health Psychology, 12,* 48–55.

Batt, R. & Valcour, P. M. (2003). Human resources practices as predictors of work-family outcomes and employee turnover. *Industrial Relations, 42*(2), 189–220.

Beehr, T. A., Johnson, L. B., Nieva, R. & Hurrell, J. J. (1995). Occupational stress: Coping of police officers and their spouses. *Journal of Organizational Behavior, 16*(1), 3–28.

Bellavia, G. & Frone, M. R. (2005). Work-family conflict. In J. Barling, E. K. Kelloway & M. R. Frone (eds), *Handbook of Work Stress*. Thousand Oaks: Sage.

Bosma, H., Stansfeld, S. A. & Marmot, M. G. (1998). Job control, personal characteristics and heart disease. *Journal of Occupational Health Psychology, 3*, 402–409.

Bronfenbrenner, U. (1977). Toward an experimental ecology of human development. *American Psychologist, 32*(7), 513–531.

Bronfenbrenner, U. (1979). *The Ecology of Human Development: Experiments by Nature and Design.* Cambridge, MA: Harvard University Press.

Bronfenbrenner, U. (1986). Ecology of the family as a context for human development: Research perspectives. *Developmental Psychology, 22*(6), 723–742.

Brotheridge, C. l. M. & Lee, R. T. (2005). Impact of work-family interference on general well-being: A replication and extension. *International Journal of Stress Management, 12*(3), 203–221.

Burke, R. J. & Greenglass, E. R. (1999). Work-family conflict, spouse support, and nursing staff well-being during organizational restructuring. *Journal of Occupational Health Psychology, 4*(4), 327–336.

Cannuscio, C. C., Jones, C., Kawachi, I., Colditz, G. A., Berkman, L. & Rimm, E. (2002). Reverberations of family illness: A longitudinal assessment of informal caregiving and mental health status in the Nurses' Health Study. *American Journal of Public Health, 92*, 1305–1311.

Carayon, P., Smith, M. J. & Haims, M. C. (1999). Work organization, job stress, and work-related musculoskeletal disorders. *Human Factors, 41*, 644–663.

Carlson, D. S. & Perrewe, P. L. (1999). The role of social support in the stressor-strain relationship: An examination of work-family conflict. *Journal of Management, 25*, 513–540.

Clark, S. C. (2002). Employees' sense of community, sense of control, and work/family conflict in Native American organizations. *Journal of Vocational Behavior, 61*, 92–108.

Cohen, S. & Williamson, G. M. (1991). Stress and infectious disease in humans. *Psychological Bulletin, 109*, 5–24.

Conway, T. L., Vickers, R. R., Ward, H. W. & Rahe, R. H. (1981). Occupational stress and variation in cigarette, coffee and alcohol consumption. *Journal of Health and Social Behavior, 22*, 155–165

Crouter, A. (1994). Spillover from family to work. *Human Relations, 37*(6), 425–442.

Demerouti, E. & Geurts, S. A. E. (2004). Towards a typology of work-home interaction. *Community, Work & Family, 7*(3), 285–309.

Duxbury, L. & Higgins, C. (2001). *Work-life Balance in the New Millennium: Where are We? Where Do We Need To Go?* Ottawa: Canadian Policy Research Networks.

Duxbury, L. & Higgins, C. (2003). Work-life conflict in Canada in the new millennium: A status report. *Australian Canadian Studies, 21*(2), 41–72.

Eagle, B. W., Miles, E. W. & Icenogle, M. L. (1997). Interrole conflicts and the permeability of work and family domains: Are there gender differences? *Journal of Vocational Behavior, 50*, 168–184.

Eby, L. T., Casper, W. J., Lockwood, A., Bordeaux, C. & Brinley, A. (2005). Work and family research in IO/OB: Content analysis and review of the literature (1980–2002). *Journal of Vocational Behavior, 66*, 124–197.

Edwards, J. R. & Rothbard, N. P. (2000). Mechanisms linking work and family: Clarifying the relationships between work and family constructs. *Academy of Management Review, 25*, 178–199.

Frazee, V. (1998). Study compares US and European work/family policies. *Workforce, 3*(1), 8.

Friedman, S. D. & Greenhaus, J. H. (2000). *Work and Family—Allies or Enemies? What Happens When Business Professionals Confront Life Choices.* New York: Oxford University Press.

Frone, M. R. (2000). Work-family conflict and employee psychiatric disorders: The National Comorbidity Survey. *Journal of Applied Psychology, 85*, 888–895.

Frone, M. R. (2003). Work-family balance. In J. C. Quick & L. E. Tetrick (eds), *Handbook of Occupational Health Psychology* (pp. 143–163). Washington: American Psychological Association.

Frone, M. R., Russell, M. & Cooper, C. L. (1992). Antecedents and outcomes of work-family conflict: Testing a model of the work-family interface. *The Journal of Applied Psychology, 77*(1), 65–78.

Frone, M. R., Russell, M. & Cooper, C. L. (1993). Relationship of work-family conflict, gender and alcohol expectancies to alcohol use/abuse. *Journal of Organizational Behavior, 14*, 545–558.

Frone, M. R., Russell, M. & Cooper, M. L. (1997). Relation of work-family conflict to health outcomes: A four-year longitudinal study of employed parents. *Journal of Occupational and Organizational Psychology, 70*(4), 325–335.

Frone, M. R., Yardley, J. K. & Markel, K. S. (1997). Developing and testing an integrative model of the work-family interface. *Journal of Vocational Behavior, 50*, 145–167.

Geurts, S. A. E. & Demerouti, E. (2003). Work/non-work interface: A review of theories and findings. In M. J. Schabracq, J. A. M. Winnubst & C. L. Cooper (eds), *Handbook of Work and Health Psychology* (pp. 279–312). Chichester: Wiley.

Goff, S. J., Mount, M. K. & Jamison, R. L. (1990). Employer supported childcare, work-family conflict, and absenteeism: A field study. *Personnel Psychology, 43*(4), 793–809.

Goode, W. J. (1960). A theory of role strain. *American Sociological Review, 25*, 483–496.

Gornick, J. C. & Meyers, M. K. (2004). More alike than different: Revisiting the long-term prospects for developing "European-style" work/family policies in the United States. *Journal of Comparative Policy Analysis, 6*(3), 251–273.

Graves, L. M., Ohlott, P. J. & Ruderman, M. N. (2007). Commitment to family roles: Effects on managers' attitudes and performance. *Journal of Applied Psychology, 92*(1), 44–56.

Greenhaus, J. H. & Beutell, N. J. (1985). Sources of conflict between work and family roles. *Academy of Management Review, 10*(1), 76–88.

Greenhaus, J. H., Collins, K. M., Singh, R. & Parasuraman, S. (1997). Work and family influences on departure from public accounting. *Journal of Vocational Behavior, 50*, 249–270.

Greenhaus, J. H. & Powell, G. N. (2006). When work and family are allies: A theory of work-family enrichment. *Academy of Management Review, 31*(1), 72–92.

Greeno, C. G. & Wing, R. R. (1994). Stress-induced eating. *Psychological Bulletin, 115*, 444–464.

Grundberg, L., Moore, S., Greenberg. E. & Anderson-Connolly, R. (1999). Work stress and self-reported alcohol use: The moderating role of escapist reasons for drinking. *Journal of Occupational Health Psychology, 4*, 29–36.

Grzywacz, J. G. (2000). Work-family spillover and health during midlife: Is managing conflict everything? *American Journal of Health Promotion, 14*, 236–243.

Grzywacz, J. G. & Bass, B. L. (2003). Work, family and mental health: Testing different models of work-family fit. *Journal of Marriage and Family, 65*(1), 248–262.

Grzywacz, J. G. & Butler, A. B. (2005). The impact of job characteristics on work-to-family facilitation: Testing a theory and distinguishing a construct. *Journal of Occupational Health Psychology, 10*(2), 97–109.

Grzywacz, J. G. & Marks, N. F. (2000a). Family, work, work family spillover, and problem drinking during midlife. *Journal of Marriage and the Family, 62*, 336–348.

Grzywacz, J. G. & Marks, N. F. (2000b). Reconceptualizing the work-family interface: An ecological perspective on the correlates of positive and negative spillover between work and family. *Journal of Occupational Health Psychology, 5*(1), 111–126.

Hammer, L. B., Cullen, J. C., Neal, M. B., Sinclair, R. R. & Shafiro, M. (2005). The longitudinal effects of work-family conflict and positive spillover on experiences of depressive symptoms among dual-earner couples. *Journal of Occupational Health Psychology, 10*(2), 138–154.

Hammer, L. B., Allen, E. & Grigsby, T. (1997). Work-family conflict in dual-earner couples: Within-individual and crossover effects of work and family. *Journal of Vocational Behavior, 50*, 185–203.

Hammer, L. B., Neal, M. B., Newsom, J. T., Brockwood, K. J. & Colton, C. L. (2005). A longitudinal study of the effects of dual-earner couples' utilization of family-friendly workplace supports on work and family outcomes. *Journal of Applied Psychology, 90*(4), 799–810.

Hanson, G. C., Hammer, L. B. & Colton, C. L. (2006). Development and validation of a multidimensional scale of perceived work-family positive spillover. *Journal of Occupational Health Psychology, 11*(3), 249–265.

Harrison, L. J. & Ungerer, J. A. (2002). Maternal employment and infant-mother attachment security at 12 months postpartum. *Developmental Psychology, 38*(5), 758–773.

Hepburn, C. G. & Barling, J. (1996). Eldercare responsibilities, interrole conflict, and employee absence: A daily study. *Journal of Occupational Health Psychology, 1*, 311–318.

Higgins, C., Duxbury, L. & Irving, R. H. (1992). Work-family conflict in the dual-career family. *Organizational Behavior and Human Decision Processes, 51*, 51–75.

Hill, E. J. (2005). Work-family facilitation and conflict, working fathers and mothers, work-family stressors and support. *Journal of Family Issues, 26*(6), 793–819.

Hughes, D. L. & Galinsky, E. (1994). Work experiences and marital interactions: Elaborating the complexity of work. *Journal of Organizational Behavior, 15*, 423–438.

Hurrell, J. J. Jr. & Kelloway, E. K. (in press). Psychological job stress. In William N. Rom (ed.). *Environmental and Occupational Medicine*, 4th edn. New York: Lippincourt-Raven.

Ingersoll-Dayton, B., Neal, M. B. & Hammer, L. B. (2001). Aging parents helping adult children: The experience of the sandwiched generation. *Family Relations: Interdisciplinary Journal of Applied Studies, 50*, 262–271.

Jones, J. W. & Boye, M. W. (1992). Job stress and employee counterproductivity. In J. C. Quick, L. R. Murphy & J. J. Hurrell (eds), *Stress and Well-being at Work*. Washington, DC: American Psychological Association.

Kahn, R. L., Wolfe, D. M., Quinn, R. P., Snoek, J. D. & Rosenthal, R. A. (1964). *Organizational Stress: Studies in Role Conflict and Ambiguity*. New York: Wiley.

Karasek, R. A. & Theorell, T. (1990). *Healthy Work: Stress Productivity and the Reconstruction of Working Life*. New York: Basic Books.

Katz, D. & Kahn, R. (1978). *The Social Psychology of Organizations*, 2nd edn. New York: Wiley.

Kelloway, E. K. & Barling, J. (1994). Stress, control, well-being, and marital satisfaction: A causal correlational analysis. In G. P. Keita & J. J. Hurrell (eds), *Job Stress in a Changing Workforce: Investigating Gender, Diversity, and Family Iissues* (pp. 241–252). Washington, DC: American Psychological Association.

Kelloway, E. K. & Day, A. L. (2005). Building healthy organizations: What we know so far. *Canadian Journal of Behavioral Science, 37,* 223–236.

Kelloway, E. K., Gottlieb, B. H. & Barham, L. (1999). The source, nature, and direction of work and family conflict: A longitudinal investigation. *Journal of Occupational Health Psychology, 4*(4), 337–346.

Kinnunen, U. & Mauno, S. (1998). Antecedents and outcomes of work-family conflict among employed women and men in Finland. *Human Relations, 51,* 157–177.

Kirchmeyer, C. (1992). Perceptions of nonwork-to-work spillover: Challenging the common view of conflict-ridden domain relationships. *Basic and Applied Social Psychology, 13*(2), 231–249.

Kirchmeyer, C. (1993). Nonwork-to-work spillover: A more balanced view of the experiences and coping of professional women and men. *Sex Roles, 28*(9/10), 531–552.

Kohn, M. L. (1969). *Class and Conformity: A Study in Values*. Homewood, IL: Dorsey.

Kopelman, R. E., Greenhaus, J. H. & Connolly, T. F. (1983). A model of work, family, and interrole conflict: A construct validation study. *Organizational Behavior and Human Performance, 32*, 198–215.

Kossek, E. E. & Ozeki, C. (1998). Work-family policies and the job-life satisfaction relationship: A review and directions for future organizational behavior-human resources research. *Journal of Applied Psychology, 83*, 139–149.

Krantz, D. S., Contrada, R. J., Hill, D. R. & Friedler, E. (1988). Environmental stress and biobehavioral antecedents of coronary heart disease. *Journal of Consulting and Clinical Psychology, 3*, 333–341.

Lee, J. A., Walker, J. & Shoup, R. (2001). Balancing eldercare responsibilities at work: The impact on emotional health. *Journal of Business Psychology, 16*(2), 277–289.

Lero, D. S., & Lewis, S., this volume.

Lundberg, U., Dohns, I. E., Melin, B., Sandjo, L., Palmerud, G., Kadefors, R., Ekstrom, M. & Parr, D. (1999). Psychophysiological stress responses, muscle tension, and neck and shoulder pain among supermarket cashiers. *Journal of Occupational Health Psychology, 4,* 245–255.

MacEwen, K. E. & Barling, J. (1994). Daily consequences of work interference with family and family interference with work. *Work and Stress, 8,* 244–254.

Marks, S. R. (1977). Multiple roles and role strain: Some notes on human energy, time and commitment. *American Sociological Review, 42,* 921–936.

Marks, N. F. (1998). Does it hurt to care? Caregiving, work-family conflict, and midlife well-being. *Journal of Marriage and the Family, 60,* 951–966.

Matthews, R. A., Priore, R. E. & Acitelli, L. K. (2006). Work-to-relationship conflict: Crossover effects in dual-earner couples. *Journal of Occupational Health Psychology, 11*(3), 228–240.

Morgan, W. R., Alwin, D. F. & Griffin, L. J. (1979). Social origins, parental values, and the transmission of inequality. *American Journal of Sociology, 85,* 156–166.

Ng, D. M. & Jeffery, R. W. (2003). Relationships between perceived stress and health behaviors in a sample of working adults. *Health Psychology, 22*(6), 632–642.

O'Driscoll, M. P., Ilgen, D. R. & Hildreth, K. (1992). Time devoted to job and off-job activities, inter-role conflict, and affective experiences. *Journal of Applied Psychology, 77,* 272–279.

O'Leary, A. (1990). Stress, emotion, and human immune function. *Psychological Bulletin, 108,* 363–382.

Parasuraman, S. & Greenhaus, J. H. (2002). Toward reducing some critical gaps in work-family research. *Human Resource Management Review, 12,* 299–312.

Parasuraman, S., Greenhaus, J. H., Rabinowitz, S., Bedeian, A. G. & Mossholder, K. W. (1989). Work and family variables as mediators of the relationship between wives' employment and husbands' well-being. *Academy of Management Journal, 32,* 185–201.

Parrott, A. C. (1995). Stress modulation over the day in cigarette smokers. *Addiction, 90,* 233–244.

Payne, N., Jones, F. & Harris, P. (2002). The impact of working life on health behavior: The effect of job strain on the cognitive predictors of exercise. *Journal of Occupational Health Psychology, 7,* 342–353.

Perry-Jenkins, M., Repetti, R. & Crouter, A. (2000). Work and family in the 1990s. *Journal of Marriage and the Family, 62*(4), 981–999.

Poelmans, S., Stepanova, O. & Masuda, A., this volume.

Rantanen, J., Pulkkinen, L. & Kinnunen, U. (2005). The big five personality dimensions, work-family conflict, and psychological distress: A longitudinal view. *Journal of Individual Differences, 26*(3), 155–166.

Rothbard, N. P. (2001). Enriching or depleting? The dynamics of engagement in work and family roles. *Administrative Science Quarterly, 46*(4), 655–684.

Rudderman, M. N., Ohlott, P. J., Panzer, K. & King, S. N. (2002). Benefits of multiple roles for managerial women. *Academy of Management Journal, 45,* 369–386.

Sahibzada, K. A., Hammer, L. B., Neal, M. B. & Kuang, D. C. (2005). The moderating effects of work-family role combinations and work-family organizational culture on the relationships between family-friendly workplace supports and job satisfaction. *Journal of Family Issues, 26*(6), 820–839.

Sauter, S. L., Murphy, L. R. & Hurrell, J. J. (1990). Prevention of work-related psychological disorders: A national strategy proposed by the National Institute for Occupational Safety and Health (NIOSH). *American Psychologist, 45,* 1146–1158.

Scharlach, A. E. (1994). Caregiving and employment: Competing or complementary roles? *Gerontologist, 34,* 378–385.

Schat, A., Kelloway, E. K. & Desmarais, S. (2005). The physical health questionnaire (PHQ): Construct validation of a self-report scale of somatic symptoms. *Journal of Occupational Health Psychology, 10,* 363–381.

Schaubroeck, J., Jones, J. R. & Xie, J. L. (2001). Individual differences in using control to cope with job demands: Effects on susceptibility to infectious disease. *Journal of Applied Psychology, 86,* 265–278.

Schwartz, J. E., Pickering, T. G. & Landsbergis, P. A. (1996). Work-related stress and blood pressure: Current theoretical models and considerations from a behavioral medicine perspective. *Journal of Occupational Health Psychology, 1*, 287–310.

Sieber, S. D. (1974). Toward a theory of role accumulation. *American Sociological Review, 39*, 567–578.

Stephens, S. A. & Townsend, A. (1997). Stress of parent care: Positive and negative effects of women's other roles. *Psychology and Aging, 12*, 376–386.

Stokols, D. (1996). Translating social ecological theory into guidelines for community health promotion. *American Journal of Health Promotion, 10*, 282–298.

Suchet, M. & Barling, J. (1986). Employed mothers: Interrole conflict, spouse support and marital functioning. *Journal of Occupational Behavior, 7*(3), 167–179.

Sumer, H. C. & Knight, P. A. (2001). How do people with different attachment styles balance work and family? A personality perspective on work-family linkages. *Journal of Applied Psychology, 86*, 653–663.

Theorell, T. & Karasek, R. A. (1996). Current issues relating to psychosocial job strain and cardiovascular disease research. *Journal of Occupational Health Psychology, 1*, 9–26.

Thomas, L. T. & Ganster, D. C. (1995). Impact of family-supportive work variables on work-family conflict and strain: A control perspective. *Journal of Applied Psychology, 80*, 6–15.

Voydanoff, P. (1988). Work role characteristics, family structure demands, and work/family conflict. *Journal of Marriage and Family, 50*, 749–761.

Voydanoff, P. (2001). Incorporating community into work and family research: A review of basic relationships. *Human Relations, 54*, 1609–1637.

Voydanoff, P. (2002). Linkages between the work-family interface and work, family, and individual outcomes: An integrative model. *Journal of Family Issues, 23*(1), 138–164.

Voydanoff, P., this volume.

Wayne, J. H., Musisca, N. & Fleeson, W. (2004). Considering the role of personality in the work-family experience: Relationships of the big five to work-family conflict and facilitation. *Journal of Vocational Behavior, 64*(1), 108–130.

Wang, J. L. & Patten, S. B. (2001). Perceived work stress and major depression in the Canadian employed population 20–49 years old. *Journal of Occupational Health Psychology, 6*, 283–289.

White, J. (1999). A matter of policy [Comparative Family Policy: Eight Countries' Stories]. *Benefits Canada, 23*(3), 13.

Williams, A., Franche, R. L., Ibrahim, S., Mustard, C. A. & Layton, F. R. (2006). Examining the relationship between work-family spillover and sleep quality. *Journal of Occupational Health Psychology, 11*(1), 27–37.

CHAPTER 12

Integrating Gender-Related Issues into Research on Work and Family[1]

Karen Korabik*, Allyson McElwain* and Dara B. Chappell†
*Department of Psychology, University of Guelph, Guelph, ON, Canada
†Department of Industrial Relations and Human Resources, University of Toronto, Toronto, ON, Canada

The purpose of this chapter is to examine the role that gender plays in the work-family (WF) interface. During every day of their lives, people's gender influences the manner in which they are expected to behave, the way that they are perceived and evaluated by others, the kinds of roles that they take on, and the possibilities that are available to them. Work and family are two domains that have long had gender-related connotations, with men being more likely to be involved in business and women in domestic pursuits in most parts of the world. Moreover, as Haas has commented, "Gender boundaries set up a hierarchical structure of constraints and opportunities which can affect work-family linkages" (1995, p. 115). In this chapter we review the research that has been carried out on the intersection of gender with the WF interface and offer suggestions for integrating gender-related issues into W-F research. First, however, it is important to understand what gender is.

GENDER

WHAT IS GENDER?

Gender refers to the psychosocial ramifications of biological sex (i.e., the implications of being a male or a female). Often gender is thought of simplistically as involving only whether someone is a man or a woman. In this paper we will use the term "demographic gender" to refer to this aspect of gender. Gender, however, is a multidimensional phenomenon (Bem, 1981) that consists of far more

---

[1]This chapter is based on a paper prepared for the Inaugural Conference of the International Center of Work and Family, International Research on Work and Family: From Policy to Practice, Barcelona, Spain, July 7–9, 2005.

Handbook of Work-Family Integration: Research, Theory, and Best Practices

than demographic gender alone. For example, according to Korabik and Ayman's (2007; see also Korabik, 1999) multiperspective model, gender-related processes can be intrapsychic, interpersonal, or sociocultural (social structural) in nature.

From the intrapsychic perspective, gender encompasses the various aspects of gender roles that a person internalizes through gender-role socialization. These include gender schemas; gender-role identity; and gender-role traits, attitudes, and values (Korabik, 1999). The interpersonal perspective focuses on how gender-related beliefs and expectations both about the self (schemas) and about others (stereotypes) influence the interactions individuals have with one another. This approach recognizes the importance of situational cues, such as the sex-typed nature of tasks and skewed gender ratios in groups, which can make gender more salient and induce priming. From the social structural perspective, gender is seen as an ascribed status characteristic that influences access to power and resources. Thus, gender is both "a hierarchical structure of opportunity and oppression as well as an affective structure of identity and cohesion and families are one of the many institutional settings in which these structures become lived experience" (Ferree, 1995, p. 125).

We can see from the above discussion that not only are gender and gender roles culturally prescribed, but gendered norms regarding social status determine much of the structure of societies around the world (Unger & Crawford, 1993). Moreover, gender is socially constructed within a historical context (Haas, 1995). In North American society, during the past four decades the social norms regarding gender-role socialization have been changing to allow greater acceptance of femininity in men and masculinity in women (Bem, 1981). Moreover, the increase in dual-earner couples has led to modifications in the traditional roles that men and women enact. Mothers now spend more time in the workforce, while fathers fulfill more responsibilities inside the home (Bellavia & Frone, 2005).

These societal transformations are tied to dramatic changes in the way that psychologists think about gender. Forty years ago, definitions of gender were based on the assumptions of biological essentialism (that men and women have essentially different natures), biopsychological equivalence (that men *should* be masculine and not feminine and that women *should* be feminine and not masculine), and gender polarization (that these differences *should* be the organizing principle for interpersonal relationships and indtrapsychic identity) (Bem, 1993). In contrast to the unidimensional models of gender that incorporated these assumptions, Bem (1974) and Spence, Helmreich and Stapp (1975) proposed bidimensional models where gender roles were viewed as consisting of two conceptually independent dimensions (masculinity/instrumentality and femininity/expressivity) that were unrelated to whether someone was a man or a woman. Much research over the last four decades has confirmed their theoretical position and extended their models to include multidimensional, multilevel, and multiperspective frameworks (see Korabik, 1999; Korabik & Ayman, 2007).

Problems with the Way Gender is Studied in the WF Literature

Despite the fact that gender is the demographic characteristic that has been studied most frequently in the WF literature (Guerts & Demerouti, 2003), most WF studies still do not include gender as a variable, combining samples of men and women for purposes of analysis. This approach is difficult to comprehend, given the dramatically different roles that men and women play both at home and at work and their unequal status in society.

Moreover, the WF research that does examine gender is riddled with problems. One of these is that most studies are either atheoretical or they are based on outdated theories of gender. Because of this, demographic gender (i.e., whether someone is a man or woman) is often used as a proxy for other aspects of gender (e.g., gender-role behaviour or gender-role attitudes). Often this approach is predicated on the mistaken assumption of biopsychological equivalence (that all men's primary orientation is work and all women's primary orientation is the family). Moreover, using demographic gender as a proxy variable is problematic because it can introduce confounds that can result in misinterpretation of research findings. In our society, demographic gender is a status marker, with men being attributed higher status than women. Because of this, what appear to be findings of gender differences can actually be due to differences between men and women in variables related to their status, for example power and authority (Korabik, 1999). Thus, it may appear that the levels of WF conflict that men and women experience are due to their demographic gender, when any differences are actually attributable to their differential access to power and resources or to their different social status.

The failure to equate men and women on confounding variables may have affected interpretations of past examinations of gender differences in WF conflict. For example, job type has a bearing on the ability to balance work and family demands. Managerial and professional jobs (which are more likely to be held by men) have more flexibility and control over work (e.g., Duxbury, Higgins & Lee, 1994; O'Neil & Greenberger, 1994), characteristics that have been related to decreased WF conflict. However, these types of jobs are also more demanding and require longer hours, which can produce higher WF conflict. Correspondingly, women's lower incomes may mean they have less money than men to pay for household helpers and other support services that would alleviate their WF conflict. Research shows that mean gender differences often disappear when the differences between men and women on such confounding variables are controlled (Korabik, 1999).

Another problem has been that the existing literature has largely focused on examining mean gender differences on variables related to the experience of WF conflict. Differences in the *relationships among* WF constructs (i.e., antecedents, role stress, and outcomes) have been neglected (McElwain, Korabik & Rosin, 2005).

As well, due to an inadequate conceptualization of gender as a variable, other important aspects of gender (gender-role traits, attitudes, etc.) have been virtually ignored in the literature. Moreover, the emphasis has been on the negative aspects of the WF interface, with WF conflict being studied to the near exclusion of WF facilitation/adaptation. In addition, most studies have employed one-shot cross-sectional designs. Finally, despite evidence that culture influences the nature of WF conflict (Joplin, Shaffer, Francesco & Lau, 2003; Ling & Powell, 2001), research has often overlooked the influence of historical context and culture.

GENDER DIFFERENCES IN WF CONFLICT

We now review the literature on gender and the WF interface, explicating the problems with specific studies as we do so. We begin with the issue of mean gender differences in WF conflict, since this is the area where almost all previous work has been done. We then move on to the issue of gender as a moderator of the relationships between WF conflict and its antecedents and outcomes. Although we use the term gender differences when discussing these studies, it should be noted that in this research gender has been operationalized solely on the basis of demographic information about whether someone is a male or female. Therefore, rather than representing all aspects of gender differences, these studies are confined to the examination of the differences between how men and women experience WF conflict.

THEORIES

There are two competing theories about why mean differences between men and women in WF conflict should exist. One is the rational viewpoint (Gutek, Searle & Klepa, 1991), which posits that the more hours one spends in a domain, the more potential there is for conflict to occur. This theory predicts that men should experience more work interference with family (WIF) than women because they spend more time at work, whereas women should experience more family interference with work (FIW) than men because they spend more time in the home.

An alternative theory is the gender role hypothesis. It proposes that, although both men and women report that their family is valued more than their work, traditional gender roles impose different levels of importance for these roles for men and women (Greenhaus, Bedeian & Mossholder, 1987). These gender roles affect perceptions of WIF and FIW such that additional hours spent in one's prescribed gender role domain (family for women and work for men) are not seen as an imposition as much as additional hours spent in the domain associated with the other gender. According to this perspective, women should report higher levels of WIF than men even when they spend the same total number of hours in paid work, and men should report higher levels of FIW than women even when they devote the same total number of hours to family activities. A recent meta-analysis of the WF literature (Byron, 2005) indicated that there was some support for each of these two rival theories.

RESEARCH ON MEAN GENDER DIFFERENCES

The research that has been carried out on the issue of whether there are mean differences between men and women in WF conflict has produced extremely contradictory findings (Voydanoff, 2002). Some studies have found that men experience more WF conflict than women (Duxbury & Higgins, 1991; Huffman, Payne & Castro, 2003; Livingstone & Burley, 1991; Yang, Chen, Choi & Zhou, 2000). But, it has also been found that women experience more WF conflict than men (Burley, 1995; Carlson, Kacmar & Williams, 2000; Hammer, Allen & Grigsby, 1997, as cited in Hammer, Colton, Caubet & Brockwood, 2002).

Other investigations have produced mixed results even within the same study. For example, Eagle, Miles and Icenogle (1997) found that men reported experiencing more strain-based FIW and time- and strain-based WIF than women, but there were no gender differences for time-based FIW. Still other studies (Gutek et al., 1991; McElwain et al., 2005) have found that women experienced more WIF than men, even when working identical hours, but that there were no gender differences in FIW. By contrast, Fu and Shaffer (2001) found that women experienced greater levels of FIW, but men experienced greater levels of WIF. Lastly, Duxbury et al. (1994) found that women reported both more WIF *and* more FIW than men.

On the whole, however, most studies have found no evidence of differences in WF conflict between men and women (Frone, Russell & Cooper, 1992; Grant-Vallone & Donaldson, 2001; Grandy & Croanzano, 1999, as cited in Hammer et al., 2002; Grzywacz & Marks, 2000; Guerts & Demerouti, 2003; Kinnunen & Mauno, 1998; Windslow, 2005). This is confirmed by a meta-analysis of 61 published studies which indicated that there were no overall mean gender differences in either WIF or FIW (Byron, 2005).

GENDER AS A MODERATOR OF RELATIONSHIPS AMONG WF VARIABLES

Relatively fewer studies have examined gender as a moderator of relationships **among** different aspects of the WF interface. This is an important avenue of research in the WF literature because an understanding of how gender differentially impacts the manner in which the antecedents and outcomes of WF conflict are related could aid in reducing the conflict and its negative consequences. The results of investigations in this area have also been mixed.

In a study of military personnel, Huffman et al. (2003) found that time demands, as measured by the number of hours worked, were more strongly related to WF conflict for men than for women. This gender difference disappeared, however, when time demands were measured via perceptions of workload. McElwain et al. (2005) used a time demands measure that was a composite of work hours and perceived job demands. They did not find any significant gender differences in the path coefficients for the relationships between worktime demands and WIF. However, there was a significant gender difference in the relationship between family demands and FIW. Specifically, women were more likely than men to experience high levels of FIW when they had high family demands. Men's levels of FIW, however, were not dependent on the amount of family demands they had. Further, McElwain et al. (2005) found that FIW was a more significant predictor of job satisfaction for men than for women. In other words, men were more likely than women to report low levels of job satisfaction when they had high levels of FIW. The relationship between WIF and family satisfaction, however, did not differ for men and women. By contrast, Duxbury and Higgins (1991) found that women were more likely than men to report low quality of work life when they had high WF conflict, whereas men were more likely than women to report low quality of family life when they had high WF conflict. Along this same line, Burley (1995) found that the relationships of WF conflict to spousal support and marital adjustment were significantly more negative for men than for women.

Hill, Yang, Hawkins and Ferris (2004) carried out a test of the Frone et al. (1992) model of WF conflict. They found that being married was more likely to reduce FIW for women than for men. In addition, having responsibility for children was associated with significantly more FIW conflict for women than for men. Moreover, the experience of WIF was more strongly related to perceptions of a lack of WF fit for women than for men.

CRITIQUE OF THESE STUDIES

Some of the discrepancies in the results of these investigations can be attributed to the differences in their methodologies. The studies have utilized many different kinds of WF conflict measures. Global measures of WF conflict or measures that confound the WIF and FIW subdimensions of WF conflict are frequently used (e.g., Bedeian, Burke & Moffet, 1988; Burley, 1995; Duxbury & Higgins, 1991; Huffman et al., 2003; Grant-Vallone & Donaldson, 2001; Yang et al., 2000). This is an important limitation because research suggests that WIF and FIW have unique role-related antecedents and outcomes (Frone et al., 1992). Even when studies employ measures that differentiate WIF and FIW, they often do not look at the time-based, strain-based, and behavior-based subdimensions of these constructs separately. In addition, Carlson et al. (2000) have expressed concern about whether scales of WF conflict have measurement invariance in regard to gender. They tested for gender differences during the development of their scale and found that women reported greater levels of time-, strain-, and behavior-based FIW, as well as greater levels of strain-based WIF than men.

Another issue is that the participants used in these studies differ considerably. Some studies have employed only managerial/professional employees (e.g., Duxbury & Higgins, 1991; McElwain et al., 2005), whereas others have used only blue collar workers (e.g., Grant-Vallone & Donaldon, 2001). Still others (e.g., Fu & Schaffer, 2001; Hill et al., 2004) have used samples that combined managerial and nonmangerial employees; despite the fact that research has shown that the experience of WF conflict is quite different depending on job type and level. For example, Schieman, Whitestone and Van Gundy (2006) found that men and women in higher status occupations experienced more WIF than those in lower status occupations.

Moreover, several investigations examining gender differences in the WF interface have used samples that have been skewed toward one gender or the other. For example, the Huffman et al. (2003) study was done with a military sample composed of 84% men. By contrast, Grant-Vallone and Donaldson's (1991) sample was composed of 70% women. Similarly, some studies have included only participants who are parents, whereas others have included only married individuals, and still others have included anyone regardless of their marital or parental status. Paying attention to sample composition is important because Byron's (2005) meta-analysis demonstrated that the percentage of men versus women in a sample, as well as the percentage of parents in a sample, moderated relationships between WF conflict and its antecedents and outcomes.

The samples of studies in this area have also differed regarding the employment status (full vs. part time) and family types (e.g., dual earner, dual career, single parent, etc.) of the participants. A particularly important aspect of this problem is that previous research on gender differences in the WF interface has been riddled with confounds because it has failed to equate men and women on key variables both in the work and family domains (Duxbury & Higgins, 1991; Huffman et al., 2003). It is, therefore, possible that some of the gender differences that have been found have actually been due to differences in the type and level of jobs men and women hold. Women tend to hold lower level jobs and work fewer hours when compared to men. All of these factors not only make it difficult to compare results across studies, they can potentially affect findings and should be controlled for.

In terms of implications for international research, a crucial issue is that the samples of most of the studies have been composed of primarily Caucasian participants from the US and Canada (Byron, 2005). The exceptions are the Kinnunen and Mauno (1998) study which was done in Finland, the Fu and Schaffer (2001) study which was done with academic employees in Hong Kong, the Yang et al. (2000) study which compared employees in China and the US, and the Hill et al. (2004) study which sampled IBM employees from 48 countries. However, with the exception of the Yang et al.'s (2000) research, these studies were not truly cross-cultural in nature and their methodologies leave something to be desired when it comes to living up to the standards of best practices for cross-cultural research set down by Gelfand, Raver and Erhart (2002). Two of the studies (Fu & Schaffer, 2001; Kinnunen & Mauno, 1998) only examined participants from one country with no between country comparisons made. Moreover, the measures used by Fu and Schaffer (2001) were *etic* in nature, having been developed in Western countries, and they were administered in English. And, although Hill et al.'s (2004) sample included participants from 48 countries, all of them worked for IBM and the measures used in the research also were *etic*. Hill et al. found little evidence of differences in the WF interface due to culture. However, they stated that this was probably due to predominance of the IBM corporate culture over the local cultures that were examined.

Thus, the generalizability of the findings of these studies to an international context can be questioned. This is particularly true in light of the evidence presented by Hurst (2004) that the most psychometrically sound measure of WF conflict (Carlson et al., 2000) demonstrates a lack of measurement equivalence for culture. Without measurement equivalence, meaningful cross-cultural comparisons can not be conducted. Certainly, more attention needs to be paid to having indigenous researchers develop *emic* measures that capture aspects of the WF interface that are particular to their cultures (see Aycan, Chapter 19 in this volume; Korabik, Ayman & Lero, 2003).

In summary, as a recent review by Bellavia and Frone (2005) concludes, there is little evidence of mean gender differences in WIF or FIW. However, more research is necessary before firm conclusions can be drawn regarding the issue of whether or not gender moderates the relationships between WIF and FIW and their antecedents and outcomes (Byron, 2005). Almost all extant research has concentrated on WF conflict and research on WF facilitation is very limited. But, what does exist suggests that gender may moderate the amount and direction of positive spillover, with women reporting slightly more positive spillover from work to family than men (Grzywacz & Marks, 2000).

OTHER ASPECTS OF GENDER

All of the studies cited thus far have focused on differences between men and women rather than on differences in gender roles. Because gender is based on culture and learned behavior, there may be greater within-sex variation than between-sex variation in gender roles (Cinamon & Rich, 2002a). We will now turn our attention to a discussion of three specific gender-role variables: gender-role orientation (e.g., masculinity/instrumentality and femininity/expressivity), gender-role attitudes (traditional/egalitarian), and gender-role values. These three intrapsychic aspects of gender influence not only individuals' identities, but also their behaviors, the roles they choose to enact and how they choose to enact them. Therefore, these aspects of gender may be better predictors of WF conflict or facilitation than whether a person is a man or a woman (Korabik, 1999). Because they are covered thoroughly in other places in this volume, we will not discuss some other aspects of gender roles—motherhood (see Chapter 13), fatherhood (see Chapter 14), gendered division of labor, or other aspects of gender-role behavior.

GENDER-ROLE IDEOLOGY/ATTITUDES

Gender-role ideology (GRI) refers to an individual's attitudes and beliefs about the proper roles of men and women. In other words, how a person judges the appropriateness of behaviors and characteristics of men and women in our society (Ayman, Velgach & Ishaya, 2005). Typically, GRI is conceptualized as falling on a unidimensional continuum ranging from traditional to nontraditional or egalitarian. Individuals with a traditional GRI believe that women should give priority to family responsibilities and men to work responsibilities. By contrast, nontraditional or egalitarian individuals believe in a more equal role distribution for men and women. The conceptualization of GRI does not make the assumption of biopsychological equivalence. That is, both men and women can have either traditional or egalitarian attitudes.

GRI and Interrole Conflict

Early research in this area examined interrole conflict in general rather than WF conflict specifically. This research demonstrated, for example, that men who had egalitarian attitudes about paid employment and housework reported higher marital satisfaction (Lye & Biblarz, 1993), were more likely to intend to have children and less likely to divorce (Kaufman, 2000), and spent less time in paid employment as the size of their family increased (Kaufman & Uhlenberg, 2000) than men with traditional gender-role attitudes. By contrast, egalitarian women reported more stress and marital conflict (Greenstein, 1995), were more likely to divorce and less likely to intend to marry or have children (Kaufman, 2000), and reported lower marital satisfaction (Lye & Biblarz, 1993) than women with more traditional attitudes. Lye and Biblarz (1993), however, found that when spouses/partners shared an egalitarian attitude toward work and family, egalitarian women had high levels of marital satisfaction and low levels of marital conflict. Furthermore, they stress the importance of controlling for spousal/partner attitudes when examining gender-role attitudes.

GRI and WF Conflict

One way that gender-role attitudes should impact on WF conflict is by influencing the extent to which people engage in traditional or nontraditional divisions of labor. Because gender-role attitudes are precursors to behavior, knowing about someone's gender-role attitudes may be more important in predicting how much WF conflict they will experience than merely knowing whether they are a man or a woman. Thus, it would be expected that women with traditional attitudes who were spending time in paid employment would experience more feelings of WIF than women who espoused egalitarian attitudes about work and family. This is because their traditional attitudes dictate that they should be putting most of their efforts into their role as a homemaker. Similarly, men with traditional attitudes who spend time with their families would be expected to experience more FIW than men with egalitarian attitudes. These men's attitudes dictate that they should spend their time providing for their family through employment.

Recently, there have been several empirical examinations of how gender-role attitudes relate specifically to WF conflict. For example, we (Chappell, Korabik & McElwain, 2005) carried out a study in Canada with 13 men and 44 women who were members of dual-earner couples with children. We measured GRI with the Sex-Role Egalitarianism Scale developed by King and King (1993). Overall, we found no significant differences between those with traditional and egalitarian GRI on either WIF or FIW. However, men with traditional gender-role attitudes reported experiencing less FIW than men with egalitarian gender-role attitudes. Moreover, egalitarian men reported higher levels of FIW than egalitarian women. Our findings are limited, however, by the fact that we did not examine the subcomponents of WIF and FIW (i.e., time-based, strain-based, behavior-based) separately.

Ayman et al. (2005) conducted a similar study involving 15 men and 11 women employed by US corporations. They found significant negative relationships between GRI and strain-based WIF, time-based WIF, and time-based FIW, indicating that egalitarian individuals experienced lower WF conflict than traditional individuals on these dimensions. They did not analyze their results separately for men and women, however. A third investigation was completed by Drach-Zahavy and Somech (2004) with 37 Israeli men and women. No significant differences in WIF and FIW were found between those with traditional and egalitarian GRI.

Using preliminary data from five of the countries involved in Project 3535[2], Poelmans et al. (2006) did a cross-cultural analysis of the relationship between GRI and WF conflict. Their participants were men and women who were employed full-time and who had a spouse/partner and child(ren). The total sample size was 324 men and 511 women and the sample sizes for each country were: India = 228, Taiwan = 121, Spain = 148, US = 62, and Canada = 276. After controlling for job sector and job level (nonmanagerial/managerial), it was found that in all countries those with traditional GRI reported greater WIF and greater FIW than those with egalitarian GRI.

Critique of these Studies

Although these preliminary studies have provided a good start to understanding the relationship of GRI to WF conflict, they suffer from a number of limitations. First, with the exception of Poelmans et al. (2006), they have had very small sample sizes. Second, none of them employed complete designs, examining the data separately as a function of gender, GRI, and the different subcategories of WIF and FIW (time-based, strain-based, etc.). Third, important confounding variables (e.g., job sector, job level, marital and parental status) were seldom controlled. The aforementioned limitations should be able to be overcome once the final data from Project 3535 have been analyzed.

GENDER-ROLE ORIENTATION

Another gender-role construct that has been overlooked in the WF literature is gender-role orientation. Because previous research has used demographic gender as a proxy for gender-role orientation, an examination of gender-role orientation might explain some of the puzzling differences between men and women that have been found in the WF literature.

Gender-role orientation is conceptualized as a bidimensional construct. The two underlying dimensions are instrumentality (also known as masculinity or agency) and expressivity (also known as femininity or communion). Individuals who are sex-typed are socialized to have more characteristics from one dimension than the other (Bem, 1974). Thus, those high on expressivity and low on instrumentality

---

[2]Project 3535 is a multinational research project on the WF interface. The Project 3535 research team is composed of (in alphabetical order): Dr. Zeynep Aycan (Turkey), Dr. Roya Ayman (US), Dr. Anne Bardoel (Australia), Dr. Tripti Pande Desai (India), Dr. Anat Drach-Zahavy (Israel), Dr. Leslie Hammer (US), Dr. Ting-pang Huang (Taiwan), Dr. Karen Korabik (Canada), Dr. Donna S. Lero (Canada), Ms. Artiawati Mawardi (Indonesia), Dr. Steven Poelmans (Spain), Dr. Ujvala Arun Rajadhayaksha (India), and Dr. Anit Somech (Israel).

are labeled feminine, while those high on instrumentality and low on expressivity are considered to be masculine. Androgynous individuals are above the medians on both dimensions, whereas undifferentiated individuals are below the medians on both dimensions (Korabik, 1999). Masculine and feminine individuals will interpret, evaluate, and organize information in terms of traditional gender-role appropriateness (e.g., women should be responsible for housework and men should financially support the family through paid employment; Bem, 1981). Androgynous and undifferentiated people have a weak gender schema and, therefore, do not categorize information according to gender appropriateness (Bem, 1981).

Livingston and Burley (1991) did not find a significant relationship between gender-role orientation and future expectations of WF conflict in a sample of university students from the US. By contrast, we examined the relationship between gender-role orientation and present experiences of WF conflict in a study conducted in Canada with 27 men and 49 women who were members of dual-earner couples with children (McElwain, Korabik & Chappell, 2004). We found no gender-role orientation differences in WIF, which was not surprising considering that all participants were employed full time. Moreover, there were no significant main effects or interactions as a function of demographic gender. Interestingly, both men and women who were high in instrumentality had significantly lower levels of FIW than those low in instrumentality. However, a significant interaction was found, indicating that the effect of instrumentality on FIW varied as a function of expressivity. Regardless of their demographic gender, feminine individuals had the highest levels of FIW, followed by masculine and undifferentiated participants. Individuals who were androgynous (high in both instrumentality and expressivity) had the lowest levels of FIW. The high levels of FIW experienced by feminine individuals could be due to the high priority these men and women put on the family domain (Thompson, 2002). However, androgynous individuals are as high in expressivity as feminine individuals, so they would also be expected to be family-oriented. But, they would likely balance this by putting an equally high priority on the work domain. Moreover, high levels of conflict and distress are atypical of androgynous individuals who are usually able to adjust to, cope with, and perform successfully in, a wide variety of social situations (Bem, 1981).

GENDER-ROLE VALUES

There has been an almost complete lack of research on gender-role values (or the relative salience of work and family roles) and WF conflict. An exception is research by Cinamon and Rich (2002a & b). Their participants were Jewish Israeli men and women who were married, had children, and were working in the computer technology or law fields. They used the Life Roles Salience Scale (LRSS) to assess gender-role values. It measures the importance of four roles (work, spousal, parental, and housework). Based on this, they divided their participants into three groups: (1) dual—those who put equal importance on their work and family roles, (2) work—those who gave high importance to the work role and low importance to the family role, and (3) family—those who gave high importance to the family role and low importance to the work role.

They found that both demographic gender and gender-role values were important to the experience of the WF interface. Their results indicated that more men than women placed greater value on work than family and more women than men placed greater value on family than work. There were no significant gender differences, however, for those in the dual category who saw work and family as being equal in importance. Moreover, men were about equally distributed over the work, family, and dual categories. But, although about 40% of women were in the dual category, among the remainder considerably more were family-oriented than work-oriented. Women were higher in level and frequency of WIF and ascribed more importance to FIW than men.

ROLE INVOLVEMENT AS A POTENTIAL MODERATING VARIABLE

There are a number of moderating variables that might be important in explaining the mixed findings in the literature on gender and the WF interface. One of these is the degree of role involvement. In terms of underlying theory, both the rational theory of WF conflict and the gender role theory make the assumption of biopsychological equivalence.[3] Thus, they are predicated on the assumption that gender differences in WF conflict are due to the acceptance by men and women of the traditional division of labor, in which the husband is the breadwinner and the wife is responsible for the family (Higgins, Duxbury & Lee, 1994). However, men's and women's roles have been changing and their degree of work and family involvement may no longer be divided along these lines. Carlson and Frone (2003)

---

[3]It should be noted that nothing inherent in either of these theories implies that an assumption of biopsychological equivalence must be made. Thus, the rational theory could be reformulated to state that individuals (regardless of whether they are men or women) who spend more time on work-related activities should experience greater WIF than those who spend fewer hours on work-related activities. Likewise, individuals (regardless of whether they are men or women) who spend more time on family-related activities should experience greater FIW than those who spend fewer hours on family-related activities.

The gender-role theory could be similarly reframed. It would then state that additional hours spent in the gender-role domain that is considered to be more important or valued more highly would not be seen as an imposition as much as additional hours spent in the domain that is considered to be less important or valued less highly. According to this perspective, individuals who value family more than work should report higher levels of WIF, whereas those who value work over family should report higher levels of FIW.

feel that the amount of involvement in work and family roles may be an important determinant of WF conflict. Involvement should be assessed both in terms of: (1) the number of hours per week spent in activities related to each domain and (2) the psychological perception of one's extent of involvement in each domain. These may differ by gender. For example, men may spend fewer hours doing housework and interacting with their children than women, but still feel the same degree of psychological role investment. Conversely, women may be highly psychologically invested in their work even though they are only employed part time.

IMPLICATIONS FOR FUTURE RESEARCH AND PRACTICE

Before we can start to understand the role that gender plays in the WF interface, there is a need for improvement in a number of areas. First, WF researchers need to develop a better understanding of theories of gender, to use more sophisticated theories in their research, and to better articulate their theoretical stance. Second, there is a need for better WF measures (see Chapter 4 in this volume). As Hurst states:

> a lack of standardized measurement exists, which has resulted in theoretical (i.e., construct clarification) and practical (i.e., comparing results from multiple studies) problems. The vast majority of measures have either been self-developed...developed without using psychometrically rigorous procedures...or failed to distinguish between either the bi directionality of the construct...or its multidimensional nature (2004, p. 4).

Not only do these problems need to be addressed, but measurement equivalence for gender and culture needs to be established for measures of WF conflict.

Third, researchers need to use more control variables in their studies to equate women and men on factors that might confound their findings (Byron, 2005). Moreover, researchers need to use more complete designs that examine both demographic gender and other aspects of gender and look at time-based, strain-based, and behaviour-based WIF and FIW separately. There is also a need for both more longitudinal research and more studies of facilitation/adaptation, instead of focusing exclusively on conflict.

Finally, there is a need for more cross-cultural research. Asian cultures, for example, may have more communal gender roles than Western ones, making it difficult to generalize results from the West to the East (Adler & Izraeli, 1994). Greater generalizability, however, may exist in regard to demographic gender as androcentrism and patriarchy (i.e., whatever is associated with men is viewed as more valuable than whatever is associated with women) still prevail in most present-day societies. Consequently, women are underrepresented in positions of power and authority throughout the world (Adler & Izraeli, 1994). Still, there are wide variations in the way that women and men enact their occupational and domestic roles in different cultures.

An increased understanding of the role that gender plays in the WF inter-face may have several practical ramifications as well. First, there are implications for individuals in that the detrimental effects of gender-role stereotyping in both the domestic and the occupational spheres should become more apparent. As a result, people should develop a greater realization of the negative impact that they produce when they judge others in terms of gender-role stereotypes. For example, they should become more aware that they should not criticize a mother who is engaged in full-time employment if she is not able to participate in her child's school field trip or if she supplies store-bought rather than homemade treats for the school party. This should impact on both men and women in that they would no longer be expected to conform to the stereotypic gender roles to which they have long been relegated. Instead, they would be given more freedom and latitude regarding the gender-role orientations, attitudes, and values that they endorse and the gender-role behaviors that they enact at home and at work.

Second, there are implications for organizations in that they also should be less likely to react to their employees in terms of gender-role stereotypes. Knowledge about gender should lead organizations to a greater understanding that WF concerns are not solely "women's issues" and that neither all women, nor all men, are the same in terms of the WF choices that they make or their needs for WF accommodations. Organizations that have developed such a realization will be more likely to embody "family-friendly" cultures and to not penalize employees (particularly men) who make use of family-friendly policies.

Finally, there are implications for society as a whole. The social structural perspective on gender emphasizes the role that patriarchy plays in maintaining the present power structure which gives women less access to influence and resources than men. If any real change is to occur within individuals, in their interpersonal interactions with one another, or in organizations, this power structure needs to change. For example, women are more likely than men to take time off from work to raise children because their lower pay means that they are the ones who bring fewer financial resources into the household. Likewise, wives have less power and influence in negotiating with their husbands around who will do the majority of the housework and childcare. And, within organizations gender is still a significant social cue that affects evaluations, resulting in biases in selection, performance evaluation, and promotion. Even though more and more women have entered formerly male-dominated professions, like medicine and law, the power of patriarchy is such that whatever is associated with women is automatically reinterpreted to be less valuable. To change these circumstances will require a complete overhaul of our present socio-cultural system. This will be incredibly difficult to bring about and will take many years, if not generations, to accomplish. Still, there is reason to be optimistic as much change has already occurred and society is continuing to change at a rapid pace.

In conclusion, in this chapter we discussed the role of gender in the WF interface. It is apparent from our review that people's gender-role traits, attitudes, and values influence the choices that they make in their work and family lives. Moreover, whether someone is a man or a woman has an impact not only on their degree of influence and their access to resources in both the employment and domestic spheres, but also on how they are evaluated and judged by others at home and at work. All of these factors contribute to the amount of WF conflict versus facilitation that men and women experience.

REFERENCES

Adler, N. J. & Izraeli, D. N. (eds). (1994). *Competitive Frontiers: Women Managers in a Global Economy*. Malden, MA: Blackwell.

Ayman, R., Velgach, S. & Ishaya, N. (2005, April). Multi-method approach to investigate work-family conflict. Poster presented at the meeting of the Society for Industrial/Organizational Psychology, Los Angeles, CA.

Bedeian, A. G., Burke, B. G. & Moffet, R. G. (1988). Outcomes of work-family conflict among married male and female professionals. *Journal of Management, 14*(3), 475–491.

Bellavia, G. M. & Frone, M. R. (2005). Work-family conflict. In J. Barling, E. K. Kelloway & M. R. Frone (eds), *Handbook of Work Stress*. Thousand Oaks, CA: Sage.

Bem, S. L. (1974). The measurement of psychological androgyny. *Journal of Consulting and Clinical Psychology, 42*, 155–162.

Bem, S. L. (1981). Gender schema theory: A cognitive account of sex-typing. *Psychological Bulletin, 88*, 354–364.

Bem, S. L. (1993). *The Lenses of Gender*. New Haven, CT: Yale University.

Burley, K. A. (1995). Family variables as mediators of the relationship between work-family conflict and marital adjustment among dual-career men and women. *Journal of Social Psychology, 135*(4), 483–497.

Byron, K. (2005). A meta-analytic review of work-family and its antecedents. *Journal of Vocational Behavior, 67*, 169–198.

Carlson, D. S. & Frone, M. R. (2003). Relation of behavioral and psychological involvement to a new four factor conceptualization of the work-family interface. *Journal of Business and Psychology, 17*(4), 515–535.

Carlson, D. S., Kacmar, K. M. & Williams, L. J. (2000). Construction and initial validation of a multidimensional measure of work-family conflict. *Journal of Vocational Behavior, 56*, 249–276.

Chappell, D., Korabik, K. & McElwain, A. (2005, June). The effects of gender-role attitudes on work-family conflict and work-family guilt. Poster presented at the meeting of the Canadian Psychological Association, Montreal, Quebec.

Cinamon, G. & Rich, Y. (2002a). Gender differences in the importance of work and family roles: Implications for work-family conflict. *Sex Roles, 47*(11), 531–542.

Cinamon, G. & Rich, Y. (2002b). Profiles of attribution of importance to life roles and their implications for the work-family conflict. *Journal of Counseling Psychology, 49*(2), 212–220.

Drach-Zahavy, A. & Somech, A. (2004, July). Emic and etic characteristics of coping strategies with WFC: The case of Israel. Paper presented at the International Congress of Cross-Cultural Psychology, Xi'an, Peoples Republic of China.

Duxbury, L. E. & Higgins, C. A. (1991). Gender differences in work-family conflict. *Journal of Applied Psychology, 76*(1), 60–74.

Duxbury, L., Higgins, C. & Lee, C. (1994). Work-family conflict: A comparison by gender, family type, and perceived control. *Journal of Family Issues, 15*(3), 449–466.

Eagle, B. W., Miles, E. W. & Icenogle, M. L. (1997). Interrole conflicts and the permeability of work and family domains: Are there gender differences? *Journal of Vocational Behavior, 50*, 168–184.

Ferree, M. M. (1995). Beyond separate spheres: Feminism and family research. In G. Bowen & J. Pittman (eds), *The Work and Family Interface*. Minneapolis, MN: National Council on Family Relations.

Frone, M. R., Russell, M. & Cooper, M. L. (1992). Antecedents and outcomes of work-family conflict: Testing a model of the work-family interface. *Journal of Applied Psychology, 77*(1), 65–78.

Fu, C. K. & Shaffer, M. A. (2001). The tug of work and family: Direct and indirect domain-specific determinants of work-family conflict. *Personnel Review, 30*(5), 502–522.

Gelfand, M. J., Raver, J. L. & Erhart, K. H. (2002). Methodological issues in cross-cultural organizational research. In S. Rogelberg (ed.), *Handbook of Research Methods in Industrial/Organizational Psychology*. Malden, MA: Blackwell.

Grant-Vallone, E. J. & Donaldson, S. I. (2001). Consequences of work-family conflict on employee well-being over time. *Work & Stress, 15*(3), 214–226.

Greenhaus, J. H., Bedeian, A. G. & Mossholder, K. W. (1987). Work experiences, job performance, and feelings of personal and family well-being. *Journal of Vocational Behavior, 31*, 200–215.

Gutek, B. A., Searle, S. & Klepa, L. (1991). Rational versus gender role explanations for work-family conflict. *Journal of Applied Psychology, 76*(4), 560–568.

Greenstein, T. N. (1995). Gender ideology, marital disruption, and the employment of married women. *Journal of Marriage and the Family, 57*, 31–42.

Grzywacz, J. G. & Marks, N. F. (2000). Reconceptualizing the work-family interface. An ecological perspective on correlated of positive and negative spillover between work and family. *Journal of Occupational Health Psychology, 5*, 111–126.

Guerts, S. & Demerouti, E. (2003). Work/nonwork interface: A review of theories and findings. In M. Schabracq, J. Winnubst & C. Copper (eds), *The Handbook of Work and Health Psychology* (pp. 279–312). Chichester, England: Wiley .

Haas, L. (1995). Structural dimensions of the work-family interface. In G. Bowen & J. Pittman (eds), *The Work and Family Interface*. Minneapolis, MN: National Council on Family Relations.

Hammer, L. B., Colton, C. L., Caubet, S. L. & Brockwood, K. J. (2002). The unbalanced life: Work and family conflict. In J. Thomas & M. Herson (eds), *Handbook of Mental Health in the Workplace*. Thousand Oaks, CA: Sage.

Higgins, C. A., Duxbury, L. E. & Lee, C. (1994). Work-family conflict: A comparison of dual-career and traditional-career men. *Journal of Organizational Behavior, 13*, 389–411.

Hill, E. J., Yang, C., Hawkins, A. J. & Ferris, M. (2004). A cross-cultural test of the work-family interface in 48 countries. *Journal of Marriage and the Family, 66*(5), 1300–1316.

Huffman, A. H., Payne, S. C. & Castro, C. A. (2003, April). Time demands, work-family conflict and turnover: A comparison of men and women. Poster presented at the 17th Annual Convention of the Society for Industrial and Organizational Psychology, Orlando, Florida.

Hurst, D. (2004, April). Cross-cultural measurement invariance of work/family conflict scales across English-speaking samples. Poster presented at the meeting of the Society for Industrial and Organizational Psychology, Chicago, IL.

Joplin, J. R., Shaffer, M. A., Francesco, A. M. & Lau, T. (2003). The macro-environment and work-family conflict: Development of a cross-cultural comparative framework. *International Journal of Cross-Cultural Management, 3*, 305–332.

Kaufman, G. (2000). Do gender role attitudes matter: Family formation and dissolution among traditional and egalitarian men and women. *Journal of Family Issues, 21*, 128–144.

Kaufman, G. & Uhlenberg, P. (2000). The influence of parenthood on the work effort of married men and women. *Social Forces, 78*(3), 931–947.

King, L. A. & King, D. W. (1993). *Manual for the Sex-Role Egalitarianism Scale: An Instrument to Measure Attitudes Toward Gender-Role Equality*. Port Huron, MI: Sigma Assessment Systems.

Kinnunen, U. & Mauno, S. (1998). Antecedents and outcomes of work-family conflict among employed women and men in Finland. *Human Relations, 51*(2), 157–177.

Korabik, K. (1999). Sex and gender in the new millennium. In G. N. Powell (ed.), *Handbook of Gender and Work*. (pp. 1–13). Thousand Oaks, CA: Sage.

Korabik, K. & Ayman, R. (2007). Gender and leadership in the corporate world: A multiperpective model. In J. C. Lau, B. Lott, J. Rice & J. Sanchez-Hudes (eds), *Transforming Leadership: Diverse Visions and Women's Voices* (pp. 106–124). Malden, MA: Blackwell.

Korabik, K., Ayman, R. & Lero, D. S. (2003). A multi-level approach to cross-cultural work-family research: A micro and macro perspective. *International Journal of Cross-Cultural Management, 3*, 289–304.

Ling, Y. & Powell, G. N. (2001). Work-family conflict in contemporary China. *International Journal of Cross-Cultural Management, 1*, 357–373.

Livingston, M. M. & Burley, K. A. (1991). Surprising initial findings regarding sex, sex role, and anticipated work-family conflict. *Psychological Reports, 68*, 735–738.

Lye, D. N. & Biblarz, T. J. (1993). The effects of attitudes toward family life and gender roles on marital satisfaction. *Journal of Family Issues, 14*, 157–188.

McElwain, A., Korabik, K. & Chappell, D. (2004, August). Beyond gender: Re-examining work-family conflict and work-family guilt in the context of gender-role orientation. Paper presented at the meeting of the International Society for the Study of Work and Organizational Values, New Orleans, LA.

McElwain, A., Korabik, K. & Rosin H. M. (2005). An examination of gender differences in work-family conflict. *Canadian Journal of Behavioural Science, 37*(4), 269–284.

O'Neil, R. & Greenberger, E. (1994). Patterns of commitment to work and parenting: Implications for role strain. *Journal of Marriage and the Family, 56*, 101–118.

Poelmans, S., Ayman, R., Korabik, K., Rajhadyaksha, U., Huang, T. P., Lero, D. S. & Pade Desai, T. (2006, August). How far is too far? Comparing Spain, Taiwan, US and Canada on work-family conflict. Paper presented at the meeting of the International Association of Cross-Cultural Psychology, Spetes, Greece.

Schieman, S., Whitestone, Y. K. & Van Gundy, K. (2006). The nature of work and the stress of higher status. *Journal of Health and Social Behavior, 47*, 242–257.

Spence, J. T., Helmreich, R. & Stapp, J. (1975). Ratings of self and peers on sex role attributes and their relation to self-esteem and the conceptions of masculinity and femininity. *Journal of Personality and Social Psychology, 32*, 29–39.

Thompson, E. H. (2002). What's unique about men's caregiving? In B. J. Kramer & E. Thompson (eds), *Men as Caregivers: Theory, Research and Service Implications* (pp. 20–47). New York, NY: Springer.

Unger, R. K. & Crawford, M. (1993). Commentary: Sex and gender – The troubled relationship between terms and concepts. *Psychological Science, 4*, 122–124.

Voydanoff, P. (2002). Linkages between the work-family interface and work, family and individual outcomes: An integrative model. *Journal of Family Issues, 23*(1), 138–164.

Windslow, S. (2005). Work-family conflict, gender, and parenthood, 1977–1997. *Journal of Family Issues, 26*(6), 727–755.

Yang, N., Chen, C. C., Choi, J. & Zou, Y. (2000). Sources of work-family conflict: A Sino-US comparison of the effects of work and family demands. *Academy of Management Journal, 43*(1), 113–123.

CHAPTER 13

Viewing 21st Century Motherhood Through a Work-Family Lens

Sarah Damaske and Kathleen Gerson

Sociology Department, New York University, New York

At the outset of the 21st century, mothers are far more likely than not to be paid workers. A demographic and social revolution has propelled most mothers and would-be mothers to join the paid labor force and establish committed work ties over the course of their lives. This irrefutable social shift has transformed the experience of motherhood and undermined mid-20th century assumptions that home and work are inherently separate, gendered spheres. Despite these vast social changes—or perhaps because of them—the idea of a "working mother" remains highly contested. Indeed, the ubiquity of the term "working mother" is telling, since it is no longer clear how such a term meaningfully distinguishes among groups of women or their life experiences. Clearly, work and family remain the two most prominent axes on which women's lives are structured, and equally clearly, they continue to be viewed as "oppositional" domains. Through a review of the burgeoning scholarship on motherhood, we consider how a work-family framework can expand our understanding of contemporary mothering and help explain and potentially resolve the contradictions in women's lives.

First, we examine contemporary variations in motherhood, with an eye to disentangling prevailing myths about past patterns from genuinely new developments. We then consider some of the persisting theoretical debates about the nature, causes, and consequences of mothering practices and beliefs, asking how these debates frame our current understanding of contemporary motherhood. Third, we ask how a work-family framework can help reframe theories, direct research, and resolve current debates. We argue that a focus on the interaction of family and work is crucial to understanding and explaining motherhood's contemporary patterns and future prospects.

PUTTING MOTHERHOOD IN PERSPECTIVE: CONTEMPORARY VARIATIONS

Since the 1960s, transformations in the institutions of marriage and work have reshaped the conditions, experiences, and ideologies of motherhood. The

Handbook of Work-Family Integration: Research, Theory, and Best Practices

increasingly impermanent and optional nature of marriage has changed the circumstances under which women make decisions about bearing and rearing
children (Cherlin, 2004; Popenoe, 1988, 1996). Close to 50% of contemporary
marriages end in divorce, compared to slightly more than 25% in the 1950s.
Similarly, the proportion of children born to unmarried women has risen from 5%
in 1960 to 26% in 1990, where it has remained (Casper & Bianchi, 2002; Giele,
1996). Although the category "unmarried women" includes never-married women,
divorced or widowed women, and women who are cohabitating, the rise in single
women means that mothers are increasingly likely to face the prospect of rearing children outside the context of lifelong marriage. In addition, the expansion
of reproductive rights, including access to an array of contraceptives and abortion
services, has given women, particularly middle-class and upper-class women, the
ability to control their reproductive lives and to delay pregnancy and motherhood.
These changes in the nature of adult commitment and reproductive control have
prompted contradictory consequences: at one end of the spectrum, more women
are bearing and rearing children on their own; at the other end, more women are
postponing and even eschewing motherhood.

These revolutionary shifts in the nature of marriage and childbearing have
been accompanied by equally dramatic changes in women's workforce participation, which has grown steadily from about 43% in 1970 to 75% today (US
Department of Labor, 1998; Hays, 2003). By 2005, women made up 46% of the
workforce and 75% of employed women worked full-time jobs (US Department
of Labor, 2005). Equally important, contemporary mothers with young children
are almost as likely as childless women to hold a paid job. Most women coming of
age at the outset of the 21st century are, or will be, juggling the often-conflicting
worlds of family and paid work throughout their adult lives.

Changes in the nature of marriage and paid work have created a diverse
array of mothering experiences and practices. While homemaking mothers persist,
they are now a distinct minority. There are more dual-earner couples today than
there were homemaker-breadwinner households in 1970 (Jacobs & Gerson, 2004).
With single mothers added to the mix, it becomes clear that no one mothering
pattern now predominates. What's more, mothers, and their children, are increasingly likely to experience change over the course of their lives, as shifts occur in
mothers' marital and work statuses (Gerson, 2002). Motherhood, as a practice and
an experience, has become increasingly diverse and fluid.

EXPLAINING MOTHERING PATTERNS: CONTENDING THEORETICAL DEBATES

Theories of motherhood have been, and continue to be, linked to social
changes and public debates about women's place. Classical sociological approaches,

formulated during the post-WW II period of domestic resurgence, argued that a gendered division between women's caretaking and men's breadwinning constituted a necessary and even optimal family arrangement in the modern context (Goode, 1963; Parsons, 1974). As the social bases of women's domesticity eroded, new theoretical approaches challenged these essentialist presumptions on several levels. Feminist historians pointed to historical shifts in family arrangements and women's fates, while sociologists and economists linked varied and changing family forms to larger social and economic contexts (Cancian, 1987). Psychoanalytically inclined feminists added another dimension to the critique of classical theories by challenging psychological frameworks that devalued women's caretaking or ignored the contexts that guide the development of gendered identities (Chodorow, 1979; Gilligan, 1984).

Early feminist challenges provided a set of powerful reformulations of classical theories of motherhood, but they did not consistently question the "dichotomous distinctions" that views women (and men) as homogenous groups (Connell, 1987; Epstein, 1988). More recent theoretical approaches, along with a host of empirical studies, have extended this early work by focusing on variations among women (and men) as well as by examining the institutional and cultural paradoxes and contradictions that leave modern mothers facing deep conflicts and dilemmas (Gerson, 2002; Hays, 1996; Lorber, 1994; Risman, 1998). Through this lens, recent research has studied the diverse and changing practices of modern and postmodern families (Coontz, 1997; Risman, 1998); the construction of a gendered division of labor in the home (Hochschild, 1990); and the ways that varied conceptions of "mothering" influence diverse family forms and political outlooks (Edin, 2000; Luker, 1984). These approaches seek to locate and understand how disparate institutional spheres are connected and how these connections pose dilemmas to which individuals must respond, often in creative ways.

An important point of departure has been to uncover differences among women that emerge from varying ethnic, race, and class subcultures, including the potential for conflicting interests between mothers and paid caretakers and the potential for exploitation of some women by others (Collins, 1991; Dill, 1988; Rollins 1985). Since the image of the "traditional" breadwinner family, in which women did not work, never applied to most non-white women, Collins (1991) argues that motherhood has always taken a different form for black women. Additionally, many working-class and working-poor families have long depended on mothers' workforce participation (Garey, 1999). This work has made it clear that only by incorporating race and class dynamics can models of motherhood encompass the full range of experiences and practices.

In addition to exploring race, class, and ethnic variation, analysts have drawn attention to the interplay between structural forces and individual strategies in shaping modern motherhood. Zimmerman and West (1987), for example, propose an interactionist perspective, in which women (and men) "do gender" in response to social contexts that expect them to perform in gendered ways (see also Butler, 1990, 2004; West & Fenstermaker, 1995). This approach takes women's active strategies seriously, but is less attentive to how social change in gendered strategies could occur. To take account of social change, Gerson advocates a developmental approach that acknowledges the roles of both childhood experiences and structural constraints, but adds a focus on "how women themselves, as actors who respond to the social conditions they inherit, construct their lives out of the available raw materials" (1985, p. 37).

Lorber (1994) and Risman (1998) also take a multidimensional approach by positing that gender is not just structured by other institutions, but is also an institution in itself. Seeing gender as an institution helps clarify the central role that gender plays at all levels in the construction of motherhood, including structural, cultural, interactional, and psychological levels. But this perspective also makes it difficult to distinguish between gender as a cause and a consequence. To overcome this difficulty, analysts have pointed to the ways that gender is structured as a series of paradoxes, contradictions, and dilemmas that leave women facing difficult, potentially irresolvable, conflicts (Hays, 1996; Lorber, 1994; Moen, 2003). Multiple, contradictory gender ideologies thus confront women with "cultural contradictions" that expect them to practice "intensive mothering" even as they take paid jobs (Hays, 1996). In this context, new generations of women have little choice but to negotiate among competing social forces and create new and varied forms of motherhood (Gerson, 2002; Risman, 1998).

UNDERSTANDING MOTHERHOOD THROUGH A WORK-FAMILY LENS

Whatever form motherhood may take, it is inescapably interwoven with work and family institutions. It is thus necessary to examine how the interactions between work and family shape women's mothering options and experiences. To do this, we first consider the current state of women's work, asking how women fare in the paid labor market as well as how occupational segregation and the gender-wage gap affect women's fate. Similarly, we examine the consequences of motherhood for women's work prospects, asking if and how a "motherhood penalty" constrains women's options. Next, we ask how women negotiate the conflicts between work and motherhood, considering current debates about the degree to which family and work remain in conflict. We also examine the changing terrain of caretaking, asking how paid caregivers experience caring for their own children and the children for whom they are hired to care. We then consider how and why women continue to assume disproportionate responsibility for housework and childcare, asking what explains persistent inequalities in the "second shift" (Hochschild, 1989). And, finally, we discuss how new and more diverse patterns of motherhood have triggered cultural controversies and political debates about the "proper place" of mothers.

Women as Mothers and Workers

It is not possible to understand women's position as mothers without also understanding their position as workers. Women's work options influence their family decisions and, for many, their family options. For most analysts, the point of departure in understanding women's attachment to the labor market has been the persistence of a gender wage gap and the shape of occupational segregation (Charles & Grusky, 2004; Kilbourne et al., 1994; Reskin & Roos, 1990). The persistence of what Charles and Grusky (2004) call "occupational ghettoes" reduces women's access to better paid work, to important job networks, and ultimately to the economic resources and work opportunities that influence their options as mothers. While work experience accounts for some of the gender wage gap, most of the gap emerges from the gendered type of occupation. Once occupations become "feminized" (with women constituting over 60% of workers), both pay and opportunity decline (Kilbourne et al., 1994).

Despite a continuing pay and opportunity gap, the influx of women into the workplace has loosened the stigma of women at work, contributed to growing workplace acceptance, and eroded male workers' (and unions') resistance to women's presence (Kanter, 1977; Reskin & Roos, 1990). With the rise of women's participation, the gender wage gap decreased from 60% in the late 1960s to 75% in the mid-1990s, when it plateaued (Blau & Kahn, 2000). Today, it is clear that women have made notable inroads into some male careers, but these inroads are not as remarkable as they once appeared. As important, they have not led to overall economic gains for women as a group. While some women can claim demonstrable gains in their earning power, not all have benefited. To the contrary, a focus on average earnings obscures the increasing variation among women, where 80% still earn less than the median male worker (Bernhardt et al., 1995). These differences in women's work opportunities have consequences for their mothering options as well.

Mothers and Workplace Inequality

Alongside occupational sex segregation and a wage gap, motherhood itself presents serious challenges to women's workplace prospects. Despite the rise of employed mothers, work structures remain organized around an "ideal worker" model that presumes unquestioned work commitment and the existence of an unpaid caretaker at home (J. Williams, 2000). It is thus no surprise that women, who remain caught between the competing demands of intensive work and intensive caretaking, face a "wage penalty for motherhood" (Budig & England, 2001). A range of possible factors—including the loss of experience at work due to maternity leave, a decline in work productivity due to childcare responsibilities, a move to more "mother-friendly" jobs, and active discrimination by employers against mothers—provide possible explanations for the link between motherhood and lower pay (Budig & England, 2001). Yet, to some extent, all of these factors reflect the ways that a growing mismatch between workplace structures and families' needs have left women caught between two worlds (Jacobs & Gerson, 2004; Moen, 2003).

Women continue to face a penalty when they leave paid jobs to raise children, even temporarily (Waldfogel, 1997). The presence of children in the household is the biggest predictor among women who report a need for leave, and women are much more likely than men to report this need, even if both parents work for pay (Gerstel & McGonagle, 1999). Taking a leave is often costly for any worker's wages and future career options, but women are much more likely to do so. The ability and need to take a leave from work is also tied to race and income. Women from working-class and poor backgrounds and women of color, particularly black women, are much more likely to say that they need to take time off than are other women (Gerstel & McGonagle, 1999). Women who choose to take part-time work instead of a full-time leave also face financial disadvantages, since part-time work has lower future returns (England, Christopher & Reid, 1999). So while the benefits of childrearing are a public good, the cost of rearing children, in the form of leave-taking or work-reduction, are paid predominantly by women (England & Folbre, 1999).

Leave-taking, however, only partially explains the motherhood wage penalty, so it is necessary to examine other possible factors. Surprisingly, there is little evidence to suggest that employment in "mother-friendly" jobs is associated with a decline in wages (Budig & England, 2001). Indeed, men who work in the "feminine" sectors of the labor market do not face the same financial penalties and may even experience a "glass escalator," in contrast to the "glass ceiling" women encounter in male-dominated occupational preserves (C. Williams, 1995). Equally important, "pink-collar" jobs and those seen as more "feminine" are *not* more family-friendly (Jacobs & Gerson, 2004). Ironically, male-dominated professions and jobs at the higher echelons of organizations often have more flexible schedules, unsupervised breaks, and paid sick and vacation leaves than do the jobs women are more likely to hold (Glass, 1990).

Some, especially among "new home economics" theorists, have argued that the motherhood penalty simply reflects mothers' lower productivity and commitment at work. They argue that increased responsibility for and attention to domestic work prompts mothers to reserve their energy for time with children and to become less productive and less attentive to their paid jobs (Becker, 1981). Yet no compelling evidence has demonstrated a productivity gap between mothers and childless women. As telling, men do not experience a wage penalty for fatherhood or a decline in work productivity, even if they take an active role in childrearing. In fact, men's wages are largely unaffected by fatherhood, and some men experience income increases after the birth of a child (Loh, 1996; Lundburg & Rose, 2000). Employer discrimination is another possible factor, but one that is difficult to measure. Budig and England argue that "researchers' inability to directly measure productivity or employer discrimination means that either may show up... as an unmeasured residual effect of motherhood on wages" (2001, p. 210). Recent qualitative research on women in male-dominated work settings nevertheless suggests that discrimination against intensive parenting, if not against mothers *per se*, leaves women disadvantaged and facing difficult choices (Roth, 2006).

To a large extent, modern work settings continue to presume an "ideal worker" model that is, in fact, a male breadwinner model (J. Williams, 2000). In a variety of ways, mobility routes at work are structured to penalize time spent in caretaking and to presume a breadwinner-homemaker household in which men can rely on an unpaid caretaker and are free to devote endless hours to their jobs (Acker, 1973; Hartmann, 1987; Jacobs & Gerson, 2004). Yet most mothers now work, and most men can no longer count on a full-time homemaking wife. And while men as well as women are experiencing new pressures and stresses, most women continue to perform the lion's share of domestic work, whether or not they hold a paid job (Garey, 1999; Greenstein, 2000; Hochschild, 1989). A lack of flexibility at work and support at home are central to understanding how and why mothers continue to face work penalties even as they make inroads at the workplace.

Negotiating between Work and Motherhood

Despite the rise of employed mothers, integrating motherhood with paid work remains a daunting challenge. Women's decisions about work and motherhood have been found to be less tied to their gender ideologies or socialization experiences and more closely linked to their varied life experiences. A package of factors, such as financial constraints, marital insecurity, and career opportunities, can induce and inspire women to seek work careers and combine them with motherhood, while contrasting experiences, such as financial support within a stable marriage and thwarted work opportunities, can send even high-aspiring women toward full-time or part-time domesticity (Gerson, 1985). Women's commitment to high-powered corporate positions, for example, depends on contingencies at work and in the home (Blair-Loy, 2003; Roth, 2006). Women who experience "positive career contingencies," such as promotions, may find themselves more committed to work, but women who experience "negative family contingencies," such as a child's illness, may turn away from work (Blair-Loy, 2003; Stone, 2007).

The "choice" between work and motherhood has always been less available to some groups of women who do not have the option to withdraw from paid work. The language of "choice," moreover, can be misleading, since, as Garey (1999) contends, work and mothering are not necessarily experienced as opposing domains. She proposes a metaphor of "weaving" to capture the ways that working-class women integrate work and motherhood in their daily lives. Yet most analysts agree that cultural ideals of intensive mothering are not compatible with the "self-interested, profit-maximizing utility" of the business world (Folbre, 2001; Harrington 1999; Hays, 1996). In this context, conflicts are difficult to avoid, and most mothers face a "balancing act" (Bianchi et al., 2006; Spain & Bianchi, 1996). Recent research on "the time divide" suggests that both perspectives provide useful analytical lenses. Women in professional careers face increased pressure to devote themselves to time-demanding jobs, while women at the other end of the educational and class spectrum may find it hard to find steady work or secure enough work hours to provide for their families (Jacobs & Gerson, 2004).

Opting Out?

Despite mothers' irrefutable move into paid jobs over the long term, recent media attention has pointed to an "opt-out revolution" among professional women who are purportedly leaving their careers to be full-time caregivers (Belkin, 2003). *The New York Times* has devoted significant coverage to this issue, and in 2006 Random House published a collection of essays about the "choice" between work and mothering entitled *The Mommy Wars*. Not only has this debate focused on a small segment of married, upper-middle-class women, it also does not accurately reflect current trends or the reasons that a small group of women may be relinquishing promising careers.

In fact, contemporary mothers face a complex array of pushes and pulls. Most mothers who have "opted out" of careers express extreme ambivalence about the decision, citing inflexible professional demands and excessively long working hours as the major culprits (Stone & Lovejoy, 2004; Stone, 2007; J. Williams, 2007). A lack of domestic and community supports also play important roles, and most "opt out" mothers cite roadblocks to finding suitable caregivers as well as reluctance on the part of husbands to relinquish career prospects or to act as primary caretakers, even when their earnings are less than or equal to their wives (Bittman et al., 2003; Stone & Lovejoy, 2004). It is thus more accurate to say that obstacles at work and in the home have "pushed" these mothers out of jobs and into the home, despite their desire to balance and integrate work and motherhood.

More important, few mothers are opting out at all. In fact, while the proportion of employed mothers with children under the age of one declined from a peak of 59% in 1998 to 55% in 2002, that figure remains vastly larger than the 31% who were in the labor force in 1976. More telling, mothers with children older than one are just as likely as other women to be working, with 72% of these mothers and 71% of childless women in the labor force. Finally, educated women are especially likely to work. The higher a woman's educational attainment, the more likely she will be a labor force participant who is either working or looking for work (and the less likely she will be unemployed) (US Department of Labor, 2005). Women who view themselves as having a "career" are more committed to the labor market than are women who view themselves as simply holding a "job" (Risman, 1998). As J. Williams (2000) points out, the depiction of professional women's departure from careers misleads far more than it illuminates.

Paid Domestic Workers and the Expansion of Caretaking

The expansion of caretaking arrangements, especially to include paid caregivers, is an important consequence of the rise of employed mothers. While few employed mothers can rely on a full-time homemaking partner, most families rely on some form of paid caretaking support either within or outside the home. In place of unpaid homemakers, paid workers perform an increasing amount of "carework" (England, 2005). As a traditionally unpaid or poorly paid tasks, carework continues to command relatively low pay, whether it is performed in a domestic or public setting (Romero, 1992). Since, as Rollins (1985) argues, women are the primary employers of most domestic workers, this practice highlights inequalities among women. Hondagneu-Sotelo (2001) adds to this analysis by showing how employment in the private sphere comes to be seen as consumption. In upper-middle class families, which are more inclined to hire domestic workers, women generally assume responsibility for consumer tasks and thus tend to downplay their position as employers in favor of interactions with nannies and housekeepers that stress personal relationships (Hondagneu-Sotelo, 2001). Women who employ domestics tend to discuss matters such as vacation days and payment as personal, rather than as business decisions—an informal approach that can intensify inequality between employer and employee (Hondagneu-Sotelo, 2001).

Many, perhaps most, domestic workers are mothers as well. Yet they are rarely allowed or expected to bring their children to work, even when they are caring for other parents' children (Collins, 1991; Ehrenreich & Hochschild, 2003; Hondagneu-Sotelo & Avila, 1997; Wrigley, 1995). Historically, domestic careworkers have thus provided childcare for others, while relying on a relative or "other mother" to care for their own children (Collins, 1991; Romero, 1992). This pattern is not new, but it has become globalized in recent years, as women from poorer nations, such as Central America and Mexico, as well as the Philippines and other Asian nations, have immigrated to the US in search of better paying jobs, often leaving their own children in the care of others (Glenn, 1986; Hondagneu-Sotelo & Avila, 1997; Romero, 1992). By leaving their children and acting as the primary breadwinner for their families, these "transnational mothers" challenge contemporary understandings of motherhood. By replacing one female caretaker with another, paid careworkers provide some women, especially those with economic resources and well-paid jobs of their own, with more work-family options, but this pattern does not challenge the social institutions that continue to rely on women as caretakers and to devalue the work that caretakers do.

Parenting Inequality and the Second Shift

Despite mothers' rising employment, women continue to do more domestic work than their partners (Deutsch, 1999; Greenstein, 2000; Hochschild, 1989). The last several decades have seen a decline in the housework gap as men's participation has increased and women's has declined. But a housework and caretaking gap nevertheless persists, and the negotiation of this process remains a complex one (Barnett & Rivers, 1996; Robinson, 1997). Gender ideologies do not consistently predict or explain the distribution of housework and childcare in a household, and egalitarian beliefs do not necessarily translate into an equal division of tasks. Hochschild (1989) finds that some couples that express an egalitarian ideology also develop an egalitarian distribution of domestic work, but most struggle with inconsistencies between their ideals and their practices.

In lieu of gender ideologies, exchange and bargaining theories suggest that economic and social resources, such as income, are more important. In this framework, spouses use economic contributions as leverage to "buy out" their responsibilities at home. Several studies have found evidence that women perform less housework (and men perform more) when women's earnings increase (Brines, 1994; Greenstein, 2000). Yet these studies also find that the distribution of housework does not necessarily become equal even when women bring in equal or higher incomes (Bittman et al., 2003; Brines, 1994; Greenstein, 2000). Rather, as a woman's earnings surpass her husband's, his contribution to household work may decrease (Bittman et al., 2003; Brines, 1994; Greenstein, 2000). As couples move away from the normative ideal of the husband as primary financial provider, some appear to compensate for this deviation in the public sphere by returning to a more gendered arrangement at home. These cases point to the need to integrate theoretical approaches that see gender as the result of social and institutional forces with those that see gender itself as a fundamental organizing principle.

Children and Employed Mothers

Despite the rise of work opportunities for women, a "continuing social mandate" still stresses fathers' responsibility to provide financially for children and mother's responsibility to care for children (Riggs, 1997). Cultural fears persist about putative harmful effects on children when mothers hold paid jobs (Coleman, 1990). These fears, no doubt, color women's experiences, no matter what choices they make. Yet decades of research have shown that children are not harmed when their mothers work (Hoffman et al., 1999). In the 1990s, a longitudinal study by the National Institute of Child Health and Human Development found that mothers' workforce participation alone did not alter the bond between mother and infant (Galinsky, 1999). A number of studies have also found that two-income households are beneficial for children (Barnett & Rivers, 1996).

Most agree that a mother's satisfaction with work and support from other care-takers (especially fathers) matters more than her work status (Galinsky, 1999; Hoffman et al., 1999).

Perhaps more surprising, but equally important, time use research shows that despite the increase in mothers' employment, today's mothers are not spending less time with their children than did those from previous decades and some have actually increased their time (Bianchi et al., 2006). Despite these findings, there continues to be an outcry of concern about the fate of children when mothers work. This contemporary nostalgia for the 1950s homemaker-breadwinner family tends to be used as a not-so-subtle effort to undermine the prospects for employed women as well as gay and lesbian families (Faludi, 1991; Stacey, 1997).

THE POLITICS OF MOTHERHOOD

The growth of alternatives to exclusive, intensive mothering has trans-formed the experiences and social circumstances of mothers in profound ways. As significant, it has fueled a set of highly contested cultural and political debates. Indeed, an intense "politics of motherhood" underlies the struggles surrounding a wide range of topics—from abortion and reproductive rights to policies regarding single mothers to the "mommy wars" depicted between employed and non-employed mothers. Despite their topical differences, all of these controversies reflect deep, persisting social and political divisions between those who welcome the expansion of women's options to rear children in diverse ways and those who wish to preserve monolithic ideals of exclusive, intensive mothering.

Debates over the social status of "working" vs "stay-at-home" mothers reflect unease on the part of most mothers about the double binds that confront all mothering strategies. Whether or not they hold a paid job, all mothers risk facing some form of social criticism. Hays (1998) points to the "cultural contra-dictions" of motherhood, in which the norm of intensive mothering pervades women's lives even as they face growing pressures to take paid jobs. Recent cri-tiques of, and some would say "attacks" on, working mothers have added a class dimension to the politics of motherhood by castigating middle-class employed mothers for relying on the carework of working-class women (Flanagan, 2006). Finally, the increase of single mothers provides another wrinkle in the ongo-ing debate about motherhood. The growth of single mothers makes it clear that motherhood is inextricably connected to notions of fatherhood (Hertz, 2006). Indeed, if men are unable to meet acceptable social standards of fatherhood, including providing income and sharing in childrearing, women are more likely to resist marriage and to choose to mother on their own (Edin, 2000). Conservatives continue to argue that all mothers should be their children's primary and even full-time caretaker and that all parents should uphold "traditional marriage." Yet they have also joined a political coalition supporting "workfare" policies that require single mothers to work. This apparently contradictory position, which requires single mothers to leave their children while simultaneously arguing that employed mothers risk harming their children, reflects the conundrums that continue to pervade views of motherhood (Hays, 2003). It is ironic that poor mothers with few job opportunities and limited childcare supports are expected to go to work, while middle-class women with more highly-honed job skills and access to higher-quality childcare are chastised for leaving their children.

With the rise of optional motherhood, employed motherhood, and single motherhood, it is not surprising that the status of mothers has become highly politicized. Since new mothering patterns are diverse, the worldviews and perceived interests of mothers and others are likely to be diverse as well. And since no one pattern can claim a cultural mandate or a secure social position, each circumstance is likely to engender discomfort and opposition among those who have followed other paths (Ginsberg, 1989; Luker, 1984). Yet there is also evidence that the uncertainty facing all contemporary mothers provides grounds for reaching across these divides. Despite findings that employed and homemaking mothers are divided (Luker, 1984), recent research also suggests that both groups hold ideals of attentive parenting that are largely shared (Hays, 1998). Across diverse situations, mothers want and need institutional and cultural avenues for crafting a variety of work-family strategies, including shared parenting with men and social supports for integrating family and work (Epstein, 1998; Gerson, 2002; Gornick & Myers, 2003; Skolnick, 2002).

IMPLICATIONS FOR FUTURE RESEARCH AND PRACTICE

A work-family lens makes it clear that the forms of motherhood, which have varied historically, have become increasingly diverse. Contemporary mothering takes many forms, from those who devote full-time to caretaking and depend on a partner's paycheck, to those who strive to combine parenting with paid work and share caretaking with others, to those who endeavor to parent on their own. What's more, the circumstances of mothers' lives are likely to change as their children grow, their adult partnerships change, and their ties to paid work shift. As an experience and an institution, motherhood has never been more diverse or fluid.

Given the changes to women's work and family lives, it is necessary to ask if women's lives have changed in other ways. Historically, a woman's class position has been highly dependent on her husband's (and, before that, her father's). But a woman's workforce participation may now be as important as, or more important than, her marital status in shaping her class position. Some women may continue to experience upward mobility through marriage or a lifelong partnership, while others may find that divorce triggers downward mobility, regardless of class position. Yet in an era of increasing economic individualism, the social status and mobility paths of most women and their children will depend as much on their ties to paid work as on their ties to a partner. It is important to understand how such changes in women's commitments to work, marriage, and family are changing the shape, direction, and dynamics of their own life trajectories as well as those of their children.

In a related way, it is crucial to chart how new generations of women are grappling with a clash between the growing ideal of work-family balance and persisting institutional obstacles, such as time-demanding workplaces and missing supports for caregiving. Contemporary women may enjoy an expanded set of options, but they also face rising uncertainty about whether and how to craft a marriage, rear children, and build a work career. While some are predicting a "return to tradition," the erosion of permanent marriage and the expansion of women's employment make it more likely that most young women will seek to combine childrearing with a substantial measure of personal autonomy and economic self-reliance (Gerson, 2007). We thus need to understand how women are crafting new patterns of motherhood amid uncharted social waters.

Amid the myriad shapes of contemporary motherhood, structural conflicts and cultural contradictions continue to pose dilemmas for all mothers. How to provide care through time and money? How to find an identity through connections to children and more public pursuits? How to divide and share the work of parenting with others? To understand the ways that mothers experience and respond to these dilemmas in their own lives, we need to focus on how work and family institutions shape women's options and mothering strategies. If we hope to improve the future prospects for mothers, we need to provide women with the social supports to enact the personal mothering strategies they deem best. Mothers cannot create these supports alone. The future of motherhood depends on collective efforts to devise new ways for workplaces, communities, and fathers to support, value, and participate in the work that mothers do.

REFERENCES

Acker, J. (1973). Women and social stratification: A case of intellectual sexism. *American Journal of Sociology, 78,* 936–945.

Barnett, R. & Rivers, C. (1996). *She Works/He Works: How Two-Income Families Are Happier, Healthier, and Better Off.* San Francisco: Harper.

Barnett, R. & Rivers, C. (2004). *Same Difference: How Myths About Gender Are Hurting Our Relationships, Our Children, and Our Jobs.* New York: Basic Books.

Becker, G. S. (1981). *A Treatise on the Family.* Cambridge, MA: Harvard University Press.

Belkin, L. (2003). The opt out revolution. *The New York Times Magazine,* October 26.

Bernhardt, A., Morris, M. & Hancock, M. S. (1995). Women's gains or men's losses? A closer look at the shrinking gender gap in earnings. *American Journal of Sociology, 101,* 302–328.

Bianchi, S., Robinson, J. & Milkie, M. 2006. *The Changing Rhythms of American Family Life.* New York: Russell Sage Foundation.

Bittman, M., England, P., Sayer, L., Folbre, N. & Matheson, G. (2003). When does gender trump money? Bargaining and time in household work. *American Journal of Sociology, 109*, 186–214.

Blair-Loy, M. (2003). *Competing Devotions: Career and Family among Women Executives.* Cambridge, MA: Harvard University Press.

Blau, F. D. & Kahn, L. M. (2000). Gender differences in pay. *Journal of Economic Perspective, 14*, 75–99.

Brines, J. (1994). Economic dependency, gender, and the division of labor at home. *American Journal of Sociology, 100*, 652–688.

Budig, M. J. & England, P. (2001). The wage penalty for motherhood. *American Sociological Review, 66*, 204–225.

Butler, J. (1990). Gender is burning. In J. Butler (ed.), *Bodies that Matter: On the Discursive Limits of "Sex"* New York: Routledge.

Butler, J. (2004). *Undoing Gender.* New York: Routledge.

Cancian, F. (1987). *Love in America: Gender and Self-Development.* New York: Cambridge University Press.

Casper, L. & Bianchi, S. (2002). *Continuity and Change in the American Family.* London: Sage Publications.

Charles, M. & Grusky, D. (2004). *Occupational Ghettos: The Worldwide Segregation of Women and Men.* Stanford, CA: Stanford University Press.

Cherlin, A. (2004). The deinstitutionalization of marriage. *Journal of Marriage and the Family, 66*, 848–861.

Chodorow, N. (1989). *Feminism and Psychoanalytic Theories.* New Haven: Yale University Press.

Coleman, J. (1990). The rational reconstruction of society. *American Sociological Review, 58*, 1–5.

Collins, P. H. (1991). *Black Feminist Thought.* New York: Routledge.

Connell, R. (1987). *Gender and Power.* Stanford: Stanford University Press.

Coontz. S. (1997). *The Way We Really Are: Coming to Terms with America's Changing Families.* New York: Basic Books.

Deutsch, F. (1999). *Halving It All: How Equally Shared Parenting Works.* Cambridge, MA: Harvard University Press.

Dill, B. (1988). Our mother's grief: Racial ethnic women and the maintenance of families. *Journal of Family History, 13*, 415–431.

Edin, K. (2000). What do low-income single mothers say about marriage? *Social Problems, 47*, 112–133.

Ehrenreich, B. & Hochschild, A. (2003). *Global Woman: Nannies, Maids, and Sex Workers in the New Economy.* New York: Metropolitan Books.

England, P. (2005). Emerging theories of carework. *Annual Review of Sociology, 31*, 381–399.

England, P., Christopher, K. & Reid, L. L. (1999). How do intersections of race/ethnicity and gender affect pay among young cohorts of African Americans, European Americans and Latino/as? In I. Browne (ed.), *Latinas and African American at Work: Race, Gender and Economic Inequality* (pp. 139–182). New York: Russell Sage Foundation.

England, P. & Folbre, N. (1999). The cost of caring. *Annals of the American Academy of Political and Social Science, 561*, 39–51.

Epstein, C. (1988). *Deceptive Distinctions: Sex, Gender, and the Social Order.* New Haven: Yale University Press.

Faludi, S. (1991). *Backlash: The Undeclared War Against American Women.* New York: Crown.

Flanagan, Caitlin. (2006). *To Hell with All That: Loving and Loathing Our Inner Housewife.* New York: Little, Brown & Company.

Folbre, N. (2001). *The Invisible Heart: Economics and Family Values.* New York: New Press.

Galinsky, E. (1999). *Ask the Children: What America's Children Really Think About Working Parents.* New York: William Morrow.

Garey, A. I. (1999). *Weaving Work and Motherhood.* Philadelphia: Temple University Press.

Gerson, K. (1985). *Hard Choices: How Women Decide about Work, Career, and Motherhood*. Berkeley: University of California Press.

Gerson, K. (1993). *No Man's Land: Men's Changing Commitments to Family and Work*. New York: Basic Books.

Gerson, K. (2002). Moral dilemmas, moral strategies and the transformation of gender. *Gender and Society, 16*, 8–22.

Gerson, K. (2007). What do women and men want? And how our system contributes to gender conflicts over work, family, and marriage. *The American Prospect*, March, A8–A11.

Gerstel, N. & McGonagle, K. (1999). Job leaves and the limits of the family and Medical Leave Act: The effects of gender, race and family. *Work and Occupations, 26*, 510–534.

Giele, J. Z. (1996). Decline of the family: Conservative, liberal and feminist views. In D. Popenoe et al. (eds), *Promises to Keep: Decline and Renewal of Marriage in America* (pp. 89–115). Lanham, MD: Rowman & Littlefield.

Gilligan, C. (1984). *In a Different Voice: Psychological Theory and Women's Development*. Cambridge, MA: Harvard University Press.

Ginsberg, F. D. (1989). *Contested Lives: The Abortion Debate in an American Community*. Berkeley: University of California Press.

Glass, J. (1990). The impact of occupational segregation on working conditions. *Social Forces, 68*, 779–796.

Goode, W. (1970). *World Revolution and Family Patterns*. New York: Free Press.

Gornick, J. & Myers, M. (2003). *Families that Work: Policies for Reconciling Parenthood and Employment*. New York: Russell Sage Foundation.

Greenstein, T. (2000). Economic dependence, gender and the division of labor in the home: A replication and extension. *Journal of Marriage and the Family, 62*, 322–335.

Harrington, M. (1999). *Care and Equality: Inventing a New Family Politics*. New York: Knopf.

Hartmann, H. (1987). The family as the locus of gender, class, and political struggles. In S. Harding (ed.), *Feminism and Methodology* (109–134). Bloomington: Indiana University Press.

Hays, S. (1996). *The Cultural Contradictions of Motherhood*. New Haven: Yale University Press.

Hays, S. (2003). *Flat Broke with Children: Women in the Age of Welfare Reform*. New York: Oxford University Press.

Hertz, R. (2006). *Single By Chance, Mothers By Choice: How Women Are Choosing Parenthood without Marriage and Creating the New American Family*. New York: Oxford University Press.

Hochschild, A. with Machung, A. (1990). *The Second Shift: Working Parents and the Revolution at Home*. New York: Avon.

Hoffman, Lois & Youngblade, L. M. with Coley, R. L., Fuligni, A. S. & Kovacs, D. D. (1999). *Mothers at Work: Effects on Children's Well-Being*. New York: Cambridge University Press.

Hondagneu-Sotelo, P. (2001). *Domestica*. Berkeley: University of California Press.

Hondagneu-Sotelo, P. & Avila, E. (1997). "I'm here but I'm there": The meanings of Latina transnational motherhood. *Gender and Society, 11*, 548–570.

Jacobs, J. A. & Gerson, K. (1998). Who are the overworked Americans? *Review of Social Economy, 56*, 442–459.

Jacobs, J. A. & Gerson, K. (2004). *The Time Divide: Work, Family and Gender Inequality*. Cambridge, MA: Harvard University Press.

Kanter, R. M. (1977) *Men and Women of the Corporation*. New York: Basic Books.

Kilbourne, B., England, P., Farkas, G., Beron, K. & Weir, D. (1994). Returns to skill, compensating differentials, and gender bias: Effects of occupational characteristics on the wages of white women and men. *American Journal of Sociology, 100*, 689–719.

Loh, E. S. (1996). Productivity differences and the marriage wage premium for white males. *Journal of Human Resources, 31*, 566–589.

Luker, K. (1984). *Abortion and the Politics of Motherhood*. Berkeley: University of California Press.

Lundberg, S. & Rose, E. (2000). Parenthood and the earnings of married men and women. *Labour Economics, 7,* 689–710.

Lorber, J. (1994). *Paradoxes of Gender.* New Haven: Yale University Press.

Moen, P. (2003). *It's About Time: Couples and Careers.* Ithaca: ILR Press/Cornell University Press.

Parsons, T. 1974. Family structure in the modern United States. In R. L. Coser (ed.), *The Family: Its Structures and Functions* (pp. 243–253). London: MacMillan.

Popenoe, D. (1988). *Disturbing The Nest: Family Change and Decline in Modern Societies.* New York: A. de Gruyter.

Popenoe, D. (1996). *Life Without Father: Compelling New Evidence that Fatherhood and Marriage are Indispensable for the Good of Children and Society.* New York: Martin Kessler Books.

Reskin, B. F. & Roos, P. A. (1990). *Job Queues, Gender Queues: Explaining Women's Inroads into Male Occupations.* Philadelphia: Temple University Press.

Riggs, J. M. (1997). Mandates for mothers and fathers: Perceptions of breadwinners and care givers. *Sex Roles, 37,* 565–580.

Risman, B. (1998). *Gender Vertigo: American Families in Transition.* New Haven: Yale University Press.

Robinson, J. (1997). *Time for Life: The Surprising Ways Americans Use their Time.* University Park, PA: Pennsylvania State University Press.

Rollins, J. (1985). *Between Women: Domestics and their Employers.* Philadelphia: Temple University Press.

Romero, M. (1992). *Maid in the U.S.A.* New York: Routledge.

Roth, L. (2006). *Selling Women ShortÚ: Gender and Money on Wall Street.* Princeton, NJ: Princeton University Press.

Skolnick, A. (2002). Grounds for marriage: How relationships succeed or fail. In M. Yalom & L. L. Carstensen (eds), *The American Couple: New Thinking/New Challenges* (pp. 149–163). Berkeley: University of California Press.

Spain, D. & Bianchi, S. (1996). *The Balancing Act: Motherhood, Marriage, and Employment among American Women.* New York: Russell Sage Foundation.

Stacey, J. (1997). *In the Name of the Family: Rethinking Family Values in the Postmodern Age.* Boston: Beacon Press.

Stone, P. (2007). *Opting Out? Why Women Really Quit Careers and Head Home.* Berkeley: University of California Press.

Stone, P. & Lovejoy, M. (2004). Fast-track women and the "choice" to stay home. *Annals of the American Academy of Political and Social Science, 596,* 62–83.

Waldfogel, J. (1997). The effect of children on women's wages. *American Sociological Review, 62,* 209–217.

West, C. & Fenstermaker, S. (1995). Doing difference. *Gender and Society, 9,* 8–37.

West, C. & Zimmerman, D. (1987). Doing gender. *Gender and Society, 1,* 125–151.

Williams, C. L. (1995). *Still a Man's World; Men Who Do Women's Work.* Berkeley and LA: University of California Press.

Williams, J. (2000). *Unbending Gender.* New York: Oxford University Press.

Williams, J. (2007). The opt-out revolution revisited. *The American Prospect,* March, A15.

US Department of Labor, Bureau of Labor Statistics. (2005). *Annual Averages and the Monthly Labor Review.* Washington, DC: Government Printing Office.

Wrigley, Julia. (1995). *Other People's Children.* New York: Basic Books.

Zimmerman, M. K., Litt, J. S. & Bose, C. (2006). *Global Dimensions of Gender and Carework.* Stanford, CA: Stanford University Press.

CHAPTER 14

Work–Life Issues for Fathers

Kerry Daly, Lynda Ashbourne and Linda Hawkins
Department of Family Relations and Applied Nutrition, University of Guelph,
Guelph, ON

INTRODUCTION

Although research on fatherhood has proliferated in recent years, much of the attention in the work-family literature is focused on challenges that women face in seeking to balance work and family responsibilities (Russell & Hwang, 2004). There are a number of possible reasons for why this is the case. First, much of the impetus for addressing work-life issues came from the entry of women into the paid labor force. Whereas men were called to make some adjustments to this, the predominant discourse was about dual-career heterosexual couples and their children, in which men carried on in their paid work and picked up some of the slack at home at their discretion. Men were called on to do their fair share and were questioned about "why they resist". By contrast, women experienced the entry into paid work as precipitating in the "double day" or "second shift" (Hochschild, 1989), where their paid work was added on top of their full-time homemaker jobs. The result was that women, more than men, faced the challenge of finding work-family balance. Not only was men's perceived resistance at home seen as part of an unchanging home culture, but women's feelings of work-life conflict in the workplace were seen as a function of an unchanging work culture that was designed for men and based on the principles of competition and loyalty (Maume & Huston, 2001).

A second important and related factor was that women entered into the workplace out of a tradition of providing primary care to family members (Dressel & Clark, 1990). In this tradition motherhood had primacy over fatherhood, and women were expected (more than men) to provide care to children, as well as husbands or partners and aging parents. This ethic of care was deeply rooted in women's experience and not easily transferred to fathers. Women taking primary responsibility for the provision of care in the home were also more likely to be held socially accountable for the provision of family care. Whereas women's experience of work-life was grounded in this care, it appeared that men's experience was rooted in the tradition of provision. For men, staying in the primary provider role precipitated fewer work and family conflicts, while women struggled more intensely with achieving work-life balance.

Handbook of Work-Family Integration: Research, Theory, and Best Practices

In spite of these viewpoints, research that examines the prevalence of work-life conflict among women and men indicates that both experience high levels of stress in their efforts to balance their work and family responsibilities. For example, there is growing evidence that men are experiencing levels of work-family conflict that are similar to women (Bond, Galinsky & Swanberg, 1998; Milkie & Peltola, 1999; Winslow, 2005) and that, for dual-career families, the gender divide regarding job family trade-offs may not be as large as assumed (Falter, Mennino & Brayfield, 2002) or that family arrangements and working conditions make juggling demands as trying for men as they are for women (Keene & Reynolds, 2005). Furthermore, the evidence suggests that work-family conflict increased for men and not women between 1977 and 1997 and this has been attributed to their changing investment in family responsibilities (Winslow, 2005).

Nevertheless, our starting point for this chapter observes the dominant perception of work-life as being more intensely experienced by women, as well as the conceptual understanding of work-life issues as profoundly shaped by a lens informed by women's experience, with important results in discourse and research. For example, parental leave is a cornerstone issue in any work-life strategy. However, with the exception of some countries who have an explicit father-leave program, this is by and large experienced as a maternity leave issue. The accompanying discourse emphasizes the discontinuity and interruption of women's careers, resulting in promotion sacrifices, and discussion of attributions that women are more unreliable due to family care responsibilities. Similarly, there is often a notion that flexibility strategies are *really* designed for women and, as a result, women's use of flexibility is perceived as unremarkable and predictable. By contrast, men's use of these policies and opportunities may be seen as unusual and subject to question and/or ridicule.

A work-life perspective that is rooted in women's experience is shaped by a number of assumptions:

- *Work for women is chosen* Conceptualizing a tension between work and family responsibilities is shaped by the reality of women having to struggle for the right to be in the paid labor force. Women earned that right, but never dropped the primary responsibility to care for children and the home, even while their work is essential to family income.
- *Women's income is secondary income* Women's paid work has been viewed as a supplement to men's paid work in "traditional" families. The increasing number of women who are the primary earners in a household is still a minority, resulting in a continued normative view of women's employment patterns as shaped by the demands of family.
- *Family life does interfere with work* Women *need* flexibility strategies in order to manage their work and care responsibilities. This assumption is rooted in the pervasiveness and unpredictability of family issues.

- *Women as primary providers of care* There is a continuing and taken for granted belief that women should take primary responsibility for the family.
- *Autonomous decision-making regarding provision of care* In light of their experience of providing primary care, women exercise more autonomy in when and how they choose to provide that care. Specifically, women do not seek "permission" from men for how to do this work and typically often do not need to negotiate with men about how to provide carework.

If we were to redirect our attention to questions of work-life using a lens that is rooted in men's experience, we might start with different assumptions:

- *The question of tension between work and life does not originate from men's experience* Men must strategically and deliberately express their entitlement to take advantage of work-life strategies, as it is not expected of them, and in accessing policies and programs they are likely to invoke questions from bosses and peers. Where men are not viewed as primary carers, their need or choice to take time away from work, or more explicitly taking time for family, may be viewed as fun, relaxation or recreation/leisure, rather than as an essential engagement. As Kugelberg (2006) has argued, in company-based discourse, fatherhood is often assumed to not affect the working life of individual men. The need for work-life opportunities for men is then rendered invisible to the workplace.
- *Men are more likely to have support at home* Men exercising use of work-life opportunities are more likely to face resistance in their workplaces, when the view is held that somehow the *women* in these men's lives are absent or not fulfilling their responsibilities sufficiently to allow men a more singular focus on work. Note that this also includes an implicit assumption that there are almost always women present who could or would take on care responsibilities. This may be part of a broader system of gender segregation that appears not only in the home in relation to housework but in the structures and processes of work organizations (Kugelberg, 2006).
- *Need to negotiate with female partners* Given that women have primary control over the running of the household and the raising of children, men's efforts to take responsibility for the provision of family care frequently involves negotiation with partners/wives/mothers about how this is to happen. Whereas women may be able to make unilateral decisions about how and when they provide care to the family, men are more likely to have to negotiate this with their female partners. This may include gate-keeping issues about when and how carework will be done, issues of trust that are rooted in perceptions of men's competency to do carework, and issues of whether women are willing to step out of their own role of being the primary provider of care.

- *Unprecedented practices and few models* Whereas women carry out their role responsibilities with a broad repertoire of models and often with socialized experiences, men are called on to create care practices anew. Although there are now new fatherhood ideals that support greater involvement (Coltrane, 1996), there continue to be questions about the continuing disjunction between the "culture" and "conduct" of fathering activity in relation to these ideals (LaRossa, 1988). Although this is challenging for fathers in all kinds of families, it may be particularly difficult when fathers occupy non-traditional fathering roles such as being a single custodial parent after separation or divorce, a gay father or a father who wishes to work part-time in order to ensure a greater proportion of time spent with the family.
- *Work-life decision-making is shaped by the experience of heterosexual dual-career families* It is important to note that accompanying this assumption is the exclusion of the experience of men who are parenting on their own, or from a non-resident position in the family, men who are in same-sex relationships, and men who are in social fathering roles. These conditions of fathering come with different kinds of responsibilities and, as a result, different kinds of needs for flexibility within the workplace.

Throughout the balance of this chapter, we have endeavoured to hold to a broader conceptualization of fathers and their experience at work and within their families. If we are to come to an appreciation of how fathers experience the personal and public challenges of work and family life, then it is important that we be attentive to the values, practices and conceptual assumptions that have shaped our way of thinking about work-life strategies.

THE VALUE OF FATHER INVOLVEMENT

What is the value of supporting and enhancing fathers' involvement in the lives of their children? While literature on child development once focused on direct effects of fathers' influence, there is a recognition of the complexity of the systems within which fathers operate, including family structure and functioning. The importance of such indirect influences of fathers is well demonstrated (Coltrane, 2004; Lamb, 1997), and include such things as father's interpersonal relations with mothers and marital quality (Cummings & O'Reilly, 1997) and fathers' participation in activities such as housekeeping (Coltrane, 2004) and providing (Christiansen & Palkovitz, 2001), as well as more direct father-child interaction.

Across age groups the importance of father participation in children's lives has been demonstrated (Allen & Daly, 2007; Coltrane, 2004; Lamb, 1997; Pleck, 1997). Positive outcomes for children of highly involved fathers include increased cognitive competence and a more internal locus of control (Lamb, 1997); higher sociability (Pleck 1997); and positive academic outcomes such as attitudes towards school, attendance, and higher achievement (Allen & Daly, 2007). Fathers' participation in household tasks also has a long-term effect on children, with increased sensitivity demonstrated in adult sons and independence in adult daughters (Coltrane, 2004). Importantly, the role of provider is crucial in the very real and complex contribution to beneficial outcomes in children's development and future life opportunities (Christiansen & Palkovitz, 2001; Coltrane, 2004).

Fathers' positive influence goes beyond demonstrations of children's emotional and social development and economic well-being, to benefit women and men in their own development as individuals and members of a family and community. For fathers, involvement includes rich and satisfying relationships with children, seeing them positively, and being attentive, more self-confident, and having greater psychosocial maturity (Allen & Daly, 2007; Palkovitz, 2002). Some evidence suggests that high involvement has a positive impact on fathers' career success (Pleck, 1997).

While fathers with children living at home are more likely to work long hours, they are also less likely to have experienced recent unemployment (Eggebeen & Knoester, 2001). Other differences between men who are fathers and those who are not include fathers as more likely to be involved in community organizations (church, service clubs, school-related organizations) (Eggebeen & Knoester, 2001; Townsend, 2002), and more generally demonstrating greater social generativity (Pleck, 1997).

The value of father involvement for women is evident, but perhaps more politically charged, when instead of doing a "fair share" of domestic carework men are perceived as adding to women's double day. Research on father participation in housework, and regular childcare tasks with children does show benefits for mothers (Coltrane, 2004), but the merit of carework, both paid and unpaid, and the connection of women's carework to workplaces is "hard won"—with resulting responsibility for revealing and encouraging men's carework and its contribution in a way that does not "detract from mothers' struggle to have their own unpaid work valued" (Doucet, 2004).

Mothers' role in facilitating father involvement is well documented, i.e., where mothers are supportive, men are more likely to be involved (Pleck, 1997; Allen & Daly, 2007), but this is not a one-way street. In heterosexual families, where women are employed, fathers' share of "total parental involvement" is greater (Pleck, 1997), describing a more equitable arrangement in these families. Lamb notes that the positive child outcomes of father involvement can perhaps be ascribed to less stereotyped attitudes of parents towards gender roles, having two adults/parents who are highly involved and providing greater stimulation, and to a family context in which both parents are able to meet their interests, career goals, and desires for relations with children (Lamb, 1997). In this way, father involvement may contribute to marital quality, where both mother-child and father-child relationships are positive, with resulting positive indirect effects on children (Cummings & O'Reilly, 1997). For women and children in families where fathers are not in residence, support continues to provide good outcomes for children through access to education, health, and nutrition. Positive adjustment after divorce in the father's relationship with the mother is noted as crucial for positive child development outcomes (Allen & Daly, 2007; Palkovitz, 2002).

Still, benefits of greater father involvement for women do not exist only in the family context, but bring "triple benefits" (Reeves, 2006). When men are more involved in childcare, heterosexual and coupled women have partners sharing the load at home, the corporate emphasis on women as the only ones with domestic responsibilities is challenged, and attitudes of men towards women's success in the workplace may be more enlightened (Reeves, 2006), benefiting all women. If our real concern in examining work-family contexts is to reveal assumptions around the gendered division of labor, and perhaps the lack of choice and fairness attributed to prescriptive social and economic roles, then the discussion alone of men's participation in all carework is a valuable and key piece to the puzzle.

Although much of the research that looks at the impact of work-life initiatives on the workplace focuses on working mothers, research that includes both women and men indicates that both are more likely to make mistakes when there are personal problems that affect their work and are more likely to quit their jobs if there aren't opportunities to address these stresses (Levine & Pittinsky, 1997). "Good dads" who are able to address these concerns were more productive and loyal to the company (Levine & Pittinsky, 1997). For the workplace, wrestling with the value of father involvement becomes added value (and a challenge) for meeting diversity and equity, particularly when using a human rights lens that sees discrimination on the grounds of family status as including men. Designed support for father-care responsibilities by workplaces contributes directly to desirable outcomes for organizations from a social justice and diversity standpoint, and may also contribute to gender-awareness around other types of unpaid caregiving currently provided primarily by women. Ultimately, the value of greater father involvement facilitated by fathers, mothers, workplaces, and communities might mean better designed and utilized workplace supports and recognition of the importance of community supports such as quality childcare.

IMPORTANCE OF CONTEXT IN UNDERSTANDING THE DIVERSITY OF FATHERS' EXPERIENCES

One of the most important contributions that recent directions in both the work-life literature and the fatherhood literature have made is highlighting the diversity of men's and women's experience within the interface of work and life. Utilizing a lens of diversity allows for particular attention to the ways in which fathers engage and live with their families and the broad range of work experience that accompanies that. In addition, a lens that premises diversity allows for an exploration of the ways in which broader social influences, cultural identity and scripts, geography and social policy, sexual identity and a diversity of family forms collectively influence the experience of work-life for fathers.

What is the *context* in which contemporary fathers experience work and family? What is the context within which contemporary North American society sees men's involvement in their roles as fathers and as workers?

HISTORICAL CONTEXT

Fathers' engagement in their family life, as well as their work-life, takes place in the face of a changing ideal for fatherhood. While much has been written in recent years about the "new" or more "involved" father, it is important to understand how much this ideal has been translated into actual behavioural change for fathers, and the standard by which they judge their own success at meeting their family responsibilities and being actively engaged in family life (Pleck, 1997; Ranson, 2001; Townsend, 2002). Individual and family changes take place within a context of the broader culture, and societal ideals or expectations regarding the "good father" and the "good worker" or "good provider" also play a significant role in how fathers engage in their family and worker roles.

While masculinity has frequently been defined in the context of men's formal paid work (Townsend, 2002), changes in the nature of employment structures (e.g., increasing numbers of "vulnerable workers", Saunders, 2006), family forms and practices within families contribute to the challenge of redefining fatherhood and identifying new practices in the absence of readily available models for men at the interface of work and family. Within a context of changing norms and forms of father involvement, peer parents can serve as role models for fathers. Masciadrelli, Pleck and Steuve (2006) found that more highly involved fathers, in particular, indicated that they learned something of value in terms of parenting from peer parents.

SOCIOPOLITICAL CONTEXT

International comparisons of policies related to work and family responsibilities, parental leave, and employer support for family care responsibilities reflect significant differences with respect to the degree to which men are supported in their parental role. These differences are reflective of a complex interaction of the cultural beliefs, norms, and practices which overlap with policy and workplace/institutional practices in various parts of the world. The ways in which "responsible fatherhood" is encouraged at a policy level in the US are quite different from the support in Sweden for fathers to take so-called "Daddy days" allowing for more time away from work and with family. The state plays a role in shaping and defining fatherhood in several ways. Policies that govern a range of areas related to parenting, from birth registration and adoption to paternity leaves, and family law governing the responsibilities of fatherhood from a perspective of both financial support enforcement and the endorsement of shared parental rights and responsibilities following marital separation, influence the ways in which "cash and care" are conceptualized relative to fathers' roles (Hobson & Morgan, 2002; Lero, Ashbourne & Whitehead, 2006). When public institutions encourage and include fathers in their programming, for example, the inclusion of fathers in prenatal and early parenting programs delivered by public health agencies at a community level, this affects the visibility of men as fathers (Lero et al., 2006).

EMPLOYMENT/WORKPLACE CONTEXT

Workplace differences contribute to the diversity of fathers' experience in meeting the needs of their families and being more or less directly involved and engaged in family life. For example, men who work what Strazdins, Clements, Korda, Broom and D'Souza (2006) refer to as "unsociable hours"—night hours, weekends—have fewer opportunities to spend time with their families, as do mothers who work such hours. In addition, fathers who are underemployed, work part-time or temporary jobs, or those who are self-employed, may lack job stability or be working more than one job and therefore may not have supports which are available to other workers in the form of extended health care benefits, paid leave for family or illness-related reasons, or unemployment insurance. Shift work and the 24-hour economy place an increased strain on families trying to manage time together around employment requirements. Those who earn a low income are potentially working longer hours for fewer resources and suffer from the combined stress of having neither sufficient financial nor time resources to share with and support their families. The local availability of work and the requirement to relocate or travel in order to obtain and maintain employment also has an impact on the amount of time that is available for fathers to spend with their families.

Specific conditions of work influence the ways in which fathers can even consider their involvement in family life and this is often compounded by similar issues of employment stability and flexibility for their partners in dual-earner households. Employment is positively related to father involvement (Christiansen & Palkovitz, 2001; Danzinger & Radin, 1990), suggesting that fathers who see that they can play a provider role through their employment also see more opportunities to be involved with their children. In fact, fathers who are not in a position to play this economic provider role may withdraw from family involvement (Christiansen & Palkovitz, 2001). If the role of provider is deconstructed as referencing more than economic provision, as encouraged by Christiansen and Palkovitz, then the responsiveness of fathers and their awareness of the needs of their children can be seen as important aspects of their involvement and engagement in fatherhood. At the same time, the measures used by employers to judge and reward success in the workforce, perhaps especially for men, may be in direct contradiction to increased involvement in family life. For example, long hours and placing work above all other commitments are associated with a "good worker" and men may be penalized when family responsibilities conflict with those of work (e.g., Butler & Skattebo, 2004). Thus, "economic" provision may be placed in jeopardy when family needs conflict with work needs, and family involvement may be reduced in the face of increased work demands. Preliminary research indicates that fathers who work non-standard shifts are less knowledgeable about their adolescent children when compared to those who work daytime shifts (Davis, Crouter & McHale, 2006). This is in part attributed to the reliance that men have on mothers for information about their children which is made difficult when spousal communication is more limited.

Workplace culture can also influence work-life practice. Levine (1996), for example, talks about a three-way collusion in workplace culture that reinforces the acceptability of women taking leave and discourages men from stepping forward. Studies of managers' perceptions of women and men taking leave have indicated that there were greater perceived detrimental effects on men taking leaves (Allen & Russell, 1999) and that male employees who took leave for birth or eldercare (in contrast with female employees) were rated as being less altruistic at work than their male counterparts who did not take leave (Wayne & Cordeiro, 2003). As this research would suggest, fathers may be less likely to use family-friendly benefits because of a fear that they will be perceived as less serious about their careers and will suffer negative career consequences. The overall result is that in spite of a number of recognized benefits associated with greater father involvement, working fathers are faced with having to make a choice between the advantages of using leave opportunities for greater family involvement and the costs associated with being perceived as a poor organizational citizen at work (Wayne & Cordeiro, 2003).

FAMILY CONTEXT

Dual-Income Families and Household Responsibilities

There is considerable evidence to indicate that in dual earner homes, mothers are more likely than fathers to be involved in carrying out activities associated with the "responsibility dimension" of parental care (Daly, 2002; Zimmerman, Haddock, Ziemba & Rust, 2001). As a result, the responsiveness of fathers to the needs of their children is frequently negotiated with mothers. When fathers are resident in the family home, household tasks and parenting are negotiated, often in the context of dual-earning couples, along with work-related tasks. Mothers are more likely to negotiate flexibility with respect to work requirements (Singley & Hynes, 2005) and to be more aware of employee family-related benefits (Baird & Reynolds, 2004). This gender difference may effectively allow fathers to take a less active and engaged role in taking responsibility for childcare and in the area of negotiating and making the work/family interface more manageable for the couple and family.

Non-Resident Fathers

When fathers are non-resident, structural aspects of the family may compound the complexity of their involvement with their children. Fathers may be, at times, rendered invisible by their non-resident status and/or lack of custody or time with their children, or their visibility may be relegated to economic provision only. One of the areas where fathers have been increasing their demand for fathers' rights to time and involvement with their children is with separated and divorced fathers.

Fathers may also be less visible in families when they are non-resident for reasons related to long or "unsociable" hours of work, or travel/geographic relocation required for work. While these men may have fewer opportunities or less time in which they can be engaged with their families, they may also be seen by mothers and children as less "essential" or "present" in the daily family activities which comprise a large part of family life.

Role of Women in Facilitating or Blocking Father Involvement

As discussed earlier, mothers may also serve a "gatekeeping" role (Allen & Hawkins, 1999) in the family, effectively limiting the involvement of fathers in activities which have traditionally been seen as belonging to mothers. In family structures where parents have new and former partners, there can be varying degrees of involvement of biological parents and step-parents/new partners. Frequently such involvement is governed by issues of residence and proximity, as well as divorce agreements, and stepmothers may continue to take on gendered and traditional caring roles of women, acting to either facilitate or block the involvement of fathers. It may be that men view such action or attitudes as either facilitating their negotiation of work and family, or as presenting obstacles to their involvement in the family.

"Single" Parenting

The "single" parent designation is used to refer to a variety of family structures. A parent may be parenting on their own, without the presence of another parent to any degree. This is a very different experience from the experience of parents who are both still living, but not residing together. These situations may range from an absent parent who is not involved at all in parental work and responsibilities, to a non-resident parent who is equally involved in the lives of their children and/or in planning regarding children's needs.

There are single fathers who, when their children are living with them, have sole responsibility for meeting their children's needs without the support or flexibility that having a resident partner affords. There are single fathers for whom time spent caring for their children is a regular and predictable "cycle" in their lives, and others who have more sporadic or unpredictable time with their children. Often non-resident fathers make arrangements to have their children stay at their home during off-work hours—e.g., weekends and evenings if he works a 9–5 weekday job. Some fathers do not have time at all with their children, and this absence from their lives may negatively impact their ability to engage and be productive workers, particularly fathers who are engaged in court processes in order to gain involvement in their children's lives. This stressor can negatively influence work involvement, in addition to often making huge demands on men's resources of time and money.

Developmental Stage of Children

In addition to the ways in which family structure, or the constellation of the family system, can influence fathers' involvement with their children, the developmental age and stage of children can also influence the nature of father involvement. Fathers may experience limited engagement or involvement in pregnancy and childbirth, or be positioned in a "secondary" role as coach or partner to the "primary" parent (Draper, 1997), but opportunities for their involvement can change over time. Fathers may be variously described by others, or see themselves as playmates, disciplinarians, coaches, or confidants, with these roles changing with their child(ren)'s age and across circumstances.

In summary, fathers are seen by themselves and others in a variety of ways and within a variety of contexts. They are engaging with their children in diverse ways that change over time and space. They are participating, to varying degrees, in parenting with current and former partners. Their work and their workplaces, their socioeconomic standing, broader cultural messages, and their partners all contribute to the degree to which they are able, and invited, to be active and engaged fathers. To conceptualize fathers' experience of work and family requires particular attention to this diversity of experience in both arenas.

FUTURE DIRECTIONS: KEY ISSUES IN WORK-LIFE INTEGRATION FOR MEN

In this chapter, we have argued that in order to understand some of the unique challenges experienced by men as they navigate their work and family lives, we must be attentive to some of the underlying assumptions about work and

family that are heavily steeped in women's experience. In order to move forward
with a conceptualization of work and family issues that is also rooted in men's
experience, we feel that it is necessary to consider a number of key issues.

First, it is evident that while men experience high levels of work-life conflict, they are less likely than women to pursue flexibility strategies as a way of
reducing this conflict. This would suggest that work-life conflict for men is more
likely to be experienced as a personal trouble rather than a public issue (to use
Mills' (1959) distinction). In other words, men feel the conflict and contend with
the competing pressures but, in general, operate in environments that rarely recognize the presence of the conflict or the need for resolution. Environments include
work cultures where men are not expected to need flexibility to respond to family needs—and the broader cultures of masculinity and fatherhood that continue
to hold mothers at the center of the parenting experience. In the absence of cultural supports for fathers to be at the center of their children's lives, work-life
balance issues for men are confined to the realm of private troubles that require
personal and private solution. If there is a desire for men to become more fully
engaged providers of care in families, it is first necessary to make the challenge of
men's work-life balance into a public issue. This is a change that must occur on
many levels including: individual men turning their private troubles into a public
issue (by speaking out about their needs and asserting their entitlement to parental leaves or flexibility strategies); work organizations opening conversations about
men's levels of work-life conflict and their needs for support; and communities
playing a greater role in recognizing the value and importance of father involvement (for children, partners, families, and community well-being).

Second, work-life challenges for fathers are as diverse as the circumstances
within which men carry out their fathering responsibilities. In thinking broadly
about work-life strategies for men it is important to recognize the many types
of fathering and the needs that might arise from those diverse experiences (e.g.,
immigrant fathers, fathers of children with special needs, single fathers). The kinds
of strategies that would effectively support fathers in being more fully involved
with their children are contingent on whether they can be truly flexible in meeting circumstances, including challenges of the age of children and daily schedules of childcare and school, the level and timing of access that the father has
when working and parenting under custody arrangements, or the nature of the
co-parenting relationship that is shaped by its own rhythms and schedules.

Third, it is important to look at men's experience of work-life within a
systemic, contextualized perspective. Given the rootedness of work-life issues in
women's experience, there is a temptation to simply extend this thinking to men's
experience—to borrow the template from women, build on the best practices and
ensure that men are provided with similar opportunities to balance their work
and family lives. However, in an effort to balance work and family lives, the issue
is not always what individual mothers or fathers need—rather the issue is how

to arrange patterns of work and family care so that family systems can function in optimal ways. When it comes down to the everyday challenge of "fitting it all in", gender differences may be over-shadowed by a picture of women and men who were working collaboratively to manage the challenges on the home and the work front (Barnett & Rivers, 1998). Fathering and mothering are seen then not as separate activities, as the experience of parenting is "created in the shared goings-on between people in the course of their lives through intervals of nego-tiating, competing, compromising and rearranging" (Matta & Knudson-Martin, 2006, p. 20). Even in families where parents are living apart, there are a variety of challenges that require collaborative efforts in order to accommodate changing schedules and respond to emerging needs.

Thinking systemically also means taking into account the centrality of wom-en's role in orchestrating family life. In contrast with an individual level question that seeks to find out "why men resist change?", a systemic question would endeav-our to look at the ways in which both women and men hold to traditional pat-terns of parenting that keep women at the center and men on the margins. Efforts to understand why men do or don't engage in work-life initiatives must take into account the underlying motives, beliefs, and values that are part of the participat-ing family system. This involves fundamental questions about whether men can be trusted to undertake the role of primary parent (e.g., with a newborn), whether men are perceived as capable and competent as mothers in carrying out the parent-ing role, and whether mothers themselves are willing to release some of their own responsibilities that are rooted in the high standards of mothering ideology.

The final issue is to think about work-family issues for men as embedded in a micropolitics of care. If part of the feminist objective was to bring public rec-ognition to the importance of paid labor for women's social status and influence, then a parallel objective in a work-family agenda for men is to bring recognition to the importance of care activity for the well-being of children, partners, and men themselves. Whereas women in our discussions seem predisposed to provide care, men must somehow learn how to provide care. By way of illustration, we are more likely to be preoccupied with how men learn to be a father (Daly, 1993), whereas for women it is taken for granted or assumed that they know how to be a mother. A micropolitics of care, as part of the work-life agenda for men, is more concerned with the ways that women and men navigate the gendered territories of mothering and fathering and work towards fairness and equity in both their relationship and their care responsibilities. It involves the degree to which co-parents choose models that are either interchangeable (based on assumptions that both parents should be able to move seamlessly into a full spectrum of parent-ing tasks) or complementary (where they decide to build on individual strengths when providing care). It involves negotiation about time and the responsibility for making decisions about family time. Partners in shared parenting bring pre-ferences about pace, rhythm, and activity to interaction and through a process of negotiation, they adjust and coordinate their activity patterns with one another. This is consistent with a relational perspective where taking responsibility for children and domestic life cannot be reduced to time allocations only, but rather involves attention to the navigation of complex, gendered caring responsibilities in relationships (Doucet, 2000). This includes not only providing care to children, but also looking at the way that fathers extend that care to their parenting partners in order to keep relationships strong (Dyck & Daly, 2006).

At the heart of the micropolitics of care is a fundamental contradiction in values about work and family: women are expected to be committed to their paid work just like men at the same time as they maintain a priority to family; men are expected to be more engaged fathers or committed to family just like women, while at the same time maintaining their role as primary provider (Daly, 1996). Getting beyond this contradiction involves recognition of the importance and value that can come from men as engaged providers of care, a greater openness to publicly address the challenges that men face in their efforts to find a better work-family balance, appreciation of their diverse needs and a willingness to consider the complex systemic dynamics that shape successful work-life initiatives.

REFERENCES

Allen, S. & Daly, K. (2007). The Effects of Father involvement: An Updated Research Summary of the Evidence. Guelph: Father Involvement Initiative Ontario Network. Retrieved November 5, 2007 from www.fira.uoguelph.ca

Allen, S. & Hawkins, A. (1999) Maternal gatekeeping. *Journal of Marriage and the Family, 61*, 199–212.

Allen, T. & Russell, J. (1999). Parental leave of absence: Some not so friendly implications. *Journal of Applied Social Psychology, 29*, 166–191.

Baird, C. L. & Reynolds, J. R. (2004). Employee awareness of family leave benefits: The effects of family, work, and gender. *Sociological Quarterly, 45*, 325–353.

Barnett, R.C. & Rivers, C. (1998). *She works, he works: How two income families are happy, healthy and thriving.* Cambridge: Harvard University Press.

Butler, A. B. & Skattebo, A. (2004). What is acceptable for women may not be for men: The effect of family conflicts with work on job-performance ratings. *Journal of Occupational and Organizational Psychology, 77*, 553–564.

Christiansen, S. L. & Palkovitz, R. (2001). Why the "good provider" role still matters: Providing as a form of paternal involvement. *Journal of Family Issues, 22*, 84–106.

Coltrane, S. (1996). *Family Man: Fatherhood, Housework and Gender Equity.* New York: Oxford University Press.

Coltrane, S. (2004). Fathers, A Sloan Work and Family Encyclopedia Entry. Boston: Sloan Work and Family Research Network. Retrieved November 2, 2006 from http://wfnetwork.bc.edu/encyclopedia_entry.php?id=236&area=academics

Craig, L. (2006). Does father care mean fathers share? A comparison of how mothers and fathers in intact families spend time with children. *Gender & Society, 20*, 259–281.

Cummings, E. M. & O'Reilly, A. W. (1997). Fathers in family context: Effects of marital quality on child adjustment. In M. E. Lamb (ed.), *The Role of the Father in Child Development*, 3rd edn (pp. 49–65). New York: Wiley.

Daly, K. J. (1993). Reshaping fatherhood: Finding the models. *Journal of Family Issues, 14*, 510–530.

Daly, K. J. (1996). *Families and Time: Keeping Pace in a Hurried Culture.* Newbury Park: Sage Publications.

Daly, K. J. (2002). Time, gender and the negotiation of family schedules. *Symbolic Interaction, 25*, 323–342.

Danzinger, S. K. & Radin, N. (1990). Absent does not equal uninvolved: Predictors of fathering in teen mother families. *Journal of Marriage and the Family, 52*, 636–642.

Davis, K. D., Crouter, A. C. & McHale, S. M. (2006). Implications of shift work for parent–adolescent relationships in dual-earner families. *Family Relations, 55*, 450–460

Deutsch, F., Lussier, J. & Servis, L. (1993). Husbands at home: Predictors of paternal participation in childcare and housework. *Journal of Personality and Social Psychology, 65*, 1154–1166.

Doucet A. (2000) "There's a huge difference between me as a male carer and women': Gender, domestic responsibility, and the community as an institutional arena", *Community Work and Family, 3*(2), 163–184.

Doucet, A. (2004). Fathers and the responsibility for children: A puzzle and a tension. *Atlantis: A Women's Studies Journal, 28.2*, 103–113

Draper, J. (1997). Whose welfare in the labor room? A discussion of the increasing trend of fathers' birth attendance. *Midwifery, 13*, 132–138.

Dressel, P. L. & Clark, A. (1990). A critical look at family care. *Journal of Marriage and the Family, 52*, 769–782.

Dyck, V. & Daly, K. (2006). Rising to the challenge: Fathers role in the negotiation of couple time. *Leisure Studies, 25*, 201–218.

Eggebeen, D. J., & Knoester, C. (2001). Does fatherhood matter for men? *Journal of Marriage and the Family, 63*(2), 381–393.

Falter Mennino, S. & Brayfield, A. (2002). Job-family trade-offs: The multidimensional effects of gender. *Work and Occupations, 29*, 226–256.

Hobson, B. & Morgan, D. (2002). Introduction. In B. Hobson (ed.), *Making Men into Fathers: Men, Masculinities and the Social Politics of Fatherhood* (pp. 1–21). Cambridge, UK: Cambridge University Press.

Hochschild, A. (1989). *The Second Shift.* New York: Avon Books.

Keene, J. & Reynolds, J. R. (2005). The job costs of family demands: Gender differences in negative family-to-work spillover. *Journal of Family Issues, 26*, 275–299.

Kugelberg, C. (2006). Constructing the deviant other: Mothering and fathering at the workplace. *Gender, Work and Organization, 13*, 152–173.

Lamb, M. (1997). Fathers and child development: An introductory overview and guide. In M. E. Lamb (ed.), *The Role of the Father in Child Development*, 3rd edn (pp. 1–18). New York: John Wiley and Sons.

LaRossa, R. (1988). Fatherhood and social change. *Family Relations, 36*, 451–458.

Lero, D. S., Ashbourne, L. M. & Whitehead, D. L. (2006). Inventory of Policies and Policy Areas Influencing Father Involvement. Guelph: Father Involvement Research Alliance. Retrieved November 2, 2006 from www.fira.uoguelph.ca

Levine, J. A. & Pittinsky, T. L. (1997). Working Fathers: New Strategies for Balancing Work and family. Reading, Mass.: Addison-Wesley.

Masciadrelli, B. P., Pleck, J. H. & Stueve, J. L. (2006). Father's role model perceptions: Themes and linkages with involvement. *Men and Masculinities, 9*, 23–34.

Matta, D. S. & Knudson-Martin, C. (2006). Father responsivity: Couple processes and the co-construction of fatherhood. *Family Process, 45*, 19–37.

Maume, D. J. & Houston, P. (2001). Job segregation and gender differences in work-family spillover among white-collar workers. *Journal of Family and Economic Issues, 22*, 177–189.

Mills, C. W. (1959). The Sociological Imagination. New York: Oxford University Press.

Milkie, M. A. & Petola, P. (1999). Playing all the roles: Gender and the work-family balancing act. *Journal of Marriage and the Family, 61*, 476–490.

Palkovitz, R. (2002). *Involved Fathering and Men's Adult Development: Provisional Balances.* New Jersey: Lawrence Earlbaum Associates.

Pleck, J. H. (1997). Paternal involvement: Levels, sources, and consequences. In M.E. Lamb (ed.), *The Role of the Father in Child Development,* 3rd edn (pp. 66–103). New York: Wiley.

Ranson, G. (2001). Men at work: Change or no change? – In the era of the "new father". *Men and Masculinities, 4,* 3–26.

Reeves, R. (2006). Dad's Army: The Case for Father-Friendly Workplaces. London: The Work Foundation. Retrieved November 2, 2006 from http://www.theworkfoundation.com/products/publications/azpublications/dadsarmythecaseforfatherfriendlyworkplaces.aspx

Russell, G. & Hwang, C.P. (2004). The impact of workplace practices on father involvement. In M. E. Lamb (ed.) *The Role of the Father in Child Development,* 4th edn. New York: John Wiley & Sons.

Saunders, R. (2006). Risk and opportunity: Creating options for vulnerable workers. *Vulnerable Workers Series No/7.* Ottawa: Canadian Policy Research Networks. Retrieved on November 2, 2006 from http://www.cprn.org

Singley, S. G. & Hynes, K. (2005). Transitions to parenthood: Work-family policies, gender, and the couple context. *Gender & Society, 19,* 376–397.

Strazdins, L., Clements, M. S., Korda, R. J., Broom, D. H. & D'Souza, R. M. (2006). Unsociable work? Nonstandard work schedules, family relationships, and children's well-being. *Journal of Marriage and Family, 68,* 394–410.

Townsend, N. (2002). *The Package Deal: Marriage, Work, and Fatherhood in Men's Lives.* Philadelphia: Temple University Press.

Wayne, J. & Cordeiro, B. (2003). Who is a good organizational citizen? Social perception of male and female employees who use family leave. *Sex Roles, 49,* 233–246.

Winslow, S. (2005). Work-family conflict, gender and parenthood, 1977–1997. *Journal of Family Issues, 26,* 727–755.

Zimmerman, T. S., Haddock, S. A., Ziemba, S. & Rust, A. (2001). Family organizational labor: Who's calling the plays? *Journal of Feminist Family Therapy, 13,* 65–90.

Zukewich, N. (1998). Work, Parenthood and the Experience of Time Scarcity. Statistics Canada, Catalogue no. 89-584-MIE. Retrieved on November 2, 2006 from http://www.statcan.ca/cgi-bin/downpub/research.cgi

SECTION III

Context, Processes, Practices & Policies

Coping with Work–Family Conflict: Integrating Individual and Organizational Perspectives

Anat Drach-Zahavy* and Anit Somech†
*Faculty of Social Welfare and Health Studies, University of Haifa,
Mount Carmel, Israel
†Faculty of Education, University of Haifa, Mount Carmel, Israel

The authors contributed equally to the chapter and are presented in alphabetical order

INTRODUCTION

Accumulating empirical evidence suggests that the ability to cope with stress arising from the simultaneous demands of work and family is a function of both the individual's capabilities and the organization's focus on a family-friendliness orientation. This chapter adopts a comprehensive perspective on coping with work-family conflict (WFC), and undertakes three complementary goals: (1) to delineate the range of coping strategies for dealing with WFC among employed parents and to test their effectiveness; (2) to identify organizational practices aimed at redesigning work and work roles for handling WFC and to probe their effectiveness; (3) to propose models for depicting the joint effects of individual and organizational coping strategies in easing work-family conflict. We start by describing the changing social context affecting the burgeoning interest in coping with WFC, and review the three main perspectives for examining this issue. Next we go through the literature on coping from the individual and the organizational perspectives. The chapter concludes with a discussion of recurring themes in the literature, and the identification of problems with the current perspective on coping with WFC. Specific suggestions for developing an integrative model combining the individual and organizational perspectives for coping, future research, and managerial implications are also made.

COPING WITH WFC IN A CHANGING SOCIAL CONTEXT

Growing demands in the last half-century in both the family and work domains led to what Kanter (1977) termed "the myth of separate worlds". Workers increasingly spend their time outside the physical precincts of their organization when they work, whether at home or "on the road" with customers and other constituents. For some individuals such practices might of course provide opportunities to cope with WFC, whereas for others such blurring of the work and family worlds might actually intensify it. Either way, questions about job and family stress, WFC conflict, and particularly coping with it by those with dual responsibilities in the work and family domains became a particular area of research, interest, and concern.

Against this backdrop of dramatic and ongoing social and workplace change, research on coping with WFC evolved. Specifically, three main perspectives came to dominate the literature: the first emphasized the individual's role, while the other two highlighted the organization's role in coping with WFC. The *individual perspective* constructed the issues emerging, especially women's issues, strictly as personal problems to be solved by the individual rather than the organization (Bailyn, 1997). The focus was on identifying normative typologies of coping strategies, namely personal coping strategies (e.g., Folkman & Lazarus, 1985; Hall, 1972), informal tactics (e.g., Behson, 2002), or characteristics of effective life management strategy (e.g., Baltes & Heydens-Gahir, 2003) that help individuals to manage WFC. These models sweepingly prescribed the optimal coping strategy for decreasing WFC across situations, context, and culture (Somech & Drach-Zahavy, 2007). Moreover, this perspective was embedded in individualistic values of self-reliance and autonomy that insisted on the individual's own responsibility to take care of his or her well-being.

Taking an *organization-calculative perspective* (committed-to-management research), several scholars suggested that the growing stress characterizing today's workplace (Dwyer & Fox, 2000; Quick, Quick, Nelson & Hurrell, 1997), coupled with spiraling health care costs (Miller, 1997) and a tightening labor market (Lewis & Cooper, 1999), had raised the incidence as well as the costs of workers' ill-health, forcing organizations to show greater concern for this issue (Behson, 2005; Pratt & Rosa, 2003; Carlson & Perrewe, 1999). The focus was on identifying organizational family-friendly supports such as the policies and practices organizations offer employees to decrease WFC. However, most research viewed coping with WFC as a means to maintain *organizational* outcomes such as effectiveness, performance, profits, and withdrawal behaviors, namely absence, turnover, and intention to leave the organization (Behson, 2005; Pratt & Rosa, 2003; Grover & Crooker, 1995).

More recently other scholars have taken an *organization-humanistic* (committed-to-participant research) point of view, asserting that workers are entitled to a more family-friendly workplace that takes care of workers' health regardless of the benefit of their occupational well-being for the organization (Wright, 2003; Wright & Cropanzano, 2000; Quick & Quick, 2004; Schaufeli, 2004). Like the organization-calculative perspective, the organization-humanistic perspective identifies family-friendly policies and practices to decrease WFC. However, the organization-humanistic approach asserts that it is the organizations' obligation to take care of workers' health in general, and easing WFC in particular. Consequently, studies taking this approach have examined the impact of workplace family friendliness on *personal* outcomes, such as employee's well-being and psychological and physical health.

COPING WITH WFC: THE PERSPECTIVE OF THE INDIVIDUAL

Coping is defined as the cognitive and behavioral efforts individuals make to manage taxing demands appraised as exceeding their personal resources (Lazarus & Folkman, 1984); it is the things people do to reduce harm from life's stressors (Aryee, Luk, Leung & Lo, 1999; Pearlin & Schooler, 1978). The relation between coping and strain was grounded theoretically in the motivational aspect of person-environment transactions (Scheck, Kinicki & Davy, 1997). In Scheck et al.s' (1997) view, stressors upset the balance in people's lives, motivating them to do something to restore it. Accordingly, theoretical models of stress recognized the importance of coping in mitigating the severity of tension and other deleterious effects of role stressors (Parasuraman & Simmers, 2001).

However, given the extensive study of coping in the stress literature (see Folkman & Moskowitz, 2004), it is puzzling to find a relative lack of research on coping in the context of work and family (Behson, 2002; Eby, Casper, Lockwood, Bordeaux & Brinley, 2005). Coping with WFC is defined here as the cognitive and behavioral efforts individuals make to manage the stresses arising from the con-flicting demands of the work and family domains. The first well-known coping typology, regarding stress, coping, and WFC, adopted Lazarus and Folkman's (1984) transactional approach to stress. Stress is transactional in that the person and the environment are viewed as being in a dynamic reciprocal relationship. The the-ory identifies two processes, cognitive appraisal and coping, as critical mediators of stressful person-environment relationships and their immediate and long-term outcomes. Cognitive appraisal is a process through which people evaluate whether a particular encounter with the environment is relevant to their well-being, and if it is, in what way. According to Lazarus (1991), in the primary appraisal process individuals evaluate whether the event is relevant, and if it is whether it represents an opportunity for growth or the potential for failure. In the secondary appraisal process individuals evaluate the coping resources available to them. A combina-tion of these two appraisals determines whether the individual perceives an event as challenging or threatening. Appraisal of the event as a challenge is accompanied by a positive feeling, making possible deployment of coping resources to prevent, reduce, control, or withstand the internal and/or external demands that arise from the stressful encounter with the environment. Appraisal of the stressful event as threatening, burdening resources, and jeopardizing well-being accelerates the strain process. Cognitive appraisal and coping are transactional variables, in that they refer not to the environment or to the person alone but to the integration of both in a given transaction (see also Folkman & Lazarus, 1988; Lazarus & Folkman, 1984).

Albeit not specifically in the WFC context, Lazarus and Folkman (1984) identified two major classes of coping strategies: emotion-focused and problem-focused. The former "does not change the objective terms of the person-environment relationship, but only how these terms are attended or interpreted" (Lazarus, 1991, p. 5). In other words, the emotion-focused strategy refers to attempts to reduce emotional distress by managing feelings and emotions via cognitive manipulations, such as reframing or positive thinking efforts. By contrast, problem-focused coping refers to efforts to define the problem and to eliminate or circumvent the source of stress (Lazarus & Folkman, 1984). Whereas all coping styles have the potential to reduce distress, research on coping with stress (e.g., Koeske, Kirk & Koeske, 1993) generally found problem-focused coping the most effective, largely owing to the importance of psychological control and self-efficacy for effective stress management (Bernas & Major, 2000; Rotondo, Carlson & Kincaid, 2003). When coping actions alter the person-environment relationship for the better, they can be instrumental in eliminating or reducing the environmental causes of stress (Behson, 2002).

Yet some studies (e.g., Bhagat, Allie & Ford, 1995) suggest that problem-focused styles, such as direct action and help-seeking, are likely to be more effective only when situations are amenable to change. When individuals have little ability to change related stressors, emotion-focused coping will be preferable. Accordingly, this kind of coping may be effective where work interferes with family due to circumstance in organizations where flexibility is unavailable or where individuals are unable to modify work-related stressors. Under these conditions, problem-focused styles are ineffective (Aryee et al., 1999; Pearlin & Schooler, 1978). Rotondo et al. (2003) found that help-seeking and direct-action coping (forms of problem-focused coping) used at home were associated with lower levels of family interference with work (FIW) conflict, but avoidance/resignation coping (forms of emotion-focused coping) were associated with higher levels of all types of WFC. However, another study, by Aryee et al. (1999), found that emotion-focused coping weakened the negative effect of FIW on job satisfaction. Hence, adapting Folkman and Lazarus' "general" coping styles to the arena of WFC yielded mixed results, and research sought a coping taxonomy pertaining particularly to WFC.

Another line of research was developed specifically for the WFC context by Hall (1972). This typology is composed of three types of coping strategy: *Type I coping* (structural role definition) involves altering external, structurally imposed expectations relative to one's role. Namely, an active attempt is made to deal directly with role senders and to lessen the conflict by mutual agreement on a new set of role expectations. *Type II coping* (personal role redefinition) involves changing one's expectations and perceptions of one's own behavior in a given role, rather than directly attempting to change the expectations themselves. With this strategy, individuals modify the meaning of the situation by changing their personal concept of role requirements or by changing self-expectations for career and family (Thompson, Poelmans, Allen & Andreassi, 2007). *Type III coping* (reactive role behavior) relies strictly on existing role behaviors (e.g., meeting all role senders' expectations) with no attempt to alter the structural or personal definition of one's roles. The Type III strategy makes relatively passive attempts to accommodate role senders.

Prior research (e.g., Hall, 1972; Kirchmeyer, 1993), which focused mainly on women, suggested that the Type III coping strategy was less effective in managing interrole conflict than the Type I and Type II strategies; while structural role redefinition (Type I) was associated with women's career satisfaction. The use of Type III coping proved negatively related to a woman's satisfaction with her life roles (Hall, 1972). Since it is unlikely that a person can ever meet all role expectations, a woman's reliance on Type III coping may produce anger, frustration, and ultimately low levels of life satisfaction. Yet the Type III strategy, whereby women attempt to be "superwomen", is apparently quite common among employed mothers (Beutell & Greenhaus, 1982). On the other hand, Kaitz (1985) suggested that structural role redefinition (Type II) is the most time-effective way of managing WFC. For example, women might shed some domestic duties, or delegate some to others, in order to have the family role accommodate the work role (referred to as family-role redefinition). However, the results of previous studies are inconsistent (Thompson et al., 2007). For example, Matsui, Ohsawa and Onglatco (1995), who studied a sample of Japanese working women, examined the effect of structural-role redefinition (work-role and family-role redefinition) on WFC. They found that family-role redefinition buffered the relationship between work-family conflict and life strain, but that work-role redefinition did not. In sum, these inconsistencies showed that adopting a certain strategy for decreasing WFC by an individual did not ensure its effectiveness, and that a more context-specific perspective is needed (e.g., one that is sensitive to gender or culture differences).

More recently, Behson (2002) introduced another typology of informal work accommodations to family which referred to a set of behaviors in which employees temporarily and informally adjust their usual work patterns in an attempt to balance their work and family responsibilities. These informal tactics may modify how, when, or where work gets done, but an individual's work output is sure to remain relatively unchanged and the work structure (total number of hours, regular work schedule, etc.) should not be permanently altered (as they would be with use of formal work-family benefits and programs).

Based on a literature review, a set of informal interviews conducted with a sample of working parents, and a series of focus groups with several samples of employees, Behson (2002) identified a set of 16 informal behaviors which represent problem-focused coping strategies used when family demands interfered with work activities. Examples are: rearranging one's work appointments to attend to a family matter (e.g., a doctor's appointment or a soccer game) that took place during regular work hours; arranging to leave work early to attend a family event; arranging for a co-worker to cover for you or switch duties in order to accommodate a family responsibility; leaving work during the day, but completing the work later that night (at home or at the office); and leaving work early to take care of family responsibilities, but coming in earlier or taking work home to accomplish the needed work. Behson (2002) found that more frequent use of these set of informal tactics attenuated the positive relationship between FIW and stress.

Finally, Somech and Drach-Zahavy (2006) introduced a new typology of coping strategies that specified and extended existing measures. By adopting an empirically driven bottom-up conceptualization of both men and women, rather than relying on researchers' professional conceptualizations, they devised a more refined and elaborate typology. It refers to specific bidirectional coping strategies—those for work interference with family (WIF) and those for family interference with work (FIW). Specifically, the authors identified eight categories denoting behavioral aspects of coping strategies that specify what individuals actually do to cope with WFC:

1 *Good enough at home*—lowering the performance of family responsibilities to a less than perfect level; for example, maintaining a reasonable level of housekeeping, cooking, and laundry.
2 *Super at home*—insisting on doing all family duties single-handedly and perfectly; for example, cooking fresh homemade meals every day, ensuring that the house is always clean, and taking care of all family members' needs.
3 *Delegation at home*—managing one's own family duties by delegating some to others; for example, utilizing paid or a relative's help to take care of the children, the cooking, or the cleaning.
4 *Priorities at home*—arranging family duties in order of priority, and undertaking only those with high priority; for example, investing in spending "quality time" with one's children at the price of a less than desirably clean house.
5 *Good enough at work*—lowering the performance of work responsibilities to a less than perfect level; for example, choosing not to stay extra hours at work and not to mingle with colleagues after office hours.
6 *Super at work*—insisting on doing all work duties single-handedly and perfectly; for example, being prepared to take on extra duties even if overloaded already, and duties that are not part of one's formal roles.
7 *Delegation at work*—managing one's own work duties by delegating some to others; for example, delegating paperwork to subordinates.
8 *Priorities at work*—arranging work duties in order of priority, and undertaking only those with high priority; for example, engaging more with customers at the expense of paperwork.

In their study, Somech and Drach Zahavy (2007) examined the effectiveness of these coping strategies on decreasing WIF and FIW with respect to sex and gender-role ideology. Although all eight styles of coping have the potential to be negatively associated with work-family conflict, the results suggest that not all styles are equally effective for managing it. Overall, these results indicate that men with traditional gender-role ideologies and women with modern or egalitarian ideologies have a similar pattern of effective practices to mitigate WFC, whereas traditional women and modern men share some coping strategies to do so. The results demonstrated that the two subgroups of modern women and traditional men balance WFC by exerting extra effort at work (*super at work*), and they tend to delegate domestic duties to others (e.g., *good enough at home* and *delegation at home*). For traditional women and modern men the picture is inverted; because they don't want their paid work to distract them from their family, they balance work and family by taking an active role at home, and they tend to delegate duties to others at work (e.g., *delegation at work* or *priorities at work*) which leads to decreased WFC. These results highlight the importance of matching the person (attitudes, values) with the preferred coping strategy.

COPING WITH WFC: THE PERSPECTIVE OF THE ORGANIZATION

How employees cope with WFC can be further examined from an organizational perspective, namely the organization's role in attempting to become family-friendly. *Workplace family-friendliness* is defined here as institutionalized structural and procedural arrangements, as well as formal and informal practices aimed to design, create, and maintain family-friendly work environments that allow individuals to balance their work and family duties within their workplace.

This definition highlights several important aspects of workplace family-friendliness. First, the definition stresses a distinction between formal and informal arrangements. The former refer to the ways organizations can "manage the situation" in such ways as childcare assistance, flexible working hours, and family leave (Allen, 2001; Clark, 2001; Veiga et al., 2004), while the latter refer to values and unspoken norms represented in the organizational culture. Research suggests that the formal arrangements of workplace family-friendliness will never be fully realized unless organizations' cultures support their use (Lobel & Kossek, 1996). Second, the definition suggests a possible gap between the potential of a family-friendly workplace to assist employees to balance their work and family duties and its effectiveness in decreasing WFC. Although on the formal level the organization might offer a vast range of family-friendly practices and arrangements to ease employees' coping with WFC, the final decision to utilize these options is the individual's. Such programs have the potential to decrease WFC, yet a variety of informal organizational norms and values might dissuade employees from participating in them (Kofodimos, 1995; Veiga et al., 2004). For example, an employee might hesitate to use the full period of parental leave due to concerns of not being promoted. On the other hand, personal values might also discourage employees from using family-friendly practices: an ambitious employee may decide to focus on his or her career and will therefore waive taking advantage of these programs (Glass & Finley, 2002). Different employees might have different needs and desires, attenuating the effectiveness of the family-friendly programs. The effectiveness of the family-friendly practices and arrangements depends on the fit between the individual's needs and the organization's solutions to meet them.

Given varying family demands and desires of individuals, family-friendly programs have been organized into three major categories: policies, benefits, and services (Neal, Chapman, Ingersoll-Dayton & Emlen, 1993; Veiga et al., 2004). *Policies* cover the formal and informal ways that employees' work and leave schedules are handled, including part-time work, job-sharing, flextime, and parental/family leave. Family-friendly policies often reduce the number of hours worked, change the place where an employee's work is done, or increase flexibility in the employee's work schedule (Veiga et al., 2004). *Benefits* cover forms of compensation that protect against loss of earnings, payment of medical expenses and vacation, personal time, or all of these. *Services* include on-site or near-site childcare centers, resource counseling and referral systems, sick leave and eldercare programs, and discounts and vouchers for a variety of support services.

How does workplace family-friendliness help in coping with WFC? Three plausible rationales provide the theoretical ground for the proposed link between workplace family-friendliness and improved work and family balance: the direct impact explanation, the effort-reward imbalance model (Siegrist & Klein, 1990), and the concept of psychological contract (Rousseau, 1998).

The *direct impact explanation* asserts that workplace family-friendliness directly impacts the work/family load, hence creates less conflict (Frone et al., 1992). For example, flexible-time arrangements allow individuals to perceive that they have greater control over their lives due, for example, to the opportunity to work at times more suited to personal needs (e.g., childcare or elderly-care obligations) or personal biological clocks (not everyone is most productive from 9.00 a.m. to 5.00 p.m.) hence creating less conflicting demands in a certain time.

According to the *effort-reward model* (Siegrist & Klein, 1990) psychological stress and mal-health occurs when there is an imbalance between what one invests in one's work (efforts) and what one gains (reward). Work efforts pertain to job demands, such as role overload, role ambiguity, and role conflict stemming from the nature of the job and the way it is structured. Work rewards include benefits the organization offers employees in return for their efforts, such as wages and salaries, esteem and recognition, promotion prospects, as well as workplace family-friendliness. The effort-reward model does not incorporate in particular work-family balance aspects, yet logically, in keeping with its basic assumptions, the same level of work efforts might lead to improved work and family balance given that employees perceive greater benefits gained (such as family-friendly policies and practices).

Finally, the so-called psychological contract is as a set of "individual beliefs, shaped by the organization, regarding terms of an exchange agreement between individuals and their organization" (Rousseau, 1998, p. 9). Although the specific content of the psychological contract is subjective, and tends to vary from one individual to another, it is reasonable that maintaining workplace family-friendliness will be a central expectation of workers, thus an important aspect of the employee's psychological contract.

According to the *psychological contract model*, perceptions of workplace family-friendliness may result in an improved balance between work and family for several reasons. First, the individual may perceive the organization's offering family-friendliness as visibly representing its concern for work and family. Employees may see this as an aspect of the psychological contract since their ability to balance multiple responsibilities is congruent with individual values about work and family (i.e., "this organization cares about people"). Second, the availability family-friendly policies and practices improves employees' perceptions about their employer and increases their overall positive feeling toward the employer, which impacts job satisfaction (Scandura & Lankau, 1997) hence might also decrease WFC. Third, employees often engage in social comparison processes (Adams, 1965) and may compare their situation with that of peers in other jobs and/or organizations that do not offer family-friendliness. Such comparisons should increase the value of employees' psychological contract with their organization.

Despite the general expectation that the use of workplace family-friendly policies will be associated with effective coping and reduced work-family conflict, little research has been conducted to examine this relationship (Eby et al., 2005; Hammer, Neal, Newsom, Brockwood & Colton, 2005; Kossek & Nichol, 1992), and the findings that do exist are not consistent. In fact, only a handful of studies have examined the effects of actual utilization of workplace family-friendliness, typically focusing on either alternative work schedules or dependent care supports (Kossek & Nichol, 1992). In addition, most studies have examined only one specific type of support at a time (e.g., Thomas & Ganster, 1995), as opposed to a wider variety, or "bundles", of supports (Perry-Smith & Blum, 2000).

Although inconsistent, the findings pertaining to the utilization of alternative work schedules have generally demonstrated relationships between utilization of alternative work schedules and outcomes such as decreased work-family conflict, increased job satisfaction, and increased performance (for reviews see Baltes, Briggs, Huff, Wright & Neuman, 1999; Hammer & Barbera, 1997; Pierce, Newstrom, Dunham & Barber, 1989).

Utilization of dependent care supports has been shown to be related to decreased turnover, decreased absenteeism, and increased organizational commitment and satisfaction (e.g., Milkovich & Gomez, 1976), pointing at enhanced coping. Other studies, however, found utilization of on-site childcare to be unrelated to work-family conflict (Somech & Drach-Zahavy, 2006), absenteeism (e.g., Goff, Mount & Jamison, 1990), and performance (e.g., Kossek & Nichol, 1992). For example, Somech and Drach-Zahavy (2006) investigated the impact of organizational coping-strategy bundles prevalent at various organizations. They found inverse patterns of findings for nonmanagers and mangers. For nonmanagers, family-friendly benefits alone decreased conflict. By contrast, for managers none of the organizational coping strategies helped in decreasing WFC conflict: the existence of a welfare policy actually raised the level of conflict.

FUTURE DIRECTION FOR COPING WITH WFC: INTEGRATING THE INDIVIDUAL AND ORGANIZATIONAL PERSPECTIVES

The above review has shown that investigating coping with WFC from the individual and organizational perspectives appeared as two distinct lines of research, only slightly overlapping. These two lines of research were led by experts from distinct areas of research, and published in separate journals: the former in the domain of occupational health psychology and clinical psychology, the latter in industrial and organizational psychology. Not surprisingly, to the best of our knowledge no study heretofore has proposed an integrated model combining these two perspectives. But such an integrated approach will generate a plethora of new questions and challenges for researchers, and also promote a host of new management issues. Specifically, from the theoretical point of view, what are the interrelationships between the individual and the organizational perspectives? Are they compensatory models in nature, namely that working in a family-friendly workplace excuses the employee from developing constructive personal coping strategies? Or the reverse: does recruiting employees well equipped with personal coping resources excuse the organization from investing in family-friendly programs? Or are the individual and organizational perspectives for coping complementary in nature, namely organizational supports and personal coping strategies act additively to decrease WFC: the more family-friendly the workplace is, and the more coping effective the employee is at coping with WFC, the lower the WFC level. Below we propose three alternative ways to capture the mutual relations between the individual and organizational perspectives, and outline several practical consequences, some beneficial and some more detrimental, of each model.

THE COMPENSATORY MODEL

The compensatory model for understanding the mutual relations of personal coping and organizational supports on decreasing WFC posits that an optimal level of coping resources is required for decreasing WFC, and additional resources beyond this level are redundant. In other words, the impact of this perspective on decreasing WFC is viewed as analogous to the influence of vitamins on physical health, with an explicit nonlinearity in the relationship (Warr, 1994). Thus, the compensatory model represents an either/or approach to considering and managing coping with work-family conflict.

Organizations might offer employees a vast range of family-friendly policies of flextime; benefits of compensations, payment of medical expenses and vacation; and *services* of on-site or near-site childcare centers, counseling and referral systems, and eldercare programs. These family-friendly supports allow the employee to cope effectively with WFC, thereby limiting his/her need to exert personal coping strategies because these efforts will not contribute to additional easing of WFC. Similarly, employees who possess effective personal coping strategies will not benefit from the workplace's family-friendly policies, benefits and services, which exceed the optimal level of coping resources needed, so organizations will not be motivated to implement such programs. Employees might sometimes even perceive these organizational efforts as a burden, as if treating them as helpless, or as if urging them precisely to compensate their organizations by working even harder. In any event, the outcome might be aggravated WFC.

This compensatory perspective has several practical consequences for organizations and employees. First, this either/or approach assumes an optimal level of required coping resources. Therefore, organizations, particularly those oriented to a cost-benefit calculation, might be tempted to rely on employees' personal coping resources, regressing toward the *individual perspective*. They may construct the issues emerging, especially women's issues, strictly as personal problems to be solved by the individual rather than the organization (Bailyn, 1997). In practice organizations might apply recruitment processes based on strict selection of employees who already possess effective coping resources. At the extreme they might choose not to recruit employees with potential WFC (e.g., mothers of young children). Organizations adopting the individual perspective might offer employees several family-friendly programs, but simultaneously convey a hidden message, that if you take advantage of these programs you should not expect "to get ahead".

In other cases organizations may well recognize that to "manage the situation" is part of their obligation. Assuming an optimal level of coping resources, it is critical that organizational supports be "tailor-made". Organizational surveys might serve to single out coping activities used by employees to deal with a variety of work and family stressors, by identifying individual differences. The need for training courses or organizational change could then be determined. If needed, organizational or training interventions could then be developed and initiated to help individuals identify, and thereafter intensify, the use of adaptive coping strategies in light of situational and individual differences (Havlovic & Keenan, 1991).

THE COMPLEMENTARY MODEL

The complementary model for understanding the mutual interrelationships between personal coping and organizational supports on decreasing WFC posits that "more is better", with an explicit linearity in the relationship. Rather than assuming an optimal level of coping resources, as in the compensatory model, this model assumes that the maximal level of resources is better for decreasing WFC. This perspective moves from a traditional, schismogenic, either/or approach to a both/and approach, making it possible to see management of WFC in genuinely new ways. The responsibility for coping with WFC relies equally on both constituencies: the organization as well as the employee. Organizations and employees alike understand their facilitative role in employees' coping with WFC. Organizations commit themselves to developing a wide range of family-friendly policies, benefits, and services; while employees are obligated to developing effective personal coping strategies for decreasing WFC. Each of those constituencies contributes independently and additively to balancing the work and family domains. Yet precisely because the two constituencies act independently, it is important to explain why each party will be motivated to do its best and invest in mitigating the conflict rather than "wait and see" what the other constituency does.

Several practical consequences of the complementary perspective for organizations and employees emerge. This both/and approach assumes the maximal level of required coping resources. Therefore, organizations that offer employees family-friendly programs also might convey a powerful message that it is legitimate for employees to use them, thereby assimilating a family-friendly culture (Thompson, Beauvais & Lyness, 1999). In their research on disabled employees' willingness to seek and utilize assistance, Baldridge and Veiga (2001) emphasized the role of supporting culture in shaping employees' assessments of image cost, anticipated compliance and appropriateness. Hence, the organizational benefits of family-friendly supports will be realized because organizations' cultures support their use. Organizations' provision of family-friendly initiatives does not lessen employees' responsibility for coping. On the contrary, organizations communicate a clear message to employees that to "manage the situation" is also part of their obligation. In sum, the complementary approach integrates supportive values with employees' autonomy and self-reliance. The possible price of taking the complementary both/and approach might be a waste of resources. Independent investment by both organization and employees in decreasing WFC might cause the organization to provide programs which are not tailor-made but are incompatible with its employees' unique and diverse needs.

THE SPIRAL MODEL

The spiral model for understanding the interrelationship of personal coping and organizational supports on easing WFC posits that each constituency's resources nurture the other's, leading to continuous improvement in the balance of the work and family domains. This model (see Figure 15.1) represents a shift from a linear conception, characterizing the complementary model, to one that emphasizes the dynamic, fluid, and progressive nature of the interaction between the organization and the employee.

The spiral model uses a cyclical approach to develop increasing coping resources culminating in incremental stages. It starts with an organization that offers its employees an extensive range of family-friendly policies, benefits, and services; these are coupled with a facilitating work culture that grants employees legitimacy to utilize these supports. This leads directly to lower levels of WFC. The spiral model assumes that besides the organization, the employee too takes an active role in the coping process; working in a family-friendly environment empowers employees to take responsibility for their conflict, being provided with available resources to devise their own coping strategies. This in turn enhances the family-friendly culture further by strengthening employees' perceptions regarding the importance of family-friendly integration issues in the organization. This cyclical process continues by feeding forward organizations and employees persistently to elaborate their repertoire for coping.

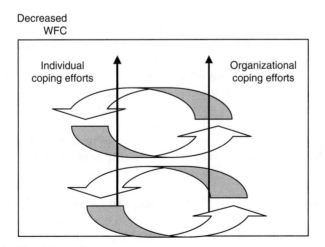

Figure 15.1 The spiral model

How does this spiral model work? How can an organization's family-friendly supports generate personal coping strategies among its employees? We suggest that employees bring personal characteristics, values, and beliefs to their work and family encounters (Somech & Drach-Zahavy, 2007), as well as earlier experiences (e.g., special training in coping with WFC, experience as employees, parents, and spouses), which help shape their individual coping behavior during the encounter. Yet organizational family-friendly supports, more particularly, where they are embedded in supportive family-friendly culture (Thompson et al., 1999; Veiga et al., 2004) can further shape these behaviors and create relatively homogeneous behaviors among employees in a specific organization. Two arguments for the mechanism described above underlie this premise: (a) the managerial argument (Borucki & Burke, 1999); and (b) the fit argument (Smith-Crowe, Burke & Landis, 2003).

The *managerial argument* maintains that societal and organizationally supportive values will bring about particular types of general and management practices; these in turn will influence employees' perceptions of the work environment and their behaviors; ultimately, individual behaviors will directly impact organizational functioning (Borucki & Burke, 1999). For example, we expect personal coping behaviors to flourish in organizations where the behaviors are supported and even rewarded, and where resources are directed to training and improving employees' coping skills.

The *"fit" argument* suggests that people strive to harmonize with their environment (Smith-Crowe et al., 2003). To achieve this, they seek information on proper behavior from their surroundings. Therefore, when the organization-promoted climate is explicit, and organizational policies, benefits, and services are directly aligned with it, people will identify and recognize what is important and display more role-fit behaviors (Burke, Borucki & Hurley, 1992). Specifically, if an organization has family-friendly programs (and culture) employees will presumably strive to display such coping behaviors by utilizing those programs, or by applying their learned coping knowledge and skills to their job.

This spiral perspective conveys several practical consequences for organizations and employees. First, like the complementary model, both constituencies, the organization and the employee, take an active role in lessening WFC. But unlike that model, this one emphasizes the interdependency of the organizations and the employees' acts, mutually feeding forward continuous elaboration of coping capacity. Hence, in contrast to the complementary approach, where joint efforts by the organization and the employees might waste resources, the practical outcome of the spiral model might lead to synergism in resource exploitation.

IMPLICATIONS FOR FUTURE RESEARCH AND PRACTICE

Coping with WFC presents a mounting challenge for organizations and employees alike. A growing number of organizations have implemented family-friendly programs to meet the needs of today's workforce, yet employees apparently hesitate to use them unless they are embedded in a supportive family-friendly culture (Veiga et al., 2004; Thompson et al., 1999). Many jobs are not suitable for alternative arrangements, like job sharing. Often the ability to cope with the stress arising from the simultaneous demands of work and family is also a function of the capabilities of the individual (Burley, 1994). Nevertheless, as our review shows, employees do not necessarily utilize the coping strategies that are most effective for easing their WFC. Moreover, the effectiveness of each strategy is contingent upon personal characteristics (e.g., gender, values, and experience), workplace characteristics (e.g., organizational role, job structure), and societal context (culture, developed versus developing countries). It is important to match the person (attitudes, values) with the preferred coping strategy.

As our review implies, despite the recent interest in examining coping with WFC authors have typically adopted either a personal perspective, identifying the individual coping strategies for reducing WFC (e.g., Hall, 1972; Lazarus & Folkman, 1984) or an organizational perspective, identifying organizational policies, benefits, and services allowing employees to manage the conflict (Veiga et al. 2004; Thompson et al., 1999). Moreover, each perspective has focused on different types of outcomes. While research based on the organizational perspective typically has been focused on the impact of the conflict on organizational outcomes such as performance, commitment, or absenteeism, studies adopting an individual perspective have typically been concerned with personal outcomes such as well-being, satisfaction, depression, and health.

The present chapter contributed to the literature by delineating three optional models, the compensatory, the complementary, and the spiral, to combine the mutual effects of individual coping strategies and organizational family-friendly supports in WFC. The compensatory model suggests an either/or relationship between the organization's and the employee's efforts in decreasing WFC; the complementary model posits a both/and relationships; the spiral model overcomes the drawbacks of these two models and suggests a synergetic relationship between the organization and the employee in coping with WFC.

The conceptualization of these integrative models sets out a rich agenda for future research. First, although our discussion of the suggested models hinted at the superiority of the spiral model for decreasing WFC, empirical research is still needed to support this assertion. Studies should examine whether the spiral model is in fact the superior one or whether the effectiveness of each model is context-specific, namely each model best fits specific circumstances. Moreover, it is important that empirical research identify the facilitating as well as the inhibiting antecedents that allow the effective models to flourish. Second, the integrative perspective may shift the focus to examining individual and organizational outcomes simultaneously in a single research framework. Research should also focus on whether the individual and the organizational perspectives have different outcomes; empirical intervention research should try to determine whether a choice has to be made between personal outcomes such as well-being and organizational outcomes such as productivity, or whether it is possible to obtain an all-encompassing well-being and productivity-promoting system.

REFERENCES

Adams, E. W. (1965). Elements of a theory of inexact measurement. *Philosophy of Science, 32*, 205–228.

Allen, T. D. (2001). Family-supportive work environments: The role of organizational perceptions. *Journal of Vocational Behavior, 58*, 414–435.

Aryee, S., Luk, V., Leung, A. & Lo, S. (1999). Role stressors, interrole conflict, and well-being: The moderating influence of spousal support and coping behaviors among employed parents in Hong Kong. *Journal of Vocational Behavior, 54*, 259–278.

Bailyn, L. (1997). The impact of corporate culture on work-family integration. In S. Parasurman & J. H. Greenhaus (eds), *Integrating Work and Family: Challenges and Choices for a Changing World* (pp. 209–219). Westport, CT: Quorum/Greenwood.

Baldridge, D. C. & Veiga, J. F. (2001). Toward a greater understanding of the willingness to request an accommodation: Can requesters' beliefs disable the Americans with the Disabilities Act? *Academy of Management Review, 26*, 85–99.

Baltes, B. B., Briggs, T. E., Huff, J. W., Wright, J. A. & Neuman, G. A. (1999). Flexible and compressed workweek schedules: A meta-analysis of their effects on work-related criteria. *Journal of Applied Psychology, 84*, 496–513.

Baltes, B. B. & Heydens-Gahir, H. A. (2003). Reduction of work-family conflict through the use of selection, optimization, and compensation behaviors. *Journal of Applied Psychology, 88*, 1005–1018.

Behson, S. J. (2002). Coping with family-to-work conflict: The role of informal work accommodations to family. *Journal of Occupational Health Psychology, 7*, 324–341.

Behson, S. J. (2005). The relative contribution of formal and informal organizational work- family support. *Journal of Vocational Behavior, 66*, 487–500.

Bernas, K. H. & Major, D. A. (2000). Contributors to stress resistance: Testing a model of women's work-family conflict. *Psychology of Women Quarterly, 24*, 170–178.

Beutell, N. J, & Greenhaus, J. H. (1982). Interrole conflict among married women: The influence of husband and wife characteristics on conflict and coping behavior. *Journal of Vocational Behavior, 21*, 99–110.

Bhagat, R. S., Allie, S. M. & Ford, D. L. (1995). Coping with stressful life events: An empirical analysis. In R. Crandall & P. L. Perrewe (eds), *Occupational Stress: A Handbook* (pp. 93–112). Washington, DC: Taylor & Francis.

Borucki, C. C. & Burke, M. J. (1999). An examination of service-related antecedents to retail store performance. *Journal of Organizational Behavior, 20*, 943–962.

Burke, M. J., Borucki, C. C. & Hurley, A. E. (1992). Reconceptualizing psychological climate in a retail service environment: A multiple-stakeholder perspective. *Journal of Applied Psychology, 77*, 717–729.

Burley, K. (1994). Gender differences and similarities in coping responses to anticipated work-family conflict. *Psychological Reports, 74*, 115–123.

Carlson, D. S. & Perrewe, P. L. (1999). The role of social support in the stressor-strain relationship: An examination of work-family conflict. *Journal of Management, 25*, 513–540.

Clark, S. C. (2001). Work cultures and work/family balance. *Journal of Vocational Behavior, 58*, 348–365.

Dwyer, D. J. & Fox, M. L. (2000). The moderating role of hostility in the relationship between enriched jobs and health. *Academy of Management Journal, 43*, 1086–1096.

Eby, L. T., Casper, W. J., Lockwood, A., Bordeaux, C. & Brinley, A. (2005). Work and family research in IO/OB: Content analysis and review of the literature (1980–2002). *Journal of Vocational Behavior, 66*, 124–197.

Folkman, S. & Lazarus, R. S. (1985). If it changes it must be a process: Study of emotion and coping during three stages of a college examination. *Journal of Personality and Social-Psychology, 48*, 150–170.

Folkman, S. & Lazarus, R. S. (1988). The relationship between coping and emotion: Implications for theory and research. *Social Science and Medicine, 26*, 309–317.

Folkman, S. & Moskowitz, J. T. (2004). Coping: Pitfalls and promise. *Annual Review of Psychology, 55*, 745–774.

Frone, M. R., Russell, M. & Cooper, M. L. (1992). Prevalence of work and family conflict: Are work and family boundaries asymmetrically permeable? *Journal of Organizational Behavior, 13*, 723–729.

Glass, J. L. & Finley, A. (2002). Coverage and effectiveness of family-responsive workplace policies. *Human Resource Management Review, 12*, 313–337.

Goff, S. J., Mount., M. K. & Jamison, R. L. (1990). Employer supported childcare, work/family conflict, and absenteeism: A field study. *Personnel Psychology, 43*, 793–809.

Grover, S. L. & Crooker, K. J. (1995). Who appreciates family-responsive human resource policies: The impact of family-friendly policies on the organizational attachment of parents and non-parents. *Personnel Psychology, 48*, 271–288.

Hall, D. T. (1972). A model of coping with role conflict: The role behavior of college educated women. *Administrative Science Quarterly, 17*, 471–489.

Hammer, L. B. & Barbera, K. M. (1997). Towards an integration of alternative work. *Human Resource Planning, 20*, 28–36.

Hammer, L. B., Neal, M. B., Newsom, J. T., Brockwood, K. J. & Colton, C. L. (2005). A longitudinal study of the effects of dual-career couples on the utilization of family-friendly workplace supports on work and family outcomes. *Journal of Applied Psychology, 90*, 799–810.

Havlovic, S. J. & Keenan, J. P. (1991). Coping with work stress: The influence of individual differences. *Journal of Social Behavior and Personality, 6*, 199–212.

Kaitz, M. (1985). Role conflict resolution for women with infants. *Birth Psychology Bulletin, 6*, 10–20.

Kanter, L. H. (1977). Can women think? *Transactional Analysis Journal, 7*, 251–252.

Kirchmeyer, C. (1993). Non-work to work spillover: A more balanced view of the experiences and coping of professional women and men. *Sex Roles, 28*, 531–552.

Koeske, G. F., Kirk, S. A. & Koeske, R. D. (1993). Coping with job stress: Which strategies work best? *Journal of Occupational and Organizational Psychology, 66*, 1–17.

Kofodimos, J. R. (1995) *Beyond Work-family Programs: Confronting and Resolving the Underlying Causes of Work-Personal Life Conflict*. Greensboro, NC: Center for Creative Leadership.

Kossek, E. E. & Nichol, V. (1992). The effects of on-site child care on employee attitudes and performance. *Personnel Psychology, 45*, 485–509.

Lazarus, R. S. (1991). *Emotion and Adaptation*. New York: Oxford University Press.

Lazarus, R. S. & Folkman, S. (1984). *Stress, Appraisal and Coping*. New York: Springer.

Lewis, S. & Cooper, C. L. (1999). The work-family research agenda in changing contexts. *Journal of Occupational Health Psychology, 4*, 382–393.

Lobel, S. A. & Kossek, E. E. (1996). Human resource strategies to support diversity in work and personal lifestyles: Beyond the "family friendly" organization. In E. E. Kossek & S. A. Lobel (eds), *Managing Diversity: Human Resource Strategies for Transforming the Workplace* (pp. 221–243). Cambridge, MA: Blackwell.

Matsui, T., Ohsawa, T. & Onglatco, M. (1995). Work-family conflict and the stress buffering effects of husband support and coping behavior among Japanese married working women. *Journal of Vocational Behavior, 47*, 178–192.

Milkovich, G. T. & Gomez, L. T. (1976). Day care and selected employee work behaviors. *Academy of Management Journal, 19*, 11–115.

Miller, S. (1997). The role of a juggler. In S. Parasuraman & J. Greenhaus (eds), *Integrating Work and Family: Challenges and Choices for a Changing World* (pp. 38–47). Westpoint, CT: Quorum Books.

Neal, M. B., Chapman, N. J., Ingersoll-Dayton, B. & Emlen, A.C. (1993). *Balancing Work and Care-giving for Children, Adults, and Elders.* Newbury Park, CA: Sage.

Parasuraman, S., Greenhaus, J. H. & Granrose, C. S. (1992). Role stressors, social support, and well-being among two-career couples. *Journal of Organizational Behavior, 13*, 339–356.

Parasuraman, S. & Simmers, C. A. (2001). Type of employment, work-family conflict and well-being: A comparative study. *Journal of Organizational Behavior, 22*, 551–568.

Pearlin, L. I. & Schooler, C. (1978). The structure of coping. *Journal of Health and Social Behavior, 19*, 2–21.

Perry-Smith, J. E. & Blum, T. C. (2000). Work-family human resource bundles and perceived organizational performance. *Academy of Management Journal, 43*, 1107–1117.

Pierce, J. L., Newstrom, J. W., Dunham, R. B. & Barber, A. E. (1989). *Alternative Work Schedules.* Boston: Allyn & Bacon.

Powell, G. N. & Graves, L. M. (2003). *Women and Men in Management* (3rd edn). Thousand Oaks, CA: Sage.

Pratt, M. G. & Rosa, J. A. (2003). Transforming work-family conflict into commitment in network marketing organizations. *Academy of Management Journal, 46*, 395–418.

Quick, J. C. & Quick, J. D. (2004). Healthy, happy, productive worker: A leadership challenge. *Organizational Dynamics, 33*, 329–337.

Quick, J. C., Quick, J. D., Nelson, D. L. & Hurrell, J. J. Jr. (1997). *Preventive Stress Management in Organizations.* Washington DC: American Psychological Association.

Reynolds, J. (2003). You can't always get the hours you want: Mismatches between actual and preferred work hours in the U. *Social Forces, 81*, 1171–1199.

Riley, F. & McCloskey, D. W. (1997). Telecommuting as a response to helping people balance work and family. In S. Parasurman & J. H. Greenhaus (eds), *Integrating Work and Family: Challenges and Choices for a Changing World* (pp. 133–142). Westport, CT: Quorum/Greenwood.

Robinson, S. L. (1996). Trust and breach of the psychological contract. *Administrative Science Quarterly, 41*, 574–599.

Rotondo, D. M., Carlson, D. S. & Kincaid, J. F. (2003). Coping with multiple dimensions of work-family conflict. *Personnel Review, 32*, 275–296.

Rousseau, D. M (1998). The "problem" of the psychological contract considered. *Journal of Organizational Behavior, 19*, 665–671.

Scandura, T. A. & Lankau, M. J. (1997). Relationships of gender, family responsibility and flexible work hours to organizational commitment and job satisfaction. *Journal of Organizational Behavior, 18*, 377–391.

Schaufeli, W. B. (2004). The future of occupational health psychology. *Applied Psychology: An International Review, 53*, 502–517.

Scheck, C. L., Kinicki, A. J. & Davy, J. A. (1997). Testing the mediating process between work stressors and subjective well-being. *Journal of Vocational Behavior, 50*, 96–123.

Siegrist, J. & Klein, D. (1990) Occupational stress and cardiovascular reactivity in blue-collar workers. *Work and Stress, 4*, 295–304.

Smith-Crowe, K., Burke, M. J. & Landis, R. S. (2003). Organizational climate as a moderator of safety knowledge–safety performance relationships. *Journal of Organizational Behavior, 24*, 861–876

Somech, A. & Drach-Zahavy, A. (2006). How to balance work-family conflict: Towards context-specific coping strategy taxonomy. Annual Meeting of the Academy of Management, Atlanta.

Somech, A. & Drach-Zahavy, A. (Forthcoming 2007). Strategies for coping with work-family conflict: The distinctive relationships of gender-role ideology. *Journal of Health Psychology.*

Thomas, L. T. & Ganster, D. C. (1995). Impact of family-supportive work variables on work and family conflict and strain: A control perspective. *Journal of Applied Psychology, 80*, 6–15.

Thompson, C. A., Beauvais, L. L. & Lyness, K. S. (1999). When work-family benefits are not enough: The influence of work-family culture on benefit utilization, organizational attachment, and work-family conflict. *Journal of Vocational Behavior, 54*, 392–415.

Thompson, C. A., Poelmans, S. A. Y., Allen, T. D. & Andreassi, J. K. (Forthcoming 2007). On the importance of coping: A model and new directions for research on work and family. In P. L. Perrewe & D. C. Ganster (eds), *Research in Occupational Stress and We-being*, Vol. 6.

Veiga, J. F., Baldridge, D. C. & Eddelson, K. A. (2004). Toward understanding employee reluctance to participate in family-friendly programs. *Human Resource Management Review, 14*, 337–351.

Warr, P. (1994). A conceptual framework for the study of work and mental health. *Work and Stress, 8*, 84–97.

Wright, T. A. (2003). Positive organizational behavior: An idea whose time has truly come. *Journal of Organizational Behavior, 24*, 437–442.

Wright, T. A. & Cropanzano, R. (2000). Psychological well-being and job satisfaction as predictors of job performance. *Journal of Occupational Health Psychology, 5*, 84–94.

CHAPTER 16

Social Support and Work-Family Conflict

Roya Ayman and Amy Antani

Institute of Psychology, Illinois Institute of Technology

When I am talking about "It Takes a Village," I'm obviously not talking just about or even primarily about geographical villages any longer, but about the network of relationships and values that do connect us and binds us together.

Hillary Rodham Clinton

In this millennium, men and women are confronted with complexities and uncertainty which are unprecedented in our society. They are encouraged to reach for their dreams and contribute to society in the arts, sciences, and industry, yet they are also expected to manage their responsibilities as parents and caregivers. In past centuries in most societies, the responsibility of work and family was divided by gender, where the men were responsible for the affairs outside of the house and the women managed the family affairs. These traditional divisions of labor are no longer the status quo. Therefore, men and women in the workplace are faced with the added stress of multiple roles and the interface of various domains in their lives.

In situations characterized by such high intensity of pressure, uncertainty, and overload, the need for buffers, coping mechanisms, and support systems increases. In collectivistic societies, where the existence of extended family prevails, the natural mode of conduct for managing these demands is the active engagement of the family and friends' social support. However, in individualistic societies where adults are expected to be self-sufficient and the nuclear family is the unit of society, the presence and use of sources of social support is not clear. As our societies become more multicultural and roles of parenting and working are not defined by gender, learning from across cultures and exploring various effective strategies and mechanisms of coping with this complex lifestyle is of great value. Therefore, the importance of social support in the lives of working parents and caregivers is the topic of this chapter.

The following is an example of how in today's society a professional woman copes with the multiple demands in her life. In a metropolitan area in the US 20 years ago, a married woman of 25 had a child, was getting a Ph.D., was working, and had a working husband. Many were at awe of how she managed her life as an active academician and professional, with many family and civic responsibilities.

Handbook of Work-Family Integration: Research, Theory, and Best Practices

Her secret was an effective use of her social support network. She decided to live where she had a group of five friends who had children of similar age. They created a pact which allowed each to work and care for their children. Each family was responsible for childcare one day a week and for cooking food for all families once a week. This arrangement provided the children with safe and familiar environments and the families were eating warm, homemade food from different ethnicities every evening. This system continued until the children started elementary school. This network of professional families became an extended family of each couple and transcended childcare in later years. Not only did this allow them to manage both work and care for children, it also created a bond among them. As they have gotten older, they have become each others' support in taking care of their aging parents and the loss of their parents.

In this chapter we review the scientific literature to define social support and the various sources of support. Subsequently, evidence is presented regarding the role that social support plays in the work-family interface and its consequences for the work and nonwork domains of life. Throughout, variances attributed to individual differences are also highlighted.

SOCIAL SUPPORT

The importance of social support in our society is evidenced by the prevalence of research on its nature and its role in people's lives. Busy workers with multiple roles, who are trying to meet numerous expectations, seem to find refuge in one form of support or another through various individuals in their social networks. With the number of dual-career families and single parents increasing, the level of stress in the typical worker's life is also intensified. The better social support is understood, the more guidance and alternatives can be provided to the stressed worker of today.

Independent of the work-family research, in stress models social support has been identified as an important coping mechanism that can reduce the negative effects of stressors (Gore, 1987; Kahn & Byosiere, 1991; Thomas & Ganster, 1995). Although there is no single, accepted definition of social support within the occupational stress literature, there is growing consensus that social support can come from both work and nonwork sources and that this support is primarily in the form of either emotional support or instrumental support (Adams, King & King, 1996; Beehr & McGrath, 1992; Gore, 1987; Kahn & Byosiere, 1991; Kaufmann & Beehr, 1986; Thomas & Ganster, 1995). However, the exact nature of the effect of social support on strains is unclear (Carlson & Perrewe, 1999; Ganster, Fusilier & Mayes, 1986; House, 1981; Kahn & Byosiere, 1991; Thoits, 1982). In the following section, presentation of the various definitions of social support is followed by an overview of the sources of support and the types of support provided. The use of support across gender and ethnicity is briefly discussed particularly as it relates to work-family conflict (WFC). Finally a discussion of the effect of social support on work-family and organizational outcomes will follow.

DEFINITIONS OF SOCIAL SUPPORT AND THEIR RELATION TO WORK-FAMILY CONFLICT

Gottlieb noted the proliferation of social support definitions or concepts when stating, "with each new study a new definition of support surfaces" (1983, p. 50). In conjunction with the various definitions, researchers have tailored measures to specifically focus on the new definition. However, underlying the various concepts of social support, three categories can be identified: social embeddedness, enactment of support, and perception of social support (Barrera, 1986). For each category various approaches to operationalization and measurement are noted in the following section.

SOCIAL EMBEDDEDNESS OR SOCIAL NETWORK

The first category has been referred to as social network resources (Vaux & Harrison, 1983; Vaux, Phillips, Holly, Thomson, Williams & Stewart, 1986), or social embeddedness (Barrera, 1986). Both terms refer to the connections that individuals have to significant others in their social environment. The first approach to assessing social embeddedness uses broad indicators of the presence of social ties (such as marital status, participation in community organizations, and contact with friends) as proxies for support. Although these indicators are not direct measures of social support, they are used with the rationale that available social ties could potentially serve as social support resources (Barrera, 1986).

The second approach to assess social embeddedness utilizes social network analysis. This involves procedures for identifying individuals who have important relationships or ties with the focal subject, determined by self-report. Methods are employed to characterize the structural properties of networks such as density (which identifies the number of network members each member knows), balance or reciprocity of the relationship, closeness, complexity, frequency of interaction, and the nature of the relationship (e.g., husband, friend) (Barrera, 1986; d' Abbs, 1982). However, just examining this component is misleading. As Wellman (1981) pointed out, when social network analysis identifies important social relationships, it is erroneous to assume that all such linkages involve the provisions of social support. Furthermore, not all linkages are voluntary, such as a possible relationship between two co-workers. They may rely upon one another for business purposes; however their "twosome" is not necessarily reciprocal or egalitarian. Finally, most social network analysis research restricts the examination to important relationships, ignoring the variability of the strength of supportive ties (Wellman, 1981).

SUPPORT ENACTMENT

This conceptualization of support involves actions that others perform when they render assistance to a focal person, known as enacted support (Barrera, 1986; Tardy, 1985). These specific supportive acts (Vaux et al., 1983; Vaux et al., 1986) were referred to as "enacted" support (Tardy, 1985) to distinguish them from "available" support that is measured by scales of perceived availability and even some measures of social embeddedness. Measures of enacted social support complement other measures by assessing what individuals actually *do* when they provide support (Barrera, 1986). Many of the typologies of social support are focused on these specific supportive acts. These acts could include childcare, or career advice, or they could include carefully listening to a person's troubles and sympathizing with their challenges or being joyful for their achievements.

PERCEIVED SOCIAL SUPPORT

This involves a subjective appraisal of support (Vaux et al., 1983; Vaux et al., 1986) and characterizes social support as the cognitive appraisal of being connected to others. In other words, there is a perception or belief that one is cared for, involved, respected, and has one's social needs met by others (Vaux et al., 1986). This is the most commonly used measure of support in research.

Measures of perceived social support incorporate two dimensions: perceived availability and adequacy of supportive ties (Holahan & Moos, 1981; Procidano & Heller, 1983; Turner et al., 1983). The goal is to capture the individual's belief that support would be available or accessible if it was needed or to characterize an environment as helpful or cohesive (Barrera, 1986). The availability of supportive ties includes looking at the number of ties in a social network and the frequency of contact with network members (Wellman, 1981). Some instruments focus solely on the perceived adequacy or satisfaction with support, as an alternative indicator of perceived support (e.g., Barrera, 1981; Sarason, Levine, Basham & Sarason, 1983). Although an important subjective appraisal, support satisfaction is a limited representation of the support appraisal construct (Vaux et al., 1986).

THE CONTENT OF SUPPORT

The above conceptualization of social support concentrated on the general nature of support. Some researchers have focused on the content of support, that is, the nature of what the support involves. The typologies proposed range from a simple duality of instrumental and emotional support (Pattison, 1977) to a categorization that encompasses four categories—directive guidance, nondirective support, positive social interaction, and tangible assistance (Barrera & Ainlay, 1983). However, common amongst the various typologies are the two main dimensions proposed early on by Pattison (1977)—instrumental support and emotional support. While different researchers have attached different labels, this duality of instrumental (i.e., tangible support) and socioemotional support has received empirical validation (King, Mattimore, King & Adams, 1995). Instrumental support is characterized by rendering of actual assistance, for example loaning money, babysitting, or help with a task. Emotional support is exemplified by sympathetic and caring behaviors.

SOURCES OF SUPPORT

Underlying all discussions of social support, emotional or instrumental, is the issue of the source of support; from whom is the focal person receiving the support? This is certainly an important question because different populations may rely on or benefit from different sources of support to different extents (Procidano & Heller, 1983).

For a working professional, it is well established that support can come from both work and nonwork sources (e.g., Adams et al., 1996; Beehr, 1995; King et al., 1995). The distinct sources that have been endorsed by many investigators are the supervisor, co-workers, and friends or family (e.g., Caplan, Cobb, French, Harrison & Pinneau, 1975; Kaufmann & Beehr, 1985; King et al., 1995), as well as support from the organization (Rhoades & Eisenberger, 2002) through policies and programs available.

WORK-RELATED SOURCES

The results of the studies on the relationship between support from work sources, such as supervisor/superior and co-workers, and stress have reached contradictory conclusions. Co-workers can provide social support by acting as confidants and giving advice about stressful work situations. They also provide information and help with work issues directly (Buunk & Verhoeven, 1991; Henderson & Argyle, 1985). The support received can reduce the stress directly or serve as a buffer. Work relationships may, however, in themselves be a source of stress (Argyle & Henderson, 1985; Buunk & Verhoeven, 1991). With supervisors and colleagues, a professional relationship exists in which individuals may not feel free to disclose feelings that might make them appear incompetent. In this situation, receiving help may increase stress as it threatens self-esteem and possible feelings of indebtedness on the part of the recipient (Buunk & Verhoeven, 1991; Hatfield & Sprecher, 1983). Recently, Hammer, Kossek, Zimmerman and Daniels

(2007) presented a multilevel conceptual model representing a system of support that is provided and perceived within the workplace.

Another area of literature that has focused on perceived social support related to the workplace is the research related to perceived organizational support (POS). This construct measures an employee's perception of the organization's instrumental support in their development and well-being (Eisenberger, Huntington, Hutchison & Sowa, 1986). Parallel to this construct, a measure of perceived supervisory support (PSS) was also developed (Kottke & Sharafinski, 1988). This defines the global perception of employees regarding the degree to which their supervisors value their contributions and care about their well-being (Eisenberger, Stinglhamber, Vandenberghe, Sucharski & Rhoades, 2002). Similar to PSS, the measurement of leader member exchange (LMX) is a measure of leadership supportive behavior. Although theoretically LMX refers to the quality of the exchange in a leader-employee dyad, based on emotional support and the exchange of valued resources (Graen & Uhl-Bien, 1995), it is measured in terms of the subordinate's perception of the leader's instrumental support and loyalty.

Although the supervisor acts as an agent of the organization, the supervisor and the organization should not be considered synonymous with one another. Therefore, it is important to the measurement of supervisor support that an employee is able to discriminate between the supervisor and the organization as sources of support. In other words, these must be perceived as two separate sources of support. In a study examining the construct validities of POS and PSS, Hutchinson (1997) found that the POS measure provided a unidimensional construct that is unique from PSS. Additionally, he also reported that POS provided a unique contribution to outcome measures from that of PSS. A study by Yoon and Lim (1999) also reported factor analytic evidence confirming the distinctiveness of supervisor support from organizational support. Correspondingly, Rhoades and Eisenberger (2002) in their meta-analysis reported a moderate relationship between supervisor support and POS. These studies provide evidence that employees distinguish between supervisors as support agents of the organization and the organization itself. In addition, Hammer et al. (2007) recently developed a more comprehensive supervisory behavior measure. The family supportive supervisory behavior (FSSB) focused on the supervisor's supportive behaviors to assist in creating work-family balance within the life of an employee.

Co-worker support is a relatively new concept, following the research that supervisors are agents of support. Researchers in this area have recognized the fact that support from co-workers also would impact organizational outcomes (Ladd & Henry, 2000; Sherony & Green, 2000; Yoon & Lim, 1999). The construct and measure have been developed based on the content of the existing constructs for perceived supervisor support and leader member exchange.

Perceived co-worker support (PCS) (Ladd & Henry, 2000) is a construct similar to perceived supervisor support and perceived organizational support; that is, PCS is the global belief employees have regarding the degree to which their co-workers value their contributions and care about their well-being (Ladd & Henry, 2000). At the same time this research also substantiates that employees are able to distinguish co-workers from other sources of support. Research in this area provided evidence of a moderate positive correlation between co-worker support and organizational support (Ladd & Henry, 2000; Yoon & Lim, 1999). In addition, this same research also reported factor analytic evidence of perceived co-worker support and perceived organizational support that indicated a clear distinction between the measurements of the two constructs.

Recently, there has been some investigation of the role of co-worker support in the work-family literature (see Warner, Slan-Jerusalim & Korabik, 2007, for a review). Co-worker support has been found to have significant effects on WFC in some studies, but to have no direct effect in others (Warner et al., 2007). These mixed results could be due to the way that co-worker support has been measured. Because there is currently no existing measure of perceived co-worker support specifically for work-family issues, general measures, like the PCS, have been used.

NONWORK-RELATED SOURCES

Social support from family has received less attention than work-related sources of social support in organizational stress literature (Adams et al., 1996). Most of the studies have operationalized nonwork support sources as a combined reference to "family and friends" and have focused on family-related stress (Adams et al., 1996). Social support from family and friends has been more strongly associated with general health and well-being and moderately associated with work-related strains. Family social support has been found to reduce the experience of stress in the family domain, such as marital-related stress (Bernas & Major, 2000; Phillips-Miller, Campbell & Morrison, 2000). In one study that did examine nonwork sources of social support separately, Kaufmann and Beehr (1989) reported that emotional support from family and friends was significantly related to job satisfaction, boredom, and depression. Family members have a unique opportunity to provide both emotional and instrumental support to the worker outside of the work environment (Adams et al., 1996).

WORK AND FAMILY SUPPORT ACROSS DOMAINS

Past research has generally studied the effect of within domain support for reducing the stress in that domain (e.g., Kauffmann & Bheer, 1986). However, it has also been noted that supportive ties in one domain may be those from which a person needs support in another domain (Wellman, 1981), such as utilizing support from co-workers for family issues or family support for work issues. As an illustrative example, an employee may come to work and seek advice or guidance from co-workers about a problem at home. Reciprocally, an employee may go home and vent to their spouse about issues at work. Anecdotally, this seems to be a common phenomenon, yet it is not well researched.

In response to this void, several studies have been conducted on the effect of received support or perceived support from work-related sources to assist with work-family conflict (Allen, 2001; Antani & Ayman, 2004; Casper, Martin, Boufardi & Erdwins, 2002; Hammer Neal, Newson, Brockwood & Colton, 2005; O'Driscoll et al., 2003). Except for Hammer et al. (2005) and Hammer et al. (2007), in most of these studies variations on Eisenberger et al.'s (1986) perceived organizational support measure were used. Allen (2001) adjusted the POS measure to focus on assisting work-family balance. Additionally, Hammer et al. (2007) included support received from the supervisor. Also, in their study Hammer et al. (2005) operationalized organizational support as both available and used.

Antani and Ayman (2004) examined both the domain-specific and the cross-domain instrumental and emotional support that was received from various work and nonwork sources. Thus, in their investigations respondents were asked to identify the sources that had provided support both within and across the domain from which the conflict or stress was occurring. Furthermore, for each domain, work, or family, statements were presented to respondents that were either instrumental or emotional in nature for that domain. For example, an instrumental support item for the work domain was, "When my job gets demanding, I can count on extra work responsibilities to be taken care of by …." An example of an emotional support item for the work domain was, "I receive encouragement about my work and career from…" An example of an instrumental support item for the family domain was, "I get help with the daily details of running a house from …" Finally, an example of an emotional support item for the family domain was, "When I am upset about family and friends, concern is expressed by …" There were two or three items for each of these types of support and domains resulting in a total of 17 statements.

The respondents identified the sources from whom they received support for each of these 17 items or stems. The sources included in the study were supervisor, co-workers, family, and friends. Ratings of the frequency of received support were made on a scale ranging from 1 to 5, where 1 = never, 5 = always and "not applicable" was coded as 0. An advantage of this measure is that the sources can be varied based on the culture of the respondents, but the item stems can stay the same. Furthermore, the items represented both types of support and support for both domains in a symmetrical format. This allows for an empirical examination of the similarities and differences of support for the two domains and the effects of various sources.

Anatani and Ayman's (2004) results indicated that the greatest use of support was from family members for both work and nonwork domain issues. Surprisingly, they also found that the more workers received support from their supervisors for family domain issues and the more they received support from their co-workers for work domain issues, the higher their family interference with work conflict (FIW). Because their data were concurrent in nature, the direction of causality is unclear. Therefore, one possible explanation is that when supervisors provide support for family issues and co-workers provide support for work issues, the fact that their families are interfering with their work lives is more salient to the workers who are receiving the support. Alternatively, it could be that when workers are experiencing stress at home (i.e., greater FIW) they look to their supervisors to make allowances for their family problems and to their co-workers to help them manage their work. An example of this would be a man who is experiencing a family situation (e.g., a divorce, or a child or spouse with a serious illness) that interferes with his ability to cope with his job responsibilities (i.e., high levels of FIW). As a result, his supervisor may provide support by being understanding of his family situation and his co-workers may provide support by helping with his workload. The more support the man receives, the more salient his family situation and how it is interfering with his work life will be to him, leading him to report high levels of FIW.

INDIVIDUAL DIFFERENCES AND SOCIAL SUPPORT

Studies examining individual differences and social support are very few. The results of these studies have shown that regardless of the type of social support, the differences due to the person's gender and ethnicity are very small. However, the subtle differences often do have practical and meaningful implications. For example, Antani and Ayman (2004), similar to Griffin, Amodeo, Clay, Fassler and Ellis (2006), found that white and African-American women did not significantly differ in the family support for family issues they received. However, within the family domain, African-American women reported significantly less social support from their co-workers, supervisor, and friends. Although neither group reported high frequency of support for family issues from these sources, white women were more likely to report support from these sources than African-American women. The effect of ethnicity on social support, therefore, seems to depend on the source of support and the domain in which support is received, further demonstrating the complexity of the construct.

Additionally, social values seem to play a role in the use of and experience with social support. Values and competencies such as low technical competency, exchange orientation, gender-role orientation, and dependence/independence have been studied to differentiate cultural and gender differences in preference for support. For example, in situations of limited competency or access to technological support and assistance, instrumental support is more appreciated (Pine, Ben-Ari, Utas & Larson, 2002). Also, Buunk, JanDoosje, Jans and Hopstaken (1993) concluded that individuals with a high exchange orientation were least happy when they did not receive social support. However, low exchange oriented individuals were not affected by the support they received. Similarly, Bheer, Farmer, Glazer, Gudanowski and Nair (2003) found that individuals high on femininity reported more strain and stress than those who were low on femininity. However, they concluded that if the stress emanates from the same source as the support, then perhaps the type of support becomes more relevant. To clarify this further, the findings of Nagurney, Reich and Newson (2004) showed that men with a high desire for independence responded negatively to social support, whereas women, regardless of their desire for independence or dependence, responded positively to support. Therefore, groups of individuals who are independent and noncommunal seem to benefit less from social support, in contrast to those who are communal. Those who are independent may even feel stressed when they receive support.

In the family domain, there is a general belief that wives receive less support than husbands. However, empirical evidence provides mixed results. Self-report studies show that wives report engaging in more supportive behaviors than husbands (e.g., Cutrona, 1996, as cited in Neff & Karney, 2005). However, observational studies have not shown any gender differences in the skill for providing support (e.g., Pasch, Bradbury & Davila, 1997; Roberts & Greenberg, 2002, as cited in Neff & Karney, 2005). Neff and Karney (2005) argue that past research, particularly observational studies, did not consider the context of the support. Examining wives' and husbands' diaries, their results showed that although men and women both may know how to give support, wives were better than husbands in giving support when the husband needed it. This study may be a further demonstration of potential gender differences in the ability to notice and respond to the subtle cues given by others and the ability to provide support. Nonetheless, with dual-career couples, the need for support regarding stress in both domains of life is heightened. These gender differences in empathy and timeliness in providing support can become a source of further stress.

THE ROLE OF SOCIAL SUPPORT IN THE RELATIONSHIP BETWEEN WORK-FAMILY CONFLICT AND ITS OUTCOMES

Four models have been identified to explain the role of social support in a stress-strain relationship, with a focus on work-family conflict (see Carlson & Perrewe, 1999; Cohen & Wills, 1985; Viswesvaran, Sanchez & Fisher, 1999). First, social support may act as an antecedent to WFC. Second, social support may act as a direct antecedent to strain. Third, social support may mediate the relationship between WFC and strain. Fourth, social support may be a moderator of the relationship between WFC and strain.

The evidence for the direct effect of social support on stress is well substantiated (Carlson & Perrewe, 1999; Fisher, 1985; Schaubroeck, Cotton & Jennings, 1989; Sullivan & Bhagat, 1992). Individuals who perceive themselves to have strong social support networks, may be less likely to perceive demands in their environment as stressors (Cohen & Wills, 1985). Wheaton (1985) also argued that support resources are mobilized when stressors are encountered.

Research suggests that perceived levels of organizational support have a negative relationship with WFC (Allen, 2001; Thompson & Pottas, 2005). Specifically, Behson (2002) demonstrated that among other organizational activities the perception of support from the organization can reduce work interference with family (WIF). It should be noted that in O'Driscoll, Poelmans, Spector, Kalliath, Allen, Cooper & Sanchez's (2003) study of New Zealand managers, the availability of family-friendly organizational policies did not relate to WFC, but perceived support did. Furthermore, Adams et al. (1996) demonstrated a reciprocal relationship between family support and WFC, where higher levels of WIF increased family support and higher levels of family support increased family interference with work (FIW).

In addition, many studies have shown the direct relationship of social support with strains within a domain. For example, studies have shown that perceived organizational support is related to high organizational commitment, high satisfaction, and lower turnover (Eisenberger et al., 2002; Harrick, Vanek & Michlitsch, 1986; Rhoades & Eisenberger, 2002; Schaffer, Harrison, Gilley & Luk, 2001; Thierry & Meijman, 1994; Thompson & Pottas, 2005). Thompson, Jahn, Kopelman and Pottas (2004) conducted a longitudinal study, which demonstrated that informal organizational family support increased retention possibilities and organizational commitment. In another longitudinal study, women were more likely to report commitment and intention to stay when they received support from the organization (Martin, Buffardi & Erdwins, 2002). Grover and Crooker (1995) also found support for relationships between organizational family support and higher commitment and lower intention to quit among employees; they further mentioned that the relationship found was stronger for intention to quit than for commitment.

On the other hand, in O'Driscoll et al.'s (2003) study of New Zealand managers, the availability of family-friendly organizational policies did not relate to psychological strain, but perceived support did. Additionally, Baruch-Feldman, Brondolo, Ben-Dayan and Schwartz (2002) found that organizational family support was related to burnout more than to job satisfaction and productivity, whereas supervisor support was more related to job satisfaction and productivity than to burnout. This array of results, although overall demonstrating a strong relationship between support and strain, also presents evidence that variance in the definition of each variable may or may not substantiate this relationship.

In summary, there is evidence that, overall, social support is strongly related to decreased strain and WFC and that WFC is positively related to strain. Due to this, there are two potential mediating models that could be considered. In Frone, Yardley and Markel's (1997) integrative model, social support was identified as a precursor to WFC. However, most empirical research on the relationship between social support and WFC has primarily been concurrent, so the direction of this relationship is not clear. With this in mind, one model could be that social support results in lower WFC, which can lead to less strain. An alternative model could be that once WFC is experienced, it leads to activation of social support, which should reduce strain. To clarify which of these models is more accurate, more longitudinal studies are needed. Also, in future studies researchers may want to consider the measure of social support employed (i.e., use, availability, or satisfaction of social support) as each of these may have a different contribution in the role of social support in the relationship between WFC and strain.

The last model to be considered is social support as a moderator of WFC and strain. The research on social support as a moderator in the stressor-strain has yielded inconsistent results (Ganster, Fusilier & Mayes, 1986; Gore, 1978; LaRocco, House & French, 1980; Viswesvaran et al., 1999). Whereas some studies have found moderating effects (e.g., Abdul-Halim, 1982; Viswesvaran et al., 1999; Witt & Carlson, 2006), others have not (e.g., Carlson & Perrewe, 1999; Ganster, Fusilier & Mayes, 1986; Haar, 2004), or have found support for a reverse or opposite moderating effect (e.g., Kaufmann & Beehr, 1986). A reverse moderating effect is found when high levels of support exacerbate rather than alleviate the effects of stressors on strains.

IMPLICATIONS FOR FUTURE RESEARCH AND PRACTICE

In this chapter we have reviewed the existing knowledge on social support and its relation to work-family conflict. It was demonstrated that while the position of and nature of the role of social support has been researched, they have not been clearly established. Among the many factors it seems that the nature of the strain under investigation matters. Three issues seem to govern the study of social support and work-family conflict: (1) the role that social support plays; (2) the operationalization of support, and (3) the nature of the strain.

The variety of operationalizations of social support reviewed in this chapter reflect its complexity and can also provide a caveat for researchers. In this chapter we discussed the potential ways social support can be measured, sources of support, and types of support. Thus, the study of the effects only of one source, one type or definition of support, or support from and within one domain can be misleading. Most measures of social support focus on within domain support, such as perceived organizational support, or supervisor support for work interference with family and its effect on work-related outcomes. In addition, some of these measures focus more on instrumental support rather than on both emotional and instrumental support. For example, perceived organizational and supervisor support, in addition to being domain specific, are primarily focused on instrumental support. This assessment is not a general criticism of the construct of perceived organizational or supervisory support, but a demonstration of its limitation when used in work-family conflict research. It is important to develop a measure representing a mix of sources, domains, and types of support.

The past studies on social support seem to show higher validity for subjective evaluations of support than for objective evaluations (Solomon, Mikulincer & Hobfoll, 1987). This may be considered as evidence that subjective measures are more effective. However, from a phenomenological perspective, it can be inferred that scholars are relying heavily on same source data, where the information about the social support evaluation and the experience of work- family conflict is gathered from the same person. Such studies would result in evidence of inflated relationships amongst variables.

Although multisource studies are ideal, in research related to stress and social support another option is to use more than one definition of support. For example, it could be that a number of support sources can relate to perceived support that together predict lower experience of work-family conflict. This added information can assist in development of the concept and implementation.

In addition, we recommend that the measure of social support used in WFC focuses specifically on support for work-family balance. Moreover, items from sources in both the work and nonwork domains should be represented. This will allow testing the fluidity of or rigidity of domain boundaries providing social support. In addition to representing both domains, the items should have a balance of emotional and instrumental support for each of these domains. Antani and Ayman (2004) have designed such an instrument to assess received support as explained earlier in this chapter. They were able to partially validate this measure of social support and its relationship with WFC.

By examining which particular work and family sources of support are related to the reduction of WIF and FIW, researchers can determine whether the support sources are domain specific or can cross domains. Certain permutations, for example a work supervisor helping with daily family chores, may seem very improbable. But, what if the supervisor permits you to come to work a half-hour late knowing that you have to drop off your child at 8:30 every morning? Would this not demonstrate the supervisor's support? Conducting empirical tests will allow for evidence to be gathered to examine the frequency of such occurrences.

From a practical perspective, the topic of social support in relation to work-family conflict is informative to individuals and organizations. From an individual standpoint, it is important that people who have active multiple domains of their lives also have large and diverse support networks. This can provide them with support that they need to feel affirmed and use when needed. Experienced co-workers may be able to provide wisdom and alternatives for managing and balancing between domains of life. Thus, although they are work sources of support, their advice may be more helpful, informative, and comforting than that of friends and family. Varied sources will provide different alternatives which can then help the person have a wider perspective regarding various options.

For example, a young woman from a traditional family may not feel support from her family to continue her career endeavors. However, a supportive manager and co-workers may provide her with empowering and informative recommendations or advice. Because of her family's traditional values, she may not get a supportive response when sharing work challenges, causing her further stress and weakening her confidence. On the other hand, a supportive work environment would consider the challenges and present her with understanding, time-management, available resources, and potentially alternative work schedules.

Therefore, organizations and managers have a responsibility in assisting their workforce to balance their work and family demands. Examining options for managing work is not new and requires courage and creativity in policy formulation at the organizational level (see Chapter 20 in this volume). The role of managers at all levels in the organization is crucial to the implementation of such policies and in providing access to various available programs.

In conclusion, the role of men and women in our society is changing and both genders are expected to be active in the work and family domains. This is by far a much more demanding situation than in the past, when the maintenance of the domains was primarily dedicated to one or the other gender. In this new evolution of our society, the two domains of life are no longer gender-typed and segregated. Men and women both can be involved and are expected to spend time in both the family and work domains, roles are not clear and require a set of norms unique to each couple. Consultation and social negotiation at all levels is needed as the responsibilities are not preset. To sustain the balance of work and family, not only do men and women need to be supportive of each other, but organizations and the various social agencies in the community also need to be developed to support this complex relationship.

REFERENCES

Abdul-Harim, A. A. (1982). Social support and managerial affective responses to job stress. *Journal of Occupational Behavior, 6*, 273–288.

Adams, G. A., King, L. A. & King, D. W. (1996). Relationships of job involvement and family involvement, family social support, and work-family conflict with job and life satisfaction. *Journal of Applied Psychology, 81*, 411–420.

Allen, T. D. (2001). Family supportive work environment: The role of organizational perceptions. *Journal of Vocational Behavior, 58*, 414–435.

Anderson, S. E., Coffey, B. S. & Byerly, R. T. (2002). Formal organizational onitiatives and informal workplace practices: Links to work-family conflict and job-related outcomes. *Journal of Management, 28*, 787–810.

Antani, A. & Ayman, R. (April, 2003). Gender, social support and the experience of work-family conflict. Paper presented at European Academy of Management, Milan, Italy.

Antani, A. & Ayman, R. (April, 2004). The relationship of ethnicity with social support and work-family conflict. Poster presented at the annual meeting of the Society for Industrial/Organizational Psychology, Chicago, IL.

Argyle, M. & Henderson, M. (1985). *The Anatomy of Relationships*. London: Heinemann.

Barrera Jr., M. (1981). Social support in the adjustment of pregnant adolescents: Assessment issues. In B. H. Gottlieb (ed.), *Social Networks and Social Support* (pp. 69–96). Beverly Hills: Sage.

Barrera Jr., M. (1986). Distinctions between social support concepts, measures, and models. *Journal of Community Psychology, 14*(4), 413–445.

Barrera, Jr., M. & Ainlay, S. L. (1983). The structure of social support: A conceptual and empirical analysis. *Journal of Community Psychology, 11*, 133–143.

Baruch-Feldman, C., Brondolo, E., Ben-Dayan, D. & Schwartz, J. (2002). Sources of social support and burnout, job satisfaction, and productivity. *Journal of Occupational Health Psychology, 7*(1), 84–93.

Beehr, T. A. (1985). The role of social support in coping with organizational stress. In T. A. Beehr & R. S. Bhagat (eds), *Human Stress and Cognition in Organizations: An Integrated Perspective* (pp. 375–398). New York: Wiley.

Beehr, T. A. Farmer, S. J., Glazer, S. Gudanowski, D. M. & Nair, V. W. (2003). The enigma of social support and occupational stress: Source congruence and gender role effects. *Journal of Occupational Health Psychology, 8*, 222–231.

Beehr, T. A. & McGrath, J. E. (1992). Social support, occupational stress and anxiety. *Anxiety, Stress, and Coping, 5*, 7–19.

Behson, S. J. (2002). Coping with family-to-work conflict: The role of informal work accommodations to family. *Journal of Occupational Health Psychology, 7*(4), 324. Retrieved January 21, 2007, from PsycARTICLES database. (Document ID: 243832191).

Bernas, K. H. & Major, D. A. (2000). Contributors to stress resistance: Testing a model of women's work-family conflict. *Psychology of Women Quarterly, 24*, 170–178.

Boyar, S. L., Maertz, Jr., C. P. & Pearson, A. W. (2005). The effects of work-family conflict and family-work conflict on nonattendance behaviors. *Journal of Business Research, 58*, 919–925.

Boyar, S. L., Maertz Jr., C. P., Pearson, A. W. & Keough, S. (2003). Work-family conflict: A model of linkages between work and family domain variables and turnover intentions. *Journal of Managerial Issues, 15*, 175–190.

Buunk, B. P., Jan Doosje, B., Jans, L. G. J. M. & Hopstaken, L.E. M. (1993). Perceived reciprocity of social support and stress at work: The role of exchange and communal orientation. *Journal of Personality and Social Psychology, 65*, 801–811.

Buunk, B. P. & Verhoeven, K. (1991). Companionship and support at work: A microanalysis of the stress-reducing features of social interaction. *Basic and Applied Social Psychology, 12*(3), 243–258.

Caplan, R. D., Cobb, S., French, J. R. P., Harrison, R. V. & Pinneau, S. R. Jr. (1975). *Job Demands and Worker Health*. Washington, DC: H.E.W. Publication No. NIOSH 75-160.

Carlson, D. S. & Perrewe, P. L. (1999). The role of social support in the stressor-strain relationship: An examination of work-family conflict. *Journal of Management, 25*(4), 513–540.

Casper, W. J., Martin, J. A., Buffardi, L. C. & Erdwins, C. J. (2002). Work–family conflict, perceived organizational support, and organizational commitment among employed mothers. *Journal of Occupational Health Psychology, 7*(2), 99–108.

Cohen, S. & Wills, T. A. (1985). Stress, social support, and the buffering hypothesis. *Psychological Bulletin, 98*, 310–357.

d'Abbs, P. (1982). *Social Support Networks: A Critical Review of Models and Findings*. Melbourne: Institute of Family Studies.

DeBrin, A. (1991). Comparison of the job satisfaction and productivity of telecommuters versus in-house employees: A research note on work in progress. *Psychological Reports, 68*, 1223–1234.

Eisenberger, R. Huntington, R. Hutchinson, S. & Sowa, D. (1986). Perceived organizational support. *Journal of Applied Psychology, 71*, 500–507.

Eisenberger, R., Stinglhamber, F., Vandenberghe, C., Sucharski, I. L. & Rhoades, L. (2002). Perceived supervisor support: Contributions to perceived organizational support and employee retention. *Journal of Applied Psychology, 87*(3), 565–573.

Fisher, C. D. (1985). Social support and adjustment to work. *Journal of Management, 11*, 39–53.

Frone, M. R., Yardley, J. K. & Markel, K. S. (1997). Developing and testing an integrative model of the work-family interface. *Journal of Vocational Behavior, 50*, 145–167.

Ganster, D. C., Fusilier, M. F. & Mayes, B. T. (1986). Role of social support in the experience of stress at work. *Journal of Applied Psychology, 71*(1), 102–110.

Gore, S. (1978). The effect of social support in moderating the health and behavioral consequences of unemployment. *Journal of Health and Social Behavior, 19*, 157–165.

Gore, S. (1987). Perspectives on social support and research on stress moderating processes. In J. M. Ivancevich & D. C. Ganster (eds), *Job Stress: From Theory to Suggestion*. New York: Haworth Press.

Gottlieb, B. H. (1983). *Social Support Strategies: Guidelines for Mental Health Practice*. Beverly Hills: Sage.

Graen, G. B. & Uhl-Bien, M. (1995). Relationship-based approach to leadership: Development of leader-member exchange (LMX) theory of leadership over 25 years: Applying a multilevel domain perspective. *Leadership Quarterly, 6*, 219–247.

Griffin, M. L., Amodeo, M,. Clay, C., Fassler, I. & Ellis, M. A. (2006). Racial differences in social support: Kin versus friend. *American Journal of Orthopsychiatry, 76*, 374–380.

Grover, S. L. & Crooker, K. (1995). Who appreciates family-response human resource policies?: The impact of family-friendly policies on the organizational attachment of parents and non-parents. *Personnel Psychology, 48*, 271–288.

Haar, J. M. (2004). Work-family conflict and turnover intention: Exploring moderation effect of perceived work-family support. *New Zealand Journal of Psychology, 33*, 35–39.

Hammer, L. B., Kossek, E. E., Zimmerman, K. & Daniels, R. (2007). Clarifying the construct of family-supportive supervisory behaviors (FSSB): A multilevel perspective. In P. L. Perrewé & D. C. Ganster (eds), *Research in Occupational Stress and Well-being* (Vol 6). *Exploring the Work and Non-work Interface* (pp. 165–204). New York: Elsevier (JAI).

Hammer, L. B., Neal, M. B., Newson, J., Brokcwood, K. J. & Colton, C. (2005). A longitudinal study of the effects of dual-earner couples' utilization of family-friendly workplace supports on work and family outcomes. *Journal of Applied Psychology, 90*, 799–810.

Harrick, E. J., Vanek, G. R. & Michlitsch, J. F. (1986). Alternate work schedules, productivity, leave usage, and employee attitudes: A field study. *Public Personnel Management, 15*(2), 159–168.

Hatfield, E. & Sprecher, S. (1983). Equity theory and recipients' reactions to help. In J. D. Fisher, A. Nadler & B. M. DePaulo (eds), *New Directions in Helping Behavior* (Vol 1), (pp. 113–141). New York: Academic.

Henderson, M. & Argyle, M. (1985). Social support by four categories of work colleagues: Relationships between activities, stress, and satisfaction. *Journal of Occupational Behaviour, 6*, 229–239.

Holahan, C. J. & Moos, R. H. (1981). Social support and psychological stress: A longitudinal analysis. *Journal of Abnormal Psychology, 90*, 365–370.

House, J. S. (1981). *Work Stress and Social Support*. Reading, MA: Addison-Wesley.

Hutchinson, S. (1997). Perceived organizational support: Further evidence of construct validity. *Educational and Psychological Measurement, 57*(6), 1025–1034.

Kahn, R. L. & Byosiere, P. (1991). Stress in organizations. In M. D. Dunnette & L. M. Hough (eds), *Handbook of Industrial and Organizational Psychology* (2nd edn), (pp. 571–641). Palo Alto: Consulting Psychologists Press.

Kaufmann, G. M. & Beehr, T. A. (1986). Interaction between job stress and social support: Some counterintuitive results. *Journal of Applied Psychology, 71*, 522–526.

Kaufmann, G. M. & Beehr, T. A. (1989). Occupational stressors, individual strains, and social supports among police officers. *Human Relations, 42*, 185–197.

King, L. A., Mattimore, L. K., King, D. W. & Adams, G. A. (1995). Family support inventory for workers: A new measure of perceived social support from family members. *Journal of Organizational Behavior, 16*, 235–258.

Kottke, J. L. & Sharafinski, C. E. (1988). Measuring perceived supervisory and organizational support. *Educational and Psychological Measurement, 48*, 1075–1079.

Ladd, D. & Henry, R. A. (2000). Helping co-workers and helping the organization: The role of support perceptions, exchange ideology, and conscientiousness. *Journal of Applied Social Psychology, 30*(10), 2028–2049.

LaRocco, J. M., House, J. S. & French, J. R. P., Jr. (1980). Social support, occupational stress and health. *Journal of Health and Social Behavior, 21*, 202–218.

Nagurney, A. J. Reich, J. W. & Newson, J. T. (2004). Gender moderates the effect of independence and dependence desires during social support process. *Psychology and Aging, 19*, 215–218.

Neff, L. A. & Karney, B. R. (2005). Gender difference in social support: A question of skill or responsiveness? *Journal of Personality and Social Psychology, 88*, 79–90.

O'Driscoll, M. P., Poelmans, S., Spector, P. E., Kalliath, T., Allen, T. D. Cooper, C. L. & Sanchez, J. I. (2003). Family responsive intervention and supervisor support, work-family conflict, and psychological strain. *International Journal of Stress Management, 10*, 326–344.

Pattison, E. M. (1977). A theoretical-empirical base for social system therapy. In E. F. Feulks, R. M. Wintrob, J. Westermeyer & A. R. Favazza (eds), *Current Perspectives in Cultural Psychiatry.* New York: Spectrum.

Phillips-Miller, D. L., Campbell, N. & Morrison, C. R. (2000). Work and family: Satisfaction, stress, and social support. *Journal of Employment Counseling, 37*, 16–30.

Pine, A. M., Ben-Ari, A. Utas, A. & Larson, D. (2002). A cross-cultural investigation of social support and burnout. *European Psychologist, 7*, 256–264.

Procidano, M. E. & Heller, K. (1983). Measures of perceived social support from friends and from family: Three validation studies. *American Journal of Community Psychology, 11*(1), 1–24.

Rhoades, L. & Eisenberger, R. (2002). Perceived organizational support: A review of the literature. *Journal of Applied Psychology, 87*(4), 698–714.

Sarason, I. G., Levine, H. M., Basham, R. B. & Sarason, B. R. (1983). Assessing social support: The social support questionnaire. *Journal of Personality and Social Psychology, 44*, 127–139.

Schaubroeck, J., Cotton, J. L. & Jennings, K. R. (1989). Antecedents and consequences of role stress: A covariance structure analysis. *Journal of Organizational Behavior, 10*, 35–58.

Shaffer, M. A., Harrison, D. A., Gilley, K. M.. & Luk, D. M. (2001). Struggling for balance amid turbulence on international assignments: Work-family conflict, support and commitment. *Journal of Management, 27*(1), 99–121.

Sherony, K. M. & Green, S. G. (2002). Co-worker exchange: Relationships between co-workers, leader-member exchange, and work attitudes. *Journal of Applied Psychology, 87*(3), 542–548.

Solomon, Z., Mikulincer, M. & Hobfoll, S. E. (1987). Objective versus subjective measurement of stress and social support: Combat-related reactions. *Journal of Consulting and Clinical Psychology, 55*, 577–583.

Sullivan, S. E. & Bhagat, R. S. (1992). Organizational stress, job satisfaction, and job performance: Where do we go from here? *Journal of Management, 18*, 353–374.

Tardy, C. H. (1985). Social support measurement. *American Journal of Community Psychology, 13*(2), 187–202.

Thierry, H. & Meijman, T. (1994). Time and behavior at work. In H. C. Triandis, M. D. Dunnette & L. M. Hough (eds), *Handbook of Industrial and Organizational Psychology* (pp. 341–414). Palo Alto, CA: Consulting Psychologists Press.

Thoits, P. A. (1982). Conceptual, methodological, and theoretical problems in studying social support as a buffer against life stress. *Journal of Health and Social Behavior, 23,* 145–159.

Thomas, L. T. & Ganster, D. C. (1995). Impact of family-supportive-work variables on work-family conflict and strain: A control perspective. *Journal of Applied Psychology, 80,* 6–15.

Thompson, C. A., Jahn, E. W., Kopelman, R. E. & Prottas, D. J. (2004). Perceived organizational family support: A Longitudinal and multilevel analysis. *Journal of Managerial Issues, 16,* 545–565.

Thompson, C. A. & Pottas, D. J. (2005). Relationship among organizational family support, job autonomy, perceived control, and employee well-being. *Journal of Occupational Health Psychology, 10,* 100–118.

Turner, R. J., Frankel, B. G. & Levin, D. (1983). Social support: Conceptualization, measurement, and implications for mental health. In J. R. Greenley (ed.), *Research in Community Mental Health.* Greenwich, CT: JAI Press.

Vaux, A. & Harrison, D. (1985). Support network characteristics associated with support satisfaction and perceived support. *American Journal of Community Psychology, 13*(3), 245–268.

Vaux, A., Phillips, J., Holly, L., Thomson, B., Williams, D. & Stewart, D. (1986). The Social Support Appraisals (SS-A) Scale: Studies of reliability and validity. *American Journal of Community Psychology, 14*(2), 195–219.

Vaux, A., Riedel, S. & Stewart, D. (1987). Modes of social support: The Social Support Behaviors (SS-B) Scale. *American Journal of Community Psychology, 15*(2), 209–237.

Viswesvaran, C., Sanchez, J. I. & Fisher, J. (1999). The role of social support in the process of work stress: A meta-analysis. *Journal of Vocational Behavior, 54,* 314–334.

Warner, M., Slan-Jerusalim, R. & Korabik, K. (in press). Co-worker support for and resentment of work-family issues. In P. Raskin & M. Pitt-Catsouphes (eds), *The WorkFamily Encyclopedia.* www. bc.edu/bc.org/avp/wfnetwork/rft/wfpedia

Wellman, B. (1981). Applying network analysis to the study of support. In B.H. Gottlieb (ed.), *Social Networks and Social Support* (pp. 171–200). Beverly Hills, CA: Sage.

Wheaton, B. (1985). Models for the stress buffering functions of coping resources. *Journal of Health and Social Behavior, 26,* 352–364.

Witt, L. A. & Carlson, D. S. (2006). The work-family interface and job performance: Moderating effect of conscientiousness and perceived organizational support. *Journal of Occupational Health Psychology, 11,* 342–357.

Yoon, J. & Lim, J. (1999). Organizational support in the workplace: The case for Korean hospital employees. *Human Relations, 52*(7), 923–945.

CHAPTER 17

Face-Time Matters: A Cross-Level Model of How Work-Life Flexibility Influences Work Performance of Individuals and Groups

Ellen Ernst Kossek[*] and Linn Van Dyne[†]

[*]Michigan State University, School of Labor & Industrial Relations, East Lansing, MI
[†]Michigan State University, Department of Management, East Lansing, Michigan

Because time at work necessarily implies time away from other activities, employees who are observed to be present at work for extended hours appear to be more committed. …it is not clear that such employees accomplish more. Face-time as an indicator of commitment, though clearly an imperfect rule, works because it unambiguously indicates that the work of the organization takes precedence over other aspects of one's life.

(Bailyn, 1993, 110)

Face-time, the visible time that employees spend at work, is a social cue that co-workers and managers use to infer employee commitment to work (Munck, 2001). Work-life flexibility options such as part-time, flextime, and telework allow individuals greater influence over the time, timing, and place of work, and have important social and group performance implications related to face-time, coordination, and motivation. Work-life flexibility occurs when employees are able to initiate flexibility in how long, when, and where they work in a manner that allows them to integrate work with other life roles such as family or leisure (Perlow, 1997).

To date, organizations have often implemented flexibility programs without adequate attention to the effects of changes in face-time on social processes in the group, coordination of work, cooperation among co-workers, and the implications for group performance. We suggest this is particularly problematic because work is increasingly being organized around groups.

Instead, research has focused on flexibility practices (such as flextime, telecommuting, and shortened work weeks) as a human resource benefit to attract and retain talent (Barnett & Hall, 2001). Even when the individual outcomes are examined, research has focused on attitudinal consequences such as satisfaction, commitment, intent to turnover, and strain over behaviors such as performance (e.g., Gottlieb, Kelloway & Barham, 1998). Very few studies consider the motivation and coordination consequences (Levine & Moreland, 1998) on individual and group performance and often overlook cross-level effects of use on groups

(Bailey & Kurland, 2002). Cross-level effects are critical because use reduces face-time and has motivational and coordination consequences for co-workers.

The limited current research and theory on the performance effects of work-life flexibility is mixed. Some scholars contend that using flexibility has many benefits such as empowering employees to have greater schedule control, and enabling them to select the most personally productive work times to implement work and family more effectively (Federico & Goldsmith, 1998; Lambert, 2000). When these outcomes occur, the company also benefits as there is likely to be improved performance and increased discretionary contributions such as higher suggestions, as well as reduced turnover, absenteeism, and interruptions from work-family conflicts (Crandall & Wallace, 1998; Hill, Miller, Weiner & Colihan, 1998; Lambert, 2000). Other research, however, is contradictory and fails to show performance benefits (Dunham, Pierce & Castenada, 1987; Hill et al., 1998; Judiesch & Lynness, 1999). In reviewing the flexibility literature, scholars have generally concluded that the potential benefits of flexibility have not been fully realized and more research is needed (Avery & Zabel, 2001; Perlow, 1997).

CHAPTER GOALS AND BOUNDARY CONDITIONS

To address these gaps, the goals of this chapter are: (1) to introduce a cross-level model that links the reduced face-time of flexibility use with in-role and extra-role individual and group-level work performance; and (2) to develop a richer conceptualization of types of flexibility by jointly examining its positive and negative effects and differentiating motivation and coordination consequences of reduced face-time for performance at multiple levels.

Our conceptualization of work-life flexibility differentiates three basic types of flexibility (time, timing, and place), highlighting the importance of light versus heavy intensity. Our model (see Figure 17.1) emphasizes individual and cross-level effects of work-life flexibility use on performance. We organize the chapter by first describing key boundary conditions. Second, we present a typology of three basic types of employee-initiated work-life flexibility. Third, we introduce our model and propositions that describe the effects of work-life flexibility use on individual and group performance and discuss its implications for research and practice.

A key boundary condition of our chapter is our focus on employee-initiated flexibility. We acknowledge that employers often initiate and require changes in the number of hours worked (e.g., temporary lay-offs or required overtime), changes in the timing of work (e.g., rotating shifts or compressed work week), and changes in the location of work (e.g., required telecommuting or split-location responsibilities). These practices require employees to be flexible about their work. These examples of required flexibility, however, are outside the domain of our model. Instead, we focus on work-life flexibility where employees influence

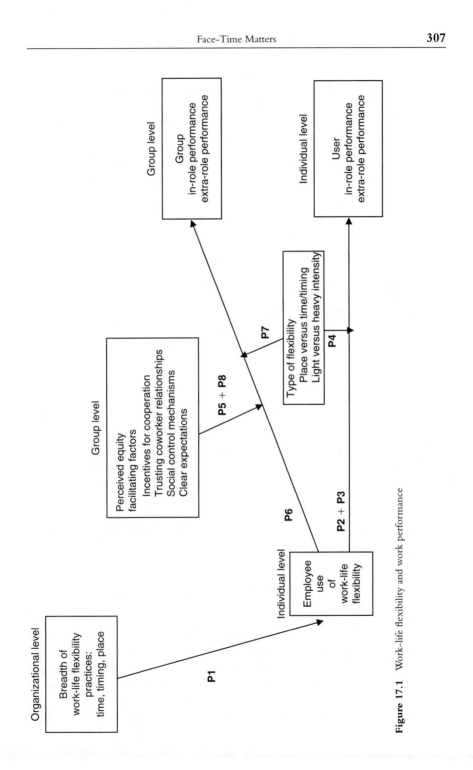

Figure 17.1 Work-life flexibility and work performance

Table 17.1

Basic types of flexibility	Employee-initiated: Time, timing, and place	Employee-initiated intensity	Empoyer-mandated: Time, timing, and place

Time flexibility
 	
Definition:
Flexibility in the *number* of hours worked
	Reduced hours
	Personal leave
	Educational leave
	Travel leave
	Family leave
	Maternity/Parental leave
	Disability leave
	Leave without pay
	Overtime limits
	Phased retirement
		Light intensity:
		  Full-time hours
		
		Moderate intensity:
		  Reduced hours
		
		Heavy intensity:
		  Extended or
		  Indefinite
		  leave of absence
			Temporary layoffs
			Temporary plant shutdown
			Reduced hours to save costs
			Required part-time hours
			Changes in overtime hours

Timing flexibility
 	
Definition:
Flexibility in *when* work occurs
	Flex-time
	Core hours flexi-time
	Total flexibility in timing
	Results-based professional work
		Light intensity:
		  Standard hours
		  (i.e., 9–5)
		
		Moderate intensity:
		  Core hours or days
		
		Heavy intensity:
		  Total flexibility;
		  no core
			Rotating shifts
			Four-day work week
			Compressed work week
			Seven-day work coverage

Place flexibility
 	
Definition:
Flexibility in *where* work occurs
	Optional telecommuting
	Occasional telecommuting
	Optional satellite office
	Flexibility to work at home
	Permanent telecommuting
		Light intensity:
		  Employer workplace
		
		Moderate intensity:
		  Occasional telework
		
		Heavy intensity:
		  Permanent telework
			Required telecommuting
			Required satellite office
			Required client office work
			Required travel
			Split-location job duties
			Job transfer

the time duration, timing, and the place of work (for examples, see Table 17.1). A second domain consideration is our assumption that work processes are interdependent and that employees must coordinate their work with others. Thus, our model, with its emphasis on face-time, has primary relevance to employees whose work is closely integrated with their work group co-workers and supervisors. It has less relevance to individual contributors and independent consultants. Our third assumption is that group performance is more than the sum of individual performance (Hackman, 1990), and thus it is important to consider face-time effects of flexibility use on group-level performance. While beyond our chapter's scope, we also wish to note that the degree to which use of work-life flexibility for individuals and their co-workers maintains or enhances individual and group performance ultimately also has implications for continued access and indirect effects on family relationships and opportunities for community involvement. Our fourth assumption is that for flexibility policies to positively affect individual and group performance, organizations must have processes that not only support the adoption of flexibility policies, but also the creation of cultures that enhance their access and use, which we refer to as embeddedness (the degree to which members feel the culture supports access and use of flexible work options) (see Andreassi & Thompson in this volume). Our fifth assumption is that although we present three types of flexibility separately (time, timing, and place) as they are often studied separately, increasingly in practice employees may be negotiating combinations such as reduced hours with more place flexibility. Although this multiple use issue is beyond our scope, future scholars should examine the performance impact of flexibility use in varying combinations.

TYPES OF WORK-LIFE FLEXIBILITY

Work-life flexibility is defined as organizational policies and practices that allow individuals to initiate flexibility in how long, when, and where they work. Flexibility provides autonomy to self-manage work-role enactment in relation to nonwork demands (Olmstead & Smith, 1997). Compared to child and eldercare benefits, which focus specifically on caring for dependents, work-life flexibility is broader and can benefit all employees across the life span. Table 17.1 provides examples of different types of work-life flexibility (time, timing, and place).

The availability of flexible work arrangements varies widely in the US according to the type of workplace and the workforce. For example, the US Bureau of Labor Statistics National Compensation Survey (2000) shows that 7% of large employers offer some flexible work arrangements compared to only 2% of small employers. Access to policies varies widely by type of employee group which creates doubt about whether organizational level studies on policy adoption provide an accurate indicator of access and use across work groups or type of job (Kossek, 2005). For example, the BLS shows that professional and technical employees were twelve times as likely as blue-collar employees and three times as likely as clerical employees to have access to flexible work schedules (BLS, 2000).

Time Flexibility

The first type of work-life flexibility is *time flexibility*—the flexibility to modify the *duration* of work relative to nonwork. Two common approaches are: (1) employee-initiated workload reduction (working less than full-time), and (2) leaves of absence. Time flexibility was initially adopted by large US employers and law/accounting firms in the 1980s, because employees often worked significant overtime (often unpaid) due to an "up or out" mentality (make partner or leave), and this time inflexibility resulted in over 20% turnover annually (Connor, Hooks & McGuire, 1997).[1]

TIMING FLEXIBILITY

The second basic type is *timing flexibility*—the flexibility to influence *when* work is scheduled. Timing flexibility, such as flextime, allows variability and temporal freedom in the *timing* or *scheduling* of work, while the number of hours worked and workload remain the same. Timing flexibility can avoid peak congestion and reduce commuting time, thus enabling more family and leisure time or more time at work (Avery & Zabel, 2001).

PLACE FLEXIBILITY

The third basic type of work-life flexibility is *place flexibility*—the flexibility to influence *where* work occurs. Place flexibility allows employees to work at home or at remote, regional, or client sites to reduce commuting and co-worker interruptions (Avery & Zabel, 2001; Bailey & Kurland, 2002). Telecommuting occurs when employees work from home and satellite teleworking occurs when employees work at a location that is remote from their main office but closer to home (Kossek, Lautsch & Eaton, 2006).

A MODEL OF WORK-LIFE FLEXIBILITY AND WORK PERFORMANCE

Our model includes consequences of work-life flexibility on individual user performance and cross-level consequences of individual use of each of these three types of flexibility on group performance. In the individual-level portion of the model we include the cross-level effects of breadth of flexibility practices on individual use. Consistent with Lambert (2000), we propose that flexibility provides motivational benefits to individual users and, extending prior work, we also identify potential coordination costs of using flexibility. When employees use flexibility (work fewer hours, work non-core hours, and work at remote locations), this reduces their face-time at work and their opportunity to coordinate work with co-workers.

We then shift to the group level where we consider cross-level effects of individual use on group performance. When employees work fewer hours, work non-core hours, or work at remote locations, this reduces their face-time at work

---

[1] This, of course, is in addition to public policies predating the 80s in many other developed countries, many of which provide maternity/parental leave; paid vacation, and disability leave.

and, based on social comparison, can raise equity issues. If co-workers feel that use is inequitable, the cross-level motivational effect on overall group performance will be negative. In contrast, if co-workers feel that use is equitable, this cross-level motivational effect will be positive and will enhance group performance. The model also incorporates cross-level coordination effects based on type of flexibility and intensity of use. Lastly, we propose four group-level facilitating factors that managers can use to manage work-life flexibility effects on group performance.

INDIVIDUAL USER CONSEQUENCES

BREADTH OF WORK-LIFE FLEXIBILITY PRACTICES (TIME, TIMING, AND PLACE)

Although designed to benefit employees, face-time concerns can cause negative reactions to flexibility (Bailyn, 1993; Kossek, Barber & Winters, 1999). For example, some employees may fear use will damage their careers (Perlow, 1997). Other employees may view lower face-time of peers negatively because flexibility policies don't benefit them personally (Grover, 1991). We suggest flexibility policy breadth (e.g., narrow practices focused on work-family needs such as child/eldercare versus broad practices including time, timing, and place options applicable to personal, community, educational, and leisure activities that can be used by all employees regardless of age, career stage, or income) may be one reason for low use of existing policies. Certainly the degree to which the culture or climate suggests attending to work and family needs, the degree to which broad flexibility options are available, and the priority put on face-time and sacrificing work over family are other informal factors that can enhance or impede the effective use of policies (see Andreassi & Thompson, this volume, and Kossek, Colquitt & Noe, 2001).

Typically, when organizations first respond to work-life issues, they offer low breadth work-family benefits (Perry-Smith & Blum, 2000). If, over time they do not expand the range of options, employees without family responsibilities may not benefit personally and may feel they are being treated inequitably (Burkett, 2000). In contrast, if flexibility practices are broad (time, timing, and place), most employees should benefit and utilization should be higher. Broadly applicable practices acknowledge that all employees juggle multiple roles and value work-life integration (Lambert, 2000) and should generate more positive reactions and less reactance than narrow practices, which benefit a more limited segment of the workforce. Broad practices support a range of life responsibilities and interests such that lower face-time is not based only on child or dependent care. In contrast, narrow policies focus attention on the lower face-time of those with the greatest family demands. We propose that broad flexibility options will lead to higher individual use, since employees may use flexibility for many different work-life reasons.

P1: Broad work-life flexibility practices that include time, timing, and place (rather than only legally mandated or work-family benefits) will enhance individual use of flexibility.

In the next sections, we differentiate motivation and coordination consequences for those who use flexibility. This extends past individual-level research, which has focused primarily on the motivational benefits to users. Drawing on Levine and Moreland (1998), we suggest that it is important to recognize both motivation and coordination consequences of flexibility.

MOTIVATION CONSEQUENCES TO USERS

When employees have options to influence how much, when, and where they work, these choices have motivational and performance implications. When organizations offer work-life flexibility options to their employees, they recognize individual differences in scheduling preferences, acknowledge diversity, and do not force all employees to conform to the same work practices. Offering a broad range of flexibility options signals that employees have unique needs and indicates that human capital is a key organizational resource (Federico & Goldsmith, 1998). Consistent with this, the research on perceived organizational support (POS) demonstrates that when employees feel they are supported by the organization, they experience an obligation to reciprocate (Eisenberger, Armeli, Rexwinkel, Lynch & Rhodes, 2001). This obligation results in higher organizational commitment and motivation to contribute to the organization in exchange for benefits received. Those who use flexibility and are able to influence the time, timing, and place of work should experience high levels of motivation.

Past work-life flexibility literature has emphasized motivational benefits of the three types of flexibility. For example, research on time flexibility demonstrates that voluntary part-time workers (e.g., job-sharers) experience psychological benefits and often work at high energy levels (Avery & Zabel, 2001). Employees who work reduced workloads report they are better able to give their best to their jobs (Lee & Kossek, 2004). Flexibility in the timing of work enhances work integration with other life commitments (e.g., childcare, eldercare, education, exercise, and financial, legal, medical appointments) and enhances job satisfaction, organizational commitment, job involvement, and motivation (Grover & Crooker, 1995; Hill et al., 1998; Kossek et al., 1999). Place flexibility cuts commuting time, reduces co-worker interruptions, and increases work concentration (Bailey & Kurland, 2002). We argue that use of time, timing, and place work-life flexibility has positive motivational consequences for employees. In work contexts, the direction, intensity, and duration of high motivation typically focus on task responsibilities (Mitchell, 1997). We propose that individual use of work-life flexibility should be personally motivating and should enhance in-role work performance.

> **P2**: *Motivational effects*: Individual use of work-life flexibility provides motivational benefits to users and enhances their in-role performance.

COORDINATION CONSEQUENCES TO USERS

When employees have options to influence how much, when, and where they work, these choices also have coordination consequences for them because they will have less face-time at work (Rapoport, Bailyn, Fletcher & Pruitt, 2002). When employees work less than full-time, work flexible hours, or work off-site, they are less proximal to their co-workers. This reduced contact and interaction can create barriers and can make it more difficult to help others with their work (Van de Ven & Ferry, 1980). We suggest that lower face-time can create coordination challenges that detract from the opportunity to engage in extra-role behavior (Brief & Motowidlo, 1986; Organ, 1988; Van Dyne, Cummings & McLean Parks, 1995). Extra-role behavior (ERB) is discretionary behavior that requires initiative, is not formally rewarded, and is not an expected role responsibility. Helping, the most commonly researched form of ERB, occurs when employees voluntarily pitch in and assist co-workers. Lower face-time, however, reduces the opportunity to help co-workers. If employees work fewer hours, at different times, or at distant locations, they may be unavailable to help when deadlines make the benefits of teamwork and cooperation particularly important. They may not be physically present to answer questions and help newcomers learn their jobs or be unaware that others need help. We propose reduced face-time creates coordination challenges that reduce discretionary helping.

> **P3**: *Coordination effects*: Individual use of work-life flexibility creates coordination challenges for users and detracts from their extra-role performance.

Moving to considering differing effects of type of work-life flexibility used (see Table 17.1), we propose that different types of flexibility have different implications for face-time, coordination, and ERB. Specifically, we argue that type of flexibility moderates the relationship between individual use and the user's ERB. We first focus on place and then on intensity.

The key aspect of place flexibility is working at a remote location. Compared to time or timing, place flexibility has the most dramatic effect on worker proximity (Wells, 2001). For example, with reduced hours (time flexibility) or flexible hours

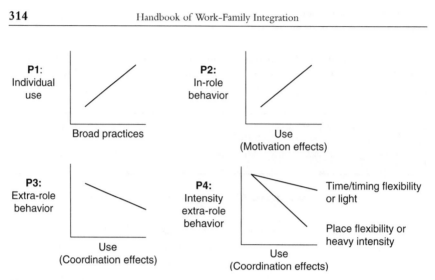

Figure 17.2   Individual work-life flexibility and individual performance

(timing flexibility), employees continue regular and ongoing contact with co-workers because they are located at the same facility. In contrast, place flexibility is more likely to have serious implications for regular face-to-face interaction. When employees work at home, at a client's office, or at a satellite facility, their access to co-workers is reduced more significantly than when they work fewer hours (time flexibility) or when they work flexible hours (timing flexibility). Those who tele-work participate in fewer informal office gatherings (lunch or coffee) and will be less aware that co-workers need their help. For example, Cooper and Kurland (2002) describe the professional isolation and reduced informal communication that occur for those who work at remote locations. Place flexibility generally makes it more difficult to offer spontaneous, discretionary help. In sum, we predict an interaction where reduced extra-role behavior (helping) will be most severe for those who use flexibility in *where* they work (i.e., place flexibility) (see Figure 17.2).

P4a: *Coordination effects*: Type of flexibility moderates the coordination effects of individual use of work-life flexibility on individual extra-role behavior, such that the relationship will be weaker for time or timing types of flexibility than for place flexibility.

UTILIZATION INTENSITY

For our second moderator, we consider the intensity of use. For each of our three basic types of work-life flexibility, we differentiate and provide examples of light, moderate, and heavy intensity. We then propose that the opportunity to perform extra-role behavior will be most severely restricted for heavy intensity flexibility.

Place Intensity

Although extreme examples of flexibility such as total flexibility of hours or permanent telework, which exemplify heavy intensity utilization, often get emphasized by the media, Bailey and Kurland's (2002) insightful conceptualization of telecommuting notes that utilization of alternate work arrangements need not be high in intensity. Although some employees telecommute 100% of the time, occasional place flexibility is more common. Light intensity *place flexibility* occurs when employees work at one central work location, except for occasional off-site meetings with suppliers or clients, etc. Moderate intensity *place flexibility* involves periodic remote work. For example, an employee who regularly works in the office might telework away from the primary work site during a special project. Teleworking 2–3 days a week allows employees to reduce commute time, work closely with clients, and accommodate personal responsibilities. In contrast, heavy intensity *place flexibility* involves long-term or permanently working away from the primary work location (Wells, 2001). This occurs when employees choose their primary or permanent place of work outside the office (home, client).

Timing Intensity

Likewise, having no core hours or working exclusively nights/weekends (heavy intensity timing flexibility) provides few opportunities for co-worker interaction, yet flextime with core hours (moderate intensity) is a more common example of timing flexibility. Light intensity *timing flexibility* occurs when employees work standard schedules such as 9–5, except for occasional school conferences, etc. Moderate intensity *timing flexibility* involves working core hours. This allows employees to influence the timing of when they start, stop, and break—as long as they are present at work during a set period of time (i.e., 9 to 3) (Olmstead & Smith, 1997). For example, working core hours but flexing starting time allows employees to meet personal obligations outside of work such as family, medical, or legal appointments. Heavy intensity *timing flexibility* allows total flexibility in hours, without core hours. This allows employees to work unpredictable hours—perhaps to satisfy irregular travel demands and client preferences for staggered or longer service hours. This includes daily flexibility with no core hours, banking hours for future time off, or a standard number of hours required in a certain period with no timing requirements.

Time Intensity

Similarly, although some employees take extended leaves for family or personal reasons (heavy intensity time flexibility), occasional or periodic reduced hours (moderate intensity) such as during school vacations or while preparing for a professional examination are more common. Light intensity *time flexibility* occurs when employees work full-time, except for occasional sick days or personal time off. Moderate intensity *time flexibility* involves voluntary workload reduction in return for reduced compensation (Lee & Kossek, 2004). Examples include working thirty hours a week, phased-in retirement or return from leave-of-absence, regular or seasonal reduced-hours, job sharing, and short increments of paid time-off (Avery & Zabel, 2001). In contrast, heavy intensity *time flexibility* includes voluntary paid or unpaid leaves of absence, where the employee takes extended time off such as leave for birth, adoption, eldercare, and education (Judiesch & Lynness, 1999).

In each of these three contrasts, heavy intensity work-life flexibility reduces opportunities for regular interaction with co-workers, while lower intensity use allows ongoing coordination and contact. Building on these distinctions, we suggest that intensity has important implications for face-time and that it will moderate the relationship between individual use and ERB. This is an important issue given contemporary trends that emphasize interdependent work processes that emphasize employees' cooperation in helping their co-workers (Ilgen, 1999). If an employee occasionally uses reduced hours, flexible hours, or off-site work (light to moderate intensity), the employee will still have regular contact with co-workers and thus can still contribute ERB.

In contrast, heavy intensity use (such as an extended leave of absence, routinely working nights, or permanently working at home) can prevent regular contact and interaction with others. Less face-time, in turn, has negative implications for user ERB. For example, employees who typically do not work the same number of hours, at the same time or in the same place, are more likely to feel cut off from peers and excluded from general interactions. They will be less aware of both work and interpersonal issues that affect their co-workers and will be less able to pitch in spontaneously and help their colleagues. Thus, we propose an interaction where intensity has coordination implications for the relationship between use and extra-role behavior (see Figure 17.2).

> **P4b**: *Coordination effects*: Intensity moderates the coordination effects of individual use of work-life flexibility on individual extra-role behavior, such that the relationship will be weaker (less negative) for light intensity than for heavy intensity.

CROSS-LEVEL CONSEQUENCES FOR THE WORK GROUP

Following the recommendations of Bailey and Kurland (2002), we now focus on cross-level effects of reduced face-time on group-level outcomes (propositions

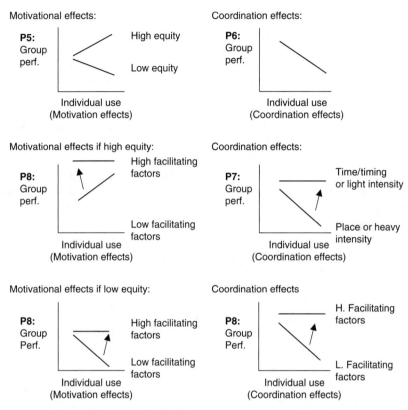

Figure 17.3   Individual work-life flexibility and group performance

5–8). For clarity, we consider motivational and coordination cross-level effects separately. (See Figure 17.3 for illustrations.)

MOTIVATIONAL FACTORS

Earlier we argued that broad work-life flexibility practices provide benefits that can be used by most employees. In this section, we suggest that peer perceptions of equitable use will moderate the cross-level motivation effects of individual use and reduced face-time on work group performance. When flexibility practices are broad, most employees can expect to benefit in the future, even though only some may benefit immediately. When peers observe co-workers using flexibility, this provides behavioral evidence (signaling) that flexibility options are real and available for use (Lambert, 2000). It also shows that the organization values employees and creates a sense of reciprocal obligations. When organizations recognize the personal lives of a broad cross-section of employees, this is motivating and facilitates reciprocity (Eisenberger et al., 2001). At the group level, equitable reduced face-time can further strengthen motivation and can lead to deviation-amplifying positive spirals (increasingly going above the norm to help out others), that enhance in-role and extra-role group performance (Lindsley, Brass & Thomas, 1995).

In contrast, if peers feel that others' use of work-life flexibility is not equitable, the cross-level motivational effects of reduced face-time on work group performance will be negative. If only a minority use flexibility (perhaps because options are narrow and not applicable to all, or because of negative career consequences), lower face-time of users becomes obvious to nonusers (Perlow, 1997). If policies focus only on work-family flexibility, those who do not have dependents may not benefit and may feel they are being treated unfairly. Here face-time can be demotivating (Burkett, 2000; Grandley, 2001) for nonusers, causing them to reduce their feelings of injustice by lowering contributions to the organization and refusing to help those who use flexibility. In extreme cases, nonusers may retaliate and punish users (exclude them from informal gatherings, withhold work-related information, or blame them for problems that occur in their absence) (Andersson & Pearson, 1998; Skarlicki & Folger, 1997). At the group level, these negative cross-level effects should further detract from motivation, leading to deviation-amplifying negative spirals, which reduce group IRB and ERB.

Combining these processes, we propose an interaction where perceived equity changes the form of the relationship between individual use and group performance, such that the relationship between individual use and group performance will be positive when perceived equity is high, but will be negative when perceived equity is low (see Figure 17.3).

> **P5**: *Motivational effects*: Perceived equity moderates the cross-level effect of individual use of work-life flexibility on group performance (both IRB and ERB), such that high perceived equity enhances motivation in the group and causes a positive relationship between individual use and group performance, but low perceived equity reduces motivation in the group and causes a negative link between use and group performance.

COORDINATION FACTORS

We also propose that individual use of work-life flexibility has cross-level effects on coordination processes in work groups (Rapoport et al., 2002). To avoid confounding relationships, we assume in this section that the motivational effects discussed above are held constant. When employees use flexibility (working fewer hours, different hours, or in a different place), their face-time is reduced and peers in the work group have additional challenges of coordinating work processes with users of flexibility. As work processes become increasingly interdependent and as managers delegate more responsibility to work groups (Ilgen, 1999), this has important implications for overall group performance. If an employee does not work the same number of hours, at the same time, or in the same location, reduced face-time influences other team members. It is not enough to create conditions where the individual is working hard—they may be working very hard, but making team dynamics work well can still be a challenge (Wells, 2001). Flexibility use by an individual can delay responses to customer requests and questions, disrupt routines of peers, create extra work for those left in the office, and cause resentment. When employees work in less proximity to each other, joint problem-solving and coordination of work processes is more difficult (IRB) and the reduced face-time makes it hard for employees to detect and respond to unexpected needs for assistance (ERB). At the group level, individual use of work-life flexibility creates coordination challenges, which lead to process losses (Steiner, 1972) and deviation-amplifying negative spirals that detract from group performance.

P6: *Coordination effects*: Individual use of work-life flexibility creates coordination challenges for peers and has negative effects on group performance (IRB and ERB).

TYPE OF FLEXIBILITY AND GROUP PERFORMANCE

We now consider the moderating role of type of flexibility in influencing the cross-level coordination effects of individual use on group performance. Extending the arguments developed to support proposition 4 (which predicted type of flexibility that would moderate the effects of use on extra-role behavior at the individual level), we propose the type of flexibility influences the relationship between individual use and group performance. We base our arguments on the criticality of coordination for both in-role and extra-role group performance.

We propose that type of flexibility used (time, timing, place) has differential cross-level implications for face-time and coordination of group outputs. We argue that individual use of place flexibility will have more extreme cross-level effects on group performance than either time or timing flexibility. This is because place flexibility (the location of work) has a more dramatic effect on worker proximity to co-workers than either time or timing. When employees work regularly from home or telework from a satellite office, they have less frequent and less regular contact with peers. This has two coordination consequences. Less face-time reduces interaction and makes group communication, problem-solving, cooperation, and coordination more difficult. Place flexibility also causes group-level process losses that detract from in-role group-level performance (Steiner, 1972).

Place flexibility and less face-time also make it more difficult for group members to know when co-workers need help and they are less likely to be present to offer help (ERB). Again, we suggest that these effects lead to deviation-amplifying negative spirals that detract from extra-role performance (Lindsley et al., 1995). Overall, we propose an interaction where type of flexibility used (place versus time/timing) changes the form of the cross-level coordination effects of individual use on group performance. When face-time is reduced the most (place flexibility), the individual use and group performance link will be stronger than for time or timing.

> **P7a**: *Coordination effects*: Type of flexibility moderates the cross-level coordination effects of individual use of work-life flexibility on group performance (IRB and ERB), such that the relationship will be weaker (less negative) for time or timing than place.

Second, we also propose that intensity (light-heavy) has differential cross-level implications for coordination of group outputs (both IRB and ERB). More specifically, we argue that face-time implications of heavy intensity (e.g., time: extended leave of absence; timing: routinely working nights; or place: permanently working at home) will change the link between individual use and group performance more than light or moderate intensity. Light intensity includes examples of time (full-time work with occasional absences), timing (a 9–5 schedule with occasional shifts in timing), and place (central work location with occasional off-site meetings). In each of these instances, employees maintain regular proximity to co-workers and thus protect their face-time and allow ongoing work coordination and discretionary helping. Similarly, moderate intensity (voluntary seasonal part-time work during school vacations, working core hours but flexing start time to avoid peak traffic, periodic remote work during a special project) allows face-time and regular contact with co-workers that, in turn, facilitates work coordination and discretionary helping. In contrast, heavy intensity interferes with IRB and ERB coordination processes in the group. When employees take an extended leave of absence from work, routinely work non-core hours, or work regularly off-site, they have little face-time. As a result, it is more challenging for the group to integrate the required and discretionary efforts of these employees. This leads to group-level process losses which detract from group-level in-role and extra-role performance (Steiner, 1972). In sum, we propose an interaction where the face-time implications of utilization intensity change the cross-level coordination effects of individual use on group performance. With heavy intensity, the relationship between individual use and group-level performance will be more negative than with light intensity.

P7b: *Coordination effects*: Intensity moderates the cross-level coordination effects of individual use of work-life flexibility on group performance (IRB and ERB), such that the relationship will be weaker (less negative) for light intensity than for heavy intensity.

GROUP-LEVEL FACILITAING FACTORS AND GROUP PERFORMANCE

We now turn our attention to group-level factors that can change the cross-level motivation and coordination effects of individual reduced face-time on group-level performance. This is a critical issue because increased coordination demands and peer concerns about flexibility abuse require careful management at the group level (Rapoport et al., 2002). In developing this part of our model, we draw on the social dilemma literature (Pruitt, 1998; Schroeder, 1995) to suggest techniques that managers can use to reduce unanticipated (and often unintended) negative consequences of individual behavior (in our case, use of work-life flexibility) on group-level outcomes (group IRB and ERB). Social dilemmas occur when individual decisions benefit the actor but also trigger costs to the group. Social dilemmas are mixed motive situations that juxtapose personal interests and collective interests (Schelling, 1978; Schroeder, 1995).

This idea of a mixed motive situation is relevant to our interest in work-life flexibility because individual use of work-life flexibility benefits the individual personally, but reduced face-time may confer motivation and coordination costs on the group. For example, propositions 5–7 describe circumstances where individuals benefit personally from the use of work-life flexibility but the cross-level motivation and coordination effects on group performance can be negative. If employees generally feel that utilization of flexibility is not equitable, this can lower motivation in the group and have negative consequences for overall group performance. Similarly, if an employee works in a different location, different hours, or fewer hours, it can be more difficult for the overall group to coordinate its work (IRB) and it can also be more difficult for peers to help each other (ERB).

The social dilemma literature provides a useful framework for thinking about managerial interventions that can reduce the group-level motivation and coordination challenges associated with reduced face-time. Pruitt (1998) suggested specific group-level facilitating factors that can be used to reduce negative cross-level effects of individual behavior on group-level outcomes. We consider four of these factors: incentives for cooperation, trusting co-worker relationships, social control, and clear expectations. According to Pruitt, each of these factors can be used to enhance cooperation among work group members. Each of these suggests managerial techniques for positively structuring and managing the cross-level effects of work-life flexibility use on overall group effectiveness. Table 17.2

Table 17.2

Group-level facilitating factors that influence work-life flexibility and group performance

Social dilemma interventions *To enhance cooperation*	Examples of practical application of social dilemma interventions
1. Incentives	
★ Tangible incentives	Provide *tangible* incentives such as *extra paid time-off* for employees who cover for co-workers. Offer greater work-life flexibility as a *reward* for high performance or as another technique for rewarding seasoned employees who have earned the maximum merit increase or are at the top of their pay range.
★ Intangible incentives	Stress *intangible* benefits, emphasizing the value of *positive relationships*, increased *social identity* with the group, and *long-term positive consequences of ongoing relationships*. Use *selection* strategies to hire self-motivated individuals with *prosocial values* who will be motivated to cooperate and support work-life flexibility.
2. Co-worker relationships	
★ Matching	Support *low-risk positive matching strategies* such as *offering to cover personally* and *asking employees* to *co-self-manage* flexibility. Encourage employees to work out *agreements to cover for each other* (e.g., I'll work for you this Saturday if you work for me next).
★ Trust	*Model trust by delegating* scheduling and coordination for specific projects to employees. Lower risks of trusting behavior by making sure that co-workers do *not have to cover for those who continually fail to follow-through* on their promises to trade time. *Intervene*, if necessary, to *curb abuse*, *reverse decisions*, or *clarify appropriate behavior*. Reinforce beliefs that *cooperation need not be identical* or zero sum in the short-run and that *all will benefit personally and collectively* from ongoing cooperation.
3. Social control mechanisms	
★ Voluntary compliance	Establish clear *norms for cooperation* and set a climate of *strong shared values*. Ask *for voluntary cooperation* and publicly *recognize* this good citizen behavior. Pair experienced employees with newcomers, as part of a *peer mentoring system* to *socialize cooperation*. Ask for *public declarations* of overall support for flexibility and future willingness to cooperate.
★ Promises/Threats	Provide clear statements of *realistic benefits* based on ongoing cooperation such as adding flexibility options for educational courses or personal travel. Provide equally clear statements of *realistic threats* for non-cooperation such as removing specific flexibility options (i.e., drop the ability to bank hours in exchange for future time off).
★ Rules	Develop *policies and procedures* for using work-life flexibility based on input from group members. Set up *web scheduling* so each employee

(continues)

Table 17.2 (*continued*)

Social dilemma interventions To enhance cooperation	Examples of practical application of social dilemma interventions
	knows everyone's schedule. *Document and publicize appropriate ways to change schedules* to support work-life flexibility.
* Approvals	Ask *group leaders or subgroups* to *administer approval* of flexibility requests. Provide *procedural justice guidelines* so that employees understand the process. Establish a *hierarchy of needs* for determining priorities and balancing responsible use over the long-term.
4. Clear expectations	Initiate conversations that *clarify expectations* for work-life flexibility use. Make sure employees *understand* the *benefits* of ongoing cooperation and the *risks* of abuse. Communicate clear expectations that work and life *situations change* and that all employees *must be flexible*. Facilitate *periodic discussions of responsible use*. Help employees *anticipate challenging situations* and *develop alternatives* for ongoing successful work-life integration. Initiate *lunch discussions* so employees better understand peer's work and lives outside of work

provides specific examples of how each facilitating factor can enhance cooperation among group members.

The first characteristic that Pruitt (1998) identified is tangible and intangible incentives that motivate cooperation. Social dilemma research suggests the importance of providing financial incentives and other rewards to support cooperation toward the attainment of group goals (Komorita & Parks, 1994) and the intangible satisfaction derived from positive work relationships (Kramer & Goldman, 1995). Specific application to work-life flexibility suggests the benefits of providing paid time off to employees who cover for co-workers who use flexibility. Another application would be offering additional flexibility options as a reward for high performance or as another incentive for those who are at the maximum of their pay ranges. Thus, managers can frame cooperation on work-life flexibility issues in terms of personal gains (financial benefits, positive relationships with others, and long-term positive consequences of ongoing relationships). Another technique suggested by the social dilemma literature is hiring employees who have a prosocial orientation. This is because those who place a high value on positive, personal relationships will derive personal satisfaction from cooperating to resolve tensions or conflict over use of work-life flexibility. These examples of tangible and intangible incentives should increase motivation to cooperate within the work group and minimize potential negative cross-level effects of individual use on group performance.

The second factor identified by Pruitt is trusting co-worker relationships, including past interactions and expectations for future behavior. Social dilemma research demonstrates that expected reciprocity increases cooperative behavior

(Van Lange, Liebrand, Messick & Wilke, 1992). For example, matching strategies (such as tit for tat) can be started and reinforced through small opening moves that carry low risk (Pruitt, 1998). This minimizes concerns about the sucker effect and enhances joint cooperation. A related technique is using trust and substitutes for trust such as making decisions reversible (allowing escape if others defect) and asking others to declare their intentions (Kramer & Goldman, 1995). Specific application to work–life flexibility suggests that managers should support low-risk, positive matching strategies such as offering to cover personally and then later asking employees to co-manage flexibility. Managers can encourage employees to develop agreements among themselves to cover for each other when work demands conflict with personal preferences to use flexibility. Enhancing expectations for matching behavior should enhance the positive effects of individual flexibility use on overall group performance. Managers can also intervene to reinforce trusting relationships, with relevance to flexibility use. They can model trust by delegating scheduling and coordination to employees. They can also intervene to make sure that no employees abuse flexibility by using it and never or rarely covering for others. These interventions include stopping inappropriate behavior and clarifying appropriate use of flexibility. Managers also can clearly communicate the belief that cooperation need not be identical or zero sum because responsible use of broad policies will allow all employees to benefit over time.

Third is social control mechanisms such as group norms for cooperation. According to Pruitt (1998), social norms are especially important for managing social dilemmas and can be divided into four basic categories: voluntary compliance, promises and threats, rules, and approvals. Applied specifically to work–life flexibility, managers can enhance voluntary compliance by asking volunteers to cooperate and then publicly recognize this behavior. They can pair experienced employees with newcomers and through peer mentoring socialize cooperation on flexibility use. Another technique is providing clear descriptions of realistic benefits of cooperation (promises) such as adding new flexibility options for education or personal travel. Similarly, managers can clearly communicate realistic threats for non-compliance (Yamagishi, 1988) such as withdrawing a specific flexibility option such as banking hours for future time off. Managers also can ask group members for input when developing new rules or procedures for flexibility. Alternatively, they might put scheduling information on a web page so that everyone has easy access to work schedules and processes for requesting schedule changes for purposes of flexibility. A final set of options relates to approvals. A manager could delegate approval of flexibility requests to a group leader or subgroup so that employees are directly involved in administrative decisions. To facilitate group decision-making, managers might provide procedural justice guidelines and a hierarchy of needs for prioritizing and balancing requests over time.

Pruitt's fourth factor is clear communication of expectations, and he describes six reasons based on prior research for positive effects on cooperation: reinforcing group norms, creating pressure for conformity, triggering public commitment, promoting group identity, encouraging expectations that others will cooperate, and promoting long-range thinking and common fate. In applying these specifically to work-life flexibility, we suggest that managers have a number of options. After clarifying initial expectations, they can make sure employees understand the benefits of responsible use and the risks of inappropriate use/abuse. They can indicate that both work and life situations change and thus signal a clear expectation that all employees must be flexible in their use and approach to flexibility. In other words, what works at one point in time, may not endure indefinitely. Periodic group discussions could reinforce appropriate use of flexibility. Finally, managers can help employees anticipate changing situations and can help the group develop alternatives for ongoing successful work-life integration for all group members.

In sum, we propose that these facilitating factors have motivation and coordination implications that will moderate the cross-level relationship between individual use of work-life flexibility and group performance, such that the negative effect of reduced face-time on group performance is weakened when facilitating factors are strong.

P8: Group-level facilitating factors (incentives for cooperation, trusting co-worker relationships, social control mechanisms, and clear expectations) moderate the cross-level motivation and coordination effects of individual use of work-life flexibility on group performance (IRB and ERB), such that the relationship will be weaker when facilitating factors are strong.

DISCUSSION

Reduced hours, flextime, and telework influence face-time at work (Bailyn, 1993; Munch, 2001). Since many organizations still use "line of sight" management styles, where visibility signals commitment and effort, face-time can have implications for performance (Wells, 2001). Building on the idea that face-time matters, we have proposed that reduced face-time has both motivation and coordination consequences for individuals and their work groups. Emphasizing the increasingly interdependent nature of work processes and work design (Ilgen, 1999), we developed a cross-level model predicting both positive and negative effects of work-life flexibility use on individual and work group performance. We suggest that acknowledging and actively managing the social and group implications of reduced face-time should help organizations improve the effectiveness of these programs, which, to date, have not been fully integrated into the workplace (Bailyn, 1993).

The two primary goals of this chapter were (1) to introduce a cross-level model that links the reduced face-time of work-life flexibility use with individual and group performance and (2) to advance work-life flexibility research by developing a richer conceptualization of types of flexibility and differentiating motivation and coordination consequences of reduced face-time for performance. Our approach differs from past perspectives by emphasizing the implications of work-life flexibility use for performance, rather than the more traditional focus on individual attitudes such as satisfaction, commitment, strain, and turnover intentions. The approach also follows the advice of Bailey and Kurland (2002) and incorporates both individual and group level effects on performance. Theoretically, the chapter provides a framework that can guide future research by providing a more precise conceptualization of the face-time implications of work-life flexibility and testable propositions for empirical analyses. Practically, the chapter suggests that type of flexibility and group-level facilitating factors can help managers implement progressive work-life flexibility programs in a manner that enhances rather than detracts from performance.

From a theoretical perspective, we provide a framework that can guide future research in two ways. First, we differentiate three types of work-life flexibility (time, timing, and place) and emphasize the importance of intensity. One of the key points of our framework is that place flexibility and heavy intensity of work-life flexibility use are especially detrimental to face-time and create more severe coordination challenges for employees. In contrast, time, timing, and light intensity are less likely to detract from group performance because they facilitate ongoing interaction among work group peers. Second, we developed an initial model of propositions depicting the effects of work-life flexibility use on performance that can be tested in future empirical analyses. In the first part of the model, we focused on consequences of use to individual users, and in the second part of the model we focused on cross-level consequences of individual use on group performance. We consider inclusion of both individual and group effects as a strength of this framework because it integrates prior work-life flexibility research that has considered individual and group levels separately.

We suggest a number of specific next steps for future research. Before firm recommendations can be made to management, it will be important to test the proposed relationships in the model. Given our emphasis on cross-level effects, this implies research that spans a number of organizations with varying breadth in their work-life flexibility practices. It also implies analysis across a range of groups so that differences between groups (such as differences in trust, incentives for cooperation, social control mechanisms, and expectations) can be assessed. Finally, testing the model will also require nested data from individuals (in work groups) who differ in their use of work-life flexibility and face-time at work. Overall, this suggests a research program that would best be accomplished by a research team, rather than by a single individual.

Another important future research consideration is the need for careful attention to the level of conceptualization and operationalization for each construct in the model. Following recommendations of Kozlowski and Klein (2000), we have explicitly incorporated two types of cross-level level relationships in our theorizing. Proposition 1 acknowledges that individuals are nested within organizations and proposes top-down, contextual effects on individual behavior. In contrast, propositions 5–8 propose a bottom-up, cross-level emergence process. Kozlowski and Klein use group performance as a classic example of emergence relationships because group performance emerges from group processes and interactions when work is interdependent. In these situations, group performance is more than the sum of individual performance. Instead, it is a cross-level collective phenomenon that is shaped by individual behavior (P6 and P7) and constrained by the context (P5 and P8). In sum, our propositions specify the level of conceptualization and operationalization for future research.

IMPLICATIONS FOR RESEARCH AND PRACTICE

The conceptual framework also has implications for practice. Given advances in information technology and the invasiveness of 24/7 work demands that exist in many organizations, the model suggests important factors for managers to consider in implementing and managing work-life flexibility programs. For example, careful attention to group-level facilitating factors should be especially relevant to managers of Generation X workers who value work-life balance more than previous generations and thus are more likely to use flexibility programs (Hochschild, 1997; Smola & Sutton, 2002). The model suggests four specific interventions based on the social dilemma literature that managers can use to enhance cooperation among group members with direct relevance to reduced face-time and successful use of work-life flexibility. This should facilitate implementation of progressive work-life flexibility programs in a manner that enhances rather than detracts from group performance. Table 17.2 described these facilitating factors and highlights specific practical applications.

Another practical implication is the importance of cross-level coordination and motivation issues. These are particularly salient in contemporary work organizations that use flexibility benefits to attract and retain highly skilled employees and that also use groups and teams to organize work. If reduced face-time seems inequitable, peers may become demotivated and may not cooperate. This can lead to negative cross-level effects on in-role and extra-role group performance. On the other hand, if organizations manage social dilemma factors proactively such that they create and reinforce cooperation, the cross-level effects of work-life flexibility use on group performance are more likely to be neutral or positive. Rapoport and colleagues (2002) described a flexibility coordination board that a high technology team used to encourage members to coordinate their use of flexibility. When members had shared values, performance improved. Increased communication and coordination helped minimize negative consequences from misreading face-time social cues and discouraged detrimentally high use.

Another practical implication of the model is the differential face-time effects of work-life flexibility based on type and intensity of use. Organizations and work groups can benefit from emphasizing time and timing flexibility as well as low-moderate types of intensity (reduced hours, flextime with core hours, periodic telework).

As for limitations of this chapter, besides the boundary conditions noted earlier, our model is incomplete. It does not include all factors (e.g., nonwork) that influence the effectiveness of work-life flexibility usage and does not include feedback loops or reciprocal effects. We view this as material for future research.

In conclusion, we have proposed that work-life flexibility programs have implications for face-time at work and important implications for individual and work group performance. Acknowledging the interdependent nature of contemporary work, we have developed a model that emphasizes cross-level relationships and factors that are most likely to increase the positive performance consequences of work-life flexibility programs. We hope that our model stimulates future research that integrates two contemporary issues in work organizations: employee preferences for increased flexibility, and the social and performance implications for work groups. To our knowledge, this is the first cross-level model to consider the challenges of managing work-life flexibility so that use enhances rather than detracts from individual and group level performance. We hope our chapter stimulates future research and serves the goal of ultimately helping employees benefit from responsible use of work-life flexibility policies while helping group members work effectively together.

REFERENCES

Andersson, L. M. & Pearson, C. M. (1998). Tit for tat? The spiraling effect of incivility in the workplace. *Academy of Management Review, 24*, 452–471.

Andreassi, J. K. & Thompson, C. A. (2008). Work-family culture: Current research and future directions. This volume.

Avery, C. & Zabel, D. (2001). *The Flexible Workplace: A Sourcebook of Information and Research*. Westport, CT: Quorum.

Bailey, D. E. & Kurland, N. B. (2002). A review of telework research: Findings, new directions, and lessons for the study of modern work. *Journal of Organizational Behavior, 23*, 383–400.

Bailyn, L. (1993). *Breaking the Mold*. New York: Free Press.

Barnett, C. & Hall, D. T. (2001). How to use reduced hours to win the war for talent. *Organizational Dynamics, 29*(3), 192–210.

Brief, A. P. & Motowidlo, S. J. (1986). Prosocial organizational behaviors. *Academy of Management Review, 11*, 710–726.

Bureau of Labor Statistics (2000). National Compensation Survey, Survey of Employee Benefits. (online). Available: www.bls.org.

Burkett, E. (2000). *The Baby Boon: How Family-Friendly America Cheats the Childless*. New York: Free Press.

Connor, M., Hooks, K. & McGuire, T. (1997). Gaining legitimacy for flexible work arrangements and career paths: The business case for public accounting and professional services firms. In S. Parasuraman & J. Greenhaus (eds), *Integrating Work and Family: Challenges and Choices for a Changing World* (pp. 154–166). Westport, CT: Praeger.

Cooper, C. D. & Kurland, N. B. (2002). Telecommuting, professional isolation, and employee development in public and private organizations. *Journal of Organizational Behavior, 23*, 511–532.

Crandall, N. & Wallace M. (1998). *Work and Rewards in the Virtual Workplace: A New Deal for Organizations and Employees*. New York: American Management Association.

Dunham, R., Pierce, J. L. & Castenada, M. (1987). Alternative work schedules: Two field quasi-experiments. *Personnel Psychology, 40*, 215–242.

Eisenberger, R., Armeli, S., Rexwinkel, B., Lynch, P. D. & Rhodes, L. (2001). Reciprocation of perceived organization support. *Journal of Applied Psychology, 86*, 42–51.

Federico, R. & Goldsmith, H. (1998). Linking work/life benefits to performance. *Compensation and Benefits Review, 30*(4), 66–70.

Gottlieb, B. H., Kelloway, E. K. & Barham, E. J. (1998). *Flexible Work Arrangements: Managing the Work-Family Boundary*. Chichester, England: Wiley.

Grandley, A. (2001). Family-friendly policies: Organizational justice perceptions of needs-based allocations. In R. Cropanzano (ed.), *Justice in the Workplace: From Theory to Practice* (pp. 145–173). Mahwah, NJ: Lawrence Erlbaum.

Grover, S. L. (1991). Predicting the perceived fairness of parental leave policies. *Journal of Applied Psychology, 76*, 247–255.

Grover, S. L. & Crooker, K. (1995). Who appreciates family responsive human resource policies? The impact of family-friendly policies on the organizational attachment of parents and non-parents. *Personnel Psychology, 48*, 271–288.

Hackman, J. R. (1990). *Groups That Work (and Those That Don't)*. San Francisco: Jossey-Bass.

Hill, E. J., Miller, B. C., Weiner, S. P. & Colihan, J. (1998). Influences of the virtual office on aspects of work and work/life balance. *Personnel Psychology, 51*, 667–683.

Hochschild, A. (1997). *The Time Bind: When Work Becomes Home and Home Becomes Work*. New York: Holt.

Ilgen, D. R. (1999). Teams embedded in organizations: Some implications. *American Psychologist, 54*, 129–139.

Judiesch, M. K. & Lynness, K. S. (1999). Left behind? The impact of leaves of absence on managers' career success. *Academy of Management Journal, 42*, 641–651.

Komorita, S. S. & Parks, C. D. (1994). *Social Dilemmas*. Madison, WI: Brown & Benchmark.

Kossek, E. (2005). Workplace policies to support families. In S. Bianchi, L. Casper & R. King (eds) *Work, Family Health and Well-Being* (pp. 97–116). Mahwah, New Jersey: LEA Press.

Kossek, E. E., Barber, A. & Winters, D. (1999). Using flexible schedules in the managerial world: The power of peers. *Human Resource Management, 38*, 33–46.

Kossek, E., Lautsch, B. & Eaton, S. (2006). Telecommuting, control, and boundary management: Correlates of policy use and practice, job control, and work-family effectiveness. *Journal of Vocational Behavior, 68*, 347–367.

Kossek, E. E., Noe, R. & Colquitt, J. (2001). Caregiving decisions, well-being and performance: The effects of place and provider as a function of dependent type and work-family climates. *Academy of Management Journal, 44*(1), 29–44.

Lee, M. & Kossek, E. (2004). *Crafting Lives that Work: A Six-Year Retrospective on Reduced Load Work in the Careers and Lives of Professionals and Managers*. An Alfred P. Sloan Study. The complete report can be downloaded at http://www.polisci.msu.edu/kossek/final.pdf

Kozlowski, S. W. J. & Klein, K. J. (2000). A multilevel approach to theory and research in organizations: Contextual, temporal, and emergent processes. In K. J. Klein & S. W. J. Kozlowski (eds), *Multilevel Theory, Research, and Methods in Organizations* (pp. 3–90). San Francisco: Jossey-Bass.

Kramer, R. M. & Goldman, L. (1995). Helping the group or helping yourself? Social motives and group identity in resource dilemmas. In D. A. Schroeder (ed.), *Social Dilemmas: Perspectives on Individuals and Groups* (pp. 49–67). Westport, CT: Praeger.

Lambert, S. J. (2000). Added benefits: The link between work-life benefits and organizational citizenship behavior. *Academy of Management Journal, 43*, 801–815.

Levine, J. M. & Moreland, R. L. (1998). Small groups. In D. Gilbert, S. Fiske & G. Lindzey (eds), *Handbook of Social Psychology* (4th edn) (pp. 415–469). Boston: McGraw Hill.

Lindsley, D. H., Brass, D. J. & Thomas, J. B. (1995). Efficacy-performance spirals: A multilevel perspective. *Administrative Science Quarterly, 20*, 645–678.

Mitchell, T. R. (1997). Matching motivational strategies with organizational contexts. In L. L. Cummings & B. M. Staw (eds), *Research in Organizational Behavior* (Vol. 19) (pp. 57–149). Greenwich, CT: JAI Press.

Munck, B. (2001). Changing a culture of face-time. *Harvard Business Review, 79*, 125–131.

Olmstead, B. & Smith S. (1997). *Managing in a Flexible Workplace*. New York: AMACOM.

Organ, D. W. (1988). *Organizational Citizenship Behavior: The "Good Soldier" Syndrome*. Lexington, MA: Lexington Books.

Perlow, L. A. (1997). *Finding Time: How Corporations, Individuals, and Families can Benefit from New Work Practices*. Ithaca, NY: Cornell University Press.

Perry-Smith, J. & Blum, T. (2000). Work-family human resource bundles and perceived organizational performance. *Academy of Management Journal, 43*, 1107–1117.

Pruitt, D. G. (1998). Social conflict. In D. T. Gilbert, St. Fiske & G. Lindzey (eds), *Handbook of Social Psychology* (4th edn) (pp. 470–503). Boston, MA: McGraw Hill.

Rapoport, R., Bailyn, L., Fletcher, J. & Pruitt, B. (2002). *Beyond Work-Family Balance: Advancing Gender Equity and Workplace Performance*. San Francisco: Jossey-Bass.

Schelling, T. C. (1978). *Micromotives and Macrobehavior*. New York: Norton.

Schroeder, D. A. (1995). *Social Dilemmas: Perspectives on Individuals and Groups*. London: Praeger.

Skarlicki, D. P. & Folger, R. (1997). Retaliation in the workplace: The roles of distributive, procedural, and interactional justice. *Journal of Applied Psychology, 82*, 434–443.

Smola, K. W. & Sutton, C. D. (2002). Generational differences: Revisiting generational work values for the new millennium. *Journal of Organizational Behavior, 23*, 363–382.

Steiner, F. F. (1972). *Group Process and Productivity*. New York: Academic Press.

Van de Ven, A. H. & Ferry, D. L. (1980). *Measuring and Assessing Organizations*. New York: Wiley.

Van Dyne, L., Cummings, L. L. & McLean Parks, J. (1995). Extra-role behaviors: In pursuit of construct and definitional clarity (A bridge over muddied waters). In B. M. Staw & L. L. Cummings (eds), *Research in Organizational Behavior* (Vol. 17) (pp. 215–285). Greenwich, CT: JAI Press.

Van Lange, P. A. M., Liebrand, W. B. G., Messick, D. M. & Wilke, H. A. M. (1992). Social dilemmas: The state of the art. In W. B. G. Liebrand (ed.), *Social Dilemmas: Theoretical Issues and Research Findings* (pp. 3–28). Oxford: Pergamon Press.

Wells, S. (2001). Making telecommuting work. *HRMagazine, 46*, 34–46.

Yamagishi, T. (1988). Seriousness of social dilemmas and the provision of a sanctioning system. *Social Psychology Quarterly, 51*, 265–271.

CHAPTER 18

Work-Family Culture: Current Research and Future Directions

Jeanine K. Andreassi and Cynthia A. Thompson
Department of Management, John F. Welch School of Business,
Sacred Heart University, Fairfield, CT
Department of Management, Zicklin School of Business, Baruch College,
One Bernard Baruch Way, New York

...our society is just about at the breaking point, especially for families who are raising children. The ones who are most likely to have a high quality of life are those without children. It's not only because of a mismatch between the old and new realities, but it's also the global economy...as well as today's technology where you're available 24/7
(Moen & Huang, in press).

The pressures facing workers today have been well documented. Long commutes, last-minute overtime requests, early morning meetings, the need to be available at a moment's notice, and the need to be in touch with co-workers, clients, and suppliers in different time zones—all wreak havoc on employees' personal lives. And often there is no one at home to pick up the slack. The number of wage and salaried employees in dual-career or dual-earner couples has increased dramatically in the last 25 years, as has the number of employees caring for elderly parents. More than 43% of the US workforce are parents of minor children (Bond, Thompson, Galinsky & Prottas, 2003). Not surprisingly, a recently released report estimates that over 50 million parents in the US are stressed because they worry about their child's welfare during the hours after school (Barnett & Gareis, 2006). Children are concerned that their parents are working too hard (Galinsky, 1999), and a recent *Wall Street Journal* article described "BlackBerry orphans," children who resent the intrusion of their parent's hand-held, go everywhere email device (Rosman, 2006).

Further evidence that workers are struggling can be seen in the increasing number of employees who say they experience a great deal of conflict between work and family. The 2002 National Study of the Changing Workforce, a study that assesses US workers' attitudes about their jobs and family lives, found that 34% of all workers report experiencing somewhat or a lot of interference between their job and family life, 35% find it somewhat or very hard to take time during the workday for personal or family matters, 28% felt that they did not have

Adapted with substantial revision from Thompson, C. A., Andreassi, J., & Prottas, D. (2005). Work-family culture: Key to reducing workforce-workplace mismatch? In S. M. Bianchi, L. M. Casper, & R. Berkowitz King (eds), Workforce/Workplace Mismatch? Work, Family, Health and Well-Being (pp. 117–132). Mahwah, NJ: Lawrence Erlbaum.
Permission by Lawrence Erlbaum Associates

enough time for their children, 40% reported not having enough time with their partner, and 53% felt that they did not have enough time for themselves (Families and Work Institute, 2004). It is likely that workers in other countries are experiencing conflict as well. In fact, women account for an increasing proportion of the labor force in the European Union, with 50% of the female population now working (van Doorne-Huiskes, den Dulk & Schippers, 1999).

To help employees cope with the competing demands of work and family, many organizations have attempted to create a "family-friendly" or "life-friendly" workplace for their employees (see Kossek & Van Dyne, Chapter 17, in this volume; Lobel & Kossek, 1996). To create such a workplace, they develop benefits, programs, and policies designed to give employees flexibility (e.g., telecommuting options), dependent care support (e.g., on-site child care centers), information (e.g., resource and referral programs), financial support (e.g., adoption assistance), and direct services (e.g., concierge services). According to the results of a national study, 55% of medium-size workplaces in the US allow employees to periodically work from home, 36% provide access to information to help locate childcare in the community, and 9% offer childcare on or near site (Galinsky & Bond, 1998). Of the workers interviewed for the 2002 National Study of the Changing Workforce (Bond, Thompson, Galinsky & Prottas, 2003), 43% reported that they were allowed to use traditional flextime (periodically change hours of work), and 23% reported that they were able to change start and stop times on a daily basis.

Despite the increased availability of work-life programs, employees are often reluctant to take advantage of these programs, especially programs that reduce their visibility to co-workers and managers. Many of these programs conflict with entrenched organizational norms such as "face time," and as a result, employees who reduce their work hours are often stigmatized (Epstein, Seron, Oglensky & Saute, 1999; Fried, 1998; Wharton & Blair-Loy, 2002). Even in Sweden, which is arguably the most advanced nation in terms of governmental work-family support, women and men have reported being discriminated against when they returned from parental leave (Nasman, 1999). In the US, researchers have found that employees who perceived unsupportive family-friendly cultures were less likely to use their employer's work-life programs, at least partly because they feared negative career consequences for using them (Allen, 2001; Thompson, Beauvais & Lyness, 1999). Evidence that their fears are not unfounded comes from a study of over 11,000 managers in a financial services firm. Judiesch and Lyness (1999) found that taking a leave of absence was associated with fewer subsequent promotions and smaller salary increases. They argued that their findings support a "gendered organizational culture" in that managers who take a leave of absence do not conform to expectations of prioritizing work over family and therefore are perceived to be less deserving of organizational rewards.

The purpose of this chapter is to discuss the role of the work environment—specifically, the culture of support for work-family balance—in understanding employees' work attitudes and behaviors, as well as their stress levels and general well-being. We will first define work-family culture and related constructs such as perceived organizational family support. We will then describe various dimensions of work-family culture that have been proposed in the literature, as well as how work-family culture has been measured. We will describe the latest research on work-family culture, including recent research using international samples, and provide several examples of what organizations are doing to create a more supportive culture. We will conclude with thoughts about future research directions and implications for practice.

WHAT IS WORK-FAMILY CULTURE?

Work-family culture has been defined as the "shared assumptions, beliefs, and values regarding the extent to which an organization supports and values the integration of employees' work and family lives" (Thompson et al., 1999; p. 394). Allen (2001) described a related construct, family supportive organization perceptions, as the "global perceptions that employees form regarding the extent to which the organization is family supportive" (p. 414). Jahn, Thompson and Kopelman (2003) described another related construct, perceived organizational family support, which taps employees' perceptions of tangible support (i.e., instrumental and informational support) and intangible support (i.e., emotional support). Finally, Lewis (1997) defined work-family culture in terms of Schein's (1985) theory of organizational culture, which distinguishes between three levels of culture (i.e., artifacts, values, and basic underlying assumptions). Lewis argued that work-life policies and programs are "artifacts," or surface level indicators of an organization's intentions to be supportive. Values underlie artifacts, and might include, for example, prioritizing work over family or family over work. Basic assumptions underlie values. For example, it is often assumed that time spent at work is indicative of productivity, despite policies to the contrary (e.g., flex-place, telecommuting). According to Lewis, it is the values and assumptions that get at the heart of workplace culture. Because values and assumptions are difficult to examine, much less change, it is usually easier for organizations to focus on surface-level change such as implementing an on-site childcare center, rather than deeper cultural changes like decreasing the importance of face time by focusing on an employee's output rather input (e.g., the number of hours logged per week).

Some definitions and operationalizations of work-family culture have included both formal (e.g., actual benefits offered, degree of schedule flexibility) and informal (e.g., perceptions of support) elements (e.g., Clark, 2001; Warren & Johnson, 1995). Jahn et al. (2003) focused on perceptions of both tangible and intangible support. Others have focused on informal or intangible aspects of culture only (e.g., Allen, 2001; Kossek, Colquitt & Noe, 2001; Thompson et al., 1999). As organizational culture has been defined in terms of employees' *perceptions* of expectations and norms for behavior at work, or what some authors have referred to as "the internal social psychological environment" (Denison, 1996), in this chapter we will focus on employees' perceptions of the informal, intangible aspects of work-family culture, while recognizing that this culture is influenced, in part, by the formal benefits offered by the organization.

DIMENSIONALITY OF WORK-FAMILY CULTURE

Most researchers have considered work-family culture to be comprised of multiple dimensions. Research by Thompson et al. (1999) suggests that work-family culture is comprised of three components: organizational time demands, career consequences for using work-family benefits, and managerial support. *Organizational time demands* refers to the extent to which there are expectations for long hours of work and for prioritizing work over family. Advertising agencies, start-up software companies, and investment banks, for example, are known for excessive time demands, with employees often working nights and weekends. *Perceived career consequences* refers to the degree to which employees perceive positive or negative career consequences for using work-family benefits. Because of norms for "face time," employees often believe that participating in work-family programs such as flexplace may damage their career progress as they will be less visible at work (Bailyn, 1993; Fried, 1998). The third component, *managerial support*, captures the extent to which individual managers are sensitive to and accommodating of employees' family needs. A supportive supervisor, according to Galinsky and Stein (1990), is someone who feels that handling family issues is a legitimate part of their role, is knowledgeable about company policies, is flexible when work-family problems arise, and handles work-family problems fairly and without favoritism.

In addition to the dimensions described above, there are most likely other relevant dimensions important for fully understanding the nature of work-family culture. For example, Kossek et al. (2001), who prefer the term "climate" to "culture," proposed that two dimensions of work climate are related to an employee's ability to balance work and family. A *work climate for sharing concerns* encourages employees to discuss family concerns with supervisors and co-workers, while a *work climate for sacrifices* entails making sacrifices in the family role to support work role performance. Kossek, Noe and DeMarr (1999) proposed that organizations have a *climate for boundary separation*: some have loose boundaries between work and family (e.g., employees can bring children to work) and some have tight boundaries (e.g., employees are not allowed to take personal calls at work). In addition, Kirchmeyer (1995) suggested that *respect* for an employee's nonwork life is an important component of a supportive organization.

Finally, there are aspects of an organization's culture that may be related to but distinct from work-family culture as currently conceptualized. In a study of Swedish working fathers, Haas, Allard and Hwang (2002) viewed culture in terms of how supportive it was of men's active participation in fatherhood, and operationalized it in terms of five company-level dimensions (e.g., a masculine ethic, caring ethic, equal opportunity ethic) and three work-group level dimensions (e.g., supervisor support for men's participation in childcare, work group norms of visibility). For example, an equal opportunity ethic captures an organization's commitment to improving the status of women in the company, which is likely related to—but not the same as—the level of organizational support for work-life balance. Their other proposed dimensions appear similar to dimensions described earlier (e.g., the caring ethic includes respect for others).

MEASUREMENT OF WORK-FAMILY CULTURE

For many years, work-life experts, journalists, and HR professionals lamented the difficulty of creating a truly family-friendly workplace, citing entrenched corporate cultures as the major barrier to real change (e.g., Kofodimos, 1995; Solomon, 1994). Early efforts to document the strength of the culture in facilitating or hindering the acceptance of work-life programs were qualitative in nature, and yielded powerful stories about the difficulties individual employees were having in their attempts to create a balanced life (e.g., Lewis & Taylor, 1996). While qualitative research is highly useful for developing a deep understanding of an organization's culture, it is limited in that it is time-consuming, labor intensive, and not usually generalizable. Further, qualitative research does not allow the researcher to test hypotheses about the nature of relationships between culture and its potential antecedents, consequences, moderators, and mediators. A quantifiable, psychometrically sound measure of work-family culture would benefit researchers who want to study the relationship between, for example, work-family culture and various outcomes important to employees (e.g., stress, life satisfaction, physical health) and employers (e.g., absenteeism, turnover, performance), as well as the extent to which these relationships are moderated by gender and mediated by work-family conflict. In addition, a quantifiable measure would enable organizations to survey its employees to get a sense of how the culture is perceived.

To facilitate research on work and family culture, several researchers have developed quantitative measures of work-family culture or related concepts (e.g., perceived organizational family support). As shown in Table 18.1, there are five measures that have been developed and used in research to date. All of these measures focus on individual perceptions of organizational culture; as such, they do not attempt to measure the degree to which these perceptions are shared among work groups or organizations as a whole (see Thompson, Jahn, Kopelman & Prottas, 2004, for an exception). Because these scales have not been used to measure shared culture, researchers must be careful to clarify the distinction between shared versus individual perceptions of culture.

Table 18.1

Measures of Organizational Support for Work-Life Balance

Author	Measure	Dimensions	Studies Using This Measure
Allen (2001)	Family Supportive Organizational Perceptions (FSOP)	One overall dimension (14 items; $\alpha = .91$)	Behson, 2002; Kikta & Tetrick, 2005; O'Driscoll et al., 2003
Bond et al., 1997; Bond et al., 2003; Reports of the National Study of the Changing Workforce	Work-family culture, 4-5 items	Items tap perceptions of negative career consequences and prioritizing work over family ($\alpha = .71$ to .75)	Anderson et al., 2002; Behson, 2004; Hill, 2005; Sahibzada et al., 2005; Thompson & Prottas, 2006
Clark (2001)	Work Culture	• temporal flexibility (5 items; $\alpha = .84$) • operational flexibility (5 items; $\alpha = .83$) • supportive supervision (3 items; $\alpha = .86$)	Dikkers et al., 2004; Lapierre & Allen, 2006
Jahn, Thompson, & Kopelman (2003)	Perceived Organizational Family Support (POFS); 10 items, including one item measuring overall family-friendliness; $\alpha = .94$	• tangible support (6 items) • intangible support (3 items)	Thompson et al., 2004; Kikta & Tetrick, 2005
Thompson, Beauvais, & Lyness (1999)	Work-family Culture (WFCult); 21 items, including one item that measures overall supportiveness for balancing work and family; $\alpha = .92$	• career consequences (5 items; $\alpha = .74$) • organizational time demands (4 items; $\alpha = .80$) • managerial support (11 items; $\alpha = .91$)	Beauregard, 2006; Behson, 2002; Bragger Lyness et al., 2005; Dikkers et al., 2004; Lyness & Kropf, 2005; Lyness et al., 1999; Mauno et al. (2005); Tay et al., 2006; Wayne et al., 2006

The measure most frequently used in research is a 20-item scale developed in 1999 by Thompson et al. As described above, this measure assesses three dimensions of work-family culture (i.e., organizational time demands, negative career consequences, and managerial support). Allen (2001) measured organizational work-family supportiveness by a 14-item unidimensional scale she named "Family Supportive Organization Perceptions." Her scale measures global perceptions of the degree to which the employee's organization is supportive of families, although Kinnunen, Mauno, Guerts and Dikkers (2005) argued that the scale seems to tap multiple dimensions (e.g., time demands, importance of separating work and family). Nevertheless, Allen's analyses did not support a multidimensional scale. Importantly, Allen (2001) did not include supervisory support in her scale as she considers organizational supportiveness and supervisory/managerial supportiveness to be separate concepts. In fact, she found that perceptions of family-supportive work environments mediated the relationship between supervisor support and work-family conflict, suggesting that supervisor support may be a precursor to a supportive work-family culture rather than an aspect of culture itself.

Clark (2001) developed a 13-item measure of work culture based on Bailyn's (1997) description of the characteristics of a family-supportive work culture: flexible work processes (what Clark called "operational flexibility"), flexible work scheduling ("temporal flexibility"), and supervisors' support for family ("supportive supervision"). However, as noted by Kinnunen et al. (2005), neither flexibility scale taps family supportiveness, although both are most likely related to an employee's ability to balance work and family.

Jahn et al. (2003) developed a measure grounded in social support theory (House, 1981) and perceived organizational support theory (Eisenberger, Huntington, Hutchinson & Sowa, 1986). Their measure, which they labeled "Perceived Organizational Family Support," is comprised of nine items which assess two dimensions: tangible support, which includes perceptions of instrumental and informational support, and intangible support, which includes perceptions of emotional support. A tenth item assesses overall family friendliness of the organization.

Finally, in its National Survey of the Changing Workforce, the Families and Work Institute includes four or five items (depending on the year of the survey) to measure perceptions of work-family culture (Bond et al., 1998; Bond et al., 2003). These items appear to tap two aspects of culture: perceptions of potential negative career consequences for tending to family needs, and the perceived importance of prioritizing work over family. Table 18.1 includes a list of researchers who have used each of these scales.

RESEARCH ON OUTCOMES RELATED TO WORK-FAMILY CULTURE

OUTCOMES RELATED TO OVERALL SUPPORTIVENESS OF THE WORK-FAMILY CULTURE

Although research investigating the impact of work-life benefits on employee attitudes and behavior has shown mixed results (see Kossek and Van Dyne's chapter in this book), research on the impact of supportive work-family cultures has been consistently positive. For example, the 2002 National Study of the Changing Workforce (Bond et al., 2003) found that employees who worked in supportive cultures were more committed to their employer, more satisfied with their jobs, and less likely to be thinking about quitting. In addition, these employees experienced less negative spillover from their jobs to their home, had better mental health, and were more satisfied with their lives.

Similarly, other research has demonstrated that perceptions of a family-supportive work environment were associated with greater job satisfaction (Allen, 2001; Sahibzida, Hammer, Neal & Kuang, 2005), positive spillover between work and family (Thompson & Prottas, 2006) and commitment to the organization (Allen, 2001; Dikkers, den Dulk, Geurts & Peper, 2005; Lyness, Thompson, Francesco & Judiesch, 1999; Thompson et al., 1999; Thompson et al., 2004). In addition, perceptions of a supportive work-family culture were related to lower levels of work stress or strain (Mauno, Kinnunen and Pyykko, 2005; Thompson & Prottas, 2006; Warren et. al., 1995), work-family conflict (Allen, 2001; Anderson, Coffey & Byerly, 2002; Behson, 2002; Mauno et al., 2005; Thompson & Prottas, 2006), and turnover intentions (Allen, 2001; Bond et al., 2003; Thompson et al., 1999). The results of a recent meta-analysis found that of five types of support (dependent care availability, work schedule and location flexibility, supervisor support, co-worker support, and work-family culture), work-family culture, followed by supervisor support, had the strongest relationship with work-family conflict (Mesmer-Magnus & Viswesvaran, 2006).

The relationship between a supportive work-family culture and positive outcomes (e.g., lower work-family conflict, commitment, lower turnover intentions) was found even when controlling for benefit availability (e.g., Thompson et al., 1999; Allen, 2001; Thompson et al., 2004). When both benefit use and work-family culture were examined together, only work-family culture was related to work-family balance (Lyness & Kropf, 2005) and work-family conflict (O'Driscoll, Poelmans, Spector, Kalliath, Allen, Cooper & Sanchez, 2003). Finally, Wayne, Randel and Stevens (2006) examined the role of individual (i.e., work and family identities), family (emotional and instrumental support), and organizational (benefit use and work-family culture) antecedents of work-family enrichment, which they defined as the positive affect that results when one role enhances the quality of life in another role. The strength of an individual's identity and informal or emotional support within a domain, rather than formal or instrumental support, were associated with greater enrichment, which, in turn, was associated with higher commitment and lower turnover intentions. Together, these results suggest that a supportive culture is more powerful than either benefit availability or usage in terms of work-related outcomes.

Outcomes Related to Organizational Time Demands

The unsupportiveness of an organization's culture is at least partially reflected in the perception that long hours are required of employees. Because the productivity of managerial and professional employees is often difficult to measure, the hours that an employee spends at work is often used as an indicator of output as well as commitment to the organization (Bailyn, 1993; Blair-Loy & Wharton, 2002). Norms regarding face time (i.e., being physically present at the workplace) create pressures for employees to work longer hours than are necessary, just to prove their dedication and commitment (Bailyn, 1993; Fried, 1998).

Research suggests that working long hours has implications for employee health and well-being (Beauregard, 2006; Major, Klein & Ehrhart, 2002; Sparks, Cooper, Fried & Shirom, 1997). For example, Major et al. (2002) found that organizational norms for how much time should be spent at work were, in fact, predictive of hours worked, which in turn were related to work-family conflict. Work time was indirectly related to psychological distress (e.g., depression) through its effect on work-family conflict. Beauregard (2006) examined potential antecedents of work-family conflict, including situational antecedents (e.g., presence of young children, perceived work-family culture, including perceived time demands) and dispositional antecedents (e.g., self-esteem, perfectionism). She found that perceived organizational time demands had the strongest relationship to work-to-family conflict. Thompson et al. (1999) also found that employees who perceived heavy organizational time demands were more likely to report higher levels of work-family conflict; this relationship held even after controlling for actual hours worked. As suggested by Greenhaus and Beutell (1985), the additional variance explained by perceptions of time demands may be due to mental preoccupation with work while at home, thus adding to the level of work-family conflict experienced. Finally, Brett and Stroh (2003) found that employees who worked the longest hours felt the most alienated from their families, and Wayne et al. (2006) found that employees who perceived heavy time demands were less likely to experience work-family enrichment.

OUTCOMES RELATED TO PERCEIVED NEGATIVE CAREER CONSEQUENCES

Anecdotal as well as empirical evidence suggests that in unsupportive work-family cultures, employees expect negative career consequences for participating in work-family programs (Soloman, 1994; Thompson et al., 1999). In the Thompson et al. study, when employees perceived fewer negative career consequences for using work-family benefits, they were less likely to think about quitting and had less work-to-family conflict. Similarly, Anderson et al. (2002) found that employees who expected negative career consequences for putting their family first reported more work-to-family conflict, lower job satisfaction, and higher turnover intentions. On the other hand, Beauregard (2006) did not find any relationship between perceived negative career consequences and work-family conflict. Taken together, however, these results suggest that even though organizations implement work-life programs to help employees balance work and family, unsupportive cultures lead employees to fear their careers will be damaged if they participate in these programs or allow their family to be a priority in their lives. These negative perceptions have consequences for the individual as well as the organization in terms of conflict experienced and intentions to quit.

Outcomes Related to Supervisory and Managerial Support

Not surprisingly, an employee's relationship with his or her supervisor is a powerful predictor of work-family balance (Galinsky & Stein, 1990). Supportive supervisors and managers likely enhance employees' sense of control, which in turn may increase employees' ability to cope with conflicting work and family demands (Major & Cleveland, 2007; Thompson & Prottas, 2006). In fact, research suggests that employees who have supportive supervisors have higher levels of "employee fulfillment" (Tay, Quazi & Kelly, 2006), lower levels of work-family conflict (Anderson et al., 2002; Frone, Yardley & Markel,1997; Lapierre & Allen, 2006; McManus, Korabik, Rosin & Kelloway, 2002; Thompson et al., 2006), and lower rates of depression, role strain, and other health symptoms (Greenberger, Goldberg, Hamill, O'Neil & Payne, 1989; O'Driscoll et al., 2003; Thomas & Ganster, 1995). Supportive supervision has also been linked to increased commitment (Allen, 2001; Greenberger et al., 1989; Thompson et al., 2004), higher job satisfaction (Allen, 2001; McManus et al., 2002; Thomas & Ganster, 1995), higher career satisfaction (Aryee & Luk, 1996), less intention to quit (Allen, 2001; Thompson et al., 1999), and lower absenteeism (Goff, Mount & Jamison, 1990). Surprisingly, in the study of Swedish fathers mentioned earlier, neither supervisor support nor top management support was related to men's decision to use parental leave, although top management support was related to actual number of days taken (Haas et al., 2002).

Allen (2001) examined the process through which supervisor support decreases work-family conflict. She found that supervisor support was directly related to employees' perceptions of organizational family support, which in turn were related to lower levels of work-family conflict. As Allen and others have noted, supervisors play a key role in determining whether or not employees are able to use work-life policies, and their willingness to be supportive influences employees' attitudes and well-being.

Additional Dimensions of Work-Family Culture

As noted earlier, Kossek et al. (2001) suggested that work climate for sharing family concerns and for sacrificing family for work might be important dimensions of the overall climate that affect employee attitudes as well as decisions about how much time and energy to devote to work. They found a climate for sharing family concerns at work was positively related to an employee's well-being and self-reports of work performance, whereas a climate for sacrificing family for work was negatively related to well-being and positively related to work-family conflict.

Kossek et al. (1999) proposed but did not test the idea that organizations might have a climate for boundary separation. Kirchmeyer (1995) examined a similar idea by investigating the effectiveness of three different organizational responses to managing work and nonwork roles: integration (organization supports combining work and family spheres), separation (the organization treats the domains as separate), and respect (the organization provides the support necessary for the individual to handle work-family demands themselves). In a sample of Canadian managers, "separation" was rated as the most common policy and was related to lower levels of organizational commitment. Integration and respect policies, although less common, were positively related to employee commitment (Kirchmeyer, 1995).

In their study of Swedish fathers, Haas et al. (2002) found that several aspects of organizational and work group culture were related to men's use of parental leave. At the organizational level, male employees who perceived that their company's values included a caring ethic (i.e., the company values empathy, helpfulness, interpersonal sensitivity) and an equal opportunity ethic (e.g., the advancement of women is valued by the company) were more likely to take parental leave. At the work group level, leave usage was related to perceptions that the culture was flexible and adaptive in responding to fathers' desire to take time off to care for children, and that performance was evaluated based on results rather than time at work. However, because individual and family factors accounted for significant amounts of variance in usage of parental leave compared to organizational culture factors, the authors suggested that the Swedish national context may render company factors less important.

WORK-FAMILY CULTURE AND BENEFIT USAGE

Researchers have begun to investigate the relationship between supportiveness of work-family culture and the extent to which employees actually *use* the work-life benefits offered. As noted earlier, even if benefits are available, they often are not used in cultures that send mixed messages about whether it is acceptable to use them (Perlow, 1995). Several recent studies found that employees were more likely to use work-life benefits when they perceived that their organizations and supervisors provided a family-supportive work environment (Allen, 2001; Dikkers, Geurts, den Dulk, Peper & Kompier, 2004; Thompson et al., 1999). For example, Dikkers et al. (2004) found that Dutch employees in a consulting firm who perceived a more supportive work culture (i.e., in terms of collegial and managerial support) were more likely to use flextime and to work from home. Interestingly, these employees also perceived negative career consequences and high time demands (two dimensions they combined and called "hindrance" factors), suggesting that they were using work-family benefits despite the possible detriment to their career. Dikkers suggested that "high support and high hindrance [might not be] two ends of the same continuum" (p. 340) and are separate factors that may co-exist.

Blair-Loy and Wharton (2002) examined possible contextual factors that may influence whether employees use work-family policies and programs. In particular, they examined whether having powerful supervisors or co-workers would increase the utilization of family-care programs and flexible work policies. They argued that a social context with powerful individuals (e.g., with men being more powerful than women in many workplaces) would provide the support necessary to reduce the potential negative career consequences associated with using work-family programs. They found that use of family care policies (e.g., daycare and paid/unpaid leave) was influenced solely by individual factors, with women, single individuals, and those with dependent care responsibilities more likely to use them. However, use of flexible policies (e.g., flextime, telecommuting) was affected by the amount of power that one's co-workers and supervisors had. For example, having a male, unmarried supervisor as compared to a female, married supervisor increased the probability of using flexible policies by 50%.

Other researchers have determined that employees who actually use work-family benefits tend to be more committed to their organization and have lower intentions to quit (Allen, 2001; Eaton, 2003; Grover & Crooker, 1995). In one study, use of work-life policies was related to increased perceptions of control, which in turn were directly related to a reduction in personal stressors and indirectly related to improved mental and physical health of employees (Thomas & Ganster, 1995). These findings highlight again the benefits of creating a supportive work culture in which employees feel comfortable using work-life benefits offered.

INTERNATIONAL PERSPECTIVE ON WORK-FAMILY CULTURE

It is increasingly recognized that national context is important for understanding work-family culture (Lewis, 1997; Korabik, Lero & Ayman, 2003). With so many organizations operating in multiple countries, it is important to understand how the culture of a country, its social norms, social policies and programs, influence formal and informal workplace support for employees with families. Research examining organizational work-family culture using international samples is limited, although the literature is growing (e.g., Beauregard, 2006; Dikkers et al., 2004; Lyness & Kropf, 2005). However, with the exception of Lyness and Kropf's study, all have been single-country studies, thus making country comparisons difficult. In the next section, we will briefly discuss findings from recent research that shed light on the relationships between country culture, organizational work-family culture, and outcomes important to individual employees and their employers.

NATIONAL CULTURE AND ORGANIZATIONAL TIME DEMANDS

In a recent cross-national study, Wharton and Blair-Loy (2002) found that Hong Kong employees were more interested in working part-time than their American and British counterparts. They attributed this finding to the Confucian culture prevalent in Hong Kong, which places family above all other concerns, including work. Americans were less likely than British or Hong Kong employees to indicate a desire to work fewer hours. The authors suggested that this finding might be due to the American tendency to equate long hours with achievement and identity. Although societal norms for working long hours likely translates into corporate norms for heavy time demands, future researchers should examine the strength of this relationship and how it varies across national cultures and across firms within these cultures.

GENDER EQUALITY AND WORK-FAMILY SUPPORTIVENESS

Gender equality refers to "the extent to which national cultures support women's development and achievements" (Lyness & Kropf, 2005, p. 34). Although the United States is seen as a relatively gender-equality-based society, the public support for gender equality is much lower than that of other nations, such as Sweden, which has nationally funded daycare and eldercare. In countries where there is more support for gender equality, workers may have greater expectations for support from the government. To test this idea, Lewis and Smithson (2001) explored the relationship between type of welfare state in the country and sense of entitlement to governmental work-family support. They conducted a qualitative study of employees from five countries (Norway, Sweden, Portugal, Ireland, and the UK), and found that employees in countries with social policies that were supportive of equality had a stronger sense of entitlement to state support for combining work and family responsibilities, compared to employees in countries with policies that were influenced by traditional gender roles. For example, in Sweden and Norway there is high gender equality, and state support was expected and taken for granted. In contrast, in Britain, Portugal, and Ireland, where gender roles are more traditional, employees were more likely to assume individual responsibility for the caring of children and did not expect state support. This sense of entitlement extended to corporations: individuals in countries with more traditional gender roles were less likely to expect corporate support for balancing work and family. Interestingly, even in countries with traditional gender roles, beliefs that one was entitled to employer work-family support increased if individuals perceived that offering work-family benefits was in the employer's economic interests. In contrast, individuals in Sweden and Norway were likely to believe that organizations should support employees' attempts to balance work and family because it was "the right thing to do." Because the sense of entitlement to receive government support was so strong, expectations for help from employers was low.

Lyness and Kropf (2005) examined whether national gender equality would be related to the work-family supportiveness of organizations, and, in turn, managers' reported ability to balance work and family. In their survey of 505 managers from 20 European countries, they found that national gender equality (measured by the United Nations' Gender Development Index) was related to higher levels of perceived organizational work-family support (measured in terms of supportiveness of work-family culture and flexible benefit availability). In turn, perceived organizational work-family support was related positively to managers' perceptions of work-family balance. As noted by the authors, these findings highlight the importance of considering the larger context—especially a nation's stance toward gender equality—in understanding work-family balance (Lyness & Kropf, 2005).

EXAMPLES OF CORPORATE ATTEMPTS TO CHANGE THE CULTURE

Because of the persistence of an overtime culture in many Western countries, solutions have been aimed at changing the perception that presence at work (including "face time") equals productivity. For example, a company in the United Kingdom implemented a "Go Home on Time Days" campaign, with employees being encouraged to work smarter, not harder. The campaign was designed to challenge the notion that time at the office is an indicator of commitment, and included management training on how to facilitate work-life balance (Brannen & Lewis, 2000). Nasman (1999) described another organization in Sweden where men take full advantage of "daddy days." Time off for children is openly promoted by men in the firm and accepted at the highest levels of the organization. In fact, company policy states that men, as well as women, have the right to take parental leave, and it stresses the company's commitment to no negative consequences for the use of these benefits.

Ernst & Young's efforts to create a more balanced work-life culture have landed it in *Working Mother* magazine's top ten list of best companies for working mothers. Instead of simply offering work-life programs and policies such as flextime or job sharing, they are attempting to change the culture by, for example changing expectations about the need to check emails on weekends and vacation, creating deployment committees to track employee work loads, and creating a travel schedule that allows employees to spend fewer nights at the client's site and more nights at home with family (Casner-Lotto, 2000; Friedman, Thompson, Carpenter & Marcel, 2001). Ernst & Young is also trying to change deep cultural assumptions that work-life balance is only for women. A recent article described a new campaign to depict flexible work schedules as "macho" by showing pictures of men in their advertisements, and by framing flexible schedules as a quality of life issue (Badal, 2006).

Changing a culture is not easy. Even with all the success that Ernst & Young has had in changing its culture, there is still resistance among many senior managers and partners. These leaders, who often rose through the ranks by sacrificing their own personal lives, find it difficult to believe that making employees happy will pay off in client satisfaction and firm growth. One of the change initiatives was to create solutions around leaders as role models, but the team in charge of this initiative gave up. While the leaders were able to improve work-life balance for their employees, they perceived that their own heavy work loads made it impossible for them to enjoy greater balance (Casner-Lotto, 2000).

Changing a culture in more traditional countries is even more difficult. In Japan and Korea, for example, corporate culture emphasizes face time, and employees are reluctant to leave work before the boss does. Further, performance is judged largely on time at work rather than the quality of work, resulting in long hours at the office during the workweek as well as on weekends. Confucian values of teamwork versus individual achievement likely add to the pressure to stay with the team until all the work is done. As a result, there is little movement toward implementing work-life strategies like telecommuting or flextime (Ihlwan & Hall, 2007), much less changing the company culture to be more family friendly.

IMPLICATIONS FOR FUTURE RESEARCH AND PRACTICE

That a supportive work-family culture is related to important organizational outcomes is well documented. However, what is not clear is the relative importance of the various dimensions of culture for predicting these outcomes. Further, it is not entirely clear that managerial or supervisor support is a component of work-family culture or a precursor. What we do know is that the dimensions examined to date are differentially related to outcomes (Anderson et al., 2002; Beauregard, 2006; Dikkers et al., 2004; Lyness et al., 1999; Thompson et al., 1999). To advance our understanding of work-family culture, we must first conduct a comprehensive study to expand our knowledge of its dimensionality. The results of such a study would enable researchers and practitioners to speak more confidently about the nature of work-family culture, as well as the aspects of culture that are most likely to impact important individual and organizational outcomes. Once the relevant dimensions have been determined, we should then invest time in developing a psychometrically sound, inclusive measure of work-life rather than work-family culture. Finally, by determining which dimensions are most predictive of positive (and negative) outcomes, organizations will be better able to focus their change efforts on aspects of culture that matter.

In addition to examining the various dimensions of culture, our knowledge would be enhanced by taking a multilevel perspective of culture (Korabik et al., 2003). To understand subcultures within an organization, for example, we need to consider how subcultures are embedded in and influenced by the larger organizational culture, which in turn is embedded in and influenced by the larger societal culture. As recommended by Gelfand and Knight (2005), we need to move beyond our individual-level focus to a more complex focus on "the multilevel terrain in which work-family issues exist" (p. 405).

Another gap in research on work-family culture is the lack of attention to how variations across organizations, occupations, and industries may impact the supportiveness of the culture. It is likely that factors such as organizational size, technology, business strategy, top management support, and national context affect the degree to which an organization's culture is supportive (Thompson & Prottas, 2005). Not surprisingly, research by the Families and Work Institute found that the extent to which an organization offered flexible work arrangements varied significantly by company size, industry, and percentage of executive positions held by women and minorities (Galinsky & Bond, 1998). There are probably similar predictors of a supportive culture, as well as additional job or work group factors such as degree of task interdependence, compensation interdependence, analyzability of the job, and level of client demand. For example, it seems likely that when an employee's compensation is highly dependent on team members, group norms for work primacy would develop (Thompson & Prottas, 2005).

Research on work-family culture would also benefit from expanding its focus beyond managerial and professional employees to blue-collar or pink-collar employees, who often work in occupations where they have little control or autonomy and are required to work overtime. These employees are often given little advance warning that they must work late, and under the Fair Labor Standards Act of 1938, employers can fire or demote workers who refuse (Perry-Jenkins, 2005). In an analysis of the 2002 General Social Survey, Golden and Wiens-Tuers (2005) found that 21% of full-time employees worked extra hours because it was required by their employer, an increase of approximately 5% since 1977. Only seven US states have passed some form of legal ban and/or right to refuse overtime.

Work-family culture studies have long excluded single employees and employees without children or eldercare responsibilities. To begin to rectify this gap, Casper, Weltman and Kweisga (2006) examined how single employees with no children viewed their organization's treatment of them. They defined a singles friendly organizational culture as "the shared assumptions, beliefs, and values regarding the extent to which an organization supports and values the integration of work and nonwork that is *unrelated to family*, and the degree to which equity is perceived in the support the organization provides for employees' nonwork lives, irrespective of family status" (p. 6). They developed a measure of a singles friendly work-life culture that included five dimensions: social inclusion, equal work opportunities, equal access to benefits, equal responsibility for nonwork, and equal work expectations. Their results suggest that single employees who perceived more social inclusion had higher levels of organizational commitment. Overall, employees who worked in a more singles friendly culture were more likely to be committed to their organization, were less likely to be thinking about quitting, and perceived their organization as supportive.

Finally, more cross-cultural research on work-life culture is needed, as many companies are growing beyond domestic borders. It is important for multinational corporations to understand how the national context might affect not only the type of work-life benefits they should offer, but the nature of the support that would be acceptable or expected. Should companies rely on a consistent set of work-family policies, or should they be tailored to the subsidiary level? Should national context be taken into consideration? It seems likely that work-family culture in subsidiary foreign locations would differ, and yet some research suggests otherwise. Researchers at IBM (Hill, Yang, Hawkins & Ferris, 2004) demonstrated that national culture, based on degree of individualism/collectivism, did not affect the way in which work and family was viewed in different countries. However, they noted that the culture at IBM may be so strong that it diluted the effect of national context on work-family outcomes. Nevertheless, it seems likely that societal cultures and state ideologies would influence the nature of work-family culture within most organizations (Gelfand & Knight, 2005).

In summary, research on work-family or work-life culture has progressed to the point that we can say with confidence that culture matters. It matters in terms of employees' ability to balance work and family, and it matters in terms of an organization's ability to recruit and retain valued employees. Researchers must now focus on expanding our knowledge of the link between national culture, type of welfare state regime, organizational work-family culture, and outcomes such as organizational commitment, benefit usage, job performance, and employee health and well-being. In addition, we must begin studying the sources or antecedents of a supportive culture versus one that requires employees to prioritize work over family. We must also broaden our focus to include a wider range of employees, including those with and without children. We should attempt to examine which dimensions of an unsupportive culture are most amenable to change, and as well study ways to increase the success of culture change efforts.

As reported in a recent *Wall Street Journal* article:

> Like the previous generation of grads, today's recruits still rate work-life balance as the No. 1 employer attribute they seek, according to Universum. But "they've taken it a step further," says Davie Huddleston, a recruiting executive at PNC Financial Services Group. Grads seem to expect flexibility without the career sacrifices that usually come with it. "This generation is pushing the envelope. They're making us re-think what it takes to be successful," says Laurie Tortorella, a recruiting executive for Intel.
>
> (Shellenbarger, February 16, 2006, pg. D1)

With younger generations demanding radical change, the time is ripe for organizations to confront the difficult task of changing their unsupportive, workaholic cultures. It is our hope that researchers will continue exploring the nature of work-family culture so that we can provide managers with the information they need to create more supportive and productive work environments.

REFERENCES

Allen, T. (2001). Family-supportive work environments: The role of organizational perceptions. *Journal of Vocational Behavior, 58*, 414–435.

Anderson, S., Coffey, B. S. & Byerly, R. T. (2002). Formal organizational initiatives and informal workplace practices: Links to work-family conflict and job-related outcomes. *Journal of Management, 28*(6), 787–810.

Aryee, S. & Luk, V. (1996). Work and nonwork influences on the career satisfaction of dual-earner couples. *Journal of Vocational Behavior, 49*, 38–52.

Badal, J. (December, 2006). To retain valued women employees, companies pitch flextime as macho. *Wall Street Journal Online*, p. B1.

Bailyn, L. (1993). *Breaking the Mold: Women, Men, and Time in the New Corporate World*. New York: Free Press.

Bailyn, L. (1997). The impact of corporate culture on work-family integration. In S. Parasuraman & J. H. Greenhaus (eds), *Integrating Work and Family: Challenges and Choices for a Changing World* (pp. 209–219). Westport, CT: Quorum Books.

Barnett, R. C. & Gareis, K. C. (2006). Antecedents and correlates of parental after-school concern: Exploring a newly identified work-family stressor. *American Behavioral Scientist, 49*, 1382–1400.

Beauregard, A. T. (2006). Organizational work-home culture and employee well-being: Direct or indirect links? Paper presented at the Annual Meeting of the Academy of Management, Atlanta, GA.

Behson, S. J. (2002). Which dominates? The relative importance of work-family organizational support and general organizational context on employee outcomes. *Journal of Vocational Behavior, 61*, 53–72.

Blair-Loy, M. & Wharton, A. (2002). Employees' use of work-family policies and the workplace social context. *Social Forces, 80*(3), 813–845.

Bond, J. T., Galinsky, E. & Swanberg, J. E. (1998). *The 1997 National Study of the Changing Workforce* (Vol. 2). New York, NY: Families and Work Institute.

Bond, T. J., Thompson, C. A., Galinsky, E. & Prottas, D. (2003). *Highlights of the 2002 National Study of the Changing Workforce*. New York: Families and Work Institute.

Brannen, J. & Lewis, S. (2000). Workplace programmes and policies in the UK. In L. Haas, P. Hwang & G. Russell (eds), *Organisational Change and Gender Equity*. London: Sage Publications.

Brett, J. M. & Stroh, L. K. (2003). Working 61 plus hours a week: Why do managers do it? *Journal of Applied Psychology, 88*, 67–78.

Casner-Lotto, J. (2000) *Holding a Job, Having a Life: Strategies for Change*. Scarsdale: Work in America Institute.

Casper, W. J., Weltman, D. & Kwesiga, E. (2006). Beyond family-friendly: Singles-friendly work cultures and employee attachment. Paper presented at the Academy of Management Meetings, August, Atlanta, GA.

Clark, S. C. (2001). Work cultures and work/family balance. *Journal of Vocational Behavior, 58*, 348–365.

Denison, D. R. (1996). What is the difference between organizational culture and organizational climate? A native's point of view on a decade of paradigm wars. *Academy of Management Review, 21*(3), 619–654.

Dikkers, J., den Dulk, L., Geurts, S. & Peper, B. (2005). Work-nonwork culture, utilization of work-nonwork arrangements, and employee-related outcomes in two Dutch organizations. In S. A. Y. Poelmans (ed.), *Work and Family: An International Perspective*. Mahwah, NJ: LEA.

Dikkers, J., Geurts, S., den Dulk, L., Peper, B. & Kompier, M. (2004). Relations among work-home culture, the utilization of work-home arrangements, and work-home interference. *International Journal of Stress Management, 11*, 323–345.

Eaton, S. (2003). If you can use them: Flexibility policies, organizational commitment, and perceived performance. *Industrial Relations, 42*, 145–167.

Eisenberger, R., Hungtington, R., Hutchison, S. & Sowa, D. (1986). Perceived organizational support. *Journal of Applied Psychology, 71*, 500–507.

Epstein, C. F., Seron, C., Oglensky, B. & Saute, R. (1999). *The Part-Time Paradox: Time Norms, Professional Life, Family and Gender*. New York: Routeledge.

Families and Work Institute (2004). *2002 National Study of the Changing Workforce Public-Use Files* (CD-ROM). New York: Families and Work Institute.

Fried, M. (1998). *Taking Time: Parental Leave Policy and Corporate Culture*. Philadelphia: Temple University Press.

Frone, M. R., Yardley, J. K. & Markel, K. (1997). Developing and testing an integrative model of the work-family interface. *Journal of Vocational Behavior, 50*, 145–167.

Friedman, S., Thompson, C., Carpenter, M. & Marcel, D. (2001). Proving Leo Durocher wrong: Driving work/life change at Ernst & Young. A Wharton Work/Life Integration Project. (http://www.bc.edu/bc_org/avp/wfnetwork/loppr/cases.html).

Galinsky, E. (1999). *Ask the Children: The Breakthroughs Study that Reveals How to Succeed at Work and Parenting*. New York: HarperCollins.

Galinsky, E. & Bond, T. (1998). *The 1998 Business Work-Life Study: A Sourcebook*. New York: Families and Work Institute.

Galinsky, E. & Stein, P. J. (1990). The impact of human resource policies on employees. *Journal of Family Issues, 11*(4), 368–377.

Gelfand, M. J. & Knight, A. P. (2005). Cross-cultural perspectives on work-family conflict. In S. A. Y. Poelmans (ed.), *Work and Family: An International Perspective*. Mahwah, NJ: LEA.

Goff, S. J., Mount, M.K., Jamison, R. L. (1990). Employer supported child care, work/family conflict and absenteeism: A field study. *Personnel Psychology, 43*, 793–809.

Golden, L. & Wiens-Tuers, B. (2005). Mandatory overtime work in the United States: Who, where and what? *Labor Studies Journal, 30*, 1–26.

Greenberger, E., Goldberg, W. A., Hamill, S., O'Neil, R. & Payne, C. K. (1989). Contributions of a supportive work environment to parents' well-being and orientation to work. *American Journal of Community Psychology, 17*(6), 755–783.

Greenhaus, J. H. & Beutell, N. J. (1985). Sources and conflict between work and family roles. *Academy of Management Review, 10*(1), 76–88.

Grover, S. L & Crooker, K. J. (1995). Who appreciates family-responsive resource policies: The impact of family-friendly policies. *Personnel Psychology, 48*, 271–298.

Haas, L., Allard, K., & Hwang, P. (2002). The impact of organizational culture on men's use of parental leave in Sweden. *Community, Work and Family, 5*, 319–342.

Hill, E. J., Yang, C., Hawkins, A. J. & Ferris, M. (2004). A cross-cultural test of the work-family interface in 48 countries. *Journal of Marriage and the Family, 66*, 1300–1316.

House, J. S. (1981). *Work, Stress and Social Support*. Reading, MA: Addison-Wesley.

Ihlwan, M. & Hall, K. (2007, March). New tech, old habits. *Business Week*, 48–49.

Jahn, E. W., Thompson, C. A. & Kopelman, R. E. (2003). Rationale and construct validity evidence for a measure of perceived organizational family support (POFS): Because purported practices may not reflect reality. *Community, Work and Family, 6*, 123–140.

Judiesch, M. & Lyness, K. (1999). Left behind? The impact of leaves of absence on managers' career success. *Academy of Management Journal, 42*, 641–651.

Kinnunen, U., Mauno, S., Guerts, S. & Dikkers, J. (2005). Work-family culture in organizations: Theoretical and empirical approaches. In S. A. Y. Poelmans (ed.), *Work and Family: An International Research Perspective* (pp. 87–122). Mahwah, NJ: Lawrence Erlbaum.

Kirchmeyer, C. (1995). Managing the work-nonwork boundary: An assessment of organizational responses. *Human Relations, 48*(5), 515–536.

Kofodimos, J. R. (1995). *Beyond Work-Family Programs: Confronting and Resolving the Underlying Causes of Work-Personal Life Conflict.* Greensboro, NC: Center for Creative Leadership.

Korabik, K., Lero, D. & Ayman, R. (2003). A multi-level approach to cross cultural research: A micro and macro perspective. *International Journal of Cross Cultural Management, 3*, 289–303.

Kossek, E. E., Colquitt, J. A. & Noe, J. A. (2001). Caregiving decisions, well-being, and performance: The effects of place and provider as a function of dependent type and work-family climates. *Academy of Management Journal, 44*(1), 29–44.

Kossek, E. E., Noe, R. A. & DeMarr, B. J. (1999). Work-family role synthesis: Individual and organizational determinants. *International Journal of Conflict Management, 10*(2), 102–129.

Kossek, E. E. & Van Dyne, L. (2007), Chapter 17 in this volume.

Lapierre, L. M. & Allen, T. D. (2006). Work-supportive family, family-supportive supervision, use of organizational benefits, and problem-focused coping: Implications for work-family conflict and employee well-being. *Journal of Occupational Health Psychology, 11*, 169–181.

Lewis, S. (1997). 'Family-friendly' employment policies: A route to changing organizational culture or playing about the margins? *Gender, Work and Organization, 4*, 13–23.

Lewis, S. & Smithson, J. (2001). Sense of entitlement to support for the reconciliation of employment and family life. *Human Relations, 55*, 1455–1481.

Lewis, S. & Taylor, K. (1996). Barriers to the effectiveness of current policies and strategies: Moving beyond policies toward culture change. In S. Lewis & J. Lewis (eds), *The Work-Family Challenge: Rethinking Employment* (pp. 112–127). London: Sage Publications.

Lobel, S. & Kossek, E. (1996). Human resource strategies to support diversity in work and personal life-styles: Beyond the 'family-friendly' organization. In E. Kossek & S. Lobel (eds), *Managing Diversity: Human Resource Strategies for Transforming the Workplace* (pp. 221–244). Cambridge, MA: Blackwell.

Lyness, K. S. & Kropf, M. B. (2005). The relationships of national gender equality and organizational support with work-family balance: A study of European managers. *Human Relations, 58*, 33–60.

Lyness, K., Thompson, C., Francesco, A. M. & Judiesch, M. K. (1999). Work and pregnancy: Individual and organizational factors influencing organizational commitment, timing of maternity leave, and return to work. *Sex Roles, 41*, 485–507.

Major, D. A. & Cleveland, J. N. (2007). Strategies for reducing work-family conflict: Applying research and best practices from industrial and organizational psychology. In G. P. Hodgkinson & J. K. Ford (eds), *International Handbook of Industrial and Organizational Psychology, 22*, 111–140.

Major, V. S., Klein, K. J. & Ehrhart, M. G. (2002). Work time, work interference with family, and psychological stress. *Journal of Applied Psychology, 87*, 427–436.

Mauno, S., Kinnunen, U. & Pyykko, M. (2005). Does work-family conflict mediate the relationship between work-family culture and self-reported distress? Evidence from five Finnish organizations. *Journal of Occupational and Organizational Psychology, 78*, 509–531.

Mesmer-Magnus, J. R. & Viswesvaran, C. (2006). How family-friendly work environments affect work/family conflict: A meta-analytic examination. *Journal of Labor Research, 27*, 555.

McManus, K., Korabik, K., Rosin, H. M., & Kelloway, E. K. (2002). Employed mothers and the work-family interface: Does family structure matter? *Human Relations, 55*, 1295–1304.

Moen, P. & Huang, Q. (Forthcoming 2007). Flexible schedule control, life course fit, and health: dual-earner middle-class couple ecologies that work. In *The Global Push for Workplace Flexibility: Tension between Market and State.* Sloan Conference Proceedings (Spring/Summer 2006).

Nasman, E. (1999). Work family arrangements in Sweden: Family strengths. In L. den Dulk, A. van Doorne-Huiskes & J. Schippers (eds), *Work-Family Arrangements in Europe* (pp. 131–149). Amsterdam: Thela Thesis.

O'Driscoll, M. P., Poelmans, S., Spector, P. E., Kalliath, T., Allen, T. D., Cooper, C. L. & Sanchez, J. I. (2003). Family-responsive interventions, perceived organizational and supervisor support, work-family conflict, and psychological strain. *International Journal of Stress Management, 10*, 326–344.

Perlow, L. A. (1995). Putting the work back into work/family. *Group and Organization Management, 20*, 227–239.

Perry-Jenkins, M. (2005). Work in the working class: Challenges facing families. In S. M. Bianchi, L. M. Casper & R. B. King (eds), *Work, Family, Health and Well-being* (pp. 453–472). Mahwah, NJ: Lawrence Erlbaum.

Rosman, K. (2006, December 8). Blackberry orphans. *Wall Street Journal*, p. W1.

Sahibzada, K., Hammer, L. B., Neal, M. B. & Kuang, D. C. (2005). The moderating effects of work-family role combinations and work-family organizational culture on the relationship between family-friendly workplace supports and job satisfaction. *Journal of Family Issues, 26*, 1–20.

Schein, E. (1985). *Organizational Culture and Leadership*. San Francisco, CA: Jossey-Bass.

Shellenbarger, S. (2006, February 16). Forget vacation time, new grads want stability and a good retirement plan. *Wall Street Journal*, p. D1.

Soloman, C. M. (1994). Work/family's failing grade: Why today's initiatives aren't enough. *Personnel Journal, 73*, 72–87.

Sparks, K., Cooper, C., Fried, Y. & Shirom, A. (1997). The effects of hours of work on health: A meta-analytic review. *Journal of Occupational and Organizational Psychology, 70*, 391–408.

Tay, C., Quazi, H. & Kelly, K. (2006). A multidimensional construct of work-life system: Its link to employee attitudes and outcomes. Paper presented at the Academy of Management Meetings, August, Oahu, HI.

Thomas, L. T., & Ganster, D. C. (1995). Impact of family-supportive work variables on work-family conflict and strain: A control perspective. *Journal of Applied Psychology, 80*, 6–15.

Thompson, C. A., Andreassi, J. & Prottas, D. (2005). Work-family culture: Key to reducing workforce-workplace mismatch? In S. M. Bianchi, L. M. Casper & B. R. King (eds), *Workforce/Workplace Mismatch? Work, Family, Health and Well-Being* (pp. 117–132). Mahwah, NJ: Lawrence Erlbaum.

Thompson, C. A, Beauvais, L. L. & Lyness, K. S. (1999). When work-family benefits are not enough: The influence of work-family culture on benefit utilization, organizational attachment, and work-family conflict. *Journal of Vocational Behavior, 54*, 392–415.

Thompson, C. A., Jahn, E., Kopelman, R. E. & Prottas, D. P. (2004). The impact of perceived organizational and supervisory family support on affective commitment: A longitudinal and multilevel analysis. *Journal of Managerial Issues, 16*, 545–567.

Thompson, C. A. & Prottas, D. J. (2006). The mediating role of perceived control on the relationship between organizational family support, job autonomy, and employee well-being. *Journal of Occupational Health Psychology, 11*, 100–118.

Thompson, C. A. & Prottas, D. J. (2005). Antecedents of a family- unfriendly culture: A tentative model. Invited paper presented at the Founding Conference of the International Center for Work and Family, IESE, Barcelona, July 2005.

van Doorne-Huiskes, A., den Dulk, L. & Schippers, J. (1999). Work-family arrangements in the context of welfare states. In L. den Dulk, A. van Doorne-Huiskes & J. Schippers (eds), *Work-Family Arrangements in Europe* (pp. 1–19). Amsterdam: Thela Thesis.

Warren, J. & Johnson, P. (1995). The impact of workplace support on work-family role strain. *Family Relations, 44*, 163–169.

Wayne, J. H., Randel, A. E. & Stevens, J. (2006). The role of identity and work-family support in work-family enrichment and its work-related consequences. *Journal of Vocational Behavior, 69*, 445–467.

Wharton, A. S. & Blair-Loy, M. (2002). The "overtime culture" in a global corporation: A cross-national study of finance professionals' interest in working part-time. *Work and Occupations, 29*, 32–64.

CHAPTER 19

Cross-Cultural Approaches to Work-Family Conflict

Zeynep Aycan

Department of Psychology, Koç University, Sariyer, Istanbul, Turkey

INTRODUCTION

Work and family—almost conflict in terms (An Australian woman)

Work and family: salt and pepper of life (A Taiwanese woman)

I work for my own personal well-being. I cannot waste my years of education (An American woman)

My family is my priority; I do everything for them—I work like crazy so that they don't have to go through the difficulties that I have gone through in life (A Chinese man)

My mother-in-law said when we had our first child, "Do the tigers give their babies to the elephants to get raised? Do the elephants ever give their babies to the lions to get raised?" I thought "Oh gosh, I better stay at home with my own kids". (An American woman; from Joplin, Shaffer, Francesco & Lau, 2003)

My mother-in-law almost fainted when I told her that I wanted to give my child to daycare. She took it as the biggest insult to herself (A Turkish woman)

Work-family conflict (WFC) is a common phenomenon of modern life in many countries and cultural contexts. However, as the above quotes demonstrate, the perception and prevalence of WFC, its antecedents and consequences tend to vary across cultures. According to Russell and Bowman, "global organizations have realized that there is a need to understand variations in work/family issues from one country or region to another, and what the key drivers of these variations are" (2000, p. 124). Understanding cultural differences in WFC is necessary not only for global organizations (e.g., MNCs), but also for domestic organizations with a multicultural workforce. To effectively manage diversity, these organizations seek to develop policies to balance work and family that are sensitive to cultural differences. Studying the influence of culture on WFC will also help managers in non-Western contexts (e.g., emerging economies), who are in need of understanding the applicability of WFC models and policies that are developed in Western industrialized societies. Cross-cultural studies, therefore, will contribute to practice and policy development, and enhance theory building by introducing the boundary conditions (i.e., cultural contingencies) in conceptualizing the WFC phenomenon and arriving at a more universal knowledge (Gelfand & Knight, 2005).

This chapter aims at providing a review of the cross-cultural literature on WFC and offering propositions to be tested by future research. In the next section the role of culture in understanding WFC will be described and the conceptual model that will guide the review will be presented. This is followed by three sections: the first will focus on the conceptualization and prevalence of WFC across cultures, the second will be on the impact of culture on demands and support mechanisms, and the third will be on the moderating effect of culture in the relationship of WFC with its antecedents and consequences.

This chapter takes a "cross-cultural", rather than an "international" perspective to explain variations in WFC. The cross-cultural perspective is a subdivision of the international perspective with a specific emphasis on the extent to which and ways in which *cultural context* influences the observed phenomenon (see Holden, 2002). As such, a cross-cultural perspective specifically requires that the researcher provides a culture-based explanation for differences observed in international comparisons. The majority of research in WFC comprises of international comparisons (e.g., WFC in China vs. US, Yang, Chen, Choi & Zou, 2000; see also, e.g., Spector, Allen, Poelmans, Cooper et al., 2005) or single country studies (e.g., WFC in Norway; Mikkelsen & Burke, 2004). In this type of research, differences or country-specific patterns are not explained particularly by the cultural context (i.e., values, assumptions, norms, belief systems). The majority of research reviewed in this chapter has not included measures of cultural dimensions in their designs. A notable exception is the cross-cultural research project (i.e., Project 3535) currently underway that tests Frone, Yardley and Markle's (1997) integrative model of WFC in ten cultural contexts (i.e., US, Canada, Spain, Australia, the Arab sect of Israel, the Jewish sect of Israel, Indonesia, India, Taiwan, and Turkey) (Aycan, Ayman, Bardoel, Desai, Drach-Zahavy, Hammer, Huang, Korabik, Lero, Mawardi, Poelmans, Rajadhyaksha, Shafiro & Somech, 2004; Korabik, Lero & Ayman, 2003; Lero, Ayman, Aycan, Drach-Zahavy, Mawardi, Pande-Desai, Huang, Rajadhyaksha, Somech, Korabik, Hammer & Bardoel, 2006). In this project, cultural dimensions including vertical and horizontal individualism vs. collectivism, monochronic vs. polychronic time orientation, gender-role egalitarianism, and coping approaches were assessed as predictors of variations in WFC and its relationship with the supports, demands, and outcomes in both work and family domains.

To fill the void in the literature in the systematic examination of the impact of culture on WFC, this chapter will offer propositions linking cultural dimensions to observed differences in the WFC process for future studies to test.

THE ROLE OF CULTURE IN STUDYING WFC

One of the most frequently cited definitions of culture in cross-cultural research is that of Kluckhohn: "culture consists in patterned ways of thinking, feeling and reacting, acquired and transmitted mainly by symbols, constituting the distinctive achievements of human groups, including their embodiments in artifacts; the essential core of culture consists of traditional (i.e., historically derived and selected) ideas and especially their attached values" (1951, p. 86). This and other commonly used conceptualizations of culture place strong emphasis on values (e.g., what is important in life?—work or family; achievement or harmony), assumptions and beliefs (e.g., what is WFC?—a problem or an inevitable life experience), and norms (e.g., how should I behave as a woman or as a man in my family?) that distinguish one human group from another. In the majority of research, cross-cultural differences in values, assumptions, beliefs, and norms are examined through cultural dimensions (e.g., individualism-collectivism). Although using cultural dimensions has a number of drawbacks (see Kagitcibasi, 1994, for a review) it is convenient, because the dimensions show validity, they are at the right level between generality and detail, they establish a link among individual, group, and societal level phenomena, and they are easy to communicate. The review of the literature suggests that cultural dimensions

Table 19.1

Cultural dimensions affecting the WFC and its relationship with its antecedents and consequences

Cultural dimension	Description
Collectivism (Hofstede, 1980)	The extent to which people place importance to extended families or clans, which protect them in exchange for loyalty. The "in-group" – "out-group" difference is salient.
Individualism (Hofstede, 1980)	The extent to which people perceive themselves as independent units separate from family and the social context and place importance in actualizing their self-interests.
Specificity (Trompenaars, 1993)	The degree to which private and business agendas are kept separated; clear, precise and detailed instructions are seen as assuring better compliance.
Diffuseness (Trompenaars, 1993)	The degree to which private and business agendas are interpenetrated; ambiguous and vague instructions are seen as allowing subtle and responsive interpretations.
Fatalism (Aycan, Kanungo, et al., 2000, p. 198)	The extent to which people in an organization or society believes that it is not possible to control fully the outcomes of one's actions.
Paternalism (Aycan, 2006)	The extent to which people in authority in the society take care of the subordinates in a manner that resembles a parent. The role of the superior is to provide guidance, nurturance, protection and care to the subordinates who, in turn, show loyalty and deference toward the superior.
Performance orientation (House et al., 1999)	The extent to which an organization of society encourages and rewards group members for performance improvement and excellence.
Gender egalitarianism (House et al., 1999)	The extent to which equal opportunities are provided to males and females in society.

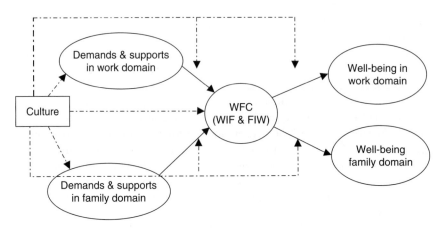

Figure 19.1   A cross-cultural model of culture and work-family conflict (based on Aycan et al., 2004, and Korabik et al., 2003)

that are the most relevant in explaining variations in WFC include individualism-collectivism, gender egalitarianism, specificity-diffuseness, fatalism, paternalism, and performance orientation (see, Table 19.1 for definitions).

How does culture influence WFC? According to Brett, Tinsley, Janssens, Barsness and Lyttle (1997) culture can be construed in two ways. The Type I hypothesis of culture treats it as the main effect; that is, culture is the main cause of the observed differences. Researchers adopting this perspective attribute mean-level differences in WFC to cultural variations. In the second approach, culture is treated as the moderator (Type II hypothesis). This approach acknowledges that constructs may be related in a non-uniform way across cultures. The model proposed in this chapter (Figure 19.1) is based on the working model of Project 3535. It depicts culture both as a main effect and a moderator. The direct links from culture to WFC, supports, and demands in the family and work domains suggest that the above-mentioned cultural values, assumptions, norms, and belief systems directly influence the prevalence of WFC as well as the type and strength of demands and supports in the work and family domains. The model also suggests that culture influences the strength of the relationship among WFC, its antecedents and consequences.

CULTURE AS THE MAIN EFFECT INFLUENCING WFC AND ITS ANTECEDENTS

IMPACT OF CULTURE ON THE EXPERIENCES AND PREVALENCE OF WFC

How is WFC construed in different cultural contexts (e.g., as a "threat" or "an opportunity for development")? How does culture influence the types of interrole conflict (e.g., "job-parent" conflict is common in Israel, whereas "job-spouse" conflict is common in Singapore)? What is the prevalence of WFC in different countries? How is the directionality of WFC influenced by the cultural context (e.g., work-to-family conflict is higher than family-to-work conflict in almost all countries, but there are cross-cultural variations in gender differences)? These are the questions that we seek to answer in this section.

There is research to suggest that WFC is construed in different ways across cultures. For example, the work and family domains are perceived to be *segmented* in the US, but *integrated* in China (Yang, 2005). Because of the perception of segmentation, work and family roles are considered to be incompatible, rather than congruent. Role incompatibility leads to experiences of *conflict* in the US, whereas role integration leads to experiences of *balance* in Hong Kong (Joplin, Shaffer, Francesco & Lau, 2003). Conflict, when experienced, is perceived as a *threat* in the US, but as an *opportunity* for development in China (Yang et al., 2000). Finally, conflict is perceived to be *inevitable* in India vs. *preventable* in the UK (United Nations Report, 2000).

Asian cultures tend to perceive work and family as different but compatible life domains enriching and balancing one's life. WFC, if it occurs, is perceived as a natural life event presenting opportunities for personal development and maturation. This is contrasted with the Anglo-Saxon perception of WFC as being "problematic", threatening to one's health and well-being, and preventable. Underlying the differences in approaching WFC could be the cultural dimensions of specificity-diffuseness, tolerance for contradictions (i.e., dialectic thinking and Confucianism; see Peng & Nisbett, 1999), tolerance for conflict (vs. preference for harmony), and fatalism.

Thus, we propose that in cultures characterized by specificity, low tolerance for contradictions, high tolerance for conflict, or low fatalism, the work and family domains are perceived to be separate, incompatible, and conflicting. The conflict is believed to be threatening and therefore something that must be prevented. By contrast, in cultures characterized by diffuseness, high tolerance for contradictions, low tolerance for conflict (high regard for harmony), or high fatalism, the work and family domains are perceived to be integrated in the unity of life, compatible in harmony, and inevitable. The conflict is believed to be an opportunity for personal development and maturation and must be accepted.

The type of interrole conflict experienced by employees also varies across cultures (Aycan et al., 2004). For example, the roles of *employee and parent* are seen as conflicting in Israel, Singapore, and India; the *employee and homemaker* roles are viewed as conflicting in the Arab sect of Israel, Singapore, and India; the roles of *employee and spouse* are seen as conflicting in Singapore and India; and the roles of *employee and social woman* (e.g., organizing and attending social events and functions) are viewed as conflicting in the Arab sect of Israel and Indonesia. The cross-cultural differences in the strength of various interrole conflicts could be a function of the salience of different roles in societies. For example, if the role of a woman in the Arab culture as a good housewife and a social woman is very strong, then it is more likely that the interrole conflict would be experienced between job and homemaker roles or between job and social woman roles. In summary, the job role conflicts with the social roles that are most salient in societies.

IMPACT OF CULTURE ON PREVALENCE OF WFC

One of the major studies on work-family pressure was conducted by Spector et al. (2005). Among the 18 countries participating in the study, Taiwan, Hong Kong, and Portugal reported the highest work-family pressure, whereas Australia, UK, and Ukraine reported the lowest. In another study comparing 8 European countries (Simon, Kümmerling & Hasselhorn, 2004), work interference with family conflict (WIF) was found to be higher than family interference with work (FIW) conflict in all countries. However, the WIF experienced by men was greater than that experienced by women in Italy, whereas the reverse was the case in the Netherlands. In a study comparing US and China, Yang et al. (2000) reported that men experienced higher levels of WFC than women did in China, whereas a gender difference did not exist in the US sample.

There may be many reasons for such cross-cultural variations, including differences in demands and supports in work and family domains (e.g., number of work hours, availability of support mechanisms and work-life balance policies). However, when all things are assumed to be equal, it appears that WFC is experienced to a greater extent in countries that are going through a rapid and continuous transition both economically and culturally, compared to those going through a less radical and rapid transition. Similarly, at the individual level, it seems that WFC is more strongly felt by men or women, depending on the strength of transition in gender roles or strength of role expansion (see Barnett & Hyde, 2001).

Thus, we would expect transitioning economies, especially those with traditional gender role stereotypes, to experience WFC to a greater extent than economically developed countries with egalitarian gender role stereotypes. Furthermore, individuals holding traditional gender role stereotypes and experiencing role expansion should be more prone to suffer from WFC, compared to those holding egalitarian gender role stereotypes.

IMPACT OF CULTURE ON DEMANDS IN WORK AND FAMILY DOMAINS

How does the cultural context influence the type and strength of demands in the work and family domains? Let us start from the demands in the work domain. Studies concur that experiences of role conflict, role ambiguity, role overload, long working hours, schedule inflexibility, work-related travel, and job insecurity are demands of work that are associated with WFC. Of course, the extent to which they are experienced may depend on the cultural and the socio-economic context. Furthermore, their impact on WFC may also vary across cultures, which will be discussed in the section on "culture-as-a-moderator" between demands and WFC.

In addition to the above, some work demands can be considered to be culture-specific. For example, in collectivistic cultures maintaining harmony and avoiding conflicts in interpersonal relationships at work is an extra demand on employees (Ling & Powell, 2001). Unresolved conflicts and tension at work may constitute emotional labor that may spill over to the family domain as strain-based WFC.

In cultures valuing achievement, high performance, and career advancement, employees should feel more demands in their work role (e.g., the pressure to be a top performer), compared to those in cultures that de-emphasize competition, achievement, and career ambition. In the former case, an ideal employee is defined as someone whose work is central to life, whereas in the latter case an ideal employee is someone who maintains harmony among work, family, and leisure. Employees in cultures characterized as the latter are less likely to experience WFC. Therefore, compared to cultures characterized by low performance orientation, in cultures characterized by high performance orientation, the pressure to be a top performer and advancement in career are expected to be among the most important work demands.

In some cultures (e.g., China) building interpersonal trust is crucial in business. In such cultures, good business requires attending frequently-occurring after-hour events, such as going out to dinner or karaoke bars with customers or business partners. In such cultures, off-work or after-hour activities to instill trust are included in work demands and these commitments pose a serious threat to work-life balance.

Finally, as a special case, women in managerial positions are more likely to experience WFC in cultures where attitudes towards women in managerial roles are negative, than in those where women in authority positions are more easily accepted and appreciated. In the former case, dealing with the negative attitudes towards women managers constitutes an extra demand in the work domain for women in those positions.

Let us now turn to the influence of culture on the type and salience of demands in the family domain. So far, studies have shown that age and number of children, occupational status of the spouse or partner, and care of elder parents are the main demands in the family domain (see Eby, Casper, Lockwood, Bordeaux & Brinley, 2005). In addition to these family demands, caring and maintaining harmonious relationships with the extended family members and live-in elders are among the most important demands for collectivistic societies. In such societies, multiple social roles, such as mother/father, daughter/son, daughter-in-law/son-in-law, neighbor, hostess in social events, wife/husband, are equally important. Perfection in all of these roles is demanded by the society. For example, offering ready-made or frozen meals to house guests is completely inappropriate in traditional societies like India, Turkey or Taiwan. A woman must prepare a rich set of food for the guests, herself, even though she is a high-status career woman or has a household helper. Thus, in collectivistic cultures, care of elderly family members and maintaining harmonious and caring relationships with the extended family are among the most important demands in the family domain.

Another demand in collectivistic societies is the *life-long* care of children. When children are at the school age, their academic achievement is the primary responsibility of the family. Children's academic status at school is considered to be the reflection of their parents' success or failure. Often times, parents have to sit down with their children to do the homework together, rather than leaving this responsibility to the children to fulfill. When children grow up, parents are again involved in their lives to find an appropriate job and a mate to marry. In fact, children have to live with their parents until they get married and parents have to take care of them emotionally and financially. When children get married and have children of their own, parents are involved in care of the grandchildren. All in all, care of the offspring is a life-long commitment for parents who are involved in their children's lives at every age and stage. For working people this is a serious responsibility and a family demand. Therefore, in collectivistic cultures, care and guidance of children at every age and stage is among the most important family demands.

IMPACT OF CULTURE ON SUPPORT MECHANISMS IN THE WORK AND FAMILY DOMAINS

The main support mechanisms at work that are cited in the literature include family-friendly organizational policies and practices and managerial support (Eby et al., 2005). In paternalistic cultures, managerial support includes managers' involvement in the nonwork lives of their employees. Aycan (2006) contends that managers in paternalistic cultures (i.e., paternalistic leaders) give advice to their employees not only for work-related problems, but also for family-related problems. Often times, they are asked to act as a mediator in resolving family disputes. Thus, in paternalistic cultures, managerial guidance and involvement in the family matters of employees who need and require it is an important source of support in the work domain.

Organizational support for family issues reflects the attitudes and policies at the national level. Based on European countries, Evans (2000) proposes four different national models. In the Nordic model (Sweden, Denmark, and Finland), family has the priority in society. There are not only well-developed public systems for childcare and eldercare, but also rules to allow flexibility at work. The second is the Continental model covering Germany, Austria, and Netherlands. In this model, family is also considered to be a premier institution in society. Although state arrangements for childcare are less common in the Continental model than in

the Nordic model, work-family reconciliation is facilitated by allowing part-time work, extended parental leaves, and large-scale social security and pension systems. Both Austria and Germany have competitions for the family-friendly organization of the year. The insular model (UK and Ireland) places an emphasis on individual freedom with little interference from the state. Women's primary responsibility is at home and there are no systems for parental leave. In this system organizational support for work-family balance is limited. Finally, the Southern European model (Italy, Greece, Portugal, Spain) emphasizes the role of the extended family as the primary support system to reconcile work and family. There are few public and organizational provisions to support work-family balance.

In summary, organizational policies and practices to enhance work-family balance are influenced by policies at the national level regarding the state's involvement in family care. In countries where care of the dependent family members is regarded as the shared responsibility between the family and the state, organizations are encouraged to make family-friendly arrangements. In countries where care of the family is completely left to the responsibility of the family members, organizational support mechanisms to work-family balance are not well-developed.

The most frequently discussed support mechanism in the family domain is the emotional and instrumental support from the spouse (Adams, King & King, 1996). However, the type and the level of support in the family domain may vary cross-culturally. Let us begin with the role of spousal support in different cultural contexts. In cultures high on gender egalitarianism (House et al., 1999), support from the male spouse or partner is more likely than it is in cultures low on gender egalitarianism. Men who do housework in traditional cultures may be called names (e.g., "light man") and looked down on as being weak and not manly. It is not unusual to observe a man washing dishes or changing diapers at home in the *absence* of family and friends (Aycan, 2004). Not only men, but also women adhere to traditional gender roles in cultures low on gender egalitarianism. Jost and Banaji (1994) explain this phenomenon with the System Justification Theory which suggests that women are the primary supporters of traditional gender roles to justify the prevailing inequalities in the social system, which they feel powerless to change. Women who internalize the traditional gender roles feel guilty for not fulfilling their wifely and motherly duties. Therefore, in cultures characterized by traditional gender role stereotypes, support from the male spouse or partner is not sought by men, women, and the society at large. Thus, support from the male spouse or partner to women is more likely in cultures high, compared to low, on gender egalitarianism. Support from the female spouse or partner to the men is more likely in cultures low, compared to high, on gender egalitarianism.

Another important source of support is the extended family. In collectivistic countries (e.g., India, Turkey, Spain) extended family support is available to working parents (see Aycan & Eskin, 2005). Grandparents or aunts of working couples are involved in childcare or care of household responsibilities (especially cooking for the family). Aycan (2004) found that emotional and instrumental support (especially support for childcare) received from the mother was more important than the spousal support for professional and managerial women in Turkey. As one of the quotes at the beginning of the chapter illustrated, care of the grandchild is both pleasure and *duty* for grandparents in collectivistic countries. If grandchildren are sent to daycare centers, grandparents may get offended believing that they are not trusted. On the other hand, in individualistic cultures privacy is a pivotal value (Ho & Chui, 1994) and involvement of third parties in family matters is not desirable. Therefore, in collectivistic cultures the extended family's involvement in care of children and management of the household is an important source of support in the family domain. By contrast, in individualistic cultures extended family support for work-family balance is not as desirable and available as it is in collectivistic cultures.

Thanks to the close social ties in the community, working parents also benefit from the support of their neighbors in collectivistic cultures. Children may stay at the neighbor's house until the parents arrive at home; neighbors may cook for each other and share food. The support from the social network (i.e., family, friends, neighbors) is free, but still comes with a cost. The cost is the obligation to reciprocate the favor. The support received, especially from the extended family, may turn into a demand in the family domain. When the extended family takes care of the children and household chores of working parents, they expect to be taken care of by them in their old age or when they get sick (Kagitcibasi, 1996). Thus, in collectivistic cultures, help received from neighbors and friends in care of children and management of the household is an important source of support in the family domain.

In addition to the support from the family and social networks, paid household help (e.g., cleaning ladies, nannies) is available and affordable in countries especially where there is large income disparity. Women from low-income groups provide cheap labor to those in high-income groups. However, the quality of support received from paid helpers is not always high and this may create an extra strain on working parents. Nannies are often women with low education and without the certification to qualify them to do the job. Nevertheless, they alleviate the family demands to some extent and help working families to maintain the work-life balance. Another source of support is the private tutors hired to help children with their schoolwork or homework. As mentioned in the previous sections, attending to children's homework is one of the important demands for families in collectivistic cultures. In summary, in countries with high income disparity and low state-sponsored institutional support, commonly used sources of support are paid household helpers, including nannies, cleaning ladies, and private tutors.

CULTURE AS THE MODERATOR OF RELATIONSHIPS BETWEEN WFC AND ITS ANTECEDENTS AND CONSEQUENCES

Cultural values may influence the strength or the direction of the relationship between work-family conflict and its predictors and outcomes. It appears that culture moderates the relationship between WFC and its antecedents more strongly than it does the relationship between WFC and its consequences (e.g., Hill, Yang, Hawkins & Ferris, 2004; Spector et al., 2005). As discussed in the previous section, cultural context has a bearing on the prevalence and the type of demands and support mechanisms at work and family domains. However, the majority of research has failed to include these variables. Therefore, cross-cultural differences observed between WFC and its antecedents may be a methodological artifact caused by the Western bias in the selection of variables included in studies. Alternatively, it can be suggested that factors *causing* WFC are more likely to vary across cultures than the *outcomes* (e.g., psychological well-being) associated with WFC.

Aryee, Fields and Luk (1999) argue that within-domain psychological processes (e.g., the relationship among stressors, involvement, conflict, life satisfaction, depression) are universal. On the other hand, there are also some interesting cross-cultural variations. For example, number of children correlates positively with work-family pressure in Australia, Romania, Sweden, and the US, but negatively in Hong Kong; in some other countries (e.g., Columbia, Portugal, Spain) the correlation was nil (Spector et al., 2005). A similar variation was found in Hill and colleagues' study (2004): the lowest correlation between the responsibility for children and FIW was found in the Eastern cultures (China, Hong Kong, India, Indonesia, Japan, Korea, Malaysia, Philippines, Singapore, Taiwan, Thailand), whereas the highest correlation was found in the US. The same pattern was replicated for the relationship between the eldercare responsibility and FIW.

Spector et al. (2005) found a significant relationship between the number of hours worked and work-family conflict among Anglos, but not among collectivistic cultures (Chinese and Latins). The authors suggest that presumably Anglos view working extra hours as taking away from their families, which results in the feeling of guilt and conflict with family members. This may not be the case in China and Latin America, where employees and their families view working long hours as a sacrifice for the family (see also Yang et al., 2000). Among other work-related demands, job workload, job travel, and job inflexibility increased WIF in a 48-country comparison of IBM workers in Hill et al.'s (2004) study.

Another important research study, conducted by Yang et al. (2000), showed that family demands (spending less time at work) had a greater impact on WFC in the US than in China, whereas work demands (spending less time in family) had a greater impact on WFC in China than in the US. The authors suggested that the difference was mainly due to cultural differences regarding the value placed on family and work time. The authors attributed the majority of the differences in the relationship between WFC and its antecedents to individualism and collectivism. However, more systematic and theory-driven research is needed to arrive at a firm conclusion.

What appears from the findings reviewed so far is that the cultural context influences the ways in which family and work demands are perceived and appraised in different societies. For example, if having children is perceived to be a "choice" or "burden" in life, childbearing responsibility aggravates WFC, compared to the situation where it is perceived to be a natural life event. Similarly, if eldercare is perceived to be a norm in society, it does not increase WFC, compared to the situation where it is perceived to be a choice or a burden. The appraisal process has a similar impact on the relationship between work demands and WFC. Time spent at work aggravates work-to-family conflict in cultures where the primary role of work is to satisfy individuals' personal needs (i.e., financial and psychological), compared to cultures where the primary role of work is to satisfy the family's needs.

In summary, cultural context moderates the relationship between demands in the family and work domains and WFC. In cultures appraising demands in a positive way such as the "norm" in society (e.g., eldercare), a "natural event in life" (e.g., having children), or a "voluntary sacrifice for the family" (e.g., working long hours), the impact of demands on WFC is expected to be lower than in cultures appraising demands in a negative way such as a "burden" (e.g., eldercare), a "choice" (e.g., having children), or a "compromise" (e.g., working long hours).

The final topic of discussion is the moderating role of culture on the relationship between WFC and its consequences. WFC has been shown to relate to negative health and life outcomes, such as increase in depressive symptoms, increase in the use of alcohol and substance abuse, decrease in life, job satisfaction, and marital satisfaction, and increase in the tendency to quit the job (Eby et al., 2005). However, there is evidence to suggest that cultural context is a moderator between WFC and its outcomes. In their 18-country comparison, Spector et al. (2005) found that work-family pressure was correlated negatively with mental and physical well-being in almost all countries. However, the magnitude of the correlations varied. The highest correlations between work-family pressure and mental well-being were obtained in Australia, Belgium, Mexico, and Ukraine (ranging from −.37 to −.47), whereas the lowest correlations were obtained in Romania, Hong Kong, Brazil, Poland, and Spain (ranging from .03 to −.18). Similarly, the relationship of work-family pressure with the physical well-being varied across cultures: it was −.01 in the UK, but −.40 in Australia. In the same study, the relationship between work-family pressure and job satisfaction was also moderated by the cultural context. In half of the countries (e.g., Belgium, China, Poland, Portugal, South Africa, UK) the correlation was near-zero, whereas in the other half it ranged from −.11 (Brazil) to −.29 (Ukraine). The authors have not provided an explanation for these differences. Indeed, it is difficult to speculate about the ways in which culture played a moderating role in these relationships without the direct assessment of the cultural values, norms, and assumptions. It is also possible that the coping mechanisms commonly may vary across cultures and this may account for the differences in the relationship between WFC and its outcomes.

In another large-scale comparative study, Hill and colleagues (2004) found that IBM employees in 48 countries experienced higher job satisfaction when there was work-family fit (i.e., the ability to integrate paid work and family life). Although, this finding appears to contradict that of Spector et al. (2005), the similarity of the relationship between work-family fit and job satisfaction across countries in Hill et al.'s study could be attributed the fact that participants were employees of the same organization.

Aryee, Fields and Luk (1999) found that the life satisfaction of Hong Kong Chinese employees was influenced primarily by WIF, while the life satisfaction of American employees was influenced primarily by FIW. The authors explained this as being due to the pivotal role that family played in Confucian societies. In such societies, the interference of work with family is seen as threatening to the family identity, whereas in individualistic countries, where people tend to identify with their work, the interference of family with work is seen as threatening to the self-identity.

Aycan and Eskin (2005) found that in Turkey WIF, but not FIW, was associated with lower psychological well-being, lower satisfaction with parental role performance, and lower marital satisfaction. They argue that because the family has a central importance in lives, the possibility of harming the family because of work responsibilities was more disturbing to Turkish dual-earner families than the possibility of harming the work due to family responsibilities.

Wang, Lawler, Walumbwa and Shi (2004) investigated the moderating role of individualism and collectivism (measured at the individual level as idiocentrism and allocentrism) on the relationship between WFC and job withdrawal intention. Findings revealed that, contrary to expectations, there was no difference in the effect of WIF on job withdrawal intentions between the US and China. However, regardless of the country, WIF was associated with higher withdrawal intentions for idiocentric (individualistic), compared to allocentric (collectivistic) individuals. On the other hand, FIW intensified the withdrawal intentions for allocentric, rather than idiocentric individuals. They suggested that perhaps, because of their loyalty to family, allocentric individuals are likely to be motivated to fulfill the family responsibilities, even if it interferes with their work performance. However, they may feel obligated to continue to work in order to ensure the well-being of the family. This dilemma is likely to intensify the stress levels and lead the individuals to consider leaving their current jobs for a less demanding or more flexible work environment. Aryee, Luk, Leung and Lo (1999) found that neither WIF nor FIW diminished family satisfaction in Hong Kong and Singapore, because work is perceived to be an activity that promotes family well-being (utilitarinistic familialism).

Finally, Aycan and Eskin (2005) introduced the concept of work-related guilt as another important outcome of WFC. In the WFC context, guilt arouses anxiety that occurs as a result of perceived failure to fulfill prescribed gender roles (see Chapman, 1987; Duxbury & Higgins, 1991). According to Staines' (1980) fixed-sum-of-scarce-resources theory, women's involvement in the work role may result in guilt regarding their performance as parents. Indeed, Aycan and Eskin (2005) found that women in Turkey experienced more employment-related guilt than men, and that guilt was more strongly associated with women's (but not men's) work-to-family conflict than family-to-work conflict.

In summary, we propose that the relationship between WFC and its outcomes varies across-cultures due to cross-cultural differences in the appraisal and coping mechanisms. Moreover, the magnitude of the impact of WFC on its outcomes depends on the ways in which WFC is perceived to harm the domain that is most important in societies. WIF is expected to be most strongly associated with negative well-being outcomes in cultures where family is the most important domain in life, whereas FIW is expected to be most strongly associated with negative well-being outcomes in cultures where work is the most important domain in life.

IMPLICATIONS FOR FUTURE RESEARCH AND PRACTICE

The aim of this chapter was to provide a theoretical framework and specific propositions linking cultural context to the WFC phenomenon. The framework suggests that culture should be treated in two ways: first, as the main effect directly influencing WFC (its prevalence, type, direction) as well as the factors leading to WFC (i.e., the magnitude and type of demands and supports in work and family domains); second, as the moderator influencing the relationship of WFC with its antecedents and consequences.

The present review alludes to a number of tentative conclusions. First, cross-cultural differences in the appraisal and coping processes (Lazarus & Folkman, 1980) seem to account for the differences in the prevalence of WFC as well as its impact on life outcomes (e.g., psychological well-being, job and marital satisfaction, turnover intention). For instance, when employees appraise WFC as a threat rather than an opportunity for development, they tend to experience greater WFC. Similarly, when WFC is appraised as a life event harming the family, which is perceived to be the most important element in life, it is associated with greater health-related problems than when it is appraised as a sacrifice for family. Therefore, one important area for future research is cross-cultural differences in appraisal and coping processes.

Second, the review suggests that there are *emic* or indigenous manifestations of some of the key constructs used in WFC research. For example, in collectivistic and high power distant cultures, managerial support may include a paternalistic approach, which can enhance work-family balance. As another example, work demands in collectivistic cultures include the pressure to maintain harmonious relationships and avoidance of interpersonal conflicts at work. The stress created by this tension at work can lead to strain-based WFC. Even the simple term "family" may mean different things in different cultural contexts. Future research should examine the culture-specific or *emic* construals of demands and supports (i.e., what constitutes demand and support) in work and family domains.

Indigenous or *emic* perspectives allow us to unfold *variform universals* (i.e., general principles hold across cultures but the form or enactment of this principle varies; Bass, 1997) and *variform functional universals* (i.e., the relationship between variables is always found but the magnitude or direction may change depending on the cultural context). As discussed by Gelfand, Erez and Aycan (2007), indigenous perspectives not only contribute to the development of more universal knowledge, but also help us to understand *our own culture and behavior.* Pruitt states that:

> ... most cultural differences are relative, rather than absolute. In other words, people across the world are capable of behaving in almost any fashion, but their preferences for one kind of behavior over another differ from culture to culture. Characteristics that are dominant in one culture tend to be recessive in another, and vice-versa... By studying other societies where these features are dominant, they can develop concepts and theories that will eventually be useful for understanding their own (2004, p. xii).

Future cross-cultural research on WFC should invest more in *emic* or indigenous perspectives in order to provide a more universal science and to unearth recessive characteristics in other cultures.

Last but not least, this review lends itself to a number of tentative implications for policy and practice. As discussed at the beginning of the chapter, understanding cross-cultural differences in WFC has important implications for diversity management. First, organizations with a culturally diverse workforce should pay close attention to the implications of their career planning for work-family balance. Employees who value the balance between work and family more than the advancement in their careers may view the promotion to a managerial position not necessarily in a positive light. For them, the promotion may even be demotivating as it is deemed to be an unnecessary compromise from the family. Second, the nature and extent of organizational and managerial support to work-life balance may be evaluated differently by employees, depending on their cultural values. Those from collectivistic and high power distant cultures are more likely to expect organizational and managerial support and guidance in their private lives, whereas those from individualistic and egalitarian cultures would consider this as an invasion of their privacy. Managers should be trained to tailor-make their approaches in handling work-family problems of their diverse workforce. Organizational support systems or benefits and allowances can also be tailor-made to fit to different needs and expectations of the diverse workforce. A cafeteria approach could be adopted in benefits and allowances to support work-family balance to include various options to choose from, such as providing support to elderly family members, helping employees to find private tutors for their children, arranging for homemade meals to take home in the evening, and organizing visits or social events for the family members.

REFERENCES

Adams, G. A., King, L. A. & King, D. W. (1996). Relationships of job and family involvement, family social support, and work-family conflict with job and life satisfaction. *Journal of Applied Psychology, 81*(4), 411–420.

Aryee, S., Fields, D. & Luk, V. (1999). A cross-cultural test of a model of the work-family interface. *Journal of Management, 25*(4), 491–511.

Aryee, S., Luk, V., Leung, A. & Lo, S. (1999). Role stressors, interrole conflict, and well-being: The moderating influence of spousal support and coping behaviors among employed parents in Hong Kong. *Journal of Vocational Behavior, 54*, 259–278.

Aycan, Z. (2004). Key success factors for women in management in Turkey. *Applied Psychology: An International Review, 53*(3), 453–477.

Aycan, Z. (2006). Paternalism: Towards conceptual refinement and operationalization. In K. S. Yang, K. K. Hwang & U. Kim (eds), *Scientific Advances in Indigenous Psychologies: Empirical, Philosophical, and Cultural Contributions* (pp. 445–466). London: Cambridge University Press.

Aycan, Z., Ayman, R., Bardoel, A., Desai, T. P., Drach-Zahavy, A., Hammer, L. Huang, T. P., Korabik, K., Lero, D. S., Mawardi, A., Poelmans, S. A. Y., Rajadhyaksha, U., Shafiro, M. & Somech, A. (2004). Work-family conflict in cultural context: A ten-country investigation. Paper presented at the 19th Annual SIOP Conference, Chicago, April.

Aycan, Z. & Eskin, M. (2005). Childcare, spousal, and organizational support in predicting work-family conflict for females and males in dual-earner families with preschool children. *Sex Roles, 53*(7), 453–471.

Barnett, R. C. & Hyde, J. S. (2001). Women, men, work, and family: An expansionist theory. *American Psychologist, 56*(10), 781–796.

Bass, B. M. (1997). Does the transactional-transformational leadership paradigm transcend organizational and national boundaries? *American Psychologist, 52*, 130–139.

Brett, J. M., Tinsley, C. H., Janssens, M., Barsness, Z. I. & Lyttle, A. L. (1997). New approaches to the study of culture in industrial/organizational psychology. In P. C. Earley & M. Erez (eds), *New Perspectives on International Industrial/Organizational Psychology* (pp. 75–130). San Francisco: New Lexington Press.

Chapman, F. S. (1987). Executive guilt: Who's taking care of the children. *Fortune*, February 16, 30–37.

Duxbury, L. E. & Higgins, C. A. (1991). Gender differences in work-family conflict. *Journal of Applied Psychology, 76*, 60–74.

Eby, L. T., Casper, W. J., Lockwood, A., Bordeaux, C. & Brinley, A. (2005). Work and family research in IO/OB: Content analysis and review of the literature (1980–2002). *Journal of Vocational Behavior, 66*(1), 124–197.

Evans, J. M. (2000). Firms' contribution to the reconciliation between work and family life. Paper presented at the Conference on Families, Labor markets, and the Well-Being of Children, Canada, June.

Gelfand, M. J., Erez, M. & Aycan, Z. (2007). Cross-Cultural approaches to organizational behavior. *Annual Review of Psychology, 58*, 479–515.

Gelfand, M. J. & Knight, A. P. (2005). Cross-cultural perspectives on work-family conflict. In S. A. Y. Poelmans (ed.), *Work and Family: An International Research Perspective* (pp. 401–415). London: Lawrence Erlbaum.

Hill, E. J., Yang, C., Hawkins, A. J. & Ferris, M. (2004). A cross-cultural test of the work-family interface in 48 countries. *Journal of Marriage and Family, 66*, 1300–1316.

Ho, D. Y. & Chiu, C. (1994). Component ideas of individualism, collectivism and social organizations: An application in the study of Chinese culture. In U. Kim, H. C. Triandis, C. Kagitcibasi, S. Choi & G. Yoon (eds), *Cross-Cultural Research and Methodology Series, Vol. 18. Individualism and Collectivism: Theory, Method and Applications* (pp. 251–266). CA: Sage.

House, R. J., Hanges, P. J., Ruiz-Quintanilla, S. A., Dorfman, P. W., Javidan, M., Dickson, M. V. et al. (1999). Cultural influences on leadership: Project GLOBE. In W. Mobley, J. Gessner & V. Arnold (eds), *Advances in Global Leadership*, Vol. 1 (pp. 171–233). Stanford, CT: JAI Press.

Joplin, J. R. W., Shaffer, M. A., Francesco, A. M. & Lau, T. (2003). The macro environment and work-family conflict: Development of a cross-cultural comparative framework. *International Journal of Cross-Cultural Management, 3*(3), 305–328.

Jost, J. T. & Banaji, M. R. (1994). The role of stereotyping in system-justification and the production of false-consciousness. *British Journal of Social Psychology, 33*, 1–27.

Kagitcibasi, C. (1994). Individualism and collectivism. In J. W. Berry, M. H. Segall & Ç. Kagitçibasi (eds), *Handbook of Cross-Cultural Psychology: Vol. 3. Social Behavior and Applications* (2nd edn) (pp. 1–49). Boston: Allyn & Bacon.

Kagitcibasi, C. (1996). *Family and Human Development Across Cultures: A view From the Other Side.* Mahwah, NJ: Lawrence Erlbaum.

Kluckhohn, C. (1951). The study of culture. In D. Lerner & H. D. Lasswell (eds), *The Policy Sciences.* Stanford, CA: Stanford University Press.

Korabik, K., Lero, D. S. & Ayman, R. (2003). A multilevel approach to cross-cultural work-family research: A micro and macro perspective. *International Journal of Cross-Cultural Management, 3*(3), 289–303.

Lazarus, R. S., & Folkman, S. (1984). Stress, appraisal and coping. New York: Springer Publishing.

Lero, D. S., Ayman, R., Aycan, Z., Drach-Zahavy, A., Mawardi, A., Poelmans, S. A. Y., Pande Desai, T., Huang, T. P., Rajadhyaksha, U., Korabik, K., Hammer, L. & Bardoel, A. (2006, July). Theory and method for studying work-family conflict in a multinational context. International Congress of Cross-Cultural Psychology, Spetes, Greece.

Ling, Y. & Powell, G. (2001). Work-family conflict in contemporary China. *International Journal of Cross-Cultural Management, 1*(3), 357–373.

Mikkelsen, A. & Burke, R. J. (2004). Work-family concerns of Norwegian police officers: Antecedents and consequences. *International Journal of Stress Management, 11*(4), 429–444.

Peng, K. & Nisbett, R.E. (1999). Culture, dialectics, and reasoning about contradiction. *American Psychologist, 54*(9), 741–754.

Pruitt, D. G. (2004). Foreword. In M. J. Gelfand, *The Handbook of Negotiation and Culture* (pp. xi–iii). Palo Alto, CA: Stanford University Press.

Russell, G. & Bowman, L. (2000). Work and Family: Current thinking, research and practice (Technical report prepared for the Department of Family and Community Services). Sydney, Australia. Macquarie University, Macquarie Research Limited.

Simon, M., Kummerling, A. & Hasselhorn, H. (2004). Work-home conflict in the European Nursing profession. *International Journal of Occupationial and Environmental Health, 10*(4), 384–391.

Spector, P., Allen, T. D., Poelmans, S. A. Y., Cooper, C. L. et al. (2005). An international comparative study of work-family stress and occupational strain. In S. A. Y. Poelmans (ed.), *Work and Family: An International Research Perspective* (pp. 71–87). London: Lawrence Erlbaum.

Staines, G. L. (1980). Spillover versus compensation: A review of the literature on the relationship between work and family. *Human Relations, 33*(2), 111–130.

Trompenaars, F. (1993) *Riding the Waves of Culture.* London: Economist Books.

United Nations (2000). *Families and the World of Work: Four Country Profiles of Family-Sensitive Policies.* Department of Economic and Social Affairs Division for Social Policy and Development Family Unit Report. New York: UN Press.

Wang, P., Lawler, J. J., Walumbwa, F. O. & Shi, K. (2004). Work-family conflict and job withdrawal intentions: The moderating effect of cultural differences. *International Journal of Stress Management, 11*(4), 392–412.

Yang, N. (2005). Individualism-collectivism and work-family interface: A Sino-US comparison. In S. A. Y. Poelmans (ed.). *Work and Family: An International Research Perspective* (pp. 287–319). London: Lawrence Erlbaum.

Yang, N., Chen, C., Choi, J. & Zou, Y. (2000). Sources of work-family conflict: A Sino-US comparison of the effects of work and family demands. *Academy of Management Journal, 43*(1), 113–123.

CHAPTER 20

Assumptions, Research Gaps and Emerging Issues: Implications for Research, Policy and Practice

Donna S. Lero[*] **and Suzan Lewis**[†]

[*]Jarislowsky Chair in Families and Work, University of Guelph, Centre for
Families, Work and Well-Being, Guelph, Ontario
[†]Professor of Organisational Psychology, Middlesex University Business School,
The Burroughs Hendon, London

This handbook on work-family integration summarizes current knowledge about many aspects related to combining paid work and family responsibilities—a field of research and policy analysis that is rich in its scope and complexity and that is expanding very rapidly. One of the exciting and very beneficial aspects of research on this topic is that it is occurring across many disciplines and in many countries. This benefit also presents two challenges. One is the challenge of synthesizing so much information coherently. The second is ensuring that we understand the meaning of findings within the context in which the research is conducted. Clearly there are vast differences between countries and between organizations in the manner in which paid work and the opportunities to combine paid work and care occur.

An additional and important challenge, especially for policy makers, is the fact that the very phenomena we are studying are, themselves, changing. A sweep across the horizon reveals that economic restructuring and globalization are producing new forms of employment and new economic pressures on companies. Employees experience more job insecurity and income instability and many spend part of their working lives in non-standard or precarious work—a situation that is likely to exclude them from access to employer-provided benefits and often from social insurance provisions. As well, families are more fluid in structure and in roles; workplaces and communities are more culturally diverse as a result of increased migration; and demographic changes are resulting from low fertility rates, delayed childbearing and population aging. These factors all complicate what is already evident: individuals, families, workplaces, and policy-makers need the best information and tools available to make decisions to address what Rapoport, Bailyn, Fletcher and Pruitt (2002) originally identified as the "dual agenda", which focuses on supporting both the integration of paid work and family and increasing workplace effectiveness—and to go even further to address what is more recently referred to as the "multiple agenda" of supporting families, workplaces, communities, and wider societies (Gambles, Lewis & Rapoport, 2006).

Handbook of Work-Family Integration: Research, Theory, and Best Practices

Our goal in this chapter is three-fold. First, we identify the importance of recognizing a wide range of assumptions that explicitly and implicitly narrow the topics we study as researchers, our interpretations of the meaning of our results, and the range of implications and options they suggest for promoting change at the individual, workplace, and policy level. Even what might appear to be fairly effective work-family reconciliation policies may require rethinking if their implementation is based on assumptions and criteria that reduce their utility and effectiveness. Secondly, and related to surfacing assumptions, is our effort to identify some significant gaps and areas where new research is needed to expand and deepen our understanding. Finally, we comment on two emerging issues—increasing migration within and across countries, and the challenges that growing numbers of workers will experience in combining work and eldercare or care for a family member with an acute or chronic health condition.

THE IMPORTANCE OF SURFACING ASSUMPTIONS IN RESEARCH, IN ORGANIZATIONS AND IN FAMILIES

The chapters in this book show how far research on work and family has progressed, and also consider some specific directions for future research and practice. Implicit in all the implications for future progress is the need to surface and challenge a whole range of assumptions—in research, in organizations, in families, in communities, and in wider societies—and to show how these assumptions impact on thinking and practice in our field. These include assumptions about what is an ideal worker, about how work should best be carried out, about the ideal mother or father, and about femininity and masculinity. In terms of research, assumptions about systems, culture, the status of so-called knowledge in the work-family field and about the nature of change may all need to be surfaced and, in some cases, challenged. Below we consider some of these assumptions and the implications for moving our field forwards.

MOVING BEYOND INDIVIDUALS TO SYSTEMIC PERSPECTIVES (ASSUMPTIONS ABOUT RESEARCH, INDIVIDUALS, ORGANIZATIONS, AND FAMILIES)

Much research in the work-family field has traditionally been carried out at the individual level, for example by looking at work-family conflict. This remains crucial for drawing attention to individual and family dilemmas, including identity dilemmas, and for challenging the still prevalent but anachronistic view of ideal employees as those who do not have, or act as though they do not have, family (or other non-work) obligations (Bailyn, 1993, 2006; Lewis, 2001; Rapoport et al., 2002). However, it is clear that there is also a need to go beyond the individual level to understand more about the social and organizational systems that can make it difficult for individuals and families to combine work and family roles. Without this wider focus there remains the danger that those who experience work-family conflict are blamed or considered non-ideal employees, rather than acknowledging the influence of workplace structures, cultures, and practices, and attempting to change them. Many of the chapters in this book, such as those on work-life policies and organizational culture and support, attest to the substantial literature on changes needed at the workplace level. Nevertheless, barriers to change remain. In many contexts work-family conflict continues to be construed as an individual or family problem rather than an organizational issue and we have seen that there is less focus on the positive outcomes of multiple roles such as enrichment and facilitation, than on conflict and stress. A more systemic approach involves questioning taken-for-granted and gendered assumptions about ideal workers and ideal ways of working that make it difficult to integrate work and family, as many of the authors in this book emphasize. Future researchers and practitioners alike need to continually challenge assumptions about work and family issues insofar as they are conceptualized as individual problems rather than organizational (and social) issues.

In fact, individual and organizational approaches to work and family are ideally interdependent rather than in conflict. Nevertheless, this distinction does raise issues about whether workplace initiatives should be tailor-made to individuals, as some authors argue, or whether we should instead focus on systemic change, that is, change for all. The argument for tailor-made initiatives is seductive because people have diverse needs and ideally there should be diverse solutions. On the other hand, individual solutions can create problems of backlash (Burke, 2005; Haar, Spell & O'Driscoll, 2005), and management discretion can create issues of perceived equity and procedural and distributive organizational justice. There is a need for research to identify aspects of wider systemic change to enable people with diverse needs to be able to work in ways that are compatible with family life; for example, opportunities for everyone to work flexibly and be valued. This often involves questioning some basic assumptions about what is an ideal (or a marginal) worker, which too often tend to keep men away from family and leave women, who are more likely to modify work for family, at the margins of work.

At the family and societal level, there is a similar need to complement individual approaches by moving beyond a focus on individual men and women or even individual families to systemic thinking. As authors in this volume acknowledge, this involves questioning the ways in which both women and men tend to cling to traditional patterns of parenting that position women as primary parents and men on the margins of families, and reflecting on the ways that this is reinforced within workplaces, communities, and public policies.

The Need for a Multilevel Systemic Approach (Assumptions About Systems)

This book highlights the complexity of work, family, and societal systems and the interactions between them. Examination of the impact of multiple layers of context and the relationships between them is critical for extending understanding of work-family processes and experiences.

Various aspects of context at the macro level are important for families. Social policies, economic and labor market conditions, historical context and cultural values all play a part, but none operate in isolation and all interact with policy and practice at the meso level, particularly the workplace and the family. Thus, although it is easier to combine work and parenting in some national contexts than others because of supportive leave policies and childcare provisions, this is not always straightforward. Workplace context (such as a "macho" culture or heavy workloads) can undermine the most "family-friendly" national policies, particularly in the face of intense global competition (Brandth & Kvande, 2002; Haas, Allardt & Hwang, 2002; Haas & Hwang, 2007). Indeed the impact of policies—whether public or organizational—is dependent upon and limited by changes, or the lack of them, on many levels (e.g., in workplaces, families, communities, and wider societal attitudes).

Changes in gender relations in the family and beyond also depend on the interaction of changes in multiple social systems and the impact that they have on gender identity and on the space for negotiation and equity. Work-family research has long focused on gender relationships (see Chapter 12) and noted both incremental changes in some contexts, but also the persistence of gendered processes at home and at work. It has often been assumed that the problem is simply that men are not increasing their contributions to family work to the extent that women have increased their paid work contributions in recent decades. Chapters within this book, however, show that the situation is more complex. Fathers' family involvement, for example, continues to be influenced not only by the family situation but also by norms and values in workplaces and wider societies (see Chapter 14). As authors in this volume have pointed out, a systems approach and theorizing, taking account of multiple influences from multiple systems, has the potential to focus on the complexities of work-family issues and to help to clarify what holds back or supports progress in practice, at all levels.

The Importance of Cross-National and Cross-Cultural Perspectives (Assumptions About Universality and Culture)

While research on work-life issues is emerging in more countries around the world, it is clear that the vast amount of research and policy analysis on work-life issues pertains to highly industrialized countries—particularly North

American, European, and Anglo countries that share comparable cultural values and economic circumstances. As Heymann (2006) reminds us, huge numbers of "Forgotten Families"—whose challenges in combining work and care are beyond what we normally consider as academics—remain invisible. It cannot be assumed that concepts developed in specific contexts can be uncritically transferred elsewhere or research findings generalized. Workplace and family systems exist within, influence and are influenced by wider social systems with their specific norms, values, policies, and practices. It is important to question assumptions about the universality of findings in work and family research and to recognize how these findings are grounded within time and place. The need to get beyond simplistic westernized concepts and recognize western biases has been emphasized in this book. Avoiding western bias is important, but there is also a need to avoid generalizing about western families and workplaces too, as there is much within-region and within-country heterogeneity (Crompton, Lewis & Lyonette, 2007).

National context tends to be highlighted and reflected upon when reporting research in many diverse countries, but is often taken as given in North American and some other western contexts. Even within the western world, national context matters in a variety of ways. There are crucial differences in public policies and the values on which they are based, and in the discourses within which work and family issues are framed or even whether these issues are articulated at all (Lewis & Smithson, 2006). This has impacts on employees' expectations and their sense of entitlement to support not only from government, but also from employers, family members, and others (Lewis & Smithson, 2001).

It is often only in carrying out cross-national (comparing national contexts) or cross-cultural (focusing on elements of culture) research that we are confronted with our own values and expectations and the prejudices that we bring to our research. Such circumstances will help us recognize that our perspective may not be universal. As work-family researchers it is valuable not only to examine the diverse influences of national contexts and cultures in comparative research, but also to reflect on how our research is influenced by our own assumptions grounded within our own experiences.

THE NEED FOR RELATIONAL APPROACHES (ASSUMPTIONS ABOUT SIGNIFICANT RELATIONSHIPS)

Several authors in this book have emphasized that relationships at home and at work are an essential aspect of work and family systems. Such relationships are affected by many factors including heavy workloads and time pressures, work schedules that fit a 24/7 economy, and technology that blurs the boundaries between work and home. The intensification of work is matched in many contexts by an intensification of the demands of parenting. Moreover, the already challenging demands of eldercare are increased by greater longevity, as well as by shifting cultural norms in some national contexts. We need to know more about the impact of current contexts on relationships between parents and children (whether it is the children or the the elderly parent who needs care), spouses, colleagues, managers, and subordinates. We also need to question the assumption that only relationships at home and at work are relevant to our field and to understand the impact of current working and caring patterns on wider relationships. If time for family is squeezed, what effect does this have on other relationships such as friendships? Moreover, if time for friendships is compromised, what is the effect on general well-being across the life course (Gambles et al., 2006; Parris, Vickers & Wilkes, in press)?

CONTEMPORARY CHANGES—SHIFTING CONTEXTS (ASSUMPTIONS ABOUT THE NATURE OF KNOWLEDGE IN THE WORK-FAMILY FIELD)

Certainly, more attention to social systems at the macro (societal) and meso (workplace) levels, as well as at the micro or individual levels, and the relationships between them, is critical for extending understanding of work-family processes and experiences. However, it is also important to recognize that social systems are not static. They are dynamic and changing, particularly in the context of globalization processes. It was changes in family systems and workplaces associated with women's greater labor force participation that first drove the development of the work-family field. Changes, as well as continuities, in families continue. However, perhaps more significant in the 21st century are the changes taking place at the workplace level in response to global competition and efficiency drives, widely discussed in this volume. These changes can exacerbate work-family dilemmas and undermine initiatives developed to support the integration of work and family life. Moreover, these changes are occurring across national boundaries as western working practices and associated work-family dilemmas are increasingly exported to countries with lower cost economies (Lewis, Gambles & Rapoport, 2007).

With the fast pace of change in both families and work it is important to question assumptions about what constitutes knowledge in the study of work and family. Such knowledge is inevitably bounded by historical time and by place. New developments rapidly make old certainties fragile and open to question. For example, adopting flexible work strategies like working from home are often recommended as ways to help people to manage their work and non-work lives. Yet, as we have seen in this volume, these can become double-edged as the pace of work and workloads intensify, increasing the possibility that flexibility in time and place become ways to enable or encourage workers to work harder and longer. Similarly, autonomous work groups or self-rostering can be a solution to work and family scheduling issues, encouraging solidarity and collaboration among working groups. Yet, with intensified workloads and team members stretched to the limit in contemporary workplaces, employees may be reluctant to work flexibly if it means overloading colleagues. Colleagues thus become agents of social control (Bäck-Wiklund & Plantin, 2007; Lewis & Smithson, 2006). Policies and practices that were appropriate in past times do not necessarily work today and are unlikely to work in the same ways in the future.

THE COMPLEX AND UNEVEN NATURE OF CHANGE AND TRANSFORMATION (ASSUMPTIONS ABOUT THE NATURE AND INEVITABILITY OF CHANGE)

Developments in the work-family field discussed in this volume also challenge simplistic assumptions about the nature of change. Firstly, sustainable change that will really make a difference to people's lives requires related changes at all levels. Such fundamental changes take time and rarely occur in a straightforward, linear and cumulative way. For example, we have witnessed dramatic changes over time in gender relations in the family and beyond. Yet, the unravelling of the "male breadwinner model" towards more egalitarian models of work-family integration within and across cultures is a complex and very slow process and gender continues to shape experiences of work and family everywhere (Crompton et al., 2007). In Europe, for example, attachment to the male breadwinner model is declining, albeit at different rates, and within different European countries a range of modern attitudinal patterns is emerging. Nevertheless, although modern patterns are more prevalent in some countries, a diversity of attitudinal patterns exists even in countries usually considered more progressive in work and family attitudes. Moreover, attachment to the male breadwinner/female carer-stay-at-home model has not totally disappeared even in countries with the most egalitarian policies (Crompton et al.).

Each level of change brings new challenges. For example, there is a strong ideological commitment to gender equity and shared parenting in Norway. Yet in one study the Norwegian women talked about the issues that greater paternal involvement raised for them, such as the reluctance of some women to finally relinquish their primary carer role, and concerns about the shared custody arrangements that inevitably followed divorce in shared parenting families (Gambles et al., 2006). Just as men have needed to change to reflect women's changing roles, progress in this direction requires reciprocal change in identity, values, and behaviors of women and again from men in an ongoing dynamic process. There are often transitional tensions along the way as changes in some individuals and some systems lag behind others (Lewis & Smithson, 2006). Longitudinal, in-depth qualitative research may be necessary to chart further changes over time and the conditions under which they are facilitated.

At the workplace level, many organizations appear to be changing to support work-family integration. Here too, however, fundamental change is slow, uneven, and often superficial. The "male model" of full-time, long-term work continues to prevail and is intensified in the contemporary settings discussed in this volume. Nevertheless, some workplaces are more supportive of work-family integration than others. This differs across national context, sector, specific type of workplace, and for different occupations, influenced by combinations of national policy and its implementation, the nature of work, and normative working practices. Moreover there are often multiple cultural layers within organizations so that while some workplace units may support working carers, others within the same workplace are more resistant to change (Bäck-Wiklund & Plantin, 2007; das Dores Guerreiro & Perreira, 2007).

We also need to clarify assumptions about the purposes of policies, practices, and initiatives designed to facilitate change in workplaces. Is the aim to support healthy families and societies or to increase workplace effectiveness, or is a dual agenda in which both sides of the equation are equally valued (Rapoport et al., 2002) really possible? If we take the latter view—that workplace effectiveness and quality of life are equally important—it may be necessary to question the inevitability of some of the contemporary changes in ways of working and particularly workloads which result from a need to compete in the global economy, discussed in this book. This, in turn, may lead to a questioning of more fundamental assumptions about the ways in which work is organized, and about the relative values placed upon profit and efficiency, or on the well-being and sustainability of employees, their families, and communities (Gambles et al., 2006; Lewis et al., 2007). Bauman, in his discussion of the human costs of globalization, suggests that "questioning the ostensibly unquestionable premises of our ways of life are arguably the most urgent service we owe to our fellow humans and ourselves" (1998, p. 5). This involves problemitizing such taken-for granted assumptions as the importance of economic growth and the logic of economic determinism. Do we really want profits to be more important than people when evidence shows that, in fact, the wealthiest countries are not the happiest (Layard, 2005)?

An alternative way of conceptualizing these issues is in terms of socially sustainable work that takes account of a multiple agenda that includes well-being at individual, family, workplace, and societal levels (Brewster, 2004; Lewis et al., 2007; Webster, 2004). Juliet Webster argues that:

> ... we now have to broaden our concerns to consider the impact of the organization of work on the wider sphere of life beyond paid employment—for the individual, for communities, for society at large. In other words, our concern must now be with enhancing the broader social sustainability of working life (2004: pp. 62–63).

The sustainability of current forms of work is in question for a number of reasons. Authors in this volume have discussed some of the impacts of contemporary phenomena such as work overload on well-being. These include rising levels of stress and sickness absence in many contexts (Back-Wiklund & Plantin, 2007).

One long-term consequence concerns declining birth rates throughout much of the industrialized world, notably in Japan and Europe. This raises issues of population sustainability and related concerns about a crisis of caring as populations age. Fertility changes in Europe have been linked with persistent gendered employment experiences, exacerbated by current forms of work (Fagnani, 2007; Hašková, 2007) which underestimate the importance of social reproduction for national economies as well as for quality of life. In Japan too there is explicit concern about sustaining a future workforce as well as future consumers. Threats to cultural traditions, some of which may be vital to sustain working families, also encourage new ways of thinking about sustainability (Gambles et al., 2006). A social sustainability approach may involve questioning some of the assumptions of current forms of competitive capitalism which value economic growth for its own sake regardless of social factors, environmental costs, and quality of life. Arguably a major challenge for work-family research in the future may be to conceptualize, theorize and experiment with work and family issues in ways that bring them from the margins to the epicentre of discussion about the future of work, families, and societies.

IMPORTANT GAPS AND OPPORTUNITIES FOR DEEPENING OUR UNDERSTANDING

It is important to identify gaps in any research area; however, sensitivity to who and what is not included or poorly represented in current research and policy planning in the work-life field is particularly important. Blind spots can mean we know little about significant numbers of individuals and families and their experiences at the work-family interface or about the conditions that affect their capacity to function effectively as a parent, in other family roles, and in the wider community. Invisibility, in turn, means that the needs and concerns of these groups are likely to be ignored in the development of good workplace practices and in policy planning. In this section, we concentrate on the need for further research on low-wage workers and low-wage families, part-time workers, and those who have non-standard work schedules. We also note the under-representation of research on work-family integration among workers in rural communities and in small businesses, and the importance of attending to specific occupations and dimensions of work beyond those that are often included in current research. In this case, we focus particularly on careworkers, both because they are a significant portion of the labor force and because access to high-quality care services (childcare, homecare, and eldercare) is so critical to the well-being of others.

WORK-FAMILY INTEGRATION CHALLENGES FOR LOW-WAGE WORKERS AND LOW-INCOME FAMILIES

Recently, work-family researchers have begun to address the unique issues that relate to low-wage workers and low-income families (Acs, Ross & McKenzie,

2001; Crouter & Booth, 2004; Perry-Jenkins, 2005). Yet it is still the case that much work-family research largely reflects the circumstances and experiences of white, middle-class, educated workers in highly industrialized countries—typically those who are organizationally employed and living in dual-earner couples. As Lambert (1999) has noted, sparse attention has been paid to the experiences of low-wage, non-professional workers and to low-income working poor families. Low-wage workers are a heterogeneous group, among whom women, minorities/recent immigrants, part-time workers, and those with limited education and skills predominate. Some have difficulty obtaining and sustaining employment because of ill-health or for family reasons; some live in regions with high unemployment; others may work full-time but receive low wages that are insufficient to support a family. A large share of children living in poverty live in single-parent, female-headed families, whose position is particularly vulnerable under regimes that provide limited financial support to them. In the US a considerable body of recent research is devoted to the impacts of welfare reform, particularly the 1996 federal Personal Responsibility and Work Opportunity Reconciliation Act that, along with state policies and funding restrictions, imposed work requirements and strict time limits for welfare recipients, but often provided only limited financial assistance to beneficiaries to improve their education or cover work expenses, including subsidized childcare (see Albelda, 2001; Clampet-Lundquist, Edin, London, Scott & Hunter, 2004; Duncan & Chase-Lansdale, 2001). According to Bernstein (2004), low-income single-parent families in the US now depend little on public assistance, relying on earnings for an average of 73% of their total income to cover all living and work-related expenses.

For low-wage workers and those who are marginally employed, work-life issues are strongly tied to concerns about income security and the provision of basic needs. Lambert and Henley (2007) direct our attention to the conditions of "low level" jobs that can affect worker and family well-being. In addition to low wages and limited wage growth, such jobs offer little security; provide workers with little control over their work schedules and continuity of work hours; often involve non-standard work hours; and provide limited access to work-family supports (Swanberg, Pitt-Catsouphes & Drescher-Burke, 2005). Most low-wage jobs offer few, if any, employer-provided benefits. The nature of the work or the limited number of work hours frequently fall outside the criteria defined by national policies or collective bargaining that would provide access to employment insurance in the event of job loss or disability, or job-protected leave in the event of childbirth, adoption, a family emergency, or even sickness. In fact, more than half of working parents with family incomes below the poverty line in the US are reported to have no paid leave—no vacation days, sick days, or personal days (Ross Phillips, 2004). This finding is particularly problematic because research demonstrates that low-income parents are more likely to experience instances of poor personal health and/or a greater prevalence of childhood illness, disability, or behavior issues that might involve school conferences or assessments and consultations with professionals (Urban Institute, 2005; Zaslow, Acs, Cameron & Vandivere, 2006, as cited in Levin-Epstein, 2006). Lack of access to paid leave days and to flexible work schedules mean that parents must take expensive unpaid time off to arrange for hours that accommodate doctors' visits and meetings with teachers, caseworkers or other personnel.

Such circumstances are not unique to the US. Many countries with progressive parental leave policies, for example, require a minimum number of hours or a specified period of time with the same employer in order to qualify for benefits. In the US, however, many low-wage workers (including one third of working parents with family incomes below the poverty line) would not qualify for coverage for unpaid leave under the Family and Medical Leave Act, and would have great difficulty taking unpaid leave even if they did (Ross Phillips, 2004). According to Bernstein's (2004) analyses, only one-third of workers with wages in the lowest quintile in the US in 2000 had access to employer-provided health insurance and less than one-fifth had any pension coverage. His analyses also suggest that over the last two decades low-wage workers lost relative bargaining power and experienced lower job quality as manufacturing jobs were lost and replaced by service-sector jobs, many of which were in the lowest paying sectors in retail and other services.

Finally, we note that low-wage jobs are often poor quality jobs in other ways. Some are physically demanding and unpleasant, leaving workers tired and strained when they return to their families. Presser (2004) points out that while non-standard hours are evident among all levels of income, the incidence of non-standard work schedules, including weekends and evening/night shifts, is disproportionately higher among workers with low incomes. Furthermore, among such common low-paying jobs as cashiers, truck drivers, waiters and waitresses, and janitors/cleaners, those who work at non-standard times receive even lower pay.

These findings suggest that beyond the economic vulnerability experienced by low-wage workers, there are other important issues of job quality such as access to benefits and public protection, physical fatigue, and the lack of control or flexibility that are important for work-family integration. Recently there have been some efforts made to identify how employers and policy-makers can support low-wage workers, enhance stable employment, and promote skill development (Litchfield, Swanberg & Sigworth, 2004; Saunders, 2006; US Government, 2007). Yet it is also true that employers who face significant economic pressures to keep costs low by reducing labor costs and potentially by outsourcing "peripheral" functions are unlikely to make such investments unless it is in their obvious interest to do so.

WORK-FAMILY INTEGRATION AND PART-TIME WORK

Working part time is an option that many women have used to enable them to participate in the labor force and contribute to their household income while having more time with young children, other family members, or in personal or community activities. Part-time work might also be used by individuals for a limited period of time to accommodate such circumstances as personal or family illness or involvement in adult education or training programs. It might also be used to smooth a transition into full-time work from a period spent out of the labor force or on leave. Currently, the literature on part-time work includes (a) descriptions and analyses of part-time work (wages and working conditions); (b) statistical analyses of the economic and employment consequences of part-time work for women; and (c) discussions of part-time work as a working time option in work-family reconciliation policy planning.

The prevalence of part-time work among women is quite variable across the OECD countries. While the average proportion of employed women working part-time across the EU countries was 33.5% in 2002, considerably lower rates were observed in the Mediterranean countries, while the highest rates of part-time work occurred in the UK (44%) and in the Netherlands, where 73% of women worked part-time, as well as 22% of men (European Foundation for the Improvement of Living and Working Conditions, 2007). Differences in prevalence reflect gender roles, welfare state policies, personal preferences, opportunities for part-time work, and more recent policy initiatives in line with the 1997 EU Directive on Part-time Work. McGinnity and McManus (2007) have noted that working part-time can have quite different long-term effects on women's wages and opportunities in countries with different institutional arrangements and policies. Their analysis of the social policy constellations in which part-time work functions in Britain, Germany and the US in what they refer to as distinct "part-time regimes" alerts us to the importance of considering the context in which different work arrangements occur.

In the US, where full-time work predominates among dual-earner couples, part-time work is often low-wage work with few benefits and, as in the UK, is likely to result in substantial wage penalties. In both countries there has been weak institutional support for part-time work; however, the UK has adopted recommendations to address issues such as providing pay equity and pro-rated benefits for those working part-time in keeping with the EU Directive on this issue. Part-time work is far more common among women in the UK than in many other countries and past research has confirmed the likelihood of negative long-term impacts on women's employment opportunities and pensions.

Three other important concerns remain about the quality of part-time work as a vehicle for work-family integration. Specifically, it appears that many part-time jobs involve non-standard work schedules with hours slotted into evenings and weekend days, particularly in the lower paying retail and service sectors. As discussed in the next section, such work schedules can be anything but child or family-friendly. Secondly, there are ongoing concerns about part-time work as an alternative that can reinforce gender inequality and occupational segregation, and impede women's long-term advancement. In particular, assumptions about ideal workers and ideal managers often reduce opportunities to work part-time without negative career consequences. Finally, it is striking that the discourse on part-time work and reduced hours as a tool for reconciling work and caregiving occurs without consideration of the needs and experiences of single parents and single caregivers of disabled or chronically-ill family members for whom part-time wages are likely insufficient and full-time work more stressful.

Discussions of part-time work figure prominently in the international literature on working time and work-family reconciliation policy (European Foundation for the Improvement of Living and Working Conditions, 2003; Gornick & Heron, 2006). Much of this policy discussion has been spurred by the 1997 EU Directive on Part-Time Work, the official purpose of which is to eliminate discrimination against part-time workers and to improve the quality of part-time work (Europa, 2004). Measures that can raise the quality of part-time work include requiring parity in pay and benefits between part-time and full-time workers and enabling workers to shift from full-time to part-time work (and vice versa) without having to change jobs. Establishing a right to good quality part-time work is seen as a way of enabling full-time workers to adjust work demands to enable a better fit with family needs and as a means to encourage women who are not employed to participate in the labor force. Policies in keeping with this Directive, while still developing and somewhat variable in implementation across the EU countries, include combinations of changes in national industrial/labor policies and collective bargaining agreements. In addition to assuring comparable treatment to full-time workers in wages and benefits, other efforts include ensuring that part-time workers have comparable social security, training, and promotion opportunities, and other rights. These actions complement earlier developments in Sweden and the Netherlands where part-time work is more firmly established as a tool to share paid work and care for young children. Of course in all these cases there is often a gap between policy and actual practice (Lewis & Smithson, 2006).

Researchers would be advised to consider various dimensions of part-time work in their research. These might include whether it is voluntary or involuntary, how it is designated in occupational schemes (e.g., regular part-time or temporary/exempt from benefits), whether part-time workers are represented adequately in collective bargaining, and their pay. Other crucial matters to consider are the number of hours worked, the duration of part-time work, work schedules and working conditions, as well as whether hours vary according to employer demand. Furthermore, how working part-time affects workers' access to other employer-provided benefits to support work-family balance, and how part-time work dovetails with other policies and institutional arrangements such as access to maternity and parental leave, and eligibility for social assistance, student loans, etc. are also important factors. Both shorter-term and longer-term consequences of working part-time for individuals and for women should be considered in diverse contexts.

WORK-FAMILY INTEGRATION AND NON-STANDARD WORK SCHEDULES

While some occupations (police and firefighters, hospital workers, public utilities) have always included some degree of non-day work, the transformation of jobs to serve a global 24/7 economy has had profound effects on workers and their families. Estimates based on US Census reports suggest that about 15% of the workforce work evenings, nights, rotating shifts, or irregular schedules (US Bureau of Labor Statistics, 2005). In Canada, it has been estimated that as many as one-third of all employees work non-standard hours and almost 1 in 5 full-time employees work on the weekend (Shields, 2002). Current estimates from the UK and Western Europe are not dissimilar (Han, 2007) and are likely to be considerably higher in large cities and in regions that depend heavily on tourism. Harriet Presser's analyses of non-standard work schedules over the last three decades consistently portray workers with non-standard work schedules in the US as more likely to be male, young, African-American, with low education and limited job skills. Many of the jobs are low-wage jobs in the service sector and in sales or personal services. Presser and others project that low-wage jobs with non-standard hours are likely to account for considerable job growth over the next ten years (Presser, 2003).

Non-standard work hours, particularly night shift work, has been associated with a variety of negative outcomes including impacts on physical health (fatigue, sleep problems, digestive problems, overweight, and increased smoking and alcohol consumption), adverse impacts on marital quality, and difficulties participating in family and social activities scheduled during the day. Finding ways to avoid or minimize such adverse affects is a concern for organizations that depend on having workers awake and alert through night shifts, both in order to get the work done, but also to avoid the possibility of injuries and industrial accidents (Rosa & Colligan, 1997).

Of particular interest for work-family researchers is the fact that non-standard work schedules (what Europeans refer to as non-social work hours) appear to be fairly prevalent in the US and Canada among dual-earner couples with young children. In fact, 1 in 4 dual-earner couples with children in the US have at least one shift worker (Presser, 2000). Often, balancing work and family responsibilities involves a complex process of organization and negotiation between partners and the use of adaptive strategies to accommodate work hours and job demands. Presser has used longitudinal data to carefully examine this fact and has confirmed that non-standard work, especially by a wife, increases the likelihood of separation and divorce (Presser, 2003).

Researchers in the US, Canada and the UK confirm that parents' participation in work scheduled outside of traditional daytime hours or on weekends reflects both "push and pull" factors. On the one hand, non-standard hours may be

a condition of the job or be the only work available. On the other hand, couples may choose to "off-shift" their work hours (work different, mostly non-overlapping schedules) in order to minimize or avoid the costs associated with non-parental childcare and/or to share parental care. Interestingly, several studies report that parents of children with disabilities or chronic health problems may use off-shifting work schedules as an adaptive strategy to enable both parents to work while ensuring consistent and responsive care for their child.

Parental off-shifting may take a variety of forms. For example, one parent may work primarily on weekend days while the other works during the week with neither working nights. Alternatively, one or both parents may work non-standard schedules, including at least one parent working a night shift. Among low-income single parents, a similar form of off-shifting may be done with a grandparent or other close relative. Recently there has been increased interest in examining off-shifting and the impacts of this arrangement on children's development and on family life. It appears that there are both costs and benefits, and that couples consciously use various strategies to maintain communication and support each other (Hattery, 2001; Pagnan & Lero, 2006). In Han's recent (2007) review of the effects of non-standard work schedules for the Sloan Work-Family Encyclopedia, she notes that seven out of 11 existing studies found negative associations between mothers working shifts and children's cognitive or behavioural outcomes, two studies find mixed relationships, and two found no significant effects. The most consistent positive finding is one of enhanced paternal involvement with children as fathers spend more time with their children than would otherwise be the case. Interviews with parents who off-shift provide evidence that the benefit of sharing care and avoiding non-parental care is highly valued, but that this pattern can be stressful and difficult or undesirable to maintain for long periods of time (Pagnan & Lero, 2006).

The potential consequences of non-standard work (temporary, part-time, on-call) and non-standard work schedules for individuals, families, and society is an important issue. The actual hours individuals work, the extent of control or flexibility available to change shifts when needed, and the extent to which off-shifting is actually a choice or a response to inadequate supports for working parents are factors that bear further examination.

OTHER GAPS AND OPPORTUNITIES FOR FURTHER RESEARCH

There are three other topics we will note in this chapter as areas that require further research and integration into our thinking about work-family reconciliation. The first is the lack of research and discourse on work-family issues in rural communities, the second pertains to individuals working in small businesses. Thirdly, we recognize the importance of studies that focus on particular occupations and professions in order to understand more specific organizational and social factors that affect workers' opportunities and constraints in integrating work and care.

There is a growing body of research on work-family issues among families in rural communities (see Leach, 1999; Mauthner, McKee & Strell, 2001; and Winson & Leach, 2002). Much of it deals with work-family integration in the context of rural economic restructuring in communities struggling to maintain their agricultural base and the productivity of family farms, while adapting to the serious economic and social challenges individuals and families experience when major local industries close or relocate. Rural communities are not homogeneous and some develop more diversified economic bases, including more cottage industries that mostly employ local women, while other communities have greater difficulty. Closure of a local plant can result in substantial economic loss and increase the need for family members (often fathers) to commute further away to maintain an adequate income. The lack of sufficient local childcare, eldercare, transportation, and healthcare resources presents additional challenges, particularly for rural women, many of whom find work in lower-pay service sector jobs (Ames, Brosi & Damiano-Teixeira, 2006). Rural communities often are also sites of out-migration, resulting in the loss of younger family members and contributing to the challenges of providing adequate support for seniors aging in place. Geographic, economic, and social factors in rural communities provide a unique context for understanding how individuals work to maintain their livelihoods, their families, and their communities.

A second area we would encourage researchers to consider further is that of small businesses as a context for work-family integration. While the criterion for what constitutes a small business can vary across countries, small businesses are typically seen as providing the largest proportion of jobs in the private sector and being the major source of job growth. In the US more than 55% of employees work in firms with fewer than 100 workers (MacDermid Hetzog, Kensinger & Zipp, 2001). In Canada, it has been estimated that more than 95% of firms have fewer than 100 employees and that almost 1 in 5 employees work in a business that employs fewer than 20 individuals (Daly, 2000; Earl, 2005). In many cases, small businesses are also family-owned and operated, which inevitably means a very strong and integral link between work and family for some employees and the firm's owner(s).

Firm size does matter, particularly in the extent to which individuals have access to employer-provided supports such as paid leave, benefits, telework options, and access to services such as employee assistance programs (Evans, 2002; Ferrer & Gagné, 2006). Assumptions about limited access to flexibility in work scheduling and the degree of support provided in the workplace, however, may or may not be warranted. In MacDermid et al.'s (2001) analyses of data from the 1997 US National Study of the Changing Force, these authors found that while workers in small businesses (<100 employees) reported lower earnings, fewer benefits and less education than their counterparts in large organizations, they also reported a better fit between their actual and desired work hours, more support-ive work environments, and less interference between work and family. Similarly, Daly (2000) found that many smaller Canadian businesses reportedly allow work-ers considerable flexibility to enable them to be productive at work while address-ing critical family concerns, even if they were less likely to provide opportunities for paid leave and other supports that would be far more expensive for small busi-nesses. Similar findings have been reported in the UK. Dex and Schreibl (2001) and Lewis and Cooper (2005) report case studies of very innovative initiatives to support work-family integration in small businesses.

In discussing work-family policies, it is important to note that in some countries employees in small firms generally are not covered under collective bar-gaining arrangements and also may be exempted from provisions in labor leg-islation that provide access to benefits such as family leave. As one important example, the US Family and Medical Leave Act exempts employers with fewer than 50 employees from the requirement of providing 12 weeks of unpaid leave. Currently in Ontario, Canada, employees working in small firms with fewer than 50 employees are not eligible to take the ten days of unpaid, job-protected emer-gency leave in case of illness, injury, and other emergencies or urgent matters that are available to workers in larger firms.

Given the large number of individuals employed in small businesses, it is important to understand and share tools that can be used to promote good practices to support work-family integration that are applicable to this context. Moreover, it is necessary to consider how national policies designed to support workers with family responsibilities can be implemented without creating serious economic hardship for employers in this sector. It is also important to recognize that in some cases it is the larger organizations that can learn from the innovative practices of smaller organizations.

Finally, we encourage researchers to be sensitive to the unique challenges and experiences that typify certain occupations and professions. Fortunately, this area of research is attracting more attention as studies are being done on work-life issues in such varied occupations and sectors as policing, law, teaching, academia, and healthcare, to name a few. In each of these, there are unique organizational and cultural contexts and stressors that affect expectations, norms, the uptake of work-family supports, and the extent of work-family conflict. Promoting positive change to enable more flexibility and support in specific occupations and profes-sions requires an in-depth understanding of the organizational and cultural norms and the constraints that operate in each case.

We wish to note one particular occupational sector that is especially rel-evant for discussions about work-family supports. The broader field of carework consists of occupations in such fields as childcare, homecare, eldercare, and care for individuals with disabilities and is associated with the broad range of health and human services that includes social work and health care (Brannen, Statham,

Mooney & Brockmann, 2007). According to the European Foundation for the Improvement of Living and Working Conditions, almost one-fifth of jobs created across the EU between 1995 and 2001 occurred in the health and human services sectors, which today amounts to almost 10% of the total workforce (2006, p. 4).

Most often analyses focus on those who provide direct care and support to individuals in a group setting, in their own home, or in the home of a child, senior, or disabled individual. Individuals employed in carework span a wide range from those who are organizationally employed and covered under formal labor standards and collective agreements to individuals working in community-based, non-profit organizations. Some careworkers are contracted by third party organizations. Careworkers who work on contract, those who provide care out of their own homes, and careworkers who are employed by individuals (nannies, domestic workers, and personal care aides) occupy a grey zone in labor policy, and often do not qualify for employment insurance or other forms of social protection. They may also be excluded from labor standards that specify maximum work hours, overtime regulations, and other statutory benefits. As described by England, Budig and Folbre (2002), both men and women careworkers pay a wage penalty for working in this sector, but the penalty is born disproportionately by women, who make up the majority of careworkers.

A particularly troubling concern is the growing number of careworkers who are immigrants and who, like native-born careworkers, find themselves working long hours for low pay in conditions where they can easily be exploited. Stewart, Neufeld, Harrison, Spitzer, Hughes and Makwarimba (2005) found that immigrant family daycare providers experienced additional challenges and lacked access to health and social services. The challenges they experienced were compounded by language difficulties, immigration, and separation from family in their home country. Participants recommended changes to policies and programs that could provide information, transportation, and access to other services and supports, and emphasized the importance of reviewing policies that affect immigration, caregiving, and access to health and social services.

Analyses of individuals working in childcare and early childhood education programs and services constitute one significant area of research designed to promote policy development. Various reports have documented a range of human resource issues (including appropriate wages, working conditions, lack of opportunities for advancement, limited access to professional development opportunities, and lack of well-defined educational and career ladders) that are affecting the capacity to attract and retain committed individuals to the early childhood education and care field—even at a time when there is a strong desire to both expand services and improve their quality (Lero, 2007; Moss, 2002). Substantial improvements in the organization, regulation and funding of services have been identified as critical for ensuring that services are both affordable to parents and are of high quality for children. Similar issues have been identified with respect to the organization of community-based homecare services to support an aging population (European Foundation for the Improvement of Living and Working Conditions, 2006), especially as demand currently exceeds supply. There is a need to ensure that such work is organized and funded appropriately to improve wages and working conditions, and to enable workers to have access to education and professional development opportunities in order to progress along a clearly defined career path. This will have a direct impact on the capacity to recruit and retain workers, the quality of care provided, and the sustainability of services that, in turn, support work-family integration for careworkers themselves and for many others.

EMERGING ISSUES AND NEW PERSPECTIVES

In this final section, we remind readers of two major demographic factors that are affecting workplaces and societies—increasing immigration and population aging. Both have profound implications for accommodating more diverse individuals in workplaces and in our communities and require forward planning, sensitivity, and the implementation of good practices and appropriate policies.

INCREASING IMMIGRATION AND WORK-FAMILY INTEGRATION

One of the major demographic factors that is changing social structures in the 21th century is international migration. According to McGovern (2007), the number of people living outside their usual country of residence has increased from 75 million in 1960 to more than 191 million in 2005. The number of countries hosting more than half a million immigrants has also doubled to more than 64 countries and there is greater diversity and visibility among recent waves of immigrants. While immigrants are seen as a welcome source of new citizens and new labor force participants in countries like Canada where fertility rates are low, immigration can also be problematic, especially when newcomers have difficulty finding appropriate employment, securing a stable income, and settling into their new community. Immigration is a central concern among policy-makers who recognize the greater prevalence of poverty and stress among recent immigrants, incidents of racial discrimination and hostility, and the likelihood of significant social exclusion reflecting an underclass of immigrants with accompanying social problems. It is also a concern of larger cities, especially when municipalities are responsible for providing appropriate health, education, social services, and settlement supports with limited funding.

A key issue that affects many immigrants, including those with post-secondary education and previous experience in a profession or business, is access to suitable employment, since recognition of their credentials is often problematic. As an example, in one recent study by Statistics Canada (2005), 70% of immigrants who settled in 2000–2001 had trouble entering the workforce and six in ten eventually took jobs outside their area of training. Moreover, recent immigrant families have been identified as one of several groups most likely to have experienced low income, and persistent low income throughout the late 1990s (Palameta, 2004). Unemployment, underemployment, and insecure low-wage work has substantial impacts on immigrants' health, opportunities, and family relationships (Shimoni, Este & Clark, 2003).

A recent study of foreign-born workers in London identifies the many tactics immigrant parents use when working long hours in low-wage work (often including non-standard schedules) and the various costs this has on their health, family relationships, and foregone opportunities for social participation in their communities (Datta, McIlwaine, Evans, Herbert, May & Wills, 2007). These authors also surface the fact that most of these jobs fail to provide job security, adequate income, representation in a union, or access to work-family or employer-provided benefits. Many of the low-wage workers interviewed, including cleaners working on contract and careworkers, are also caught in a confusing array of policies that limit access to public assistance benefits, education opportunities, and other services that would be helpful for themselves and their families.

A separate literature exists that indicates that workplaces need to adapt to a far move diverse workforce and customer base to be successful. Respecting each individual's cultural background, religion, and values and assuring fair and equitable hiring and promotion policies become essential good practices in workplaces and benefit everyone. Often this includes recognition of diverse work-family contexts and needs (Rana, Kagan, Lewis & Rout, 1998).

To date there is limited research on work-family conflict and work-family enrichment that includes an analysis of cultural differences, including differences in gender role ideology that might contribute to higher levels of stress in families. Further research may suggest that immigrant workers' attitudes and values about their role as providers and parents, about the extent to which families should accommodate work demands, and about the extent to which they rely on social support from kin and neighbors are important variables in predicting how they experience the work-family interface. Given possible attitudinal and behavioural differences, one might also see different rates of take-up of family-supportive benefits in workplaces among immigrants and native-born workers. On the other hand, research indicates that immigrants may have difficulty accessing information about health and social services in their communities and be reticent to use formal services.

POPULATION AGING, ELDER CARE AND WORK-FAMILY INTEGRATION

Population aging has been described as one of the most important demographic factors that will shape policy and influence workers' lives during this century (Wilmoth & Longino, 2006). Projections of growth in the population aged 65 and older and aged 80 or 85 or older are common and quite significant across most developed countries including the EU, the US, and Canada. Growth estimates in the proportion of seniors result from the aging of the baby boom generation born between 1946 and 1964, lower fertility rates, and longer life expectancy. Fortunately, in most countries, seniors are living healthier lives, with increased opportunities for living more years independently without serious disability or impairment. The number of working-age adults will shrink, however, even if retirement is delayed for a few years, and consequently a higher proportion of workers will simultaneously and/or sequentially be involved in combining paid employment with providing care and support to a child, ailing spouse or partner, parent, in-law or other older relative, or a close friend.

The implications for workplaces and workers are two-fold: first, many workplaces are or will be adapting to the need to retain older workers. In areas where labor is in short supply or skills are specialized, the retention of older workers will be a significant concern. Many older workers have a preference for part-time work or will find flexible hours an attractive option.

Secondly, more workplaces will experience firsthand the concerns of employees with eldercare responsibilities and will need to adapt appropriate practices and policies to support these workers. According to the most recent figures available, in 2002 more than 1.7 million Canadians aged 45–64 provided some care on a regular basis to an elderly person with long-term disabilities or physical limitations, and 7 out of 10 of these caregivers were also employed. This works out to about 16% of the workforce in this age group (Pyper, 2006). As the population ages, this proportion will grow. Moreover, a national survey of over 31,000 employees in large and medium-sized workplaces in 2000–2001 indicated that slightly more than 1 in 4 employees reported experiencing a high level of caregiver strain (physical, financial, and mental stress attributable to caregiving demands along with feelings of being overwhelmed) that were most directly predicted by the number of hours spent providing eldercare per week (Duxbury & Higgins, 2005). While approximately equal numbers of employed men and women provide at least some level of eldercare, women provide considerably more hours of care, more personal care (assistance with bathing, feeding, dressing, etc.) and report higher levels of caregiver strain.

In 1998, Marks studied the effects of caregiving for children, spouses, parents, and other kin and non-kin among employed midlife workers. Caregiving was a strong predictor of high family to work spillover and stress for both men and women. In turn, the amount of work-family conflict employees experienced affected the extent to which caregiving resulted in distress, hostility, and poorer health. How do employed caregivers cope with significant care responsibilities for a senior or a chronically-ill family member? According to Statistics Canada data, many employees adapt their work schedules, while others take a period of unpaid leave, which can be quite problematic, especially for low-wage workers. Caregiving for an older family member is more likely to be a reason for withdrawal from the labor force among women than men. In 2002 more than 21% of retired women aged 45–64 who provided eldercare but only 8% of men caregivers who retired said that the need to provide care was one of the reasons they retired. Among currently employed caregivers, it is estimated that as many as 1 in 5 women and 1 in 10 men could retire sooner than planned because of caregiving responsibilities. These statistics are important early warning signals that policy makers' interests in extending the number of years individuals work may be on a collision course with the realities of trying to maintain employment while providing eldercare. Pavalko and Henderson (2006) report that women are more likely to quit their jobs than to cut back or try to work things out with their employer, unless their employer has made it clear that flexibility is possible. In such cases, "women who report access to flexible hours had 50% greater odds of still being employed two years later than those who did not have access to this benefit" (Pavalko & Henderson, p. 366).

In addition to providing flexibility to workers, other supportive measures that will need to be in place in countries which have not yet developed such initiatives, are provisions for paid caregiving leave similar to parental leave policies, homecare, respite services, financial assistance (especially for low-income caregivers and those who incur significant financial costs), and information and supports to enable employees to plan ahead and to access information and support in a timely fashion. Carers' leave already exists in the UK and in a number of other European countries, but careful analysis of these policies, their take-up, and use is not available. Major studies in Canada and the US have begun to identify good business practices and appropriate policy supports to help ease the pressures of combining work and eldercare, which are also applicable to providing care supports for individuals with a seriously or acutely ill spouse/partner. Given current population trends and the number of employees already experiencing eldercare and family care concerns, further development of policies and practices should not be delayed. Care should also be taken to reduce the costs to women as primary caregivers and to low-income earners who are not covered under policies that could otherwise be more effective in promoting the integration of work and care responsibilities.

CONCLUSIONS

Work-family research has made tremendous strides since it began in the late 1960s. Nevertheless, there clearly remain many new and emerging challenges. Not the least of these challenges is to be inclusive in policy and practices across a wide range of work and care situations; to reflect on and be responsive to the changes occurring in families, workplaces, communities, and beyond. It is critical to reflect on our assumptions, to address current gaps, and to be aware of emerging issues as we move forward.

Research such as that summarized in this handbook is a critical tool for understanding the complex, multifaceted, and dynamic issues that influence the potential to successfully integrate paid work and family life. This is no longer a private concern, but one that affects economic prosperity and social well-being around the globe. It deserves our full engagement as we strive to influence behaviours, policies, and practices that will make a difference to individuals, families, workplaces, and communities in our increasingly interconnected world.

REFERENCES

Acs, G., Ross, K. & McKenzie D. (2001). Playing by the rules, but losing the game: Americans in low-income working families. In R. Kazis & M. Miller (eds), *Low-Wage Workers in the New Economy* (pp. 21–44). Washington, DC: Urban Institute Press.

Albelda, R. (2001). Welfare-to-work, farewell to families? US welfare reform and work/family debates. *Feminist Economics, 7*(1), 119–135.

Ames, B. D., Brosi, W. A. & Damiano-Teixeira, K. M. (2006). "I'm just glad my three jobs could be during the day": Women and work in a rural community. *Family Relations, 55,* 119–131.

Bäck-Wiklund, M. & Plantin, L. (2007). The workplace as an arena for negotiating the work-family boundary: A case study of two Swedish social services agencies. In R. Crompton, S. Lewis & C. Lyonette (eds), *Women, Men, Work and Family in Europe* (pp. 171–189). London: Palgrave Macmillan.

Bailyn, L. (1993). *Breaking the Mold: Women, Men and Time in the New Corporate World.* New York: Free Press.

Bailyn, L. (2006). *Breaking the Mold: Redesigning Work for Productive and Satisfying Lives.* Ithaca, NY: Cornell University Press.

Bauman, Z. (1998). *Globalisation: The Human Consequences.* Cambridge, UK: Polity Press.

Bernstein, J. (2004). The low-wage labor market: Trends and policy implications. In A.C. Crouter & A. Booth (eds), *Work-Family Challenges for Low-Income Parents and their Children* (pp. 3–34). Mahwah, NJ: Lawrence Erlbaum.

Brandth, B. & Kvande, E. (2002). Reflexive fathers: Negotiating parental leave and working life. *Gender, Work and Organization, 9*(2), 186–203.

Brannen J., Statham, J., Mooney, A. & Brockmann, M. (2007). *Coming to Care: The Work and Family Lives of Workers Caring for Vulnerable Children.* Bristol, UK: Policy Press.

Brewster, J. (2004). Working and living in the European knowledge society: The policy implications of developments in working life and their effects on social relations. Report for the project "Infowork". Department of Sociology, Trinity College, Dublin.

Burke, R. (2005). Backlash in the workplace. *Women in Management Review, 20*(3), 165–176.

Clampet-Lundquist, S., Edin, K., London, A., Scott, E. & Hunter, V. (2004). "Making a way out of no way": How mothers meet basic family needs while moving from welfare to work. In A. C. Crouter & A. Booth (eds), *Work-Family Challenges for Low-Income Parents and their Children* (pp. 203–241). Mahwah, N.J.: Lawrence Erlbaum.

Crompton, R., Lewis, S. & Lyonette, C. (eds) (2007). *Women, Men, Work and Family in Europe.* London: Palgrave Macmillan.

Crouter A. C. & Booth, A. (2004). *Work-Family Challenges for Low-Income Parents and their Children* (pp. 3–34). Mahwah, N.J.: Lawrence Erlbaum.

Daly, K. (2000). Work-life practices and flexibility in small businesses: A Canadian research report. Guelph, ON: Centre for Families, Work and Well-Being. http://www.worklifecanada.ca/resources/small_businesses1.pdf

Das Dores Guerreiro, M. & Pereira, I. (2007). Women's occupational patterns and work-family arrangements: Do national and organisational policies matter? In R. Crompton, S. Lewis & C. Lyonette (eds), *Women, Men, Work and Family in Europe* (pp. 190–209). London: Palgrave Macmillan.

Datta, K., McIlwaine, C., Evans, Y., Herbert, J., May, J. & Wills, J. (2007). From coping strategies to tactics: London's low-pay economy and migrant labour. *British Journal of Industrial Relations, 45,* 404–432.

Dex, S. & Schreibl, F. (2001). Flexible and family-friendly working arrangements in small and medium-sized businesses: The business case. *British Journal of Industrial Relations, 38,* 411–431.

Duncan, G. & Chase-Lansdale, P. (2001). *For Better and for Worse: Welfare Reform and the Well-Being of Children and Families.* New York: Russell Sage Foundation.

Duxbury, L. & Higgins, C. (2005). Report Four: Who is at risk? Predictors of work-life conflict. Public Health Agency of Canada. http://www.phac-aspc.gc.ca/publicat/work-travail/report4/index.html

Earl, L. (2005). Are small businesses positioning themselves for growth? A comparative look at the use of selected management practices by firm size. Statistics Canada, Science Innovation and Electronic Information Division working paper. Catalogue no. 88F0006XIE – No. 010.

England, P., Budig, M. & Folbre, N. (2002). Wages of virtue: The relative pay of carework. *Social Problems, 49*(4), 455–473.

Europa (2004). Activities of the European Union. Summaries of legislation, part-time working. http://europa.eu/scadplus/leg/en/s02307.htm

European Foundation for the Improvement of Living and Working Conditions (2003). A new organization of time over working life. Retrieved July 20, 2007 from www.eurofound.eu.int.ef0364.en.pdf

European Foundation for the Improvement of Living and Working Conditions (2006). Employment in social care in Europe. Retrieved July 10, 2007 from http://www.eurofound.europa.eu/pubdocs/2006/50/en/1/ef0650en.pdf

European Foundation for the Improvement of Living and Working Conditions (2007). Part-time work in Europe. Retrieved September 5, 2007 from http://www.eurofound.europa.eu/ewco/reports/TN0403TR01/TN0403TR01.pdf

Evans, J. (2002). Work/family reconciliation, gender wage equity and occupational segregation: The role of firms and public policy. *Canadian Public Policy. XXVIII* (Special Supplement), S187–S216.

Fagnani, J. (2007). Fertility rates and mothers' employment behaviours in comparative perspective: Similarities and differences in six European countries. In R. Crompton, S. Lewis & C. Lyonette (eds), *Women, Men, Work and Family in Europe* (pp. 58–75). London: Palgrave Macmillan.

Ferrer, A. & Gagné, L. (2006). The use of family friendly workplace practices in Canada. Institute for Research in Public Policy. IRPP working paper series no. 2006-02.

Gambles, R., Lewis, S. & Rapoport, R. (2006). *The Myth Work-Life Balance: The Challenge of Our Time for Men, Women, and Societies.* London: Wiley.

Gornick, J. C. & Heron, A. (2006). The regulation of working time as work-family reconciliation policy: Comparing Europe, Japan, and the United States. *Journal of Comparative Policy Analysis, 8*(2), 149–166.

Haar, J., Spell, C. & O'Driscoll, M. (2005). Exploring work-family backlash in a public organization. *International Journal of Public Sector Management, 18,* 604–614.

Haas, L., Allardt, K. & Hwang, P. (2002). The impact of organizational culture on men's use of parental leave. *Community, Work and Family, 5*(5), 319–342.

Haas, L. & Hwang, P. (2007). Gender and organizational culture: Correlates of companies' responsiveness to fathers in Sweden. *Gender, Work and Organization, 21,* 52–79.

Han, W. (2007). Non-standard work schedules and work-family issues. Sloan Work and Family Research Network Work-Family Encylopedia. Boston College. http://wfnetwork.bc.edu/encyclopedia.entry.php?id=5854&area=All

Hašková, H. (2007). Fertility decline, the postponement of childbearing and the increase in childlessness in Central and Eastern Europe: A gender equity approach. In R. Crompton, S. Lewis & C. Lyonette (eds), *Women, Men, Work and Family in Europe* (pp. 76–85). London: Palgrave Macmillan.

Hattery, A. J. (2001). Tag-team parenting: Costs and benefits of utilizing non-overlapping shift work in families with young children. *Families in Society, 82*, 419–427.

Heymann, J. (2006). *Forgotten Families: Ending the Growing Crisis Confronting Children and Working Parents in the Global Economy*. New York: Oxford University Press.

Lambert, S. (1999). Lower-wage workers and the new realities of work and family. *Annals of the American Academy of Political and Social Science, 562*, 174–190.

Lambert, S. & Henley, J. R. (2007). Low-level jobs and work-family studies. Sloan Work and Family Research Network Work-Family Encyclopedia. Boston College. http://wfnetwork.bc.edu/encyclopedia.entry.php?id=4254&area=All

Layard, R. (2006). *Happiness. Lessons From a New Science*. London: Penguin.

Leach, B. (1999). Transforming rural livelihoods: Gender, work and restructuring in three Ontario communities. In S. Neysmith (ed.), *Restructuring Caring Labour: Discourse, State Practice and Everyday Life* (pp. 209–225). Toronto: Oxford University Press.

Lero, D. S. (2007). Investing in quality: Policies, practitioners, programs and parents. Report of the Expert Panel on Quality and Human Resources. Ontario Ministry of Children and Youth Services. http://www.children.gov.on.ca/NR/CS/Publications/QHRReport_en.pdf

Levin-Epstein, J. (2006). Getting punched: The job and family clock. CLASP Center for Law and Social Policy. www.clasp.org

Lewis, S. (2001). Restructuring workplace cultures: The ultimate work-family challenge? *Women in Management Review, 16*, 21–29.

Lewis, S. & Cooper, C. L. (2005). *Work-Life Integration: Case Studies of Organizational Change*. London: Wiley.

Lewis, S., Gambles, R. & Rapoport, R. (2007). The constraints of a "work-life balance" approach: An international perspective. *International Journal of Human Resource Management, 18*(3), 360–373.

Lewis, S. & Smithson, J. (2001). Sense of entitlement to support for the reconciliation of employment and family life. *Human Relations, 55*, 1455–1481.

Lewis, S. & Smithson, J. (2006). *Final Report of the EU Framework Five Study, Transitions: Gender, Parenthood and the Changing European Workplace*. RIHSCH, Manchester Metropolitan University, UK.

Litchfield, L., Swanberg, J. & Sigworth, C. (2004). Increasing the visibility of the invisible workforce: Model programs and policies for hourly and lower wage employees. Report 31 of the Boston College Center for Work and Family, Carroll School of Management, Boston College.

MacDermid, S. M., Hertzog, J. L., Kensinger, K. B. & Zipp, J. F. (2001). The role of organizational size and industry in job quality and work-family relationships. *Journal of Family and Economic Issues, 22*, 191–216.

Marks, N. F. (1998). Does it hurt to care? Caregiving, work-family conflict and midlife well-being. *Journal of Marriage and the Family, 60*(4), 951–966.

Mauthner, N., McKee, L. & Strell, M. (2001). *Work and Family Life in Rural Communities*. York, UK: Joseph Rowntree Foundation.

McGinnity, F. & McManus, P. (2007). Paying the price for reconciling work and family life: Comparing the wage penalty for women's part-time work in Britain, Germany and the United States. *Journal of Comparative Policy Analysis, 9*(2), 115–134.

McGovern, P. (2007). Immigration, labour markets and employment relations: Problems and prospects. *British Journal of Industrial Relations, 45*(2), 217–235.

Moss, P. (ed.) (2002). Care work in Europe: Current understandings and future directions. Mapping of care services and the care workforce. Working paper 3. Retrieved March 15, 2006 from http://144.82.35.228/carework/uk/reports/index.htm

Pagnan, C. & Lero, D. S. (2006). What do we know about dual-earner couples and their experiences with off-shifting? Presented at the 2006 Conference of the National Council on Family Relations, Minneapolis, Minn.

Palameta, B. (2004). Low income among immigrants and visible minorities. *Perspectives on Labour and Income*. Statistics Canada, Catalogue no. 75-001-XPE (April, 2004), 12–17

Parris, M., Vickers, M. & Wilkes, L. (in press). Friendships under strain: The work-personal life integration of middle managers. *Community, Work and Family*.

Pavalko, E. K. & Henderson, K. A. (2006). Combining care work and paid work: Do workplace policies make a difference? *Research on Aging, 28*(3), 359–374.

Perry-Jenkins, M. (2005). Work in the working class: Challenges facing families. In S. M. Bianchi, L. M. Casper & R. B. King (eds), *Work, Family, Health, and Well-Being* (pp. 453–472). Mahwah, NJ: Lawrence Erlbaum.

Presser, H. B. (2000). Non-standard work schedules and marital instability. *Journal of Marriage and the Family, 62*, 93–110.

Presser, H. B. (2003). *Working in a 24/7 Economy: Challenges for American Families.* New York: Russell Sage Foundation.

Presser, H. B. (2004). Employment in a 24/7 economy: Challenges for the family. In A. C. Crouter & A. Booth (eds) *Work-Family Challenges for Low-Income Parents and their Children* (pp. 83–106). Mahwah, NJ: Lawrence Erlbaum.

Pyper, W. (2006). Balancing career and care. *Perspectives on Labour and Income*. Statistics Canada Catalogue no. 75-001-XIE (November 2006), 5–15.

Rana, B., Kagan, C., Lewis, S. & Rout, U. (1998). British South Asian women managers and professionals: Experiences of work and family. *Women in Management Review, 13*, 221–232.

Rapoport, R. Bailyn, L., Fletcher, J. & Pruitt, B. (2002). *Beyond Work-Family Balance: Advancing Gender Equity and Work Performance.* Chichester, UK: Wiley.

Rosa, R. R. & Colligan, M. J. (1997). Plain language about shift work. US Department of Health and Human Services. National Institute for Occupational Health and Safety.

Ross Phillips, K. (2004). Getting time off: Access to leave among working parents. Urban Institute. Retrieved June 5, 2007 from http://www.urban.org/publications/310977.html

Saunders, R. (2006). Risk and opportunity: Creating options for vulnerable workers. Ottawa: Canadian Policy Research Networks, Inc. http://www.cprn.org

Shields, M. (2002). Shift work and health. *Health Reports, 13*, 11–33.

Shimoni, R, Este, D. & Clark, D. (2003). Paternal engagement in immigrant and refugee families. *Journal of Comparative Family Studies, 34*(4), 555–568.

Statistics Canada (2005a). Longitudinal survey of immigrants to Canada: Progress and challenges of new immigrants in the workforce. Available at http://www.statcan.ca

Stewart, M. J., Neufeld, A., Harrison, M. J., Spitzer, D., Hughes, K. & Makwarimba, E. (2005). Immigrant women family caregivers in Canada: Implications for policies and programmes in health and social sectors. *Health and Social Care in the Community, 14*(4), 329–340.

Swanberg, J., Pitt-Catsouphes, M. & Drescher-Burke, K. (2005). A question of justice: Disparities in employees' access to flexible schedule arrangements. *Journal of Family Issues, 26*, 866–895.

Urban Institute (2005). Low-income working families: Facts and figures assessing the New Federalism. http://www.urban.org/url.cfm?ID=900832.

US Bureau of Labor Statistics (2005). Workers on flexible and shift schedules in May 2004. US Department of Labor. Cited in W. Han (2007). Non-standard work schedules and work-family issues. Sloan Work and Family Research Network Work-Family Encylopedia. Boston College. http://wfnetwork.bc.edu/encyclopedia.entry.php?id=5854&area=All.

US Government, General Accounting Office (2007). Women and low-skilled workers: Other countries' policies and practices that may help these workers enter and remain in the workforce. Retrieved August 25, 2007. www.gao.gov/cgi-bin/getrpt?GAO-07-817

Webster, J. (2004). Working and living in the European knowledge society: The policy implications of developments in working life and their effects on social relations. Report for the project "Infowork". Department of Sociology, Trinity College, Dublin.

Wilmoth, J. M. & Longino, C. F. (2006). Demographic trends that will shape US policy in the twenty-first century. *Research on Aging, 28*(3), 269–288.

Winson, T. & Leach, B. (2002). *Contingent Work, Disrupted Lives: Labour and Community in the New Rural Economy.* Toronto: University of Toronto Press.

Zaslow, M., Acs, G., Cameron, M. & Vandivere, S. (2006). Children in low-income families: Change and continuity in family context and measures of well-being. Paper presented at the Urban Institute and Child Trends Roundtable discussion: Trends and policies that affect low-income children: What are the next steps? Jan 12, 2006.

APPENDIX

Work-Family Websites, Resources, and Organizations

Australian Centre for Research in Employment and Work (ACREW)
    http://www.buseco.monash.edu.au/mgt/research/acrew/
Australian Workplace
    http://www.workplace.gov.au
Berkeley Center for Working Families
    http://wfnetwork.bc.edu/berkeley/index.html
Boston College Center for Work & Family
    http://www.bc.edu/centers/cwf
Canadian Database on Time Pressure, Stress and Health (University of Waterloo, Canada)
    http://www.lifestress.uwaterloo.ca/
Canadian Policy Research Networks
    http://www.cprn.org/index.cfm?l=en
Case Studies of Flexible Work
    http://www.flexibility.co.uk/cases/index.htm
Catalyst
    http://www.catalyst.org/
Center on Aging & Work: Workplace Flexibility at Boston College
    http://agingandwork.bc.edu/template_index
Center for Families, Purdue University
    http://www.cfs.purdue.edu/CFF/pages/about/index.html
The Rosabeth Moss Kanter Award for Excellence in Work-Family Research (through Center for Families above)
    http://www.cfs.purdue.edu/CFF/pages/kanter/index.html
Center for Families, Work and Well-being, University of Guelph, ON, Canada
    http://www.worklifecanada.ca/
Center for Gender and Organizations, Simmons School of Management, Boston MA
    http://www.simmons.edu/som/centers/cgo/index.shtml

Handbook of Work-Family Integration: Research, Theory, and Best Practices

Center for Law and Social Policy (CLASP)
www.clasp.org
Center for Time, Work and the Family, The Ackerman Institute
http://www.ackerman.org/centers_time.htm
Center for Work and Family Research (Penn State)
http://cwfr.la.psu.edu/index.html
The Center for Work Life Law
www.worklifelaw.org
The Clearinghouse on International Developments in Child, Youth and Family
Policies (Columbia University)
http://www.childpolicyintl.org/
Community, Families & Work Program (Brandeis University)
http://www.brandeis.edu/centers/cfwp/
Cornell Employment and Family Careers Institute
http://www.human.cornell.edu/che/BLCC/Research/Publications/
workingpapers.cfm
The Council on Contemporary Families
http://www.contemporaryfamilies.org/
Drago (Robert) – Work-Family Listserve
Email Dr. Drago at drago@psu.edu to join
Employee Benefits Research
www.ebri.org
European Foundation for the Improvement of Living and Working Conditions
http://www.eurofound.europa.eu/
European Industrial Relations Observatory On-line
http://www.eurofound.europa.eu/eiro/
Families and Work Institute
http://familiesandwork.org
Flexible Work and Well-Being Center (University of Minnesota)
http://flexiblework.umn.edu
Great Place to Work Europe
http://greatplacetowork-europe.com/
Health and Safety Executive
http://www.hse.gov.uk/
The Health Communication Unit
http://www.thcu.ca/Workplace/Workplace.html
Institute for Research on Labor and Employment, University of California, Berkely
http://www.irle.berkeley.edu/index.html
International Labour Organization (United Nations agency)
http://www.ilo.org/global/lang--en/index.htm
International Center of Work and Family (ICWF)
http://www.iese.edu/en/RCC/ICWF/Home/Home.asp

JobQuality.ca
  http://www.jobquality.ca/
Kossek, Ellen, Ph.D. Website
  http://www.msu.edu/~kossek/
Labor Project for Working Families
  http://www.working-families.org/
Luxembourg Income Study (LIS)
  http://www.lisproject.org/
Organization for Economic Co-operation and Development (OECD)
  http://www.oecd.org/home/
The Population, Work, and Family Policy Research Collaboration (PWFC/CPTF)
  http://policyresearch.gc.ca/page.asp?pagenm=PWFC_index

SLOAN CENTERS ON WORKING FAMILIES

Sloan Work and Family Research Network, Boston College
  http://wfnetwork.bc.edu/
The Employment and Family Careers Institute, Cornell University
The Center on Parents, Children and Work, the University of Chicago
  http://wf.educ.msu.edu/
The Center for the Ethnography of Everyday Life (CEEL), University of Michigan
  http://ceel.psc.isr.umich.edu/
The Center on Myth and Ritual in American Life, Emory University
  http://www.marial.emory.edu/
The Center on Working Families, University of California, Berkeley (1998–2002)
  http://wfnetwork.bc.edu/berkeley/
The Center on the Everyday Lives of Families (CELF), UCLA
  http://www.celf.ucla.edu/pages/about.php

SLOAN CENTERS ON THE WORKPLACE

MIT Workplace Center
  http://web.mit.edu/workplacecenter

SLOAN CENTERS ON WORKPLACE FLEXIBILITY

The UC Faculty Friendly Edge (A University of California Berkeley initiative, assisted by the Sloan Center, to support workplace flexibility within the academy).
  http://university of california, familyedge.berkeley.edu/

Workplace Flexibility 2010 (An Alfred P. Sloan Initiative at Georgetown University Law Center to support the development of a comprehensive national policy on workplace flexibility at the federal, state and local levels).
http://www.law.georgetown.edu/workplaceflexibility2010/index.cfm
Families and Work Institute
http://familiesandwork.org/site/research/main.html
The Alfred P. Sloan Awards for Faculty Career Flexibility
http://www.acenet.edu/AM/Template.cfm?Section=Leadership&Template=/CM/HTMLDisplay.cfm&ContentID=13294
Sloan Awards for Business Excellence in Workplace Flexibility
http://familiesandwork.org/3w/awards/index.html

SLOAN RELATED PROGRAMS AND SERVICES

Sloan Work and Family Research Network (Boston College)
http://wfnetwork.bc.edu/
Work-Family Research Newsletter
http://wfnetwork.bc.edu/The_Network_News/1-1/winter99/index.html.

TakeCareNet
http://www.takecarenet.org/
Vanier Institute
www.vifamily. ca
Work and Family Balance (Saskatchewan Labour Department, Canada)
http://www.workandfamilybalance.com/
Work/Family Newsgroup
http://Iser.la.psu.edu/workfam/history.htm
Work-life Balance in Canadian Workplaces (Human Resources and Social Development Canada)
http://www.hrsdc.gc.ca/en/lp/spila/wlb/01home.shtml
Work Life and Human Capital Solutions
http://www.workfamily.com/
Work Life Law, University of California, Hastings College of the Law
http://www.uchastings.edu/?pid=3624
Work Life Research Centre
http://www.workliferesearch.org/wl_site/hp_main.htm
Working Mother: 100 Best Companies for Working Mothers
http://www.workingmother.com/?service=vpage/106

AUTHOR INDEX

A

Abbott, A., 97, 115
Abdel-Halim, A.A., 298
Abramovitz, M., 18, 27
Acker, J., 239
Acs, G., 379, 381
Adams, E.W., 275
Adams, G.A., 291, 293, 297, 361
Adler, N.J., 228
Ainlay, S.L., 291
Albelda, R. 77, 380
Allard, K., 334, 340, 341, 374
Allen, S., 252, 253, 254, 258
Allen, T.D., 65, 148, 148, 150, 152, 157, 158,
    159, 160, 161, 162, 165, 170, 192, 198, 199,
    200, 201, 202, 203, 271, 273, 294, 297, 332,
    336, 337, 338, 340, 341, 342, 354, 358, 363,
    364, 365
Allie, S.M., 270
Alliger, G.M., 147
Almeida, D.M., 147
Altucher, K.A., 101, 112
Alwin, D.F., 195
Ames, B.D., 386
Amick, B., 113
Amodeo, M., 295
Anderson, S.E., 158, 164, 338, 339, 345
Anderson-Connolly, R., 191
Andersson, L.M., 318
Andreassi, J.K., 148, 150, 207, 271, 309, 311
Aneshensel, C.S., 81, 111
Antani, A., 294, 295, 299
Antonucci, T.C., 99
Argyle, M., 291
Armeli, S., 312, 317
Arora, R., 127
Artis, J.E., 111
Aryee, S., 62, 65, 67, 130, 150, 158, 159, 161,
    168, 193, 195, 201, 269, 270, 340, 365
Ashbourne, L., 16, 83, 256
Avery, C., 306, 310, 312, 316
Avila, E., 241

Aycan, Z., 195, 222, 354, 357, 360, 361, 362,
    365, 366, 367
Ayman, R., 216, 222, 223, 224, 294, 295, 299,
    342, 346, 354, 357

B

Bacharach, S.B., 129, 130, 131, 135
Bachman, K., 164
Bachu, A., 87
Backon, L., 23, 126, 135
Bäck-Wiklund, M., 377, 3778
Badal, J., 345
Bailey, D.E., 306, 310, 312, 315, 326
Bailyn, L., 277, 305, 311, 313, 318, 321, 325,
    327, 334, 337, 339, 371, 373
Bainbridge, T.J., 197, 198, 206
Baird, C.L., 258
Bakker, A.B., 145
Baldridge, D.C., 273, 274, 278, 280, 281
Bales, R.F., 78
Balter, M., 114
Baltes, B., 165, 198, 268, 275
Bamberger, P., 129, 130, 131, 135
Banaji, M.R., 361
Bandura, A., 116
Barak, M.E.M., 169
Barber, A.E., 275, 311, 312
Barbera, K.M., 275
Bardoel, A., 354, 357
Barham, E.J., 305
Barham, L., 165, 166, 199
Barling, J., 165, 191, 195, 197, 198, 201, 202, 208
Barnett, C., 305
Barnett, K.A., 168
Barnett, R.C., 47, 76, 79, 80, 81, 83, 84, 85, 88,
    130, 131, 133, 135, 141, 142, 187, 192, 193,
    194, 195, 200, 201, 207, 242, 261, 331, 358
Barrah, J.L., 165
Barrera, M. Jr., 289, 290, 291
Barsness, Z.I., 355
Baruch, G.K., 81, 130, 135, 193

Handbook of Work-Family Integration: Research, Theory, and Best Practices

Baruch-Feldman, C., 169, 297
Basham, R.B., 290
Bass, B.L., 62, 64, 68, 149, 198, 200, 201
Bass, B.M., 367
Batt, R., 165, 207
Bauer, T.N., 163, 164, 165
Beatty, C.A., 158
Beaujot, R., 13, 16, 17
Beauregard, A.T., 339, 342, 345
Beauvais, L.L., 148, 153, 278, 280, 281, 332, 333, 334, 336, 338, 339, 345
Becker, G.S., 238
Becker, P.E., 113
Bedeian, A.G., 162, 195, 218, 220
Beehr, T.A., 208, 288, 291, 293, 296, 298
Beham, B., 142, 153
Behson, S.J., 268, 269, 270, 271, 297, 338
Belkin, L., 89, 240
Bellavia, G., 57, 58, 59, 64, 96, 105, 192, 195, 199, 200, 201, 202, 204, 205, 206, 207, 216, 222
Bellman, S., 110
Bem, S.L., 216, 225, 226
Ben-Ari, A., 295
Ben-Dayan, D., 169,
Berkman, L., 198
Bern, S.L., 215
Bernard, J.S., 78
Bernas, K.H., 270, 293
Bernhardt, A, 237
Bernstein, J., 178, 380, 381
Beutell, N.J., 50, 58, 59, 96, 129, 130, 133, 135, 160, 193, 195, 198, 271, 339
Bhagat, R.S., 270, 297
Bhuian, S.N., 162
Bianchi, S., 14, 15, 95, 107, 177, 178, 179, 180, 181, 234, 239, 243
Biblarz, T.J., 223
Bielby, D.D., 65
Bielby, W.T., 65
Bird, G.W., 129, 131, 135
Bittman, M., 240, 242
Bivens, J., 20, 30
Blair-Loy, M., 180, 239, 332, 339, 342, 343
Blau, F.D., 237
Blau, G., 159
Block, R.N., 19, 23, 26, 27
Blood, R.O., 157
Blossfeld, H.-P., 107, 111, 112
Blum, T.C., 275, 311
Boey, K.W., 159

Bogenschneider, K., 27
Bohen, H.H., 58, 129, 131
Boles, J.S., 58, 158, 159, 162, 165, 166
Bolino, M.C., 163
Bond, J.T., 14, 18, 19, 22, 23, 24, 30, 31, 76, 85, 88, 126, 127, 135, 141, 179, 250, 331, 332, 337, 338, 346
Bongers, P., 113
Bonoli, G., 24
Boorsboom, R., 162
Booth, A., 101, 380
Bordeaux, C., 203, 204, 207, 269, 359, 360, 364
Boris, E., 17, 18, 20, 26, 28
Borucki, C.C., 280
Bosma, H., 110, 113, 191
Boudreau, J.W., 159, 169
Boushey, H., 89
Bowen, G.L., 49
Bowman, L., 353
Boyar, S.L., 163, 164, 165
Boye, M.W., 191
Bradbury, K., 89
Bragger, J.D., 163
Brandth, B., 374
Brannen, J., 344, 387
Brass, D.J., 318, 320
Brayfield, A., 148, 152, 153, 250
Brennan, R.T., 47, 81, 83, 88
Brett, J.M., 41, 130, 134, 339, 356
Bretz, R.D. Jr., 159, 169
Brewster, J., 378
Brief, A.P., 313
Briggs, T.E., 275
Brines, J., 101, 242
Brinley, A., 203, 204, 207, 269, 359, 360, 364
Brisson, C., 113
Brockmann, M., 388
Brockwood, K., 131, 195, 196, 197, 219, 275, 294
Brondolo, C., 169, 297
Bronfenbrenner, U., 37, 106, 194
Broom, D.H., 256
Brosi, W.A., 386
Brotheridge, C.I.M., 199, 203
Brownfield, E., 19, 23, 31, 126, 135
Bruck, C.S., 157, 158, 159, 160, 161, 165, 192, 198, 199, 200, 201, 202
Budig, M.J., 237, 238, 239, 388
Buehler, C., 135
Buffardi, L.C., 57, 58, 59, 160, 294, 297

Bumpus, M., 126
Burke, B.G., 220
Burke, M.J., 280
Burke, R.J., 199, 200, 201, 354, 373
Burkett, E., 311, 318
Burley, K.A., 219, 220, 226, 281
Burr, J.A., 109
Butler, A.B., 143, 146, 147, 161, 162, 192, 197, 257
Buunk, B.P., 291, 295
Bycio, P., 163
Byerly, R.T., 158, 164, 338, 339, 345
Byosiere, P., 288
Byron, K., 50, 59, 219, 221, 222, 228

C

Cameron, M., 381
Campbell, N., 293
Canadian Center for Policy Alternatives, 20
Cancian, F.M., 103
Cannuscio, C.C., 198
Canu, R.G., 47
Caplan, R.D., 291
Caplow, T., 87, 88
Carayon, P., 191
Carlson, D.S., 58, 59, 61, 62, 63, 65, 66, 68, 70, 90, 142, 144, 146, 147, 148, 158, 159, 168, 169, 194, 219, 221, 222, 227, 268, 270, 288, 296, 297, 298
Carmeli, A., 160, 162
Carnicer, M.P.d.L., 160
Carnoy, M., 178
Carpenter, M., 344
Carr, D., 16
Casner-Lotto, J., 344, 345
Casper, L., 178, 181, 234
Casper, W.J., 160, 203, 204, 207, 269, 294, 297, 346, 359, 360, 364
Castenada, M., 306
Castro, C.A., 219, 220, 221
Catsouphes, M., 380
Caubert, S., 131, 219
Cavanaugh, M.A., 23
Chait Barnett, R., 96
Chan, K.B., 159
Chapman, F.S., 366
Chapman, N.J., 274
Chappell, D.B., 204, 219, 220, 221, 224, 226
Charles, M., 237

Chase-Lansdale, P., 380
Chatman, C., 101
Chaudry, A., 179, 180
Chay, Y.W., 168
Chen, C.C., 219, 220, 222, 354, 358
Chen, J.J., 25
Cherlin, A., 234
Chermack, K., 96
Chesley, N., 96, 102, 104, 106, 107, 108, 109, 112, 114
Chi-Ching, E.Y., 161
Chodorow, N., 235
Choi, J., 219, 220, 222, 354, 358
Christiansen, S.L., 77, 252, 253, 256, 257
Christopher, K., 238
Chudakoff, H.P., 97
Chui, C., 362
Cinamon, G. 223, 226
Ciscel, D.H., 15, 17, 18
Clampet-Lundquist, S., 380
Clark, A., 249
Clark, D., 390
Clark, R., 85, 86
Clark, S.C., 43, 203, 207, 273, 333, 337
Clarkberg, M., 102, 107, 108, 112
Clay, C., 295
Clemens, J., 27
Clements, M.S., 256
Cleveland, J.N., 340
Cobb, S., 291
Coffey, B.S., 158, 164, 338, 339, 345
Coghill, D., 125
Cohen, A., 61, 163, 164, 165, 166, 168, 169
Cohen, S., 191, 296, 297
Colditz, G.A., 198
Coleman, J., 242
Colihan, J., 306, 312
Colligan, M.J., 384
Collins, K.M., 65, 66, 67, 166, 205
Collins, P.H., 235, 241
Colquitt, J.A., 161, 162, 311, 333, 334, 340
Colton, C.L., 61, 62, 131, 144, 168, 194, 195, 196, 197, 205, 219, 275, 294
Coltrane, S., 15, 80, 252, 252, 253
Conger, R.D., 107
Conley, S., 129, 131, 135
Connell, R., 235
Connolly, T.F., 58, 129, 130, 195
Connor, M., 310
Contrada, R.J., 191

Conway, T.L., 191
Cooke, R.A., 131, 132, 135
Coontz, S., 235
Cooper, C.D., 314
Cooper, C.L., 96, 148, 170, 194, 195, 196, 268,
    294, 297, 338, 339, 340, 354, 357, 363, 364,
    365, 387
Cooper, G.L., 110
Cooper, M.L., 58, 130, 133, 134, 135, 138, 143,
    167, 198, 199, 201, 219, 274
Cordeiro, B., 257
Cordeiro, L., 159
Corden, A., 24
Cotton, J.L., 297
Coverman, S., 129, 131, 132, 133, 135, 138
Covey, M.C., 150
Covey, S.R., 150
Cowan, C.P., 83
Cranford, C.J., 24
Crawford, M., 216
Cregan, C., 197, 198
Crittenden, A., 18
Crompton, R., 375, 377
Crooker, K.J., 268, 297, 312, 342
Cropanzano, R., 268
Crosby, F.J., 79, 81
Cross, W., 1010
Crouter, A.C., 15, 61, 85, 96, 101, 126, 142, 143,
    144, 159, 192, 201, 203, 257, 380
Csikszentmihalyi, M., 182
Cullen, J.C., 194
Cummings, E.M., 252, 254
Cummings, L.L., 313

D

d'Abbs, P., 289
D'Souza, R.M., 256
Dahlin, E., 114
Daly, K.J., 16, 18, 83, 95, 179, 252, 253, 254,
    257, 261, 262, 386, 387
Damaske, S., 16
Damiano-Teixeira, K.M., 386
Daniels, R., 291, 292, 294
Dannefer, D., 110
Danzinger, S.K., 256
das Dores Guerreiro, M., 378
Datta, K., 390
Davies, M., 81
Davis, K.D., 257
Davy, J.A., 269

Day, A.L., 191, 205, 209
de Jonge, J., 113
de Lange, A.H., 45
Deater-Deckard, K., 80
DeBord, K., 47
Deckman, M., 66
Del Campo, D.S., 168
Del Campo, R.L., 168
Delage, B., 25
DeLamater, J.D., 86
DeMarr, B.J., 151, 164, 334, 341
Demerouti, E., 131, 132, 133, 145, 158, 192, 193,
    199, 200, 203, 204, 207, 217, 219
Dempster-McClain, D., 111
den Dulk, L., 332, 338, 341, 345
Denison, D.R., 334
Dennis, W.J., 25
Dentinger, E., 107, 108, 112
Desai, T.P., 354, 357
Desmarais, S., 191
Deutsch, F., 242
Dex, S., 387
Dickson, M.V., 361
Dikkers, J.S.E., 159, 168, 336, 337, 338, 341,
    342, 345
Dill, B., 235
Donaldson, S.I., 219, 220, 221
Donnelly, B.W., 84
Donofrio, H.H., 158
Doress-Worters, P., 198
Dorfman, P.W., 361
Dormann, C., 152
Doucet, A., 253, 262
Doumas, D.M., 145
Douvan, E., 81
Downey, G., 101
Downs, B., 76
Drach-Zahavy, A., 224, 268, 272, 273, 276,
    280, 354, 357
Drago, R., 77
Draper, J., 259
Drescher-Burke, K., 380
Dressel, P.L., 249
Drobnič, S., 107, 111, 112
Drory, A., 158
Duncan, G., 111, 380
Dunham, R.B., 275, 306
Durik, A.M., 86
Duxbury, L., 22, 125, 126, 127, 133, 135, 192,
    197, 200, 203, 204, 205, 206, 207, 208, 217,
    219, 220, 221, 227, 366, 391

Dwyer, D.J., 268
Dyck, V., 262
Dyer, J., 132

E

Eagle, B.W., 219
Eardley, T., 24
Earl, L., 386
Eaton, S.C., 162, 166, 310, 342
Eby, L.T., 203, 204, 207, 269, 275, 359, 360, 364
Eccles, J., 101
Eddleston, K.A., 160, 273, 274, 280, 281
Edin, K., 235, 243, 380
Edwards, J.R., 46, 61, 90, 144, 146, 157, 162,
    194, 205
Eggebeen, D., 253
Ehrhart, M.G., 339
Eisenberg, M., 80
Eisenberger, R., 152, 291, 292, 294, 297, 312,
    317, 337
Elder, G.H. Jr., 96, 97, 99, 100, 101, 107, 111, 115
Eliason, S., 115
Ellis, M.A., 295
Ellroy, D.F., 130
Emes, J., 27
Emlen, A.C., 274
England, P., 237, 238, 239, 240, 241
Epstein, C.F., 235, 244, 332
Erdwins, C.J., 160, 294, 297
Erez, M., 367
Erhart, K.H., 222
Eskin, M., 362, 365, 366
Essex, M.J., 85, 86
Este, D., 390
Ettner, S.L., 108
Europa, 383
European Foundation for the Improvement
    of Living and Working Conditions,
    382, 383, 389
Evandrou, M., 111
Evans, J.M., 360, 386
Evans, Y., 390
Ezra, M., 66

F

Fagnani, J., 379
Falter Mennino, S., 148, 152, 250
Faludi, S, 243
Families and Work Institute, 332

Farmer, S.J., 295
Farrell, M.P., 81
Fassler, I., 295
Fazio, E.M., 111
Federico, R., 306, 312
Fenstermaker, S., 236
Ferree, M., 83, 216
Ferrer, A., 386
Ferris, M., 67, 170, 220, 222, 347, 363, 365
Ferry, D.L., 313
Fields, D., 195, 365
Fields, J., 16
Finegold, D., 168
Finley, A., 274
Fisher, C.D., 297
Fisher, J., 296, 298
Flanagan, C., 243
Fleeson, W., 61, 64, 142, 147, 149, 150, 168,
    195, 204, 205
Fletcher, J., 313, 318, 321, 327, 371
Folbre, N., 238, 240, 388
Foley, S., 158, 166
Folger, R., 318
Folkman, S., 46, 268, 269, 270, 281, 366
Foner, A., 102
Ford, D.L., 270
Forster, N., 110
Fox, M.L., 268
Francesco, A.M., 218, 338, 345, 353, 357
Franche, R.L., 146, 149, 200
Frankel, B.G., 290
Frazee, V., 208
Freeman, R.B., 89
French, J.R.P. Jr., 291, 298
Fried, M., 332, 334
Fried, Y., 339
Friedler, E., 191
Friedman, S.D., 197, 344
Froberg, D., 145
Frone, M.R., 57, 58, 59, 60, 61, 64, 67, 96, 105,
    130, 131, 132, 133, 134, 135, 138, 142, 143,
    147, 161, 167, 192, 193, 194, 195, 196, 198,
    199, 200, 201, 202, 204, 205, 206, 207, 216,
    217, 222, 227, 274, 298, 340, 354
Fu, C.K., 219, 221, 222
Fusilier, M.F., 288, 297

G

Gabel, J.T.A., 24
Gagné, L., 386

Galinsky, E.M., 14, 19, 23, 30, 31, 76, 84, 86, 88,
126, 127, 135, 141, 179, 203, 242, 243, 250,
331, 332, 334, 337, 338, 340, 346
Gallagher, S., 104
Gambles, R., 371, 376, 377, 378, 379
Ganster, D.C., 164, 205, 275, 288, 297, 340, 342
Garbarino, J., 101
Gareis, K.C., 47, 81, 84, 96, 331
Garey, A.L., 19, 235, 239
Gavanas, A., 16
Gelfand, M.J., 222, 346, 347, 354, 367
Gentry, J.W., 159, 166
George, L.K., 108
Germano, L.M., 22, 23
Gerson, K., 14, 16, 18, 24, 28, 76, 101, 102, 127,
178, 180, 234, 235, 236, 238, 239, 240, 244,
2458
Gerstel, N., 104, 238
Geurts, S., 131, 132, 133, 158, 159, 168, 192,
193, 199, 200, 203, 204, 207, 217,
219, 336, 337, 338, 341, 345
Giele, J.A., 115, 234
Gignac, M.A.M., 163, 164
Gilley, K.M., 165, 166, 297
Gilligan, C., 235
Gillis, J., 181
Ginsberg, F.D., 244
Gjerdingen, D., 145
Glaser, K., 111
Glasgow, N., 112
Glass, J., 238, 274
Glazer, S., 295
Glenn, 241
Glezer, H., 25
Godbey, G., 179
Godshalk, V.M., 160
Goff, S.J., 197, 276, 340
Goldberg, W.A., 340
Golden, L., 346
Goldin, C., 89, 180
Goldman, L., 323, 324
Goldsmith, H., 306, 312
Gomez, L.T., 276
Good, L.K., 159, 166
Goode, W.I., 104, 129, 131, 193, 235
Gore, S., 82, 288, 297
Gornick, J.C., 102, 208, 244, 383
Gottlieb, B.H., 163, 164, 165, 166, 199, 289, 305
Graen, G.B., 292
Grandey, A.A., 159, 163, 164, 165, 318

Grant-Vallone, E.J., 219, 220, 221
Graves, L.M., 197
Gray, M., 127, 135
Green, S.G., 292
Greenberg, E., 191
Greenberger, E., 85, 217, 340
Greenglass, E.R., 199, 200, 201
Greenhaus, J.H., 50, 58, 59, 60, 61, 62, 63, 64,
65, 66, 67, 90, 96, 129, 130, 133, 135, 141,
142, 144, 145, 146, 162, 166, 169, 192, 193,
195, 196, 197, 198, 199, 202, 205, 206, 218,
271, 339
Greeno, C.G., 202
Greenstein, T.N., 223, 239, 242
Greif, G.L., 80
Griffin, L.J., 195
Griffin, M.L., 295
Grigsby, T., 198, 219
Griswold, R.L., 77
Grover, S.L., 268, 297, 311, 312, 342
Grundberg, L., 191
Grusky, D., 237
Grzywacz, J.G., 50, 61, 62, 63, 64, 65, 66, 67, 68,
70, 90, 134, 142, 143, 144, 146, 147, 148,
149, 168, 169, 192, 193, 194, 195, 197, 198,
199, 200, 201, 202, 204, 205, 206, 207, 219,
222
Gudanowski, D.M., 295
Guelzow, M.G., 129, 131, 133, 135
Guiom, R.M., 163
Gutek, B., 58, 86, 129, 134, 218, 219

H

Haar, J.M., 298, 373
Haas, L., 18, 25, 26, 216, 334, 340, 341, 374
Hackett, R.D., 163
Hackman, J.R., 308
Haddock, S.A., 257
Hagestad, G.O., 100, 101
Haims, M.C., 191
Hall, D.T., 268, 270, 271, 281, 305
Hall, K., 345
Hamill, S., 340
Hammer, L.B., 61, 62, 131, 144, 163, 164, 165,
168, 194, 195, 196, 197, 198, 205, 219, 275,
291, 292, 294, 338, 354, 357
Han, S.-K., 100, 101, 102, 104, 107, 111
Han, W., 384, 385
Hancock, M.S., 237

Hanges, P.J., 361
Hang-yue, N., 158, 166
Hansen, K.V., 19
Hanson, G.C., 61, 62, 63, 144, 168, 194, 196, 197, 205
Hardy, M., 115
Hareven, T.K., 97, 107
Harrick, E.J., 297
Harrington, M., 18, 239
Harris, P., 191
Harrison, D., 289
Harrison, D.A., 165, 166, 297
Harrison, L.J., 195
Harrison, M.J., 388
Harrison, R.V., 291
Hartmann, H., 239
Hašková, H., 379
Hasselhorn, H.-M., 358
Hatfield, E., 291
Hattery, A.J., 385
Hawkins, A.H., 170
Hawkins, A.J., 67, 220, 222, 258, 347, 363, 365
Hawkins, L., 16, 83
Hays, S., 108, 234, 235, 236, 239, 243, 244
Head, M., 126
Health Canada, 31
Heath, J.A., 15
Heilman, M.E., 25
Heinz, W.R., 97, 103
Hellen, D., 147
Heller, K., 290, 291
Helmreich, R., 216
Henderson, K.A., 392
Henderson, M., 291
Henley, J.R., 380
Henretta, J.C., 102, 110
Henry, R.A., 292, 293
Hepburn, C.G., 165, 198
Herbert, J., 390
Heron, A., 383
Herscovitch, L., 160
Herst, D.E.I., 157, 158, 159, 160, 161, 165, 192, 198, 199, 200, 201, 202
Hertz, R., 19, 243
Hertzog, J.L., 386
Heuveline, P., 16
Heydens-Gahir, H.A., 198, 268
Heymann, J., 375
Hicks, L., 87, 88
Higginbottom, S.F., 165, 197, 198

Higgins, C., 22, 125, 126, 127, 133, 135, 192, 197, 200, 203, 204, 205, 206, 207, 208, 217, 219, 220, 221, 227, 366, 391
Hildreth, K., 194
Hill, D.R., 191
Hill, E.J., 64, 67, 159, 168, 170, 180, 192, 199, 204, 207, 220, 222, 306, 312, 347, 363, 365
Hill, M., 111
Hill, R., 95
Ho, D.Y., 362
Hobfoll, S.E., 299
Hobson, B., 256
Hochschild, A.R., 15, 19, 21, 127, 181, 187, 235, 236, 239, 242, 249, 327
Hochwarter, W.A., 159
Hofferth, S.L., 76, 179
Hoffman, L.W., 76, 242, 243
Hoffman, S., 111
Hogan, N.L., 159
Holahan, C.J., 290
Holden, K.C., 30
Holly, L., 289, 290
Holt, A., 19
Hom, P.W., 162, 164, 166
Hondagneu-Sotelo, P., 241
Hoogstra, L., 181
Hooks, K., 310
Hoontan, H., 150
Hopstaken, L.E.M., 295
Houkes, I., 170
House, J.S., 288, 298
House, R.J., 361
Houtman, I., 113
Howard, W.G., 158
Huang, Q., 106, 112, 115, 331
Huang, T.P., 354, 357
Hudson, K., 25
Huff, J.W., 275
Huffman, A.H., 219, 220, 221
Hughes, D., 101, 203
Hughes, K., 388
Hunter, V., 380
Huntington, R., 292, 294, 337
Hurley, A.E., 280
Hurrell, J.J. Jr., 202, 205, 208, 209, 268
Hurst, D., 222, 228
Huston, T.L., 65
Hutchinson, S., 292, 294, 337
Hwang, C.P., 249
Hwang, P., 334, 340, 341, 374

Hyde, J.S., 79, 80, 85, 86, 142, 194, 200, 207, 358
Hynes, K., 107, 112, 257

I

Ibrahim, S., 146, 149, 200
Icenogle, M.L., 219
Ihlwan, M., 345
Ilgen, D.R., 194, 316, 319, 325
Indovino, L., 163
Ingersoll-Dayton, B., 197, 274
Irving, R.H., 205
Ishaya, N., 223, 224
Izraeli, D.N., 227

J

Jackson, S., 129
Jacobs, J.A., 14, 16, 18, 24, 28, 76, 82, 102, 127,
     178, 180, 234, 238, 239, 240
Jahn, E.W., 297, 333, 335, 337, 338, 340
James, J.B., 88
Jamison, R.L., 197, 276, 340
JanDoosje, B., 295
Jans, L.G.J.M., 295
Janssen, P.P.M., 170
Janssens, M., 356
Jarvis, L.H., 180
Jaskar, K.L., 79
Javidan, M., 361
Jeffery, R.W., 200
Jenkins, M., 159
Jennings, K.R., 297
Jiménez, M.J.V., 161
John, R.S., 145
Johnson, E.M., 65
Johnson, J., 159
Johnson, L.B., 208
Johnson, P., 333, 338
Jones, C., 198
Jones, F., 191
Jones, J.R., 191
Jones, J.W., 191
Jong, J., 170
Joplin, J.R.W., 170, 218, 353, 357
Joseph, G., 112
Jost, J.T., 361
Judge, T.A., 159, 169
Judiesch, M.K., 306, 316, 332, 338, 345

K

Kacmar, K.M., 58, 61, 62, 70, 90, 142, 145, 147,
     148, 158, 159, 168, 169, 219, 221, 222
Kagan, C., 390
Kagitcibasi, C., 355, 362
Kahn, L.M., 237
Kahn, R., 193
Kahn, R.L., 99, 102, 157, 193, 198, 288
Kaitz, M., 271
Kalleberg, A.L., 25
Kalliath, T., 294, 297, 338, 340
Kandel, D.B., 81
Kanter, L.H., 267
Karasek, R., 113, 191
Karney, B.R., 296
Katz, D., 193
Katz, J., 89
Katz, L.F., 89
Kaufman, G., 223
Kaufmann, G.M., 288, 291, 293, 298
Kavey, A., 101
Kawachi, I., 198
Kawakami, N., 113
Keene, J., 250
Kelley, E., 45
Kelloway, E.K., 45, 163, 164, 165, 166, 191, 197,
     198, 199, 202, 205, 209, 305, 340
Kelloway, K., 165
Kelly, E., 96, 99, 101, 114
Kelly, E.L., 26
Kelly, K., 340
Kelly, R.F., 130
Kensinger, K.B., 386
Kerpelman, J., 47
Kessler, R.C., 79, 81
Keyes, C.L.M., 115
Khan, R.L., 128, 129, 130, 135, 138
Kiewitz, C., 159
Kilbourne, B., 237
Kim, S.S., 19, 23, 31, 126, 135, 179
Kincaid, J.F., 270
King, D.W., 224, 291, 293, 297, 361
King, L.A., 224, 291, 293, 297, 361
King, S.N., 142, 150, 152, 194, 197
Kingston, P.W., 179
Kinicki, A.J., 162, 164, 166, 269
Kinnunen, U., 159, 168, 195, 196, 204, 219,
     222, 336, 337, 338

Kirchmeyer, C., 61, 62, 63, 65, 142, 144, 145, 150, 163, 164, 165, 166, 192, 204, 207, 208, 271, 334, 341
Kirk, S.A., 270
Klein, D., 274
Klein, K.J., 327, 339
Klein, M.H., 85, 86
Klepa, L., 58, 86, 129, 218, 219
Kluckhohn, C., 354
Knight, A.P., 346, 347, 354
Knight, P.A., 147, 204
Knoester, C., 253
Knudson-Martin, C., 261
Ko, Y.C., 159
Koball, E.H., 129, 131, 135
Kodz, J., 127
Koeske, G.F., 270
Koeske, R.D., 270
Kofodimos, J.R., 65, 274, 335
Kohli, M., 95, 97, 103
Kohn, M.L., 195
Kollar, M., 164
Komarovsky, M., 129
Komorita, S.S., 323
Kompier, M.A.J., 159, 168, 341, 345
Kopelman, R.E., 58, 129, 195, 297, 333, 335, 337, 338, 340
Korabik, K., 204, 216, 217, 219, 220, 221, 222, 223, 224, 226, 293, 340, 342, 346, 354, 357
Korda, R.J., 256
Kossek, E.E., 19, 151, 158, 159, 161, 162, 163, 164, 165, 166, 198, 199, 273, 275, 276, 291, 292, 294, 309, 310, 311, 312, 316, 332, 333, 334, 337, 340, 341
Kottke, J.L., 292
Kozlowski, S.W.J., 327
Kramer, R.M., 323, 324
Krantz, D.S., 191
Krecker, M.L., 96
Kropf, M.B., 338, 342, 343, 344
Krüger, H., 97, 100, 103
Kuang, D.C., 198, 338
Kugelberg, C., 251
Kulik, C.T., 197, 198
Kulka, R.A., 81
Kümmerling, A., 358
Kurland, N.B., 306, 310, 312, 314, 315, 326
Kutcher, E.J., 163
Kuziemko, I., 89

Kvande, E., 374
Kweisga, E., 346

L

Ladd, D., 292, 293
Lai, G., 159
Lamb, M.E., 252, 253
Lambert, E.G., 159
Lambert, S.J., 65, 141, 306, 310, 311, 317, 380,
Landis, R.S., 280
Landsbergis, P.A., 191
Lang, M.M., 14
Lankau, M.J., 275
Lapierre, L.M., 340
Lareau, A., 180
LaRocco, J.M., 298
LaRossa, R., 252
Larson, D., 295
Larson, R., 182
Lau, T., 218, 353, 357
Lautsch, B.A., 162, 166, 310
Lawler Dye, J., 15, 17
Lawler, J.J., 170, 365
Layton, F.R., 146, 149, 200
Lazarus, R.S., 46, 268, 269, 270, 281, 366
Leach, B., 386
Lee, C., 217, 227
Lee, E., 112
Lee, J.A., 206
Lee, J.C., 101, 103
Lee, M., 312, 316
Lee, R.T., 199, 203
Lein, L., 81
Leisering, L., 98
Lero, D.S., 25, 208, 222, 256, 342, 346, 354, 357, 385, 388
Leung, A., 130, 158, 269, 270, 365
Levin, A., 169
Levin, D., 290
Levine, H.M., 290
Levine, J.A, 254
Levine, J.M., 305, 312
Levin-Epstein, J., 22, 24
Lewin, A., 187
Lewis, C.H., 17, 18, 20, 28
Lewis, S., 25, 26, 96, 132, 268, 333, 335, 342, 343, 344, 371, 373, 375, 376, 377, 378, 379, 383, 387, 390

Liebrand, W.B.G., 324
Lim, J., 292, 293
Lindsley, D.H., 318, 320
Ling, Y., 218, 359
Linton, R., 127
Litchfield, L., 381
Livingston, M.M., 219, 226
Lo, S., 130, 158, 269, 270, 365
Lobel, S.A., 273, 332
Lockwood, A., 203, 204, 207, 269, 359, 360, 364
Logan, J.R., 112
Loh, E.S., 238
Loi, R., 158, 166
London, A., 380
London, B., 101
Longino, C.F., 391
Loperst, P., 178, 181
Lorber, J., 235, 236
Lovejoy, M., 16, 18, 27, 240
Lowe, G.S., 20
Lui, S., 158, 160, 161
Luk, D.M., 165, 166, 297
Luk, V., 65, 130, 158, 161, 168, 195, 269, 270,
    340, 365
Luker, K., 235, 244
Lundberg, S., 238
Lundberg, U., 213
Lüscher, K., 96, 99
Lye, D.N., 223
Lynch, P.D., 312, 317
Lyness, K.S., 148, 153, 159, 160, 278, 280,
    281, 306, 316, 332, 333, 334, 336,
    338, 339, 342, 343, 344, 345
Lyonette, C., 375, 377
Lyons, S., 22
Lyttle, A.L., 355

M

MacDermid, S.M., 57, 58, 59, 64, 65, 66, 67,
    86, 129, 171, 386
Macdonald, C., 19
MacEwan, K.E., 165, 195, 197, 198
Macmillan, R., 115
Maertz, C.P. Jr., 163, 164, 165, 170
Maes, S., 45
Magennis, R., 96
Major, D.A., 22, 23, 270, 293, 339, 340
Makwarimba, E., 388
Malin, M.H., 19

Mangione, T.W., 82
Mansfield, N.R., 24
Maoz, E., 41
Marcel, D., 344
Margolin, G., 145
Markel, K., 130, 131, 132, 133, 134, 135, 143,
    161, 195, 200, 297, 340, 354
Marks, N.F., 50, 62, 63, 67, 112, 143, 146, 147,
    148, 149, 192, 193, 194, 195, 198, 199, 200,
    202, 204, 206, 207, 219, 222, 391
Marks, S.R., 21, 42, 65, 66, 67, 86, 129, 142,
    146, 193, 198
Marmot, M.G., 110, 191
Marshall, K., 15
Marshall, N.L., 81, 85, 194
Marshall, V.H., 103
Martin, J.A., 160, 297
Martin, S.P., 17
Martins, J.A., 294
Martins, L.L., 160
Masciadrelli, B.P., 255
Massagli, M.P., 109
Masuda, A., 90, 194, 197
Matheson, G., 240
Matsui, T., 271
Matta, D.S., 261
Matthews, K.A., 80
Mattimore, L.K., 291
Mattingly, M.J., 107, 179
Maume, D.J., 249
Mauno, S., 159, 204, 219, 222, 336, 337, 338
Mauthner, N., 386
Mawardi, A., 354, 357
Maxham, J.G.I., 158, 159, 162, 163
May, D.C., 149, 150
May, J., 390
Mayer, K.U., 97, 111, 114
Mays, B.T., 288, 297
McCartney, K., 80
McDonald, D.A., 147
McElwain, A., 204, 217, 219, 220, 221, 224, 226
McGinn, D., 89
McGinnity, F., 382
McGonagle, K., 238
McGovern, P., 389
McGrath, J.E., 288
McGuire, T., 310
McHale, S., 126, 257
McIlwaine, C., 390
McKee, L., 386

McKenzie, D., 379
McLanahan, S., 14, 15, 17, 27
McLean Parks, J., 313
McManus, K., 340, 382
McMurrian, R., 58, 159, 162, 165, 166
McRae, J.A., 81
Meersman, S.C., 111
Meijman, T., 297
Meiksins, P., 115
Menaghan, E.G., 13, 18, 20
Menguc, B., 162
Mesmer-Magnus, J.R., 59, 158, 163, 164, 165, 338
Messick, D.M., 324
Meyer, J.P., 160
Meyer, J.W., 95, 97, 101, 102
Meyers, M.K., 102, 208
Michlitsch, J.F., 297
Mikkelsen, A., 354
Mikulincer, M., 299
Miles, E.W., 219
Milkie, M.A., 14, 15, 65, 66, 83, 95, 177, 179, 180, 243, 250
Milkovich, G.T., 276
Miller, B.C., 306, 312
Mills, C.W., 260
Mishel, L.R., 178
Mitchell, T.R., 313
Moen, P., 88, 95, 96, 98, 99, 100, 101, 102, 103, 104, 106, 107, 108, 109, 110, 111, 112, 113, 114, 115, 180, 236, 238, 331
Moffet, R.G., 220
Mohrman, S., 168
Moje, E., 101
Mooney, A., 388
Moore, S., 191
Moos, R.H., 290
Moreland, R.L., 305, 312
Morgan, D., 256
Morgan, H., 29
Morgan, W.R., 195
Morris, M., 237
Morrison, C.R., 293
Mortimer, J.T., 99, 100, 101, 103
Moskowitz, J.T., 269
Moss, P., 388
Mossholder, K.W., 162, 195, 218
Motowidlo, S.J., 313
Mount, M.K., 197, 276, 340
Muhonen, T., 110, 115

Mullen, J., 45
Munck, B., 305, 325
Murphy, L.R., 205, 209
Musisca, N., 61, 64, 142, 147, 149, 150, 168, 195, 204, 205
Mustard, C.A., 146, 149, 200
Mutchler, J.E., 109
Myers, M., 244

N

Nagurney, A.J., 295
Nair, V.W., 295
Nasman, E., 332
National Center for Health Statistics (NCHS), 87
National Survey on Drug Use and Health, 109
Neal, M.B., 194, 195, 196, 197, 198, 274, 275, 294, 338
Neff, L.A., 296
Nelson, D.L., 268
Netemeyer, R.G., 58, 59, 158, 159, 162, 163, 165, 166
Neufeld, A., 388
Neugarten, B.L., 100, 101
Neuman, G.A., 275
Newsom, J.T., 195, 196, 197, 275, 294,, 296
Newstrom, J.W., 275
Ng, D.M., 200
Ngo, H., 158, 160, 161
Nichol, V., 162, 164, 275, 276
Nielsen, M., 178
Niemiec, C.P., 65
Nieva, R., 208
Nippert-Eng, C.E., 43, 151
Nisbett, R.E., 357
Nissly, J.A., 169
Nock, S.L., 179
Noe, R.A., 23, 151, 161, 162, 311, 333, 334, 340, 341
Nomaguchi, K.M., 14, 179
Nunnally, J., 67
Nydegeer, C.N., 97

O

O'Driscoll, M., 142, 148, 170, 194, 294, 297, 338, 340, 373
O'Leary, A., 191

O'Neil, R., 85, 217, 340
O'Neill, G., 16
O'Rand, A.M., 96, 110, 111
O'Reilly, A.W., 252, 254
Oglensky, B., 332
Ohlott, P.J., 142, 150, 152, 194, 197
Ohsawa, T., 271
Oliker, S.J., 103
Olmstead, B., 309, 315
Onglatco, M., 271
Ono, H., 82
Oppenheimer, V.K., 82, 87
Organ, D.W., 313
Organization for Economic Co-operation and
    Development (OECD), 127
Osterle, S., 100
Ozeki, C., 158, 159, 161, 163, 164, 165,
    198, 199
Ozer, E.M., 81, 83

P

Padavic, I., 77
Paden, S.L., 135
Pagnan, C., 385
Palameta, B., 390
Palkovitz, R., 77, 252, 253, 254, 256, 257
Pande Desai, T., 354
Panzer, K., 142, 150, 152, 194, 197
Parasuraman, 60, 141, 160, 166, 192, 195, 205,
    269
Parcel, T.L., 13, 18, 20
Parks, C.D., 323
Parris, M., 376
Parrott, A.C., 191
Parsons, T., 77, 78, 235
Patten, S.B., 191
Patterson, J.M., 45
Pattison, E.M., 290, 291
Pavalko, E.K., 102, 107, 109, 111, 115, 392
Payne, C.K., 340
Payne, N., 191
Payne, S.C., 219, 220, 221
Pearlin, L.I., 111, 269
Pearson, A.W., 163, 164, 165
Pearson, C.M., 318
Peeters, M.C.W., 170
Peltola, P., 65, 66, 83
Peluchette, J.V.E., 160

Peng, K., 357
Peper, B., 338, 341, 345
Pérez, M.P., 161
Perlow, L.A., 305, 306, 311, 318, 341
Perreira, I., 378
Perrewe, P.L., 159, 194, 268, 288, 296, 297, 298
Perry, G., 80
Perry-Jenkins, M., 15, 85, 201, 203, 346, 380
Perry-Smith, J.E., 275, 311
Peter, R., 113
Petola, P., 250
Phillips, J., 289, 290
Phillips-Miller, D.L., 293
Pickering, T.G., 191
Pienta, M., 109
Pierce, J.L., 275, 306
Piktialis, D., 29
Pillemer, K., 112
Pine, A.M., 295
Pinneau, S.R. Jr., 291
Piotrkowski, C., 42, 43
Pitt-Catsouphes, M., 30
Pittinsky, T.L., 254
Pittman, J.F., 47
Pixley, J., 101
Plantin, L., 377, 378
Pleck, J.H., 81, 82, 85, 252, 253, 255
Poelmans, S., 90, 142, 148, 150, 151, 153, 170,
    194, 197, 225, 271, 294, 297, 338, 340, 354,
    357, 358, 363, 364, 365
Popenoe, D., 234
Porter, A., 28
Posthuma, R.A., 170
Powell, G.N., 50, 61, 62, 63, 90, 142, 144, 145,
    146, 168, 192, 193, 196, 197, 199, 202, 205,
    206, 218, 359
Pratt, M.G., 268
Presser, H.B., 21, 22, 177, 178, 180, 381, 384
Preston, M., 145
Procidano, M.E., 290, 291
Prottas, D., 14, 76, 126, 127, 146, 148, 149, 152,
    158, 168, 169, 297, 331, 332, 335, 337, 338,
    340, 346
Pruitt, B., 313, 318, 321, 323, 324, 327, 371
Pulkkinen, L., 195, 196
Pullig, C., 158, 159, 162, 163
Purohit, Y.S., 160
Pyper, W., 391
Pyykko, M., 338

Q

Qu, L., 127, 135
Quazi, H., 340
Quick, J.C., 268
Quick, J.D., 268
Quinn, R.P., 128, 129, 130, 135, 138, 157, 193, 198

R

Rabinowitz, S., 195
Radcliffe Public Policy Center, 88
Radin, N., 256
Rahe, R.H., 191
Rajadhyaksha, U., 354, 357
Raley, S.B., 107
Ramachandran, N., 152
Rana, B., 390
Randel, A.E., 338, 339
Ranson, G., 255
Rantanen, J., 195, 196
Rapoport, R., 53, 134, 313, 318, 321, 327, 371, 373, 376, 377, 378, 379
Ratcliff, K.S., 83
Raveis, V.H., 81
Raver, J.L., 222
Reeves, R., 254
Reich, J.W., 295
Reichart, E., 102, 104, 107, 108, 112, 114
Reid, L.L., 238
Reilly, A.H., 41
Rennan, R.T., 96
Repetti, R.L., 15, 80, 81, 82, 85, 110, 201, 203
Reskin, B.F., 25, 77, 237
Rexwinkel, B., 312, 317
Reynolds, J.R., 250, 258
Rhoades, L, 291, 292, 297, 312, 317
Rich, Y., 223, 226
Riggs, J.M., 242
Riley, M.W., 97, 102
Rimm, E., 198
Rindfus, R.R., 111
Risman, B.A., 80
Risman, B.J., 14, 235, 236, 241
Rivers, C., 187, 242, 261
Robinson, J.P., 15, 95, 177, 179, 180, 182, 242, 243
Robison, J., 111

Rodriguez-Srednicki, O., 163
Roehling, P., 95, 98, 103, 104, 110, 180
Rogers, S.J., 149, 150
Rohwer, G., 112
Rollins, J., 235, 241
Romero, M., 241
Roos, P.A., 237
Rosa, J.A., 268
Rosa, R.R., 384
Rose, E., 238
Rosenberg, S.D., 81
Rosenfeld, R.A., 111
Rosenman, R.H., 82
Rosenthal, R.A., 128, 129, 130, 135, 138, 157, 193
Rosin, H.M., 217, 340
Rosman, K., 331
Rosner, E., 163
Ross Phillips, K., 380, 381
Ross, K., 379
Roth, L., 239
Rothbard, N.P., 42, 43, 46, 61, 90, 144, 146, 157, 162, 167, 168, 169, 192, 193, 194, 198, 202, 205
Rotondo, D.M., 270
Rousseau, D.M., 131, 132, 135, 274, 275
Rout, U., 390
Rowan, B., 97
Rubin, B.A., 148, 152, 153
Ruderman M.N., 142, 149, 150, 152, 194, 197
Ruiz-Quintanilla, S.A., 361
Russell, G., 249, 353
Russell, M., 58, 130, 133, 134, 135, 138, 143, 167, 194, 195, 196, 198, 199, 201, 219, 274
Russo, N.F., 81
Rust, A., 257
Ryff, C.D., 115

S

Sahibzada, K.A., 198, 338
Sakai, K., 23, 126, 135
Sánchez, A.M., 161
Sanchez, J., 148, 170, 294, 296, 297, 298, 338, 340
Sandberg, J.F. 179
Sarason, B.R., 290
Sarason, I.G., 290
Sarfati, H., 24

Saunders, R., 255, 381
Saute, R., 332
Sauter, S.L., 205, 209
Sauvé, R., 18
Sayer, L.C., 15, 240
Scandura, T.A., 275
Scarr, S., 80
Schafer, C., 27, 28
Schaffer, M.A., 297
Scharlach, A.E., 198
Schat, A., 191
Schaubroeck, J., 191, 297
Schaufeli, W.B., 145, 268
Scheck, C.L., 269
Schein, E., 333
Schellenberg, G., 20
Schelling, T.C., 321
Schieman, S., 111, 221
Schippers, J., 332
Schmitt, J., 178
Schoepflin, U., 97, 114
Schooler, C., 269, 270
Schor, J.B., 127
Schreibl, F., 387
Schroeder, D.A., 321
Schuler, R., 129
Schultz, K.S., 165
Schwartz, J., 169, 297
Schwartz, J.E., 191
Schwartz, P., 83
Scott, E., 380
Searle, S., 58, 86, 129, 218, 219
Segal, N., 107
Seron, C., 332
Settersten, R.A. 95, 97, 101, 111
Shaffer, M.A., 165, 166, 218, 219, 221, 222, 353, 357
Shafiro, M., 194, 354, 357
Shamir, B., 158
Shanahan, M.J., 99, 101, 108, 110
Shanock, L.R., 152
Sharafinski, C.E., 292
Sharlicki, D.P., 318
Sharp, D.C., 15
Sharp, S., 115
Shaw, J.D., 65, 66, 67
Shaw, S.M., 178
Sheldon, K.M., 65
Shellenbarger, S., 347
Sherony, K.M., 292

Shi, K., 170, 365
Shields, M., 384
Shimoni, R., 390
Shirom, A., 339
Shoup, R., 206
Shulman, S., 77
Sieber, S.D., 43, 61, 129, 142, 144, 193, 198
Siegrist, J., 45, 113, 274
Sigworth, C., 381
Silverstein, L.B., 16
Simmers, C.A. 269
Simmons, T., 16
Simon, M., 358
Simons, R., 79, 80
Sinclair, R.R., 194
Singh, R., 166, 205
Singley, S.G., 112, 257
Sisler, G.F., 159, 166
Skattebo, A., 161, 162, 257
Skolnick, A., 244
Slan-Jerusalim, R., 293
Smith, B., 109, 111
Smith, C.R., 130
Smith, M.J., 191
Smith, S., 309, 315
Smith-Crowe, K., 280
Smithson, J., 343, 375, 377, 383
Smola, K.W., 327
Smyer, M.A., 30
Snoek, J.D., 128, 129, 130, 135, 138, 157, 193, 198
Snyder, K., 187
Solomon, C.S., 335, 339
Solomon, Z., 299
Somech, A., 224, 268, 272, 273, 276, 280, 354, 357
Sommer, S.M., 58, 61
Sowa, D., 292, 294, 337
Spain, D., 240
Sparks, K., 339
Sparrow, P., 22
Spector, P.E., 148, 158, 162, 170, 294, 297, 338, 340, 354, 357, 363, 364, 365
Spell, C., 373
Spence, J.T., 216
Spencer, D., 96, 110, 114
Sperling, J., 81, 83
Spitze, G., 112
Spitzer, D., 388
Spratlin, J., 30

Sprecher, S., 291
Spreitzer, G.M., 168
Srinivas, E.S., 150, 158, 159, 168, 193, 201
Stacey, J., 243
Staff, J., 101, 103
Staines, G.L., 366
Stanley, D.J., 160
Stansfeld, S.A., 110, 191
Stanton, D., 127, 135
Stapp, J., 216
Statham, J., 387
Statistics Canada, 20, 23, 127, 389
Stein, P.J., 334, 340
Steiner, F.F., 319, 320
Steiner, R.L., 168
Stepanova, O., 90, 194, 197
Stephens, G.K., 58, 61
Stephens, S.A., 197
Steuve, J.L., 255
Stevens, J., 338, 339
Stewart, D., 289, 290
Stewart, M.J., 388
Still, S., 110
Stinglhamber, E., 292, 297
Stokols, D., 195
Stolz, H.E., 165
Stone, P., 16, 18, 27, 239, 240
Story, L., 89
Strazdins, L., 256
Strell, M., 386
Stroh, L.K., 41, 130, 134, 339
Stuenkel, C.P., 187
Sucharski, I.L., 292, 297
Suchet, M., 202
Sullivan, S.E., 297
Sumer, H.C., 147, 204
Sutton, C.D., 327
Sutton, M., 157, 158, 159, 160, 161, 165, 192,
     198, 199, 200, 201, 202
Swanberg, J.E., 76, 86, 88, 127, 131, 179, 250,
     337, 380, 381
Sweet, S., 96, 100, 101, 112, 115
Swicegood, C.G., 111
Swisher, R., 96, 101, 112
Swope, J.E., 180

T

Tan, H.H., 158, 159, 168, 193, 201
Tardy, C.H., 290

Taris, T.W., 159, 168
Tay, C., 340
Taylor, K., 335
Tenbrunsel, A.E., 41
Teng, W., 47
Tetrick, L.E., 57, 58, 59
Theorell, T., 113, 191
Thierry, H., 297
Thoits, P.A., 79, 85, 115, 288
Thomas, J.B., 318, 320
Thomas, L.T., 164, 205, 275, 288, 340, 342
Thomas, W.I., 97
Thompson, C.A., 14, 76, 126, 127, 146, 148,
     149, 150, 152, 153, 158, 168, 169, 207, 271,
     278, 280, 281, 297, 309, 311, 331, 332, 333,
     334, 335, 336, 337, 338, 339, 340, 344, 345,
     346
Thompson, D.E., 159, 160
Thompson, E.H., 226
Thompson, L., 78
Thomson, B., 289, 290
Timberlake, J.M., 16
Tinsley, C.H., 356
Tompson, H.B., 149, 163, 169
Topolnytsky, L., 160
Torkelson, E., 110, 115
Townsend, A., 197
Townsend, N., 253, 255
Tummers, G.E.R., 170
Turner, R.J., 290
Turnley, W.H., 163
Twenge, J.M., 88
Tyre, P., 89

U

Uhl-Bien, M., 292
Uhlenberg, P., 102, 223
Umberson, D., 112, 115
Unger, R.K., 216
Ungerer, J.A., 195
United Nations, 357
Urban Institute, 381
US Bureau of Labor Statistics, 13, 14, 17, 18, 20,
     22, 23, 24, 25, 27, 76, 87, 309, 384
US Census Bureau, 31, 77, 87, 89
US Department of Labor, 17, 20, 21, 23, 28, 29,
     30, 76, 87, 126, 234, 240
US Government
Utas, A., 295

V

Valcour, P.M., 165, 207
Van de Ven, A.H., 313
van der Doef, M., 45
van Doorne-Huiskes, A., 332
Van Dyne, L., 313, 332, 337
Van Gundy, K., 221
van Hooff, M.L.M., 159, 168
Van Lange, P.A.M., 324
Vandenberghe, C, 292, 297
Vandivere, S., 381
Vaneck, G.R., 297
Vaux, A., 289, 290
Veiga, J.F., 160, 273, 274, 278, 280, 281
Velgach, S., 223, 224
Verhoeven, K., 291
Verma, A., 103
Veroff, J., 81
Vickers, M., 376
Vickers, R.R., 191
Viswesvaran, C., 59, 158, 163, 164, 165, 296, 298, 338
Viveros-Long, A., 58, 129, 131
Vosko, L.F., 24
Voydanoff, P., 42, 51, 52, 69, 84, 130, 133, 179, 180, 195, 199, 202, 219
Vuolo, M., 101

W

Waite, L.J., 178
Wakefield, S., 101
Waldfogel, J., 84, 238
Waldron, I., 80, 82
Walker, A.J., 78
Walker, J., 206
Wallis, C., 89
Walumbwa, F.O., 170, 365
Wambold, S., 159
Wang, J.L., 191
Wang, P., 170, 365
Ward, H.W., 191
Warner, M., 293
Warr, P., 80, 277
Warren, J., 333, 338
Watson, D., 147
Wattenberg, B.J., 87, 88
Way, N., 101

Wayne, J.H., 61, 62, 64, 70, 90, 142, 144, 147, 148, 149, 150, 168, 169, 195, 204, 205, 257, 338, 339
Webster, J., 378
Weiner, S.P., 306, 312
Weitzman, M., 67
Wellman, B., 289, 290, 293
Wells, S., 315, 319, 325
Weltman, D., 346
Werner, J.M., 149, 163, 169
West, C., 235, 236
Westman, M., 145
Weston, R., 127, 135
Wethington, E., 79, 81, 101, 107, 112
Weymann, A., 114
Wharton, A.S., 180, 332, 339, 342, 343
Wheaton, B., 97, 297
White, J., 208
Whitehead, D.L., 256
Whitestone, Y.K., 221
Wiens-Tuers, B., 346
Wilke, H.A.M., 324
Wilkes, L., 376
Wilkie, J.R., 83
Williams, A., 146, 149, 200
Williams, C.L., 238
Williams, D., 289, 290
Williams, J., 16, 237, 239, 240, 241
Williams, J.C., 107
Williams, K., 112, 115
Williams, K.J., 147
Williams, L.B., 101, 112
Williams, L.J., 58, 158, 159, 219, 221, 222
Williamson, G.M., 191
Wills, J., 390
Wills, T.A., 296, 297
Wilmoth, J.M., 391
Wing, R.R., 202
Winslow, S., 16, 219, 250
Winson, T., 386
Winters, D., 311, 312
Witt, A., 62
Witt, L.A., 298
Wittig-Berman, U., 160
Wolcott, I., 25
Wolfe, D.M., 128, 129, 130, 135, 138, 157, 193, 198
Wood, J.A., 159
Woodbury, S., 102, 107, 109

Wright, J.A., 275
Wright, T.A., 268
Wrigley, J., 241

X

Xie, J.L., 191
Xie, W., 101

Y

Yamagishi, T., 324
Yang, C., 170, 220, 222, 347, 363, 365
Yang, N., 219, 220, 222, 354, 357, 358
Yardley, J., 130, 131, 132, 133, 134, 135, 143,
    161, 195, 200, 297, 340, 354
Yoon, J., 292, 293

Youngblade, L.M., 242, 243
Yu, Y., 108, 109, 180

Z

Zabel, D., 306, 310, 312, 316
Zapf, D., 152
Zaslow, M., 381
Zedeck, S., 96
Zhou, Y., 219, 220, 222, 354, 358
Ziemba, S., 257
Zierk, K.L., 81
Zimmerman, K., 291, 292, 294
Zimmerman, M.K., 235
Zimmerman, T.S., 257
Zipp, J.F., 386
Znaniecki, F., 97
Zukewich, N., 24

SUBJECT INDEX

500 Family Study: methodology, 181–2, 187
7 *Habits of Highly Effective Families* (Covey), 150

A

absenteeism: enhanced coping and, 276; role
    overload and, 135; work-family conflict and,
    163–5
African-American women, 82, 295
ageism, 21
aging population: adequate funds for, 29;
    care provisions for, 19, 198; eldercare and,
    376; growth of, 19; policy supports for,
    392; 'sandwich generation,' 19, 197;
    work-family integration and, 390–2;
    work opportunities for, 21; workplace issues
    for, 29, 391
Alfred P. Sloan Center on Parents, Children and
    Work, 181
algorithm: and work-family balance, 67
altruism, 257
American Dream, 98
androgyny, 226
Arab culture: interrole conflict in, 357
Asian cultures: work-family conflict in, 357
assumptions: workplace culture and, 333
artifacts: of organizational support, 333
Australia, 110, 127, 358, 363–4
Austria, 360

B

'balancing act,' 240
Belgium, 111, 364
benefits: employer-sponsored, 30; exclusion from,
    371; family-friendly, 274, 341 flexibility,
    311–12, 317
biographical pacing, 100–01. *See also* time
    convoy
'BlackBerry orphans,' 331
BLS: *See* Bureau of Labor Statistics (BLS)
blue-collar work: changing nature of, 21;
    flexibility and, 309; overtime and, 346
boundaries. *See* work-life boundaries

Brazil, 364
Britain. *See* United Kingdom
Bureau of Labor Statistics (BLS): 309
burnout, 297

C

Canada: childcare, 26; employee benefits, 24;
    employment insurance, 28; fertility rates,
    17; gender-role ideology, 224; health care,
    31; industrial growth, 20; labor force, 14,
    197; National Work Life Study, 127; parental
    leave, 19, 26; role overload, 125; unions, 23;
    welfare reform. 28; 384, 386–7, 391–2; work
    hours, 127
Canada Health Act, 31
Canada Pension Plan (CPP): 30
Canadian Centre for Policy Alternative, 20
capital: forms of, 108
caregiving, 241; coping strategies, 391–2;
    eldercare, 108; men and women's roles in,
    103–4; well-being and, 198
careworkers: increase in, 387–9; lack of benefits
    to, 388
career: planning across cultures, 367; progression,
    22; satisfaction and work-family conflict,
    158–9; work-family benefits and, 334
'career mystique,' 95, 98
CASA: *See* National Center on Addiction and
    Substance Abuse (CASA)
cell phones, 106, 126
childcare: benefits, 25–6; cultural variations in,
    360, 362–3; in European Union, 27; father
    involvement in, 254, 258–9; human resource
    issues in, 388; provision of, 18; time spent
    on, 15; in US and Canada, 26; use in US, 76
children: family functioning and, 203; working
    mothers and, 242
China, 111–12, 170, 222, 357–9, 363, 365
Clinton, Hilary Rodham, 287
cognitive appraisal: of stressful events, 269–70
Colombia, 363
commitment: to work and family, 86
commuting: and role overload, 136–7

compensatory model: for coping with work-family conflict, 277–8

complementary model: for coping with work-family conflict, 278

computers, 22

Confucian values, 343, 345, 357, 365

contingent workers, 24

contracting out, 20, 24

control cycles, 108–9, 109f

convergence, 110–11

converging divergences, 110–11, 114. *See also* life course

cooperation: enhancement of, 322–3f, 323–4; face-time and, 321

coping: defined, 269; strategies, 270–3; integrated models of work-family conflict and, 276–80; social support and, 288

coping strategies: behavioral model, 272–3; compensatory model, 277; complementary model, 278; emotion-focused, 270; problem-focused, 270–2; spiral model, 279; Type I (structural role redefinition), 270–1; Type II (personal role definition), 270–1; Type III (reactive role behavior), 271

co-workers: as sources of support, 148, 291–3

CPP: *See* Canada Pension Plan (CPP)

crossover: of stress and satisfaction, 145

culture: definitions of, 354–5; dimensions of, 355f; family demands and, 359–60; family-friendly policies and, 360–2; interrole conflict and, 357–8; perceptions of work and, 357, 364; Project 3535, 225, 354, 356f; spousal support and, 361; Type I and II hypotheses of, 356; work demands and, 357; work-family conflict and, 355f, 355–6, 356f, 364

'cultural contradictions': of motherhood, 243

D

'Daddy days,' 256, 334

decision-process theory, 151

deindustrialization, 20

delayed childbearing, 17

demand-control mode, 45. *See also* ecological systems theory

'demographic gender,' 215, 217

Denmark, 112, 360

depletion theory, 157. *See also* role-conflict theory

depression. *See* well-being, stress

direct impact explanation: of family-friendliness, 274

discrimination, 21; against mothers, 237

divergence, 110–11

diversity, earning power of, 18; examples of, 17; in the workplace, 21

DOL: *see* US Department of Labor (DOL)

domain-specific overload, 130–1

domestic workers, 241, 362

'double day,' 246

downsizing, 21, 22

'dual agenda,' 371

dual-earners: benefits of, 83; changing gender roles of, 216; children's well-being and, 84; combined income of, 14; crossover between, 145; distribution of family time and, 182–4; father involvement and, 83, 256; household tasks and, 187, 242, 257–8; necessity for 17–18; non-work issues and, 134; off-shifting of work hours, 385; response to family needs, 107–8; rise of in US, 76, 102; social support and, 296; stress and, 14; time squeeze and, 179; work-family balance and, 249; work-life integration and, 178; workloads of, 126

E

Early Childcare Research Network, 76

ecological systems theory: framework of, 37–41; work-family interface and, 194

education: gender equity in, 17

effort-reward model: of family-friendliness, 274

eldercare. *See* aging population

emic perspectives: of work-family demand and support, 367

emotional intelligence (EI), 160

emotional support, 291; of family, 293–4

employee-initiated flexibility, 306

employees: decrease in benefits for, 24; and work-family-interface, 208; motivation and flexibility, 312

employers: family benefits and, 19; health coverage, 31; relationship with employees, 22

employment: inequality in opportunities for, 21

employment insurance, 28–9

enacted support, 290

enhancement, 142, 148f

enrichment: caregiving and, 198; definitions of, 61, 141, 169; dimensions of, 144–5; enhancement of, 152; informal or emotional support and, 338; job commitment and, 338; measure of, 63–4; multiple roles and, 373; reciprocal model of, 196–7, skill variety and, 147; types and benefits of 144f, 145; work-family roles and, 199–200. *See also* work-family interface, spillover

ERB. *See* extra-role behavior (ERB)

Ernst and Young, 344–5

ESM. *See* experience sampling method (ESM)

etic measures: of gender, 222

ethic of care, 249

European Foundation for the Improvement of Living and Working Conditions, 388

European Union, 332

exosystem, 38, 194–5. *See also* ecological systems theory

expansion hypothesis, 142, 193–4

Expansionist Theory of Women, Men, Work, and Family, An, 79–80

experience sampling method (ESM), 182

extra-role behavior (ERB): face-time and, 313–14, 316; place flexibility and, 313; work-life flexibility and, 318

F

face-time: career progress and, 334; commitment and, 305, 339; concerns regarding, 311; group performance and, 316–25, 317f, 322–3f; intensity level and, 314f, 316; social dilemmas and, 321–2, 322–3f; work coordination and, 308, 313; facilitation: definition of, 61–2; problematic measures of, 64; work-family interface and, 192

Fair Labor Standards Act, 346

Families and Work Institute, 346

family: care roles, 197–8; changes practices of, 235; children and, 203, demands and role overload, 134–5; diversity, 16; ideal worker and parent, 16; resilience, 45; return to traditional roles, 14; as source of social support, 293–4; supports to enhance flexibility, 44–5. *See also* dual-earner, single parents, single mothers

family characteristics: work-family conflict and, 202–3

family/dyadic effects: of work-family conflict, 201–2

family-friendly: cross-cultural policies, 360–2; organizational culture, 278; policies and practices, 115, 268; psychological contract model, 275; workplace models, 273–5, 332

family interfering with work (FIW): absenteeism and, 163–5; career outcomes and, 160–1; cross-cultural variations in, 358; gender and, 218–20, 224; in-role performance and, 161–2; job satisfaction and, 158–9; organizational citizenship behavior and, 162–3; organizational commitment and, 159–60; organizational support and, 294; role conflict and, 129; social support for, 294–5; turnover and, 165–6. *See also* work-family conflict (WFC)

Family Medical Leave Act (FMLA), 26

family supportive organization perceptions, 336

family supportive supervisory behavior (FSSB), 292

family time: with children, 179–80; emotional dimensions of, 184–5, well-being and, 181; 186f; work-family balance and, 185, 186f

family-to-work conflict (FTW): gender-role attitudes and, 224; increase in, 193; psychological distress and, 195–6; family-to-work enrichment, 145

fatherhood: culture and conduct disjuncture, 252; men's wages and, 238; policy and, 256–7; work-family culture and, 335

father involvement, 15; children's developmental stage and, 259; dual-earner couples and, 83; mother's role in, 253; positive outcomes for, 252–4; social norms and, 374; strategies for future of, 259–62; the workplace and, 254, 256–7

fathers: childcare and, 15, 80; leisure time and, 15; non-resident, 258; as primary parents, 261; work hours and, 256. *See also* multiple roles

feminine mystique, 98

feminism, 235

feminized occupations, 237

fertility rate, 17, 26, 87, 379

Finland, 222, 360

fit argument: for spiral model of coping with work-family conflict, 280

FIW. *See* family interfering with work (FIW)

flexible time (flextime): approaches to, 309–10; formal program of, 27; supervisory power

and, 342; US workers using, 332; as
work-family balance strategy, 49; flexibility,
250; benefits of, 306; control mechanisms
for cooperation, 324–5; costs on IRB and
ERB of, 321–2; as double-edged, 376–7;
employee commitment and, 312; employee
groups and, 309; expectations around,
334–5; group performance and, 319,
324; operational, 337; options for, 305,
311–12, 315; organizational culture and,
309; temporal, 337. *See also* work-life
flexibility
FMLA. *See Family Medical Leave Act* (FMLA)
France, 19
FSSB. *See* family supportive supervisory behavior
(FSSB)
FTW. *See* Family-to-work conflict (FTW)

G

Gallup poll, 88
gender: convergence, 14; contract, 26;
    cross-cultural comparisons of, 222;
    228; cultural contradictions and, 236;
    definitions of, 215–16; equity and
    work-family support, 343; ideological
    attitudes to, 88, 223; inequities, 374;
    intrapsychic perspective of, 216;
    multidimensional approach to, 236,
    216–17; power and, 229; rational
    viewpoint theory of, 218; as a research
    variable, 217–18, 220–2, 228–9; social
    contexts of, 236; social norms and, 216;
    social support and, 295–6; stereotypes,
    229; wage gap, 237; work-family conflict
    and, 204, 217
Gender Development Index, 344
gender-role ideology (GRI): interrole conflict
    and, 223–4; orientation characteristics,
    225–6; work-family conflict and, 224–6
gender-role stereotypes: 229; cross-cultural, 358
gender-role values: and work-family
    conflict, 226
General Social Survey, 346
Germany, 111, 360, 382
'glass ceiling,' 18, 238
'glass escalator,' 238
globalization, 21, 371
'Go Home on Time Days,' 344
'good worker' model, 257

government: and work-family support, 208
GRI. *See* gender-role ideology (GRI)
group performance: shaped by behavior and
    context, 327

H

health. *See* mental health, well-being.
health care: access to in US and Canada, 31
hindrance factors, 342
Hong Kong, 166, 222, 343, 357–8, 363–5
housework, 253, 258
Hungary, 111

I

IBM: workers' study, 170, 222, 363–4
ideal parent, 16
'ideal worker' model, 16, 239, 359, 372–3, 383
immigrants: labor pool and, 17, 241, 388
incentives: tangible and intangible, 323
India, 159, 168, 357, 361, 363
individual stress theory, 37
Indonesia, 357, 363
industry: associated with 'good jobs,' 20;
    deindustrialization, 20
in-role behavior (IRB): work-life flexibility
    and, 318
integrative model: of social support, 298
intensity: group performance and, 320
institutional convoy, 100. *See also* time convoy
instrumental support, 291; of family, 293–4
integration: organizational support and, 341; of
    work-life boundaries, 151; interactionist
    perspective, 235–6
interrole conflict: across cultures, 357–8
intrapsychic perspective, 216. *See also* gender
IRB. *See* in-role behavior (IRB)
Ireland, 361
Israel, 357
Italy, 111, 358

J

Japan, 127, 271, 345, 363, 378–9
job autonomy: and positive spillover, 146
job satisfaction: decrease in, 22–3; family-friendly
    policy and practice and, 275; flexibility
    and, 312; measures of work-family conflict
    and, 158–9; positive spillover and, 150; role

overload and, 135; social support and, 297; work-family fit across cultures and, 365
job security, 24, 115; low-wage workers and, 380

K

Kirchmeyer scale, 62–3
Korea, 345, 363

L

labor force: aging, 29–30; cost of, 20; decline in, 17, 20; gender proportions in, 14, 17; mothers in, 14
labor standards: and family-friendly policy, 208
leader member exchange (LMX), 292
leave of absence: penalties for, 332
life course: adaptive strategies for, 105f, 106–8; age and gender stratification of, 102–3; aging workforce and, 103; caregiving and, 103–4 'converging divergences' and, 110; early development of concept, 98; family-work strategies in Europe and China and, 111–12; gender and, 98–9; institutional change and, 114; levels of meaning, 97; policy and research issues in, 112–15; public vs economic policy around, 99; 'structural lag' and, 102–3; theoretical implications of, 101; toxic social ecologies and, 101; work-family conflict and, 104, 105f
Life Roles Salience Scale (LRSS), 226–7
'light man,' 361
linkages: in social relationships, 289
LMX. See leader member exchange (LMX)
low-income families: job security and, 380; time squeeze and, 187; work-family research and, 379–80
loyalty, 292
LRSS. See Life Roles Salience Scale (LRSS)

M

macrosystem, 38–9; 194–5
Malaysia, 363
managerial argument: for spiral model of coping with work-family conflict, 280
managerial support: for work-family culture, 334
marriage: childbearing decisions and, 234; quality of, 82–3; postponement of, 87, 104, 234;

roles in, 78; maternity leave, 19; early return to work and, 76
measurement: algorithmic, 67–8; Kirchmeyer scale, 62–3, Marks and MacDermid scale, 67, MIDUS scale, 62–3, multiple item, 67; of work-family balance, 69
Medicaid, 31
Medical Care Act, 31
men: caregiving and, 251; flexible work options of, 27; gender-role attitudes and, 220, 223–4; housework and, 15; job satisfaction and, 159; labor force participation in US, 13; non-traditional fathering roles and, 252; paternal involvement, 15–16; role-overload predictors for, 136; well-being and, 80, 109; work-family conflict and, 250–1; work-life stress of, 16. *See also* family, father involvement, fathers
mental health, 80–1, 85. *See also* well-being
mesosystem, 38–9, 194–5
Mexico, 170, 241, 364
micropolitics of care, 261–2
microsystem, 38–9, 194–5
MIDUS scale: as measure of work-family interface, 62–3. *See also* spillover: positive
migration: international, 389–90; rural-urban, 19–20
MNCs. *see* multinational corporations (MNCs)
Mommy Wars, The, 240
motherhood: choice between work and, 239; class issues and, 243; diverse patterns of, 104, 234, 244–5; feminist reformulations of, 235; 'new home economics' theorists and, 238; primacy of, 249, 261; race and class variations in, 235; reshaping of since 1960s, 233–4; shared ideals of, 244; as social construct, 236; wage penalties for, 237–8; women's jobs and, 237
'motherhood penalty,' 236
mothers: gains in parenting time of, 15; household work and, 242; labor force participation of, 14; 233; maternity leave, 19; nonmarital childbearing, 15; time spent with children and, 243. *See also* family, single mothers, women
motivation: flexibility and, 213
multiple roles: benefits and limits of, 80–5; 198, 373; biology and, 78; decision-process theory and, 151; effects of, 78–80; early attitudes to, 75, 77–8; reinforcement of,

86–7; role quality and, 85–6; stress and, 178; well-being and, 85, 200–1; work-family conflict and, 86. *See also* dual-earners, men, women
multinational corporations (MNCs), 353
'multiple agenda,' 371
multitasking, 23

N

National Center on Addiction and Substance Abuse (CASA), 177
National Compensation Survey, 309
National Institute for Occupational Safety and Health (NIOSH), 205
National Institute of Child Health and Human Development (NICHD), 76, 242
National Study of the Changing Workforce, 168, 331, 337–8
National Study of Employers, 19
National Survey on Drug Use and Health, 109
National Work-Life Study, 125, 127; and role-overload, 135–7
negative family contingencies, 239
Netherlands, 111, 145, 159, 168, 170, 341, 358, 360, 382
networks, 289
New Zealand, 127, 162, 297
NICHD. *See* National Institute of Child Health and Human Development (NICHD)
NIOSH. *See* National Institute for Occupational Safely and Health (NIOSH)
nonmarital childbearing, 15
non-resident fathers, 258
nonwork demands,133
Norway, 344
nuclear family, 16; dominant view of, 78

O

OCB. *See* organizational citizenship behavior (OCB)
occupational ghettoes, 237
occupational stress theory, 37, 45
OECD. *See* Organization for Economic Co-operation and Development (OECD)
off-shifting, 385
opt-out revolution, 240
'organizational anorexia,' 126
organizational citizenship behavior (OCB): work-family conflict and, 162–3

organizational commitment, 159–60, 203, 276, 297
organizational culture: dimensions of, 333
organizational support, 291–3; gender equity and, 344; job satisfaction and, 338; need for systemic thinking around, 373; respect and, 334; retention and, 297; role overload and, 137; work-family conflict and, 297. *See also* work-family culture, work-family support
organizational time demands: work-family conflict and, 339; work-family culture and, 334
organization-calculative perspective, 268
Organization for Economic Co-operation and Development (OECD): 126–7
organization-humanistic perspective, 268–9
organizations: flexibility programs in, 305; gender-role stereotypes and, 229; as source of support, 291–2; supportive work-family culture and, 137, 148, 152, 273; tangible and intangible support of, 333; workplace policy and, 207
outsourcing, 24
overload dilemmas, 134. *See also* role overload

P

parental leave, 19, 26, 250, 341, 381
parenting: collaborative, 261; equitable models of 261–2; traditional patterns of, 373
part-time work, 381–3
PCS. *See* perceived co-worker support (PCS)
peer mentoring, 324
pension plan, 30
perceived career consequences: of work-family benefits, 334
perceived control, 108
perceived co-worker support (PCS), 292–3
perceived equity: and group performance, 318
perceived organizational support (POS), 292, 333, 337
perceived social support, 290
perceived supervisory support (PSS), 292
Personal Responsibility and Work Opportunity Reconciliation Act (PRWORA), 27
personal role definition, 270
Philippines, 241, 363
pink-collar jobs, 238, 346
place flexibility, 310, 314f; group performance and, 219–20; intensity of, 315
Poland, 364

policy (policies): assumptions 378; contexts at
macro level and, 374; family-supportive,
22, 268–9, 274, 277; flexible workplace,
27, 207; 309, 311–12; maternal and
parental leave, 19, 25; to reduce negative
spillover, 151; roots of work-family, 25–6;
shifting norms and, 21; small business
exemptions from, 387; welfare, 27–8;
work-family balance and, 148; 'politics
of motherhood,' 243
Portugal, 358, 363–4
POS. *See* perceived organizational support (POS)
positive career contingencies, 239
positive spillover. *See* spillover: positive
postpartum depression, 85–6
poverty, 111
problem-focused coping strategies, 271–2
productivity gap, 238
professionalized parenting, 15
Project 3535, 225, 354, 356, 356f
provision of care, 18, 249, 251
PRWORA. *See* Personal Responsibilities and Work
Opportunity Reconciliation Act (PRWORA)
PSS. *See* perceived supervisory support (PSS)
'psychological contract,' 22, 275
psychological rewards: definition of, 43. *See also*
ecological systems theory

Q

quality time, 187
quiet revolution, 76

R

rational viewpoint theory, 218
relationships: social network analysis of, 289
reproductive rights, 234
resilience theory, 37
respect: and organizational support, 334, 341
retention: cross-cultural differences in, 365;
organizational support and, 297
retirement: adequacy of funds for, 29–30; of
baby boomers, 17, 103, 391; eldercare
and, 392
role accumulation: expansion hypothesis and,
193–4; positive outcomes of, 145
role-conflict theory: 128, 130–1, 193
role overload: 1960s role-conflict theory
and, 128, 130–1; absenteeism and, 135;
in Canada, 125; defined, 125; detrimental

outcomes of, 134–5, 141; gender-related
predictors for, 136–7; non-work demands
and, 133; risk factors for, 132; role conflict
and strain as components of, 129, 131;
terms and concepts for, 128–30; as
time-based conflict, 130; total role
overload model and, 131; well-being and,
135; work demands, and 126; work-life
conflict and, 138
role performance, 42–3
role quality, 85
role theory, 193–4
Romania, 363–4
rural communities: work-family issues for, 386

S

'sandwich generation,' 19, 197
scarcity hypothesis, 193
'second shift,' 15, 236, 249
segmentation: of work-life boundaries, 151
separation: and organizational support, 341
service-oriented jobs, 20–1
services: family-friendly, 274
Sex-Role Egalitarianism Scale, 224
shift work, 21, 84, 180, 257, 384
Singapore, 357, 363, 365
single employees, 346
single mothers: childcare challenges of, 15, 18;
rise in, 234; US households headed by, 16,
380; work issues of, 243
single parents: examples of, 258; fathers as, 259;
rise in, 16; work-family demands and,
178–9; work hours and, 180–1
Sloan Work-Family Encyclopedia, 385
small business: benefits and, 386–7; work life
integration and, 386
social clock, 100–1. *See also* time convoy
social convoy: concept of, 99; linked lives and,
100. *See also* time convoy
social dilemmas: face-time and, 223–3f;
reciprocity and, 323–4
social embeddedness, 289
social network analysis, 289
social network resources, 289
social security benefits, 30
social support: in collectivist societies, 287–8;
effect on stress of, 297; emotional and
instrumental, 291; ethnicity and, 294; family
and, 293–5; gender identity and, 295–6;
integrative model of, 298; measures of, 299;

need for, 288; perceived availability of, 290; social embeddedness and, 289; support enactment and, 290; theory of work-family culture, 337

social systems: dynamism of, 376

South Africa, 364

Spain, 111, 361, 363–4

spillover:

negative: reduction of, 151; work-family conflict and, 142–3; well-being and, 201

other types of, 144

positive: attitude and, 150; benefits of, 149f, 150; bidirectional model of, 143f; gender and 204; job satisfaction and, 168; measures of, 62, 69; theoretical framework of, 197; turnover intentions and, 169; well-being and, 197, 200–1; work-family enhancement and, 142; work-family interface and, 61; work-life factors and, 146. *See also* work-family interface

psychological, 42

spiral model: of work-family conflict coping, 279–80, 279f

spousal support, 361

strain-based demands, 42, 47

strategic selection: and life-course fit, 107, 113

Statistics Canada, 20, 23, 127, 389

stress: coping with, 269; effect of social support on, 294; model of job stressors, 205; work-family conflict and, 199, 201. *See also* well-being

structural lag, 102–4

structural role definition, 270

supervisory support, 291–2, 340

support enactment, 290

supportive supervision, 148, 337

Sweden, 19, 112, 256, 334, 341, 344, 360, 363

System Justification Theory, 361

T

Taiwan, 358, 363

technology: nature of work and, 21–2, 24, 132, 141; role overload and, 126. *See also* work-family conflict

telework, 22, 314–15

Thailand, 363

time-based demands: characteristics of, 41, 47; family life and, 95; increased work-life conflict and, 132–3, 135–6. *See also* role overload

time convoy: biographical pacing transitions, and 100; social clock and, 100; as social or institutional convoy, 99–100; 'time divide,' 240

time flexibility: approaches to, 309–10

time squeeze, 104, 179, 187. *See also* dual-earners, single parents

timing flexibility, 310; intensity of, 315

total role overload, 131

toxic social ecologies, 101, 109. *See also* life course

trade deficit, 20

traditional family, 235

'transnational mothers,' 241

travel: and role overload, 136

'triple benefits,' 254

Turkey, 361–2, 365

turnover: enhanced coping and, 276; work-family conflict and, 165–6

U

Ukraine, 358, 364

unemployment insurance. *See* employment insurance

unions: decline in US and Canada, 23; workplace change and, 208

United Kingdom, 344, 357–8, 361, 364, 382, 384, 387, 392

United Nations Declaration of the Rights of the Child, 25

United States: aging population, 19, 391–2; contingent workers, 24; dual-earners, 14–15, 76; employee benefits, 24; fertility rates, 17; health care, 31; labor force, 14; marriage demographics, 87; parental leave, 26; part-time work in, 382; population increase, 21; retirement plans, 29–30; self-employment, 25; social security benefits, 30; unions, 23; wages, 18; 89; welfare reform, 27; women and well-being, 81; women's labor-force participation, 17, 76–7; work-family conflict in, 170, 358, 363, 365; work flexibility, 309, 332; work hours, 126–7; working at home, 22

Universal Child Care Benefit, 26

'unsociable hours,' 256, 258, 384. *See also* work hours

US Bureau of Labor Statistics, 13–14, 17–18, 22–8, 76, 384
US Bureau of the Census, 77, 87, 89, 384
US Department of Labor (DOL), 20–1, 29–30, 76, 87, 126, 234
US Family and Medical Leave Act, 387
US National Study of the Changing Workforce, 126f
US Panel Study of Income Dynamics, 111

V

values: workplace culture and, 333

W

wage gap, 18, 89, 236–7
wage penalty: for motherhood, 237–8
Wall Street Journal, 347
welfare: mothers, 28; move to work and, 178; reform in US and Canada, 27–8
well-being: cost of, 200; decrease in, 44–5; family support and, 293; family time and, 185, 186f; job stressors and, 205; men's, 80; occupational, 268–9; perceived stress and, 199; related to work-family balance, 50; resources and needs gap, 108; role overload and, 135; women's employment and, 79–80; work and health links to, 109–10, 113; work-family conflict and, 200, 364. *See also* spillover: positive
Western Collaborative Group Study, 82
WFC. *See* work-family conflict (WFC)
WIF. *See* work interfering with family (WIF)
Wisconsin Maternity Leave and Health Project, 86
women: depression and, 81, 85–6; domestic work share and, 239; dual role of, 16; employed with children, 87; family balance and, 15; fertility rates of, 17; flexible work options and, 27; gender-role attitudes and, 223–4; immigration and, 241; income of, 18, 250; job satisfaction and, 159; labor force participation of, 13–14, 75–6, 77, 89, 234, 237; management and, 17, 359; post-secondary education and, 17, 88–9, 240; poverty and, 29; provision of care and, 249, 251; reproductive rights and, 234; role-overload predictors for, 136; 'second shift,' 15; traditional roles for, 77; welfare

and, 28; well-being and, 79–80, 85; work and status of, 245; work-family demands and, 220; 250. *See also* motherhood, mothers, single mothers
work: allocation of time to, 14; career progression, 22; changing boundaries of 268; changing nature of, 13, 19, 24, 132; choice between motherhood and, 239; coordination and face-time, 308; culture-specific demands of, 359; factors affecting blue-collar, 21; high-involvement systems of, 207; from home, 22; job loss, 20; part-time, 381–3; socially sustainable, 378; stressors and well-being, 191–2. *See also* multiple roles, policy, work hours
work climate: for boundary separation, 334; for sacrifices, 334; for sharing concerns, 334. *See also* organizational support
work efforts, 274
work-family balance: 500 Family Study and, 183; assessment of and strategies for, 48–9; conceptualization of, 64–5; as a consequence of equality, 65; decreased role overload and, 137; family time and, 177, 185–6, 186f; job autonomy and, 180; job satisfaction and, 168; measurement strategies of, 66–8; organizational support and, 152; role satisfaction and, 65–6; supervisory support and, 340, 345. *See also* work-family fit
work-family border theory, 37, 43
work-family conflict (WFC): absenteeism and, 163–5; Asian cultures and, 357; balanced approach to, 205; career-related outcomes of, 160–1, 167; coping strategies, 272–3, 277–80; cultural bidirectional model of, 143f, 192; culture and, 170–1, 353–4, 355, 356f, 357–8, 366; as distinct phenomenon, 59–60; family-friendly workplace and, 273–4; gender roles and, 358; guilt and, 366; implications for research in, 60; integrated models of coping and, 276–80; intensification of, 141; job performance and, 161–2; life-course fit and, 105; measures of, 60; 220–2; model of, 50–2, 51f, 105f; occupational conditions and, 180; as an organizational issue, 373; organizational outcomes and, 268; organizational policy and, 268–9; 277; reports of, 331–2; social support and, 294,

297–8; turnover and, 165–6; well-being and, 200–1. *See also* family-to-work conflict (FTW), work-to-family conflict (WTF)

work-family culture: definitions of, 333; dimensions of, 334; gaps in research, 346; international samples of, 342–4; measures of, 335–6, 336f; organizational outcomes and, 345; positive work outcomes and, 338; shared vs individual perceptions of, 335; use of benefits and, 341

work-family enrichment. *See* enrichment

work-family facilitation, 50–2, 51f, 142

work-family fit: conceptual model of, 46–7, 48f, 105f; cross-cultural research on, 170–1; quality of life and, 200; strategies for, 49; work-family balance relationship and, 52. *See also* ecological systems theory

work-family integration: career outcomes and, 168; changes toward, 377; diverse attitudes to, 378; earliest mentions, 13; earning/caring dichotomy, 16; evolution of, 13; factors affecting experience of, 3; multi-level approach to, 4; part-time work and, 382; provision of care and, 18

work-family interface: contemporary implications for, 52–3, 70, 106; demands and resources related to, 40; ecological model defined, 38, 39f; ecological systems theory and, 194–5; enrichment and, 199; gender and, 204, 227, 254; integrative perspective of, 64–5; job attitudes, and 168; job strain and, 203; linkages between domains of, 38, 41, 43, 46, 142, 143f; negative perspective on, 58; outcomes of model, 40; positive constructs related to, 60–1; range of characteristics, 37; role conflict and, 193; role involvement and, 227–8; study methodologies, 171; support for, 44; theoretical framework of, 37; trends in, 141; well-being and, 198–201. *See also* life-course fit, work-family conflict, work-family fit

work-family policies: implications for, 46; leave and benefits, 25–6

work-family research: blind spots in research and policy around, 379; future development of, 68–70; measurement concepts, 57; western biases in, 375

work-family support: career consequences of use, 339–40, 342

work-family values, 275

'workfare,' 244

work hours: actual and ideal, 178–9; alternative, 275; children's well-being and, 84; 'continental hours,' 23; face-time norms and, 339; increase in US, Canada, and New Zealand, 127; non-social, 384; non-standard, 384; off-shifting of, 385; role overload and, 126; shift work, 384; well-being and, 339, 384; work-life conflict and, 132–3, 135–6; 180

working day: diversity in structure, 21. *See also* shift work

Working Mother magazine, 344

'working scared,' 21

work interfering with family (WIF): absenteeism and, 163–5; career outcomes and, 160–1; cross-cultural variations in, 358; gender and, 218–20, 224; in-role performance and, 161–2; job satisfaction and, 158–9; organizational citizenship behavior and, 162–3; organizational commitment and, 159–60; organizational support and, 297; role conflict and, 129; turnover and, 165–6. *See also* work-family conflict

work-life boundaries: blurring of, 375; effect of technology on, 141; segmentation and integration of, 151

work-life flexibility: benefits and costs of, 306, 310–11; cooperation and, 323; multinationals and, 347; negative reactions to, 311; options for, 305; stigmatization for use of, 332; types of, 308f, 309–10, 326; work performance and, 307f, 308f

workplace: diversity in, 21; flexibility in, 27; family-positive culture in, 207, 273–4; values and assumptions in, 333

work rewards, 274; supports and, 291–3

work-to-family conflict (WTF): increase in, 192, psychological distress and, 195. *See also* family interfering with work (FIW); family-to-work conflict (FTW), work-family conflict (WFC), work-interfering with family (WIF)

work-to-family enrichment, 144–5

work trends: self-employment, 24–5; service-oriented jobs, 20–21; temporary work, 24; time spent in labor force, 15; working at home, 22

World War II, 13, 18, 75, 77, 103

WTF. *See* work-to-family conflict (WTF)